The authors use these principles both to organize the text overall and to drive discussions within chapters.

Real World, Real Speakers: A New Way to Teach Public Speaking

Presentations in Everyday Life **is a briefer, hands-on, and practical text focused on the real-world communication contexts in which many students already find themselves.**

The book's real-world focus reflects responses from a survey of presenters and professionals from business, health care, education, government, and social services. These responses guided the authors to include unique material, to have a more modular book-wide organization, and to emphasize practice based on theory. They also confirmed the authors' overriding goal: to give students practical advice about creating powerful presentations in an encouraging, accessible way.

Presentations in Everyday Life **teaches speakers how to speak.**

Rather than telling readers to make sure they speak loud enough, the text explains *how* to increase volume, *how* to speak with or without a microphone, and *how* to adjust to different surroundings. It also explains *how* to select effective strategies for achieving a specific, informative purpose. Teaching speakers *how to* goes well beyond *what* because it gives them a repertoire of communication strategies and skills that can be adapted to any speaking situation.

Presentations in Everyday Life **goes beyond describing what speakers do. It explains how to select the best strategies and master the most critical skills needed to become a highly effective speaker.**

Focus on Strategies: A strategic decision-making system based on seven principles of presentation speaking—purpose, audience, logistics, content, organization, credibility, and performance—helps students develop and deliver effective presentations.

Based on recommendations from the survey and from extensive research, we provide:

Sample speeches and text examples drawn directly from business and "real-world" situations that offer an honest picture of potential speaking experiences students are most likely to encounter;

A **no-nonsense, approachable style** that will engage diverse student populations, especially underrepresented students and adult learners;

Concise **how-to advice** on issues such as building presentation confidence, choosing a purpose and topic, using introductions and conclusions to maximum effect, gaining and maintaining audience interest, and other such topics that research has shown students need the most;

Acknowledgment of the **impact of technology** and electronic communication in collecting, preparing and presenting information;

A **flexible, modular chapter configuration** that recognizes the realities of today's campuses and lets instructors easily choose the topics best suited to their students' needs.

Chapter features:

▶▶ **Common Questions** which provide a road map to the chapter, and the **Chapter Summary** repeats the questions and gives a brief answer to each based on chapter content.

> ▶▶ **What do I need to know about the place where I'll be speaking?**
> ▶▶ **What materials and equipment should I use?**
> ▶▶ **How long should I speak?**
> ▶▶ **Should I change my presentation for different occasions?**
> ▶▶ **What should I wear?**

▶▶ **TIPs** provide insider information drawn from the authors' extensive experience, such as "Never tell your audience that you're nervous," "Practice in bite-sized chunks," or "Present More Message and Less Information."

NEVER TELL AN AUDIENCE THAT YOU ARE NERVOUS

Some novice speakers take sharing a little too far—they figure that if friends will be supportive of their fears, most audiences will be, too. Unfortunately, sharing your anxieties with the audience tends to backfire. It only makes audience members more aware of your nervousness and makes you feel more self-conscious. Don't describe or discuss your speaking anxiety with your audience. Don't apologize before, during, or after your presentation. Don't tell your audience that you haven't prepared well enough. Don't burden them with all the problems you've had getting ready. If you are well prepared and have practiced your presentation, there won't be any need to apologize. Talk privately with your friends or instructor about presentation anxiety. Speak confidently to your audience.

USING A MICROPHONE

You may be thinking, "Well, if people can't hear me, why can't I just use a microphone to amplify my voice?" You can, but don't jump at every chance to use an amplification system. Most microphones don't reproduce a natural-sounding voice. Therefore, you may have to speak more slowly, articulate more clearly, and make sure that the system can accommodate changes in your volume. Microphones tend to be preset for one volume. If you speak too loudly, it may sound as though you are shouting at your audience. If you speak too softly, the "mike" may not pick up everything you say. An audience might forgive a few lost words under non-miked circumstances, but they will be less forgiving when you use a microphone, since they will expect to hear you very well.

Sometimes, though, a microphone is essential. An audience or a room may be so large that you won't be heard without one. Or you may find yourself in a situation where microphones have already been set up for each speaker. Regardless of how you end up in front of a microphone, make the most of the technology.

The trick is to go against your instincts. If you want to project a soft tone, speak closer to the microphone and lower your volume. Your voice will sound more intimate and will be able to convey subtle emotions. If you want to be more forceful, speak further away from the microphone and project your voice. This technique minimizes distortions and will make your presentation sound more powerful.

Familiarize yourself with the specific microphone you'll be using.

▶ If you can, test the mike ahead of time. Ask someone to sit at the back of the room and monitor your amplified voice. Can you speak at a normal volume, or do you need to be louder?

▶ Determine whether the microphone is sophisticated enough to capture your voice from various angles and distances or whether you'll need to keep your mouth close to it.

▶ Microphones work best when placed about five to ten inches from the speaker's mouth. If you are using a hand-held microphone, hold it below your mouth at chin level.

▶ If you are using a clip-on lavaliere microphone (wired or wireless), test it carefully. Once it's clipped on, it can be difficult to readjust.

▶ Focus on your audience, not on the microphone. Stay near the mike, but don't tap it, lean over it, keep readjusting it, or make the *p-p-p-p-p* "motorboat sound" as a test. Experienced speakers make all the adjustments they need during the first few seconds that they hear their own voices projected through an amplification system.

▶ When your microphone is well adjusted, and you're feeling comfortable, speak in a natural, conversational tone.

Sometimes the *p* sound comes popping through a microphone, particularly if you speak straight into it instead of at an angle. Adjusting the position of the microphone usually eliminates the popping sound. If you hear the painful squeal of sound system feedback, try moving away from the speakers; you may be too close to them. Last, keep in mind that a microphone will not only amplify your voice; it will also amplify other sounds—coughing, throat-clearing, the shuffling of papers, or the tapping of a pen.

Learn to avoid these common microphone problems, and you'll sound like a pro! Microphones can be a valuable tool once you learn how to use them effectively.

➡ **Mini-modules** provide step-by-step instruction on optional presentation techniques many books gloss over, such as "Conducting Audience Surveys," "Using a Microphone," or "Handling Hostile Questions."

➡ **Real World, Real Speakers** offer stories and examples from survey respondents, the authors, and professionals that show presentation principles and strategies in action.

REAL WORLD, REAL SPEAKERS

Rosa Vargas, Human Resources Manager for The Topps Company in New York City, was introduced to team presentations in graduate school. She wrote:

During my MBA studies, I was part of a team, and our purpose was to launch a new product to market. I feel that preparation and rehearsal are key to a successful team presentation. I was nervous in the beginning of our presentation (we presented to a panel of professors and students), but as the presentation progressed, I relaxed a bit. Our group had practiced, and I know this helped us give a more focused presentation.

Another respondent was less fortunate. She wrote that her work-based team presentation was unsuccessful because "people hadn't gotten together beforehand, and hence there was unnecessary repetition in the group presentation." Successful team presentations must be meticulously planned and practiced.

➡ Slides, modeled after presentation software, preview and summarize core principles and strategies covered in major sections.

PRINCIPLES OF PRESENTATION SPEAKING

Purpose

Audience

Logistics

Content

Organization

Credibility

Performance

---

and sentences. Speaking in a monotone limits your expressiveness. In English, we tend to use a rising inflection when we ask questions, express uncertainty, or stress a word or syllable.[9] We tend to use downward inflections at the ends of phrases and sentences or when we're depressed or under stress. "I can't cope anymore" would not end with a rising inflection unless you were doing a "Valley Girl" imitation, in which almost every statement would end on the upswing.[10]

Inflection both helps you to avoid having a monotone voice and allows you to emphasize an important or meaningful word or phrase. When you're speaking from a manuscript, we recommend that you underline words that should receive extra stress or emphasis. More often than not, varying pitch sets a word apart from the rest of a sentence. A single change in inflection can change the entire meaning of a sentence, as is illustrated in the following examples.

I was born in New Jersey.   (You, on the other hand, were born in Maryland.)

I **was** born in New Jersey.   (No doubt about it!)

I was **born** in New Jersey.   (So I know my way around.)

I was born in **New Jersey**.   (Not in New York.)

Inflection may not seem very important, since the resulting change in pitch can be a fraction of a note. Yet, like the effects of any strong spice in a recipe, a small rise or drop in inflection can change the entire meaning of a sentence or the quality of your voice. Inflection is a key ingredient in making your voice more interesting, exciting, emotional, and emphatic.

Fluency

Fluency is the ability to speak smoothly without tripping over words or pausing at awkward moments. Although an audience might not notice how fluent you are, they *will* notice when something interrupts the flow of your speech.

The more you practice your presentation, the more fluent you will become. Practice will alert you to words, phrases, and sentences that look good in your notes but sound awkward or choppy when spoken. You'll find out if you have included any words that you have trouble pronouncing. Practice lets you work on volume, rate, pitch, and articulation. With adequate practice, your voice will sound fluent.

Filler Phrases. Many people have the habit of using filler phrases, a very common fluency problem. Annoying filler phrases, you know, like a, okay, break up, um, your fluency and, uh, drive your audience, right, like crazy. Everyone knows how annoying and distracting it can be to listen to a presentation loaded with filler phrases. Who hasn't sat in the back of a classroom or auditorium and counted the number of times a speaker said, "You know" or "okay"? Unfortunately, most speakers don't even know they're doing it.

In addition to filler words and phrases such as "you know," "okay," "like," and "right," some speakers have their own personal phrases—"Got it?" "There!" "Yup," and the unwarranted giggle that appears when it absolutely shouldn't. It doesn't matter what the phrase is. It only matters that you become aware of how often you use it and then try to stop.

FAQ HOW DO I AVOID SAYING UM AND UH SO OFTEN? First, let's get one misconception out of the way about *ums* and *uhs*. Not all filler phrases are equally bad. There is nothing wrong with an occasional *uh* or *um*, particularly when you're speaking informally or impromptu. Even the most eloquent and experienced speakers may insert an occasional *uh* or *um* into their presentations to make themselves sound more natural and spontaneous. In fact, *um* seems to become part of our vocabulary before the age of three.

An *um* can mean that you're thinking about the way to phrase the next sentence or that you're searching for a word. In a presentation, it is perfectly okay to have a few of these short filler phrases—not three or four per sentence, but an occasional interruption that makes your speech sound natural and conversational. With worries about saying an occasional *uh* and *um* put aside, you can start eliminating some of your more annoying filler phrases as well as excessive use of *uh* and *um*.

Tape-record one of your practice sessions or an actual presentation and listen for filler phrases. Sometimes they appear only during your actual presentation, when you are most nervous and least aware of the extra phrases that can sneak into your speech. Then comes the hard part. In order to break the filler phrase habit, you must slow down and listen to yourself as you practice. At first, you will be less fluent, stopping at almost every phrase, correcting yourself. Monitor your performance and practice as well as your everyday speech. Filler phrases cannot be turned off at the beginning of a presentation and allowed to reappear afterwards. As in breaking any habit, going "cold turkey" requires saying *no* to filler phrases in *all* speaking situations.

Run-on Sentences. The second cousins of filler phrases are run-on sentences. Sometimes, because a speaker is nervous and is trying hard to maintain fluency, she or he may have a tendency to connect all sentences with *and* or *uh* and keep going, even though there may have been several natural places to stop and begin another sentence during the speech. Notice how the last sentence could have ended after *uh* but instead used the word *and* to keep going. In a few cases, student speakers have managed to utter a seven-minute sentence rather than give a seven-minute presentation.

As with breaking the filler phrase habit, you need to slow down and listen to yourself. Even better, tape-record your practice sessions and listen for run-on sentences. For practice purposes, write out a few sections of your presentation in manuscript form to make sure that your sentences are short. Practice those sections in order to get a feel for speaking in smaller units. Then apply that feeling to your entire presentation.

Clarity and Correctness

A strong, well-paced, optimally pitched voice that is also fluent and expressive may not be enough to ensure the successful delivery of a presentation. Clarity and correctness also matter. A million-dollar vocal instrument will have little value if you mumble and mispronounce words. Proper articulation and pronunciation are just as important as volume, rate, pitch, fluency, and inflection.

➡ **FAQs** (Frequently Asked Questions) provide short answers to some of the most commonly asked questions, such as "Can I fake charisma?," "What should I do with my hands?," or "What if I need more time to say something important?"

➡ **Web Site Screens** include screen shots and URLs for Web sites that may serve as an additional resource to help students understand communication strategies and master speaking skill

The Instructor's Resource Manual,

by Dianna Wynn and Isa Engleberg, can be adapted to a variety of course formats and teaching styles. The Instructor's Resource Manual includes the following elements:

▶ Sample **syllabi**

▶ Chapter-by-chapter **test bank** and **exercises**

▶ Ready-to-use **speaking assignments, writing assignments,** and **assessment instruments**

▶ Photo-ready **graphics** for use as transparencies or handouts

▶ **Guidelines** for using the manual

▶ Techniques for **videotaping** and **assessing** student presentations

Additional instructor's ancillaries include:

▶ A **Computerized Test Bank**, available in both PC and Mac formats, with all the testing items from the Resource Manual.

▶ A *PowerPoint* **Presentation Program**, including all the "Slides" from the text.

▶ A **Companion Web Site** includes links to all chapter screen shots, as well as research sites and exercises.

▶ **Student Speeches Videos** and the **Contemporary Great Speeches Video**, along with other video opportunities.

▶ **Blackboard and WebCT** Course Cartridges, which contain text-specific resources including lecture outlines, suggested classroom activities, and assignments.

Student resources include:

▶ The **Speech Preparation Workbook**, which contains activities and outline formats for the major presentations discussed in the textbook and assigned in the Instructor's Resource Manual.

▶ The **Multicultural Activities Workbook for the Public Speaking Classroom.**

▶ A student-focused **Companion Web Site** includes exercises and activities to further develop student skills, such as:

A Cyber Evaluation (ACE) online chapter quizzing, hot links to research sites, and links to all screen shots found in the text.

▶ The **Real Deal Upgrade CD** is a student study aid CD-ROM available for free with the text.

About the Authors

Dr. John Daly, Liddell Professor of Communication and TCB Professor of Management at the University of Texas-Austin, has won eight teaching awards while teaching for the University including the Distinguished Teaching Professor Award. He has published over 90 scholarly articles, edited two academic journals, and authored five academic textbooks. Dr. Daly has devoted his academic life to the field of communication and served as President of the National Communication Association in 1998 during which time he worked to enhance the credibility and visibility of communication nationwide. In addition to his academic work, Daly has been an active communication consultant with more than 300 public and private organizations.

Dr. Isa Engleberg is a Professor of Speech Communication at Prince George's Community College in Maryland where she serves as Vice President of Advancement and Planning. She has written two college textbooks and over three dozen articles on communication studies and higher education. In 1996, she was appointed as the first community college chairperson of the National Communication Association's Research Board, served three terms on the Legislative Council, and chaired the NCA's Community College Section. Engleberg was honored as the Outstanding Community College Educator by the NCA and won the highest honor granted by Prince George's Community College, the President's Medal.

Presentations in Everyday Life

Strategies for Effective Speaking

Presentations
in Everyday Life

Strategies for Effective Speaking

John A. Daly
University of Texas, Austin

Isa N. Engleberg
Prince George's Community College

Houghton Mifflin Company   Boston   New York

Executive Editor: George Hoffman
Sponsoring Editor: Adam Forrand
Associate Editor: Jennifer Wall
Basic Book Editor: Karla Paschkis
Senior Project Editor: Tamela Ambush
Senior Production/Design Coordinator: Jennifer Meyer Dare
Senior Manufacturing Coordinator: Marie Barnes
Marketing Manager: Stephanie Jones

Library of Congress Catalog Card Number: 00–104949

ISBN: 0–395–88819-0

2 3 4 5 6 7 8 9 - VH - 04 03 02 01

Brief TOC

Contents

FAQS

TiPS

Mini-Modules

Preface

For all of our adult lives, each of us has studied, taught, consulted, coached, and written about human communication. We enjoy speaking in front of groups and look forward to listening to good presentations. We remain in awe of people whose presentations have the power to inspire and inform. Great speakers move people and nations–they can change the world with their words.

We both became interested in communication in high school, when we competed on our respective schools' debate and public speaking teams. In college, we both discovered that we could continue to compete and even take classes in speech communication! We knew that learning to speak comfortably in front of groups was more than a competitive skill; it was a survival tool.

Whether we were speaking to classmates, professors, colleagues, friends, or the public, our speaking ability helped determine whether we achieved personal and career success, whether we were respected by those around us, and whether we were included in the social and political life of our community. By the time we entered graduate schools, our career paths were clear. Both of us became communication professors. John Daly now teaches communication at the University of Texas at Austin. Isa Engleberg is a vice president at Prince George's Community College in Largo, Maryland, where she holds the title of professor of speech communication.

We also find ourselves seeking opportunities outside the classroom to help people become better speakers. While most people don't make many presentations, the ones they do make are often critical to their personal and professional success. From our more than fifty combined years as communication instructors and speech coaches, we know that most people can become more effective presenters with study and practice.

Very simply, we wrote this book because we are passionate about the importance of good speaking. The challenge of helping speakers decide what to say and how to say it still excites and interests us. And it's something we want to share.

We Focus on Student and Speaker Needs

Presentations in Everyday Life: Strategies for Effective Speaking integrates the scholarship and theory of presentation speaking with the needs of today's diverse college students. Our research and writing have been guided by an overriding principle that asks, "What do speakers want and need to know?" Although we recognize that what speakers *want* ("I want to get rid of my nervousness") may not be what they *need* (to learn how to reduce and adjust to the natural consequences of presentation anxiety), we have honored their expressed concerns and provided practical, time-tested answers to their questions. At the same time, we have made a concerted effort to apply the best communication theory and research to practical strategies and skills.

Questions asked by students, colleagues, clients, and public speakers led us to pose a critical question to ourselves: What do real people want and need to know about presentation speaking? This question both inspired us to write this book and planted the seeds of the real-world approach we take to the subject of presentation speaking. We actualize our real-world focus in two significant ways. We explain *how* to use communication strategies and skills when making a presentation, and we respond to the needs of real-world speakers.

Emphasizing *How* to Speak. Unlike textbooks that primarily describe *what* to do when making a presentation, *Presentations in Everyday Life* teaches speakers *how* to do it. For example, rather than telling readers to make sure they speak loud enough, we explain *how* to increase volume, *how* to speak with or without a microphone, and *how* to adjust to different surroundings (see Chapter 14). Rather than just listing a variety of ways to organize an informative presentation, we explain *how* to select effective strategies for achieving a specific, informative purpose (see Chapter 17). Teaching speakers *how* goes well beyond *what* because it gives them a repertoire of communication strategies and skills that can be adapted to any speaking situation.

Surveying Real-World Speakers. Most students take a speech course for a semester, yet are real-world speakers for the rest of their lives. Understanding this reality, we teamed up with Houghton Mifflin to design, conduct, and analyze some non-traditional market research: We sent surveys to individuals from all walks of life who had bought books on speaking over the past year. We asked them what they wanted to learn about presentation speaking and which communication strategies and skills they relied on the most in their professional lives. We also asked them to volunteer stories about their successes and frustrations as presenters.

The results of this research were both predictable and surprising. For example, although respondents acknowledged concerns about their delivery skills and speech anxiety, they were much more interested in learning how to prepare substantive, engaging presentations. Their insights and needs helped us link communication scholarship to the real world of presentation speaking. The stories they shared provide an added dimension to the textbook. Not only do they give us genuine and often amusing examples, they also reveal a sophisticated appreciation of the importance and consequences of effective communication.

We Combine Tradition and Innovation

We fully recognize that like us, the majority of instructors who adopt this textbook have strong opinions about course content as well as tried-and-true teaching methods. We know that a textbook is no substitute for the professional mastery that comes from years of teaching. At the same time, we know that some instructors will be new to the teaching profession and that their choice of textbooks may influence their development into seasoned professionals. In order to serve the needs of both types of instructors, we have retained the content and logical sequence of topics that can be found in other textbooks while adding several innovative features.

Tradition. Like most other textbooks in the field, ours begins with an introduction to the basic principles of presentation speaking and moves through considerations of topic selection, audience analysis, supporting material, organization, delivery, and the application of communication principles to informative, persuasive, and special occasion presentations. Our chapters, however, are modular in design, providing instructors with the flexibility to make assignments that mix different chapters in different ways, depending on their goals.

As a way of focusing on *how* to speak and the needs of real-world speakers, we have split several traditional chapters into smaller units. For example, whereas other textbooks may devote only one or two chapters to delivery, our Part V includes four brief chapters. One focuses on preparation and practice, the second addresses vocal delivery, the third highlights physical delivery and adapting to mediated presentations, and the fourth explores developing and using presentation aids. The appearance of twenty-one chapters should neither alarm instructors nor hinder instruction. Well-established course competencies and teaching techniques will work just as well with these smaller, more precise chapters. Our modular approach also enables us to cover the traditional topics and simultaneously provide a "home" and focus for materials that are missing from or randomly scattered throughout other textbooks.

Innovation. In addition to including traditional content, several innovations demonstrate our *how* focus for real-world speakers. For example,

- We emphasize *presentation* speaking rather than public speaking. As we see it, presentation speaking is a broader term that refers to any time a speaker generates meaning and establishes relationships with audience members. Public speaking more narrowly focuses on less common, more formal speeches delivered to *public* audiences in *public* settings.

- We develop a Dynamic Presentation Model that focuses on the realities of real-world presentation speaking. Chapter 1 introduces the seven basic encoding principles of the model, which are reinforced throughout the textbook and applied to all types of presentations.

- In Chapter 2, "Critical Thinking and Listening," we both link these skills to one another and demonstrate their applicability to speakers and listeners alike.

- In Chapter 3, "Building Presentation Confidence," we rely on current research in communication apprehension to help students understand and deal with presentation anxiety.

- In a special section of Chapter 9, "Organizational Tools," we present alternative methods (beyond outlining) for discovering and organizing the key points and supporting material in a presentation.

- At the center of the textbook, Chapter 11, "Speaker Credibility and Ethics," connects these concepts to one another and to the basic principles of presentation speaking.

- Chapter 12, "Generating Interest," was created in response to the number one concern of our survey respondents: "How can I make my speeches more interesting?" This unique, pivotal chapter focuses on the effective use of language, stories, humor, and audience participation and serves as a bridge to the applied chapters in the remainder of the book.

- In Chapter 17, "Developing Informative Presentations," we recommend rhetorical strategies for informative speaking based on matching audience analysis with appropriate organizational patterns, supporting material, and explanatory techniques.

- In Chapters 18 and 19, we cover theoretical and practical approaches to persuasion, including clear explanations of critical theories and how they can be applied to everyday examples of persuasive communication.

- We include a final chapter, "Speaking in Groups," that applies the textbook's basic encoding principles to public groups, teams, and working groups.

Our Pedagogy Keeps the Focus on the Real World

To help readers understand and master materials presented in this textbook, we have developed special pedagogical features that reflect our teaching styles and professional expertise. The questions that open each chapter and those that appear in the Frequently Asked Questions (FAQs) features emerged from recurring questions we have been asked by our students, survey respondents, and real-world speakers. The TIPs reflect "trade secrets" and "insider information" we share with our students and clients. All of these features help students master the content because they are based on many years of successful teaching, scholarly research, and personal experiences. We know these features work because we have used them to great advantage with thousands of speakers.

- **Opening Questions.** Every chapter opens with a set of questions commonly asked by students, instructors, and/or survey respondents. The chapter content answers these questions and the end-of-chapter summaries repeat them, this time with brief answers based on the chapter's content.

- **FAQs (Frequently Asked Questions).** We provide short answers to frequently asked questions such as "How many key points should I include?" (Chapter 9), "How do I avoid saying *um* and *uh* so often?" (Chapter 14), "What should I do with my hands?" (Chapter 15), and "How do I find common ground?" (Chapter 18).

- **TIPs.** Advisory paragraphs provide "insider information," cautionary notes, or reminders, such as "Never tell an audience that you are nervous" (Chapter 3), "Appeal to varied learning styles" (Chapter 16), and "Evidence can change attitudes" (Chapter 19). TIPs provide sound advice in an encouraging tone.

- **Real World, Real Speakers.** Real-world stories told by respondents to our survey, the authors, students, and fellow speakers appear throughout the text to illustrate communication principles and strategies. The stories also reinforce the power of narratives as a rhetorical device and capture the tone and perspectives of our storytellers.

- **Mini-Modules.** Most chapters include a Mini-Module, a brief, boxed discussion of an optional technique often ignored by other textbooks, such as "Interviewing for Information" (Chapter 7), "Telling Stories" (Chapter 12), "Using a Microphone" (Chapter 14), and "Handling Hostile Questions" (Chapter 20).

- **Slides.** Every chapter includes several summary and preview lists of core principles and strategies, such as "Top-Ranked Speaking Skills" (Chapter 1), "A Purpose Statement Should Be . . ." (Chapter 4), "Tests of Supporting Material" (Chapter 7), and "Benefits of Eye Contact" (Chapter 15). These are also available as downloadable PowerPoint slides from the companion Web site.

- **Web Site Screens.** Screen shots and URLs for Web sites such as www.gallup.com (Chapter 5), www.libraryspot.com (Chapter 12), www.clipart.com (Chapter 16), and www.intellectualcapital.com (Chapter 18) provide an added resource to help students understand communication strategies and master speaking skills such as audience adaptation, researching supporting material, using presentation aids, and analyzing arguments.

We Support Varied Learning Styles

We took on the challenge of adapting our textbook to the varied learning styles of our readers. We know, for example, that some students learn better by reading about the principles and strategies of good speaking. Others need real-world examples to demonstrate the principles in action. Some learners always pose questions that must be answered before they can master a skill.

We have tried to practice what we preach about audience adaptation:

- For students who learn best by reading about communication principles, we offer detailed explanations of both theories and speaking strategies, supported by multiple examples.

- For those experiential learners who need to see principles in action, we have included many excerpts from student and real-world presentations throughout the textbook and seven complete presentations in Appendix A.

- For learners with a visual orientation, we have included summary and preview slides, charts, tables, photographs, diagrams, drawings, Web site screens, and highlighted FAQs and TIPs.

And to keep all of our readers interested and engaged, we have included scenarios, dialogues, outlines, real-world stories, Mini-Modules, and short questionnaires written in clear, vivid language and even with a sense of humor. These strategies, which we also recommend in Chapter 12 for generating interest, are more than good writing principles. They help us capture reader attention and ultimately enhance interest, understanding, and learning.

We Offer a Complete Package for Instructors and Students

By enlisting the resources of our publisher, we provide a full range of ancillary materials for both instructors and students.

The comprehensive **Instructor's Resource Manual,** by Dianna Wynn and Isa N. Engleberg, can be adapted to a variety of course formats and teaching styles. Features that often appear at the end of textbook chapters are included in the manual. Our rationale for moving this information to the manual is twofold. First, many end-of-chapter features are not used by instructors or students. We would rather devote our space to chapter content and let instructors decide which features to include or use in class. Second, many end-of-chapter features (instruments, exercises, evaluation forms) are difficult to use in class because they are part of the textbook. By putting these features in photo-ready form in the manual (and providing textbook adopters with an easy-to-modify computer disk), we enable instructors to adapt and use the material more easily. They also can decide which resources best meet the needs of a particular class. The Instructor's Resource Manual includes the following elements:

- Sample **syllabi**

- A chapter-by-chapter **test bank** of objective and essay questions

- Ready-to-use **speaking assignments** for every chapter

- Ready-to-use **writing assignments** for every chapter

- Ready-to-use **assessment instruments,** including presentation evaluation forms, student feedback forms, and self-evaluation forms

- Chapter-by-chapter **exercises** with accompanying teaching tips

- Photo-ready **graphics** for use as transparencies or handouts

- **Guidelines** for using the manual and its pedagogical features

- Techniques for **videotaping** and assessing student presentations

Other instructor's ancillaries include:

- A **Computerized Test Bank**, available in both PC and Mac formats, includes all the test items from the Instructor's Resource Manual.

- A ***PowerPoint* Presentation Program** includes all the "Slides" from the text in addition to other downloadable assets.

- A **Companion Web Site** includes links to all screen shots shown within the chapters, as well as research sites, exercises, the "Slides," and other ancillary materials for instructors and students alike.

- A **Contemporary Great Speeches Video** and a compilation of **Student Speech Videos**, in addition to other video opportunities, are available to textbook adopters. Ask your Houghton Mifflin representative for details.

- **Blackboard and WebCT** Course Cartridges, which contain text-specific resources including lecture outlines, suggested classroom activities, and assignments.

Student resources:

- The **Speech Preparation Workbook** contains activities and skeleton outline formats for the major presentations discussed in the textbook and assigned in the Instructor's Resource Manual.

- The **Multicultural Activities Workbook for the Public Speaking Classroom**.

- A student-focused **Companion Web Site** includes exercises and activities to further develop student skills, such as **A Cyber Evaluation (ACE)** online chapter quizzing, hot links to research sites, and links to all screen shots found in the text.

- The **Real Deal Upgrade CD** is a student study aid CD-ROM available for free with the text.

Acknowledgments

We extend our sincere appreciation to the following reviewers, whose excellent suggestions and comments helped shape the final form of *Presentations in Everyday Life*:

Tim Borchers, *Moorhead State University;* Harold Borden, *El Camino College;* Audrey Boxman, *Merrimack College;* R. D. Britton, *Suffolk Community College;* Jeff Butler, *University of Central Florida;* Lori A. Byers, *Spalding University;* Robert E. Gwynne, *University of Tennessee—Knoxville;* David S. Hopcroft, *Quinebaug Valley Community Technical College;* Kimberly Howard, *Walla Walla College;* Karen Huck, *Central Oregon Community College;* Richard Ice, *St. John's University;* Charles J. Korn, *Northern Virginia Community College—Manassas;* Rick Maxson, *Tennessee Technical University;* Janette Kenner Muir, *George Mason University;* Terri Reherman, *San Juan College;* Kellie W. Roberts, *University of Florida;* Cameron Smith, *Community College of Southern Nevada;* Glynnis Holm Strause, *Coastal Bend College (formerly Bee County College);* Jennifer Van Kirk, *University of Illinois at Urbana-Champaign;* Karin A. Wilking, *Rochester Community and Technical College;* Dianna Wynn, *Midland College.*

Although the title page of this book puts our names front and center, the project would never have seen the light of day without the work of a special trio of professionals: George Hoffman, Karla Paschkis, and Dianna Wynn. George, our sponsoring editor, helped us transform a bare-bones vision into a fully realized textbook. We also thank George for delivering us into the capable hands of Adam Forrand, who took the helm of this project when George was promoted—quite deservedly, we would add—to Executive Editor, Business and Communication. We bless the day Karla Paschkis became our developmental editor. Her good humor, professionalism, common sense, and genius helped us improve our ragtag manuscript. Rounding out the invincible trio is Dianna Wynn, a colleague and speech communication instructor at Midland College in Texas, who did more than her share as a reviewer while co-authoring the excellent Instructor's Resource Manual that accompanies this textbook.

If it takes a village to raise a child, it takes a team of publishing professionals to create a textbook. We extend heartfelt thanks to Walter Cunningham, Pamela Laskey, Stephanie Jones, Jennifer Wall, Henry Rachlin, Ann Schroeder, Jennifer Meyer Dare, Tamela Ambush, and Sarah Godshall, whose contributions in researching, marketing, designing, photo researching, art development, and production personified the principle of group synergy. We also thank Houghton Mifflin's College Division president, June Smith, for making a major commitment to us by delegating such exceptional talent to this project.

John A. Daly

Isa N. Engleberg

THE BASICS

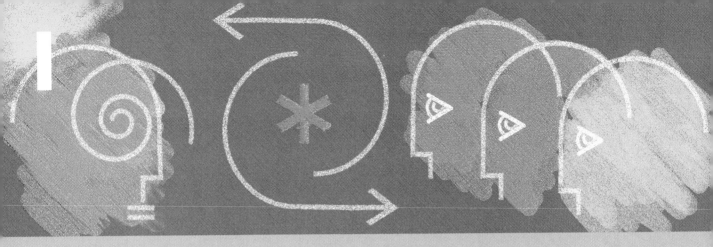

Presentation Speaking

- ▶▶ What do real-world speakers want to know about presentation speaking?
- ▶▶ What's the difference between a presentation and a public speech?
- ▶▶ What basic principles underlie all types of presentation speaking?
- ▶▶ How do speakers and listeners work together to communicate?
- ▶▶ How can a theory make me a better speaker?

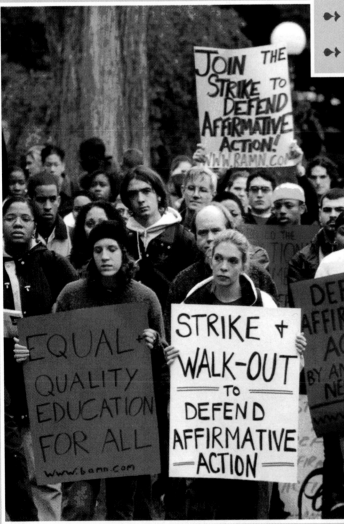

There are dozens of public and presentation speaking books on the shelves of most retail bookstores. Some of their titles are practical—*Speaking Your Way to the Top, Writing Great Speeches, High-Impact Presentations.* Other titles are somewhat bizarre—*I Can See You Naked, I'd Rather Die than Give a Speech,* and *What to Say When You're Dying on the Platform.* Both types of titles provide some insight into their topics. The practical titles presume a compelling need for presentation speaking skills in business and career settings. The "weird" titles tap into the underlying anxiety that often accompanies the prospect of having to speak in front of an audience. Both sets of titles have merit. Most people will have to make presentations, even though making them can create anxiety.

By calling our book *Presentations in Everyday Life: Strategies for Effective Speaking,* we are placing it squarely in the practical category. Our subtitle—*Strategies for*

Effective Speaking—indicates that being an effective speaker requires strategic decision making about everything from organizing your content to developing a strong and clear speaking voice. To become an effective speaker, you must go well beyond the books that offer "secrets," "tips," "checklists," and "recipes for success." We believe that effective communication—be it between two people or in front of thousands—requires an understanding of communication theory and research. To that end, we dedicate ourselves to backing up our advice with that of the best communication scholars and researchers we know. *Presentations in Everyday Life* does more than offer advice about *what* to do when you have to speak—it explains *how* to speak and *why* the advice works.

The Real World of Presentation Speaking

What do real people want to know about presentation speaking? This question prompted us to write this textbook. In cooperation with the Market Research Department of our publishers, Houghton Mifflin Company, we designed and conducted a national survey aimed at answering this question. Instead of surveying faculty or students, we sent a questionnaire to people at business addresses who had bought one or more commercially available books on public speaking within a one-year period. We wanted to learn which topics were most important to consumers beyond the college classroom. After all, you may be a student speaker for only one brief semester—and a "real-world" speaker for the rest of your life!

Our questionnaire included a checklist and one open-ended question: "Can you tell us about a situation in which you had to prepare and deliver a speech or presentation and why you think it was successful or unsuccessful?" The respondents' answers are gems. We have stories about speaking triumphs and disappointments. People shared their "secrets" of good speaking as well as their anxieties. We discovered that even the most experienced and successful speakers are still looking for ways to improve. You will find some of these real-life stories throughout this book and, we hope, will identify with the challenges these speakers faced and learn from the ways in which they met those challenges.

What Matters to Our Real-World Speakers

Without going into significant detail, we would like to share a few notable results from our survey. But please do not draw any broad conclusions. Remember that this survey was sent to a specific type of audience—working professionals who had purchased a book on public speaking during a one-year period. And as with any other opinion survey, there are no "right" answers. Rather, our results give a rough sketch of what motivated book buyers wanted to learn about becoming better speakers.

What do you think mattered most to our book buyers? The top six concerns are listed to the right.

Many students enter public speaking classes filled with anxiety, and if you're one of them, you may wonder why overcoming nervousness didn't make the top of the list. We wondered, too, but figured it out when we analyzed our results. Our respondents reported that they *do* feel anxious but have learned to compensate for or mask their anxiety

TOP-RANKED SPEAKING SKILLS

1. **Keeping your audience interested**
2. **Beginning and ending your presentation**
3. **Organizing your presentation**
4. **Selecting ideas and information for your presentation**
5. **Deciding what to say (choosing a topic or an approach)**
6. **Understanding and adapting to your audience**

by being well prepared. In this light, the lower rating for speaking anxiety is understandable. Learning *how* to speak was more important to our group of book buyers than overcoming anxiety. And as we'll see in Chapter 3, "Building Presentation Confidence," becoming a skilled speaker is actually one of the more effective means of reducing nervousness.

We drew one more conclusion from analyzing the results of our survey and thinking about our own students' needs. Regardless of his or her level of speaking experience and ability, everyone has questions about how to become a better speaker. Sometimes the questions are enormous in scope: Where do I start? Sometimes they're very specific: What should I do with my hands when I speak? Because the answers to questions like these can make a big difference in a presentation's outcome, we have structured the entire book around asking the questions our students ask us most often and exploring their answers.

Why Speaking Skills Matter to You

A few years ago, an article appeared in the *New York Times*[1] with the headline "Meek and Mumblers Learn Ways of Getting a Word In." The article describes how more and more people are devoting time, money, and energy to improving their speaking skills. Why? The article's examples demonstrate how important presentation speaking has become for achieving personal and career success.

▶ One 14-week public speaking course offered by Dale Carnegie & Associates, Inc., attracted 117,000 students and garnered $100 million in revenue.

▶ Toastmasters International, the best-known nonprofit organization whose mission is to improve public speaking, has enjoyed a 7 percent annual increase in membership for the last decade.

▶ An estimated 45 percent of all medium and large corporations provide some public speaking training for their employees.

▶ Corporate clients can pay up to $3,000 per day for one-on-one instruction and $15,000 for group lessons in public speaking.

▶ Special medical clinics offer 16-week treatments for presentation anxiety, that can cost $800 to $2000 per person.

Speech training has become a big business for good reasons. Real people in the real world give real presentations. In fact, despite and because of our increased interaction with technology and media, we have more opportunities to speak today than we had only a decade ago. In the introduction to her book *Simply Speaking*, Peggy Noonan, who was one of President Ronald Reagan's speechwriters, notes:

The changes that have swept modern businesses have contributed to a talking boom. As more and more businesses become involved in the new media technologies, as we become a nation of fewer widgets and more Web sites, a new premium has been put on the oldest form of communication: the ability to stand up and say what you think in front of others. At the business conference, in the teleconference and the seminar, businessmen and businesswomen are increasingly called on to speak about their industry, their plans, the realities within which they operate, what govern-

TIP GET THE MOST OUT OF YOUR PRESENTATION There is more to a presentation than meets the eye (and ear) of your audience. Since you *will* have to speak, why not take full advantage of the opportunity? In addition to sharing a message, presentations are a way to stand out personally. Robert Pike, a communication consultant and trainer, puts it this way: "We live in a competitive world. An effective presentation allows you, as well as your knowledge, talent, and abilities, to stand out from the rest of the crowd."[1] He also says, "How you [give presentations] will either raise or lower your credibility and make a difference in your ability to influence others."[2]

1. Robert W. Pike, *High-Impact Presentations* (West Des Moines, IA: American Media, 1995), p. 9.
2. Pike, p. 8.

Bobby Drozek, a student at Marlboro College in Vermont, argues for the installation of cable television at a monthly town meeting where students and faculty each have a vote.

ment is doing or not doing to make things better or worse. And they're not alone. Teachers and professors and reporters and doctors are out there too.[2]

In short, no matter what your current or future profession may be, it will most likely require you to make presentations. Thus, learning to become an effective presenter is a wise personal investment.[3] Since you *will* give presentations, be prepared to do them well—and use them as a professional development tool.

What Is Presentation Speaking?

Perhaps you are sitting in a college course titled Public Speaking and wondering why we've been talking so much about *presentation* speaking. We chose this term deliberately because we believe that *presentation speaking* is a broader, more inclusive term than *public speaking*. The key word here is *public*.

The American Heritage Dictionary of the English Language defines *public* as "of, concerning, or affecting the community or the people; participated in or attended by the people or a community; connected with or acting on behalf of the people, community, or government." In brief, the word *public* refers to the "community or people as a whole."[4] When you hear the term *public* or *public audience*, what do you envision? A staff meeting? Probably not. You probably see a lone figure standing on a stage facing a large audience. Now, what do you think of when you hear the term *presentation* or *presentation speaking*? A political rally? Probably not. You probably see a professional person addressing a group of colleagues in a meeting or someone talking to an informal group of interested listeners.

As we see it, **public speaking** is a special type of presentation speaking that occurs when speakers address public audiences in community, government, and/or organizational settings. Public speeches are usually open and accessible to the public and press and have the potential, if not the purpose, of affecting people beyond the immediate audience. **Presentation speaking** is a broader term and refers to *any* time speakers use verbal and nonverbal messages to generate meanings and establish relationships with audience members, who are usually present at the delivery of a presentation.[5] We prefer the term *presentation speaking* for three reasons:

> ## PRESENTATIONS
> - **Are more common than public speeches**
> - **Are less formal than public speeches**
> - **Are more important to employers**

Presentations Are More Common

Most of you will make many presentations but few public speeches. Your presentations will *not* be directed to the community or to "people as a whole." Of course, there are exceptions. If you decide to run for office or to become active in community issues, you will have to speak in front of public audiences. If you become famous—as either an expert or a celebrity—you will be invited to make public speeches. But in general, you are much more likely to be asked to make a presentation in smaller, private settings.

As we've indicated, *presentation speaking* is a broad term. It encompasses everything from small, intimate talks in private settings to major speeches in front of large public audiences. By using the broader term, we can cover more kinds of speaking situations and still zero in on the kinds of presentations you will be asked to make.

Presentations Are Less Formal

Generally, a public speech is more formal than a private presentation. Usually, presentations are delivered from notes rather than written out and delivered word for word. Given the workplace setting of most presentations, you are also more likely to use visual aids during a presentation. And although some politicians and public figures are increasing their use of visual aids, most public speakers go solo.

Presentations usually allow and even encourage more interaction between the speaker and the audience. Both the speaker and the audience members may question each other. There may even be a brief pause for a discussion among listeners. On the other hand, in public speaking, the speaker speaks, the audience listens, and questions come only after the speech is finished.[6]

Presentations Are More Important to Employers

In 1997, the Business–Higher Education Forum, in affiliation with the American Council on Education, conducted a study in which employers were asked how best to prepare college students for the world of work. The subsequent report placed (oral) communication skills at the top of the list.[7] In 2000, the National Association of Colleges and Employers conducted a survey in which employers were asked to rank, in order of importance, a list of ten skills they seek in college graduates. The results: oral communication skills were first on the list.[8]

Businesses need good presenters, not public orators. When employers are asked about the skills they are looking for in new employees, *public* speaking is not at the top of their lists. What does emerge, however, is a clear preference for communication skills, including the ability to present ideas and information to colleagues and clients. In fact, most business settings use the term *presentations* rather than *public speaking*. When we work as consultants, we are never asked to prepare a public speaking seminar. Instead, we are asked to provide training sessions that focus on presentation skills. The titles of many popular books on speaking also reflect this business orientation: The American Management Association publishes *How to Prepare, Stage & Deliver Winning Presentations*. Career Press publishes *Secrets of Power Presentations*. Robert W. Pike, a nationally recognized communication trainer, is the author of *High-Impact Presentations*.[9]

Chita Roa-Marquez, a nurse from New Jersey, understands the difference between presentation speaking and public speaking. In her response to our survey, she wrote: "As a nurse supervisor by profession, I make a lot of presentations (about new procedures, trends, and in-service training). As founding president of a nonprofit organization, I do a lot of public speaking (welcoming addresses, keynote speeches, or being the mistress of ceremonies at a public event)."

Other Forms of Communication

Presentation speaking is only one way to communicate with an audience. You can also reach an audience by writing articles for newspapers, creating advertisements for electronic and print media, producing films, sending messages to a listserv, recording music, and writing and distributing memos to colleagues at work. We see and hear hundreds of communications every day. We read the newspapers with our morning coffee, we listen to the car radio on the way to work or school, we read reports and memos at work, and we watch many hours of television.

What makes presentation speaking different from other forms of communication? The presence of a speaker makes it different—a real and usually visible person who is responsible for creating and delivering the message. Even an official spokesperson who represents a company or a government agency is still a single person who must speak and adapt to an audience. The speaker is as important as the message. What a speaker says is directly affected by who the speaker is and how she or he communicates. Effective presentations require strategic decision-making, serious preparation, and skilled delivery.

Speaking and Writing.   Writing for readers is not the same as speaking to an audience. The major difference is that a reader can go back and reread a written message, whereas an audience member cannot go back and rehear a presentation unless it has been taped or distributed in written form. In most speaking situations, a listener is required to "get the message" as it is spoken. Once it's out of the speaker's mouth, it's gone. You must consider this unique "now you hear it; now you don't" quality of presentation speaking in every decision you make about a presentation. If you load your talk with technical details, your audience may struggle to understand what you are saying. If you use long, complicated sentences, you run the risk of losing the audience's attention and interest. If you speak too softly or too fast, your audience cannot turn up the volume or reduce your speed as you speak. Your decisions must take into account the fact that a presentation is a one-shot opportunity to inform or influence an audience.

Writing for readers and speaking to an audience require different skills. Certainly, good writing can help you to become a good speaker. Good speakers often are good writers. The key is knowing what *kind* of writing is best for readers and what kind is best for speaking. How many times have you sat through a long and

REAL WORLD, REAL SPEAKERS

I once worked for a man who seemed to have two personalities—one for conversations and one for presentations. His conversational speaking style was very friendly and relaxed, with a great sense of humor. Colleagues looked forward to talking with him because he made them feel so comfortable. You were his equal in all discussions. Everyone thought he was a great boss. His presentation speaking style, however, was totally different. He'd get up in front of a group, and his voice would go down in pitch. He'd use lots of technical terms. He'd become stiff and formal. He'd even research jokes to tell. Although he had strong interpersonal communication skills, he was an awful speaker. He didn't seem like himself. He put people off. Even his jokes were bad. Only those who worked with him knew this wasn't what he was really like. Unfortunately, he lost several top management jobs because he came across as cold and technical when speaking in front of groups. It's too bad he didn't trust using the conversational speaking style that everyone knew and liked.

Isa Engleberg

boring presentation that was little more than someone reading a written report? The speaker would have been better off giving everyone a copy of the report and letting the audience read it silently.

Presentation Speaking and Conversational Speaking.   People who spend hours talking to their friends, family members, and coworkers often freeze up when they're asked to give a five-minute presentation. A manager who can drop in on a colleague to discuss a new project may panic when asked to give a talk explaining that project to a group of vice presidents. A neighbor who complains about the condition of the street may back off when asked to describe those conditions at the weekly city council meeting. Why is it that we treat presentation speaking and conversational speaking so differently? We devote Chapter 3 to one reason—presentation anxiety. Fear of speaking in front of groups can turn ordinarily confident people into nervous wrecks.

There is, however, another reason why people regard presentation speaking and conversational speaking as different forms of communication. A lot of people think that presentation speaking requires a very different kind of speech—different vocabulary, a different way of talking, different physical behavior. Experienced speakers know that using a conversational speaking style can create a friendly atmosphere in which audience members are comfortable and motivated to listen. We will see in Chapter 12, "Generating Interest," that choosing the style and language that best suit your audience is a critical part of presentation speaking. In general, effective speakers rely on words that are simple, short, and direct rather than on the more formal language used in a term paper or business report.

You don't have to become a different person when you speak in front of an audience. However, that doesn't mean you should use exactly the same style for both conversational and presentation speaking. There are some differences. For a presentation, you should make sure that you are speaking loudly enough to be heard. You should also spend more time preparing. At the same time, don't give up a speaking style that has worked for you for years in most other communication situations. Trust yourself and let your personality be an important part of your speaking style.

CHOOSING THE BEST FORM FOR YOUR MESSAGE

Before you begin to prepare a presentation, you need to make your first and most basic decision: Should you speak or should you write? Presentations are more appropriate in some situations than in others. In your opinion, which form of communication would be more effective for each of the messages listed below?

	Speaking	Writing
Describe how to assemble a bicycle.	_____	_____
Warn preteens about the long-lasting effects of drug abuse.	_____	_____
Convince your teacher to change your grade.	_____	_____
Complain about a defective product to a company.	_____	_____
Share a recipe for lemon poppy-seed pound cake.	_____	_____
Explain how to repair a broken light switch.	_____	_____
Persuade nonvoting friends to vote.	_____	_____
Coax a frightened speaker to speak.	_____	_____
Teach someone how to meditate.	_____	_____

What do the topics that lend themselves to speaking have in common? What about the topics that lend themselves to writing? Can you definitely say that one form is always better than another for certain messages or kinds of topics?

The following questions can help you decide whether a presentation is the best or only way to convey your message:

▶ *Is a presentation requested or required?* You may be asked to address a graduating class, present a report at a staff meeting, offer a toast at a wedding, or introduce a guest speaker. In such cases, not only does the nature of the event require a presentation, the audience also expects certain qualities in the presentation—inspiration for a commencement speech, clarity and brevity in a report, good cheer at a wedding, and background information about a guest speaker.

▶ *Is immediate action needed?* If an unexpected problem arises, there may not be time to write a memo or publish a report. If an audience must be made aware of a problem in order to take immediate action, a presentation may be the best way to respond. If a crisis requires that everyone be told about a situation as quickly as possible, a presentation would be much more effective than a written report.

▶ *Is the topic controversial?* Confronting a controversy in person can often produce better results than trying to deal with the problem in writing. A face-to-face situation gives a speaker the opportunity to explain the problem and correct misunderstandings as they arise. Audience members can listen, ask questions, and challenge ideas. Although this kind of speaking can be difficult and even intimidating, audiences would prefer to hear about most controversies from a speaker. The exceptions are topics that can be too upsetting to discuss before a large audience, such as news about a personal tragedy or announcements about budget cuts. In these cases, written messages or one-to-one conversations can soften the blow.

▶ *Will the audience have questions?* Any subject, whether it's controversial or not, may prompt audience questions. A new or complex procedure may best be introduced in a presentation that encourages audience questions and comments. In a controversial or emergency situation, answering audience questions may be the most important part of a presentation. A presidential press conference, for example, may begin with a short statement about a new or ongoing crisis and be followed by the many and varied questions of the White House press corps.

▶ *Will YOU make a difference?* It is difficult to ignore someone talking to you face to face. It is much easier to ignore an email, a memo, or a report. The emotion in a speaker's voice and the physical energy of a presentation are difficult to capture in a written message. Audiences know that you're taking a bigger risk when you put yourself and your message in front of them rather than communicate through the safety and distance of a written message. A presentation can be the most effective form of communication simply because *you are there.* Your willingness to "put yourself on the line" makes your message more personal and important. The more your message depends on you, the more you need a presentation.

Basic Principles of Presentation Speaking

At the heart of this textbook is a decision-making system based on a few carefully chosen communication principles. These principles can help you make critical decisions about your presentation from the minute you find out you will have to speak to the minute you've said your last word. By applying these principles, you should be able to make effective decisions about what to say, be able to explain the reasons why your decisions make sense, and be able to evaluate your decisions by assessing the success of your presentation.

The Seven Principles

The basic principles of presentation speaking include seven decision-making points that encourage critical thinking. We have selected a single word to represent each principle. Are the principles represented by these seven words all you need to know about effective speaking? No. As you can see from the upcoming chapter headings, we cover many more than seven topics in this textbook. The seven principles, however, represent the most basic decisions you will have to make when preparing and delivering a successful presentation. Each principle answers key questions about presentation speaking.

> **PRINCIPLES OF PRESENTATION SPEAKING**
>
> Purpose
> Audience
> Logistics
> Content
> Organization
> Credibility
> Performance

Purpose: Why are you speaking?   When determining the purpose of your presentation, ask yourself these questions: What do I want my audience to know, think, believe, or do as a result of my presentation? Given my purpose, how do I focus and narrow my topic?

Audience: Who is in your audience?   To understand your audience, ask yourself: How do the characteristics of my audience—such as demographics, interests, and attitudes—affect my purpose? How can I learn more about my audience? In what ways can I adapt to my audience in order to improve my presentation?

Logistics: Where and when will you speak?   When considering the location and occasion of a presentation, ask yourself: Why am I speaking to this group at this time in this place? How can I plan for and adapt to the logistics of the place where I will be speaking? Does the occasion require special adaptations?

Content: What ideas and information should you include?   When searching for and selecting materials for your presentation, ask yourself: Where and how can I find good ideas and information for my presentation? How much and what kind of supporting material do I need? Have I found the best sources? Which ideas and information should I include?

When Secretary of State Madeleine Albright testifies, her credibility enhances her effectiveness.

Organization: How should you arrange your content?   When organizing your presentation, ask yourself: Is there a natural order to the ideas and information I want to include in my presentation? What are the most effective ways to organize my presentation in order to adapt it to my purpose, audience, logistics, and content? How should I begin and end my presentation? How do I link its major sections?

Credibility: Are you believable?   Presentations can enhance your credibility. Ask yourself: How can I become associated with my message in a positive way? What can I do to demonstrate my expertise on this topic? What will assure the audience that I am worthy of their trust? Am I an ethical speaker?

Performance: How should you deliver your presentation?   Asking yourself questions about delivery before you get up to speak can improve the quality of your performance. Ask yourself: What form of delivery is appropriate for my purpose, audience, and setting? What delivery techniques will make my presentation more effective? How much and what should I practice?

Applying the Seven Principles

The answers to these questions are more than a "To Do" list for effective speaking. Each principle affects the others. For example, even the best-organized presentation won't achieve its purpose if it offends the audience or uses words they don't understand. Likewise, a flawlessly prepared but poorly delivered presentation may not capture its audience's attention. Any decision made about one principle will have an impact on the others.

Moreover, later decisions can affect earlier ones. If, while practicing your presentation, you discover that you've gone far over the time limit, you should go back and reduce the amount of information in your presentation or cut some of the key points. If you can't find the information you need, or if your research doesn't prove the point you want to make, you may need to modify or change your purpose.

How Communication Works

The seven principles of presentation speaking work for a reason: They have emerged from centuries of studying what communication is and how it functions. These definitions and functions can be expressed in **communication models,** which identify and name the steps or components involved in the communication process. Models also show how these components relate to and interact with each other. And they can help explain why a communication did or did not achieve its intended purpose—or even predict whether or not it will.[10]

How do these models characterize the interaction between speakers and listeners? They begin with a **message,** the content of the presentation itself. As the **source** of that message, the speaker **encodes** it with specific words and actions and then sends that message out into the world. The **channel** is the medium (sight and sound) through which the message travels. The message, though, doesn't really mean anything until it arrives at a **receiver,** a person who **decodes** the message and decides what it means.

The speaker (source) and the audience (receiver) rely on each other to give messages their meaning. Communication is not a one-way street. Rather, it is a transaction between a speaker and one or more listeners. In a business transaction, we exchange money for goods. In a **communication transaction,** we exchange messages in order to share meaning.

Finally, all communication takes place in a **context**—a surrounding environment that can affect every aspect of the communication process. Context can be physical—the size of a room, the lighting, the attractiveness or comfort of the setting. Context can also be psychological—the mood of the audience, the temperament of the speaker, the unsettling effects of a recent event. All presentations occur in a certain setting at a certain time under certain conditions. All of these factors contribute to a context that affects how we speak and listen to one another.

The Dynamic Presentation Model

In the same way that communication models represent the interaction between communicators, a model of presentation speaking that we have developed reflects the dynamic relationship between your presentation and your audience. We use the word *dynamic* to signify the fact that presentation speaking is a complex, compelling, and even chaotic process. During a presentation, many things happen at once. Figure 1.1 "freezes" a presentation to illustrate our model's interacting components.

The Presentation.   Let's start with the left "wheel," representing a speaker's presentation. At the center or hub of the wheel is the first and most important decision-making point: determining the purpose of your presentation. All subsequent decisions you make will connect to and revolve around this point. The spokes on the wheel represent the remaining six principles.

Purpose should guide the ways in which you adapt to your audience and to the logistics of your presentation. Purpose likewise should influence your decisions about gathering, selecting, and organizing the ideas and information you will include in that presentation. All the "purposeful" choices you make in the planning stages in turn will affect your decisions about how to present yourself as a credible source and how best to deliver your message. All these spokes connect the hub (purpose) to the outer "surface" or "rim" of the wheel, the presentation itself. Thus, a well-prepared speaker delivers a message that reflects strategic decisions about every principle.

The presentation wheel is a dynamic representation of what happens when a speaker encodes a message. However, having a purpose is not enough; the hub of a wheel won't get you anywhere. Successful encoding also involves deciding how to construct and place each spoke of the wheel on the hub so that the wheel is strong and headed in the right direction. Keep in mind that a missing spoke or a weak one can cripple a wheel. Likewise, failing to consider one or more principles can prevent a speaker from reaching an audience and achieving the presentation's purpose.

The Audience.   At the center or hub of the audience's wheel is its response. In an ideal communication transaction, the speaker's purpose and the audience's response would be the same. For example, if your purpose is to persuade audience members to donate five dollars to the local Red Cross chapter, you have a successful transaction when everyone in the audience donates five dollars. However, in the real world of presentation speaking, perfect transactions are extremely rare. More than likely, some audience members will donate nothing, some will give you their pocket change, others will produce the $5 bill, and a few inspired listeners may give you more than five dollars.

Chapter 5, "Audience Analysis and Adaptation," explores the factors represented by the spokes of the audience wheel. By considering and adapting to these factors, a speaker has a better chance of matching purpose and response—the message the audience "gets" is the message the speaker intended.

Figure 1.1   The Dynamic Presentation Model

The source of the message—you—is represented by the wheel on the left.
The receiver—your audience—is represented by the wheel on the right.

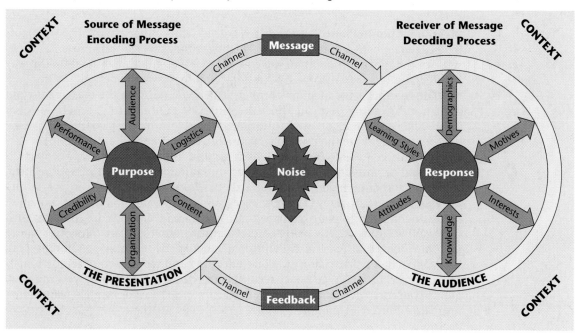

13

Feedback works both ways. The success of this jazz musician's workshop depends on his ability to respond to student feedback when he speaks and performs—and on his giving appropriate feedback to students when they speak and perform.

The audience wheel is a dynamic representation of what happens when audience members decode a message. Depending on the spokes of the audience wheel (demographics, motives, interests, knowledge, attitudes, and learning styles), listeners may interpret, evaluate, and respond to a message in a variety of ways that have little to do with the speaker's intended message. On the other hand, when a speaker considers the audience "spokes," the speaker and the audience may share a common meaning.

Message, Channel, and Feedback.   There are three other essential components in the Dynamic Presentation Model. The first is the message—the presentation itself. Your message is more than the content of a presentation; it includes the way in which you have transformed your purpose into words and action.

The channel is the medium through which you transmit the message to your audience. Anything that can affect the senses of sight, hearing, touch, taste, or smell can be used as a communication channel. In most speaking situations, hearing and sight are the principle channels used to transmit a message.

The third element, **feedback**, is critical to a speaker's success. Feedback is any verbal or nonverbal response from your audience that you can see or hear. Are your audience members smiling or frowning, leaning forward or falling asleep, taking notes or raising their hands, applauding or grumbling, asking questions or challenging your conclusions? Audience feedback helps you to assess how well your message is being received and whether you are likely to achieve your purpose. Feedback is also a critical element in the meaning-creation process; it is your audience "speaking" to you—encoding and sending you their own messages. If you "listen" to audience feedback and decode its meaning, you can even adjust your message and delivery while you are speaking. We strongly believe that feedback-induced adaptation is critical to a speaker's success.

Noise

Presentation speaking is not, unfortunately, a perfectly predictable or reliable process. As the wheels in our model turn and interact, they may encounter "bumps" and obstacles in their path that can inhibit a message from reaching its receivers as it was intended to do. **Noise** is a communication term used to describe these inhibiting factors. Noise can be external—such as a police siren outside the window, a soft speaking voice, or a difficult-to-understand accent. Noise can also be internal and psychological. Psychological noise occurs when a listener is preoccupied with personal thoughts and therefore misses or misinterprets a message.[11] Psychological noise affects speakers, too. For example, the "noise" of worrying about how you look or focusing on an audience member who is frowning may inhibit your ability to speak effectively.

Effective speakers are as sensitive to potential and real noise as they are to audience feedback. If noise is physical, they can try to reduce or eliminate it—for example, by closing a window or speaking with more volume and clarity. If noise is psychological, they can try to overcome their internal or audience distractions. Noise is an unpredictable and ever-present phenomenon in every speaking situation.

In an ideal speaking situation, the speaker has a clear central purpose and strong "spokes" to support a presentation. The message the presentation conveys moves through a channel without any interfering noise. Listeners receive a message that takes their feedback into account and adapts to the characteristics represented by the audience wheel's "spokes." And most critically, in an ideal speaking situation, the speaker's purpose and the audience's response overlap into a mutually beneficial transaction, as Figure 1.2 on the following page shows. Effective speakers accept the fact that they may never create or deliver a perfect presentation. At the same time, they never stop trying to reach that ideal.

Figure 1.2   A Successful Communication Transaction

A speaker's purpose and the audience's response are brought together by a message and feedback-induced adaptation.

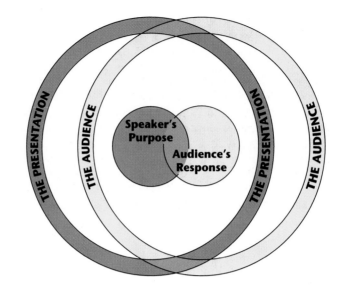

Becoming an Effective Speaker

A presentation can often be the most efficient and effective way to communicate. Presentation speaking can make immediate and personal contact with an audience in a way that cannot be duplicated by writing and can reach many people with an efficiency that cannot be matched in one-to-one conversations.

Reading this textbook will not make you a better speaker. Speaking will. Like many skills, presentation speaking requires knowledge *and* practice. It also requires as much preparation as a lawyer gives to an important case, as a tennis pro gives to a championship tournament, and as a great chef gives to a royal banquet. Some speakers are luckier than others. They seem to have an instinct that tells them when and how to achieve their goals through presentation speaking. Most of us are not that fortunate. We need to consciously learn the strategies and skills of preparing and delivering effective presentations. However, you *can* become a confident and successful speaker, and we're here to help. For starters, you should understand the value of theories, strategies, and skills as well as the need to communicate ethically and the importance of making strategic decisions.

Theories, Strategies, and Skills

Communication theories, strategies, and skills are inseparable. Mastering isolated skills will not help you to plan your presentation strategically, nor can you choose the best strategies for your presentation without understanding why those strategies work.

Theories.   **Theories** are statements that explain how the world works. They try to interpret or predict something. The philosopher Karl Popper described theories as "nets to catch what we call 'the world': to rationalize, to explain, and to master it."[12] Communication theories have emerged from extensive observation, empirical research, and rigorous scholarship. They help us to understand why some speakers succeed and why others fail to achieve their purposes. Learning these theories in isolation, however, will not make you a more effective speaker. Theories do not necessarily tell you what to do or what to say. Nevertheless, without theories, we would have difficulty understanding why or how a particular speaking strategy works or how strategies and skills interact.

Strategies. **Strategies** are the specific plans of action you select to help achieve the purpose of your presentation. The word *strategy* comes from the Greek word *strategia* and refers to the office of a military general.[13] Thus, like a general, a speaker marshals his or her "forces" to achieve a specific purpose. Throughout this textbook, you will encounter many communication strategies—from ways to analyze and adapt to your audience to techniques for organizing the key points of your presentation. Learning about strategies, however, is not enough. Effective strategies are often based on theories. If you don't understand theory, you won't know why strategies work in one situation and fail in another. Strategies based on theory give you a way to understand when, where, why, and how to use a particular strategy most effectively.

Skills. **Skills** are the tools you use to prepare and perform a presentation. They range from writing talent to performance ability. Skills also include the ability to do research, think critically, create an outline, and even use computer technology. Like strategies, skills are most effective when grounded in theory. Without that grounding, you may not understand when and why to use a particular tool to its best advantage.[14] In our eagerness to make an effective presentation, we may grab ready-made, easy-to-use "tricks of the trade" that do not adapt to the audience or help us to achieve our speaking goal.

Let's look at one of the seven basic principles for making a presentation—speaker credibility—to see how theory, strategies, and skills interact. As you will learn in Chapter 11, "Speaker Credibility and Ethics," communication theorists claim that audiences judge a speaker's believability and credibility by assessing his or her character, competence, and charisma. Knowing this theory and its related research, for example, does not necessarily tell you how to become more believable. Strategies do. Deciding on a strategy that will enhance your charisma, however, won't necessarily tell you how to convey the energy and enthusiasm characteristic of dynamic speakers. Skills do. The effectiveness of any skill depends on understanding the strategy it supports. Moreover, choosing the best strategy for a specific presentation's purpose, audience, and logistics depends on understanding the underlying theory that explains why that strategy works.

Communicating Ethically

Sadly, the strategies and skills in this textbook can be used and have been used for less-than-honorable purposes. Unscrupulous speakers have misled trusting citizens and consumers. Bigoted speakers have used hate speech to oppress those who are "different." Self-centered speakers have destroyed the reputations of their rivals with public pronouncements.

Chapter 11 devotes a major section to the ethical obligations of a good speaker. Here we emphasize that ethical communication is essential for becoming an effective and respected speaker. The National Communication Association (NCA) provides us with an appropriate credo for ethical communication.[15]

In Latin, the word *credo* means "I believe." Thus, an ethics credo is a belief statement about what it means to be an ethical communicator. We strongly believe that an effective and credible communicator must be an ethical communicator. The NCA credo sets clear standards for all communicators and has specific

In addition to posting the communication ethics credo, the Web site, www.natcom.org, of the National Communication Association, the largest professional organization of communication scholars, educators, and practitioners, is a rich source of information about association activities and discipline.

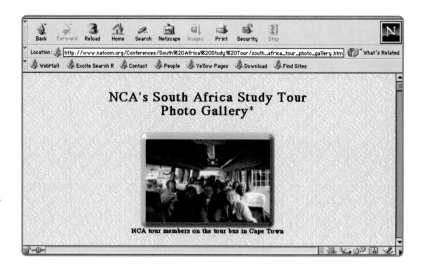

NCA's South Africa Study Tour Photo Gallery*

NCA tour members on the tour bus in Cape Town

applications to presentation speaking. The NCA Credo for Ethical Communication begins with the following preamble:

> Questions of right and wrong arise whenever people communicate. Ethical communication is fundamental to responsible thinking, decision making, and the development of relationships and communities within and across contexts, cultures, channels, and media. Moreover, ethical communication enhances human worth and dignity by fostering truthfulness, fairness, responsibility, personal integrity, and respect for self and others. We believe that unethical communication threatens the quality of all communication and consequently the well-being of individuals and the society in which they live.

The credo goes on to endorse specific principles and practices for ethical communication, including truthfulness and honesty, freedom of expression, tolerance, and respect. It condemns coercive communication and hate speech. It encourages all communicators to take responsibility for the consequences of their communication and expect the same of others. We agree with this credo and its underlying assumption that ethical communication is a vital ingredient in a civil and democratic society. (See Appendix B for the entire NCA Credo for Ethical Communication.)

Making Strategic Decisions

We wrote this book to help you make strategic decisions about preparing and delivering a successful presentation. We don't ask you to memorize tons of communication theory or research. Rather, we apply theory and research to all aspects of the presentation speaking process. Seeing theory in action will help you to make your own decisions as you develop and deliver your presentations. As most experienced speakers know, there's more to speaking than simply following a set of rules. Effective speaking depends on the ability to think critically and to make strategic decisions at key points in the presentation speaking process. In this textbook, we apply the best of communication theory and research to the real-life speaking situations you will face in your future.

Summary

◆✦ What do real-world speakers want to know about presentation speaking?

They want to know how to keep an audience interested, how to begin and end a presentation, how to select and organize appropriate content, how to choose a good topic, and how to adapt to an audience.

◆✦ What's the difference between a presentation and a public speech?

Presentation speaking occurs any time speakers use verbal and nonverbal messages to generate meanings and to establish relationships with audience members. Public speaking is a type of presentation speaking that occurs when speakers address public audiences in community, government, and/or organizational settings.

◆✦ What basic principles underlie all types of presentation speaking?

The following questions represent seven basic principles to consider when preparing a presentation: (1) What is your purpose? (2) Who is in your audience? (3) What are the logistics? (4) What content should you include? (5) How should you organize your content? (6) How can you enhance your credibility? (7) How should you practice and deliver your presentation?

◆✦ How do speakers and listeners work together to communicate?

Speakers and audiences rely on each other to give messages their meaning. In an ideal speaking situation, the speaker's purpose and the audience's response overlap in a mutually beneficial transaction.

◆✦ How can a theory make me a better speaker?

Although theories do not tell you what to say during a presentation, they can help you to understand why and how a particular speaking strategy works and which skills are needed to make a presentation more effective.

Key Terms

channel 12

communication model 12

communication transaction 12

context 12

decoding 12

encoding 12

feedback 14

message 12

noise 15

presentation speaking 5

public speaking 5

receiver 12

skills 17

source 12

strategy 17

theory 16

Notes

1. "Meek and Mumblers Learn Ways of Getting a Word In," *New York Times*, 29 May 1989, pp. 1 and 24.

2. Peggy Noonan, *Simply Speaking: How to Communicate Your Ideas with Style, Substance, and Clarity* (New York: HarperCollins, 1998), p. x. Copyright © 1998 by Peggy Noonan. Reprinted by permission of HarperCollins Publishers, Inc.

3. Thomas Leech, *How to Prepare, Stage & Deliver Winning Presentations* (New York: AMACOM, 1993), pp. 9 and 17.

4. *The American Heritage Dictionary of the English Language*, 3rd ed. (Boston: Houghton Mifflin, 1992), p. 1464. Copyright © 1996 by Houghton Mifflin Company. Reproduced by permission from *The American Heritage Dictionary of the English Language, Third Edition*.

5. The Association for Communication Administration's 1995 *Conference on Defining the Field of Communication* produced the following definition: "The field of communication focuses on how people use verbal and nonverbal messages to generate meanings within and across various contexts, cultures, channels, and media. The field promotes the effective and ethical practice of human communication." See *www.natcom.org/publications/Pathways/5thEd.htm*.

6. Leech, p. 4.

7. Business–Higher Education Forum, *Spanning the Chasm: Corporate and Academic Cooperation to Improve Work-Force Preparation* (Washington, DC: Business–Higher Education Forum in affiliation with the American Council on Education, January 1997), p. 5.

8. National Association of Colleges and Employers, *Job Outlook, 2000*. See *www.jobweb.org/pubs/pr/pr11800.htm*.

9. Thomas Leech, *How to Prepare, Stage & Deliver Winning Presentations* (New York: AMACOM, 1993); Marjorie Brody, *Speaking Your Way to the Top: Making Powerful Business Presentations* (Boston: Allyn & Bacon, 1998); William Hendricks et al., *Secrets of Power Presentations* (Franklin Lakes, NJ: Career Press, 1996); Robert W. Pike, *High-Impact Presentations* (West Des Moines, IA: American Media, 1995). There are many other commercially available, business-oriented books on speaking that use the terms *presentations* and *presentation speaking* rather than *public speaking*.

10. Rob Anderson and Veronica Ross, *Questions of Communication: A Practical Introduction to Theory*, 2nd ed. (New York: St. Martin's, 1998), p. 68.

11. Dominic A. Infante, Andrew S. Rancer, and Deanna F. Womack, *Building Communication Theory*, 2nd ed. (Prospect Heights, IL: Waveland, 1993), p. 32.

12. Karl R. Popper, *The Logic of Scientific Discovery* (New York: Basic Books, 1959), p. 59.

13. *The American Heritage Dictionary*, p. 1775.

14. Peter M. Senge et al., *The Fifth Discipline Fieldbook: Strategies and Tools for Building a Learning Organization* (New York: Doubleday, 1994), p. 31.

15. The credo for ethical communication was developed at the 1999 Communication Ethics Credo Conference sponsored by the National Communication Association. The credo was adopted and endorsed by the Legislative Council of the National Communication Association in November 1999. The complete credo is available in Appendix B and on the NCA Web site *www.natcom.org/aboutNCA/Policies/Platform.html*. Used by permission of the National Communication Association.

Critical Thinking and Listening

- ◆◆ How do I apply critical thinking to the presentation speaking process?
- ◆◆ Is everyone equally able to think critically?
- ◆◆ Is there more than one way to listen?
- ◆◆ How can I become a better listener?
- ◆◆ How do I "listen" to an audience?

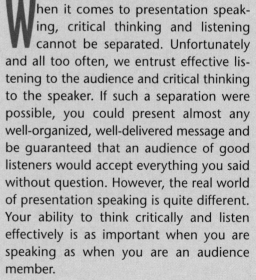

When it comes to presentation speaking, critical thinking and listening cannot be separated. Unfortunately and all too often, we entrust effective listening to the audience and critical thinking to the speaker. If such a separation were possible, you could present almost any well-organized, well-delivered message and be guaranteed that an audience of good listeners would accept everything you said without question. However, the real world of presentation speaking is quite different. Your ability to think critically and listen effectively is as important when you are speaking as when you are an audience member.

As a speaker, you need to think critically in order to analyze what you learn about your audience before and during a presentation. Only then can you make strategic decisions about how to achieve your purpose. As an audience member, you should think critically about what you see, hear, and feel about a speaker and his or her message. Only then can you decide what to do or what to believe. Both kinds of critical thinking require effective listening.

What Is Critical Thinking?

Although critical thinking has strong links to listening, it is not the same thing. Nor is critical thinking the same as day-to-day, "automatic" thought. Rather, **critical thinking** is the particular kind of thinking we use to analyze what we read, see, or hear in order to arrive at a justified conclusion or decision. It is a conscious process that when effective, always has an outcome. It can result in a conclusion, decision, opinion, or behavior. It can even result in a presentation.[1]

After many years of teaching, coaching, and speaking, we have learned that the best and brightest speakers tend also to be excellent critical thinkers. Whereas actors perform lines written by a playwright, speakers write their own lines. Whereas athletes may model their behavior after superstars and Olympic medal winners, good speakers develop their own styles. Whereas an author can spend days, weeks, or years writing a significant article or book, speakers are often required to get up and make a significant presentation with little advance notice. To succeed, speakers must be able to think critically.

At every stage of the encoding process, you will need to make critical decisions: What is the purpose of my presentation? How should I adapt to my audience? What is the best way to arrange the room in which I will be speaking? How much research do I need to do? How should I organize my content? How can I make my presentation interesting? What form of delivery should I use? Critical thinking skills can help you answer these questions. Those answers in turn can help you develop a presentation that achieves your purpose, meets your audience's needs, and thus establishes and enhances your credibility.

Audience members must be critical thinkers, too. Otherwise, they may misunderstand messages or be deceived and exploited by speakers. Critical thinkers intelligently evaluate speakers and their messages. They recognize the differences between fact and fiction, between valid and invalid arguments, between credible experts and biased sources, and between skilled persuasion and intimidating coercion. When one audience member does not think critically, the consequences are unfortunate for that particular listener. When most audience members, television viewers, and citizens do not think critically, the consequences can undermine the foundation of a democratic society.

Learning to Think Critically

We've established that critical thinking is a way of analyzing information to arrive at a well-reasoned conclusion about its value and validity. But you may be wondering how to go about it. The key lies in analyzing, *systematically*, what you're being asked to believe—the claim—and then determining if the reasons given for that belief—the argument—are sound.

Brooke Noel Moore and Richard Parker, the authors of *Critical Thinking*, define a *claim* as a statement that is either true or false.[2] When you hear someone make a claim—"We had chicken for dinner," "Teenagers have difficulty identifying emotions by looking at facial expressions," "Audiences like to hear personal stories about a speaker"—you can react in several ways. You can challenge the claim or ignore it. You can dismiss or defend it. Usually, though, what we do is "determine whether to accept it (that is, believe it), reject it (believe that it is false), or suspend judgment about it (possibly because we don't have enough information at the time to accept or reject it)."[3] How we make these decisions requires a deeper understanding of what makes audience members believe some claims and reject others.

Building and Analyzing an Argument

An **argument** is not a disagreement between two people; it is a claim supported by evidence and reasons for accepting it. Stephen Toulmin, a philosopher and the author of *The Uses of Argument*, developed a way of looking at arguments that has become a mainstay in communication studies.[4]

This model is a useful way for both speakers and listeners to understand the basic structure of an argument. The Toulmin model says that a claim is only one part of a complete argument. To be complete, an argument also requires evidence, a warrant, backing, reservations, and qualifiers.[5]

> **COMPONETS OF AN ARGUMENT**
>
> **Claim**
> **Evidence**
> **Warrant**
> **Backing**
> **Reservations**
> **Qualifiers**

DOES CRITICAL THINKING REQUIRE CRITICIZING?

A common confusion about critical thinking is that it means criticizing. Definitions of the word *criticize* include "to find fault with" and "to judge the merits and faults of."[1] The word *critical* is a broader, less fault-finding term. *Critical* comes from the Greek word for critic (*kritkos*), which means to question, to make sense of, to be able to analyze.[2] Critical thinking is a way of analyzing what we read, see, and hear in order to make intelligent decisions about what to do or believe. It is *not* a way to tear down an argument or criticize a speaker. Critical thinking requires specific skills: You need to be able to identify what you're being asked to believe or accept and to evaluate the evidence and reasoning you're given in support of the belief. You need the ability to judge the credibility of sources. You should be able to develop and defend a position on an issue, to ask appropriate questions, to be open-minded, and to draw reasonable conclusions.[3]

1. *The American Heritage Dictionary of the English Language*, 3rd ed. (Boston: Houghton Mifflin, 1992), p. 443. Copyright © 1996 by Houghton Mifflin Company. Reproduced by permission from *The American Heritage Dictionary of the English Language, Third Edition.*
2. John Chaffee, *Thinking Critically*, 4th ed. (Boston: Houghton Mifflin, 1994), p. 51.
3. Robert H. Ennis, "Critical Thinking Assessment," *Theory into Practice* 32 (1993): 180.

Claim.   The **claim** is the conclusion or position a speaker advocates in a presentation. It is the idea a speaker wants the audience to believe or accept. For example, a speaker could claim that "keeping a food-intake diary is the best way to monitor a diet," that "communication skills are the most important characteristics to look for when recruiting new employees," or that "capital punishment deters criminals." A good critical thinker tries to determine whether these claims are true or false and whether they merit belief.

Evidence.   Speakers support and prove the claims they advocate by providing information, data, and opinions as evidence. **Evidence** answers the questions "How do you know that?" and "What do you have to go on?" A sound argument relies on strong evidence, which can range from statistics and multiple examples to the advice of experts and generally accepted audience beliefs. For example, if you claim that keeping a food-intake diary is the best way to monitor a diet, you might share the results of a study conducted at a major medical school which concluded that food-intake diaries produced the best results. Or you might tell stories about how your many attempts to lose weight failed until you spent two months keeping a food-intake diary. You might even distribute examples of food-intake diaries to the audience to show them how easy it is to surpass a 30-gram fat allowance during a "day of dieting." Without good evidence, critical thinkers in your audience may be reluctant to accept your claims.

Although supporting a claim and proving an argument require some form of evidence, not all evidence is logical or substantive. For instance, a speaker may use evidence based on audience knowledge and beliefs. Remember the first question that evidence tries to answer in an argument: "How do you know that?" Sometimes, when an audience "knows that," you can use their beliefs as evidence. For example, doesn't "everyone know that" a 150-pound person who rarely exercises will gain weight if he or she consumes 4,000 calories a day? Doesn't "everyone know that" running five miles a day is a more vigorous form of exercise than walking a half mile? By using such audience beliefs as evidence, you can claim that restricting calories combined with vigorous exercising will help you lose weight.

A speaker may also use his or her expertise about the topic or the expertise of an information source as evidence. For example, if we recommend an exercise for improving the quality of your speaking voice, we hope that you will take our advice because we are professors and authors who have spent most of our professional lives studying communication. Sometimes, to strengthen a claim, we will also provide a quotation from a study or a book written by other communication experts.

In many cases, your audience's beliefs, knowledge, and sympathies can be powerful forms of ready-made evidence. For example, if you have learned that most members of your audience believe that controlling guns will reduce violent crime, you can use that belief as evidence to support a gun-control argument. When appealing to audience members familiar with the findings of a government task force or a renowned psychologist on the impact of gun violence, you can use their knowledge to support your argument. You could also quote a well-known and sympathetic victim of gun violence such as James Brady, who in 1981, was shot and paralyzed in an assassination attempt on President Reagan and then became an advocate of gun control. In Toulmin's model, evidence can take many forms: audience motives, values, and beliefs; speaker credibility or source expertise; and traditional forms of supporting material such as statistics and examples.

Warrant. Strong claims supported by good evidence, however, may not be enough to make an argument believable. The third component in Toulmin's argumentation model is the warrant. The **warrant** explains why the evidence is relevant and why it supports the claim. For example, the warrant might say that the author of the article on food-intake diaries has been recognized as one of the country's leading nutrition experts. Rather than asking, "What do you have to go on?" the warrant wants to know "How did you get there?" and "What gives you the right to draw that conclusion?" Figure 2.1 illustrates how the Toulmin model represents the evidence, warrant, and claim of an argument.

The previous argument, then, would sound like this: "Want to lose those extra pounds for good? Keep a food-intake diary. Dr. Nathan Carter, the lead researcher in a medical school study, has reported that patients who kept food-intake diaries were twice as likely to lose weight as were patients who used any other method." Warrants can demonstrate the logical relationship between the evidence and the claim. They can also prompt audiences to move from the evidence to the claim on the basis of the speaker's expertise or on the basis of their shared beliefs. Evidence and claims will remain separate unless warrants build a mental bridge between them.

Backing. **Backing** provides support for the argument's warrant. Backing is not needed in all arguments, but it can be crucial if an audience questions why the warrant should be accepted as the link between the evidence and the claim. While the warrant answers the question "How did you get there?" the backing answers the question "Why is this the right way to get there?" Backing can be in

Figure 2.1   Basic "T" of the Toulmin Model

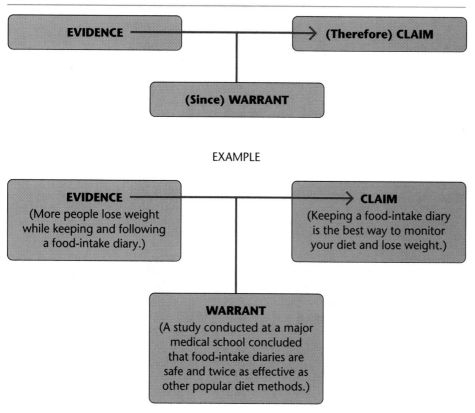

EXAMPLE

the form of more information about the credibility of a source: "Dr. Nathan Carter and his colleagues received two national awards for their contributions to weight-loss research." Backing can also describe the methodology used in the weight-loss study that determined the effectiveness of food-intake diaries.

Reservations.   Not all claims are true all of the time. The **reservation** component of the Toulmin model recognizes exceptions to an argument or indications that a claim may not be true under certain circumstances. For example, a food-intake diary is only as good as the limits placed on daily food intake. Setting a limit of 4,000 calories and 100 fat grams a day for a 150-pound person won't do it. Moreover, there are some people whose weight problems have hormonal or genetic causes. The reservations could be stated this way: "Food-intake diaries must be well-calibrated and may not work if there are genetic or hormonal causes of obesity. In such cases, keeping a standard food-intake diary may not be sufficient." Not only does a reservation make an argument more reasonable, it can also serve as an exception to an argument because it acknowledges that under certain circumstances, a claim may not be warranted.

Qualifiers.   When the argument contains reservations, the speaker may have to qualify it. The **qualifier** states the degree to which a claim appears to be true. Qualifiers usually include the words *likely*, *possibly*, or *probably*. This could be a claim with a qualifier: "Unless there are medical reasons for seeking other therapies, using and following a food-intake diary calibrated to your own dietary goals is *probably* the best way to lose weight." Speakers need qualifiers when the evidence or warrant is less than certain and when audience members are likely to have doubts. Qualifiers soften a claim and therefore can make an argument more acceptable to a skeptical audience. Figure 2.2 maps out a complete argument.

You can use the Toulmin model to think critically about the basic components of any argument. When you develop a presentation, this model can help you test your own claims and arguments to determine whether they need to be strengthened or qualified. By recognizing that situations may alter the certainty of a claim, you can advocate more reasonable positions and thereby help audience members decide what to do or believe about your message.

The Toulmin model also supplies audience members with questions to ask about a speaker's claims. It can help listeners recognize when a speaker makes an unsupported claim that they may reject for lack of evidence. If the speaker provides evidence, the model helps listeners question the evidence's relevance and whether it warrants the claim.

Adapting to Different Ways of Thinking

Imagine that you and a friend have gone to a talk on natural medicines, a topic you're both interested in. As you leave the hall, you say to your friend, "Wasn't that great? I love the way the speaker built up her argument about vitamin C by showing how medical doctors have ignored a lot of good research on its beneficial effects." Your friend gives you a blank stare and replies, "What do you mean? I thought that was a really confusing presentation! She never said what she believed. She just kept bringing up all those other people's ideas. I couldn't tell which one was right!" You wonder to yourself if you and your friend were at the same talk. In a sense, you weren't—or at least you didn't come away from it with

Figure 2.2   The Toulmin Model of an Argument

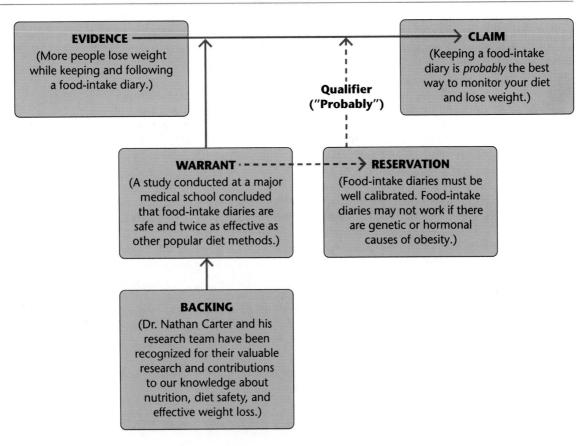

the same message. Why not? Critical thinking is relatively easy for some audience members and difficult for others. One way of understanding why can be found in research on intellectual development.

In the 1970s, Harvard University professor William Perry interviewed students at several points in their college careers to find out how critical thinking develops over time.[6] On the basis of these interviews, Perry determined that it progresses gradually through several stages. Thinkers in early stages saw issues in yes-or-no terms: Every question had just one right answer. In later stages, thinkers understood that often there are multiple answers whose "rightness" depends on context and personal circumstances.

Perry's research has been hugely influential in work on critical thinking. At the same time, we must note that Perry looked at only a rather privileged group of students—white males of traditional college age at Harvard University. What about women at other types of schools and of different ages? Mary Belenky and her colleagues looked at this question and found four categories of intellectual development that help to explain how and why people respond so differently to the "job" of critical thinking.[7] We have applied these four levels to explaining one of the reasons why listeners can respond so differently to the same presentation.

Level 1: Received Knowledge. At this level, listeners trust facts. Learning simply means remembering the facts that a speaker presents. Ideas are either correct or incorrect. Speakers are authority figures who present knowledge, suggest opinions, and recommend behavior. For Level 1 thinkers, the notion of questioning a so-called fact or challenging a speaker's opinion makes little sense. "She wouldn't be speaking if she didn't know," they conclude. Or "The speaker knows what is right and true, and if we listen carefully, we'll also know what's right and true." Audience members who prefer to receive knowledge are passive. They want to be told what to think and what to do. They are not critical thinkers.

Level 2: Subjective Knowledge. At this level, listeners acknowledge that unknowns, contradictions of facts, and uncertainties exist. As a result, one opinion may seem just as good as another. Rather than seeking the truth, these audience members rely only on their own instincts and intuition to decide what is right or wrong, true or false.[8] These listeners think: "No one can know what's *really* true. Everyone has a right to his or her own opinion!" Audience members who rely on subjective knowledge to make decisions are often willing to accept everything that "makes sense" while denying the power of critical thinking.

Level 3: Procedural Knowledge. At the third level, listeners begin to understand that some opinions are better than others. They have learned that claims should be supported with evidence and reasoning. They test facts and opinions by using a variety of critical thinking tools—they test the logic of arguments; they verify facts by researching the work of other experts; they experiment. Audience members who rely on procedural knowledge have a toolbox full of techniques for analyzing what they hear. However, they rely on these tools without question or compassion. They may carefully analyze their thinking and the thinking of others, but they do not embrace critical thinking as a way of clarifying and understanding their lives and the world around them.

The judges at the World Court in The Hague, Netherlands, must be excellent critical thinkers who go beyond testing facts and opinions in order to make crucial far-reaching decisions.

Level 4: Constructed Knowledge. At this highest level of intellectual development, listeners take a position and make commitments. They are excellent critical thinkers. They go beyond the objective testing of facts and opinions to draw personal conclusions. They understand that a presentation's context and audience have as much to do with the meaning of a message as the speaker's intentions. Even when such audience members are well aware that other facts and opinions exist, they are satisfied that their critical thinking has found a position that is reasonable for them. Perry describes how such a listener thinks: "I must . . . fight for my values yet respect others, believe my deepest values [to be] right yet be ready to learn."[9]

So what does this mean to you, the speaker? Audience members at the Received Knowledge level do *not* think critically. They are likely to accept whatever facts and opinions you share with them. If, however, your audience includes members at the Subjective Knowledge level, and your position runs counter to their feelings or beliefs, there may be very little you can do to influence them. They rely on their own instincts. Your audience members at the Procedural Knowledge and Constructed Knowledge levels think critically about your message and can become involved in it and be empowered by it. Nevertheless, a well-prepared, well-presented message will make a lasting impression on audience members at all four levels. In Chapter 5, "Audience Analysis and Adaptation," we explore how audience analysis can help you adapt your presentation to your audience's needs and characteristics.

What Is Listening?

We define effective **listening** as the ability to understand, analyze, respect, and appropriately respond to the meaning of another person's spoken and nonverbal messages.[10] At first, listening may appear to be as easy and natural as breathing. After all, everyone listens. In fact, just the opposite may be closer to the truth. Although most of us can *hear*, we often fail to *listen* to what others have to say. Hearing and listening are not the same thing. Hearing requires only physical ability; listening requires thinking ability. People who are hearing-impaired may be better listeners than those who can hear the faintest sound.

Listening is what audiences are supposed to do when speakers talk. In fact, listening is our number-one communication activity. Although percentages vary from study to study, Figure 2.3 shows how most of us divide up our daily communication time.

One study of college students found that listening occupies more than half of their communicating time.[11] In the corporate world, executives may devote more than 60 percent of their workday listening to others.[12]

Yet despite all of the time we spend listening, most of us aren't very good at it. For example, immediately after listening to a short talk, most of us cannot accurately report 50 percent of what was said. Without training, we listen at only 25 percent efficiency.[13] And of that 25 percent, most of what we remember is distorted or inaccurate.[14]

As a speaker, you must learn to adjust to and compensate for the poor listening habits of your audience. As an audience member, you will find that your listening ability affects whether you understand and accurately interpret what you hear in a presentation. This dual responsibility on the part of the speaker and audience ensures that presentations achieve their purpose. As we indicated in Chapter 1, a successful communication transaction occurs when a speaker's purpose and an audience's response are brought together by a message. Without effective listening, the transaction will fail to produce shared meaning.

Figure 2.3   Time Spent Communicating

Communication Activity	Percentages
Listening	40–70%
Speaking	20–35%
Reading	10–20%
Writing	5–15%

Source: Isa Engleberg and Dianna Wynn, *Working in Groups*, 2nd ed., p. 112. Copyright ©2000 by Houghton Mifflin Company. Reprinted with permission.

Types of Listening

Listening is a complex behavior. Researchers have identified several types of listening, each of which employs unique listening skills.

> **TYPES OF LISTENING**
>
> **Comprehensive listening**
> **Empathic listening**
> **Analytical listening**
> **Appreciative listening**

Comprehensive Listening.   Comprehensive listening answers this question: What does the speaker mean? **Comprehensive listening** focuses on accurately understanding the meaning of a speaker's spoken and nonverbal messages. Later in this chapter, we discuss how to "listen" to nonverbal communication—the messages speakers send without using words.

Comprehensive listening involves two basic steps. First, make sure you accurately hear what is said while simultaneously paying attention to nonverbal cues such as facial expressions, gestures, posture, and vocal quality. Second, make sure that you accurately interpret the speaker's meaning. Can you identify the key points as well as the claims and evidence she uses to support an argument? After all, if you don't comprehend what a person says, you can't be expected to respond in a reasonable way.

Suppose a speaker is trying to persuade you to participate in a voter registration drive. As a comprehensive listener, you may wonder whether "Join the voter registration drive" means that you (1) should, in general, support voter registration, (2) should volunteer and help register voters, or (3) should register to vote. The way in which you interpret the meaning of a single comment can determine your response to the whole presentation.

Audience members aren't the only ones who need strong comprehensive listening skills. During a question-and-answer session, speakers need to understand audience questions. In addition, comprehensive listening can be just as important before you speak. It's the type of listening you should use when someone asks you to speak so that you can be sure that you understand the presentation's purpose, audience, logistics, and occasion.

Empathic Listening.   Empathic listening answers this question: How does the speaker or audience feel? **Empathic listening** goes beyond understanding what a person means; it focuses on understanding and identifying with a person's situation, feelings, or motives. Can you see the situation through the speaker's eyes? To put the question another way, how would you feel in a similar situation?

By not listening for feelings, you may overlook the most important part of a message. Even if you understand every word a person says, you can still miss the anger, enthusiasm, or frustration in a speaker's voice. An empathic listener doesn't have to agree with or feel the same way that a speaker does, but he should try to understand the type and intensity of feelings that the speaker is experiencing. For example, suppose a speaker says that voting is a waste of time. An empathic listener may wonder whether the speaker means that (1) she is stressed and may have more important things to think about, (2) she is frustrated because there aren't any good candidates to vote for, or (3) the line is usually so long at the polling station that standing in it wastes her precious time.

Audience members can be empathic listeners in simple ways. For instance, smiling and nodding at someone who is speaking communicates attention and interest. What's more, if you act as though you're listening, you may actually end up listening more effectively and retaining more information!

Analytical Listening. Analytical listening answers this question: What's my opinion? Of the four types of listening, **analytical listening** most closely relates to critical thinking because it focuses on evaluating whether a message is reasonable. Analytical listening asks you to make a judgment based on your evaluation of the speaker's arguments. Is the speaker right or wrong, logical or illogical? Good analytical listeners apply critical thinking skills and understand why they accept or reject a speaker's ideas and suggestions.

A speaker makes the following proposal: "Suppose we post signs and offer free rides to the voting polls." An analytical listener might have questions such as these: (1) Will voters misinterpret the ride as pressure to vote for a particular candidate? (2) Wouldn't voters want to check to see that all drivers have adequate car insurance? (3) Is there enough time to design, print, and post the signs before the election?

Figure 2.4   Questions for Analytical Listening

Purpose Questions:
____Is the speaker's purpose clearly stated? If not, what is the speaker trying to achieve?
____Could the speaker have a hidden or an ulterior motive?
____Did the speaker achieve his or her purpose?
____Was achieving the *speaker's* purpose worth the time *you* spent listening?

Audience Questions:
____Does the speaker seem to understand the nature and characteristics of the audience?
____Does the speaker appear to understand and respect the audience's attitudes and beliefs?
____Does it seem as though the speaker is trying to take advantage of the audience in any way?
____Could this presentation be delivered to *any* audience, or has the speaker made an effort to adapt it to this audience's interests and needs?

Logistics Questions:
____Has the speaker stayed within the time limit? If not, what has been the effect of too little or too much speaking?
____Has the speaker adapted to the setting of the presentation (considering the size of the room and the audience, using amplification, using presentation aids)?
____If the presentation is taking place on a special occasion, has the speaker adapted to that occasion?
____Could this presentation be delivered to any audience in any setting, or has the speaker effectively adapted to this setting and occasion?

Content Questions:
____Does the speaker seem well informed?
____Is the information relevant to the topic or purpose of the presentation?

____Does the speaker identify her or his sources of information?
____Does the information seem reasonable and believable? If not, what is the problem?
____Does the speaker appear to be misleading the audience?

Organization Questions:
____Is the presentation clear and easy to follow?
____Are the key points identified and well supported?
____Does the speaker go off on tangents that have little to do with the purpose or the key points of the presentation?

Credibility Questions:
____As far as you can determine, is the speaker well informed about the topic?
____Does the speaker seem to be sincere and trustworthy?
____Does the speaker appear to be genuinely interested in the topic and the audience?
____Do you trust and believe this speaker?
____Would you invite this speaker to address an audience of colleagues or friends?

Performance Questions:
____Was the speaker's delivery effective?
____Could you hear and understand what the speaker said?
____Did the speaker's gestures, posture, and dress enhance the presentation?
____Did the speaker use equipment and presentation aids well?
____Did the speaker look directly at the audience?
____To what extent did the speaker's delivery affect your opinion of his or her message?

A listener needs analytical listening skills in order to judge the validity of an argument and the factors that separate credible sources from biased ones. To listen analytically, you can apply the Toulmin model discussed earlier in this chapter: Identify the speaker's claim; assess the evidence, warrant, and backing; and be alert to reservations and qualifiers. You can also evaluate presentations by testing the ways in which they apply the seven basic principles of presentation speaking, as Figure 2.4 shows. Using either method, analytical listeners can assess the strength and merit of a speaker's ideas and opinions.

Appreciative Listening. Appreciative listening answers this question: Do I like, value, or enjoy what the speaker is saying? **Appreciative listening** applies to *how* speakers think and speak—the ways in which they choose and use words and their ability to use humor, tell stories, argue persuasively, or demonstrate understanding. Appreciative listening can reward a speaker who is able to capture and eloquently describe a complex concept or proposal. When a speaker's words, stories, or sense of humor delight us, we listen appreciatively. Appreciative listening skills can help us enjoy and acknowledge good presentations.

Planning to Listen

What if we told you that next week you will have to make a presentation that really matters to a very important group of people. We bet that you would spend a lot of time planning that talk. Now, suppose we told you that next week you will be attending a meeting to listen to an important presentation. How much time would you spend preparing? Our guess is that you would spend much less time preparing to listen. We believe that planning to listen can be just as important as planning to speak. Here are five suggestions that can help you plan to listen:

▶ *Do some prior study.* The more you know about a topic, the more you will get out of hearing a presentation about it. In some classes, communication instructors ask students to announce their topics a week in advance so that listeners can start thinking about what they will be hearing.

▶ *Identify your listening goals.* In a general sense, ask yourself this question: What do I want to get out of listening to this presentation? If you can find a personal reason for listening, you will be a better listener.

▶ *Match your listening style to the presentation's purpose.* Thomas Leech, a communication consultant, suggests that "by knowing which listening hat to wear, listeners can get more out of the presentation and properly direct their own efforts."[1] For example, if you're attending a presentation designed to entertain, you probably won't need to listen analyti-

cally. However, you would want to listen analytically to a speaker who was trying to persuade audience members to change their opinions or behavior. At an informative presentation filled with detailed facts and figures, you would apply your comprehensive listening skills. And if you're listening to someone tell a good story or read a passage from literature, empathic and appreciative listening may be most appropriate. Good listeners can rely on any and all of the four listening styles when necessary.

▶ *Generate some questions in advance.* When you go to a presentation with questions in mind, you will listen better because you'll be paying attention to whether or not the speaker answers them. If you discover that the speaker has avoided or has not not developed the topic you were curious about, ask your question during a question-and-answer session. The audience may appreciate your question and benefit from the answer.

▶ *Share the message.* After the presentation ends, make a point of telling someone else what you heard. If you know in advance that you will be reporting on what you have heard, you will have to listen more carefully. Also, by reporting, you will have to repeat the message and will be more likely to remember what was said.

1. Thomas Leech, *How to Prepare, Stage, & Deliver Winning Presentations* (New York: AMACOM, 1993), p. 266.

Suppose that a speaker suggests there is no greater duty in a democracy than that of expressing your opinion at the polling booth on Election Day. An appreciative listener might think that (1) the speaker phrased that idea eloquently; (2) when seen as a patriotic duty rather than as a time-consuming chore, voting seems worthwhile; or (3) the tone of the speaker's voice communicated genuine sincerity.

Learning to Listen

You *can* learn specific listening skills, and as we'll soon see, most of them apply two basic principles: (1) use your extra thought speed and (2) apply the "golden listening rule." Once you understand and apply these principles as overriding listening strategies, you can begin to work on specific listening skills.

Use Your Extra Thought Speed.   Most people talk at about 125 to 150 words per minute. According to Ralph Nichols, a respected listening researcher and author, if thoughts were measured in words per minute, most of us could think at three or four times the rate at which we speak.[15] Thus, we have about 400 words' worth of spare thinking time for every minute during which a person talks to us.

Thought speed is the speed (words per minute) at which most people can think, compared to the speed at which they can speak. So what do we do with all that extra thinking time? Poor listeners use their extra thought speed to daydream, engage in side conversations, take unnecessary notes, or plan how to confront a speaker. Good listeners use their extra thought speed productively when they

▶ Identify and summarize key points

▶ Pay more attention to nonverbal behavior

▶ Analyze arguments

▶ Assess the relevance of a speaker's comments

Conscientious audience members don't waste their extra thought speed—they use it to enhance comprehensive and analytical listening.

Comprehending and respecting speakers on both sides of a controversial question require the application of the *golden listening rule:* Listen to others as you would have them listen to you.

Apply the Golden Listening Rule.   The **golden listening rule** is easy to remember: Listen to others as you would have them listen to you. Unfortunately, this rule can be difficult to follow. It asks you to suspend your own needs in order to attend to someone else's.

The golden listening rule applies to the speaker, too. As a speaker, you know your material, but your audience is hearing it for the first time. You may have spent hours crafting your message; your audience may not have given much thought to the issue. You may believe what you're saying; the listener may be skeptical.[16] Conscientious speakers understand and adapt to the ways in which audience members listen to a presentation.

Listening Skills

Although using your extra thought speed and applying the golden listening rule are basic listening principles, ways to practice them may not be obvious. The following five skills can improve your listening ability and help you apply the two basic principles of effective listening. When and how you use these skills depend on whether you are the speaker or an audience member, whether you are speaking to a large or small group, and whether you have the flexibility to interact with the speaker or audience members during or after a presentation.

> **LISTENING SKILLS**
>
> **Overcome distractions**
> **Listen for the big ideas**
> **"Listen" to nonverbal behavior**
> **Paraphrase**
> **Listen before you leap**

Overcome Distractions.   Distractions can take many forms.[17] Loud and annoying noises, uncomfortable room temperature and seating, frequent interruptions, distracting decor, and outside activities are environmental distractions. A speaker's delivery can also be distracting. It's hard to listen to a speaker who talks too softly, too rapidly, or too slowly or who speaks in a monotone or with an unfamiliar accent. Even a speaker's mannerisms and appearance can be distracting. Remember the concept of noise in our communication model? Reducing the noise—physical or psychological—that interferes with the communication process can improve your entire audience's ability to listen to your message.

One important form of psychological noise is listener bias. A bias can be either of two things: your own prejudice or an unfair attitude which you hold that stems from prior experience. Bias can also be a preference that inhibits you from making an impartial judgment.[18] If, for example, you "know" you disagree with a viewpoint that is going to be discussed, either you won't listen or you'll spend your time criticizing the speaker. Pro-life audiences may not want to listen to a pro-choice speaker—and vice versa. A gun-control advocate may not have an easy time getting a group of gun owners to listen. Please understand that there's nothing wrong with criticizing a speaker *after* you've listened comprehensively and analytically to a presentation. The problem results when you let your bias prevent you from listening as a responsible audience member.

When a distraction is environmental, you are well within your rights as a listener or speaker to shut a door, open a window, or turn on more lights. In large groups you may need to ask permission to improve the group's surroundings.

REAL WORLD, REAL SPEAKERS

At a recent communication convention, I was sitting in a packed, standing-room-only meeting room in which communication researchers were making their presentations. Within a few minutes, the body heat and cramped quarters began affecting the room's temperature. At first, no one seemed to mind. By the time the third speaker began, the room temperature was well into the 80s. One of the other presenters began fanning herself with her research paper. Another caught my eye and silently mouthed, "It's hot!" Soon audience members were taking off suit jackets and sweaters.

Finally, I couldn't stand it anymore. No one was listening; everyone was preoccupied with the hot room. I stood up and had to excuse myself across a tightly packed row of people. Several people scowled at me for my disruptive behavior. Then I had to make my way through the standing audience members. At the back of the room, I reached my goal—the thermostat. The temperature was 90 degrees. I flicked on the air conditioning switch and set the thermostat at 72. Cool air came roaring through the room vents.

I then went back to my seat. Those who had scowled at me were now saying, "Thank you." The speaker who had silently mouthed, "It's hot" sent a silent thank-you my way. You would think that in a room full of people, someone in the back would do something to overcome the distraction of 90-degree heat.

Be a hero. Help an audience listen by taking action to overcome distractions whenever possible.

Isa Engleberg

Depending on the circumstances and setting of a presentation, you may be able to take direct action to reduce distractions. If an audience member's behavior is distracting, you may be well within your rights to ask that person to stop talking or moving around. After all, if she is distracting you, the person is probably also distracting others. If a presenter speaks too softly or uses visual aids that are too small, a conscientious audience member may ask him to speak up or to explain what is on a visual.

Listen for the Big Ideas.   This is where the critical thinking skills discussed earlier really kick in! Good listeners can identify a speaker's purpose, central idea, and key points. They can tell the difference between fact and opinion and between evidence and claims. On the other hand, poor listeners tend to listen for and remember isolated facts.

Admittedly, sometimes the fault lies with the speaker. When faced with a disorganized speaker who keeps talking long after making a point, listeners may lose track and drift off. In a small group setting, a good listener who senses such problems could interrupt the speaker and ask, "Could you help me out here and summarize your point in a couple of sentences?" Such an interruption is not rude when it is the only way to get the speaker to clarify an important issue. There's also a big difference between asking for a summary and yelling out, "Hey, what's your point?" Although it is tempting for listeners to blame poor speakers when they can't figure out the message, good listeners try to cut through facts and irrelevant comments in order to identify the most important points and main ideas.

One way to listen for "big" ideas is to borrow a plan-to-listen tip. Plan to tell someone else what you've heard. We know that when people believe they have to report back on what they've heard, their comprehension increases significantly. Ask yourself the audience's side of the purpose question: What does the speaker want me to know, think, believe, or do after hearing this presentation? Then try to list the key points or ideas the speaker used to achieve that purpose.

"Listen" to Nonverbal Behavior.   Speakers don't always put everything that's important into words. Very often, you can understand a speaker's meaning by noting and interpreting nonverbal communication. **Nonverbal communication** is a general term used to describe the messages that we send without using words. It applies to body language, physical appearance, facial expression, and eye contact as well as to the emotions and emphasis communicated by the tone of a person's voice. Good listeners know that nonverbal behavior can communicate as much as or more meaning than words alone. They pay attention to the "mismatch" between verbal and nonverbal messages, such as when a speaker says, "I'm delighted to see you here today" while cringing and turning toward the door.

A change in a speaker's vocal tone or volume may be another way of saying, "Listen up; this is very important." A presenter's sustained eye contact may be a way of saying, "I'm talking to you!" Facial expressions can reveal whether a thought is painful, joyous, exciting, serious, or boring. Even gestures can be used to express a level of excitement that words cannot convey.

If, as research indicates, more than half of our meaning is conveyed nonverbally,[19] we are missing a lot of important information if we fail to "listen" to nonverbal behavior! Even Sigmund Freud suggested that "he that has eyes to see and ears to hear may convince himself that no mortal can keep a secret. If his lips are silent, he chatters with his fingertips; betrayal oozes out of him at every pore."[20] No wonder it is difficult to conceal what we mean and feel during a live presentation.

Correctly interpreting a speaker's nonverbal responses can tell a listener as much as or more than the spoken words. At the same time, the nonverbal reactions of listeners (head nods, smiles, frowns, eye contact, and sitting posture) can affect the quality, quantity, and content of a speaker's message. Even the setting of a presentation (a nonverbal aspect) can communicate a wealth of meaning about the status, power, and respect given to speakers and listeners.

Paraphrase. Paraphrasing is the ability to restate what people have said in a way that indicates that you understod them. Too often we jump to conclusions and incorrectly assume that we know what a speaker means and feels. Paraphrasing is a listening check that asks, "Am I right? Is this what you mean?"

Paraphrasing requires finding new words to describe what you have heard, rather than repeating what a person has said. In addition to rephrasing the meaning of the speaker's message, a paraphrase usually includes a request for confirmation. Paraphrasing can be used for many purposes:

To clarify meaning: "When you said that you weren't going to the conference, did you mean that you want one of us to go instead?"

To ensure understanding: "I know that you said you approve, but I sense you're not happy with the outcome. Am I way off?"

To summarize: "What you seem to be saying is that it's not the best time to change this policy. Am I right?"

By rephrasing what we have heard and requesting confirmation, we can use paraphrases to help confirm our perceptions. Effective paraphrasing requires us to use our extra thought speed to produce a statement that follows the golden listening rule.

REAL WORLD, REAL SPEAKERS

A highly respected and successful courtroom attorney told a story about how audience feedback let him know that his client had no chance of avoiding jail time. He was defending one of four suspects in an armed bank robbery. Right after the robbery, the police followed a lead to a city row house and found four men matching the descriptions of the bank robbers asleep in one bedroom. Under one bed they found the exact amount of money stolen from the bank. The lawyer's client contended that he lived at the house and that three of his friends had asked to crash for the night. The lawyer made these final arguments to the jury: My client is the unfortunate victim of circumstance.

Because he let his buddies crash at his house, he has been accused of a crime he didn't commit. Just because there were four bank robbers doesn't mean that my client is one of them.

As he spoke, the jury's chairwoman nonverbally "told" him that he would lose his case. A small, amused smile crept across her face as the lawyer spoke. Almost imperceptibly, her head moved back and forth in a "no." When he said that his client had no idea that a bank had been robbed, another juror raised one eyebrow with a look that said, "Okay, you've done your best to defend your client, but you and I know he's guilty as sin." Sure enough, the jury found all four suspects guilty as charged.

Listen Before You Leap. One of the most often quoted pieces of listening advice to come from Ralph Nichols's writings is that "we must always withhold evaluation until our comprehension is complete."[21] Good listeners make sure that they understand a speaker before reacting either positively or negatively.

Sometimes when we become angry, friends may tell us to "count to ten" before reacting. Taking the same precaution is also good advice for listening. Counting to ten, however, implies more than withholding evaluation until you understand completely. You may comprehend a speaker's words perfectly but be infuriated or offended by what you hear. If an insensitive speaker refers to the women in the audience as "girls," it may take your counting to twenty to allow you enough time to collect your thoughts and maintain your ability to listen comprehensively. If a speaker tells an offensive joke, you may have a double reaction—anger toward the speaker and disappointment with those who laugh. Try to understand the effects of offensive comments and emotionally laden words without losing your composure or concentration.

When you listen before you leap, you are not approving of or condoning what someone says. Instead, you are using your extra thought speed to decide how to react to controversial, prejudiced, or offensive comments. Listening before you leap gives you time to adjust your reactions in a way that will help clarify and correct a statement rather than offend, disrupt, or infuriate a speaker or other audience members.

Listening to Your Audience

One of the most important and difficult speaking skills to learn involves "listening" and adapting to your audience during a presentation. Here, we are not talking about listening to their comments or questions after your presentation.

Instead, we are talking about watching and listening for their feedback *during* your presentation. As we indicated in Chapter 1, feedback is the verbal and non-verbal responses audience members communicate as they listen to a speaker. Feedback tells you a great deal about whether your audience is responding positively or negatively to your presentation.

Everyone in an audience reacts in some way. Sometimes that reaction is crystal clear. Audience members may smile or frown. They may nod "yes" or "no" as they listen. They may break into spontaneous applause or refuse to applaud. They may sit forward at full attention or sit back and look bored. At other times, they may stare at you with blank faces or appear distracted. Feedback can help you determine the kind of effect that you are having on your audience.

As you speak, look at and listen to the ways in which audience members react to you. Do they look interested or bored, pleased or displeased? If you can't see or hear reactions, ask for feedback. There is nothing wrong with stopping in the middle of a presentation to ask audience members if they understand you. Not only does such feedback help you adapt to your audience; it also tells listeners that you are interested in their reactions. Asking for feedback also helps your audience listen. By asking the audience questions or seeking confirmation, you are helping everyone understand and respond to the same message.

Adjusting to Audience Feedback

As important as it is to "listen" to your audience, it is just as important to listen to yourself. The ability to monitor and understand the effects of what you say will make you a more successful speaker. Two skills can enhance your ability to listen to yourself. First, translate feedback into useful information about the way you speak and listen so that you can answer questions such as these:

▶ Are audience members actively listening to me, or do I seem to be talking to a blank wall?

▶ Do audience members seem to understand what I am saying, or do they seem confused by my remarks?

▶ Do I feel my voice rising and my heart racing when I talk about an emotional issue or address an argumentative audience member?

Good speakers silently ask and answer these questions as they speak. Then they use a second important skill—they make mid-presentation corrections. If an audience seems confused, the speaker may slow down and re-explain a concept. If the audience looks bored, the speaker may add an interesting or amusing story to rekindle their interest. If the audience seems hostile, the speaker may try to defuse the tense atmosphere by acknowledging the legitimacy of the audience's concerns, announcing a question-and-answer session scheduled for *after* the talk, or beginning with an amusing story about how another speaker handled an inhospitable audience.

Learning to "listen" as a speaker is just as important as learning to listen as an audience member. Both skills require critical thinking, a willingness to withhold evaluation until comprehension is complete, and the courage to make mid-performance adjustments as you speak.

Adapting to Different Listeners

Just as audience members have different backgrounds and abilities, they also have different ways of listening. Remember the levels of intellectual development we discussed earlier? Audience members will listen quite differently, depending on

On Houghton Mifflin's Public Speaking Web site, www.hmco.com/college/communication, you'll find video clips of major presentations by speakers with different backgrounds and perspectives. How do such differences affect the way you listen to a speaker's message?

whether they are at the first level (Received Knowledge) or at the highest level (Constructed Knowledge). At the first level, audience members may only listen for and remember a few facts. They may not be able to identify or analyze your central idea or key points because they may have underdeveloped empathic, analytical, or appreciative listening skills. On the other hand, audience members at the Constructed Knowledge level may be skilled at almost all forms of listening.

Listening behavior may also differ between men and women. Researchers tell us that men may be more likely to listen to the content of what is said, while women may focus more on the relationship between the speaker and the audience. Males tend to hear the facts, while females are more aware of the mood of the communication. In other words, men tend to focus on comprehensive and analytical listening, while women are more likely to be empathic and appreciative listeners.[22]

Cultural differences can also influence the ways in which audience members listen and respond to a presentation. One study concluded that international students perceive U.S. students to be less willing and less patient as listeners than those from African, Asian, South American, or European cultures.[23] Myron Lustig and Jolene Koester, communication professors and the authors of *Intercultural Competence,* offer an explanation of such perceived differences in listening behavior. English is a speaker-responsible language in which the speaker structures the message and relies primarily upon words to provide meaning. Japanese, however, is a listener-responsible language in which speakers indirectly indicate what they want listeners to know. Listeners must rely on nonverbal communication and an understanding of the relationship between the speaker and the listener to interpret meaning.[24] Thus, an English-speaking listener may feel as though a Japanese speaker is leaving out important information whereas the Japanese listener may think that the English speaker is overexplaining or talking down to him or her. Such misunderstandings and perceived discourtesy are due to speaking and listening differences rather than substantive disagreement.

Adapting your presentation to the diverse listening styles of audience members can be a complicated and challenging task when you take intellectual development stages, gender, and cultural differences into account. Fortunately, critical thinking and listening are skills that can be taught, learned, practiced, and mastered. Not only are these skills essential to encoding and decoding presentations; they are also critical elements in *all* forms of communication.

Summary

●▶ **How do I apply critical thinking to the presentation speaking process?**

Speakers and listeners should learn to analyze the claims, evidence, and warrants used to justify a speaker's position in a presentation. They also should ask critical questions about the purpose, audience, logistics, content, organization, credibility, and performance of a presentation.

●▶ **Is everyone equally able to think critically?**

Depending on their level of intellectual development, some people have difficulty thinking critically. Those who think critically go well beyond the objective testing of facts and opinions to decide what they know, believe, and value.

●▶ **Is there more than one way to listen?**

Depending on the circumstances, you can use one or more of the following types of listening: comprehensive, empathic, analytical, and appreciative.

●▶ **How can I become a better listener?**

In addition to using your extra thought speed to analyze what you hear and applying the golden listening rule, the following skills can enhance your ability to listen: overcoming distractions, listening for the big ideas, "listening" to nonverbal behavior, paraphrasing, and listening before you leap.

●▶ **How do I "listen" to an audience?**

You "listen" to an audience by looking for and responding to feedback. Responding and adapting to audience feedback have the added advantage of helping your audience listen to and understand your message.

Key Terms

analytical listening 30
appreciative listening 31
argument 23
backing 24
claim 23
comprehensive
  listening 29

critical thinking 22
empathic listening 29
evidence 23
golden listening rule 33
listening 28
nonverbal communica-
  tion 35

paraphrasing 35
qualifier 25
reservation 25
thought speed 32
warrant 24

Notes

1. For other definitions and discussions of critical thinking, see Brooke Noel Moore and Richard Parker, *Critical Thinking,* 5th ed. (Mountain View, CA: Mayfield, 1998); John Chaffee, *Thinking Critically,* 6th ed. (Boston: Houghton Mifflin, 2000); Richard W. Paul, *Critical Thinking: How to Prepare Students for a Rapidly Changing World* (Santa Rosa, CA: Foundation for Critical Thinking, 1995).
2. Moore and Parker, p. 5.
3. Moore and Parker, p. 5
4. Stephen Toulmin, *The Uses of Argument* (London: Cambridge University Press, 1958). *Note:* Many of the popular critical thinking books on the market do not consider Toulmin's notions of warrant, reservation, or qualifier. They also fail to acknowledge authoritative warrants (expert testimony and speaker credibility) or motivation warrants (audience beliefs, attitudes, and values) as forms of evidence. Using Toulmin provides a sophisticated mechanism for analyzing different kinds of arguments, including those based on logical reasoning, source credibility, and audience motivations, beliefs, and experiences.
5. We have taken liberty and departed from some of Toulmin's terminology for the layout of an argument. We also have used elements of the Toulmin model as modified by Douglas Ehninger and Wayne Brockriede to explain the different types of proof that can be used to support an argument. See Douglas Ehninger and Wayne Brockriede, *Decision by Debate* (New York: Dodd, Mead, 1963), Chapters 8–11. Also see Douglas Ehninger and Wayne Brockriede, *Decision by Debate*, 2nd ed. (New York: Harper & Row, 1978), Chapters 4–6. Also see Sonja K. Foss, Karen A. Foss, and Robert Trapp, *Contemporary Perspectives on Rhetoric* (Prospect Heights, IL: Waveland Press, 1985), Chapter 4.
6. Kelvin L. Seifert, Robert J. Hoffnung, and Michelle Hoffnung, *Lifespan Development*, 2nd ed. (Boston: Houghton Mifflin, 2000), p. 447.
7. Joanne Gainen Kurfiss, *Critical Thinking: Theory, Research, Practice, and Possibilities,* ASHE–ERIC Higher Education Report No. 2 (Washington, DC: Association for the Study of Higher Education, 1988), pp. 51–58.
8. Kurfiss, p. 54.
9. William G. Perry, Jr., "Cognitive and Ethical Growth: The Making of Meaning," in *The Modern American College,* ed. Arthur W. Chickering and Associates (San Francisco: Jossey-Bass, 1981), p. 79.
10. Sections of this chapter are based on Chapter 6 of Isa N. Engleberg and Dianna R. Wynn, *Working in Groups: Communication Principles and Strategies,* 2nd ed. (Boston: Houghton Mifflin, 2000).
11. Larry L. Barker et al., "An Investigation of Proportional Time Spent in Various Communication Activities by College Students," *Journal of Applied Communication Research* 8 (1980): 101–109.
12. Andrew D. Wolvin and Carolyn G. Coakley, *Listening,* 5th ed. (Madison, WI: Brown & Benchmark, 1996), p. 15.
13. Ralph G. Nichols, "Listening Is a 10-Part Skill," *Nation's Business* 75 (Sept. 1987): 40.
14. S. S. Benoit and J. W. Lee, "Listening: It Can Be Taught," *Journal of Education for Business* 63 (1986): 229–232.
15. Nichols, p. 40.
16. Alan M. Perlman, *Writing Great Speeches* (Boston: Allyn & Bacon, 1998), p. 91.
17. Madelyn Burley-Allen, *Listening: The Forgotten Skill,* 2nd ed. (New York: Wiley, 1995), pp. 68–70.
18. *The American Heritage Dictionary of the English Language,* 3rd ed. (Boston: Houghton Mifflin, 1992), p. 181.
19. Mark L. Knapp and Judith A. Hall, *Nonverbal Communication in Human Interaction,* 4th ed. (Fort Worth, TX: Harcourt Brace, 1997), p. 466.
20. As cited in Knapp and Hall, p. 391.
21. Ralph G. Nichols, "Do We Know How to Listen? Practical Help in a Modern Age," *Speech Teacher* 10 (1961): 121.
22. See Deborah Tannen, *You Just Don't Understand: Women and Men in Conversation* (New York: William Morrow, 1990), pp. 149–151; Diana K. Ivy and Phil Backlund, *Exploring Gender Speak* (New York: McGraw-Hill, 1994), pp. 206–208 and 224–225.
23. Wolvin and Coakley, p. 125.
24. Myron W. Lustig and Jolene Koester, *Intercultural Communication Across Cultures,* 3rd ed. (New York: Longman, 1999), p. 249.

3

Building Presentation Confidence

- Where does presentation anxiety come from?
- What makes some speakers look so confident?
- How can preparation reduce presentation anxiety?
- Do relaxation techniques really work?
- How can breaking the rules help me to become a more confident speaker?
- How do practice and focus build confidence?

Whether you call it presentation anxiety, communication apprehension, stage fright, or talking terror, you wouldn't be human if the thought of giving a speech or presentation didn't make you a bit nervous. On the first day of a public speaking class at our respective institutions, we often ask students what their goals are for the course. An overwhelming number of students only give answers related to fear of speaking. No other answer comes close. Students write that they want to "gain confidence," "overcome anxiety," "stop being nervous," "get rid of the jitters," and "calm down."

In fact, about 75 to 85 percent of the U.S. population experiences some form of anxiety when faced with the prospect of making a presentation.[1] In study after study, Americans report that they fear public speaking more than heights, death, financial difficulties, and snakes.[2] Even people such as Barbra Streisand, Billy Graham,

Jane Fonda, and Lily Tomlin who are known for their public performances and presentations have reported that they suffer from extreme stage fright.[3] It's hard to believe that people would rather fall off cliffs, die, lose their jobs, or be thrown into a snake pit than make a presentation. Most people probably would choose to give a speech rather than suffer any of the previously mentioned horrors. Nevertheless, for many Americans the *thought* of making a presentation is incredibly frightening. In this chapter, we focus on the causes of presentation anxiety and what you can do to reduce it and become a more confident speaker. This last sentence is an important one. As we've indicated, most people experience some anxiety when they make an important presentation. It would be unnatural not to. In fact, that "keyed up" feeling is a positive and normal reaction to speaking and demonstrates that you care about what you have to say. The issue, then, is not whether you experience presentation anxiety, but rather how you label it and transform it. And that is the focus of this chapter.

What Is Presentation Anxiety?

Presentation anxiety is a natural reaction to a unique kind of social situation—the task of getting up to speak in front of a group of people. Speakers cite many reasons for getting nervous—such as "I could forget what I want to say," "My audience will hate me," or "I'll make a huge, embarrassing mistake." However, the probability of any of these things happening is very small. It's *imagining* their happening that creates anxiety.

Presentation anxiety is also a physiological response to stress. Physical symptoms such as sweaty palms and a perspiring forehead, a fast pulse, shallow breathing, cold extremities, flushed skin, nausea, trembling hands, quivering legs, and "butterflies" in the stomach are the body's reaction to the release of stress hor-

---

HOW CONFIDENT ARE YOU?

To assess your level of communication confidence, complete this brief questionnaire:

Presentation Confidence Survey*

For each statement please indicate whether you (1) strongly agree, (2) agree, (3) neither agree nor disagree, (4) disagree, or (5) strongly disagree.

1. I have no fear of making a speech.   1 2 3 4 5

2. I feel relaxed when giving a speech.   1 2 3 4 5

3. Giving a speech really scares me.   1 2 3 4 5

4. My thoughts become confused and jumbled when I'm giving a speech.   1 2 3 4 5

5. I face the prospect of giving a speech with confidence.   1 2 3 4 5

Now score yourself using this formula: Your score = 12 minus (items 3 + 4) plus the sum of (items 1 + 2 + 5). If your score is quite high (the possible range is from 5 to 25), you're probably very nervous about making presentations in most situations. If your score is quite low, you have a low level of anxiety when planning or making a presentation. Most scores fall in the middle range—indicating a moderate level of speaking anxiety. Regardless of your level of anxiety, however, you will still have to make presentations. Thus, it's important to learn how to deal with your apprehensions in various settings.

* There are longer, more sophisticated instruments for assessing your level of communication apprehension and stage fright. See Richmond and McCroskey in the Notes section.

mones such as adrenaline.[4] Yet these symptoms also resemble those that accompany many *positive* experiences. Suppose you're waiting for the exciting conclusion of a football game, the ending of an adventure movie that has had you at the edge of your seat, or the arrival of a loved one whom you haven't seen for many years. How would you feel? You'd be physically aroused, just as you are when making a presentation—pounding heart, shortness of breath, flushed skin. Many of the physical sensations of excitement are the same as those of anxiety. It's the way in which you interpret them that is important. You can think of making a presentation as an exciting adventure or as a frightening, even horrifying event. It all depends on how you choose to label it. Let's look at what the "anxiety" label means.

Presentation anxiety is a speaker's individual level of fear or anxiety that is associated with either real or anticipated communication to a group of people or an audience.[5] What does this mean? First, look at the phrase *a speaker's individual level of fear or anxiety*. All this says is that some speakers are more frightened than others. Some people look forward to presentation speaking; others would do almost anything to avoid it.

Second, note the phrase *real or anticipated communication*. This says that anticipating all the things that could go wrong makes some people more nervous than making an actual presentation, while others are most nervous *during* a presentation. In fact, for many speakers, less than a minute after beginning a presentation, their anxiety subsides as their heart rates begin a gradual and fairly steady decline.[6]

Third, see how the definition mentions a *group of people or an audience*. This means that some people are just as nervous when speaking to a small group of three people as others are in front of an audience of thousands. Again, those anxious feelings are perfectly natural in either setting—and may be as much a sign of excitement as of nervousness.

Sources of Presentation Anxiety

One of the keys to building presentation confidence is to understand the sources of the nervousness and discomfort that you may feel when speaking to a group or an audience. While everyone has his or her own personal reasons for being nervous, researchers have identified some of the key fears that underlie presentation anxiety.[7] See if you can recognize yourself in any of the sections that follow.

> ### THE "BIG SEVEN" SOURCES OF PRESENTATION ANXIETY
>
> Fear of failure
>
> Fear of disapproval
>
> Fear of the unknown
>
> Fear of the spotlight
>
> Fear of the audience
>
> Fear of breaking the rules
>
> Fear of fear

Fear of Failure.   Virtually everyone fears failure, especially public failure. Presentations happen in public, in front of an audience that watches and evaluates you. Some researchers maintain that the fear of a negative evaluation is the number-one cause of speaking anxiety.[8] In part, presentation anxiety anticipates the possible anguish and embarrassment of being evaluated as a poor speaker—of failing.

Before a presentation, you may worry about what audience members will think of you and your talk. During a presentation, you may experience heightened anxiety if you begin to think that your audience is not interested or approving. And afterwards you may be haunted by worries about audience members' final judgments. "Did they like it?" and "How'd I do?" are not idle or innocent questions; they are ways of determining whether you have succeeded or failed.

So how do you turn the fear of failure on its head? Scan your audience for positive reactions—a nod, a smile, or an alert look. When you find them, focus on them: Seeing positive feedback generally reduces presentation anxiety. When you sense that your listeners like you and your message, that reaction means your presentation is succeeding.

Fear of Disapproval.   Most of you have probably heard the saying "Children should be seen and not heard." Let's hope you didn't hear it in your own home too often. In homes where silence is rewarded and talk is punished, children learn that speech is something to avoid. Staying quiet is safe. Speakers who have learned and believe that their talking is grounds for disapproval are rarely confident speakers. Virginia Richmond and Jim McCroskey, experts in the study of communication apprehension, found that a person's level of presentation anxiety is determined in part by the extent to which she or he was rewarded for or deterred from communicating as a child.[9] So how do you break this cycle? One way is to understand that your anxiety is based on a childhood habit rather than on an adult response. Another way is to use the same strategies that work for those who fear evaluation. Use your audience's feedback as a reality check. Their positive reactions can reassure you that it's okay to be seen *and* heard.

Fear of the Unknown.   Most people fear the unfamiliar, and making a presentation falls into that category for many inexperienced speakers. Even if you have had some experience making presentations, you may still become anxious if you don't know much about your audience or topic. In unfamiliar settings, the size and shape of a room, unexpected background noises, the ways in which lights and microphones operate, and whether and where audience members will sit all have the potential to unnerve a speaker. Even a familiar room and audience can look quite different from the podium.

The switch to an uncommon or unexpected role can transform a usually confident person into a tangle of nerves. Imagine that you are asked to stand up and explain a new procedure or introduce a guest in the audience. If you were attending an event or a meeting and expecting to be a listener, being called on to switch roles and to be a presenter instead could be unsettling, to say the least.

So how do you reduce your fear of the unknown? For starters, remind yourself that since you're taking this course, presentation speaking *won't* be an unknown anymore! If you're asked to give a presentation, whether months or moments in advance, you'll know what to do.

Fear of the Spotlight.   One of the primary reasons many people give for having presentation anxiety is knowing that they will be the main focus of their audience's attention. While a little attention may be flattering and pleasurable, standing alone in the spotlight makes many people nervous. In such a situation your audience is watching everything that you do; they are there to hear what you have to say. It's hard to imagine anything more conspicuous. Moreover, feeling conspicuous can lead to excessive self-consciousness, which in turn may cause you to focus on yourself rather than on your message. The more self-focused you are, the more likely you will experience nervousness.

Since excessive self-focus can limit your effectiveness as a speaker, try this trick to break the habit: Focus your attention on a few friendly faces in the audi-

REAL WORLD, REAL SPEAKERS

In our classes we often ask students to describe how they feel when asked to make a presentation. We've received responses that range from a sense of empowerment to total terror, as the following illustrate:

- Giving a speech makes me feel powerful. Although nervousness enters the picture, so does a feeling of power. The thought of having everybody's full attention and being able to convey my point of view makes me feel as though I'm in charge.

- Giving a speech makes me feel scared. I feel as though people aren't listening to me but instead are looking at my shoes or clothes, so I worry that I have both earrings in or that my blouse is buttoned correctly. You're on the spot with twenty pairs of eyes staring at you.

- I'm very quiet and shy in front of most people, especially people I don't know. Because I'm a quiet person, I'm not comfortable with just coming out and speaking to someone—which is just like giving a speech because you are speaking to people you've never met.

- Giving a speech makes me feel extremely nervous. My heart starts racing so fast that it makes me breathless. My knees, and the rest of my body, start to tremble, and I feel like I'm going to lose control. I've tried taking deep breaths to calm myself when I feel this way. I've also tried medication, but it doesn't work. The last time I enrolled in a speech class, I dropped out because I was so nervous about giving a speech and embarrassing myself.

We are pleased to report that all four of these students did quite well in the course.

John Daly and Isa Engleberg

---

ence rather than on your notes or on yourself. Not only will this technique make you less self-conscious, but it will also engage your audience in your presentation and focus their attention more on your message—and less on you!

Fear of the Audience.   Sometimes the characteristics of the audience can heighten a speaker's anxiety. Talking to two people is quite different from speaking to two thousand, so it's no surprise that large audiences arouse more anxiety than small ones.

Large audiences also tend to be composed of people with varying backgrounds, interests, and purposes—and this diversity can make some speakers nervous. They may worry that adapting to one part of a diverse audience means running the risk of excluding another part. More likely, though, fear of the audience relates to the fear of the unknown we discussed earlier. If you don't know much about your audience—and what you do know is that you don't have much in common with them—you're likely to feel somewhat apprehensive.

One way in which you may differ from your audience is in your status. A junior-level financial officer suddenly asked to present a major report to a group of senior vice presidents would probably be more anxious about speaking than if she were assigned to talk to a group of beginning finance students. Why? Because of the relative imbalance between her status level and her audience's.

As we discuss in Chapter 5, "Audience Analysis and Adaptation," you can learn a lot about your audience and use the information that you gather to develop a presentation uniquely suited to their needs. You may find areas of common interest, reducing the perceived gaps between you and your audience. And you may find that you have been invited to present because you know more about a given topic than your "higher status" audience does. Increasing your knowledge about your audience can decrease your anxiety.

Fear of Breaking the Rules.   Many speakers experience presentation anxiety because they are burdened with too many rigid rules and misconceptions about what makes a presentation good or bad. The rules of speaking are not like the rules of baseball or the laws of physics. "Three strikes and you're out" works in baseball; this rule doesn't apply to presentations. "What goes up must come down" is fine in applied physics but not in presentations. Unfortunately, some speakers believe that the "rules" they find in textbooks or learn about in a communication class are hard and fast. At best, the rules are generalizations that can be applied to many situations. At worst, some rules are wrong. We wish we had a dollar for every student who has been told to look at a spot on the back wall above the heads of the audience rather than to establish direct eye contact. For fear of saying "uh" or "um" in a presentation, speakers have overrehearsed to the point of sounding like robots.

Novice speakers sometimes take all the rules about a good presentation too seriously. They become anxious because as they are speaking, they find themselves not adhering to every rule. Experienced speakers know, however, that no two presentations are alike and understand that rules are only rough guides. They know that sometimes these rules should be bent or broken.

Fear of Fear.   One of the biggest problems with presentation anxiety is that it grows upon itself. If, for example, you start feeling a slight tremor of fear, you may become more conscious of that feeling, which in turn can generate even more anxiety. Don Green, who applies the techniques of sports psychology to helping musicians overcome performance anxiety, suggests a quick and simple method for breaking the fear cycle: Give a name to your fear; then tell "Pete" or "Ruth" to scram![10] We explore other methods for ending this cycle in the rest of this chapter.

Sources of Confidence

Successful speakers know two very important facts about presentation anxiety: They know that it's very common, and they know that it's usually invisible. Remember that 75 to 85 percent of the U.S. population experiences presentation anxiety. This means that most audience members will understand your feelings, wouldn't want to trade places with you, and might even admire your courage for being up there. If you do appear a bit nervous, most listeners will know how you're feeling and won't let it interfere with their impression of you or your presentation. Despite most people's worst fears, audiences tend to be kind to speakers. They are willing to forgive and forget an honest mistake. Since no one in your audience expects you to be perfect, why should you? Indeed, audiences are usually on your side.

Also, remember that in most cases your anxiety is invisible. Audiences cannot see or hear your fear. They cannot see a pounding heart, an upset stomach, cold hands, or worried thoughts. They do not notice small changes in a voice or remember occasional mistakes. In fact, most speakers who describe themselves as being nervous appear confident and calm to their audiences. Many speakers think that they display far more anxiety than audience members actually report seeing. Even experienced speech teachers, when asked about how anxious a speaker is, seldom accurately estimate the speaker's anxiety.[11]

If you find yourself feeling a little anxious before your next presentation, remind yourself of these two vital facts. They can help you transform your anxiety into presentation confidence.

> **REMEMBER: PRESENTATION ANXIETY IS . . .**
>
> **shared by your audience**
> **and**
> **usually invisible**

Becoming a Confident Speaker

A good side effect of presentation anxiety's being so common is that psychologists and communication researchers have developed many effective methods for helping anxious speakers cope. We hope you find some that can work for you in the pages that follow![12]

> **BUILD YOUR PRESENTATION CONFIDENCE:**
>
> **Prepare**
> **Relax**
> **Adapt**
> **Practice**
> **Focus**

Prepare

"Be prepared" is more than the Boy Scouts' motto; it is one of the guiding maxims of successful speakers. Not only does conscientious and thorough preparation make your presentation better, it also makes you a better presenter. Why? Remember that fear of the unknown contributes to presentation anxiety. Preparation is one way of changing something unfamiliar into something familiar. Novice speakers often report that a symptom of their nervousness is their feeling lost and confused as they speak. Preparation can replace this sense of confusion with confidence.

Good preparation requires that you know as much as possible about where and to whom you are speaking, what you are going to be talking about, and how you are going to deliver your message. We urge you to check out the place where you will be speaking beforehand, choose a familiar topic, and avoid taking on more than you can handle.

Check It Out. Pilots check out their airplanes before taking off, champion golfers check out the course before playing a round, and good speakers check out

REAL WORLD, REAL SPEAKERS

Lilly Walters, the author of *Secrets of Successful Speakers*, advocates hours of preparation as a way of reducing stage fright. To make her point, she tells stories about several famous speakers and their preparation of formal and impromptu speeches (which are spur-of-the-moment comments). Mark Twain, one of the highest-paid speakers of his era, said, "It takes me at least three weeks to prepare an impromptu speech." A friend of Winston Churchill, England's great prime minister, wrote, "Winston has spent the best years of his life writing impromptu speeches." Churchill estimated that it took him six to eight hours to prepare a forty-five-minute speech. For an important presentation, you may need to spend as much as one hour preparing for each minute of the presentation.[1]

1. Lilly Walters, *Secrets of Successful Speakers* (New York: McGraw-Hill, 1993), pp. 32–33. Her information about Winston Churchill is taken from William Manchester, *The Last Lion: Winston Spencer Churchill* (New York: Dell, 1983), p. 32.

the places where they will be speaking before they speak. Check out the seating, the microphone, the lighting, and the equipment *before* you speak. That way you make the unfamiliar familiar—*and* you don't have to worry about technical difficulties during your presentation. Make sure that you can see your notes and have a place to put them. Make sure the lectern isn't too high or too low. If you can, you may want to rearrange the audience's seating. Practice a few sentences of your presentation before anyone gets there, so that you'll have a feel for the sound of the room. Checking out the setting beforehand can help you feel more confident about approaching the podium and your audience when it's time to do the real thing.

If you can't get to the place where you will be speaking in advance, ask the person who invited you about the facilities, equipment, and other logistical details. As Chapter 6, "Logistics and Occasion," discusses in more detail, knowing about where, when, and why you're speaking reduces the novelty of the speaking situation and can help to reduce your anxiety.

Speak About a Familiar Topic.   Speakers who know what they're talking about feel more comfortable and less anxious. If you have ever made a presentation about something you knew little about, you know what it feels like to be unprepared. You may fear questions you can't answer, fear that you don't have enough to say, and even fear that you are wrong about something you do say. You can nip nervousness in the bud by picking a topic that you already know and care about. If you do this, you'll find it's much easier to prepare your presentation, and you'll feel more confident delivering it. You won't have to worry that audience members will think you're uninformed or that questions following your talk will be ones that you can't answer. Your interest in your topic will show and will engage your audience.

Begin in Your Comfort Zone.   If you aren't a confident swimmer, you probably won't jump into the deep end of a pool. If you aren't an experienced midwife or physician, you should be reluctant to deliver a baby. And if you aren't a confident speaker, you shouldn't talk in dangerous territory. Try to begin by speaking

Exhibitors at trade shows repeatedly make the same presentation on topics they know well, growing more confident and competent each time.

in your comfort zone. If your level of anxiety is high, don't deliver your presentation for the first time to an audience of 2,000 people. Instead, try it out on a group of friends or coworkers first. If your topic is complicated, make sure that the beginning of your presentation is clear and well rehearsed. Tell a story you know very well, or make sure the beginning of your presentation is the one part that you know best. By starting in "shallow water," you can gradually make your way into deeper water without fear of drowning.

Relax

One well-accepted way of reducing presentation anxiety is to learn how to relax and minimize its symptoms. Relaxation techniques reduce nervous feelings by substituting feelings of calmness. You can begin this process by learning simple relaxation exercises that lessen many of the physical symptoms of presentation anxiety—rapid heartbeat, stomachache, shaky hands and legs, and trembling voice. Many of the books and courses that teach meditation and relaxation techniques can help you prepare for any situation that makes you nervous or anxious. However, some meditation techniques require time and privacy. Since you cannot excuse yourself from an auditorium stage to meditate right before your presentation, try to develop a set of short tension-reducing techniques that you can use in the few minutes or seconds before speaking. (See the TIP on page 51.)

Systematic Desensitization. A technique of behavioral therapy called **systematic desensitization**[13] can be especially effective as a relaxation technique for reducing performance anxiety. Sometimes we associate fear with certain situations, things, or experiences such as flying, insects, elevators, snakes, or presentation speaking. One way of breaking the fearful response bond is to learn a new, relaxed response to the same situation.[14] Systematic desensitization begins by training speakers to achieve deep muscle relaxation. In this relaxed state, they are then asked to imagine themselves in a variety of communication situations—ranging from one that is very comfortable to those that produce more anxiety. Karen Dwyer, author of *Conquering Your Speechfright,* has noted "When you can visually imagine yourself in all the steps in the speechmaking process and maintain deep relaxation at the same time, you will have broken your fearful response to public speaking."[15] Systematic desensitization is a therapy developed by psychologist Joseph Wolpe to help clients with phobias and serious anxieties. Clients are taught to visualize a series of anxiety-provoking situations while maintaining a state of relaxation and, as a result, weakening the bond between the anxiety and the feared object. To accomplish this goal, clients are asked to imagine an item from a sequence of increasingly fear-provoking situations called a *desensitization hierarchy*.[16]

How would this technique apply to presentation speaking? Figure 3.1 shows a hierarchy of presentation speaking situations.

Systematic desensitization works amazingly well. The underlying notion is that presentation anxiety arises when you mentally associate fear with speaking. After your successful treatment, a sense of relaxation will arise when you think about making a presentation. Any number of studies confirm that the technique works.[17] It is also a method used by almost every professional sports team to aid players in coping with "clutch" moments. Watch a basketball game. A "clutch" moment occurs when, for instance, a game is tied, and one team has one free throw left that will allow it to win if a basket is made. The player making the shot may "choke"—shoot the ball and entirely miss the hoop. If she does, there's no win. Watch carefully how this player acts as she prepares to take the shot. Note how relaxed she is. Every muscle appears to be almost limp. What you are seeing is systematic desensitization at work. The player has learned that the more nerve-wracking the situation, the more relaxed she has to be.

Figure 3.1   A Desensitization Hierarchy for Presentation Anxiety

Even anxious speakers would feel comfortable thinking about the first few items of this hierarchy. As the process progresses, however, the situations become more anxiety-producing. By trying to relax even when visualizing these situations, the anxious speaker can slowly learn to associate presentation speaking with relaxation rather than with nervousness.

1. You are reading a newspaper article about a politician's speech.
2. You are watching a television newscast in which speakers are shown speaking at a meeting.
3. You are listening to someone give a presentation at work.
4. You learn that you will have to give a presentation at work next month.
5. You are starting to gather ideas and information for your presentation.
6. You are learning a lot about the size and composition of your audience.
7. You are preparing your notes for the presentation.
8. You are practicing your presentation in private.
9. You are practicing your presentation in front of a good friend or family member.
10. You see yourself arriving at the place where you will present your talk.
11. You see yourself walking to the podium and preparing to speak.
12. You see yourself beginning your presentation.

Understanding how systematic desensitization works can help you overcome presentation anxiety. The big idea here is that if you can teach yourself to relax, you'll be less nervous. Certainly this is easier said than done. But try deep breathing, peaceful meditation, stretches, or other tension-releasing techniques before your next presentation. They should help.

Cognitive Restructuring.   Whereas systematic desensitization assumes that a relaxed body will relax your mind, cognitive restructuring goes a step further. **Cognitive restructuring** assumes that presentation anxiety is caused by worrisome, irrational, and nonproductive thoughts (cognitions) about speaking. Thus, reducing anxiety, fear, and nervousness requires changing or restructuring those cognitions.[18]

Consider the following transcript of a cognitive restructuring session between a teacher and a student.

Teacher: Well, why are you so scared about making a presentation?

Student: I don't know . . . maybe because I know people will laugh at me if I make a mistake.

Teacher: Now, let's think about that. Why do you think you'll make a mistake . . . a mistake that will make people laugh at you?

Student: I just know I could.

Teacher: Sure you could, but the walls in this office could collapse, too. So let's assume you make a mistake, as rare as that might be. What's the harm?

Student: I'd be embarrassed.

Teacher: You're right. Embarrassing things happen to all of us—even when we're not making presentations. We survive, don't we?

Student: Yeah, but I would feel bad.

Teacher: Sure you would, but only for a little while . . .

USE THE SILENT REEELAAAX

Break the word *relax* into two syllables: *re* and *lax*. Breathe in slowly through your nose while saying the sound *re* (ree) silently to yourself, holding the long *e* sound all the while you are inhaling. This should take just about three seconds. Then breathe out slowly, also for about three seconds, thinking the sound *lax* (laks) silently to yourself, and hold the *a* sound while exhaling. Inhale and exhale, thinking, "REEE-LAAAX" four or five times. By the time you finish this thirty-second relaxation exercise, your pulse should be slower and, hopefully, you will also feel calmer. A word of caution, though: If you inhale and exhale too deeply and for too long, you could end up feeling lightheaded or faint rather than relaxed and calm. Try to find the pace that helps you relax before beginning your presentation.

If using the word *relax* doesn't work, try *calm down* or *no fear*. As long as there are vowels to hold for three seconds, any two-syllable phrase that suggests tension reduction can work. If repeating a word or phrase doesn't work for you, try something simpler. A small yawn or quiet sigh right before you speak can relax your neck and throat muscles. Tensing and relaxing your stomach muscles before you speak can squeeze a lot of tension out of your body. Find the relaxation exercise that works for you, and you'll be rewarded with a calmer body and mind.

As you can see, the process tries to change the speaker's unrealistic beliefs about making a presentation. Most of the time, you won't make big mistakes. Most of the time people won't laugh at you, and even if they do laugh, it isn't the end of the world.

Jerry Lynch, a sports psychologist, works with athletes who become anxious or fearful when it's time to perform.[19] He recommends that they adopt affirmations to restructure the way that they think. "Watch what you say," he cautions. "When you say, 'I can't,' you lose power. Your body immediately backs down." Lynch urges his athletes to write and repeat strong positive statements about their performances. The same technique can work for speakers. The next time that you feel anxious, try telling yourself these positive statements: "My message is important." "I am a well-prepared, skilled speaker." "Apprehension gives me extra energy."

The thing to remember about cognitive restructuring is that it helps you to become more realistic about what will happen when you make a presentation. The experience won't be all that bad. You'll survive. And remember this, writes speechwriter Peggy Noonan: "Every great speaker in history has flopped some-where along the way, most of them more than once. So relax. It's only a speech."[20] Challenge and then banish the irrational, negative beliefs that get in the way of speaking success.

Visualization.   Closely related to cognitive restructuring is **visualization,** a procedure that encourages people to think positively about presentation speak-ing by taking them through the entire speechmaking process.[21] Many profes-sional and Olympic athletes use visualization to improve their performance. Dr. Marcia Middel, a psychologist and former All-American swimmer, helps athletes and musicians to overcome performance anxiety through visualization.[22] They are told to find a quiet place where they can relax and visualize a picture of them-selves in competition. For example:

> Create a mental picture of yourself diving into the pool. Now, enter that pic-ture; hear the sounds you usually hear; smell the air; feel the sweat on your body; tune into what the diving board feels like under your feet or the water around your body. If you are hoping to improve a particular technique, then remember a time [when] you did it very well. Recreate that moment, then carefully perform the technique until you have executed it flawlessly in your head. Rehearse this image for a few minutes each day.[23]

Speakers can use visualization to overcome presentation anxiety. Before you make your presentation, sit back and picture the entire event. Imagine walking into the room with confidence and energy. Think about how many smiles you'll receive as you talk, think about the heads nodding in agreement, think about the looks of interest you'll see in the eyes of your audience, think about how smoothly you will deliver your message, and think about your successful conclu-sion. And then congratulate yourself. Many speakers find visualization a power-ful method of building confidence.

Like professional and Olympic athletes, speakers can use visualization to enhance their performance and confidence.

Sharing Your Fears with Friends. Discussing and sharing your anxieties with others can have several positive results. Because a majority of people fear presentation speaking, you will discover that you are not alone. It's also easy to believe that your fears are worse than anyone else's until you begin talking about them. You'll probably find that even the most confident-looking speakers can have upset stomachs and moments of panic. Remember that presentation anxiety is natural. You may not like the feeling of it, but it's one you share with most other people.

Discussing your speaking fears with others can also help you to correct misperceptions you may hold about your presentations. If you tell a friend or your instructor that you stumble over your words, you may find out that they've never noticed it. What seems like a major stumble to you may be nothing more than a pause to your audience. If you think that your voice shakes while you are speaking, you may find out that your listeners don't hear any shakiness. Remember that audiences can't see most symptoms of presentation anxiety. Likewise, confirming that your symptoms are invisible to your audience can be very reassuring.

Last, sharing your anxieties can help you to substitute positive thoughts for negative ones. If you tell your friends you were afraid that your audience noticed your shaky hands, they may tell you that everyone was too far away to notice and that, in fact, you looked poised. Rather than thinking, "I was a nervous wreck," substitute the thought "My friends tell me I look calm."

NEVER TELL AN AUDIENCE THAT YOU ARE NERVOUS

Some novice speakers take sharing a little too far—they figure that if friends will be supportive of their fears, most audiences will be, too. Unfortunately, sharing your anxieties with the audience tends to backfire. It only makes audience members more aware of your nervousness and makes you feel more self-conscious. Don't describe or discuss your speaking anxiety with your audience. Don't apologize before, during, or after your presentation. Don't tell your audience that you haven't prepared well enough. Don't burden them with all the problems you've had getting ready. If you are well prepared and have practiced your presentation, there won't be any need to apologize. Talk privately with your friends or instructor about presentation anxiety. Speak confidently to your audience.

Adapt

A presentation is not a permanent, written document. Unexpected events, questions from audience members, and late-breaking news may mean that you have to modify your well-prepared presentation on the spot. Doing this can be difficult for anxious speakers, who may be too busy concentrating on their own feelings to veer away from their planned presentations. However, anticipating potential problems and bending or breaking rigid rules can help even the most nervous speaker become more flexible and confident.

Anticipate and Address Potential Problems. Related to checking out your physical surroundings (see page 47) is assessing, in advance, what might create problems for you during a presentation. Once you've identified what makes you conscious of your nervousness or what could lead an audience to conclude that you're nervous, you can devise strategies to mask or modify these difficulties.

For instance, suppose that you notice that your hands shake when you hold your notes during a presentation. The sense that everyone might see them trembling might raise your anxiety level. The solution is simple: Eliminate the display of shaking. How? Since flimsy paper will shake in speakers' hands, no matter how comfortable they are about speaking, use stiffer note paper or lay your notes on a lectern or clipboard to eliminate much of the noticeable shaking. Or what should you do if a visible rash creeps up your neck whenever you speak? Again, the answer is simple: Mask it. Wear a buttoned-up shirt, a turtleneck, or a scarf. Thinking ahead about potential problems gives you the time to resolve them. Don't wait until you're speaking to deal with things that hinder your performance.

Bend or Break the Rules. Many years ago, a psychologist at UCLA, Mike Rose, researched why people experienced writer's block.[24] After watching many writers, he found that those with writer's block had rigid rules about writing. They believed, for example, that you had to have a perfect first sentence before you could go on to write the next sentence. These writers slaved over that first sentence for hours, often feeling that they would "never get it right." Writers who didn't suffer from writer's block knew that an opening sentence was important but decided not to worry about it if nothing immediately came to mind. The difference between "blocked" and comfortable writers was that the former group let the rules run them, while the latter group ran the rules. Don't be too tied to beliefs that you might have about what a "good" speaker looks and sounds like.

There are no "must" rules of speaking. This book is, of course, filled with advice. But every piece of advice should be adapted to *your* purpose, *your* audience, and *your* situation. Is it sometimes all right to put your hands in your pockets while speaking? Yes. Is it acceptable, in some situations, to sit down rather than to stand when speaking? Sure! Rules are best understood as guidelines for speaking, not as commandments. Sometimes breaking a commonly accepted rule can make your presentation more interesting and memorable. Smart speakers use rules when they aid their presentations and dismiss them when they get in the way.

Apprehensive speakers can be reluctant to abandon the "safety" of their rules, yet they may also feel more confident in communication contexts with fewer rules. For instance, most people are far more comfortable answering questions than they are making presentations. You'd think it would be the opposite, since a speaker has to think "on her feet" when answering questions, whereas she can do most of her thinking about a presentation beforehand. Because people have far fewer rigid rules about what good question-and-answer sessions ought to be like, they find them less nerve-wracking. On the other hand, almost everyone has strong notions of what presentations should be like. Drop the rules if they don't produce the results you want.

Practice

If you're good at something, you will usually be more confident when doing it, and the best way to become good at something is to practice. Knowing how to make effective presentations is the best way to ensure that you will succeed with

Michelle Crawford practiced her lines and prayed with her mother before speaking to the Wisconsin Legislature about how the state's new welfare program had transformed her life. Governor Tommy G. Thompson beams at Ms. Crawford's success.

REAL WORLD, REAL SPEAKERS

Peggy Noonan, who was one of President Reagan's speechwriters, describes herself as being near-phobic about speaking in front of groups. After having a horrible experience in seventh grade—she had been asked to read aloud from "The Song of Hiawatha" and was in such a panic that she lost her voice and nerve—she didn't give another speech until she was forty years old. An interesting thing happened to her about halfway through that presentation:

> But what I remember most, the key thing, is that about halfway through the speech I improved, became more focused and more sure, because my mind fastened on what I was saying, and I wanted to be understood. . . . I realized: When you forget yourself and your fear, when you go beyond self-consciousness because your mind is thinking about what you are trying to communicate, you become a better communicator. . . . This is the beginning of the end of self-consciousness, which is the beginning of the end of fear.[1]

1. Peggy Noonan, *Simply Speaking: How to Communicate Your Ideas with Style, Substance, and Clarity* (New York: HarperCollins, 1998), p. 8. Copyright © 1998 by Peggy Noonan. Reprinted by permission of HarperCollins Publishers, Inc.

them. In fact, the best piece of insider information we can give to anyone learning a skill is this: practice, practice, practice. If you've spent time practicing your presentation, you have less reason to be nervous. You know that you can make it through the presentation, no matter how anxious you are. Don't memorize your entire speech (what if you forget it?); just practice it often. Even though both of us have made thousands of presentations to hundreds of different groups, we still practice before going "on stage." Our secret of success is that there is no secret. Although it takes valuable time to practice, the payoff is a confident and seemingly effortless presentation.

Focus

Experienced speakers know that one of the best ways to build presentation confidence is to concentrate on the message and audience rather than on themselves. Speakers who worry about how they look and sound often feel more anxious than speakers who concentrate on what they have to say. Just as professional athletes and musicians channel their nervous energy into the sport or the music, excellent speakers convert nervousness into energy that focuses on their message.[25] Focusing on getting your message across to your audience means that you won't have enough time to think about your fears. Conveying that you care about your message gives your presentation an added measure of courage, conviction, and confidence. Janice Bryant, a nurse and social worker with Home Hospice in Sherman, Texas, discovered this effect when making a presentation to a local United Way board about hospice care. "It was very successful," she wrote, "because for the first time I was able to put aside my nervousness and convey the true emotions of my topic."

If you want to torture someone involved in a sport, ask the athlete to think of every movement he or she makes while playing. Ask a tennis player to note where his arms and legs are as he serves. Ask him to think about how high the ball goes before he hits it. Very quickly, any serve he would make would be ruined if he applied this focused self-attention during a match. The same is true during a presentation. If you concentrate all of your attention on how you look and sound rather than on what you have to say, you can be guaranteed a less-than-wonderful presentation and a higher level of anxiety. On the other hand, speakers who focus on achieving their purpose report low tension levels.

This observation explains why research studies have found that people with high levels of presentation anxiety find it hard to remember very much about their audience, the room they were in, or even what they said. They can recall, however, the negative feelings and worries they had during the presentation.[26] Giving less thought to yourself and more thought to reaching the audience with your message can reduce your level of anxiety and improve the quality of your performance and presentation.

Just Do It

Experience is a great teacher. One of the best ways to change presentation anxiety into presentation confidence is to speak. It's like learning to swim. You can read about how to tread water and listen to all the advice that your swimming instructor and friends may give you, but in the end you have to get in the water and try it. So take your first plunge with a positive mental attitude. Learn to say, "I can do it, and I will do it" rather than "I'm scared." And remember this: Always give your talk. No matter how frightened you are, you *can* do it. Making the decision to give a speech is the first step in building skills and confidence.

We're not saying it's easy. Building confidence will take conscientious work on your part. Moreover, it won't happen overnight. You'll have to practice the various skills we've described, a number of times, with a variety of presentations in different situations. Eventually, they'll become second nature. Practice will give you the tools to project confidence in yourself and in your message.

Summary

◆▸ Where does presentation anxiety come from?

Sources of presentation anxiety include fear of failure, fear of disapproval, fear of the unknown, fear of the spotlight, fear of the audience, fear of breaking the rules, and fear of fear.

◆▸ What makes some speakers look so confident?

Successful speakers may be just as nervous as unsuccessful speakers, but they also know that presentation anxiety is natural and usually invisible. They also know how to cope with anxiety by using a variety of methods that help them prepare, relax, adapt, practice, and focus.

◆▸ How can preparation reduce presentation anxiety?

Preparation helps to reduce fear of the unknown. Preparation strategies that help to reduce presentation anxiety include checking out the place where you will be speaking in advance, speaking about a familiar topic, and beginning in a comfortable setting.

◆✦ **Do relaxation techniques really work?**

Relaxation techniques help to reduce nervous feelings by substituting feelings of calmness. Effective relaxation techniques include systematic desensitization, cognitive restructuring, and visualization.

◆✦ **How can breaking the rules help me to become a more confident speaker?**

Some speakers become too tied to rigid rules that prevent them from adapting to their purpose, audience, and logistics.

◆✦ **How do practice and focus build confidence?**

Practice can improve both skills and confidence. Focus teaches you to concentrate on your message rather than on yourself. Conveying that you have practiced your presentation and care about your message gives your presentation an added measure of courage, conviction, and confidence.

Key Terms

cognitive restructuring 51
presentation anxiety 43
systematic desensitization 49
visualization 52

Notes

1. Michael T. Motley, *Overcoming Your Fear of Public Speaking: A Proven Method* (Boston: Houghton Mifflin, 1997), p. 3; Virginia P. Richmond and James C. McCroskey, *Communication: Apprehension, Avoidance, and Effectiveness,* 4th ed. (Scottsdale, AZ: Gorsuch Scarisbrick, 1995).
2. In *Conquer Your Speechfright* by Karen Kangas Dwyer (Fort Worth, TX: Harcourt Brace, 1998), Dwyer cites *The Book of Lists* by Wallenchinksy, Wallace, and Wallace (New York: Bantam Books, 1977), in which fear of public speaking ranks as the number-one "common fear" in America. Similar data can be found in The Bruskin Report, *What Are Americans Afraid Of?* (Research Report no. 53, 1973).
3. Motley, p. 3.
4. Sharon S. Brehm, Saul M. Kassin, and Steven Fein, *Social Psychology,* 4th ed. (Boston: Houghton Mifflin, 1999), p. 510.
5. This definition is based on James McCroskey's definition of *communication apprehension:* "an individual's level of fear or anxiety associated with either real or anticipated communication with another person or persons." See Richmond and McCroskey, p. 41.
6. Motley, p. 27.
7. We have tried to summarize some of the considerable research related to communication apprehension. Four available sources that report the results of this research are: John A. Daly and James C. McCroskey, eds., *Avoiding Communication: Shyness, Reticence, and Communication Apprehension* (Thousand Oaks, CA: Sage, 1984); Richmond and McCroskey, *Communication;* Dwyer, *Conquer Your Speechfright;* and Motley, *Overcoming Your Fear of Public Speaking.*
8. See Dwyer, p. 23.
9. Richmond and McCroskey, p. 64.
10. Ralph Blumenthal, "First Divers, Now Divas: Exorcising the Jitters," *New York Times,* 18 August 1999, pp. B1 and B4.

11. Lori J. Carrell and S. Clay Willmington, "The Relationship between Self-Report Measures of Communication Apprehension and Trained Observers' Ratings of Communication Competence," *Communication Reports* 11 (1998): 87–95.

12. Also see John Daly and Isa Engleberg, "Coping with Stagefright: How to Turn Terror into Dynamic Speaking," *Harvard Management Communication Letter* 2 (June 1999): 1–4.

13. For more on systematic desensitization, see Richmond and McCroskey, pp. 97–102, and Dwyer, pp. 73–86. A narrated audiotape on deep muscular relaxation is also available: Larry L. Barker, *Listening to Relax: A Deep Relaxation Guide from Head to Foot* (Fort Worth, TX: Harcourt Brace, 1996).

14. Dwyer, p. 40.

15. Dwyer, p. 40.

16. Douglas A. Bernstein et al., *Psychology,* 5th ed. (Boston: Houghton Mifflin, 2000), pp. 571–572.

17. See Mike Allen, John E. Hunter, and William A. Donohue, "Meta-Analysis of Self-Report Data on the Effectiveness of Public Speaking Anxiety Treatment Techniques," *Communication Education* 38 (1989): 54–76; Gustav Friedrich et al., "Systematic Desensitization," in John A. Daly et al., *Avoiding Communication: Shyness, Reticence, and Communication Apprehension* (Creskill, NJ: Hampton, 1997), pp. 305–329.

18. Dwyer, p. 40 and pp. 53–72; Richmond and McCroskey, pp. 102–105.

19. Delaine Fragnoli, "Fear of Flying," *Bicycling* 38 (1997): 46–47.

20. Peggy Noonan, *Simply Speaking: How to Communicate Your Ideas with Style, Substance, and Clarity* (New York: HarperCollins, 1998), p. 205. Copyright © 1998 by Peggy Noonan. Reprinted by permission of HarperCollins Publishers, Inc.

21. Joe Ayres and Tim S. Hopf, "Visualization: Is It More than Extra-Attention?" *Communication Education* 37 (1989): 1–5; Joe Ayres and Tim S. Hopf, "Visualization: Reducing Speaking Anxiety and Enhancing Performance," *Communication Reports* 5 (1992): 1–10; Joe Ayres and Tim S. Hopf, *Coping with Speech Anxiety* (Norwood, NJ: Ablex, 1993); Joe Ayres, Brian Heuett, and Debbie Ayres Sonandre, "Testing a Refinement in an Intervention for Communication Apprehension," *Communication Reports* 11 (1998): 73–84.

22. Wendy DuBow, "Do Try This at Home," *Women's Sports and Fitness* 19 (1997): 78.

23. DuBow, p. 78.

24. Mike Rose, "Rigid Rules, Inflexible Plans, and the Stifling of Language: A Cognitivist Analysis of Writer's Block," *College Composition* 13 (1980): 389–401.

25. Blumenthal, p. B1.

26. John Daly, Anita Vangelisti, and Samuel Lawrence, "Public Speaking Anxiety and Self-Focused Attention," *Personality and Individual Differences* 10 (1989): 903–913.

PREPARATION

Purpose and Topic

❯❯ Can a presentation have more than one purpose?

❯❯ How do I refine my purpose?

❯❯ Can the type of presentation help me find a good topic?

❯❯ How can I interest my audience in the things that most interest me?

❯❯ How do I narrow my topic to fit the time limit?

tudents in public speaking classes and presentation training seminars often ask their instructors, "What should I talk about?" The question is important but may be unique to a communication class. "What should I talk about?" is rarely asked by presenters outside of the classroom. While almost all college-level public speaking textbooks devote an entire chapter to choosing a topic, most commercial books on making presentations ignore this subject. Why? They do so because of the special nature of teaching and training sessions. Whether you are taking a three-credit college course or are enrolled in a one-day seminar on presentation skills, the goal is learning *how* to develop and deliver effective presentations. Outside of the classroom, though, the goal is achieving a specific purpose *through* an effective presentation.

Presentations outside of the classroom are a means to an end. In the classroom, they are the subject of study and the graded end product. Because most presentations take place outside of the class-room, this chapter explores how to determine your purpose and topic from both perspectives.

Topic Versus Purpose

In the world outside of the communication classroom or training seminar, pre-senters usually choose or are invited to speak because they are experts on a sub-ject, because events call for a presentation on a particular topic, or because they are recognized celebrities. What they should talk about is rarely a concern. A noted scientist invited to give a commencement address at a college graduation would know that a highly technical presentation would be inappropriate. The same speaker, if asked to make a presentation at a chemical engineering conven-tion, would know that the audience would expect a discussion of complex scien-tific data.

Famous people—a U.S. president, a Nobel Peace Prize winner, or a distin-guished writer or actor—may not be asked to speak on a specific topic. Groups consider themselves lucky to get such speakers to agree to make an appearance. These speakers know how to use such opportunities for their own benefit. The president can offer a new policy option or defend his administration's actions; the prize winner can champion a political cause; a distinguished artist can sup-port a charitable project or promote a new book or film.

Within the walls of a college classroom or a training seminar, your speaking situation is unique. You aren't being asked to speak because you're an expert or because the audience is eager to hear your presentation. In fact, you probably have been given a speaking assignment by an instructor who wants to teach you how to apply communication principles.

Like many other students, you may find choosing a topic for an in-class pres-entation difficult. Unless your instructor specifies a topic area, you have a world of topics from which to choose. The wide range of choices can be overwhelming and bewildering. As a result, many students ask a common and understandable question: What should I talk about?

Presenters outside of the classroom are less concerned with this question. In-stead, they focus their attention on *how* to achieve a specific goal in front of a specific audience. You can do the same: Shift your focus to the goal you want your presentation to achieve, and let that goal guide your topic choice.

Determining Your Purpose

Asking, "What do I want to achieve as a result of my presentation?" is *not* the same as asking, "What should I talk about?" **Purpose** asks, "What do I want my audience to know, think, feel, or do as a result of my presentation?" Purpose fo-cuses on *why*: Why am I speaking, and what outcome do I want? We believe that identifying your purpose is the critical first step in developing an effective pres-entation. In Chapter 1, the Dynamic Presentation Model indicates that decisions about your purpose are at the center or "hub" of the encoding process.

Determining your purpose is similar to deciding where you want to go on a trip. As one communication consultant put it, "If you don't know where you are going, it is difficult to decide how to get there."[1] You must know *why* you are speaking before you can select or develop a topic. Even if your only reason for speaking is that your instructor has assigned the task, your decisions about a topic

REAL WORLD, REAL SPEAKERS

At an annual ProMax media convention in Toronto, Canada, actor Christopher Reeve, who had been paralyzed in a horseback-riding accident, was invited as a keynote speaker. Almost every one of the several thousand professionals working in the field of radio, television, and film promotion attended the session. Sitting in his wheelchair at center stage and speaking in the slow, halting voice his breathing apparatus required, Mr. Reeve talked about how his accident had changed the way he viewed his past, his present, and his future life. A hush fell over the audience during the entire presentation. Many listeners were moved to tears by the speaker's courage and determination. When invited to speak, Christopher Reeve can talk about anything he wants to. To his credit and with enormous credibility, he uses such opportunities to garner support for spinal injury research and to champion the rights of the disabled.

should be influenced by the nature and potential outcomes of that assignment. In order to illustrate the difference between purpose and topic, we offer two brief scenarios—one between a client and a communication consultant, the other between a student and a communication instructor.

Client and Consultant Scenario

Speaker: I have to make a presentation to the production department.

Consultant: Why?

Speaker: You mean *what,* don't you? On what topic?

Consultant: No. I mean *why.* Why are you making the presentation?

Speaker: Because I've been told to.

Consultant: Why?

Speaker: Because management wants our employees to keep better track of customer questions and complaints.

Consultant: Why?

Speaker: Because better records tell us how well the product works and what problems customers are having with it.

Consultant: So why are you speaking?

Speaker: To convince the production department to keep better records of customer input so we can improve services and make a better product.

Consultant: Congratulations. That's your *purpose.*

Student and Instructor Scenario

Student: I've been asked to give a talk to new students in our department.

Instructor:	Why?
Student:	Why have *I* been asked, or why do the new students need to hear a talk by a fellow student?
Instructor:	Both.
Student:	Well, I guess they chose me because I've been very involved in the department—between classes and cocurricular activities, I practically live in the department.
Instructor:	Not to mention that you're a pretty good speaker. But why do new students need to hear *you* talk? Why not a faculty member?
Student:	I know the kinds of questions students have. After all, I'm one of them. New students might feel more comfortable asking me a question than they would asking a professor.
Instructor:	Does this suggest a purpose and topic area?
Student:	I sure don't want to talk about the official stuff! They can bore themselves by reading that in the catalog and the department handbook.
Instructor:	So what's your purpose?
Student:	To give new students the inside scoop—the unwritten rules, the unofficial tips.
Instructor:	Does this purpose suggest a topic?
Student:	How about "Department Survival Guide"?
Instructor:	Good. That's a presentation they'll appreciate.

DON'T SPEAK WITHOUT A CLEAR PURPOSE Dr. Terry L. Paulson, psychologist and author of *They Shoot Managers, Don't They?*, warns speakers about the hazards of speaking without a purpose: "There are so many messages and memos being hurled at today's business professionals [that] they are in information overload. It's like sipping through a fire hydrant. Don't unnecessarily add to the stream by including unnecessary fill, facts, and fluff. Volume and graphs will not have a lasting impression; having a focus will. Ask yourself early in the process: What do I want them to remember or do three months from now? If you can't succinctly answer that question, cancel your presentation."[1]

1. Quoted in Lilly Walters, *Secrets of Successful Speakers* (New York: McGraw–Hill, 1993), pp. 3–4.

What question did the consultant and the instructor keep asking? "Why?" And why did they keep asking it? Because presentation speaking is a means to an end. By first asking yourself *why* you are speaking, you determine your strategic goal. You focus on what you want to accomplish, and this establishes a *purpose* for speaking. Use your purpose to pinpoint the outcome you want to achieve, not the information you want to include.[2]

Having a clear purpose does not guarantee that you will achieve it. But without a purpose, little can be accomplished. In the workplace, the average employee spends a lot of time listening to other people, attending meetings, and reading memos or reports. If all that time spent doesn't accomplish something, it's obvious the communicators didn't spend enough time asking "why" questions. They didn't know their purpose.

Public and Private Purposes

There can be more than one answer to the question "What is my purpose?" The student speaker in the scenario who wanted to "give students the inside scoop" in the "Department Survival Guide" had a clear purpose. However, that same student may also have wanted to please the faculty members who requested the presentation or to use the speaking opportunity as a way to meet new students. Wanting to share the unwritten rules in a department survival guide is a *public purpose.* Wanting to please faculty members or to meet new students is a *private purpose.* Skilled speakers understand the absolute necessity for a public purpose, the advantages of a private purpose, and most important, the difference between the two.

If you were asked to state the goal of your presentation for a newsletter announcement or to a communication class instructor, you would be stating your **public purpose.** You may not need or even want to share your **private purpose,** the personal goal of your presentation. For example, many companies sponsor volunteer speakers bureaus, programs in which company employees volunteer and are scheduled to speak to community groups. Let's say that the volunteer speakers bureau of a local utility company publicly announces that its chief engineer will give an informative talk on ways to conserve energy. The presentation's public purpose will attract an audience. The private purpose, however, can explain why the utility company wants an audience in the first place: It wants to create goodwill and convince the public that the utility is interested in helping them conserve energy. An audience that likes the utility company is less likely to make a fuss when the company raises its rates. Though the company is not likely to announce this private purpose in a newsletter, the private purpose often underlies the public purpose. Corporations spend millions of dollars to create a positive corporate image through speakers bureaus, public service projects, and donations to charities.

Why would a company employee volunteer for a speakers bureau, though? It's extra work, there is rarely extra pay, and the assignment could subject the speaker to harassment from a hostile audience. When we have asked such volunteer speakers why they are willing to do all that extra work, we have heard a variety of personal reasons. Most express private purposes that focus on personal and career goals. Some employees volunteer because their service looks good on their résumés or will help them when it's time for a promotion. Others do it to improve their presentation speaking skills and to take advantage of the training provided by the company.

In a communication class that requires presentation speaking, private purpose can take a variety of forms. Some students choose the same topic for a presentation as they do for a term paper in another class. Here, the private purpose is to "kill two birds with one stone" by researching one topic rather than two. The private purpose has nothing to do with the speech topic; it only enables the speaker to save time and energy.

In a communication class, the private purpose often relates to the speaker's academic goals. By carefully following the instructor's advice and guidelines for an assignment, a student is more likely to get a good grade. If your instructor requires that you use statistics in your presentation, your chances of getting an A diminish if you don't include them. If the time limit is eight minutes, don't speak for thirteen minutes or for three. All speaking situations have limits and unwritten rules such as time restraints and appropriate dress. Use your speaking opportunity for achieving your private purposes—an A, the personal admiration of your class, a future recommendation from your instructor, and even improved speaking skills.

Don't miss the opportunity to get the most out of your presentation. As long as the different purposes don't conflict or undermine each other, there is nothing wrong with a presentation that tries to achieve both a public and a private purpose.

FAQ

Is It Ethical to Have a Private Purpose?

As the preamble to the communication ethics credo in Chapter 1 indicates, "questions of right and wrong arise whenever people communicate," and that includes whenever speakers make presentations. Becoming a "good" speaker involves more than delivering a well-organized presentation. A good speaker is committed to preparing and presenting an ethical presentation that is honest, fair, and beneficial to both the speaker and the listeners.

One of the most important ethical questions to ask yourself is this: Who will benefit if I achieve my purpose—will I, my audience, or my audience *and* I? If your public and private purposes conflict or undermine each other, you may be on shaky ground. If you would be hesitant or embarrassed to tell your audience your private purpose, this may be a sign that it's ethically questionable. There is nothing wrong with having a private purpose such as wanting to get a good grade on your presentation or wanting to impress the boss with your speechmaking success. However, there *is* something wrong if achieving your private purpose would hurt or deceive your audience. As the ethics credo in Chapter 1 notes, truthfulness and honesty, freedom of expression, tolerance, and respect are essential to the integrity of communication. Both of us share that belief and apply it to every presentation we make or hear.

REAL WORLD, REAL SPEAKERS

Many presentations do not have both a public and private purpose. I once asked a utility company speaker why he volunteered to join the speakers bureau. He said it was because he wanted to help people conserve energy. When I asked whether he had any private reasons such as impressing his boss or getting free speech training, he said *no*. He told me that he was just very concerned about the country's energy resources, and the volunteer speakers program gave him the opportunity to tell other people how to conserve energy. That was his one and only purpose.

Likewise, a student who tries to persuade other students to register to vote may have no motive other than a belief that voting is the most important act of a citizen in a democracy. The public and private purpose can be the same.

Isa Engleberg

We want to emphasize that a presentation should have only one public purpose but may have several private purposes. Figure 4.1 illustrates some of each.

Private purposes are not in and of themselves unethical, but deceptive purposes are. Keep asking yourself, "Who will benefit if I achieve my private purpose—will I, my audience, or my audience *and* I?" Be honest with yourself about your purpose, and even more important, be honest with your audience.

Figure 4.1   Public Purpose, Private Purposes

Public Purpose	Private Purposes
I want to persuade my audience to visit the National Gardens in June to see the largest display of late flowering azaleas in America.	(1) I want to attract more visitors to the gardens in order to increase our entry fee receipts. (2) I want to impress my boss by showing her how in my new role as assistant director of public services, I can attract more visitors to the gardens.
I want to inform my audience about the nature of the electromagnetic spectrum and its implications for AM and FM radio advertising.	(1) I want to demonstrate why our company can reach more listeners by advertising on both AM and FM stations. (2) I want to remind listeners that I am well qualified to discuss technical issues.
I want to persuade my audience that all children should be immunized before starting kindergarten.	(1) I want my research on the need for immunization to help me as I prepare a booklet for the clinic where I work. (2) Given the instructor's comments about her young children, I hope this topic will interest her and will help me earn a good grade.

The Purpose Statement

When you know *why* you want to speak, you're ready to state your purpose and, in the process, figure out if it's a good basis for a presentation. Writing a **purpose statement** that clearly specifies the goal of your presentation will help give your purpose a reality check. "My purpose is to tell my audience all about my job as a phone solicitor" is too general and is probably an impossible goal to achieve in a time-limited presentation. "My purpose is to make my audience aware of two common strategies used by effective phone solicitors to overcome listener objections" is better. Effective purpose statements share three characteristics: They are specific, achievable, and relevant to audience needs and interests.

A PURPOSE STATEMENT SHOULD BE . . .

Specific

Achievable

Relevant

Specificity.   A general or vague purpose statement won't help you prepare your presentation. A specific statement, though, can give you both scope and direction. Think of your purpose statement as the description of a destination. Telling a friend, "Let's meet in New York City" is too general and vague. "Let's meet at the Gramercy Park Tavern at 5:30 P.M. on Tuesday" is a more specific statement that will make sure that both of you end up in the same place at the same time. A specific purpose statement ensures that both you and your audience know where you're going.

Achievability.   A purpose statement should establish an achievable goal. Inexperienced speakers often make the common mistake of trying to cover too much ground or asking too much of their audiences. A presentation is a time-limited event. An audience of less-than-perfect listeners can absorb only a limited amount of information. Changing audience attitudes about a firmly held belief can take months rather than minutes. Both of us have advised well-meaning students and clients to scale down the goals of their presentations. What is the likelihood that a student speaker can convert a class to his religion during a ten-minute presentation? What is the likelihood that a speaker can convince every person at a rally to donate $100 to the campaign of a relatively unknown political candidate? A purpose statement can be specific, but it may not be achievable.

Rather than seeking to convert the whole class to your religion, you may be more successful if you try to dispel some misconceptions about it. Rather than asking for $100 for a candidate's campaign, you may ask audience members to take home campaign flyers or to consider signing up as campaign volunteers. Achieving one small step may be much more realistic than attempting a gigantic leap into unknown or hostile territory.

Relevance.   Even if your purpose statement is specific and achievable, you may still have difficulty reaching your goal if your topic is irrelevant to your audience's needs or interests. Describing the characteristics of semiconductors or the different varieties of tree toads may fascinate you, but if you can't find a reason why the topic would be relevant or interesting to your listeners, you may find yourself talking to a bored or annoyed audience. Political candidates usually focus their attention on the issues that matter to a particular audience. Advocating

Several ministers answered our survey and reminded us of the importance of purpose in developing a presentation. The Reverend Bill D. Nickell, who has been a pastor of the First Assembly of God Church in Canyon, Texas, for twenty years, told us that he has to prepare four sermons a week. The Reverend Glenn Ridall, Jr., pastor of the Stewartstown Baptist Church in Stewartstown, Pennsylvania, wrote that he delivers two to three sermons a week and other presentations for special occasions and holidays.

In both cases, the pastors have found the Bible a rich source of topics on which to base a sermon. The key, however, is finding the passage or story that illustrates a message of importance to a congregation. The purpose of the sermon—strengthening the family, accepting the word of God with absolute faith, opening one's heart to others—is supported by and based on scripture. The Bible is not necessarily the topic but is the foundation and means of helping the ministers achieve their purposes.

tax breaks for new businesses may not be of much interest to (and may even antagonize) a group of parents who want more funding for public schools.

Drafting a specific, achievable, and relevant purpose statement is not an academic exercise; it is a means of producing an invaluable tool that can help you determine how to prepare and organize your presentation. All elements of your presentation should be specifically related to your purpose statement.[3] As we indicate in our Dynamic Presentation Model in Chapter 1, all encoding decisions related to the audience, logistics, content, organization, credibility, and performance should be driven by your purpose. You will save yourself time and effort by staying focused on a clear and achievable goal.

From Purpose to Topic

Purpose asks, "What do I want my audience to know, think, feel, or do as a result of my presentation?" Topic completes the previous question by adding "about what?" Your **topic** is the subject matter of your presentation.

Presentation topics can range from rap music to repairing refrigerators to religion. A topic is often a simple word or phrase: *rap music*. Yet two presentations that discuss the same topic can be different because they have opposing purposes. Purpose is a sentence that describes the goal of your presentation. "I want my audience to understand and appreciate rap music" is quite different from "I want my audience to boycott recording companies that promote rap music with violent and offensive lyrics."

Always make sure your purpose and topic are specific, achievable, and relevant to your audience—no matter what their age may be.

Topics for Classroom Presentations

The somewhat artificial nature of the classroom setting can make it difficult to decide upon a purpose and topic for a class presentation. For example, your assignment tells you only that you have to give an informative presentation on a topic of your own choosing, organized or delivered in a certain way, in a specific number of minutes. You're not making a presentation because the situation demands it (a condition that would help you identify the purpose) but because your instructor does! When choosing a topic to meet these unique demands, begin by asking several questions.

> **QUESTIONS FOR CHOOSING A TOPIC**
>
> 1. **What type of presentation is assigned?**
> 2. **What topics interest me?**
> 3. **What do I know about these topics?**
> 4. **What will appeal to my audience?**

Inside and outside a classroom, these questions can be the key to finding a good topic when the choice is yours. By considering each question, you should be able to find a topic that suits you, your audience, and your purpose.

Study Web, www.studyweb.com, provides hundreds of possible topics in general subject categories and for every letter of the alphabet.

Topics for Different Presentation Types

Another way to determine your purpose and to select an appropriate topic is to understand the type of presentation you are being asked to make. Traditionally, presentations have been divided into three types.

Informative Speaking. An **informative presentation** is designed to instruct, explain, describe, enlighten, demonstrate, clarify, correct, or remind. Teachers spend most of their lecture time trying to inform students. Sometimes an informative presentation explains a complex concept or demonstrates a new procedure. Sometimes it updates old information or clears up misunderstandings. Informative presentations can take the form of a report to a committee or a formal lecture to a large audience. Informative presentations tend to be uncontroversial; they concentrate on sharing information. We cover informative presentations in more detail in Chapter 17, "Developing Informative Presentations."

Persuasive Speaking. A **persuasive presentation** is designed to change audience opinions and/or behavior. These changes may be directed toward an idea, a person, an object, or an action.

Idea: Kindness should be the golden rule.

Person: Lincoln was our greatest president.

Object: Broccoli is the perfect food.

Action: Wear seat belts.

Advertisers try to persuade customers to buy their products. Political candidates do their best to persuade audiences to elect them. Persuasive presentations occur in courtroom arguments, in religious services, in blood donation drives, around the dinner table, and in daily conversations.

The information provided by a crewman's brief presentation can reassure passengers and prepare them for an emergency.

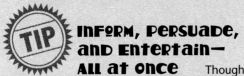

TIP

INFORM, PERSUADE, AND ENTERTAIN— ALL AT ONCE Though determining your purpose will help you decide whether you should be trying to inform, to persuade, or to entertain, it's not always an either/or decision. Some skilled speakers, regardless of their purpose, will try to do all three. For example, the purpose of a college professor's lecture usually is to inform. In order to inform, however, a good teacher also may try to persuade students that the information is important, relevant, and interesting. Such persuasion can motivate students to listen and learn. The professor may also try to entertain students so that they will pay better attention to an informative lecture. Regardless of which type of presentation you have been assigned or have chosen to make, there may be benefits to including components that inform, persuade, and entertain. Presentations that only inform or persuade or entertain are rare. Make your presentation more interesting and compelling by considering how you can include all three types of speaking.

Different types of persuasive presentations have different goals. Some try to strengthen or weaken an existing attitude; others are designed to change audience attitudes. Some persuasive presentations try to create positive or negative feelings; others attempt to whip an audience into an emotional frenzy. A persuasive presentation can convince an audience to take action, or it can encourage an audience to consider unpopular viewpoints. Chapters 18, "Understanding Persuasion," and 19, "Developing Persuasive Presentations," provide more detail on persuasive presentations. For now, just remember that different types of persuasive presentations require different strategies and seek different outcomes.

Entertainment Speaking. A presentation that entertains often takes place in informal settings. As the name implies, **entertainment speaking** tries to amuse, interest, divert, or "warm up" an audience. Stand-up comedy is a form of entertainment speaking. After-dinner speakers amuse audiences too full to move or to absorb serious ideas and complex information. Speakers at a retirement party often "roast" a coworker to the delight of colleagues, friends, and family.

Make sure that you understand the type of presentation you have been asked to prepare and deliver. If your audience or instructor wants an informative presentation, relying on a series of jokes or emotional pleas won't impress your listeners or meet audience expectations. If your audience wants to be entertained, a complex statistical analysis or a series of persuasive arguments will not amuse them. First and foremost, make sure that you know what kind of presentation is expected and then meet those expectations.

Topics That Interest You

Sometimes when we ask students what topics interest them, we are greeted with blank stares. What do you like to do, we ask—on the job, in your spare time, with your family or friends? It hasn't occurred to them that a topic they find interesting could also interest an audience. When asked, "What do you like to do in your spare time?" students often tell us that they're too busy to have spare time. They eat, sleep, go to classes, study, work, and may even have families to raise. Yet as busy as all of us are, there is always something that we enjoy doing above and beyond the daily grind—a sport, a hobby, an activity. What do we look forward to when the schoolwork is done, when the kids are out or in bed, when we've left work?

The enormous range of interests in one class can be astounding—from mountain climbing to nineteenth-century German philosophers. In one semester, for instance, we heard student presentations on the topics listed in Figure 4.2.

There are several ways to get in touch with the ideas, things, and people you find interesting. Answering the "leading questions" in the TIP on page 73 can help, or you can do some brainstorming. Create a chart in which you list potential topics under broad headings—sports, food, hobbies, places and destinations, famous people, art and music, important events, personal goals, public and community issues, objects and things, theories and processes, natural and supernatural phenomena, campus concerns. By the time you finish filling in your interests on such a chart, you may have dozens of good topics for a presentation. You might even try mind mapping, an organizational technique described in Chapter 9, "Organizational Tools," as a way to get your creative juices flowing.

Figure 4.2   Topics Based on Student Interests

71

From Purpose to Topic

Interpretation of Dreams	Exercise and Long Life
The Elvis Cult	Haunted Houses
Investment Strategies	Being a Big Brother/Big Sister
The Perfect Chocolate Chip Cookie	Afro-Cuban Jazz
Reading Poetry	Financial Planning
Collecting Baseball Cards	Total Quality Management
Genealogy and Your Family Tree	Sign Language and Fingerspelling
Wine Tasting	Restoring Cars

What Do You Know About These Topics?   Everyone is good at something. Everyone knows more about a few things than most other people do. Almost everyone can claim to be an expert in some area. A fruitful source of topics is your work experience. The following scenario is based on a conversation one of us had with a student who was searching for a suitable topic:

Student: But my job isn't interesting—to me or to an audience.

Prof: What do you do?

Student: Phone solicitation. You know, when someone calls you at dinner-time and asks you to subscribe to a newspaper or magazine you don't want.

Prof: I hate those calls, especially during dinner.

Student: I know. Most people do. So there's no way I can use this as a topic for my presentation.

Prof: Are you good at your job?

Student: I've been doing it part-time for three years. I always go beyond my quotas.

Prof: How come?

Student: Well, there's a knack to it. I know what works—how to get people to listen—how to get over their objections.

Prof: You mean you've become an expert at getting people to listen to your pitch and to buy your product over the phone?

Student: Expert? I don't know about that. But I sure know the tricks of the trade.

Prof: Are the tricks a company secret?

Student: No. We're trained, but we also develop our own styles.

Prof: I know I can't speak for the rest of the class, but I'd like to know more about the strategies you use when you call.

Student: Really?

Prof: Absolutely. You have the makings of a terrific presentation.

Many of the best presentations are based on personal experiences. Don't underestimate your experiences and skills. Rely on your expertise and enlighten

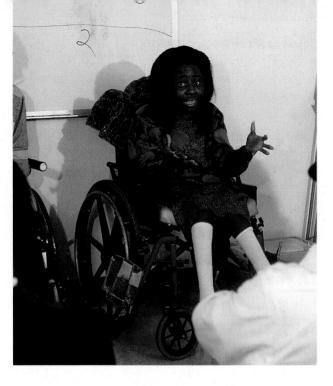

Bus drivers listen to a speaker whose experience and expertise help her explain how to assist disabled passengers.

your audience. That's what some of our former students did. Their topics are listed in Figure 4.3.

What Will Appeal to Your Audience?   Questions about your audience are more difficult to answer than questions about your own interests and expertise. The interests of your listeners can differ in as many ways as there are people in the audience. Chapter 5, "Audience Analysis and Adaptation," will discuss audiences and audience analysis in detail. As you consider potential topics, try to think of how to make each one appeal to your audience. If you are interested in the interpretation of dreams, relate the theories to the kinds of dreams most people have experienced. If your topic is haunted houses, you can make it more immediate by describing ghostly sightings in *local* haunted houses. And if you plan to compare recipes you've collected in your search for the perfect chocolate chip

Figure 4.3   Topics Based on Personal Experience

Shoeing a Horse	Drawing Blood
Volunteering for Suicide Hotlines	Duties of a Night Watchman
Teaching a Parakeet to Speak	Spiking a Volleyball
Doing Missionary Work in China	Brewing Beer
Playing the Cello	Instructing in Aerobics
Editing a Video	Growing Tomatoes
Closing a Sale	Butchering a Side of Beef
Therapeutic Massage	Weight Lifting

cookie, you should share the most delicious samples with your audience. Find the links between your interests and those of your audience.

Narrow the Topic

So you've found a presentation topic that clearly has an informative, persuasive, or entertaining purpose that interests you, appeals to your audience, and draws on your expertise. But have you found a topic that you can manage? If, as we have recommended, you have written a specific, appropriate, and relevant purpose statement, your topic should be well focused and ready for further development. However, you may still need to narrow or modify your topic in order to achieve your purpose or to adapt to your listeners' needs. There's an old saying: "Don't bite off more than you can chew." For presentations, the saying should read instead: "Don't bite off more than your audience can digest."

Although you may be an expert on your topic, your audience may be hearing about it for the first time. Don't bury them under mounds of information. Ask yourself: If I only have time to tell them one thing about my topic, what should it be? Chances are that conveying a single important idea will be enough to achieve your purpose.

Let's say your purpose is to demonstrate the difficulty and danger of serving as a volunteer firefighter, but you don't have enough speaking time to explain all the risks of firefighting. You could narrow your topic by focusing on how hard it is to break down a fire-engulfed door or on the skills needed to safely carry a victim from a burning building. Although you would like to share more information, you can still achieve your purpose by choosing a narrow, specific topic.

Look at how these students narrowed some broad, general topic ideas into better topics for classroom presentations:

Broad: The History of Rock Music
Better: Chuck Berry and the Twist

Broad: A Review of Greek Mythology
Better: The Origins of Aphrodite

Broad: Preparing a Five-Course Dinner for Eight
Better: Setting the Table for a Formal, Five-Course Dinner

Broad: Converting the Class to My Religion
Better: Explaining the Purpose of Baptism

Broad: Advances in Semiconductor Technology
Better: What Is a Semiconductor Device?

As we indicated in Chapter 2, "Critical Thinking and Listening," most listeners will not remember most of what you say. In fact, audience members are more likely to remember their impression of you rather than the details of your presentation. Consider who's listening as you narrow your topic to achieve your purpose.

ASK YOURSELF SOME LEADING QUESTIONS

You don't have to be the world's greatest expert to give a presentation; you just have to be interested enough to begin collecting ideas and information. Completing the following statements may help you find a topic worth researching:

I've always wanted to know more about . . .

If I had to read one book of nonfiction, it would be . . .

If I had an unexpected week off, I'd . . .

I've always wanted to be able to . . .

If I could give away a million dollars, I would . . .

If I could make one new law, I would . . .

Developing these statements can help you answer the question: What topic interests you?

Summary

◆◆ **Can a presentation have more than one purpose?**

All presentations should have a public purpose, a stated goal that can be shared with an audience. Presentations can also have a private purpose that achieves a personal goal.

◆◆ **How do I refine my purpose?**

Ask yourself, "What do I want my audience to know, think, feel, or do as a result of my presentation?" Make sure your purpose statement is specific, achievable, and relevant.

◆◆ **Can the type of presentation help me find a good topic?**

Presentations to inform, persuade, or entertain have different goals that require different types of preparation.

◆◆ **How can I interest my audience in the things that most interest me?**

In choosing a topic for an assignment, try to answer the following questions: (1) What type of presentation is most appropriate? (2) What topics interest me? (3) What do I know about these topics? (4) What topics will appeal to my audience?

◆◆ **How do I narrow my topic to fit the time limit?**

Narrow your topic by asking: If I only have time to tell my audience one or two things about my topic, what should they be?

Key Terms

entertainment speaking 70

informative presentation 69

persuasive presentation 69

private purpose 64

public purpose 64

purpose 61

purpose statement 66

topic 67

Notes

1. Christina Stuart, *How to Be an Effective Speaker* (Chicago: National Textbook, 1998), p. 7.
2. Gerald M. Phillips and Jerome J. Zolten, *Structuring Speech* (Indianapolis: Bobbs-Merrill, 1976), p. 70.
3. Thomas Leech, *How to Prepare, Stage, & Deliver Winning Presentations* (New York: AMACOM, 1993), p. 46.

5

Audience Analysis
and Adaptation

➡➤ How do I focus my presentation on a particular audience?

➡➤ What do I need to know about my audience?

➡➤ How can I gather useful information about my audience?

➡➤ How do I effectively analyze and adapt to the results of my audience research?

➡➤ What techniques can help me adapt to my audience during a presentation?

The presence of a living, breathing audience makes presentation speaking different from most other forms of communication. Whereas writers have little control over when, where, or why they are read, speakers often can decide when, where, or why they speak. Writers, filmmakers, and TV producers do not usually see their audience's immediate reactions (although they may hear or read about them later). However, speakers not only see their audience's immediate reactions, they can also adapt to the responses. The writer writes alone, and the reader reads alone; the speaker and the audience work together and form a unique relationship. Audiences make presentations unpredictable, anxiety-producing events. They also make speechmaking one of the most personal, exciting, and empowering forms of communication.

Audience-Focused Communication

You've spent hours of time and thought determining your purpose and narrowing the topic of your presentation. You know what you want to accomplish. Now it's time to develop the presentation itself. Right? Not necessarily. Instead, now you need to focus your attention on your audience. It's time to put their interests and needs above yours. Because a presentation is *not* a presentation unless it has an audience, being a truly effective speaker requires understanding, respecting, and adapting to the people who will be listening to you. Always remember that presentations are made to and for audiences.

Audience-focused communication is all around you. In advertising and marketing, it's called *targeting.* Each ad for a product takes aim at a target market: sweetened breakfast cereals for kids, athletic shoes for teenagers, convenience foods and detergents for homemakers, beer for sports fans. In marketing, the primary purpose is to sell the product, but the means and methods of selling can be as different as the customers in the audience. In a presentation, this process is called audience analysis and adaptation.

As we indicated in Chapter 1, the process of developing a presentation begins with identifying your purpose. The second principle to consider in that process is analyzing the people in your audience. **Audience analysis,** the ability to understand and adapt to listeners, separates good speakers from great ones and is critical to improving your presentation. A thoughtful, deliberate analysis of the audience and their likely responses to your presentation can help you plan what to say and how to say it.[1] How you go about achieving your purpose should depend on your audience. The examples you include in your presentation, the words you use, and even your delivery style should be adapted to your audience's interests and needs.

The goals of audience analysis are to find out something about your audience, to interpret those findings, and as a result, to select appropriate strategies that will help you achieve the purpose of your presentation. Fortunately, there are some fundamental audience analysis steps that can help you attain this goal. As obvious as these steps may seem, they can require hours of research and thinking to complete. But if you don't address them, your presentation may miss the mark.

> **AUDIENCE ANALYSIS STEPS**
>
> 1. **Ask relevant questions about your audience**
> 2. **Gather information that answers audience research questions**
> 3. **Analyze the researched information about your audience**
> 4. **Adapt your presentation on the basis of your audience analysis**

Understanding and adapting to your audience has several practical advantages beyond those linked to achieving your purpose.[2] A thorough understanding of your audience can help you focus your presentation and decide how to narrow your topic. If, for example, you discover that your audience is very familiar with the business philosophy Total Quality Management, you don't have to explain its basic tenets. An audience-focused approach can also simplify and shorten your preparation time by using the audience as a criterion for deciding what to include or exclude. You would give different examples of how TQM can improve the operation of an organization to an audience of college administrators than you would to an audience of automobile manufacturers. Putting the audience at the center of your thinking can help you customize your presentation. Also, by focusing your presentation on the audience, you are likely to feel more comfortable and confident when you finally address them face to face.

Researching Your Audience

You get to know your audience by asking relevant research questions about its members. Six basic questions apply to all audiences. In some cases, the answers may be obvious, particularly when you know the people in the audience or have addressed them before. In other cases, you will have to spend a lot of time and effort answering these following questions.

AUDIENCE RESEARCH QUESTIONS

Who are they?

Why are they here?

What do they know?

What are their interests?

What are their attitudes?

What are their learning styles?

Audience Characteristics

Answering these audience research questions can help you paint a portrait of your audience's characteristics—a combination of their demographics, motivations, knowledge, interests, attitudes, and learning styles. As our Dynamic Presentation Model in Chapter 1 shows, these characteristics are found in every audience and are well worth knowing.

Who Are They?   Answers to this question reveal many audience characteristics. Are the people in your audience predominantly male or female, old or young, rich or poor? You should be trying to gather as much **demographic information** as you can about the people who will be watching and listening to you.

You can collect both general and specific demographic information about your audience. Considering general demographic characteristics such as the ones listed in Figure 5.1 can help you think about your presentation in broad terms.

Figure 5.1   **General Demographic Characteristics**

Age	Gender	Marital Status
Race	Religion	Ethnic Background
Occupation	Income Level	Place of Residence

H°w Can I ADapt WithºUt Steree- TYPiNG?

Too often we form "one-size-fits-all" opinions about people based on visible or obvious demographic characteristics such as their age, race, gender, occupation, nationality, or religion. These oversimplified conceptions, opinions, or images of a person or a group of people are called **stereotypes.*** Stereotyping can inhibit effective audience analysis and adaptation. So how do you avoid it? First, there are the obvious suggestions—never use racial slang terms; don't tell sexist or racist jokes; don't use stereotyped references. Second, don't try to mimic or look like the members of a cultural group to which you don't belong. You'll only look and sound foolish and probably will be resented by your audience. Third, don't make universal assumptions about your audience: They will live in mostly white neighborhoods if they're white and in mostly black neighborhoods if they're black; they will like chow mein if they're Chinese and fried green tomatoes if they're Southern.

Avoiding stereotyping requires a deeper understanding and respect for others. If a person dislikes the music, political candidates, clothes, and hobbies that you like, you should make every effort to respect these differences of opinion rather than ridicule the person for having such opinions. Learn as much as you can about your audience and acknowledge the differences you discover. Then concentrate on communicating a message designed to share meaning with your audience.

*For a more detailed understanding of stereotyping and other obstacles to intercultural competence, see Myron W. Lustig and Jolene Koester, *Intercultural Competence: Interpersonal Communication Across Cultures,* 3rd ed. (New York: Longman, 1999), p. 149–160, and Guo-Ming Chen and William J. Starosta, *Foundations of Intercultural Communication* (Boston: Allyn & Bacon, 1998), pp. 32–57. For insights into the effects of stereotyping, see Alberto Gonzalez, Marsha Houston, and Victoria Chen, eds., *Our Voices: Essays in Culture, Ethnicity, and Communication,* 2nd ed. (Los Angeles: Roxbury, 1997).

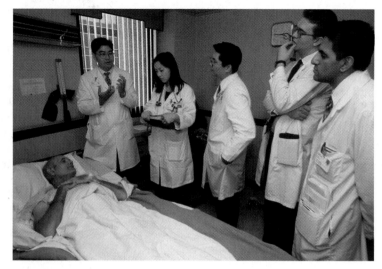

As this teaching physician discusses the patient's condition, he must be sensitive to the ways in which his message could affect each of his audiences (the medical students and the patient) very differently.

If you know that the audience is composed of a particular group or will be meeting for a special reason, you can gather more specific demographic information such as the characteristics listed in Figure 5.2. An audience of college undergraduates will differ from an audience of airline pilots. A group of homeowners will differ from a group of students living in a dormitory.

Whether they are general or specific, knowing something about the demographic characteristics of your audience helps you to target your presentation. For example, you can assume that everyone in an audience of college students has earned the equivalent of a high school diploma. You probably can conclude that a Baptist youth group will be more familiar with the New Testament than the members of a Jewish or Muslim youth group would be. If the people in your audience are members of a single group or organization, think about the characteristics that brought them together. What do they have in common? Are they all taking the same class? Do all of them have children in the daycare center you're working with? Do they own or manage local businesses?

Figure 5.2   Specific Demographic Characteristics

Health and Physical Characteristics	Career Goals
Hobbies	Common Interests
Working Hours and Conditions	Recreational Activities
Dress and Appearance	Political Affiliations
Club/Association Memberships	Choice of Vacations
Newspaper/Magazine Subscriptions	Choice of Automobiles
Employment Positions	Military Experience

When adapting to audience demographics such as age, gender, nationality, race, education level, and socioeconomic background, you must strive to understand and respect the differences you discover. Be careful not to stereotype audiences according to their demographic characteristics. Stereotyping audience members (Asians are good students; all women want children; New Yorkers are aggressive) can do more harm than good.

Considering demographic characteristics goes well beyond race and ethnic background. For example, consider age. We know that, in general, younger audiences are more susceptible to persuasion than older audiences, whose members are often more set in their ways. Yet knowing the audience's ages may not be enough to tell you how to approach the group. Try persuading a teenage audience that opera is a higher art form than the music they listen to and love. But show an older audience a way to save money on taxes, and we'll show you audience members willing to change their ways!

We are not suggesting that you ignore an audience characteristic such as age, but rather that you also consider other factors such as education, income, political affiliations, interests, and occupations. Asking how differences in audience characteristics are relevant to your purpose and topic matters most. Moreover, remember that *your* own age, nationality, race, education level, and socioeconomic background may be just as critical in determining how well an audience listens to you.

Why Are They Here?   Asking why an audience is assembled is not the same as asking about their demographic characteristics. As much as you may want your audience to be there because they are interested in you and your presentation, this is not always or even usually the case. Answers to the question "Why are they here?" can tell you a great deal about your audience that will help you meet them where *they* are rather than where *you* are. Audiences attend meetings and presentations for many different reasons, as Figure 5.3 illustrates.

Needless to say, the audience members who are interested in the topic or who stand to benefit from attending a presentation will be quite different from those who don't know why they are there or who are required to attend. Each type presents its own special challenges for a speaker. A highly interested and well-informed audience demands a compelling, knowledgeable, well-prepared speaker.

Figure 5.3   Why Are They Here?

Reason for Attending	Examples
Audience members are required to attend.	A college class, a mandatory training session, a talk by a supervisor
Audience members always attend.	A monthly service club meeting, a weekly staff meeting, a popular social event
Audience members are interested in the topic.	A topic related to their personal and/or professional interests
Audience members are interested in the speaker.	A political candidate, a celebrity, a newly hired executive or manager
Audience members will be rewarded.	Earn "points" with the speaker, boss, or instructor; paid to attend; receive credit for professional development
Audience members are not sure why they are attending.	Accompanying a friend, taking notes for a colleague or boss, substituting as a group representative, having nothing else to do

ADAPT TO KEY AUDIENCE MEMBERS

Sometimes an audience may be so varied that it's impossible to find a best way to reach everyone. In such cases, it helps to identify and concentrate on key audience members—the people who have the authority or ability to make things happen. They may be opinion leaders or other respected audience members. Other audience members may take their cues from the ways in which these people react to a presentation or speaker. If key people seem interested and responsive, others will mimic their behavior. If they seem bored or annoyed, others will be, too. If you cannot reach everyone in an audience, try to reach those who have influence. How do you find out who these key audience members are? Check the nonverbal communication of audience members: Who gets the most handshakes? Who is given a prominent seat or is accompanied by an entourage? Who commands attention? If you can't tell who is most important by observing an audience, ask. Ask the person who invited you about audience members who have influence or hold senior-level positions. You may even discover that the most important and influential person in the audience is the person who invited you.

An audience required or reluctant to attend a presentation may be pleasantly surprised and influenced by a dynamic speaker who has the ability to give audience members a reason to listen. Moreover, entire audiences rarely fit into one type of group. You may find yourself speaking to an audience that includes several people representing each reason for attending.

What Do They Know?   Because audience members possess various levels of education and knowledge, figuring out what they know about your topic is an important step in determining what to include in your presentation. Audience knowledge is based on several factors: educational level, demographic characteristics, and interest or expertise in a topic. Assessing your audience's knowledge level can be challenging, particularly when you are addressing a diverse audience.[3] You can meet this challenge by asking yourself several questions:

▶ How much do they know about the topic?

▶ How much background material do I need to cover?

▶ Will they understand my vocabulary and specific, topic-related terminology or jargon?

▶ Have they heard any of this before?

Answering these tough questions is essential to matching your presentation to an audience's level of understanding and knowledge. As Michael Hattersley, a columnist for the *Harvard Management Update,* maintains, "nothing is more boring to audiences than a rehash of overly familiar information, and nothing more frustrating than trying to decipher a presentation pitched way over their heads."[4]

The level of education completed can tell you something about your audience's general knowledge and vocabulary. Demographics can tell you something about their experiences and expertise in areas as diverse as childcare, religious training, and firsthand experience with cultural and historical events. An audience being introduced to a new management theory or scientific concept—regardless of their education levels, demographic characteristics, or interests—may need a carefully worded and basic-level introduction to a complex topic.

What Are Their Interests?   Answering these questions—Who are they? Why are they here? What do they know?—can help you gauge your audience's interests, which are often what bring people to hear a presentation. Ignoring this important factor can result in a less-than-effective presentation. As we see it, there are two types of audience interests: self-centered interests and topic-centered interests.

Self-centered interests are aroused when a presentation can result in personal gain or loss. A political candidate's position on tax increases can result in more or fewer taxes for audience members. A proposal to restructure a company or an organization can result in more or less power for employees. A talk by a personnel director can provide information about how to get a more desirable job. In all of these cases, the listener stands to lose or to gain something as a result of the presentation or its outcome.

Audience members also have topic-centered interests—subjects they enjoy hearing and learning about. Topic-centered interests can include hobbies, favorite sports or pastimes, or subjects loaded with intrigue and mystery. However, topic-centered interests often tend to be personal. A detailed description of a Civil War battle may captivate the Civil War buffs in the audience but bore the other members. The presentation of a new approach to management may intrigue those who enjoy management theory but alienate the hands-on administrators who find such theories restrictive and impractical in real-world settings. Whether self-centered or topic-centered, listener interests have a significant effect on how well an audience pays attention to you and your message.

What Are Their Attitudes?   When you ask about **audience attitudes,** you are asking whether the people in your audience agree or disagree with your purpose statement, how strongly they agree or disagree, and what you can do to influence their opinions and/or behavior. There can be as many opinions in your audience as there are people. Some audience members will already agree with you before you begin your presentation. Others will disagree no matter what you say. Some audience members will be neutral or have no opinion; they will neither agree nor disagree. Figure 5.4 on the following page shows a wide range of opinions that can be found in an audience listening to the same presentation. In Chapters 18, "Understanding Persuasion," and 19, "Developing Persuasive Presentations," we focus on ways of adapting a persuasive presentation to listeners who agree with you, to those who disagree, and to those who are neutral. Once you understand why an audience agrees or disagrees with you, you can begin the decision-making process of matching persuasive strategies to audience attitudes.

When Knight Ridder, Inc., bought the *Kansas City Star,* CEO Anthony Ridder had to consider audience attitudes and reactions when he announced the big purchase to a group of anxious employees.

Figure 5.4   Spectrum of Audience Opinions

The speaker's stated purpose is "to convince the audience that imposing longer jail sentences will deter and reduce crime." Audience members may hold a variety of opinions on the issue.

Strongly Agree	Agree	Neutral	Disagree	Strongly Disagree
If criminals know they won't be back on the streets within a short period of time, longer jail sentences will deter them and reduce crime.	Because criminals are sometimes released before they have served their sentences, longer jail sentences may help deter and reduce crime.	There are good, strong arguments on both sides of the issue. *or* I don't know very much about this issue.	Because longer jail sentences cost more and are unfairly given to poor and minority defendants, longer jail sentences may not be a wise course of action.	Longer jail sentences do not deter or reduce crime; they only create more hardened, dangerous criminals.

To make matters even more complicated, there can be many different reasons why people have the same opinion. For example, audience members who oppose longer jail sentences for convicted criminals may do so for various reasons:

▶ The jails are too crowded now, and there's no money or public support to build new ones.

▶ Longer sentences do not prevent or stop crime.

▶ Rehabilitation should be stressed instead of jail time.

▶ Rich people will get off; the poor will be the ones who spend more time in jail.

▶ Long sentences are cruel and unusual punishment for some crimes.

▶ Longer jail sentences won't work if criminals can get out on early parole.

Not only can a wide range of opinions be found in one audience; an equally wide range of *behaviors* may also be present, as Figure 5.5 shows.

As with opinions, there can be many different reasons why people behave in certain ways. For example, audience members who volunteer to work on Robin Brown's campaign may do so for several reasons. One audience member may like Brown's position on education; another may want to see her shake up the old guard; a third may hope that she will appoint active campaign workers to government and community board positions.

Adapting to audience knowledge, interests, and attitudes can produce a winning combination for most speakers. Ignoring these factors can lead to failure. Here are two examples in which presenters ignored these factors:

▶ A student speaker tried to convince her class to join her church and to become born-again Christians. She warned the audience that failure to embrace her religion would condemn their souls to hell. The result: Although the speaker was sincere in her beliefs, listeners of different religions and other Christian denominations resented her talk and were offended by her warning.

▶ A new, eager manager decided to use his time during a staff meeting to describe the principles and value of Total Quality Management. He gave a highly informative presentation that included the history of TQM, studies demonstrating its value, and recommendations for ways it should be used by his col-

Figure 5.5   Spectrum of Audience Behavior

The speaker's purpose is "to convince the audience that Robin Brown is the best candidate for mayor because she supports zero tolerance of crime." Audience members may behave quite differently, depending on their attitudes about an issue.

Strongly Agree	Agree	Neutral	Disagree	Strongly Disagree
Because I don't feel safe in my own neighborhood, I will volunteer my time to work on Brown's campaign.	Because crime in our city is on the rise, I will vote for Brown on Election Day.	I don't know whether crime is a voting issue. *or* I still don't know whether I'll vote for Brown or D'Angelo.	Because I think there are more pressing issues facing our city than crime, I will vote for D'Angelo on Election Day.	Because I think "zero tolerance for crime" is just a code phrase for licensing police brutality, I will volunteer my time to work on D'Angelo's campaign.

leagues. What he failed to realize was that the audience had been through two years of TQM training and probably knew more about the topic than he did. The result: The other managers, who had looked forward to welcoming a new member to their team, were disappointed with his presentation and disturbed by his arrogance in assuming that he knew more than they did about TQM.

What Are Their Learning Styles?   You can go beyond audience characteristics and opinions to ask one additional question that relates to how audiences react to a presentation: How do they learn and process information? Some people can learn more if they read, while others learn more by listening. Why can some people understand complex theories and abstract concepts with little difficulty, while others never seem to grasp the essence of such models? People have several different ways of learning and processing information.

Psychologist David Kolb is best known for his theory of "experiential learning," which classifies learning preferences as four learning styles. Depending on whether people learn from concrete (real-world) experiences, reflective observations about the world around them, contemplation of abstract ideas and theories, or active experimentation in which they test what they have learned, they are classified as "divergers," "assimilators," "convergers," or "accommodators."[5] Each person in your audience reflects at least one type of learning style in the experiential learning process.

- *Divergers* learn through "concrete experience and transform it through reflective observation. Their major strength is their imaginative ability."[6] They like looking at ideas and information from difference perspectives; they are people oriented and emotional. They also are more likely to major in or enjoy studying the humanities and the liberal arts.

- *Assimilators* learn by creating and analyzing abstract ideas. They like to take ideas and information and transform them into theoretical models. They are less interested in people and practical ideas.

- *Convergers* like to take an assimilator's abstract idea and experiment with it to see if it really works. They like to find answers and immediate solutions in the ideas and information they read or hear about. They are relatively unemotional and prefer dealing with things rather than with people.

ADAPT TO CRITICAL THINKING AND LISTENING ABILITY

Chapter 2, "Critical Thinking and Listening," devotes all of its attention to critical thinking and listening. Not only are these abilities essential skills for speakers, they also influence an audience's ability to learn. Audience members at the Received Knowledge level of intellectual development are not critical thinkers—they only listen for and believe facts. Audience members at the Constructed Knowledge level go beyond facts and draw personal conclusions. If your only goal is getting an audience to remember facts, you don't have to worry about what kind of critical listeners are sitting before you. If, however, your goal is to get audience members to make a strong commitment to a controversial position, you will have a difficult time adapting to listeners who lack critical thinking ability. The same kind of analysis and adaptation needs to be made in regard to your audience's ability to listen. If audience members don't listen comprehensively, you will have difficulty sharing your meaning with them. If your audience doesn't listen analytically or empathically, you will have a hard time getting them to support an important but emotional issue. Although you cannot change an audience's ability to think or listen, you can *adapt to* their learning, thinking, and listening styles.

Accommodators learn by doing and by having new experiences. They often use trial and error to solve problems and can become quite impatient with theories that don't make sense or have an obvious use. They are risk takers and are skilled at adapting (accommodating) to different situations.

Not surprisingly, people's college majors or career choices often reflect their learning styles. According to Kolb, business majors tend to be accommodators—they have little time for or patience with abstract theory. Engineers tend to be convergers—they want to use information to find practical and hands-on solutions. History, English, psychology, political science, and probably quite a few communication studies majors tend to be divergers—they're good at generating ideas, brainstorming, and working with people. Those with interests in mathematics, chemistry, and economics tend to be assimilators—they ask questions, collect and analyze data, and develop or find a theory to explain their findings.[7] As distinct as these styles may be, we urge you to exercise caution when drawing conclusions about an audience. Avoid stereotyping. Not all historians are divergers, and not all engineers are convergers.

All speakers need to take their audience's learning styles into account. We recommend that unless you are quite sure that there are only one or two learning styles in your audience, you should ensure that your presentation has aspects that will appeal to all four learning styles. Present facts and real-world examples for those who need and want concrete details. Try to demonstrate how theory matches those facts and successfully explains the way things work. Link facts and theory to personal examples or interesting stories about people. Offer solutions for those who need them without closing the door on alternative options. Fortunately, you can enhance audience comprehension by using what you know about learning styles to guide the development of your presentation.

In our own teaching, each of us uses a variety of delivery techniques: We talk, write on the board, use overheads, display presentation software slides, and/or provide handouts so that our listeners will have several different types and sources of information. When we lecture, we try to make our lectures as organized as possible for those who need a clear presentation of fact or theory. We include numerous examples that are relevant, timely, and in some cases, personal to demonstrate our own involvement. In addition, we try to break up the class period or seminar with group discussions or activities for those who learn by doing. This variety makes our presentations more dynamic and also accommodates the range of learning styles in our audiences.

Gathering Audience Information

We've been talking about the basic research questions you should ask about your audience. But how do you gather that information? There are several ways, ranging from simple observation to using sophisticated survey methods. The method that will work best for you depends on how much time and energy you can devote to the audience analysis process. In general, though, two very basic techniques can tell you a great deal about your audience: Learn to look and listen.

Look.   The simplest method is to observe your audience or to imagine what they will look like and try to answer as many questions as you can on the basis of their appearances. What percent of your audience will be male or female? Will there be a wide age range? Is the audience likely to be racially diverse or fairly uniform? Do you picture audience members as formally or casually dressed?

Looking at your audience will tell you more about their characteristics than about their opinions. Nevertheless, you can draw a few conclusions about your audience's opinions and behavior from their appearances or their group member-ship. A young audience may be more likely to support a tax on social security income than an audience of senior citizens. A group of well-dressed corporate exec-utives may be more conservative than an audience of community activists.

You also may want to observe their behavior. Are they restless, or do they ap-pear eager to listen? Are they smiling or frowning? Do they look wide awake or tired? From your conclusions about their behavior, you may want to inject more or less energy into your presentation. You may want to shorten it or add more ex-amples. Because audience feedback can send powerful messages to a speaker, your success may depend on how well you pay attention and adapt to such messages.

Listen.   Simply put, ask questions about the people in your audience and listen to the answers! You won't always have the opportunity to look at your audience before your presentation. When that's the case, use the Listen technique.

You can get valuable information about your audience from the person who invited you to speak or from someone who has previously spoken to this group. If you can, arrange to talk to several audience members before you are scheduled to speak. Talk to as many people as you can, listen for common characteristics as well as for information about their opinions and behaviors, and take some notes about your conclusions. But be careful when asking about opinions. One person's opinion may be atypical.

The Look and Listen techniques are streamlined enough that you can even apply them during the few minutes you have before speaking. As you're waiting to speak, quickly scan the room. What audience characteristics and behaviors leap out? You will be able to see how many men and women are in your audi-ence. You can quickly judge whether all ages seem to be represented or whether the audience consists of one age group. You can see how they're dressed.

Christina Stuart, a popular and widely published communication consult-ant, describes the benefits of prepresentation small talk as an audience analysis technique:

> It always surprises me to see how speakers fail to chat with their audience at coffee breaks and mealtimes. I find these times an invaluable source of mate-rial and will often refer to a conversation which I have had with a member of the audience prior to my talk. For example, saying, "Someone was telling me during the coffee break that . . ." can lead to my next point. It has the advan-tage of showing the audience that you are approachable and that you can re-late to their problems and experiences. And you benefit from speaking face to face with the individuals who are your audience. It is also more relaxing than trying to fit in a final mental rehearsal.[8]

Analyzing and Adapting to Your Audience

Everything you learn about your audience tells you something about how to pre-pare your presentation, but you have to analyze what you have learned in order to apply it effectively. This step is not always easy, particularly if you're saturated with tons of information about your audience. How do you separate the useful

CONDUCTING AUDIENCE SURVEYS

In most speaking situations, you will only have time to look at your audience and listen to the answers to questions about them. There is, however, another way to get valuable information about your audience: using an audience survey. A **survey** is a series of written questions designed to gather information about audience characteristics and opinions. These simple guidelines can help you write a useful audience survey.

▶ A good survey should tell you something you need to know, something you don't already know about your audience. Don't use a survey to ask obvious questions: Is drunk driving a problem? Should the U.S. oppose terrorism? Do you want to earn more money? Any answer other than "yes" to questions like these would be so unusual that you would wonder about the person's motives or sanity.

▶ A good survey should give you information you can use. Don't use a survey to ask questions unrelated to your purpose or questions that don't help you understand an audience's answers. A question such as "Do you exercise regularly?" does not tell you whether "regularly" means twice a day, week, or month.

▶ A good survey should be fair. If you don't word your questions carefully, you won't get an accurate picture of your audience. *Yes* or *No* questions often leave out audience members who don't know the answers or who are undecided. Questions such as "Are you against gun control?" or "Do you favor stricter prison sentences?" don't leave room for answers like "It depends on the circumstances" or "I haven't made up my mind."

▶ A good survey should be confidential. People are less likely to give you information about themselves, their opinions, and their behavior if you also ask for their names.

▶ A good survey should look professional. Audiences are more likely to give serious thought to one that looks professional than to one that has been scribbled and slapped together at the last minute.

▶ A good survey should be short. Find out only what you need to know. Most people don't like taking the time to answer a long questionnaire. A long questionnaire also gives away too much about your presentation and can ruin the effect you are trying to achieve.

When you create a survey, try to figure out which kinds of questions will give you accurate, useful, and fair information about your audience. Survey questions can be divided into two broad types: open-ended and close-ended. Open-ended questions allow

from the useless? You go back to your purpose statement and apply to it the answers to your audience questions. Identify which audience factors can help you to achieve the purpose of your presentation.

Let's look at how two speakers applied their audience research to two very different types of presentations—an informative presentation on growing tomatoes and a persuasive presentation on the harmful effects of television violence. Note how the answers to our six audience questions affected the ways in which each speaker modified her preliminary purpose into one that better suited her audience.

Preliminary Purpose: To provide information on growing tomatoes.

Who are they? They are twenty women and eight men who belong to the local garden club. All but three are over forty. They have known one another for many years.

Why are they here? They are attending a monthly club meeting at which they discuss group-selected topics. Many attend for social reasons, too.

What do they know? They already know a lot about growing tomatoes but want to improve the health and output of their plants.

What are their interests? They are very interested in plants of all kinds, but a few may be more interested in growing flowers than in growing tomatoes.

The Gallup polling organization's Web site, www.gallop.com, provides detailed information about many audience characteristics—from product preferences and social interests to audience knowledge of and opinions about political issues and candidates.

respondents to provide specific or detailed answers. Write these questions to include phrases such as "What do you like most about . . . ?" or "Please explain why. . . ." On the other hand, close-ended questions force audience members to choose an answer from a limited list. Allow your respondents to check off whether they agree with, disagree with, or are neutral toward a statement. Ask multiple-choice questions to assess your audience's knowledge about a topic. Present a checklist to gauge attitudes or behaviors related to a topic. Have audience members rate a statement on a 1 to 5 scale or rank a list of options in order of preference to determine the strength of their opinions.

Next, determine the best way to distribute and collect your questionnaires. If you are speaking to a classroom audience, you can hand out your survey before class and pick it up at the end of class. Alternately, the instructor may set aside part of one class period for this process. It is much more difficult to distribute and collect a survey outside of a classroom setting. You must have the permission and cooperation of the group or organization that you will be addressing, and you must have plans in place to collect the responses. You may want to provide stamped, pre-addressed envelopes so that respondents can send their questionnaires directly to you. Unfortunately, response rates to such surveys tend to be quite low, so you may want to see if the group that invited you to speak would be willing to distribute and collect the survey for you. Regardless of what method you choose, the effort is well worth your time and attention because a good survey can provide the keys to understanding, respecting, and adapting to the people in your audience.

Fortunately, the group picked the topic, a factor indicating their high level of interest.

What are their attitudes? They are avid gardeners, but they may be a bit wary about *my* ability to tell them something new and interesting about tomatoes.

What are their learning styles? Like most audiences, they will represent a variety of learning styles. My guess is that they will be hands-on, concrete learners who like listening to details and who also enjoy sharing their own experiences and opinions.

Revised Purpose: To share my knowledge of the latest and best research on improving the health and output of a tomato plant in this growing region.

Preliminary Purpose: To warn the class about the effects of television violence.

Who are they? They are twenty-five college students, the majority of whom range in age from eighteen to twenty-nine. Three are over thirty; two are over forty. They are taking a required communication course. About 50 percent have younger siblings; 20 percent are the parents of young children. Most of those without children say they plan to have children in the future.

Why are they here? They are in class because attendance is required. They may be preoccupied with thoughts about their own presentations or about personal matters.

What do they know? They have probably read or heard about the effects of television violence but may not be familiar with specific studies. They are aware of the television rating system.

What are their interests? Most of them are mildly interested; those with children are more interested.

What are their attitudes? Most of them believe that television violence is something of a problem, but their positions are not very strong. A few have strong opinions—believing either that television violence is very harmful or that controlling television content could ban many of the programs they enjoy.

What are their learning styles? I know most of my classmates. The most common majors are computers, engineering, and nursing. The computer and engineering majors will need lots of concrete examples—and maybe some statistics. The aspiring nurses have probably seen young victims of violence in their clinical internships—they might appreciate understanding how television contributes to such tragedies. Generally, college undergraduates learn best from concrete experiences and examples.

Revised Purpose: To urge listeners to support measures that protect children from the harmful effects of frightening TV shows and movies using examples and research from Dr. Joanne Cantor's television violence study.[9]

Candace Gingrich, half-sister of former Congressman Newt Gingrich, addresses a Gay Rights rally on the front steps of the State Capitol in Pennsylvania. Although she knew that her immediate audience was sympathetic and friendly, she also wanted to reach an audience that was not as friendly nor as supportive of her cause.

Although these answers are used merely as illustrations, they demonstrate that different topics and different audiences produce very different responses to audience questions. Good analysis selects and uses those responses that provide insight into preparing a presentation that adapts to audience interests and needs.

Your willingness to research, understand, and respect your audience can mean the difference between failure and success. Georganne Millard, a motivational speaker and radio talk-show host in Purchase, New York, describes how she successfully speaks to audiences of older adults: "Most of my speeches are given to an elderly audience, and as I am in midlife, it's obvious there is a generation gap. Therefore, I preface all my presentations with stories about my 'grandma' and her trials and tribulations. That way everyone understands and can then relate to my topic."

Mid-Presentation Adaptation

Thus far, we have explored ways of gathering and analyzing audience information and ways to adapt to audiences *before* you speak. Just as crucial is having the confidence to engage in these important activities *during* a presentation. Sometimes, no matter how well you've prepared for an audience, you run into the unexpected. What if an audience of engineers or top executives bring their spouses or families to your presentation? Do you ignore the unexpected guests or acknowledge and adapt to them? What if the chief executive officer or company president shows up at a training workshop for clerical workers? Do you continue the presentation that you planned, or do you try to adjust it in a way that would make participants feel more comfortable in the presence of their boss? What if your carefully researched and well-organized presentation doesn't seem to be working? If your audience members seem restless, bored, or hostile, how can you adjust to that negative feedback? And finally, what do you do if you are informed, at the last minute, that your twenty-minute presentation must be shortened to ten minutes in order to accommodate another speaker?

Expect the Unexpected

The confidence to make midcourse changes depends on good advance preparation. If you have prepared well and have practiced your presentation, you should be able to deviate from your plan with little trouble. Remember that one of the ways in which a presentation differs from written communication is in the presenter's ability to adapt to a living, breathing audience right on the spot. Speakers who stubbornly stick to their outlines or manuscripts and refuse to accommodate or adapt to their audiences will never be highly successful. Those who see their presentation as a game plan that can be modified before and during the game are much more likely to achieve their purpose.

To effectively adapt to your audience during a presentation, you need to do three things at once: deliver your well-prepared presentation, correctly interpret the feedback you receive from the audience, and successfully adapt your presentation on the basis of your interpretation. Interpreting feedback requires that you look at your audience members, read their body language, and sense their moods. As one writer puts it: "Want to know how you're doing? Look at your audience."[10] Are they looking directly at you with interest? Do they look bored or distracted? Watch how they interact with each other. Are they nodding and smiling or having side conversations? Audience members who sit forward as they listen tend to be more interested than those who sit back.

REAL WORLD, REAL SPEAKERS

Tim Norbeck, the chief executive officer of the Connecticut Medical Society, provided us with his real-world advice about paying attention to audience reactions during a presentation: "I speak to groups frequently, usually on specific subjects related to health care. Although people tell me that my talks are well received, I know that this is the case by watching their reactions during a speech. If the audience stays riveted, you know that you have connected. I strongly believe that to keep the audience's interest, you must use interesting and relevant stories and humor—to connect them to the points you are trying to make. If a speaker is observant, he or she will always know whether a speech is successful or not."

Let the Audience Help You

If audience feedback suggests that you're not getting through, don't be afraid to interrupt your presentation by asking **comprehension questions.** A question such as "Would you like more detail on this point before I go on to the next one?" does more than get your audience's attention. It also involves your audience, assesses their understanding, and keeps you in control of the situation.[11]

Think about adjusting your presentation in the same way in which you would adjust your conversation with a friend. If your friend looks confused as you speak, you might ask what's wrong. If your friend interrupts with a question, you probably will answer it or ask if you can finish your thought before answering. If your friend tells you that he has a pressing appointment, you are likely to shorten what you want to say. The same is true with an audience. If the faces and body language of audience members indicate that they're confused, re-explain what you're saying. Unless you're in a very formal setting, you can ask them why they seem puzzled. You can even encourage them to ask questions during your presentation if time allows. However, if you choose this tactic, make sure that their questions don't detract from the message you want to share.

Finally, if your talk is running too long, or the audience is becoming restless, don't ignore the problem; adapt to it. Cut your presentation, highlight the key points, or choose to cover one important point rather than two. And be gracious. Don't abuse the time limit and run the risk of annoying your audience or host.

The whole point of audience analysis is putting your listeners first. They are why you are there. Ron Hoff, the author of several trade books on presentation speaking, has said it as well as anyone: "Here's the point: the minute you start to worry about yourself—how much *you've* got to cover, how late *you* already are, whatever—thereby ignoring the condition of your audience, you're headed for deep trouble. Audiences inevitably put *their* needs ahead of *your* needs. It's not even close."[12] Effective audience analysis and adaptation ensure that the audience's needs are first, and always first, in the heart and mind of a presenter.

Summary

❖❖ How do I focus my presentation on a particular audience?

Audience-focused presentations depend on effective audience analysis, which includes researching your audience, analyzing the results of your research, and adapting your presentation to that analysis.

❖❖ What do I need to know about my audience?

You need to know useful information about audience demographics, the reasons why they are attending, and their levels of knowledge as well as their interests, attitudes, and learning styles.

❖❖ How can I gather useful information about my audience?

Methods for gathering information about your audience range from very simple observational techniques to sophisticated survey methods. The technique that will work best for you is often determined by the amount of time and energy you can devote to the audience analysis process.

❖❖ How do I effectively analyze and adapt to the results of my audience research?

When analyzing the results of audience research, go back to your purpose statement and integrate the answers to your audience questions into your goal. Then adjust your presentation in a way that adapts to the audience's characteristics, interests, and needs.

❖❖ What techniques can help me adapt to my audience during a presentation?

Learn to read, interpret, and adapt to the feedback that you receive from an audience during your presentation.

Key Terms

audience analysis 76

audience attitudes 81

comprehension questions 90

demographic information 77

stereotypes 78

survey 86

Notes

1. Michael Hattersley, "The Key to Making Better Presentations: Audience Analysis," *Harvard Management Update* 2 (Oct. 1996): 5.

2. See Dennis Backer and Paula Borkum Backer, *Powerful Presentation Skills* (Chicago: Irwin, 1994), p. 1. The authors include the results of an unattributed national survey: "Knowledge of the listeners was cited as one of the most important pieces of information necessary to prepare and present a speech."

3. Thomas Leech, *How to Prepare, Stage, & Deliver Winning Presentations* (New York: AMACOM, 1993), p. 51. Leech provides a series of excellent quotations from experienced speakers highlighting the importance of taking audience knowledge into account. Examples: "Perhaps the single most important thing in making a presentation is understanding . . . the degree of knowledge and interest by principal audience members. My own observation is that very few people who make presentations understand that. . . . People don't do much homework regarding the sophistication of audiences. . . . If audience members can't understand your language, don't relate to your references, or can't follow your line of discussion, it is highly unlikely that they will grasp your message."

4. Hattersley, p. 6.

5. A short but well-documented summary of Kolb's theory and its applications to different types of learners can be found in Charles S. Claxton and Patricia H. Murrell, *Learning Styles: Implications for Improving Educational Practices* (Washington, DC: Association for the Study of Higher Education, 1987), pp. 25–33. An interesting study by Karen Kangas Dwyer in *Communication Education* 47 (1998): 137–150 has linked communication apprehension and learning style preferences on the basis of Kolb's theory.

6. Claxton and Murrell, p. 27.

7. Claxton and Murrell, pp. 27–28. Also see David A. Kolb, "Experiential Learning Styles and Disciplinary Differences," in *The Modern American College,* Arthur W. Checkering and Associates, eds. (San Francisco: Jossey-Bass, 1981), pp. 232–255.

8. Christina Stuart, *How to Be an Effective Speaker* (Chicago: National Textbook, 1988), p. 119.

9. See Joanne Cantor, *Mommy, I'm Scared: How TV and Movies Frighten Children and What We Can Do to Protect Them* (San Diego: Harcourt Brace, 1998).

10. Ron Hoff, *I Can See You Naked* (Kansas City, MO: Andrews and McMeel, 1992), p. 169.

11. Stuart, p. 115. The author recommends using comprehension questions for smaller audiences as a way of remaining in control by confining your comments to the material you have already presented.

12. Hoff, p. 210.

Logistics and Occasion

6

◆▶ What do I need to know about the place where I'll be speaking?

◆▶ What materials and equipment should I use?

◆▶ How long should I speak?

◆▶ Should I change my presentation for different occasions?

◆▶ What should I wear?

People make presentations for many different reasons at a variety of times and locations, in front of different sizes of audiences, using a wide range of media. Just as every audience is different every time you speak, so too are the occasion and the place where you speak. And just as you need to understand and adapt to your audience, you need to understand and adapt to the logistics and occasion of your presentation.

Why Place and Occasion Matter

As important as determining the purpose of your presentation and adapting to your audience are, it can be easy to overlook a critical interim step—analyzing and adapting to the occasion and the place where you will be speaking. You need to investigate and analyze important questions about where, when, how, why, and to whom you are speaking. Asking and answering these questions lets you tailor your presentation to the occasion and can minimize the risk that something unexpected or unwanted will get in the way of its effectiveness.

Why do couples spend so much time searching for the ideal wedding site? Why do filmmakers scout for the perfect location? Why do advance staff check and recheck every detail before a politician gives a speech? The answer is this: They want to make sure that the location not only matches the purpose and tone of the occasion but also adds value and impact to the event. They do their best to ensure that nothing goes wrong. Your presentation can benefit from the same kind of "advance" work.

Logistics

Whether you are speaking at a family barbecue or a formal banquet, a prayer meeting or a party, take a critical look at the place where you will be speaking *before* you begin deciding what you want to say. Adapting to the place where you will be speaking requires critical thinking about logistics. The term **logistics** comes from the military and describes the strategic planning, arranging, and use of people, facilities, time, and materials relevant to your presentation.

Proper attention to the logistics of your presentation can help ensure its success. As management communication consultant Thomas Leech put it, "When presentations go smoothly, audience members scarcely notice anything about the mechanics; when something goes wrong, that may become the most dominant and lasting impression: *'I don't recall anything he said, but I'll never forget what he did.'*"[1] Although there is a great deal to consider about the logistics of every presentation, answering four general questions can make your presentation more effective.

> **LOGISTICS QUESTIONS**
>
> **People:** *Who* and how many people are in the audience?
> **Facilities:** *Where* will I be speaking?
> **Time:** *When* will I speak?
> **Materials:** *How* will I display materials?

Who?

Answering the first question—Who is in my audience, and how many people will be there?—helps you determine how the size of your audience could or should affect the preparation and presentation of your message. If there are only fifteen people in your audience, you probably don't have to worry about whether they

REAL WORLD, REAL SPEAKERS

I once had a major presentation to deliver at a convention in Denver. I spent months researching and preparing the project. I had written a paper and duplicated it so that every seminar participant would have a copy. I'd put the main points of my presentation on well-designed overhead slides. I had had my favorite "power" suit dry cleaned. I had carefully packed my suitcase and had rechecked to make sure that I'd included the packet of papers and overheads.

The plane left the East Coast on time. Then disaster struck. Bad weather delayed the plane's landing in Chicago, so I had only ten minutes to change planes for a connecting flight. Although the second plane reached Denver on time, my luggage wasn't on it. No papers, no overheads, no suit. My only clothing option was a less-than-professional set of plane-wrinkled clothes.

The lesson? If you have to travel to make your presentation, make sure to put papers, handouts, overheads, or disk copies of your presentation slides in your carry-on luggage. As for clothing, make sure that you're dressed appropriately for a same-day presentation. Anticipating what could go wrong can help you avoid disaster. Now I know!

Isa Engleberg

---

can hear you. If there are five thousand people in your audience, though, you should plan to use a microphone and will need to make sure it's supported by a good sound system. In Chapter 14, "Vocal Delivery," we include a mini-module on how to use a microphone most effectively.

Knowing the size of your audience also helps you figure out what kinds of presentation aids might work best. If there are five hundred people in the audience, projecting images onto a large screen would be more effective than using a small chart or demonstrating a detailed procedure. If you want to distribute handouts, passing them out is fine for a small audience. For a large audience, it would be better to leave a stack by the doorway for audience members to take as they enter or leave the room.

The size of an audience also affects the amount of eye contact you can establish, the extent to which you can ask an audience to interact with you, and the amount of time it takes an audience to get settled.

Where?

Make sure you know as much as you can about the facility in which will you be speaking. Will you speak in an auditorium, at a barbecue, in a classroom, or on television? Figure 6.1 on the following page lists some of the questions to consider when thinking about where you will be speaking.

With answers to the questions listed in Figure 6.1, you're ready to take the next step: figuring out how to adapt to the place where you will be speaking. You can make the logistics work *for* you rather than against you. If you have the opportunity to control the physical arrangements of the place where you will be speaking, take full advantage of it. Adjust the seating arrangements, lighting, and sound system to match your needs as a speaker.

Figure 6.1   Find Out About Your Facilities

▶ Will the presentation take place inside or outside?

▶ What are the size and shape of the room?

▶ Will the room be formal or informal (a ballroom, an auditorium, a locker room, a community center, an art gallery)?

▶ Does the room have good ventilation (heating, air conditioning, air circulation)?

▶ Will the audience sit or stand?

▶ If the audience is seated, what are the seating arrangements (rows, tables)?

▶ Will the audience fill the space or be scattered?

▶ What kind of lighting will there be?

▶ Will there be a speaker's platform (podium, lectern, table for materials or equipment)?

▶ Will there be a public-address system?

▶ Will there be any distracting sights or sounds?

Seating Arrangements.   Ask in advance about the seating arrangements for your audience. Will they be seated in a theater-style auditorium, around a long conference table, or at round tables scattered throughout a seminar room? If, for example, an audience of one hundred people is expected in an auditorium that can seat eight hundred, you may want to request that the balcony or side sections be closed off so that the audience will be seated in front of you.

If you will be asking audience members to read handouts or to write, try to set up a seminar-style arrangement in which every listener has a desk arm or table to write on. If you intend to involve the audience in small-group discussions during or after the presentation, make sure the chairs are movable. However, if you have a lot of information to share in a short period of time and need your audience's undivided attention, straight rows of chairs or auditorium seating can reduce the interaction among audience members.

Seating arrangements can also affect where you stand and where you put any equipment or presentation aids. Something as basic as placing a screen in front of an audience can divert or focus the "spotlight" on the speaker.

TIP **Don't Leave Them In The Dark**   While adjustable lighting has considerable advantages over simple on/off switches, use it carefully. If you are going to display videotapes, overhead transparencies, or computer-generated slides, turn the lights down, but don't leave your audience in the dark. You never want the lights any dimmer than they need to be. If the room is too dark, your audience may drift off to slumberland in the glow of your beautiful slides. If you intend to turn off your overhead projector when you're not displaying a slide, remember that the room will become even darker without that light source. Another problem can arise if you dim the lights sufficiently to let everyone see your slides or overheads. The room may become too dark for you to read your notes.

Obviously, you need to find a middle ground—partially dimming the lights might be one solution, but getting a lectern with a light would be better. The more you know about the lighting system in a room, the better you can plan how to speak and how to use your presentation aids.

Lighting.   In many speaking situations, you can't do much about lighting. Most lights can only be turned on or off, with no options in between. In more sophisticated settings, you may be able to dim lights as required for a slide presentation or to use theater lights to spotlight your location.

Remember that electricity isn't the only source of light. Windows let in natural light during the day, so if there aren't any curtains, you may have trouble displaying projected images. If the room is too dark, you may have just as much difficulty keeping your audience's attention focused.

Sound.   Different rooms have different acoustics. The term **acoustics** refers to the science of sound. Good acoustics help your voice carry and sound strong and natural. Poor acoustics

Positioning a Screen

If you intend to use a screen, don't place it in the center of the room. Don't angle it toward the audience on the left side of the room (from the audience's point of view), either. Instead, angle the screen toward the audience on the right side. Why? For one thing, you, not your presentation aids, should be the center of the audience's attention. If your screen is in the center of the room, you will be stuck on either the right or the left side of the room, unable to move across the room without walking in front of the screen. You will be "cornered." So why put it on the right side but not the left? There are two reasons, both having to do with the fact that people read English from left to right. When readers scan an image, they generally start at the left side and move toward the right. Consequently, your audience's attention will be drawn to a screen on the left rather than to you in the middle. What is more important, however, is that when you point at a screen on the left side, you will be forced to point to the ends of sentences, phrases, or words rather than to the beginnings. When the screen is placed on the right side (from the audience's perspective), you will be able to point to the beginnings of items—the points where your audience's eyes will naturally be focused. Figure 6.2 shows a floor plan for correct screen placement.

Figure 6.2   Placing the Screen

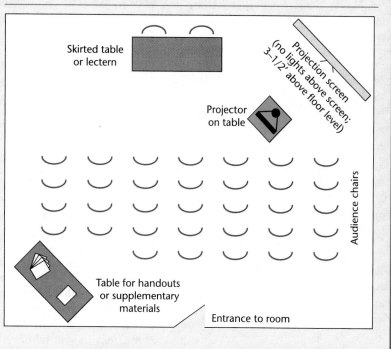

may make your voice echo, may distort it as it bounces off multiple surfaces, and can create "dead zones" where you can barely be heard at all. Although you can rarely change a room's acoustics, you can adapt to them. If your voice will not carry to the far reaches of the audience, arrange for the use of a microphone or ask your audience to move closer to you.

If the room has a strange echo or distorts your voice, consider moving away from the podium and closer to your audience. Since you can't move the walls of the room, move yourself to a position that improves the carrying power and quality of your voice. If you're lucky, there may be a technician available to test your voice and to adjust the room's sound system *before* the audience arrives as well as *during* your presentation. Paying attention to the acoustics of a room can help you decide how to deliver your presentation and whether to arrange for a sound system support.

When?

When will you be speaking—in the morning, during a busy workday, before a ceremony, or after a meal? Are you scheduled to speak for five minutes or for an hour? Asking questions about the time and duration is essential to planning a

WHAT IF I NEED MORE TIME TO SAY SOMETHING IMPORTANT?

Although we often give advice about staying within a time limit, many speakers dismiss our warning. "But I have something really important to say, and I *have* to talk longer!" they exclaim. What these speakers fail to understand is that just because *they* believe that their message is important or interesting, this doesn't mean it's important or interesting to the audience. Part of your responsibility as a speaker is to spark that interest and focus the listeners' attention.

If you often exceed your time limit, try this exercise. Imagine that you've just been told that you have to give your presentation in half the time you were promised. Which sections or subsections of your presentation would you cut? Ask yourself whether anyone would miss what you've cut. Ask yourself whether you can still achieve your purpose without the material you've cut. Now, take another look at your presentation. You may discover that the shortened version is crisper and more focused. Don't add back what you've cut unless the material is absolutely essential. Do your best to stay within the time limit you've been given. Doing so demonstrates respect for your audience, and they will appreciate your self-discipline and kind consideration.

successful presentation. After all, if you've prepared an hour's worth of material and then discover that you have only ten minutes to speak, what do you cut? Figure 6.3 lists some questions concerning when you will be speaking.

Your answers to the questions in Figure 6.3 may require that you make major adjustments to your presentation. Say you're scheduled to speak at 8 A.M. Because your audience may not be fully awake, adjust your presentation so that it's crisp and clear as well as kind and gentle to help them ease into the day. However, if you're scheduled for a 4:30 P.M. presentation, your audience may be very tired after a long day's work. If that's the case, plan on using a more energetic speaking style to perk up your audience. And if you have to speak to an audience after a five-course banquet, you may find that a short or humorous approach is the only way to compete with their desire for an after-dinner nap. Speaking before or after a dinner or social event can put you in a difficult spot. You must gain your audience's attention and interest right from the start to counter the distraction of what came before your presentation or what's going to happen after it.

Of all the questions to consider about when you will speak, perhaps the most important and, unfortunately, the most ignored one is how long you are *scheduled* to speak. Make sure that you know how much time you've been given and adjust your presentation accordingly. Unless you're a famous celebrity or an extraordinary speaker, most audiences will become impatient if you exceed the time limit. Whether you're scheduled for five minutes or for an hour, never add more than 10 percent to your allotted time. Better yet, aim for 10 percent less!

Plan your presentation so that it fits well within your time limit. Time yourself, keeping in mind that real presentations often take longer than the one you have practiced. Put a watch right next to you when you speak. Ask someone to give you a signal when it's time to begin your conclusion. And when that signal comes, don't ignore it, even if it means skipping major sections of your presentation. Your audience gave you their time; don't take more than you've been given.

Common sense and an alert eye on the audience can help you adapt to timing issues as they arise. If you're the third speaker on a panel, and the first two

Figure 6.3   **Ask About Time and Duration**

- ▶ At what hour will I be speaking?
- ▶ For how long am I scheduled to speak?
- ▶ How long do I want to speak?
- ▶ What comes before or after my presentation (other speakers, lunch, entertainment, cocktails, questions and answers)?
- ▶ Is there anything significant about the date or time of my presentation (birthday, holiday, anniversary)?

have spoken for so long that they've used up most of your time, don't be stubborn and also speak too long. Be honest and fair with your audience. If they're scheduled to be somewhere else in fifteen minutes, tell them you will shorten your presentation to accommodate them and do just that. If, on the other hand, an audience doesn't want to let you go and keeps asking for more, give it to them. Use your common sense. Watch and analyze your audience's feedback. If they're squirming in their seats, checking their watches, or beginning to slip out of the room, cut to your conclusion. If you use your time wisely, you will be using it well.

How?

Once you've considered the audience size as well as the setting and the time of your presentation, you're ready to make decisions about the materials and equipment you will need and how best to integrate them into your presentation. Materials and equipment include lecterns, projection screens, and microphones. You'll also have to make decisions about the clothes you will wear (which we discuss a little later in this chapter) or arranging for technical assistance.

Figure 6.4 lists some questions to consider when deciding what materials and equipment you'll need for a presentation.

Knowing where you will be speaking also enables you to make decisions about the materials and equipment you may need and how to adapt accordingly. Although you may have a great set of slides to show, there may not be a screen or a convenient place to put or to plug in a slide projector or computer. Although you may like using a lectern, some places cannot provide one. It's best to know in advance what is—and just as important, what isn't—available at your presentation's location so that you can consider those factors during the planning stages.

When planning how to use equipment and presentation aids, make the necessary physical arrangements and then prepare yourself to make do with less in the unlikely event that your arrangements fall through. It is possible to be heard by an audience of one thousand people without a microphone. It is possible to describe a procedure if your demonstration video malfunctions. If a media technician doesn't show up, you should know how to run the equipment on your own. But why make it difficult for yourself when careful logistical planning and preparation can provide what you need?

SHOULD I USE A LECTERN? Before

answering this question, we want to clarify two terms that are frequently but mistakenly used interchangeably: *lectern* and *podium*. A **lectern** is "a stand that serves as a support for the notes or books of a speaker," whereas a **podium** is "an elevated platform, as for an orchestra conductor or a public speaker."[1] You approach and stand on a podium. You put your notes on (and may be tempted to clutch the edges of) a lectern. If the lectern is small, and you know you will need a glass of water or a place to put a display object, find a table to put next to the lectern.

Generally, you will need a lectern if your presentation is formal or to be made before a large audience. For more informal talks and presentations to small groups, you may have nothing more than an assigned place to stand or sit. Chapter 15, "Physical Delivery," provides advice on how to take advantage of a lectern and how to avoid using it as a crutch or barrier between yourself and your audience.

1. *The American Heritage Dictionary of the English Language,* 3rd ed. (Boston: Houghton Mifflin, 1992), pp. 1026 and 1396. ©1996 by Houghton-Mifflin Co. Used by permission from *The American Heritage Dictionary of the English Language,* 3rd ed.

Figure 6.4   Do an Equipment Check

> ▶ What equipment, if any, do I need to be seen and/or heard?
>
> ▶ What equipment, if any, do I need for my presentation aids to be seen?
>
> ▶ Is there a lectern (adjustable, with a built-in light or microphone, big enough to hold my notes)?
>
> ▶ Are there any special arrangements that I need to make (requests for water, a timer, special lighting, or a media technician)?

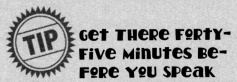
Assuming that everything you need is in the room in which you will be speaking, make sure that each piece of equipment is working. Turn on every machine. Boot up your computer and click through a few slides (and don't forget to backtrack to the beginning of your presentation). Make sure that you know how to operate any unfamiliar equipment. Don't forget the small things, and don't assume they will be where you expect them to be on the day of your presentation. Are there pens, pointers, cords, and even extra batteries and bulbs available? A good friend of ours recently made an important training presentation. He carefully prepared his overheads, arrived long before his scheduled speaking time, made sure that the overhead projector was plugged in, and then, after he was introduced, discovered that there was no screen on which to project his slides!

Once you've checked out the equipment and the room from your vantage point, walk to the back of the room and see what the most distant members of your audience will be seeing. Do you need to angle the flip charts or the screen in a particular direction? Is the projector in focus? Are the chairs arranged in a way that will allow everybody to see you and the screen clearly? Are there any barriers that will block the view of some audience members?

All of these preparatory steps take time. In the same way that bands do a sound check before a concert begins, experienced speakers always check the room and equipment *before* their presentations and never assume that everything is in working order.

Occasion

When either of us is asked to make a presentation, our first questions do not focus on whether the audience expects a PowerPoint presentation or whether we'll have a lectern for our notes. Instead, we usually ask, "What's the occasion?" Once we know *why* an audience will be assembled, we can ask better questions and make better decisions about logistics.

When you're a student preparing a speaking assignment for a class, you don't have to worry much about the occasion or the setting of a presentation. You know where you will be speaking (the classroom), when you will be speaking (the date and time of the class), and how long you can speak. You also know what type of presentation your speaking assignment requires. Given that you're probably in the same room every time your class meets, you even know what materials and equipment you can use to enhance your presentation. You know the audience, the instructor's expectations, and the criteria that will be used to determine your success.

Real-world speakers do not have the luxury afforded student speakers or seminar participants. Not only do speakers outside of the classroom have to spend time planning for the logistics of a presentation; they also must give serious consideration to the occasion of a presentation. When we use the term **occasion,** we mean the reason why an audience has assembled at a particular place and time. The occasion for a presentation can be as public and formal as witnessing the inauguration of a U.S. president or as routine as giving a brief status report at a staff meeting. Certainly, the logistics of these occasions differ, but so do the speaker's motivation, tone, and role. Whereas logistics ask about *who, where, when,* and *how,* occasion asks *what* and *why.*

At a political forum in New Hampshire, Vice President Gore had to adapt to a variety of logistics. He juggled his attention among many factors: the TV lights and cameras, the TV audience, the forum moderators, the public audience in front and behind him, well-known people in the live audience, and questioners, as well as the reactions of his opponent, former New Jersey senator Bill Bradley.

Would you give the same presentation at a memorial service as at a pep rally? Of course not. Because each occasion dictates a very different type of presentation, considering the nature of the occasion is important. You must take into account the nature and significance of the event as well as the circumstances that motivated the audience to attend the presentation.

> **OCCASION QUESTIONS**
>
> **Motive: Why is the audience assembled?**
>
> **Speaker: Why are *you* speaking on this occasion?**
>
> **Expectations: What is expected for this occasion?**
>
> **Protocol: What is appropriate for this occasion?**

What's the Occasion?

Every occasion exists for a reason. College classes or training seminars provide occasions during which student speakers can improve their ability to make effective presentations. The workplace presents numerous speaking occasions. One day, you may be given a few minutes with a group of senior managers to explain why you want to hire a new employee. On another day, you may be required to present a quarterly report to your department. The agendas for these staff meetings dictate the kinds of presentations you may be required or may need to make. On a larger scale, you may choose to attend a public forum in which you are given three minutes to explain your position on a particular issue. Or you may ask or be invited to speak at the memorial service of a family member, a good friend, or a colleague. In all of these cases, the occasion has as much to do with how you prepare and present your remarks as it does with your purpose and audience.

If you were to tell someone about having to make a presentation, and she then asked, "What's the occasion?" what would you say? Whether you answer, "Oh, it's just an assignment I have to do for my speech class" or "I've been asked to testify on behalf of legislation protecting disabled adults," make sure that you understand the reason for the event and what kind of presentation best suits the occasion.

Why Me?

Is your audience assembled because they want to hear *you* or because they are interested in your topic? Are you speaking because you were assigned the task or because you were invited to speak? In some cases, a group may want you to speak because they have heard that you're an expert on a topic they're interested in. Sometimes, you may be chosen to speak because you've won an award, because you're well known, or just because you're available and won't say no when asked. For example, if you're the chair of an awards committee, or you know the award recipient, you may be asked to present an award at a banquet. If you're a marketing expert, you may be asked to address the sales force to broaden their understanding of your company's marketing goals and product development efforts.

Speakers are not picked randomly. They are chosen because they are the most knowledgeable, most able, or most appropriate persons to make presentations. So when you're chosen to make a presentation, always ask yourself, "Why have *I* been invited to speak to *this* audience in *this* place and on *this* occasion?"

What Does the Audience Expect?

The occasion of a presentation also reveals something about your audience's expectations. Are they assembled for a mandatory training session, to be entertained, to kill time, or to learn a new skill or principle? Successful speaking involves adapting to the audience's expectations. (Chapter 5, "Audience Analysis and Adaptation," discusses this in detail.) If you've been asked to give a toast at a wedding, don't bemoan the high divorce rate. If asked to talk about methods of lowering taxes, don't spend your time campaigning for a political candidate.

Utah Jazz forward Karl Malone proudly points to the logo for his new charity, the Karl Malone Foundation for Kids, during a press conference. As founder of the charity, he was the most appropriate speaker for this occasion, and the audience expected to hear his comments.

The occasion also raises audience expectations about the way a presentation will be delivered. Business audiences often expect speakers to pepper their presentations with sophisticated, computer-generated graphics and visual aids. Audiences at political events have become accustomed to the sound bite on television and expect to hear short, crisp phrases in live public speeches, too. Think about what style of presentation *you* would expect to hear at a particular occasion. Then try to match your speaking style to those expectations.

What's Proper?

Events or gatherings often have specific rules of protocol. **Protocol** is a term that refers to the expected format of a ceremony or the etiquette observed at a particular type of event. In diplomatic circles, the rules of protocol are written down and taken very seriously—addressing everything from where to seat a dignitary at dinner to how to address a member of the monarchy. In other circumstances, the "rules" of protocol are less formal or are part of a tradition. Thus, we expect a certain tone at a graduation ceremony and a very different tone at a political rally. At a funeral, a eulogy may be touching or funny, but it's almost always very respectful and short.

When inquiring about the protocol of an occasion, you are asking what customs or rules may require special adaptation on your part. Understanding customs or rules of delivery style, timing, language, or dress can help you plan what you want to say, organize your message, choose the most appropriate delivery style, and even select what to wear for your presentation.

How do you determine the protocol of an occasion? Unless you've been to a similar event, you should ask those who have invited you to speak or those who have attended before. We naturally ask such questions when we are invited to a wedding, an awards banquet, or a fundraising event. Is the wedding formal? Is the awards banquet a black-tie event? Is the fundraiser a casual daytime event or a Saturday-evening extravaganza? For example, if you have never been to a christening, a bar mitzvah, or the breaking of a fast during the month of Ramadan, you would probably ask several questions about how to behave—such as when to arrive, what to wear, and whether you should bring a gift. Before you begin researching, writing, or rehearsing a presentation, make sure that you know about any customs or "rules" that may apply.

Dress and Appearance

Deciding how to dress for a presentation requires an understanding of the occasion: why an audience is assembled, why you are the speaker, what the audience expects for the occasion, and what the "rules" of protocol are. In short, your clothes should fit the occasion.

In a college classroom or training seminar, a few speakers may carefully select what they will wear on the days when they are scheduled to speak, particularly if the speaker's outfit is part of the presentation. For example, demonstrating your martial arts skills is much easier if you're wearing your karate outfit and your hard-earned black belt. Wearing your uniform may add emphasis to your presentation about joining the National Guard. Yet for the most part, students and trainees do not give a lot of thought to what they will wear when they speak in class. Outside of the classroom, however, speakers devote significant attention to what they wear and to the impression their appearance will create for their audience.

We are often asked, "What should I wear when I make a presentation?" Our answer is always this: Dress to create a positive impression. Long before an

REAL WORLD, REAL SPEAKERS

An experienced speaker who asked to remain anonymous told us the following story: "Once, at the last minute, I was asked to sit on a large stage with several other speakers who were scheduled to speak to an audience of about five hundred people. When I walked on stage, I knew I had worn the wrong dress. It was a button-all-the-way-down-the-front dress, and it was short. Sitting on the stage created an immediate problem. In a seated position, the dress rode up several inches above my knees, and the button at the hem of the dress opened a slit another two inches. I had to keep one hand on the base of the dress so it wouldn't be more revealing. Before I knew it, my name was being called to speak. I found myself feeling unusually flustered and agitated as I walked to the lectern. It should have been an easy-to-give presentation. Instead, my concern about a dress prevented me from being fully prepared and fully composed."

audience hears what you say, they will see you, so wear something that will match the purpose and tone of your presentation. What you wear can affect your audience's initial and lasting impressions of you and your message.

Dress for Success

John T. Molloy, the well-known author of *New Dress for Success,* emphasizes how important it is for your clothes to fit the occasion. Given that the first and often most important statement a speaker makes to an audience is a nonverbal one, Molloy urges presenters to dress to fit audience expectations. He contends that if you dress inappropriately for an audience, you will lose them for the first few minutes. Rather than focusing on you and your message, they will be criticizing or be distracted by what you are wearing.[2]

Your appearance is part of your presentation, and like everything else, it benefits from planning. If your clothes don't match your purpose or the occasion, you can send a mixed message. For instance, how would you react to a student giving a graphic and emotional speech about child abuse while wearing a T-shirt with a large yellow "happy" face on the front? Would you believe a speaker talking about "get-rich-quick" investment opportunities who showed up in a wrinkled, poorly tailored suit? In both cases, the message and the outfit conflict. Your clothing should help you achieve your purpose, not distract you or your audience from it.

Wardrobe Guidelines

The clothes you wear for a presentation are more important in some settings than in others. A well-tailored suit may be perfect for an important corporate presentation but inappropriate for a company picnic, a talk on bass fishing, or a cooking class. What you normally wear to work will usually be perfectly appropriate for a presentation in a staff meeting. However, the clothes you usually wear to class may be too casual or inappropriate for an important, graded presentation. Your clothes don't have to be expensive, and they don't have to make a fashion statement. What matters most is that they reflect your purpose, fit your audience and the occasion, and are appropriate and comfortable for you.[3]

Be Comfortable.   Rarely will either of us wear brand-new clothes or shoes when we are scheduled to make a presentation. We know that if your shoes hurt, you won't move about naturally, and you'll be preoccupied with pain. If you discover when you stand up to speak that your new clothes have become creased and crumpled, you may find yourself worrying about it rather than concentrating on your presentation. An outfit that looks and feels good while you're standing in front of a store's three-way mirror may be constricting and unattractive when you are sitting on a stage or are at a lectern. If you perspire a great deal, wear cool fabrics and colors that mask wet stains. Presentations are stressful enough as it is, so don't wear something that adds another source of discomfort.[4]

Be Appropriate.   You can use what you've learned about your audience to select an outfit that fits the style and customs of the occasion. For example, one of us once addressed a group of academic administrators in Singapore, an Asian city-state only a few miles from the equator. The year-round temperature and humidity were near 90. Some buildings lacked air conditioning. Wearing a tailored suit would have been stifling. Cotton-blend pants and skirts with loose-fitting shirts and blouses were perfectly acceptable and appropriate.

Generally, it's a good idea to wear standard business clothing for a presentation. For men, that means a dark business suit or a conservative sports coat with an appropriately matched pair of pants. In more casual settings, a light-colored sports jacket is fine. You can always remove your jacket and tie if that's necessary.

Women have a tougher time when it comes to choosing a presentation wardrobe. In formal settings, a two-piece suit is always appropriate. Solid colors, high necklines, and comfortable high heels are safe bets. Tailored suits and dresses are more authoritative and professional than frills and cute prints. There's nothing wrong with wearing a pant suit or slacks and a blouse if you've determined beforehand that such outfits are going to be predominant in your audience.

One of our colleagues recently moved from a faculty position at a large East Coast college to a communication department at small college in a ranching and oil-rich section of Texas. During her first year at the new college, one of her students showed up for his first major speech wearing a nice cowboy hat, pressed jeans, a dress shirt, and polished Western boots. She started to dock him points for his attire but quickly realized that what he wore was perfectly appropriate and professional for many business settings in that part of the country. The overall impression mattered, not specific "dress-for-success" rules.

If there is a rule of thumb about selecting appropriate clothing, it is this: Be as conservatively dressed as the key members of your audience. If you know in advance that everyone will be wearing cowboy boots, exercise outfits, or fishing clothes, use your best judgment and consider joining them. Your wardrobe should enhance your presentation, not hurt it.

Be Yourself.   Despite all of the advice on how to dress for a successful presentation, the objective is to look appropriate and professional—but not to look like a clone. If you look better in light colors and like to wear them, don't buy a dull, dark suit. But please understand that for many men, the classic dark suit is a "power garment" that helps establish authority, credibility, and likableness.[5]

At the same time, don't abandon a signature piece of clothing or accessory. Some of our most distinguished colleagues wouldn't look right without these unique items. Sam would not be Sam without his bow tie. Judith would look unusual in anything but bright colors and high heels. Ellen needs her dark eyeglass frames. A special suit style, a set of complementary colors, a type of eyeglass frame, or a "signature" tie is not inappropriate if it is part of someone's unique personality. Being yourself means finding clothes and colors that fit *your* style,

REAL WORLD, REAL SPEAKERS

Dan Alexander is Neiman Marcus's top salesman. He works at the Tyson's II Galleria store in northern Virginia. A native Washingtonian, he has been in the garment business for forty years. In 1998, he was more than the company's top African American salesman; he was the number-one associate, ringing up two million dollars in sales. In addition to working with customers, he has conducted seminars on the art of sales. How does he dress for such occasions? On the day he was interviewed for the business section of the *Washington Post*,[1] he wore a three-button navy suit with working buttonholes on the sleeves. His white shirt had French cuffs and a point collar. He wore a deep blue silk tie with a subdued diamond pattern, and a pale blue handkerchief tucked discreetly into the breast pocket of his jacket. His trousers were cuffed and broke gently over a pair of black Oxfords, which were brilliantly shined but not to a flashy military sheen. "You want to look like what you do," he said.

1. Robin Givhan, "Secrets of a Supersalesman," *Washington Post*, 6 December 1998, pp. H1 and H12.

your body shape, and *your* coloring. Looking professional does not mean that you must copy the latest look in a fashion magazine. Find the outfit that enhances your presentation and your credibility.

When preparing for your presentation, give your clothes the kind of attention that supersalesman Dan Alexander does (see Real Word, Real Speakers above). In fact, a salesperson and a speaker have a lot in common. Both have a purpose; both have an audience; both adapt to the interests and needs of their listeners. Like the supersalesman at Neiman Marcus, a good speaker should look appropriate for the purpose, audience, and occasion of a presentation.

Grooming and Accessories

As important as clothing is to your appearance, so also is something even closer to you—your body. Hair that falls in your face and requires rearranging throughout a presentation will annoy you and your audience. If you have long hair, put it up or pull it away from your face for a tighter, tailored look. An unshaven face, unwashed hair, and smeared makeup have no place in most speaking settings. If you're wearing a suit or sports jacket, button one of the coat buttons when you stand to speak. Take things out of your pockets, whether they're pens in your shirt pocket or the change and keys in your pants pocket. Women should leave their purses with a friend or colleague.

If you wear makeup, it should look natural. As tempting as it may be to wear bright lipstick, heavy eye shadow, blush, and thick dark eyeliner around your eyes, resist the temptation. At the very least your makeup should be understated and carefully applied.

As is the case with your presentation wardrobe, there is a rule of thumb about grooming and accessories. Nothing on your body should draw attention to itself. If you wear bracelets, they shouldn't clang together. If your earrings dangle and reflect light, they could be distracting. If your tie displays a big pattern of cartoon characters, it may not be appropriate. Your presentation should be the center of an audience's attention. If something about your appearance could distract your listeners, fix it or leave it far from the lectern.

Although the way in which you dress can have a significant impact on your presentation, your message matters more. An expensive suit and perfect hair cannot camouflage a poorly prepared presentation.

Link Purpose, Audience, and Place

At this point in the preparation process, you should have identified your purpose (Chapter 4, "Purpose and Topic"), analyzed your audience (Chapter 5, "Audience Analysis and Adaptation"), and decided how you will adapt to the occasion and place where you will be speaking. All of these decisions should be made before you begin preparing the content of your presentation. At the same time, we urge you to be flexible. As you do your research, you may discover that your purpose will change, due to audience expectations or the time limit you've been given. As you organize your content and plan your speaking strategies, you may find that you will need more presentation aids (or none) to make your point. If, as you practice, you discover that you are more comfortable using extensive notes, you may need to make sure that a lectern will be available at the front of the room.

Purpose, audience, logistics, and occasion are linked. Devoting attention and critical thinking to all four will, in the long run, save you time and help you develop and deliver a more effective presentation.

Summary

❖❖ What do I need to know about the place where I'll be speaking?

You should know enough about the place's logistics to be able to plan for and adapt to the people, facilities, time allotted for, and materials relevant to your presentation.

❖❖ What materials and equipment should I use?

Make sure that you know what materials and equipment will be available before you decide whether to use them in your presentation. Rather than being caught unaware, arrive far in advance to make sure that everything you need is present and in good working order.

❖❖ How long should I speak?

Speak for as long as you are scheduled to speak. Be prepared to shorten your presentation if circumstances require doing so.

❖❖ Should I change my presentation for different occasions?

Adapt your presentation to the nature of the occasion, the reason why you are the speaker, the expectations of the audience, and the protocol of the occasion.

❖❖ What should I wear?

Your clothes should be comfortable, appropriate for the setting and occasion, and in a style that suits your personality and purpose.

Key Terms

acoustics 96   logistics 94   podium 99

lectern 99   occasion 100   protocol 103

Notes

1. Thomas Leech, *How to Prepare, Stage, & Deliver Winning Presentations* (New York: AMACOM, 1993), p. 170.
2. John T. Molloy, *New Dress for Success* (New York: Warner, 1988), pp. 358–359.
3. Leech, pp. 220–222.
4. Leech, p. 220.
5. Molloy, p. 62.

CONTENT AND ORGANIZATION

7

Supporting Material

Imagine that you're at a party chatting about aerobic exercise with a person you've just met. This person says, "You really ought to give up step classes and take Tai Bo instead." You ask why, and all she can say is, "Because I read it's better." You think to yourself, "Why should I listen to her if she can't give a better reason than that?" Often, audiences find themselves in a similar situation: A presenter offers some new information or asks them to do something, and unless the speaker can back up the information or request, chances are the audience won't pay much attention.

A good presentation not only makes a point but also backs up that point with relevant, interesting, and accurate supporting material. As soon as you know the purpose of your presentation, you should begin collecting ideas and information that support it. This entire process can be as simple as spending a few hours thinking about your purpose or as all-encompassing as spending months doing research. In this chapter we look at different forms of supporting material and where and how to find them.

Support Your Ideas

Expert speakers are information specialists. They know their subjects well and can recite names, dates, statistics, stories, and sayings about their topics. Just as devoted baseball fans know their team's statistics, expert speakers know their subjects and can tailor their presentations to suit a variety of audiences, occasions, and purposes.

Most speakers aren't experts, though, and need to search for supporting material. **Supporting material** consists of ideas, opinions, and information that help to explain and/or advance a presentation's main ideas and purpose. Facts, opinions, statistics, and stories are just a few of the forms of supporting material speakers use in their presentations.

Types of Supporting Material

Information comes in many different forms. You will find definitions in dictionaries, background and historical information in encyclopedias, facts and figures online and in almanacs, true-life stories in magazines and on home pages, and editorial opinions in newspapers and online newsletters. The best presentations use a mix of supporting material; they don't rely on just one type. Why? Most audiences would find an unending list of statistics boring. They might find a speaker who tells story after story frustrating, particularly if there's no clear reason for his telling the stories. Variety is the spice of life, and different forms of information can give a presentation added life and vitality. Let's explore the options available to you and look at situations in which different types of supporting material work particularly well.

> **TYPES OF SUPPORTING MATERIAL**
>
> **Facts**
> **Statistics**
> **Testimony**
> **Definitions**
> **Analogies**
> **Descriptions**
> **Examples**
> **Stories**

Facts. A **fact** is a verifiable observation, experience, or event known to be true. "*Shakespeare in Love* won the 1998 Oscar for Best Picture" is a fact, but "*Saving Private Ryan* should have won" is an opinion. Facts can be personal ("I went to the 1999 Kentucky Derby") or the official record of an event (the 1999 Kentucky Derby winner failed to capture the Triple Crown). They are usually short statements that can be proven true or false. Most presentations—regardless of their purposes—are supported to some extent by facts. Facts provide support by using something certain or knowable to demonstrate or prove something less well-known. Facts are most effective when the audience has no trouble accepting them as true. When an old-time TV detective asked for "just the facts, ma'am," he was looking for factual material to support his case. In the following example, a speaker links factual information about a fairly well-known disease to the recent appearance of a new form of it.

> Hepatitis types A and B have been around and well known by doctors for many decades. But hepatitis C was not identified until quite recently—1989 to be exact.[1] And unlike the case with the A and B versions, very few hepatitis C victims survive.

Statistics. **Statistics** organize, summarize, and analyze numerical information that has been collected and measured. Statistics are also used to predict events ranging from economic trends to the winners of football games. Although many people equate statistics with facts, statistics are factual only if they have been collected and analyzed fairly. Even if all of your friends prefer chocolate to vanilla ice cream (a fact), you cannot conclude that 100 percent of the population prefers chocolate (a statistic). To draw conclusions about the ice cream flavors most people prefer, you would have to survey a larger and more representative group of people. In a presentation, statistics are effective support when you want to describe what a population is like as well as what a population likes. Note how the student speaker in the following excerpt uses statistics to bolster her point about geographic illiteracy.

> The *Los Angeles Times* reported on a survey conducted by a California State University professor in which students were told to name and locate the leading trading partner with the United States. The students named Japan, but then none could find it. The leading trade partner to the United State is Canada, and only 29 percent of those students located Canada on a map.

Testimony. **Testimony** refers to statements or opinions that someone has said or written. In advertising, testimony from celebrities associates a product with a famous person (if I buy X, I'll be like that person), while testimony from "real" people associates a product with someone "just like me." Testimony in a presentation works the same way and can add believability to your presentation. In Chapter 18, "Understanding Persuasion," we describe how celebrity endorsements work to persuade audiences.

You can support your presentation with testimony from books, speeches, plays, magazine articles, radio or television, courtroom testimony, interviews, or home pages. You can quote real people—politicians, scientists, celebrities, experts—living or from years gone by. Sometimes a quotation, whether it comes from the president of the United States or from Big Bird on "Sesame Street," can make your point better than you can. In the following example, a student uses an expert's testimony to support her point.

> My own childhood experiences may not be enough to convince you that something should be done to control media violence viewed by children. Instead, listen to the words of Dr. Joanne Cantor, a communication professor and author of the recent book *Mommy, I'm Scared.* "From my 15 years of research on mass media and children's fears, I am convinced that TV programs and movies are the number-one preventable cause of nightmares and anxieties in children."[2]

Definitions. **Definitions** explain or clarify the meaning of a word, phrase, or concept. A definition can be as simple as explaining what *you* mean by a word or as detailed as an encyclopedia or unabridged dictionary definition. Use definitions when your presentation includes words or ideas that your audience may not know or may misunderstand. In the following excerpt, a speaker uses two very different definitions of the same term to talk about the musical form known as "the blues."

> Not sure what the blues are? The *New Encyclopedia Britannica* defines the blues as an African American "vocal and instrumental style characterized by expressive pitch inflections (blue notes), unique tonal qualities, a text-phrase construction based on a three-line stanza and, typically, a 12-measure form." Well, that's okay for some, but have you ever heard Muddy Waters sing "You Can't Lose What You Never Had?" The encyclopedia definition just doesn't cut it. That's why I like to use an old bluesman's definition: "The blues ain't nothin' but the facts of life."

ADD IMPACT WITH PRESENTATION AIDS

Presentation aids can enhance the impact of supporting materials by conveying ideas and information in memorable ways. For example, rather than trying to define or describe the blues, playing a Howlin' Wolf or Muddy Waters recording can accomplish the same objective. A piece of sheet music for a blues song would show exactly what a three-line stanza and a twelve-measure form look like. Not only can presentation aids help audiences remember the information in your presentation; they can also be an effective source of information on their own. We focus on presentation aids in Chapter 16, "Presentation Aids."

Analogies. **Analogies** identify similarities. In a sense, they compare definitions of one concept to another. Analogies can identify similarities in things that are alike—"If the traffic plan worked in San Diego, it will work in Seattle." Analogies also can identify similarities in things that are not really alike—"If a copilot must be qualified to fly a plane, a U.S. vice president should be qualified to govern the country." Analogies are a useful way of describing a complex process or relating a new concept to something the audience understands very well. Here's how Jesse Jackson, a masterful speaker, used an analogy to define the Rainbow Coalition, a political group committed to fostering diversity:

> America is not like a blanket—one piece of unbroken cloth, the same color, the same texture, the same size. America is more like a quilt—many patches, many pieces, many colors, many sizes, all woven and held together by a common thread.[3]

Descriptions. **Descriptions** help to create a mental image of a scene, a concept, an event, an object, or a person. They provide more details than definitions by offering causes, effects, historical background information, and characteristics. In the description that follows, a speaker expands the definition of the blues by describing the musical style's origins and essence.

> The impact of the blues goes well beyond the Mississippi Delta and the urban blues of Chicago. The *New Grove Dictionary of Music and Musicians* describes the influence and importance of the blues as follows: "From obscure and largely undocumented rural, (African) American origins, it became the most extensively recorded of all folk music types. . . . Since the early 1960s blues has been the most important single influence on the development of Western popular music." Not bad credentials for a musical form that's too often called the devil's music.

Examples. An **example** provides a reference to a specific case or instance in order to make an abstract idea more concrete. We've used examples throughout this book to clarify, emphasize, and reinforce our points. Examples can be brief descriptions or detailed stories. By choosing examples carefully, you can customize your presentation for a particular audience. The first example that follows supports a claim about the popularity of Muzak; the second contrasts the contributions of male and female blues singers.

> No wonder Muzak has so many fans—fans like AT&T, IBM, and Xerox.

Today most of us associate the blues with male performers—Muddy Waters, Howlin' Wolf, B. B. King, and Buddy Guy. In the 1920s, the blues stars were women—Ma Rainey, Bessie Smith, Victoria Spivey, and Alberta Hunter.[4]

Stories. **Stories** are accounts or reports about something that has happened. Audiences often remember a good story, even when they can't remember much about a presentation. Stories should be interesting, but what's more important is that they reinforce your point. Almost nothing else has the impact of real stories about real people in the real world. Here, Vivian Hobbs, a former attorney who recently lost her fight to survive a crippling disability, used a personal story in the beginning of a commencement address about the triumph of human will:

> I was in an automobile accident just after high school, which left me in a wheelchair. I was trying to deal with that, a new marriage, and other personal and financial problems, not the least of which was an uncertainty about what I could do—about the extent of my own potential.[5]

In Chapter 12, "Generating Interest," we devote a major section to the value and the techniques of telling good stories during a presentation.

Vary Your Supporting Materials

Try to use at least three different forms of supporting materials in a presentation. To see why, consider the following selection from an article titled "The Shadow Epidemic," about hepatitis C, a form of liver disease. The article appeared in *The New Yorker* magazine and was written by Dr. Jerome Groopman, a cancer and immunology specialist.

> Approximately four million Americans, nine million Europeans, and a hundred and seventy million people worldwide are infected with hepatitis C. In contrast, about a million Americans are thought to be HIV positive. Some 4 percent of people between the ages of thirty and fifty are believed to carry the virus; among black American men, it's 10 percent. Each year, there are an estimated thirty thousand new infections and ten thousand deaths. There is no broadly effective treatment, and if none is developed over the next decade, the death rate from hepatitis C could rise to thirty thousand a year—a mortality rate roughly equal to that of AIDS in 1996.[6]

If you were to hear someone read the previous paragraph in a presentation, would you understand and remember most of the statistics? Would you be able to separate the statistics on hepatitis C from those on HIV infections? Certainly, the epidemic appears to be serious, but the long list of medical statistics makes the nature of the epidemic and its frightening outcome difficult to grasp. Don't misunderstand us—this is excellent and compelling information. But if you want to include Dr. Groopman's data about hepatitis C in a presentation, you should try to combine it with other types of supporting material such as examples, testimony from patients and other doctors, descriptions of the disease, and even the use of presentation aids to display and compare statistics.

Test Your Supporting Materials

Speakers use supporting materials to enhance their presentations and to demonstrate their depth of knowledge about their topics. However, information that's not accurate and up-to-date undermines this function. Test every piece of supporting material before adding it to your presentation. Is it the *best* information? Is it valid? **Valid** means that the ideas, opinions, and information are well founded, justified, and true. Do 75 percent of American families recycle cans, bottles, or paper? Are the history and evolution of the blues really separate from those of jazz? Five questions can help you test your information to determine its validity.

> **TESTS OF SUPPORTING MATERIAL**
>
> 1. **Is the source identified and credible?**
> 2. **Is the information recent?**
> 3. **Is the information consistent?**
> 4. **Is the information relevant?**
> 5. **Is the statistical method valid?**

Is the Source Identified and Credible?   This is the first and most important question to ask when you're trying to determine your information's validity. Although you may not know what percentage of Americans recycle, there are sources that do know. References such as *The Information Please Almanac, The World Almanac,* or the *New York Times Almanac* have been in business for many years. Their continued success depends on their ability to collect and publish information that is true and up-to-date. Also, check newspapers. Their reputations depend on their ability to publish accurate information. There are, however, big differences among newspapers. The sensational and often bizarre *National Enquirer* may be fun to read, but the *Wall Street Journal* is more likely to contain reliable information.

Also, make sure that you use objective sources of information. A source can be **biased,** meaning that it states an opinion so slanted in one direction that it may not be objective or fair. As a researcher, you must be alert to potential bias. If the source has a strong opinion or will gain from your agreement, be cautious. For years, tobacco companies publicly denied that cigarette smoking was harmful, even though their own research told them otherwise. Now, we recognize that the tobacco companies' pronouncements were biased and untrue. What biases do you think special interest groups such as the National Rifle Association, Pro-Choice or Pro-Life groups, NORML (National Organization to Reform Marijuana Laws), the AARP (the American Association of Retired Persons), and the Teamsters Union may have? The information that they publish could be incorrect; the opinions may be unfounded. However, just because sources are biased, doesn't necessarily mean they aren't telling the truth.

No matter where you get your information, you must be able to identify its source and determine whether that source is qualified and credible. If you're using an article, what magazine does it come from, and who wrote it? Always note your source as completely as possible, including the date of publication and page number. Is the author a recognized authority on the subject? Is the person a recognized expert, a first-hand observer, a scientist, or a respected journalist?

Is the Information Recent?   Ask yourself this question if the information you're considering will be subject to change or if you will be using it to make claims about events or to predict outcomes. In these cases, you would probably be better off using magazine or newspaper articles and reliable Web sources rather than books. Health books written before 1985 won't have much to say about AIDS. Books written in the early 1990s on how to use a library will not contain much advice about the use of computerized index systems, the Internet, or CD-ROMs. But if your topic is philosophical, historical, or timeless, there is nothing better than using an old book to discover new information. When you are collecting and recording information, note the source's publication date. In this rapidly changing information age, your data can become old news in a matter of hours.

Is the Information Consistent?   Check to ensure that the information you want to include reports facts and findings similar to other information on the same subject. Another way to look at this question is to ask whether the information makes sense. If every doctor and medical expert tells you that penicillin will *not* cure a cold, why believe a friend who recommends it as a treatment? If the evidence clearly shows that cigarette smoking is dangerous, the fact that your grandmother smoked two packs a day and lived to be eighty-five doesn't mean you should ignore the warnings.

At the same time, information that is different can be interesting and worth noting. If most reports indicate that cutting down on salt and animal fats will reduce cholesterol and high blood pressure, you may be suspicious of a study that says salt and fat intake are okay. Yet some studies that compared U.S. salt intake with that in other countries concluded that salt may not be as dangerous as once was thought. When a French study reported that drinking red wine dampens the dangerous effects of fat intake, liquor stores began providing free copies of the study to their wine-drinking customers. Despite such studies, however, it may be wiser to wait for more information before making a presentation that recommends abandoning a low salt/low fat diet and taking up a red wine diet.

Is the Information Relevant?   Make sure that the information is related to your purpose and topic. Say you were speaking about the divorce rate of American marriages. Just because Elizabeth Taylor has been married eight times does not demonstrate that stable marriages are on the way out. As the U.S. Census Bureau knows, fifty million Americans marry and stay married to one person. If you're trying to persuade an audience that "Seinfeld's" high TV ratings as a network program in the 1990s justify its selection as the best commentary on life in the last decade of the twentieth century, your evidence may be irrelevant to the millions of people who can't relate to the New York City lifestyle depicted on "Seinfeld."

Is the Statistical Information Valid?   Interpreting statistics is an art and a science. Most of you probably don't know how to use the sophisticated research methods required to produce valid statistical results. Instead, you have to rely on the numbers reported by others. The problem with choosing and using the best statistical information is that you may have no idea whether the research that produced the statistics is valid. For example, if 100 percent of the physics professors at one college are African American and 100 percent of the physics professors at a neighboring college are European American, you may wonder whether a charge of discrimination could be justified—until you learn that there is only one physics professor at each college.

Incorrect statistics can come from poorly designed research or from people who misinterpret the numbers. Statistics can be informative, dramatic, and convincing. They also can mislead, distort, and confuse. Use them carefully.

Research Strategies

You may have a general idea of which forms of supporting materials you want to use, but finding the specific pieces requires research. **Research** is a systematic search or investigation designed to find useful and appropriate supporting material. Even if you already know something about your topic area, good research can make you look and sound a lot better. For example, you may know that Americans watch a lot of television; research lets you know that the average American watches TV more than four hours a day.[7] Although everyone may know that communication skills are important for business success, research lets you know that many managers rank communication skills first in importance of all the skills needed to succeed in business.[8]

A good researcher with a good research strategy becomes an effective investigator who has a systematic plan for searching the available sources of information in the same way in which a detective searches for clues. The information you need is out there; you just have to find it. Investigative research involves knowing how to uncover valuable resources. That said, the research process starts with *you*.

You Are a Source

Yes, you! When speakers ask us whether they can use their personal experiences and knowledge as a form of support, we encourage them to do so. In fact, if you are an expert on a topic, have a unique background or life experience, or work in an unusual job or field, you may be the best source of ideas and information about it. A stamp collector, a carpenter, a musician, and a refugee from Kosovo or East Timor will all be able to share stories and information that can be new and interesting to an audience.

You can be a good source of ideas, even if you're not an expert. The reason why you are speaking, the experiences you have had, your ethnic or religious background, your job or hobby, or your strong beliefs and opinions are valuable sources of ideas as well as information. If you're going to make a presentation about drunk driving, you might want to describe an accident you witnessed or were involved in that was caused by a drunk driver. Note how this student used his own experiences as supporting material for his presentation:

> Even though I'm a guy, I wanted to make a presentation about how to avoid rape. I admit that rape isn't something I thought about much—that is, I didn't think about it at all until last month, when my older sister called me in tears to tell me that she'd just narrowly escaped a sexual assault. Visions of a stranger trying to attack my sister in the dark of night flashed through my

A once-in-a-lifetime safari in Africa can provide a speaker with dozens of unique stories and examples for a presentation.

mind. But was I ever wrong—the attack took place at lunchtime, and the attacker was a man she'd been dating for a few weeks. Turns out that what little I thought I knew about rape was wrong!

We give, however, a word of caution about relying on yourself as a resource. If you use your own ideas and opinions, make sure that they are based on fact. You may believe that capital punishment deters criminals, yet your additional research may reveal that criminologists who have studied this question disagree. You may believe that colds are caused by working up a sweat in damp, cold weather; research may tell you that exposure to a virus is the cause of a cold, regardless of the weather. Although you may be an excellent source of ideas and information, you should also check some other sources to reinforce your views. That's where libraries and online research come in.

Libraries

Before leaping to the World Wide Web, we want to reinforce the value and techniques of doing library research. For those of you who may think that libraries are becoming obsolete, think again. From your local branch library to the Library of Congress, libraries contain valuable information you can't find anywhere else. Learn to use libraries to their fullest potential.

> **USING THE LIBRARY**
> - **Find the right library**
> - **Get facts and figures from the reference collection**
> - **Get recent material from periodicals and newspapers**
> - **Get background and general information from books**

Find the Right Library.   Not all libraries are alike, so before you start your library research, make sure you're in the right one! Your local public library may have everything you need if your topic and audience are general. You'll be able to find popular magazines, local and national newspapers, encyclopedias, and general interest books in most public libraries. In some large cities, the central branch of a public library can be as comprehensive as a college or university library.

A second type of library—college and university libraries—tends to be larger than most public libraries and holds vast collections of academic resources. Whereas a public library might have a few dozen books on music, a university with a strong music department will have in its library shelves books and recordings that deal with almost every form of music. Academic libraries subscribe to specialized journals covering topics from accounting to zoology in such great detail that these publications may be too technical for your needs.

A third kind of library, the special collections library, can be found at museums, professional schools, performing arts centers, corporations, government agencies, or nonprofit organizations. As the name implies, these libraries hold highly specialized collections of books, magazines, and special documents related to specific fields. If you need highly specialized information and cannot find it at a college library, contact a special library for permission to visit and conduct your research. Most public and college libraries have a directory that you can consult to find special collections libraries in your area.

A fourth type of library is much closer to home. In fact, it *is* your home. The books, magazine, and newspapers you have in your home may contain valuable supporting material. As soon as you have determined your purpose and topic, start looking for ideas and information right at home. You may find a vital piece of information in a newspaper or magazine article that you overlooked before selecting your topic. If your home has an encyclopedia, you can do some general reading to prepare yourself for your trip to a public, college, or special collections library. Some people have in their homes their own "special collections" built around interests, beliefs, and hobbies. Our friend Karla loves 1950s fashion magazines and probably has a better "collection" than most libraries. Our friend Sid loves to fish and has just about every magazine and guidebook on bass fishing that exists. And, as you might have guessed, one of us has an extensive collection of blues music and literature. For some information, there's no place like home.

Get Facts and Figures from the Reference Collection.   All libraries have a reference collection. Reference books are just what their name suggests—you refer to them, consult them, skim through them. They are not meant to be read in their entirety. Unfortunately, you cannot check them out of the library. Even so, they are one of the first places to look for supporting material.

Reference materials can give you a broad overview of a topic or very specific information. The information is there; it is your job to find it. Reference books and CD-ROMs are available on almost every subject. Figure 7.1 lists and describes some of the different types of references, many of which are also on CD-ROM, that you can find in most libraries.

Figure 7.1 gives you only a brief description of some of the many resources in a library's reference collection. Encyclopedias and almanacs are most useful for finding general background information and specific facts. A popular reference book like Bartlett's *Familiar Quotations* can give you access to thousands of famous passages, phrases, and proverbs to use as testimony in your presentation. But

Figure 7.1   Reference Collection Resources

Encyclopedias	Contain information on almost all subjects; they are a good place to start your research. (*Encyclopedia Americana, International Encyclopedia of Social Studies*)
Yearbooks	Summarize the events of one year; they can cover many subjects or specialize in one field of study. (*Britannica Book of the Year, Yearbook of Science and the Future*)
Dictionaries	Provide information about words—their spelling, meaning, pronunciation, origin, and use. (*The American Heritage Dictionary of the English Language, Anchor Bible Dictionary, Roget's Thesaurus*)
Almanacs & Abstracts	Collect up-to-date facts and statistical information. (*Statistical Abstract of the United States, The Information Please Almanac*)
Handbooks & Manuals	Provide broad, factual information on one subject. (*Occupational Outlook Handbook, Chilton's Auto Repair Manual*)
Atlases	Contain a collection of maps, some with statistical charts and special maps showing population, climate, and so forth. (*The Time Atlas of the World, Atlas of the Oceans*)
Biographical References	Provide brief articles or background information about noteworthy and famous people. (*Who's Who in America, Contemporary Authors*)

ASK THE RIGHT KIND OF LIBRARIAN

This tip could begin and end with the following piece of advice: Ask a librarian for help. If you do, you will spend your research time more efficiently because you will be guided by a person qualified to help you find the information you need and to direct you to the best source for it. But make sure you ask the right kind of librarian. Not everyone who works in a library is a trained professional with a degree in library science. The person who checks out books may only be a clerk or a student intern.

Look for or ask to talk to a reference librarian—someone who helps library patrons find what they need. Be prepared to tell the librarian the purpose and topic of your presentation as well as to give a brief description of the audience and the place where you will be speaking. By providing the librarian with specific information, you will gain a partner who can help and direct you. Not only can librarians assist you with your research; they also can show you the best way to use their library. Rather than wander aimlessly through rows of shelving, you can ask a librarian to point you in the right direction and guide you through your search.

remember that the information you gather from a library's reference collection is only the raw material for your talk. A presentation is much more than a list of famous quotations and interesting facts.

Get Recent Material from Periodicals and Newspapers.
Whereas reference collections contain factual and background information, periodicals and newspapers provide recent, up-to-date information. Periodicals include scholarly journals as well as the most current and popular magazines. Newspapers can give you the local, national, and international news of the day along with feature articles, commentary, and editorial opinions.

In order to find articles on specific subjects in periodicals, you should use the library's periodical index. Today, almost all such indexes can be found on CD-ROM. Depending on your choice of library, you may find different systems in use. Computerized indexes can contain references to hundreds of magazines as well as listings for national newspapers.

One of the richest sources of current information is the newspaper. Here, too, there are special indexes. There is a *New York Times Index*, a *Washington Post Index*, a *National Newspaper Index*, and the *NewsBank*. Again, depending on the library, you may find that all of these indexes are on CD-ROM. Many large libraries also subscribe to newspaper and news organization Web sites on which you can find daily updates of news stories and feature articles. Look up *www.nytimes.com* or *www.cnn.com* to see for yourself.

Get Background and General Information from Books.
It may surprise you to find books listed at the end of a list of library resources. But there is no point in searching for books if you're in the wrong library or haven't checked the available references and periodicals. Choose books carefully and avoid checking out a pile of them that may not contain what you need.

Books are marvelous resources, particularly when you need background information on a general topic or a thorough understanding of a writer's theory or research. There are, however, drawbacks to using books as your *only* source of information. Books can become dated very quickly. Between the time an author writes a book and the time you check it out of the library, several years can pass.

A second drawback to using books as a sole resource is the amount of time it can take to find the piece of information you need. You don't have to read an entire book while researching a presentation. Just read those parts that relate to your topic. Review the table of contents at the front of the book and the index at the back to focus your search on a few relevant sections or pages. Does this mean that books should not be read cover-to-cover? Of course not. Good books are always a delight to read. But if you have a presentation to research and can't take the time to read an entire book, don't feel guilty about skipping large sections in order to find the supporting materials you need.

Computerized, online library catalogs have made the process of selecting books much easier. Now you can use key words in a computer search to find library books related to your topic. In most libraries you can print a list of book titles and their authors, publishers, dates, call numbers, and library locations. The printout can also include whether the books are available, on loan, or in the reference collection. Libraries, like computers, have become user friendly.

At this point you may be feeling overwhelmed. It may seem as though there are so many places to look for information that you could spend your whole life

LANGUAGE TOOLS

SEE OUR SITES:
iTools!
Find-It!
Research-It!

SEE MORE ABOUT:
your awards
advertising here
write to us

Research-It!

JUMP TO SECTION:
LANGUAGE . LIBRARY . GEOGRAPHICAL . FINANCIAL . SHIPPING . INTERNET

SEARCH THROUGH	SEARCH TEXT	ACTION	USAGE
Dictionary			
English (Merriam-Webster)		look it up!	word ? * are wild
Computing (FOLDOC)		look it up!	word
Rhyme (Rhyming Dictionary)		look it up!	word
Pronounce (CMU Pronouncing Dict.)		look it up!	word or sentence
Law (Law.com Dictionary)		look it up!	word or sentence
Thesaurus			
English (Merriam-Webster)		look it up!	word ? * are wild
Translator			
Universal (LOGOS)	Word in any language [parlez] Will translate to/from: English, French, Danish, Spanish, Swedish, German, Italian, Turkish, Portuguese, Dutch, Russian, Czech, Slovenian, Romanian, Latvian, Serbian, Croatian, Polish, Greek, Chinese,	look it up!	word

Research-It! calls itself a one-stop reference desk. This versatile Web site, www.itools.com/research-it, can help you define and translate words, find biographical information, locate places on maps, look up ZIP codes, follow the stock market, and more.

researching and run out of time to prepare your presentation. But that is exactly why it's important to use the library systematically. Match the type of information you're seeking with the appropriate kind of source material. Efficient and productive research will turn up materials uniquely suited to your presentation's purpose, topic, audience, and occasion.

With the advent of the Internet and the extraordinary reach of the World Wide Web, some speakers have abandoned libraries. Don't join the exodus. Libraries are still gold mines of information in which, if you are a skilled researcher, you can find most of the supporting materials you need for a presentation. At the same time, the World Wide Web is a rich source for finding information on almost any conceivable topic. Use both—you'll double your chances of finding the best supporting material for your presentation.

Electronic and Online Research

Most of the resources available in libraries are also available online. The Internet puts the world at your fingertips. We do not have the space in this book to teach you how to use the Internet—and besides, it changes so quickly that we would surely be guilty of providing out-of-date information. So rather than describe how to get information from the Web, we will instead concentrate on some advantages and disadvantages of online research.

Advantages. The advantages of searching the World Wide Web for supporting materials are apparent to anyone who has tried. For example, when we were looking for up-to-date information on the issue of plagiarism from online sources, we went online and found what we needed in minutes.

DiFFerentiate Between Your Primary and Secondary Sources When conducting research and deciding which supporting materials to use, consider whether you need or are using primary or secondary sources of information. A **primary source** is the document, testimony, or publication in which information first appeared. For example, a journal article that contains the results of an author's original research would be a primary source. A magazine or newspaper that reports on the original research or writing done by someone else is a secondary source. **Secondary sources** report, repeat, or summarize information from one or more other sources. Look carefully at secondary sources of information to determine, if possible, the primary source. Publications like *Newsweek, USA Today,* and *Parade Magazine* rarely conduct their own research. As secondary sources, they publish information they have obtained from primary sources.

There are millions and millions of Web sites out there. Finding the ones that meet your research needs can be a mind-boggling challenge. At first you may be tempted to engage a search engine in pursuit of a single word. Single-word searches will give you thousands of sites, most of which will be totally useless. A better idea is to do a what is called a **Boolean search** to target the research material you need.*

- Use *AND* (or, in some cases, a + sign) if you want *both* words to appear in a document: blues AND Chicago.

- Use *OR* if only one of the words must appear in a document: blues OR zydeco.

- Use *NOT* (or in some cases a − sign) in front of words that must *not* appear in a document: blues NOT zydeco.

- Use quotation marks to specify a multi-word phrase: "rhythm and blues," "devil's music," "jump blues."

- Use an asterisk as a substitute for letters that might vary: "juke*joint," "jook*joint."

- Use parentheses to group a series of possible terms and combine it with another term: (blues OR zydeco) AND "recording companies."

* There are many sources of information describing how to use Boolean operators with search engines or in computerized library indexes. Named after the nineteenth-century mathematician George Boole, Boolean operators provide a way of narrowing your search and reducing the number of "hits" you get. Try entering "Boolean operators" or "Boolean + operators" on any major search engine, and you'll find several thousand Web pages giving you everything from simple to highly complex explanations of Boolean operators.

You will find thousands of databases, personal Web pages, publications, research, and visuals online.[9] Fortunately, there are a number of online search services that provide indexes and access to all this specialized information. General directories such as the *Internet Public Library* (www.ipl.org) at the University of Michigan or *The Library of Congress* (www.lcweb.loc.gov) and popular search engine directories such as Yahoo! (www.yahoo.com) often provide directories of selected sites related to specific topics.

Most of you are familiar with one or more **search engines** such as AltaVista, Excite, Lycos, HotBot, InfoSeek, WebCrawler, and Yahoo! These Web "catalogs" help you find what you need by matching key words to Web sites that include those terms. For example, Yahoo!, one of the most popular search engines, can be used in two ways: Type in a term or click on one of many indexed topics that have proved popular. Of course, unless you carefully select your key terms, you can end up with thousands of sites that have little to do with your topic.

Metacrawler (www.metacrawler.com) searches other search engines, combing the results into a single list. By the time this textbook has been published, there may be many more sophisticated search engines that are even easier to use and more efficient in targeting the information you need.

Disadvantages. Despite the enormous benefits of electronic research, there are significant disadvantages. The first problem is that the sources on the Internet do not cover all possible kinds of information (at least they don't today, but who knows what the future will bring?). If you want the latest news or very current information, using the Internet may be your best bet. But if you're looking for commentary on a classic novel, specialized research reports on an academic topic, or a reliable explanation of a political issue or historical movement, Internet sources may not be comprehensive or objective enough to meet your research needs.

A second disadvantage to using the Internet for research is that it can be difficult to test the validity of the information you find. Some trustworthy Web sites include those of major newspapers and magazines, professional associations, government agencies, libraries, legitimate media outlets, and well-known experts. Unfortunately, there are also highly biased sources. Because no one can possibly screen everything on the Internet for accuracy, it can be difficult to separate reliable from unreliable sources. Both of us have listened to student presentations in which all of the information was taken from highly questionable sources found on the Internet. Using less-than-credible Web sources can jeopardize the believability of an entire presentation. William Miller, president of the Association of College and Research Libraries, notes, "Much of what purports to be serious information [on the Web] is simply junk—neither current, objective, nor trustworthy."[10]

In addition to the questions asked about any type of information (see page 115), there are special questions to consider when evaluating Internet information and its sources. Anyone can put anything on the Internet. Make sure that your sources are trustworthy and that your information is valid. Always test information that you have found on the Internet by asking these four additional

INTERVIEWING FOR INFORMATION

Print and online sources are excellent for some kinds of information, but sometimes asking an expert can give you material you won't get any other way. Once you know the purpose and topic of your presentation, start looking for someone who can tell you more about it—a professor, a police officer, a lawyer, a store manager, a chef—and see if you can schedule an interview with the person. Call or write to set up an appointment with someone you want to interview several days or weeks before you would like to meet with him or her. Indicate what you would like to discuss and how long you expect the interview to last. Setting up an appointment in advance demonstrates your respect for the interviewee and gives you time to prepare.

As with any presentation (and yes, an interview *is* a kind of presentation), careful planning is the key to success. Ask yourself these questions:

▶ *Why am I conducting this interview?* Narrow the focus of your information-gathering interview by pinpointing what you want or need to know that you cannot find some other way.

▶ *Whom am I interviewing?* The more you know about the person you are going to interview, the more prepared you will be. Make sure that you know your interviewee's area of expertise and job functions. Think about your interviewee as a one-person audience and apply the techniques discussed in Chapter 5, "Audience Analysis and Adaptation," to gather background information.

▶ *What do I want or need to know?* You will need to do some background research before your interview. Find out about the organization for which that person works. The more you know about your topic before the interview, the easier it will be to understand and appreciate the interviewee's comments.

▶ *What questions should I ask and in what order?* No matter whom you are interviewing, come prepared with a series of questions. Begin with a general question such as "What interests or abilities led you to this job?" Then, move on to specific questions that will give you detailed information. What you learn in the first few minutes can tell you which of your specific questions to use. You can ask for lists of achievements, most difficult problems, or suggestions for change. However, don't interview to get information you've already found through research. Use the interview to learn something new.

▶ *How can I get the interview off to a good start?* Treat your interview as an important event. Show up at the appointed time appropriately dressed. Have your questions typed on clean paper. At the beginning of the interview, remind your interviewee why you need his or her information and advice. This can take the form of a thank-you—"Thanks so much for taking twenty minutes out of your day to talk with me about your company's commitment to community service. I know you're the driving force behind it, and I'm looking forward to hearing about what got you started." Demonstrating what you know about the topic and why you want to interview this person shows that you are well prepared and professional.

▶ *How do I keep the interview running smoothly?* Your behavior during the interview should be as professional as your dress and your level of preparation and planning. When you speak, make sure that your voice is clear and easy to hear. Establish eye contact with the person whom you are interviewing throughout the course of the interview. Keep track of the time, dropping a few of your questions if you're running overtime. And remember that it's okay to smile, gesture, lean forward, take notes, and even frown if it's appropriate. Your engaged, animated responses will keep the interview moving.

▶ *Do I need to follow up?* When your interview is over, there's one more step to remember. Send a thank-you email or note. Call with a follow-up question that gives you a chance to personally thank your interviewee. Not only will you be doing the right thing and making a good impression, but you will also be ensuring your ability to return to your interviewee for more information.

Interviewing is as much an art as a skill. One of the keys to conducting a successful interview is good listening. Good listening will tell you if your questions have been answered before you ask them. Good listening can also give you new insights that can lead to new questions. Listen carefully and modify your questions according to the answers you hear. If all goes well, all your questions will be answered as you have a fascinating discussion with an interesting and cooperative expert.

Why not bookmark Metacrawler, www.metacrawler.com? In addition to offering a very large directory and a great search engine, a search of "great speeches" will lead you to some excellent Web sites.

questions: (1) Who put the information on the Net? (2) Why did they post it? (3) When was the information written versus when was it posted? (4) Do other published sources verify this information?

Documentation

All forms of supporting material used in a presentation (including information from Internet sources and interviews) should be documented. **Documentation** is the practice of citing the sources of your supporting material in a presentation. In-speech documentation enhances your credibility as a researcher and communicator and informs listeners about the sources and validity of your information and ideas.

Even if an author or a Web site grants you permission to reproduce material for personal use, you still must give the source of that information credit in your presentation.[11] Getting permission can become a complicated process requiring that you pay a publisher or an author for the right to use his or her material. In most college settings, permission doesn't obligate you to pay an author, but it does require you to include an acknowledgment of the rightful author and the source in your presentation or references.

Documenting Your Sources in Writing

In a written report, documentation follows one of several accepted formats such as Modern Language Association (MLA) style, American Psychological Association (APA) style, the prescriptions of *The Chicago Manual of Style* (published by the University of Chicago Press), or many others. The documentation section in any of these organizations' manuals will provide models of how to format a reference, endnote, or footnote. Depending on which style manual you use, there are very specific rules for documenting electronic sources.

Documenting electronic sources is much like documenting print sources. One difference is that there are two types of electronic sources. There are those that change, such as Web sites or online resources. Then there are those that don't change, such as a computer program or a database stored on a CD-ROM.

This is an important distinction. If you are using an electronic source that changes, make sure that you provide the date on which you used the source. Why? Because the information could be different on the following day. When working with a permanent CD-ROM, treat it like a book or journal and make sure that you provide the date of publication, not the date on which you used the source. Here are two examples of citations from online sources:

Julie J. C. H. Ryan, Student Plagiarism in an Online World, *Prism,* http://www.asee.org/prism/December/html/ student_plagiarism_in_an_onlin.htm, December 1998.

Web Weaves New Concerns About Plagiarism, *Purdue News,* http://www.purdue.edu/UNS/html14ever/9809. Offenbach.plagiarism.html, October 1998.

Always be prepared to provide a list of the references you used to prepare your presentation—just as you would for a written report. In most speaking situations, you will not be required to provide such a list. We recommend, however, that you keep a list of your references for your own use. If nothing else, it will remind you of which sources you used in the event that you are challenged about information or asked to repeat or to update your presentation. There are situations, however, in which you may be asked to provide your references—either for your instructor or for informing audience members and colleagues.

Documenting Your Sources in Presentations

In a presentation you should document the sources of supporting material "out loud." We are not suggesting that you read complete citations to your audience. Imagine how strange it would be to read aloud the previous examples of online citations on plagiarism. Think how awkward it would sound to provide the detail required by any of the publication manuals in the middle of your presentation. The last thing you want to do is to clutter your talk with complete citations or long Internet addresses. What you should provide is enough oral information to credit the sources of your information. If you believe that your audience should have access to the information you have used, you may provide a handout listing your references.

Not Documenting Your Sources Is Plagiarism

Why does documentation matter? Because without it you could fall into the trap of plagiarizing your source materials, intentionally or not. To **plagiarize** is to "to use and pass off (the idea or writing of another); to appropriate for use as one's own passages or ideas from (another)."[12] The word *plagiarism* comes from a Latin term, *plagium,* which means "kidnapping." Thus, when you plagiarize, you are stealing or kidnapping something that belongs to someone else. Simply put, when you plagiarize, you fail to document and give credit to the sources of your information. Unfortunately, some speakers believe that prohibitions against plagiarism don't apply to them. Others know that they apply but think they can get away with it. Still others plagiarize without even realizing that they are doing it.

Plagiarism Hurts Everyone.   Although most speakers don't intend to commit "literary theft," plagiarism occurs more often than it should, often with serious

So What Should I Say to Document Supporting Material?   Your spoken citation should include just enough information to allow an interested listener to find the original source you're citing. Generally, it's a good idea to provide the name of the person (or people) whose work you are using, say a word or two about that person's credentials, and mention the source of the information: "Dr. Joanne Cantor, a University of Wisconsin professor, drew this conclusion in her book *Mommy, I'm Scared*: 'Media violence. . . .'" When the information is time-sensitive, you should include the date of publication or posting. Sometimes, when a person or reference is well known, you don't have to do much more than say, "In his last State of the Union Address, President Clinton said . . . " or "As the great psalm begins, 'The Lord is my shepherd; I shall not want. . . .'" To document electronic sources orally, you could say, "An article on plagiarism in the *Purdue News,* found at *www.purdue.edu,* reports that. . . ." You could also display the complete Web site addresses on a slide (as long as you give listeners enough time to copy them). If you want your audience to have complete citations, prepare a bibliography as a handout.

Is it ever okay to "borrow" a phrase or an idea?   It's one thing to slip in a quotation and pretend it's your idea and wording. It's another thing to use a familiar phrase in a new context to support an idea. For instance, politicians often use phrases borrowed from other sources. So do writers. Throughout this textbook, we have alluded to phrases taken from literature and popular sources. For example, on p. 119 we wrote that for some information "there's no place like home." Anyone who's seen *The Wizard of Oz* knows that Dorothy used that magic phrase in order to get back home to Kansas. Using a familiar phrase like this in other contexts can make an idea more interesting and memorable. Besides, think how awkward the following acknowledgment would be: "For some information, 'there's no place like home,' as Dorothy said to her family and friends in the 1939 movie *The Wizard of Oz*." Making an allusion to a famous quotation is not plagiarism as long as the phrase is well known and is used to interest or inspire audience members who will recognize the phrase.

consequences. In colleges, students have failed classes, been expelled from programs and schools, or been denied a degree when caught plagiarizing. In the publishing business, authors have been sued by writers who claimed that their ideas and words had been plagiarized. Well-respected scientists, politicians, university officials, and civic leaders have been tarnished with charges of plagiarism.

Avoiding Plagiarism.   Most speakers don't set out to plagiarize. Ignorance, however, is no excuse. Almost every teacher has had students who turned in entire articles from magazines or encyclopedias as their original work. "But," say the accused students, "we were told to find and share research." This is true, but presenting someone else's work as your own is not research—it's plagiarism. Give credit where credit is due. The person who published or posted those original ideas spent a lot of effort creating them and should be recognized for that effort.

The key to avoiding plagiarism is to identify the sources of your information in your presentation. A second key is understanding that changing a few words of someone else's work is not enough to avoid plagiarism. If they're not your original ideas, and most of the words are not yours, you are ethically obligated to tell your audience who wrote or said them and where they came from.

This requirement applies equally to material you find on the Web. The World Wide Web has added a new dimension to the problem of plagiarism. In an article in *Prism,* a publication of the American Society for Engineering Education, author Julie Ryan explains that "the proliferation of Web pages and electronic publications makes plagiarism easier to accomplish and harder to recognize."[13] She describes the problem as follows:

> A few words typed into a Web search engine can lead a student to hundreds, sometimes thousands, of relevant documents, making it easy to "cut and paste" a few paragraphs from here and a few more from there until the student has an entire paper-length collection. Or a student can find a research paper published in one of the hundreds of new journals that have gone online over the past few years, copy the entire text, turn it into a new document, and then offer it up as original work without having to type anything but a cover page. Even recycling efforts and ghost writers have gone global with Web sites offering professionally or student-written research papers for sale, some even with a money-back guarantee against detection."[14]

Fortunately, the Web also provides instructors with the same access to information. Given time and a good search engine, many would-be plagiarizers have been caught and appropriately punished.

The bottom line is this: Plagiarism is not just unethical and illegal; it represents the theft of a person's hard work and good ideas. Diana Hacker, author of *The Bedford Handbook,* expresses this idea quite eloquently when she explains that any writing you do (whether for a research paper or for a presentation) is a collaboration between you and your sources: "To be fair and ethical, you must acknowledge your debt to the writers of these sources."[15]

A presentation is more than a collection of statistics, examples, quotations, stories, and famous phrases from other sources. Supporting material helps you explain, clarify, convince, and interest your audience. Use it to spice up your presentation, demonstrate a principle, or prove a point. Don't use information in place of ideas. Use information to support ideas. And when you use it, give the person who wrote it or the publication that printed it the credit it deserves for supplying you with the raw materials you needed for your presentation.

Summary

◆✦ **What forms of supporting material should I use?**

Select the best quality of material and use more than one type of the following forms of supporting material for your presentation: facts, statistics, testimony, definitions, analogies, descriptions, examples, and stories.

◆✦ **How can I tell if my supporting materials are valid?**

Test your supporting material by asking whether the information you want to use is credible, recent, consistent, relevant, and statistically accurate.

◆✦ **Can I use personal knowledge as support?**

You may be an excellent source of information, as long as you make sure that your facts are accurate and your opinions well founded.

◆✦ **How do I find good supporting material in a library?**

After making sure you have found the right library and sought the services of a professional librarian, look for materials in the reference collection, in periodicals and newspapers, and in appropriate books.

◆✦ **How do I conduct research online?**

Use an appropriate search engine to help yourself find the material you need. Narrow your search to a very specific term or phrase in order to maximize the efficiency and effectiveness of your research.

◆✦ **How much credit should I give to the sources of my supporting material?**

Provide enough information about your sources so that a listener could locate that information. To be fair and ethical, you must acknowledge your debt to those who wrote the ideas and information you have used in a presentation.

Key Terms

analogy 113	example 113	secondary source 121
biased 115	fact 111	statistics 112
Boolean search 122	plagiarism 125	stories 114
definition 112	primary source 121	supporting material 111
description 113	research 116	testimony 112
documentation 124	search engine 122	valid 114

Notes

1. Jerome Groopman, "The Shadow Epidemic," *The New Yorker,* 11 May 1998, pp. 48–49.
2. Joanne Cantor, *Mommy, I'm Scared: How TV and Movies Frighten Children and What We Can Do to Protect Them* (San Diego: Harcourt Brace, 1998), p. 5.
3. Jesse Jackson, Rainbow Coalition speech given at the 1984 Democratic Convention, 17 July 1984. For an analysis and complete text of the speech, see James R. Andrews and David Zarefsky, *Contemporary American Voices* (New York: Longman, 1992), pp. 355–362.
4. Daphne Duval Harrison, *Black Pearls: Blues Queens of the 1920s* (New Brunswick, NJ: Rutgers University Press, 1988).
5. Vivian Hobbs, Commencement Address at Prince George's Community College, Largo, Maryland, 1991. See Appendix A for complete address.
6. Groopman.
7. *New York Times 1999 Almanac* (New York: Penguin, 1998), p. 395.
8. Jerry L. Winsor, Dan B. Curtis, and Ronald D. Stephens, "National Preferences in Business and Communication Update," *Journal of the Association for Communication Administration* 31 (1997): 170–179.
9. A useful compilation of subject-specific library resources and Web sites can be found in Diana Hacker, *Research and Documentation in the Electronic Age,* 2nd ed. (Boston: Bedford Books, 1999). In addition to general advice on Internet research, the booklet lists sources in the humanities, history, social sciences, and sciences and features a large section on how to document sources according to different style manuals.
10. Quoted from *Chronicle of Higher Education,* 1 August 1997, p. A44, in Ann Raimes, *Keys for Writers,* 2nd ed. (Boston: Houghton Mifflin, 1999), p. 73.
11. Diana Roberts Wienbroer, *The McGraw-Hill Guide to Electronic Research and Documentation* (Boston: McGraw-Hill, 1997), p. 26.
12. *The American Heritage Dictionary of the English Language,* 3rd ed. (Boston: Houghton Mifflin, 1992), p. 1383. Copyright © 1996 by Houghton Mifflin Company. Reproduced by permission from *The American Heritage Dictionary of the English Language, Third Edition.*
13. Julie J. C. H. Ryan, "Student Plagiarism in an Online World," *Prism,* December 1998, p. 1, as retrieved online at *http://www.asee.org/prism/*.
14. Ryan, p. 2.
15. Diana Hacker, *The Bedford Handbook* (Boston: Bedford Books, 1998), p. 570.

8

Organization

Many popular books on presentation speaking include a three-step guide to organization that we call the "Tell 'em Technique." It goes like this: "Tell 'em what you're gonna tell 'em—tell 'em—then, tell 'em what you told 'em." As simple as the Tell 'em Technique seems, it does capture three important tips about how to organize a presentation. Audiences benefit if they know what the main ideas of a presentation will be. They also benefit if they hear the main ideas more than once. And finally, a summary of the main ideas helps them remember what they have heard. There is, however, more to good organization than the Tell 'em Technique, which tells you *what* to do but not *how* to do it. How do you select the best ideas and information for your presentation? How do you arrange those ideas? There's no one right way, but there *are* many ways in which you can use organizing principles to help yourself get the most out of your speaking opportunities. We explore these principles in this chapter.

Why Organization Matters

Years of teaching, coaching, and communication consulting have led us to conclude that most speakers underestimate how important organization is to the success of their presentations.

As an audience member, you already know how much it matters. You no doubt find a well-organized presentation easier to listen to and remember than a poorly organized one. You probably find it difficult to understand and remember the words of a speaker who rambles and doesn't connect ideas. In fact, you may never want to hear that speaker again. Researchers confirm that audiences react positively to well-organized presentations and speakers and negatively to poorly organized ones.[1]

This idea is not new. Cicero, the great Roman senator and orator, identified two initial tasks required of every effective speaker. The first was to determine the key points; the second was to put those key points into an orderly sequence. Cicero used the Latin word *inventio* to describe the speaker's attempt "to find out what he should say."[2] He identified the second step, *dispositio*, as the task of arranging ideas and information for a presentation in an orderly sequence. The selection and arrangement of ideas and information can help audience members make decisions about important issues and select a course of action. For example, if a speaker is trying to help audience members assess the benefits of competing insurance plans, a disorganized presentation will neither describe each plan clearly nor help the listeners decide which plan is best or which to choose. They may feel even more confused after hearing the presentation than before they heard it.

ORGANIZATION HELPS THE AUDIENCE

Understand the message
Remember the message
Decide how to react

Organization also helps you as a speaker. If you are well organized, you are much more likely to achieve the purpose of your presentation. Organization helps you to decide how many and what kinds of research and supporting materials you will need for your presentation. If, for example, your purpose is to report on the need for repairs at the community swimming pool, you do not have to spend time researching the hourly pay rate of lifeguards.

Organization also helps you to determine a clear and effective arrangement of the content that you want to include. Not only does it tell you which ideas should come first or last, but organization also keeps you focused on the development of each idea. Equally important and not surprisingly, well-organized speakers are seen as more competent and confident than disorganized speakers.

ORGANIZATION HELPS THE SPEAKER

Gather ideas and information
Arrange those ideas strategically
Enhance his or her credibility

REAL WORLD, REAL SPEAKERS

How to Get Organized

Building a strong presentation is like building a house, and organization is the blueprint. Collecting ideas and information for your presentation is similar to choosing and collecting the materials you would need to build a house. Although just about every house includes wood, nails, windows, doors, siding, wiring, and plumbing, piling all those building materials on a home site would not give you a house. You would still need a detailed blueprint or plan to tell you what you're building, what you need to build it, and how to put the pieces together. Similarly, most presentations have a purpose and supporting materials that advance and support them—but just "piling up" your ideas won't result in an effective presentation. The **organization** of a presentation helps you to stay focused on your purpose while you're deciding what to include in your talk and how to put it all together in an effective way. Your purpose and the needs and interests of your audience help you decide what to include on your "blueprint."

Before you can put all the pieces of a presentation into a pattern, structure, or order, though, you must decide which pieces to use. Considering your purpose, your audience, the occasion, and the logistics of the situation can help you make these decisions.

- *Consider Your Purpose.* When deciding what to include in your presentation, always begin with your purpose (see Chapter 4, "Purpose and Topic"). Include ideas and supporting material that will help you to achieve your purpose. Leave out anything that's not relevant. If your purpose is to teach new employees how to fill out a performance evaluation form, you won't need to talk about the history of the evaluation system. If, however, your purpose is to explain why the performance evaluation form is so complicated, information about its history and development might be just what you need.

- *Consider Your Audience.* Having analyzed your audience (see Chapter 5, "Audience Analysis and Adaptation"), you're in a good position to select ideas and supporting material that will interest and influence its members. Say your purpose is to gain support for a tax increase. To an audience of government employees, you might explain how a tax increase could prevent staff layoffs. To members of a neighborhood organization, you might explain that a failure to increase revenues through taxes would result in fewer police patrols.

▶ *Consider the Logistics and Occasion.* Use what you know about where, when, and why you will be speaking (see Chapter 6, "Logistics and Occasion") to guide your selection of ideas and supporting material. Let's say that you know you will have only ten minutes to speak, and you have five advertising campaigns that you want to describe as examples of a marketing company's effectiveness. You likewise would know that you would have time to focus on only one or two of them or to provide a brief highlight of each campaign.

Considering these factors will help you to determine what ideas to include, in a general sense. Now it's time to get specific and think about how to shape those ideas into a well-organized, effective presentation.

Select Your Key Points

At this point in the preparation process, you may have heaps of excellent ideas and supporting material but no plan for organizing them. The first step in organization requires answering a single question: What are the key points that I want to cover in my presentation? The **key points** of a presentation represent the most important issues or the main ideas that you want your audience to understand and to remember during and after your talk. Finding and selecting your key points (Cicero's *inventio*) are the first step in developing a clear organizational format for your presentation. So how do you do this? Look for a pattern or a natural grouping for your ideas and information.

Depending on your purpose and topic area, this can be an easy task or a huge puzzle. Inexperienced speakers often feel overwhelmed by what seem to be mountains of unrelated facts and figures. Don't give up! Finding a pattern is similar to assembling a patchwork quilt or planting a flower garden. You have all the pieces or plants; now it is time to look for similarities in shape and color as well as to figure out how all the pieces can be combined to create a complete picture.

One way to begin your search for a pattern is to apply the "4Rs of Organization" to the ideas that you're considering for inclusion. The 4Rs represent a series of critical thinking steps that can help you find an effective organizational pattern for your presentation.

This speaker uses a flip chart to clearly list key points of her presentation to a Spanish-speaking audience on preventing depression.

THE 4Rs OF ORGANIZATION

Review

Reduce

Regroup

Refine

Review.   Find an uninterrupted block of time and a quiet place and bring all of your ideas and supporting material to the table. Reread and critique what you've written or collected. Does the information you've collected support your purpose, or is it marginal or irrelevant? Have you determined the key points that you want to make in your presentation? Evaluate the amount of supporting material you've gathered. Is there enough? Or is there too much to include in your presentation? What common ideas have appeared in most of your research? Which ones seem most interesting, relevant, and important? Will you need some vital statistics or dramatic testimony to back them up?

By thinking critically and unemotionally about your material, you may find that certain ideas and information jump out as must-include "keepers," whereas others can be put aside for another day. Both of us have found that a way of organizing the ideas and information that we have collected for a presentation often emerges during the process of carefully reviewing our materials.

Reduce.   Once you have reviewed your ideas and information, try to boil the "keepers" down to their essential points. In a presentation, less can be more. Rather than risk overwhelming your audience with too much information, choose a few key items that they will notice and remember. Great chefs know that reduction is the secret of a great sauce. In cooking, reduction is more than just boiling off water—it's a way of intensifying flavors and changing the chemical composition of the other ingredients. The same is true in a presentation. Reduction looks for and organizes the essence of a presentation; it boils away the extras. Finding the essence of your presentation will help you create an organizational pattern that will give you and your message more impact.

Regroup.   Try regrouping the ideas and relevant supporting material that you want to include in your presentation into different categories. If you plan to talk about a problem, you may want to put illustrative stories about the problem into one group and statistics and research that analyze the problem into another. Or you might consider categorizing the problem along a timeline—how did it start, when did it become serious, what's the current status, and what will happen if the problem is not solved? If your presentation will focus on a set of accomplishments by your organization, you could try several different groupings—achievements that have won awards, the impact of selected accomplishments on groups of people or organizations, a history of the organization's achievements, or the practical value of encouraging outstanding efforts by employees. Regrouping your ideas and information may help you to identify an organizational pattern that will best suit the purpose of your presentation.

Refine.   Once you have reviewed, reduced, and regrouped your material, it is time to refine—time for the finishing work. Sometimes this can be the most important step because it puts your key points into a form that will make your presentation more memorable. If, for example, you were listing the accomplishments of an organization, you might group them in terms of how *ready, willing,* and *able* the organization is to serve its public.

Very often, refining means rewording an idea in a creative way. Refining can also help you to find a useful or familiar "hook" on which to hang your key points. For example, the 4Rs of Organization use a common first letter to help you to remember how to use this technique. Labeling each section of a presentation about the organization's accomplishments with *ready, willing,* or *able* uses a popular saying as the basis for refining your ideas.

Link Your Key Points and Central Idea

Now that you've discovered and selected your key points, you must directly link them to your central idea. A house that does not connect the framing to the foundation will not stand. Similarly, a presentation that does not connect its key points to the central idea will not achieve its purpose.

Your purpose and your central idea may not be the same. Your purpose states what you want your audience to know, think, believe, or do as a result of your presentation. Your **central idea** is a sentence or thesis statement that summarizes the key points of your presentation. The central idea also can provide a brief preview of the organizational pattern you will follow to achieve your purpose. As the overall structure of your presentation emerges during the *regrouping* stage, you should connect your key points to your central idea. If you find that it takes more than one sentence to state your central idea, go back to the drawing board. You may be trying to do too much, or you may not have a clear purpose or organizational pattern. The following three examples illustrate how topic area, purpose, and central idea are different but closely linked to one another.

Topic Area:	Growing tomatoes
Purpose:	To teach the audience how to grow healthy tomatoes
Central Idea:	Growing healthy tomatoes requires good soil, bright sun, plenty of water, and a watchful eye.

Topic Area:	Refugee families
Purpose:	To increase donations to the church's refugee assistance program
Central Idea:	Because the church's refugee families program has been a blessing for all of us—the families, our church, and you—please continue to make financial contributions to our ministry.

Topic Area:	Muzak
Purpose:	To make the audience more aware of the purpose and power of Muzak
Central Idea:	The next time that you hear Muzak playing your song, you will remember how pervasive it is, how it originated, and how it tries to lift your spirits and productivity.

Notice how the statement of the central idea in the examples above identifies the topic area and the purpose of a presentation while previewing the organizational pattern. As you review, reduce, regroup, and refine your material, your central idea may go through many revisions. But by the time you are ready to speak, the central idea should be clear and should state what you are going to say and in what order you will say it to achieve your purpose.

Several years ago both of us attended an address by a well-respected colleague. The presentation got off to a good start, but after twenty minutes the audience began to get restless. Just then, the speaker announced that he would conclude by sharing ten major recommendations with us. You could almost hear the audience groan. It was just too much! As the presentation dragged on, the recommendations merged into one another. We left the assembly without a clear understanding of what had been said. We had to read the address in printed form before we could begin to appreciate the speaker's message and key points. The presentation was neither simple nor clear, and as a result, it did not achieve its purpose.

Isa Engleberg and John Daly

Keep It Simple

Even the best listeners in your audience will not be able to remember everything that you say. Keeping your overall structure simple and clear will improve the chances that your audience will retain your central idea, a few of your key points, and the best pieces of supporting material that you include. Television news reports and news magazines structure their material so that a sixth-grader can follow a story. Approach your presentation in the same way. Don't be tempted to include ten reasons for change, two hundred years of history, or twenty-five charts just because that material is available. Instead, pick out the most important reasons, the key events, or the most dramatic charts.

At this point in the organizational process, you may be wondering how to consolidate your key points into a clear and coherent presentation. If a clear organizational pattern doesn't emerge as you review, reduce, regroup, and refine your material, you may be able to apply one or more commonly used patterns to meet your organizational needs.

Organizational Patterns

Even the most polished presentation speakers sometimes find it difficult to see how their ideas and information fall into an organizational pattern. If you're in a similar position, do not despair. Several commonly used organizational patterns can help you clarify your central idea and find a format for your presentation.

Arrange by Subtopics

Topical arrangement involves dividing a large topic into smaller subtopics. Subtopics can describe reasons, characteristics, techniques, and procedures. For example, you could divide the topic of alcoholism into its

ORGANIZATIONAL PATTERNS

- Topical
- Time
- Space
- Problem-Solution
- Causes and Effects
- Stories and Examples
- Comparison-Contrast
- Memory Aids

symptoms and treatments, or you could devote your entire presentation to describing available treatments. For a presentation on growing tomatoes, you could divide the topic into different types of tomatoes or growing techniques. You could support a political candidate by describing his or her stand on different issues or by listing the candidate's qualifications and contributions to the community. If your ideas and information can be divided into discrete categories, topical arrangement can provide a clear pattern of organization. For example:

Topic Area: Facial expressions in different cultures

Purpose: To appreciate that some facial expressions don't always translate between cultures

Central Idea: Americans and native Japanese often misinterpret facial expressions depicting fear, sadness, and disgust.[3]

Key Points: A. Fear

      B. Sadness

      C. Disgust

Sequence in Time

Some topics lend themselves to a **time arrangement,** which orders information according to time or calendar dates. Most step-by-step procedures begin with the first step and continue sequentially through the last step. Giving recipes, listing assembly instructions, and describing technical procedures often require a time arrangement, as do presentations on historical events. You also can use time arrangement for a past-present-future pattern or for a before-after pattern. For example:

Topic Area: Running meetings

Purpose: To explain how to use meeting time effectively and efficiently

Central Idea: Well-run meetings have a definite beginning, middle, and end.

Speakers often use time arrangement when demonstrating the steps of a recipe or cooking technique. The chicken must be prepared and properly trussed before it can be roasted.

Key Points: A. Convening the meeting
B. Giving the opening remarks
C. Providing direction to the group
D. Ending the meeting

Position in Space

Observing where people and places are located as well as where events take place may help you alert your audience to your key points. **Space arrangement** is not used as often as time arrangement, but it's just as obvious a pattern for certain topics. If your information can be placed in different locations, you may want to use space arrangement as an organizational pattern. Travel books often divide a map into sections in order to describe different regions of a country. A proposed highway system is hard to describe unless you can show where it will go and what it will displace. You can use space arrangement to discuss a topic involving different locations, such as city, state, and federal taxes or national holidays in Canada, Mexico, and Brazil. Here is an example of spatial organization:

Topic Area: Brain structure

Purpose: To explain how different sections of the brain are responsible for different functions

Central Idea: A guided tour of the brain begins in the hindbrain, moves through the midbrain, and ends in the forebrain, with side trips through the right and left hemispheres.

Key Points: A. The hindbrain
B. The midbrain
C. The forebrain
D. The right and left hemispheres

Present Problems and Solutions

A **problem-solution arrangement** can be used to describe a situation that is harmful (the problem) and then offer a plan to solve the problem (the solution). Problems can be as simple as a squeaking door, a burned cookie, or a misunderstood procedure or as serious and as widespread as drunk driving, poor quarterly earnings, African famine, low employee morale, or acid rain. Solutions likewise can be just as different, ranging from oiling a door hinge to airlifting tons of food and medicine to another continent. As Chapter 19, "Developing Persuasive Presentations," discusses in more detail, problem-solution patterns work especially well for persuasive presentations. They can also be used in informative presentations, as this outline shows:

Topic Area: Poor participation in meetings

Purpose: To provide suggestions for solving common "people problems" in meetings

Central Idea: Learning how to deal with a few common behavioral problems in groups will improve a group's performance.

Key Points: A. Nonparticipants
B. Loudmouths
C. Interrupters
D. Whisperers
E. Latecomers and early leavers

REAL WORLD, REAL SPEAKERS

On April 19, 1995, the Alfred P. Murrah Federal Building in Oklahoma City was blown up. Federal intelligence linked Timothy McVeigh and Terry Nichols to the crime. Imagine what it must have been like for prosecutors in the 1997 Terry Nichols trial to win their case. They had to prove that Nichols, a man with an ironclad alibi for the day of the Oklahoma City bombing, was a co-conspirator with convicted bomber Timothy McVeigh. Although there was, in the words of prosecutor Beth Wilkinson, "an avalanche of evidence" against Nichols, most of it was circumstantial. Nothing put him at the scene of the crime; no one testified that he had planned or had taken credit for the bombing.

At the beginning of her three-hour summation to the jury, Ms. Wilkinson presented a large poster on which, in the upper left-hand corner, the Alfred P. Murrah Federal Building was pictured *before* the bombing. In the lower right-hand corner, there was a photo of the building *after* the bombing. Prosecutor Wilkinson organized her summation by taking the jury on a journey along a winding road that connected the two buildings. At critical "stops" along the road, she focused on key pieces of evidence—Nichols's purchase of fertilizer, his theft of bomb-making materials, his phone calls to McVeigh. She walked her jury from one piece of evidence to another—all leading to the bombing that claimed 168 lives. Not only did she use a spatial arrangement pattern to help her lead the jury clearly and logically to the picture of the bombed building, but she also led them to find Nichols guilty.

Show Causes and Effects

A **causes and effects arrangement** either presents a cause and its resulting effect, or details the effects that lead to a cause. In cause-to-effect, you describe or identify a situation, object, or behavior that results in another situation, object, or behavior. We have heard speakers claim that eating red meat causes disease and depression, that lower taxes result in more business investment and personal savings, and that large classrooms, inadequate discipline, and low teacher salaries explain the decline in educational achievement. In effect-to-cause, you can describe situations, behavior, or objects and then identify their causes—the reasons why they occur. We have heard speakers claim that sleepiness or lack of energy can be caused by an iron deficiency, that the decrease in lake fish is caused by acid rain, and that low voter turnout may be due to the belief that voting doesn't make a difference anymore. As these examples show, causes and effects arrangements work particularly well when you want to establish a relationship among occurrences or to justify a course of action or conclusion.

Be careful with causes and effects, though. The fact that one occurrence follows another does not mean that the first causes the second. Perhaps a third factor is to blame. Sleepiness or lack of energy can also be caused by too many late-night parties. The decrease in lake fish can also be caused by too much fishing. Remember that there was a time when people believed that bad luck was caused by walking under ladders, breaking mirrors, or having a black cat cross their path. In the following outlines, a speaker identifies the causes (biological and environmental) of an effect (overeating).

Celebrating a decades-long struggle to protect the American bald eagle from pesticides and encroachments on its habitat, President Clinton announces the ultimate effect of this thirty-year effort: saving the living symbol of the United States from extinction.

Topic Area: Overeating

Purpose: To understand the multiple factors that influence eating habits

Central Idea: Identifying the causes of overeating can help you begin to minimize its effects.

Key Points: A.   Biological causes

B.   Environmental causes

In the next example, a speaker contends that television has harmful effects on children.

Topic Area: Children and television

Purpose: To describe the harmful effects that television has on children

Central Idea: Television has a negative influence on children and their families because it displaces time that could be spent on more important activities.[4]

Key Points: A.   Television has a negative effect on children's physical fitness.

B.   Televison has a negative effect on children's school achievement.

C.   Televison is a hidden competitor for more important activities.

D.   Television watching may become a serious addiction.

Tell Stories and Give Examples

Sometimes a series of dramatic stories can be so compelling and interesting that they can easily become the backbone of a presentation. Such stories can be used as an organizational pattern or, as we indicated in Chapter 7, "Supporting Material," they can be used as supporting material for presentations organized in other ways.

Sometimes selecting a series of appropriate stories or examples is all you need to do to organize your presentation. Television commercials use this technique.

You see a series of people who have been made happy, rich, beautiful, healthy, sexy, or clean by a product. In a presentation, you tell stories or provide a series of examples to support your point. Dramatic stories about successful artists or professionals who escaped from youthful poverty and prejudice can be the key points of your presentation, as this outline illustrates:

Topic Area: Leaders and adversity

Purpose: To convince listeners that disabilities are not a barrier to success

Central Idea: Many noteworthy leaders have lived with disabilities.

Key Points: A. Franklin D. Roosevelt, president of the United States

B. Jan Scruggs, disabled soldier and Vietnam Memorial founder

C. Helen Keller, deaf and blind advocate

Compare and Contrast

A **comparison-contrast arrangement** shows your audience how two things are similar or different. This pattern works well when an unfamiliar concept is easier to explain by comparing it to a familiar concept or when you are trying to demonstrate the advantages of one alternative over another. For example, you can compare and contrast the features of one car to those of another in its price class. You can compare and contrast the rate of growth and yield of tomato plants grown with or without fertilizer. You can compare and contrast the story of a refugee family helped by a church assistance program to that of a family who relied on government services. For example:

Topic Area: Family sedans

Purpose: To recommend a way of evaluating medium-sized cars

Central Idea: Comparing performance, comfort, fuel economy, and reliability can help you to select and purchase a new mid-sized car for your family.

Key Points: A. Performance

B. Comfort

C. Overall fuel economy

D. Predicted reliability

A special form of the compare-contrast arrangement is called a **figurative analogy.** As discussed in Chapter 7, an analogy is a description that shows the ways in which two things are similar and suggests that what is true about one thing will also be true about the other. A figurative analogy notes similarities in two things that are not obviously comparable. The following example compares student success to horse racing.

Topic Area: Student success in college

Purpose: To identify the multiple factors that affect student success in college

Central Idea: Predicting student success is like picking the winning horse at the racetrack and must include considerations of a student's high school record, parents' education, teachers, and advisers as well as the college's type of campus.

Key Points: A. High school grades and test scores = Track record

B. Parents' education = Horse's breeding record

C. Teacher = Trainer

D. Adviser = Jockey

E. Type of campus = Track conditions

Use Memory Aids

Journalists use the Who, What, Where, When, and Why questions to remind themselves of the key parts of a news story. First aid instructors teach the ABCs of First Aid—Open the *Airways*, check for *Breathing*, and check for *Circulation*. Music teachers have their 3Bs (Bach, Beethoven, and Brahms), and the 4-H Club has used its name to remind members of its fourfold aim of improving head, heart,

ORDERING THE KEY POINTS

Once you have identified the key points that will directly support your central idea and have chosen the organizational pattern that you want to use, you may find yourself faced with a very common question: Which key points should go first, second, or last?

In many cases, the organizational pattern you've chosen will dictate the order of your key points. If, for example, you are using time arrangement, the first step in a procedure should come first. If you are looking at a historical event, you can begin at the beginning and work your way forward to the finish.

But what if your format does not dictate or suggest an order? In these cases, identify and place your strongest ideas in strategic positions. Do you "put your best foot forward" and lead with your strongest idea? Or do you "save the best for last"? Unfortunately, there is no single answer. Your answer depends on many factors, such as the audience's attitude toward you and your message, the occasion of the presentation, and the strategies you intend to use to achieve your purpose. That said, we offer some tips related to these factors:

▶ *Strength and Familiarity.* If one of your ideas is not as strong as others, place it in the middle position. For example, in illustrating the Stories and Examples organizational format, we used the example of a presentation on leadership and physical disabilities that featured examples—stories about President Roosevelt, Jan Scruggs, and Helen Keller. Whereas most audiences would have some familiarity with the first and third individuals, they probably wouldn't recognize Jan Scruggs (who, by the way, is a disabled Vietnam veteran who founded the Washington Vietnam Veterans Memorial and authored *To Heal a Nation*[1]). Thus, we put the least

familiar story in the middle of the presentation, so as to start and end with better-known examples.

▶ *Audience.* Whether you lead from strength or "end with a bang" depends on your best judgment about how to achieve your purpose, given what you've learned about your audience. If your audience wants information about current projections, make sure that you satisfy that need early. Other points related to future sales projections can come later. If an audience is not very interested in your topic, don't begin with your most technical, detailed point. You may be better off beginning with a point that explains why understanding the topic is important. If you are facing a hostile audience or speaking about a controversial topic, you may want to begin with a key point that focuses on the background of an issue or on the reasons why there is a need for change.

▶ *Logistics.* In addition to audience factors, the logistics of a situation can affect the order of key points. If you're one of a series of presenters, you may end up with less time to speak than was originally scheduled. Plan your presentation so that your most important key points come first. That way, if you *do* have to shorten your presentation, your audience will still have heard the main thing you came to say.

There aren't any hard and fast rules about ordering your points. Just make sure that they follow a logical progression and are ordered in a way that helps your audience to understand and remember what you tell them.

1. Jan C. Scruggs and Joel L. Swerdlow, *To Heal a Nation: The Vietnam Veterans Memorial* (New York: HarperCollins, 1992).

hands, and health. Throughout this textbook you have already seen and will continue to see **memory aids** such as these used as organizational patterns and as ways of helping you remember what you've read. You can use them alone to organize your presentation or in combination with any of the other organizational patterns we've been discussing. Here's an example:

Topic Area:	Organizing a presentation
Purpose:	To provide an effective method for selecting the key points of a presentation
Central Idea:	The 4Rs represent a series of critical thinking steps that can help you develop an effective organizational pattern for your presentation.
Key Points:	A. Review
	B. Reduce
	C. Regroup
	D. Refine

Please note that these commonly used patterns of organization are neither strategies nor solutions to organization problems.[5] They are only arrangements to consider when looking for an effective organizational pattern. And even though many presentations will fit one or more of these common formats, there is nothing wrong with coming up with your own original pattern.

Match the Format to the Content

A little earlier in this chapter, we introduced you to the 4Rs of Organization. Let's look at how this technique can be applied to matching an organizational pattern to the content of a presentation. Suppose you wanted to give a talk on the uniquely American musical form known as the *blues*. As you *review* the material you've gathered, you may discover that a lot of it focuses on famous blues musicians—that emphasis would imply a topical arrangement that lists individual artists and describes their contributions. You can now *reduce* the number of influential artists you will talk about and *regroup* them by years, areas of the country, or special contributions. You could further *refine* your topical arrangement by using a famous song title as the heading for each key point.

On the other hand, your *review* of your research might instead suggest a causes and effects arrangement that would demonstrate how the blues influenced other forms of music such as the rock revival of the 1960s and rap music in the 1990s. Again, think about how to *reduce* these influences to the major forms of music, *regroup* them by era or type, and *refine* your presentation by labeling each form.

In a third *review* of your research, you might note that the blues migrated from the Mississippi Delta region to cities such as Memphis and Chicago. You then might try space arrangement that follows the railway lines moving north and northeast. *Reduction* would limit your consideration to major migration routes. *Regrouping* could organize your material by early and late migrations or East Coast versus Midwest migrations. *Refining* might suggest the names of famous northbound trains as headings for each section of your presentation.

FAQ ISN'T ORGANIZING THE SAME AS OUTLINING? Leonard Rampulla, a New York architect who also serves as president of a professional organization, told us: "[Although] there is a comfort level using my voice and gestures and answering questions, my delivery was more successful when I was well organized and used an outline." Mr. Rampulla understands the value of organization and the utility of an outline. He also understands that they are not the same thing.

Organizing a presentation requires careful attention to selecting key points and appropriate supporting material and then to putting all the pieces of a talk in their proper place and order. Organization provides a strategic framework that links your purpose to the audience's willingness and ability to listen, understand, and respond to your message. Organization is a strategy. Outlining, on the other hand, is a technique, as you will see in Chapter 9, "Organizational Tools."

Choose the approach—the contributions of individual musicians, the influence of the blues on contemporary music, or the migration of the blues—that best adapts to your purpose, the people in your audience, and the logistics and occasion of your presentation.

There are many ways to organize the content of your presentation. You may find that one format is perfect or that a combination of patterns is best. It's important to note that there are many other organizational patterns such as advantages-disadvantages, using famous quotations as key points, do's and don'ts, and checklists. In Chapter 19, "Developing Persuasive Presentations," and Chapter 20, "Developing Special Presentations," we suggest additional patterns of organization for different types of presentations.

One of the reasons why both of us spend so much of our preparation time thinking about and experimenting with ways to organize our remarks is that the time is so well spent. Remember that deciding how to organize is part of the overall strategy for making a presentation. Organization provides you with a framework that can tell you what to include in your presentation, in what order to include it, and for what effect.

Summary

◆◆ Why is organization so important?

Organization helps a speaker gather ideas and information, develop a rhetorical strategy, and enhance credibility. Organization also helps an audience understand, remember, and react to what you say.

◆◆ How do I select the key points for a presentation?

Consider your purpose, the audience, the occasion, and the logistics of the situation. Then apply the 4Rs of Organization—review, reduce, regroup, and refine.

◆◆ How do I link my purpose, central idea, and key points?

Make sure that your central idea summarizes the key points of your presentation and, if appropriate, provides a brief preview of the organization you will follow to achieve your purpose.

◆◆ Are there established organizational formats that I can follow?

Common organizational patterns include topical arrangement, time arrangement, space arrangement, problem-solution, causes and effects, stories and examples, comparison-contrast, and memory aids.

Key Terms

causes and effects arrangement 138

central idea 134

comparison-contrast arrangement 140

figurative analogy 140

key points 132

memory aids arrangement 142

organization 131

problem-solution arrangement 137

space arrangement 137

time arrangement 136

topical arrangement 135

Notes

1. Some of the best research on the value of organizing a presentation was done in the 1960s and 1970s. See Ernest C. Thompson, "An Experimental Investigation of the Relative Effectiveness of Organizational Structure in Oral Communication," *The Southern Speech Journal* 26 (1960): 59–69; Ernest C. Thompson, "Some Effects of Message Structure on Listeners' Comprehension," *Speech Monographs* 34 (1967): 51–57; James McCroskey and R. Samuel Mehrley, "The Effects of Disorganization and Nonfluency on Attitude Change and Source Credibility," *Communication Monographs* 36 (1969): 13–21; Arlee Johnson, "A Preliminary Investigation of the Relationship Between Organization and Listener Comprehension," *Central States Speech Journal* 21 (1970): 104–107; Christopher Spicer and Ronald E. Bassett, "The Effect of Organization on Learning from an Informative Message," *Southern Speech Communication Journal* 41 (1976): 290–299.

2. One of the best overviews of Cicero's contributions to rhetoric appears in Lester Thonssen and A. Craig Baird, *Speech Criticism: The Development of Standards for Rhetorical Appraisal* (New York: The Ronald Press, 1948), pp. 78–91. Also see James L. Golden, Goodwin F. Berquist, and William E. Coleman, *The Rhetoric of Western Thought,* 4th ed. (Dubuque, IA: Kendall/Hunt, 1989).

3. Steve Emmons, "Emotions at Face Value," *Los Angeles Times,* 9 January 1998, pp. E1 and E8.

4. See Marie Winn, "The Trouble with Television," in *Taking Sides: Clashing Views on Controversial Issues in Mass Media and Society,* ed. Alison Alexander and Jarice Hanson, 5th ed. (Guilford, CT: Duskin/McGraw-Hill, 1999), pp. 22–28.

5. Katherine E. Rowan, "A New Pedagogy for Explanatory Public Speaking: Why Arrangement Should Not Substitute for Invention," *Communication Education* 44 (1995): 236–250.

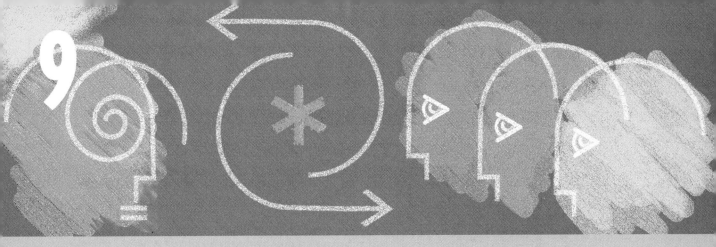

9

Organizational Tools

- ➤ How do I go about shaping my ideas into a presentation?
- ➤ How can outlining help me organize my presentation?
- ➤ How do I connect one idea to another?
- ➤ Can I be both creative and well organized?

Determining and ordering the key points of a presentation are two different but related functions. Chapter 8, "Organization," describes strategies for surveying the ideas and information you have collected to determine the key points that will best suit your purpose. Ordering involves arranging the specific parts of a presentation in an effective sequence. Do you recall the two basic tasks Cicero required of every effective speaker? Creating a well-organized presentation requires both of them: determining the key points (*inventio*) and putting those points into an orderly sequence (*dispositio*). We explored *inventio* in Chapter 8. Now, we will look at *dispositio* in more detail.

Fortunately, there are several techniques or tools for arranging your ideas and information in a well-organized presentation with a clear beginning, middle, and end. These tools can shape your content and strengthen your message. Although they are not unique to speech making, these techniques can prove invaluable when you're deciding how to sort and where to strategically place the key points of a presentation.

Getting Ready to Outline

Almost every presentation and public speaking book ever written advocates outlining as a means of organization. So do we, yet we also recognize that outlining has its limits and appreciate that not everyone finds outlining equally useful. Outlining is a planning tool, not an end in itself. Outlining helps you organize and order your ideas. Thomas Leech, a communication consultant and executive speech coach, observed that "presenters sometimes say that they don't outline because it will constrain their thought process and take away their natural flow. Yet a presentation must be constrained. It must be tightly packaged, with all the extraneous ideas and materials excluded. An audience deserves and will insist upon a concisely organized message that achieves its goals in the least possible time."[1]

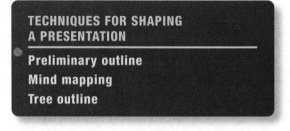

TECHNIQUES FOR SHAPING
A PRESENTATION

Preliminary outline
Mind mapping
Tree outline

Preliminary Outlines

Outlines give you a clear and logical framework on which to hang your ideas and supporting material. They are not born fully grown during the speechwriting process with every detail and subpoint in place. Outlines grow. They begin in a preliminary form with a few basic building blocks. An informal **preliminary outline** puts the major pieces of your message in a clear and logical order. In its simplest form, a preliminary outline looks like this:

    I. Introduction

    II. Body of Presentation

    III. Conclusion

Figure 9.1 shows an expanded preliminary outline for a presentation that you can use as a model.

You can use this model to organize almost any presentation. Naturally, you would modify the outline, depending on the number of key points and the types and amount of information you would be using as supporting material. There should be at least one piece of supporting material under each key point. If you think that you know what your key points will be, try developing the details of your presentation according to this model.

Figure 9.1   Model Outline

Topic Area:
- I. **Introduction**
  - A. Purpose/Topic
  - B. Central Idea
  - C. Brief Preview of Key Points
    1. Key Point #1
    2. Key Point #2
    3. Key Point #3 (or more)
- II. **Body of the Presentation**
  - A. Key Point #1
    1. Supporting Material
    2. Supporting Material
  - B. Key Point #2
    1. Supporting Material
    2. Supporting Material
  - C. Key Point #3
    1. Supporting Material
    2. Supporting Material
- III. **Conclusion**

Mind Maps

Not everyone is skilled at outlining. Moreover, a preliminary outline may not be the best way to *begin* organizing a presenta-

REAL WORLD, REAL SPEAKERS

When we introduce the model outline to a class or seminar, listeners often challenge our assertion that it can be used to organize almost any presentation. We challenge them right back, saying, "Give us any topic you can think of, one minute to organize our thoughts, and the right to make up supporting material." Then one of us declares, "I will deliver a presentation on your topic with a complete introduction, a central idea and preview, a well-developed body that includes between two and four key points, and a memorable conclusion."

At first, audience members look at us as though we have lost our minds. Then, the fun starts. Suggestions for topics start flying. We've done this demonstration using topics that ranged from shoelaces to shuttle diplomacy, from swimwear fashions to fly fishing, and from world music to world religions.

We have never disappointed our listeners. Why? Because the model outline is imprinted in our brains (and we have been doing this for over twenty-five years). During our one-minute preparation period, we come up with two to three key points and relate them to a central idea. Just before speaking, we decide upon an attention-getting introduction. As we speak, we fill in the supporting material blanks with made-up statistics, quotations, examples, stories, and other forms of support. The result: a well-organized presentation.

Of course, as we mention after speaking, the central idea may not be true, the key points may be fiction, and the supporting materials are made up. That is not the point. The point is that a ready-made model outline can serve you well when you're required to prepare a well-organized presentation—even if you have only one minute.

Isa Engleberg and John Daly

---

tion, particularly when a linear, logical progression of ideas may be difficult to develop or may not be the ideal way to achieve your purpose.

We recommend that you use a technique called **mind mapping** because it encourages the free flow of ideas and lets you define relationships among the ideas. Rather than forcing your content into a predetermined organizational pattern, you can discover connections that suggest one or more organizational patterns for your presentation.

How do you mind map? Start with a clean sheet of paper. Write your subject at the top or center of the page. Then, write down the ideas you hope to cover in your presentation. Don't be afraid to fill the page. Neatness doesn't count. What is important is that you have a one-page conglomeration of the ideas that you want to include in your presentation. If possible, put related ideas near each other on the page and draw a circle around that group of ideas. If groups of ideas are related, let your circles overlap or draw lines between those circles.

Figure 9.2 shows a mind map for a presentation on Muzak created by Julie Borchard, a student who was preparing to compete in an informative speaking contest. It's a hodgepodge of words, phrases, lists, circles, and arrows. After completing such a mind map, you can label circled ideas as key points and put them in a logical order. The entire text of Julie's presentation is included in Appendix A.

Because there was so much interrelated material to be included, Julie found the mind map a useful way to begin the organizational process. Note how almost every idea on the mind map in Figure 9.2 is included in the presentation.

Figure 9.2   Muzak Mind Map

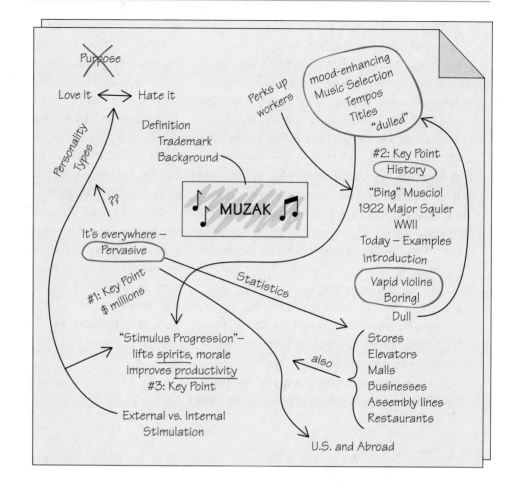

Mind mapping is a very useful tool when you have lots of ideas and information about a topic but are having trouble deciding how to arrange the ideas for a presentation. Mind maps let you see all of your ideas without superimposing an organizational pattern on them. They also let you postpone the need to arrange your ideas in a pattern until you have collected enough information to think about how you want to organize the content of your presentation.

Tree Outline

If you can't outline with ease, don't think mind mapping would work for you, or need more help sorting your ideas and information, you might want to try another organizational technique. It's known by a variety of similar names: tree outlines, idea trees, organization trees.

Let's start with the most lifelike example—the **tree outline.** Although an outline and a tree are not alike, there are some characteristics that have similar functions and relationships. You can think of your central idea as the tree's trunk, your key points as its limbs, and your supporting materials as branches extending from each limb. Your words are the leaves. Figure 9.3 shows a tree outline.

In a tree outline, all of the limbs (key points) are directly attached to the trunk (central idea). All branches (supporting material) are attached to respective limbs, and all leaves (words) are attached to branches. A limb cannot be attached to a branch or a leaf. Note that the tree outline follows the model preliminary outline (see p. 146).

I. Introduction
    A. Central Idea = Trunk
    B. Preview of Key Points = Limbs #1 and #2
II. Body of Presentation
    A. Limb #1
        1. Branch and Leaves
        2. Branch and Leaves
    B. Limb #2
        1. Branch and Leaves
        2. Branch and Leaves
III. Conclusion

Your tree may look quite different, depending on the organizational pattern that you use. For example, suppose that you have decided to give a presentation on the need to support local refugee families. After reviewing your material, you decide that telling a series of dramatic stories about real-life refugee families would be the most effective way to present your message. In such a presentation, there would be only one central idea: People should help support the refugee families in your community. Thus, instead of having several limbs with branches attached, you would go straight from the trunk to the branches for your supporting material. As Figure 9.4 shows, this tree outline would resemble a pine tree.

Organizational Patterns _Do_ Grow on Trees. Using the tree outline is a great way to experiment with different organizational patterns. For example, if you were using a problem-solution format, your tree might have just two limbs—one labeled "problem" and one labeled "solution." After reviewing your material, however, you might discover the need for a third limb, labeled "causes." Causes are neither the problem nor the solution; rather, they explain why there is a problem or why there isn't a solution. So what began as a tree with two mighty limbs has become one with three limbs (problem, causes, solution).

By experimenting with a tree outline, you may find that you have limbs with no branches and/or branches with no limbs. You may have planned to compare the safety of fossil fuel energy to the dangers of nuclear energy but find you have no branches (supporting material) for the "fossil fuels are safe" limb. Or you might have lots of branches on rubber production, but they don't belong on a tree trunk (central idea) labeled "How to Change a Tire."

The Organization Tree. An **organization tree** is a more structured version of the tree outline. Although it doesn't look like a tree, it still maintains the relationships

Figure 9.3   Tree Outline

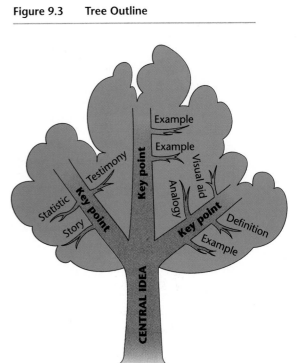

Figure 9.4   Pine Tree Outline

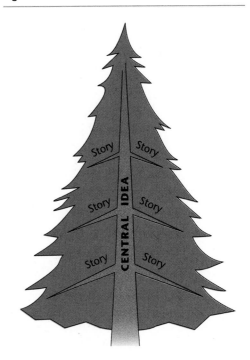

depicted in the tree outline. Figure 9.5 is a worksheet for preparing an organization tree and was developed by Marya Holcombe and Judith Stein, the authors of *Presentations for Decision Makers.*[2]

How do you use this worksheet?

1. On the far left of the organization tree worksheet, fill in your central idea—the one concept that you want the audience to understand and remember.

2. In the center section, fill in your key points—those ideas that would be the major branches on a tree outline. Each key point should be separate and should not be a subtopic of another key point.

3. To the right of each key point, add detailed supporting material. Make sure that each piece of supporting material is directly linked to the key point to which it is attached.

Figure 9.5   Organization Tree Worksheet

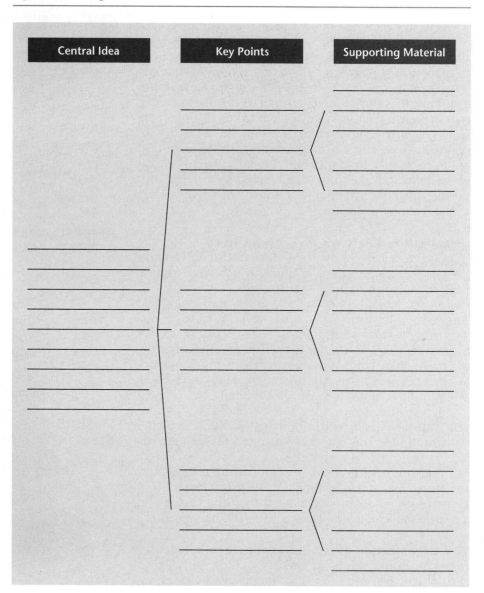

Not only does the organization tree add more structure than a mind map does; it also puts the ideas and information in a hierarchical order. The central idea is more fundamental than each of the key points. The key points are more prominent than the supporting material. An organization tree provides a pattern for your presentation. It shows you whether or not your key points directly relate to your central idea and whether or not you have adequate supporting material for each key point.[3]

The Formal Outline

Preliminary outlines, mind maps, and tree outlines help you to develop and arrange your ideas into a sketch of a presentation. Refining these sketches into your actual presentation often requires the creation of a formal outline. A **formal outline** is a comprehensive written framework for a presentation that follows established conventions concerning content and format. Whereas informal outlines help you plan your presentation—particularly while your key ideas are still evolving—a formal outline helps you create the first complete draft of your presentation. Once you identify your key points and feel confident about the way in which you want to arrange and support them, a formal outline can ensure that your presentation is logical, well organized, and clear.

Formal Outlining Principles

Just about everyone knows what an outline is. You probably learned how to outline from a series of English teachers and composition textbooks.[4] These techniques also apply to presentation outlines. Here we offer three basic rules of outlining and note the exceptions that apply to presentation speaking.

Use Numbers, Letters, and Indentation. All parts of a formal outline are systematically indented and numbered or lettered.[5] This system reflects the hierarchy of your material. Roman numerals (I, II, III) signify the largest major divisions at the top of the hierarchy. In an outline for a presentation, we recommend using a Roman numeral *I* for your introduction, Roman numeral *II* for the body of the presentation, and Roman numeral *III* for the conclusion. This suggestion breaks a rule that you will find in most composition textbooks: Leave the introduction and conclusion out of the outline. We disagree. Because these two sections are vital parts of a successful presentation's structure, we recommend including them in a formal outline.

After using Roman numerals to establish the major sections of a presentation, follow standard outlining rules about letters, numbers, and indentation: Indented capital letters (*A, B, C*, and so forth) are used for subtopics that fit under a major division. In a presentation, capital letters can be used to designate the key points. Further indented Arabic numbers (*1, 2, 3*, and so forth) are even more specific. In a presentation, Arabic numbers can be used to list supporting material, evidence and reasoning, or any other subdivision of a key point. If you need a fourth level, you would indent and use lowercase letters (*a, b, c*, and so forth). As you move from Roman numerals to capital letters to

HOW MANY KEY POINTS SHOULD I INCLUDE? Including

too many ideas or key points is one of the most common mistakes speakers make when outlining their presentations. Not surprisingly, then, one of the questions we hear most often is this: How many key points should I include? We wish there were a definitive answer. Generally, we suggest that there should be at least two key points and no more than five. Three are ideal. Of course, there are exceptions. Remember the pine tree outline? That presentation advocating community help for refugees focused on dramatic stories that supported a single central idea which was also the key point.

If you have too many key points, try to boil them down. Audiences usually seem able to understand and remember three key points better than four or five. Ask yourself these questions: Which ideas are the most essential? Which ones will help me achieve my purpose? Which ones are most likely to interest and affect my audience? Apply the 4Rs technique discussed in Chapter 8. Carefully review, reduce, and, if possible, regroup your key points. It's better to cut one of your key points than to sacrifice your whole presentation to a bored or restless audience.

Arabic numbers to lowercase letters, your information should become more and more specific. Remember the tree outline. You start with a single trunk, move to limbs (*A, B, C*), then to branches (*1, 2, 3*), and finally to small twigs and leaves (*a, b, c*).

Divide Your Subpoints Logically.   Each major subpoint should include at least two points indented under it or none at all. If there is an A, there must be a B; for every 1, there must be a 2. In other words, all headings or subpoints must have at least two parts because you cannot logically divide something into just one part. Why? Think of it this way: Can you cut a piece out of a cake with only one slice from the middle to the edge? No. Instead, you need two cuts to remove a slice (or none at all if you want a really big piece—the whole cake!).

Wrong: I.
                A.
             II.

Right: I.
                A.
                B.
             II.

Keep the Outline Consistent.   Use either a topic, a phrase, or a full sentence for each key point in your outline rather than mixing styles. When you get to the Arabic number level, you may need more than a word or a phrase to record supporting material, but you should try to use a consistent style to label each level throughout the outline. Also, use a consistent grammatical form: If you begin each subpoint with a verb, don't switch to beginning with nouns halfway through the outline. Don't change styles or grammatical forms in the same outline. Not only will consistency make your outline easier to read and use; it will also force you to work on finding the best and most precise words, phrases, and/or sentences for each section.

Wrong: I. Consistent Style
             II. Use a consistent grammatical form.

Right: I. Keep the outline consistent in style.
             II. Use a consistent grammatical form.

Right: I. Consistent style
             II. Consistent grammatical form

Why, you may ask, are there such strict rules? The reason has little to do with the obsessions of English teachers. These rules can help you to create a clear and useful outline. Consistent headings, consistent style, and consistent grammatical structure keep your outline clear and provide a dependable structure for organizing your presentation.

The Benefits of Outlining

A formal outline is a planning tool, a blueprint for your presentation. It tells you where every piece of your presentation goes—from the introduction through the conclusion. However, its benefits don't stop there. Besides helping you organize your presentation, a formal outline also serves other important functions.

OUTLINING HELPS YOU

Select and order your supporting material

Enhance your word choice

Change and adapt your presentation

Check your structure

Reveal flaws in logic

Selecting and Ordering Supporting Material. A formal outline helps you pull together the results of your gathering and ordering ideas and information. With your key points in place, you can then insert your related supporting materials, identifying each by its form under each key point. A quick scan of your formal outline will reveal at a glance whether you have too many statistics and not enough testimony or stories. If this is the case, you can modify the presentation by substituting different forms of supporting material in your outline.

Enhancing Word Choice. A formal outline also requires that you use very specific word choices when writing the beginning of your presentation, stating your central idea, labeling your key points, and even making a smooth transition from one section to another. Ideally, you should include the exact wording of your central idea and key points on your formal outline. Also include references to or the exact wording of the supporting material that you intend to use. By paying careful attention to wording, you can make sure that it's consistent, clear, and memorable. Unless you are reading your presentation from a manuscript (something we discuss in Chapter 13, "Performance and Practice"), a formal outline may be the only written record of your presentation.

Making Changes and Adaptations Easier. In the same way that builders modify blueprints as they work, you can adjust your formal outline. A formal outline allows you to make changes in any part of your presentation quite simply. For instance, once you have your key points outlined, you can easily test different organizational patterns for them by arranging the sections and their related subsections in different sequences. If you find a great piece of supporting material at the last minute, you can just add an Arabic number for it under the appropriate capital letter. A formal outline allows you to update material at the last minute without disturbing the outline format. With a few quickly drawn arrows to guide your way around a section that should be cut, an outline can help you modify your presentation at the last minute.

Checking Structure. A formal outline lets you check each subpoint against its key point and each key point against your central idea. As you construct a formal outline, keep asking yourself questions such as these: Do subpoints 1 and 2 support the major A point? Do the A and B points support the central idea? If they don't, you may not be well organized, or you may

PROCEED WITH CAUTION WHEN USING PRESENTATION SOFTWARE Just a dozen or so years ago, few speakers used sophisticated software to prepare and give their presentations. Today colleges and corporations are demanding that everyone learn to use one or more **presentation software** packages such as PowerPoint, Corel Presentations, or Freelance. Most of these packages encourage beginners to use the software's fill-in-the-blank outline. Perhaps you've already tried this and are wondering why we're spending so much time talking about outlining a presentation when there are already programs that will do it for you. The answer is that these packages *don't* organize! Rather, they convert material that you input into outlines or convert your outline into a storyboard of visual aids.

You can't rely on software packages to organize your presentations for you. Unless you have reviewed, reduced, regrouped, and refined your materials (see Chapter 8), you'll most likely end up with a flashy but fragmented presentation. Presentation software may help you put on a good-looking show, but it's no substitute for good organization.

not have selected appropriate supporting material for your presentation. If, for example, your list of key points (A, B, C, D, E, F, G, and so forth) begins to look like alphabet soup, find a way to consolidate those ideas into a few major categories with more subcategories. If, on the other hand, you are straining to find a B point to follow an A point, your first key point may be too broad. Remember: A well-developed outline provides and checks the structure of your message.

Revealing Flaws. Outlines can also help you look for errors, flaws, and digressions. The outline of a presentation can reveal whether a section is lacking supporting material. It can also reveal whether two sections are saying the same thing and whether every section is relevant to your central idea.[6] An added advantage of having a formal outline is that you can share it with someone else before you speak. In reviewing your outline, a helpful reader may find phrases that are unclear, terms that are ambiguous, or supporting material that doesn't support a main idea.

A good formal outline is more than an organizational tool. It is a safety net that helps you arrange and rearrange ideas and supporting materials, and catch and correct errors. It also forms the basis for flexible speaking notes that you can use to rehearse and deliver your presentation. Using a formal outline can shape your content, strengthen your message, and enhance audience understanding.

Presentation Outlines

Formal outlines provide a great way to organize your material and to double-check the content of your message. Formal outlines are not, however, the same as speaking notes. The notes that you use during a presentation should not be as long or detailed as a formal outline. Generally, we like using a short outline—one that includes little more than a list of key points and reminders of supporting material. Other speakers whom we know use full sentence outlines in which each key point is written out word for word. Rarely, however, do speakers use a complete formal outline as speaking notes. Figure 9.6 shows a simplified complete sentence outline for a presentation on the importance of customer service. Note that the introduction, central idea, key points, and conclusion are written out, whereas reminders about the type and substance of supporting material are put in parentheses.

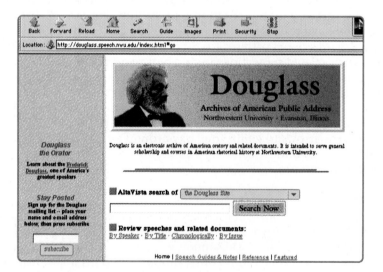

The Douglass Archives of American Public Address Web site at Northwestern University, http://douglass.speech.nwu.edu, provides numerous examples of historic American speeches on a variety of issues.

Figure 9.6   Complete Sentence Outline

I. Introduction

   A. Question: What will be the most important factor for competitive business success in the year 2000 and beyond? (Gallup Poll of CEOs, owners, and company presidents)

   B. Answer:

      18% said operating efficiency

      25% said product/service quality

      27% said *customer service*

   C. Central Idea: Become a service-centered business if you want to succeed.

II. Body

   A. Your job security and business success depend on how valuable you are to your customers. (Stories, statistics, and descriptions of successful employees and businesses)

   B. Customers will replace you with better service providers. (When the product and price are the same, service is the only area in which you can be different from the competition. Ask audience for examples.)

   C. Develop a reputation for responsiveness. (Nordstrom, Saturn, Ritz Carlton Hotels, the local hospital)

III. Conclusion

Customers are the lifeblood of your business. They are not dependent on you; you are dependent on them. So remember the secret of keeping good customers: Exceed their expectations! And you'll succeed in business!

Presentation outlines rarely conform to all the rules of formal outlining. Rather, speakers use these rules as guidelines to help them create a clear and compelling presentation. Figure 9.7 shows the detailed outline for Julie Borchard's presentation on Muzak (see p. 148 for her mind map). The outline provides a lot of detail because it was used to prepare a manuscript version of the presentation. You can read the complete text of this award-winning presentation in Appendix A.

Notice that this outline does not conform to all of the outlining rules we cited. Although it does use numbers, letters, and indentation, it is not consistent in style or in grammatical form. Because the speaker used parts of the outline as her speaking notes for a well-rehearsed presentation, she needed only a word or phrase to remind her where she was. Nevertheless, she wrote her central idea and preview of key points as entire sentences to make sure that she got the wording exactly right. In addition, she identified the different types of supporting material in her outline to make sure that a variety of types were included in the presentation.

Connecting Your Key Points

Even though an outline shows how you've structured and developed your key points, it's missing the "glue" that attaches the key points to each other. **Connectives** are this glue and include the internal previews, internal summaries,

Figure 9.7   Complete Presentation Outline

MUZAK

I. **Introduction**

  A. Play a sample of Muzak on a tape recorder to gain audience's attention.

  B. Provide descriptions

  1. By creators: sonorous design, sound energy

  2. By the public: spineless melodies, vapid violins

  C. Muzak

  1. Trademarked brand name for background music (definition)

  2. Muzak dominates the field (quotation from the president of Muzak)

  D. Central Idea and Key Points

  1. You can become more enlightened about Muzak

  a. By understanding how pervasive Muzak is

  b. By understanding how it originated

  c. By understanding how it lifts spirits and increases productivity

II. **Body**

  A. Key Point #1: Pervasive (*USA Today* article)

  1. Statistics: Size of business, number of listeners

  2. Poll results: People like Muzak

  3. Statistics: American companies using Muzak

  B. Key Point #2: Origins and Development

  1. 1922: Major George O. Squier

  2. 1937: "Fatigue and Boredom in Repetitive Work" (Wyatt and Langdon Study)

  3. 1945: 75% of World War II industries (Nye Study)

  4. 1972: Studies of Muzak and worker productivity (Manhattan Blue Cross/Blue Shield Study)

  C. Key Point #3: Lifts Spirits and Improves Productivity

  1. Work patterns and "stimulus progression" (*USA Today* article)

  a. Tempos

  b. Titles

  2. Music Forms: "Dulled" recordings (quotation by Muzak executive)

  3. Uses

  a. Major corporations and the federal government (examples)

  b. Restaurants, supermarkets

  c. Hospitals (St. Joseph's Hospital)

  4. Personality Types and Muzak

  a. Need for external stimulation (study by Mose)

  b. Need for quiet (quotation from Perpetual Savings and Loan executive)

III. **Conclusion**

  A. Size and Success of Muzak

  B. Quotation: "Bing" Muscio, former President of Muzak

  C. The sound of Muzak is here to stay

transitions, and signposts that connect the pieces of your presentation to form a coherent whole. Without them, even a well-organized presentation can sound choppy and awkward.

Just as the chapter titles and headings in this textbook help you understand and follow what is being discussed, connectives help your audience follow, understand, and remember your message. In fact, connectives matter far more in spoken than in written communication.[7] A reader can go back to see how a writer connects ideas. Listeners don't have that luxury. They need wording such as "my next point is," "on the other hand," or "it's time to talk about solutions" to alert and prepare them for important ideas in a presentation. Connectives help link one part of a presentation to another, clarify how one idea relates to another, and identify how supporting material bolsters a key point.

CONNECTIVES
- **Internal previews**
- **Internal summaries**
- **Transitions**
- **Signposts**

Internal Previews

One of the first connectives likely to appear in a presentation is the internal preview. In the introduction of a presentation, an **internal preview** reveals or suggests your key points to the audience. It tells them what you are going to cover and in what order. In the body of a presentation, an internal preview describes how you are going to approach a key point. Depending on your topic and your audience, you may need an internal preview only in your introduction. If your key points are complex with many subpoints, however, you may also want to include internal previews within the body of your presentation.

Here's how one student internally previewed his presentation on weight loss:

> How do researchers and doctors explain obesity? Some offer genetic explanations; others psychological ones. Either or both factors can be responsible for your never-ending battle with the bathroom scale.

Internal Summaries

Internal summaries are closely related to internal previews. The obvious difference is that a summary ends a section, whereas a preview begins one. **Internal summaries** are a useful way to reinforce important ideas. They also give you an opportunity to pause in a presentation and repeat critical ideas or pieces of information. Here's how the same student concluded a section on the genetic factors that influence overeating:

> So remember, before spending hundreds of dollars on diet books and exercise toys, make sure that your weight problem is not influenced by the number and size of your fat cells, your hormone level, your metabolism, or the amount of glucose in your bloodstream.

Transitions

The most common type of connective is the **transition**—a word, number, brief phrase, or sentence that helps you move from one key point or section to another. Transitions act like lubricating oil to keep a presentation moving smoothly. Transitions can be quite simple and can consist of little more than a word or phrase. They can also be one or two complete sentences that help you move from one major section of a presentation to another. We underline some common transitions in the following examples:

<u>Yet</u> it's important to remember . . .

<u>In addition</u> to metabolism, there is . . .

<u>Next</u>, we'll see . . .

<u>On the other hand</u>, some people believe . . .

<u>Of equal importance</u> is . . .

<u>Another reason why</u> he should be elected is . . .

<u>Finally</u>, a responsible parent should . . .

As simple as these transitions may seem, they can serve an important purpose by helping you and your audience move smoothly through a presentation.

Transitions can also function as mini-previews and mini-summaries that link the conclusion of one section to the beginning of another. For example:

Once you've eliminated these four genetic explanations for weight gain, it's time to consider several psychological factors.

Signposts

A final type of connective is the signpost. Quite simply, **signposts** are short phrases that, like signs on the highway, tell or remind your listeners where you are in a presentation. For example, the previously mentioned student said he would discuss four genetic explanations for weight gain, so he began each explanation with numbers—first, second, third, and fourth: "Fourth and finally, make sure your glucose level has been tested and is within normal levels. . . ." Not only did his audience know that he had reached the fourth explanation; they also knew that he was concluding the "genetics" section and was moving on to the "psychological" explanations for overeating.

Along with alerting you of a destination, road signs also can make you aware of road hazards and even scenic outlooks. Signposts within a presentation can do the same thing. They can focus attention on an important statistic or idea. They can also highlight an eloquent phrase or special insight. For example: "Even if you can't remember his every accomplishment, please remember one thing: Alex Curry is the only candidate who has been endorsed by every newspaper and civic association in this county." Here's another example: "As I read this section of Toni Morrison's novel, listen carefully to how she uses simple metaphors to describe the cemetery scene."

Generally, audiences like to hear internal previews, internal summaries, transitions, and signposts during a presentation. Just as most travelers like to know where they are, where they've been, how they got there, and where they're going, audiences likewise appreciate a speaker who uses connectives well. Using connectives effectively requires you to pay careful attention to the places in your presentation that need links to other sections. In a short, uncomplicated talk, simple transitions may be all that is needed. However, in an important and complex presentation, you may need to use all four kinds of connectives. Either way, connectives will make your presentation much easier to understand and much easier to deliver with confidence.

Creative Organization

These two chapters have emphasized how important it is to have a clear plan for organizing the ideas and supporting material you wish to include in your presentation. We have suggested a variety of reliable organizational formats and have recommended several tools to help you explore and then organize your content. At this point, good organization may seem to be like a jigsaw puzzle in which your ideas and supporting material are dropped into the "right" pattern or outline. But we don't see it that way. Rather, we see these formats and tools as avenues to creativity. Creativity plays an important role in discovering and arranging the ideas that you want to include in a presentation.

What Is Creativity?

If you want your presentation to be both unique and memorable, try thinking creatively about its organization. Lee Towe, president of Innovators International, Inc., defines **creativity** as consisting of two parts: creative thinking and creative output.[8] *Creative thinking* is the process of searching for, reviewing, reducing, and regrouping ideas *without* making judgments. Mind mapping is a good example of creative thinking in action. When you mind map, you begin with a blank page rather than with a formal organizational pattern. Once you have put your ideas on paper, you also have a flexible tool to review, reduce, and regroup them. Finally, a mind map allows you to reserve judgment about how to refine and organize your ideas until your mind map is finished.

Creative output is the second component of creativity and consists of connecting and combining previously unrelated elements. For example, the circles and arrows you draw on a mind map allow you to combine ideas from various points on your page. Mind mapping, however, isn't the only way to think creatively about organization. Creativity requires a mental flexibility that allows you to mix thoughts and ideas from many different sources.

Creative Applications

A presentation on growing tomatoes can be ordered topically and creatively. How can you improve upon the following organization pattern? "You can grow healthy tomatoes by (1) planting them in a sunny place, (2) giving them plenty of fertilizer and water, and (3) keeping pests and weeds under control." What about comparing tomatoes to caring for a newborn baby? "You can be the proud parent of healthy tomato plants by (1) making their garden 'nursery' safe and comfortable, (2) giving them special food and formula that will help them grow up strong and healthy, and (3) seeing that they don't come down with the usual diseases." The tomatoes/newborns analogy makes the organizational pattern more interesting and more memorable. However, remember that using analogies is not the only way to produce creative organizational patterns.

On the other hand, creativity runs some risks. For example, suppose that the audience

Alison Horton, director of the Michigan chapter of the Sierra Club (accompanied by Roger the Roadkill Deer) covers five key points about Michigan's environmental record. She refers to the state's environmental legislation as "roadkill," saying lawmakers have lost touch with citizens' values.

REAL WORLD, REAL SPEAKERS

Patricia Phillips, a customer services expert who lives in Alexandria, Virginia, uses excerpts from popular songs to begin each major section of her training seminar. Notice how each of the following song titles lends itself to customer service: "I Can't Get No Satisfaction" by the Rolling Stones, "Help" by the Beatles, "Respect" by Aretha Franklin, "Don't Be Cruel" by Elvis, and "Don't You Come Back No More" by Ray Charles. These well-known songs give Pat an upbeat and creative way to move into each new section of her seminar.

Another speaker, who works in a human relations department, uses the Bible's Ten Commandments to describe a company's work rules: "Thou shalt have no other jobs other than this one." In other words, if you're caught working at a second full-time job, you may be fired. He worded another rule as "Honor thy supervisor that thy days may be long with this company."

members were unfamiliar with the songs that Patricia Phillips (above) referred to? They might find her presentation more confusing than memorable. What if using the Ten Commandments as a creative organizational pattern offended Christian and Jewish members of the second speaker's audience? If you wanted to use such a pattern, what could you say or do to avoid misunderstandings and people's taking offense?

Although there are potential dangers and costs to using creativity, almost nothing else more effectively enhances your credibility and promotes your audience's willingness to listen and learn. Using other creative organizational patterns such as a series of famous quotations, colors, or visual aids as signposts to the key points of your presentation can help an audience remember and thus help you achieve your purpose.

Despite its benefits, many speakers are reluctant to embrace using creativity as a means of discovering the best way to organize a presentation. Lee Towe suggests that many of us are not creative because we are guided by three noncreative habits: inertia, instruction, and imitation.[9] Some of us suffer from inertia (we've always organized presentations this way, so why change?), instruction (this is how we were taught to organize a presentation, so why do something different?), or imitation (we've heard good speakers organize their presentations this way, so we'll stick with these models). Instead, try a dose of innovation (by thinking creatively, we'll find interesting, effective, and unique ways to organize our presentations).

We are not suggesting that you abandon everything we've included in Chapters 8 and 9 in a quest to be creative. Instead, use the principles of organization to give yourself a firm foundation for exploring creative alternatives. Before you can "think outside the box" about organizing a presentation, you ought to know exactly what that box is and why most speakers stay within its reliable and useful confines.

Remember Cicero's initial tasks for every effective speaker. The first (*inventio*) requires a search for main ideas; the second (*dispositio*) involves putting those ideas into an orderly sequence. If using creativity helps you to find the best ideas and supporting material for your presentation and helps you to put your content into an effective and orderly sequence, don't hesitate to release your creative talents.

Summary

◆◆ How do I go about shaping my ideas into a presentation?

Techniques that can help you shape your ideas and information into an effective presentation include preliminary outlines, mind mapping, tree outlines, and organization trees.

◆◆ How can outlining help me organize my presentation?

Outlining is only one of many ways to begin the organizational process. A formal outline, however, effectively concludes the organizational process by packaging your message in a concise manner that excludes extraneous ideas and materials.

◆◆ How do I connect one idea to another?

Using connectives such as internal previews, internal summaries, transitions, and signposts will join the pieces of your presentation to form a coherent whole.

◆◆ Can I be both creative and well organized?

Creativity can enhance your ability to review, reduce, regroup, and refine good ideas for a presentation that is organized and interesting.

Key Terms

connectives 155
creativity 159
internal preview 157
internal summary 157
formal outline 151

mind map 147
organization tree 149
preliminary outline 146
presentation software 153

signposts 158
transitions 157
tree outline 148

Notes

1. Thomas Leech, *How to Prepare, Stage, & Deliver Winning Presentations* (New York: AMACOM, 1993), p. 97.
2. Marya W. Holcombe and Judith K. Stein, *Presentations for Decision Makers: Strategies for Structuring and Delivering Your Ideas* (Belmont, CA: Lifelong Learning Publications, 1983), p. 35.
3. Holcombe and Stein, pp. 36–37.
4. The rules of outlining contained in this chapter represent a composite of guidelines and conventions found in various handbooks for writers. See Ann Raimes, *Keys for Writers: A Brief Handbook*, 2nd ed. (Boston: Houghton Mifflin, 1999); H. Ramsey Fowler and Jane E. Aaron, *The Little, Brown Handbook*, 7th ed. (New York: Longman, 1998); Diana Hacker, *The Bedford Handbook*, 5th ed. (Boston: Bedford Books, 1998); Melinda G. Kramer, Glenn Leggett, and C. David Mead, *Prentice-Hall Handbook for Writers*, 12th ed. (Englewood Cliffs, NJ: Prentice-Hall, 1995); Lynn Quitman Troyka, *Simon and Schuster Handbook for Writers* (Englewood Cliffs, NJ: Prentice-Hall, 1987).
5. Troyka, p. 40.
6. Troyka, p. 37.
7. Jo Sprague and Douglas Stuart, *The Speaker's Handbook*, 4th ed. (Fort Worth, TX: Harcourt Brace, 1995), p. 137.
8. Lee Towe, *Why Didn't I Think of That? Creativity in the Workplace* (West Des Moines, IA: American Media, 1996), p. 7.
9. Towe, p. 14.

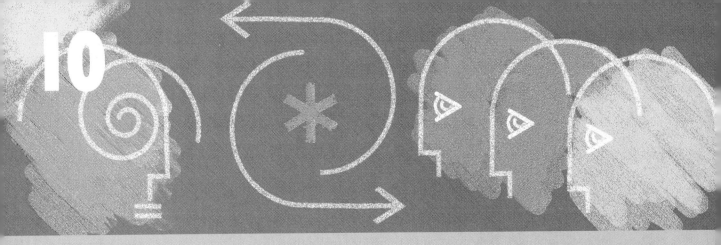

10

Introductions and Conclusions

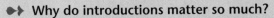

- ▸▸ Why do introductions matter so much?
- ▸▸ How do I link my introduction to my topic?
- ▸▸ How can I acknowledge the speaking situation in my introduction?
- ▸▸ What do good conclusions do?
- ▸▸ What's the best way to end my presentation?

Real estate agents know that first impressions can sell a house. They call this "curb value" and tell sellers to mow their lawns, paint the front door, and bake fresh-from-the-oven chocolate chip cookies before hosting an open house. Movie promoters hire teams of creative artists to design posters and previews to entice potential audiences to see their productions. Large corporations invest millions of dollars in designing annual reports to make a strong first impression that communicates success to investors. First impressions definitely count.

Most of us try to make a good first impression. We make sure that every detail of our clothing is perfect for an important meeting or job interview. We clean up our homes for visits from bank appraisers, our bosses, or our parents. We work on our appearances from head to toe in order to make a splash at a party or club. Some people even practice their handshakes to make sure that they communicate just the right combination of confidence and sincerity. First impressions count in our profes-sional and in our personal lives. They also count in presentations. What you say, how you say it, and how you look contribute to an audience's initial reaction to you. Making a good first impression is one of the most important components of an effective presentation.

By the same token, last impressions also last. Why do political candidates of-ten jockey to be the last speaker at a rally? Why do films run the best songs and soundtrack tunes in the final credits? Why do elegant restaurants hire pastry chefs and teams of bakers to make sure that their desserts are as beautiful as they are delicious? The answer is that politicians, filmmakers, and restauranteurs know that we tend to pay attention to and remember the last thing that we see or hear. Be-cause first and last impressions are critical, we discuss them separately from the rest of a presentation.

Introductions as Mini-Presentations

The introduction to your presentation is so important that it deserves almost as much attention as an entire presentation does. If you find the first chapter of a book confusing, you may not read any further. If the first few minutes of a TV movie bore you, you may zap to a new channel. If a salesperson offends or ig-nores you, you may leave the store. And if the beginning of your presentation isn't interesting, you may lose your audience. Although they may not walk out on you, they might tune you out, misunderstand you, forget you, or even worse, remember you as a poor speaker. On the other hand, a good beginning can create a positive, lasting impression and pave the way for a presentation that achieves your purpose.

Psychologists describe the power of first impressions as the **primacy effect.** They note that we recall items that are presented first. The primacy effect is most powerful at the beginning of a presentation, the point at which audience atten-tion to some new stimulus is at its peak.[1] The best introductions capitalize on the primacy effect.

To create an effective introduction for your presentation, you must first un-derstand what it can and should accomplish. Not only does the beginning of your presentation introduce you and your topic to the audience; it also intro-duces your audience to you. Your introduction gives the audience time to adjust, to settle in, to block out distractions, and to focus its attention on you and your message. At the same time, it gives you a chance to get a feel for the audience, to calm down, and to make any last-minute adjustments to what you want to say and how you want to say it. A good introduction establishes a relationship among three elements: you, your message, and your audience. It can also set the emotional tone for the rest of your presentation.

EFFECTIVE INTRODUCTIONS

1. **Focus audience attention**
2. **Put *you* in your presentation**
3. **Preview your message**
4. **Set the emotional tone**

Focus Audience Attention

Focusing audience attention may be *the* most important goal for the beginning of a presentation. In order to learn from or act on your presentation, your audience has to listen to it! So how do you focus your audience's attention? As we'll see shortly, you might begin with a direct question, report an unusual example or statistic, or tell a fascinating story. No matter which technique you use, your goal is to use the first few seconds of your presentation to focus the audience on you and your message.

You can gain an audience's attention by exploding a firecracker, but once the smoke clears, your audience may be more frightened than interested. The best way to capture your audience's attention is to relate your purpose and topic to your audience's characteristics, motives, interests, needs, and attitudes. Give your listeners a selfish reason to listen to you by explaining how your presentation will help them. Tell a story about how people have benefited from listening to what you have to say. Your goal is to get your audience focused on and interested in what you are about to say.

Put *You* in Your Presentation

You can craft an attention-getting and interesting introduction that doesn't put *you* in your presentation. But why not make a good beginning better? If you can link yourself to your topic or purpose, your audience is much more likely to pay attention and stay interested. You can give an informative presentation about baseball, but your audience will listen more intently if they know that you are or have been a baseball player, a lifelong fan, an umpire, or a baseball-card collector. If you are trying to convince an audience to stay sober while driving, your message will be much more persuasive if your audience learns that you are a drug abuse counselor or a recovering alcoholic or were the victim of a drunk driver. However, you don't need direct experience with your topic to put yourself in your presentation. Putting *you* in your introduction involves personalizing your message. If your audience sees that the topic affects you, they are more likely to let it affect them.

We devote most of Chapter 11, "Speaker Credibility and Ethics," to ways of putting *you* into your *entire* presentation. What your audience members think about your competence and character can be just as important as what they think about the content of your message. Right at the beginning of your presentation, an audience starts to decide whether you know what you're talking about and if you can be trusted.

Preview Your Message

Use the beginning of your presentation to give your audience a sneak preview about the subject of your talk. Better yet, give them a clear idea of how you are going to develop your central idea. As Chapter 8, "Organization," discusses, you can state your central idea and briefly list the key points or steps that you will take to achieve your purpose. You also can introduce your topic by making sure that any stories, examples, or statistics that you share in the introduction relate directly to your topic. In most presentations, your audience should know right from the start what you will be talking about.

Set the Emotional Tone

There is one other goal that speakers often overlook when crafting an introduction. Look at your introduction and think about the mood you want to create when you begin. Do you want your audience to be amused? relieved? worried?

concerned? curious? Patrick Collins, author of *Say It with Power and Confidence,* urges speakers to make sure that their introductions set an appropriate emotional tone that suits their purposes.[2]

You set the emotional tone of your introduction with the language that you use and the way in which you deliver your presentation. Is a joke an appropriate introduction to a presentation on child abuse? If your audience has assembled to hear about a controversial issue, will they patiently listen to a long opening story? If you're launching a new product or program, your words and mood should be positive and upbeat right from the start. If you're sharing tragic or disappointing news, your opening words should be clear and your mood respectful and somber. Select a style for your introduction to your presentation that matches the emotional tone of what's to come.

Even though introductions can be extremely effective for focusing audience attention, establishing speaker credibility, previewing the message, and setting the emotional tone, many inexperienced speakers don't prepare them with enough care. Why not? Speaking anxiety may be part of the reason. Chapter 3, "Building Presentation Confidence," notes that many speakers are most nervous during the first few seconds of their presentations. A well-planned, well-delivered introduction may be the last thing on their list of worries. It should be one of the first. Planning and practicing an effective introduction can do more than make a good first impression; it can also reduce anxiety. The first few seconds of a presentation need and deserve a lot of attention and thought. After all, you can't make a first impression a second time.

Ways to Begin

There are almost as many ways to begin a presentation as there are speakers, topics, and audiences. We have divided several of the most common methods into two types. **Topic-specific introductory methods** rely on topic-related supporting material to capture attention, gain interest, enhance the speaker's credibility, focus on the topic, and set the appropriate mood. **Situation-specific introductory methods** rely on the speaker's adapting to the interests and concerns of a specific audience in a particular setting or situation.

Topic-Specific Introductory Methods

There are many topic-specific methods for beginning a presentation, but among the most successful are those that immediately start with a piece of supporting material that captures the audience's attention. These methods can be used separately or in combination with one another.

TOPIC-SPECIFIC INTRODUCTIONS

- Use an interesting example or statistic
- Quote someone
- Tell a story
- Ask a question
- Use a presentation aid

Use an Interesting Example or Statistic.   Sometimes your research will turn up an example or a statistic that is unusual or dramatic. When presented all by itself, a good piece of research can gain an audience's attention and interest. Here's how one student began his speech on America's "growing" population:

> America is overweight. Approximately fifty million Americans are carrying around millions of extra pounds of fat. And it's getting worse. Several years ago, Yankee Stadium lost 9,000 seats during renovation because the new seats had to be three inches wider just to fit the "growing" population of America.

Beginning with an interesting example or statistic can prompt your audience to start thinking about your topic. The image of fat Americans squeezing into stadium seats is likely to stay with an audience.

Quote Someone.   There are many great speakers and writers. Careful research can uncover a dramatic statement or eloquent phrase that is ideal for the beginning of your presentation. Rather than trying to write the perfect beginning, you may find that someone else has already done it for you. But remember to give the writer or speaker full credit.

Sometimes a good quotation can help an audience overcome their doubts, especially when the writer or speaker is a highly respected and expert source of information. In the following example, a student uses two quotations to begin his presentation about the use of marijuana.

> "Marijuana, in its natural form, is one of the safest therapeutically active substances known to man." And "marijuana is about the safest drug you can give for treating the side effects cancer patients have to endure from chemotherapy." Who made these statements? The first was made by Francis Young, the chief administrative law judge of the Drug Enforcement Agency. The second was made by Dr. Lester Grinspoon, a professor of medicine at Harvard University.

Tell a Story.   Speakers can have great success by beginning a presentation with stories about their personal hardships or triumphs. They also can share stories they read about or hear from others. Sometimes stories are private and personal; at other times they are fictional and designed to illustrate a concept or an idea. An eighteen-year-old student shares a very personal story in the following introduction:

> When I was 15, I was operated on to remove the deadliest form of skin cancer, a melanoma carcinoma. Even though a plastic surgeon performed the surgery, I had horrible scars. My doctor injected 10 shots of steroids into each scar every three weeks to stop the scars from spreading. One year and two operations later, I was told it would be impossible to do anything to correct the scars until I am at least 25 years old. I now know that it wasn't worth a couple of summers of being tan to go through all that pain and suffering. Take steps now to protect yourself from the harmful effects of the sun.

Ask a Question.   Asking a question can attract your audience's attention and interest. Why? Because it encourages them to think about the answer.

> Why is it hotter in the summer than in the winter? When twenty-three Harvard students were asked this question at their graduation, only two were able to give a correct answer.

The Quotable Quotes Web site, www.quotablequotes.net, is just what it claims: "Your resource for all things quotable." The topic-based categories can help you find an appropriate quotation to use in the introduction of your presentation.

Asking a question is an effective way to begin a presentation, particularly if the question has a direct effect on the audience. A variation of *ask a question* is *let them guess*. Rather than leaving audience members thinking, "Yes, I've often asked that question" or "Yes, those are important questions," this method should elicit a response such as "I have no idea!"

> Which of the following eight products are owned by American companies and made in America: Bic pens, Arrow shirts, Godiva chocolates, Vaseline petroleum jelly, Firestone tires, Holiday Inns, and Tropicana orange juice? All? Half? The answer is *one*. Godiva chocolate is made and sold by the Campbell Soup Company.[3]

Use a Presentation Aid. A presentation aid such as a productivity chart, a cartoon, a product display, or a piece of taped music can help an audience focus its attention at the beginning of a presentation. In the following example, the student whose presentation on Muzak was outlined in Chapter 9, "Organizational Tools," began by playing a tape-recorded selection of some very smooth but dull music. After ten long seconds of recorded music, she began to speak.

> It's been referred to by its creators as "sonorous design" and "sound energy, attractively arranged." On the other hand, to much of the American public, this product more often conjures up images of "spineless melodies" with "vacant volumes of vapid violins." In short, it's Muzak. And what you're hearing is an actual demonstration tape of Muzak. But Muzak isn't just any old song. According to its creators, it can reduce your stress, boredom, and fatigue and can increase your productivity.

Situation-Specific Introductory Methods

As successful as the topic-specific methods for beginning a presentation may be, situation-specific methods can give you an added advantage. They let your audience know that you understand their specific interests and needs. Adapting your introduction to the characteristics of the audience, the nature of the occasion, or the circumstances of a situation demonstrates that your presentation is custom-made.

SITUATION-SPECIFIC INTRODUCTIONS

- **Refer to the place or occasion**
- **Refer to a recent or well-known event**
- **Directly address audience interests and needs**
- **Establish a personal link**

Refer to the Place or Occasion. An obvious, situation-specific way to begin a presentation is to refer to the place in which you are speaking or the occasion for the gathering. Consider this excerpt by General Douglas MacArthur, who led U.S. troops in the Pacific during World War II and the early years of the Korean War. Due to disagreements with fellow officers and President Harry S. Truman, he was relieved of his duties as general. On April 19, 1951, he addressed a joint session of Congress. He began his speech by referring to the place in which he was speaking rather than to himself:

> Mr. President, Mr. Speaker, and distinguished Members of the Congress, I stand on this rostrum with a sense of deep humility and great pride—humility in the wake of those great American architects of our history who have stood here before me, pride in the reflection that this forum of legislative debate represents human liberty in the purest form yet devised. Here are centered the hopes, and aspirations, and faith of the entire human race.[4]

A dozen years after General MacArthur's address, another famous American spoke in Washington, D.C. On August 28, 1963, Dr. Martin Luther King Jr. made his famous "I Have a Dream" speech on the steps of the Lincoln Memorial. By referring to the "shadow" of Abraham Lincoln, he was able to link his message to the man who signed the Emancipation Proclamation. Even his first few words echoed Lincoln's famous Gettysburg Address that began "Four score and seven years ago." Dr. King began his speech as follows: "Five score years ago, a great American, in whose symbolic shadow we stand, signed the Emancipation Proclamation."[5]

Garrison Keillor, creator and host of the radio show "Prairie Home Companion," establishes a personal link with his live audience by making sure his opening monologue includes references to and stories about the city he is visiting.

Refer to a Recent or Well-Known Event. Events that have occurred shortly before your presentation or in the recent past can provide a means of gaining audience attention and interest. This method also applies to events that might occur even seconds before you speak. In formal speaking situations, you often will hear speakers begin by referring to what was said by the person who introduced them, particularly if the introducer has told a friendly or humorous story about the speaker or has praised her. This technique can make the speaker seem more human after a lengthy introduction.

You cannot, however, rely on being introduced or on thinking up a good line on the spot to follow an introduction. It's better to plan a strong beginning that refers to an event known to your audience. For instance, in the following introduction, a student refers to a recent local news story.

> Last Friday, a front-page article in the *Journal* told a terrifying story: "Firefighters searching the burned-out shell of a popular all-night coffee shop made a grisly discovery early yesterday in the aftermath of a raging fire: the bodies of two male employees shot to death near a rear exit and, nearby, a third employee, critically wounded." Like you, I was horrified and shocked by this tragedy so close to home. But why, I wonder, does it take such a terrifying event to make us sit up and take notice of the crime problem in our own backyard?

The "recent event" technique is a big part of political speechmaking. If you listen carefully to the news or watch the president's State of the Union address, you are bound to hear references to well-known recent events. President Franklin D. Roosevelt's words provide a famous example: "Yesterday, December 7, 1941—a date which will live in infamy—the United States was suddenly and deliberately attacked by naval and air forces of the empire of Japan."[6]

Directly Address Audience Interests and Needs. When there is a crisis, you need to address the problem at the outset. If budget cuts will require salary reductions, audience members will want to hear the details. They won't want to hear a humorous story, a clever question, or an unusual statistic. When a person's job or future is threatened, no time should be spent on clever beginnings. In fact, such introductions may even make the audience hostile. Get right to the point. Here's an example:

> As you know, the state has reduced our operating budget by 2.7 million dollars. It is also just as important that you know this: All of you will have a job here next year—and the year after. There will be no layoffs. Instead there will be cutbacks in nonpersonnel budget lines, downsizing of programs, and, possibly, short furloughs.

This speaker went directly to the central idea and the preview section of her presentation. Having first reassured employees that no one would be fired, she could then explain how the budget cutbacks, downsizing, and shorter furloughs would be implemented.

Establish a Personal Link. Use your introduction to link your background and experiences to those of your audience. Even though you may not know or may be quite different from the members of your audience, your experiences may be similar. For instance, a Jewish student told the following story at the beginning of a presentation on race relations to a predominantly African American audience.

> When I was eight years old, I stayed home for a Jewish holiday in September. After I went to synagogue, my parents let me go outside to ride my bike. As I rode through the neighborhood, I encountered a group of kids coming home from school. Because I wasn't dressed for school and was riding my bike, they rightfully assumed I was Jewish. At first they began taunting me with the most terrible derogatory names imaginable. Then one of the kids picked up a two-by-four and tried to knock me off my bike. Even though he landed several direct blows, I kept pedaling until I outraced him. By the time I arrived home, I could barely walk. My back was badly bruised and my spine was damaged. To this day, I attribute my recurring back pains to that terrible day. And to this day, I am reminded of the pain that stays with you when people and prejudice breed hatred.

Mix Your Methods

Many speakers combine introductory methods to begin their presentations. For instance, this student began her introduction to a persuasive presentation on

SHOULD I SAY "LADIES AND GENTLEMEN"? Perhaps you've noticed that speakers often begin formal presentations with phrases such as "Ladies and gentlemen" or "Mr. President, distinguished faculty members, students, alumni, and friends." Is this kind of acknowledgment necessary? It depends on the audience, the place, and the occasion. Very formal public settings pretty much require mentioning the officials or groups of people in attendance. Most ceremonial occasions— a major convention, a graduation, an acceptance speech, a televised address—likewise call for formal behavior. Using these introductory formalities is a way of thanking those who have invited you to speak and honoring the important people and groups who have come to listen to you. Even in somewhat less formal circumstances, such as speaking on a stage after having been introduced by someone else, you may want to formally acknowledge that person and others on the stage.

But sometimes formality can be out of place. Addressing a group of coworkers or peers in an informal setting as "Ladies and Gentlemen, distinguished colleagues . . ." could seem stiff and unfriendly.

geographical illiteracy with a familiar rhyme, a statistic, a question, and the worrisome results of a survey.

"In fourteen-hundred and ninety-two Columbus sailed the ocean blue and found this land, land of the free, beloved by you, beloved by me." Or so the historical rhyme reminds us. But, according to the National Geographic Society, over 48% of Americans don't know where Columbus landed. Do you? In fact, five to fifteen percent of Americans believe that Columbus set sail to find Europe.

mini module

BEGINNING WITH A JOKE

Many public speaking books recommend beginning a presentation with a joke. As much as we enjoy a good laugh, we don't necessarily agree. Just because you've heard a good joke doesn't mean it would work as the introduction to your presentation. The audience may remember the joke but forget your message. Introductory jokes are great when they are perfectly matched to the topic and the audience. But if they aren't, save them for your friends.

Avoiding jokes doesn't mean avoiding humor in an introduction—an amusing example, a strange statistic, a funny story, or a great line from a comedian can work wonderfully. Some of the best speakers use humor in their introductions because they know that it's a sure way to gain audience attention and that it can give an audience a hint about the mood and direction of a talk. Some of the worst speakers use humor in their introductions because they can't think of any other way to begin. Because such speakers don't give their introductions a great deal of thought, their humor can be unrelated to the topic and, even worse, in poor taste.

Using humor effectively is more difficult than it seems, but these three guidelines always apply:

▶ First, the humor should be related to the topic or the speaker. When it is, humor can even be used to make a serious point. Note how this student began her presentation by comparing silly state laws to those controlling hand guns and assault weapons.

There ought to be laws against some laws. In Weaverville, North Carolina, it's illegal to walk an unleashed miniature pig in public. On South Padre Island, Texas, it's illegal to wear socks or ties. In Topeka, Kansas, you can run afoul of the law if you put alcohol in a teacup. And in Ridgewood, New Jersey, you can't play with Silly String—in the summer.[1] Yet in all of these states, it's perfectly legal to own and use certain types of guns—weapons that have no other function than shooting people.

▶ Second, the humor in your introduction should be appropriate for the people in the audience. In 1983,

Senator Jesse Helms was invited to be the commencement speaker at Grove City College. Like most other commencement speakers, the senator knew that his audience had probably heard many boring commencement addresses. Thus, he began:

Mr. President, distinguished faculty members, alumni, friends of Grove City College—and, most especially, members of the graduating class, while it is an honor to have been invited to share this memorable occasion with you, I suppose that there have been few commencement speakers who have not contemplated the remark made by an irreverent classmate who speculated that if all the commencement speakers in America were laid end-to-end—that would be fine.[2]

▶ Third, it must be well delivered! We devote an entire section of Chapter 12, "Generating Interest," to using humor in a presentation.

In the previous examples, the speakers made light of their audience's expectations about them or their topic. They didn't tell jokes, yet their introductions gained the audience's attention and set a mood for what followed. If you're considering a humorous introduction, make sure that it relates to your topic. You might even test your introduction on a few friends— just give the introduction and then ask them what they think your presentation's topic is. If their guesses are too far afield, your introduction probably is, too.

Make sure that your introduction is appropriate. Give special consideration to the diversity of your audience and how different audience members might react to humor. Last, be sure to deliver your humor flawlessly. How? As the native New Yorker replied to the tourist who asked, "How do I get to Carnegie Hall?"—Practice, practice, practice.

1. "Banned in the U.S.A.," *Time*, 6 July 1998, p. 32.

2. For the complete text of Helms's commencement address plus commentary, see James R. Andrews and David Zarefsky, *Contemporary American Voices: Significant Speeches in American History, 1945–Present* (New York: Longman, 1992), pp. 317–321.

Regardless of how you begin your presentation, always ask yourself whether the method you're using will gain audience attention and interest, will put *you* in your presentation, will introduce your purpose or topic area, and will set the appropriate emotional tone. No matter how funny your joke, how inspiring your quotation, or how startling your statistic, your opening remarks won't accomplish anything unless they are linked to these introductory goals.

Starting Strong

In their eagerness to get going, some speakers don't give their introduction enough attention. Rather than applying the time-tested introductory techniques we've been exploring, they may fall into one or more common traps. If you know what these traps are, you can avoid them—and start strong!

Plan the Beginning at the End

Simply put, don't plan the introduction to your presentation before you've developed the body of it. There are many decisions to make when preparing a presentation; how to begin should not be the first. Because a strong introduction can help you achieve your purpose, it should be adapted to your audience and should relate to the content of your presentation. You have to know what the content is before you can preview your key points.

There's No Need to Apologize

Wouldn't it be strange if an actor came out onto the stage before a play to tell the audience that he hadn't memorized his lines very well and that he'd had a lot of trouble singing the first song in the second act? Why, then, do speakers apologize for their presentations before they give them? Too often, speakers begin with apologies or excuses. "I don't speak very often, so please excuse my nervousness." "I wish I'd had a few more days to prepare for this presentation, but I just found out that I had to make it on Tuesday." Comments like these do not accomplish very much. If your presentation is wonderful, the audience may be confused by your excuses. If it's awful (or you just think it is), let the audience draw their own conclusions. A presentation should start with a strong beginning and should not make excuses or apologize for the level of preparation or quality of delivery.

Avoid Using "My Speech Is About . . ."

Beginning statements such as "I'm going to talk about . . ." or "My topic is . . ." may be true, but they don't help you gain the audience's attention or interest. And even though they may introduce your topic, such statements will not necessarily make that important connection between your purpose and your audience.

Nevertheless, like all other rules, this one has exceptions. "I'm going to talk about how I was surrounded by killer sharks and survived" would probably make the most jaded audience

HOW LONG SHOULD MY INTRODUCTION BE? Generally, we recommend that your introduction should take no longer than 10 percent of your presentation time. If it takes more than that amount of time, audience members may begin to think, "Get on with it" or "Okay, okay, I catch your drift—now show me!" There are, of course, exceptions to the 10 percent guideline. If you are facing a distrustful or hostile audience, you may need more time to establish your credibility or to establish common ground with your audience. **Common ground** is a term we use to describe a belief, attitude, or experience shared by the speaker and the audience—a place where both you and your audience can "stand" without disagreement. In some situations, a speaker may need a longer introduction to create a more hospitable mood or to reduce audience concerns about the topic. In most cases, however, 10 percent of a presentation is ample time for achieving the goals of an introduction.

listen! "My talk will be about the budget crisis and how it will affect your jobs" will likewise hold audience attention and interest. But you should usually try to avoid such beginnings. They communicate a lack of confidence and originality. Unless you have a good reason for choosing "My speech is about . . ." as a beginning, try not to use this method.

You Need More than a Great Beginning

A great beginning can accomplish a great deal. It can excite your audience and make them eager to hear more about you and your topic. But if the rest of your presentation doesn't live up to it, you can be headed for trouble. Remember the real estate agent's "curb value"? A newly mowed lawn won't make up for a leaky roof. Remember the movie poster that promises adventure and romance? No matter how eye-catching the poster, the movie had better live up to its image. A successful presentation can survive a less-than-great beginning, but a great introduction cannot save a poor presentation.

Last Impressions Last

What is true of introductions is also true of conclusions. Whether you like it or not, the final thing you say to an audience can determine how they think and feel about you and your presentation. It's no wonder that songs at the end of a concert are often the ones the audience has been waiting for. It's no wonder that the finalé of a Broadway musical is often the most exciting number in the show. Even on a personal level we often worry about the last impression we make. For example, we send thank you notes to show our gratitude or save a great dessert for the end of a meal. We know that last impressions can count just as much as first impressions and that last impressions last.

Remember the primacy effect and its implications for introductions? Psychologists have a similar term for explaining why we more accurately recall items presented last. It's called the **recency effect** and indicates that recall is even higher for items at the end of a list than for those at the beginning.[7] Final words can have a powerful and lasting impact on your audience. A good ending can ensure that the audience will remember the most important part of your message.

Conclusions as Mini-Presentations

What you say and do during the last few seconds of your presentation can determine whether and how well you achieve your purpose. Have you ever been disappointed by the ending of a book or a movie? Have you ever had a bad dessert ruin a decent meal? And have you ever squirmed in your seat when a speaker went on and on with a long, rambling conclusion?

The first step in deciding how to end your presentation is to understand its goals. Like the introduction, a conclusion should establish a relationship among three elements: you, your topic, and your audience. Like the beginning of a presentation, the ending should try to accomplish specific goals.

EFFECTIVE CONCLUSIONS SHOULD

1. Be memorable
2. Be clear
3. Be brief

Be Memorable

The most important goal of your conclusion is to make you and your message memorable. Before drafting your conclusion, ask yourself this question: "What is the one thing that I want my audience to remember at the end of my presentation?" Is it your central idea? Is it an image, a story, or a statistic? Audiences rarely remember all the details of a presentation. Instead, they remember a few ideas and a few images. The conclusion of your presentation gives you the opportunity to shape that idea or image into a lasting memory.

One way to make your conclusion memorable is to link your purpose to your audience's interests and needs. Give them a reason to remember you and your presentation. Show them how your message has affected you personally or how it can affect them as well.

Also, try to end on an emotional note that matches your message. If your presentation focuses on how to do something, try to get the audience excited about giving it a try. If your presentation gives your listeners a lot of new information, show them how to remember it and why they should. If you're trying to change your audience's attitude, show them how that change will help others, will solve a serious problem, or will make them feel good. But no matter what method you decide to use, you will want your audience to remember good things about you and your message.

Be Clear

Being clear is just as important as being memorable. The last thing that you want your audience to do is to leave your presentation wondering what it was all about. What's the point of using a beautiful quotation or telling a funny story if it's not clear how it relates to your message? Again, ask yourself, "What is the one thing that I want my audience to remember at the end of my presentation?" Make sure that your conclusion repeats that one thing as clearly as possible. You may have to make that point more than once or word it several different ways in order to be sure that it's clear. Don't use the conclusion to add new ideas or to insert something that you left out of the body of the presentation. Use it to reinforce your central idea and to make your message sharp and clear.

Be Brief

When trying to make the ending of your presentation memorable and clear, you may be tempted to make it long. Resist this temptation! How do you react when you hear a speaker say, "And in conclusion . . ." and then take twenty more minutes to finish? The announced ending of a presentation should never go beyond two or three minutes, no matter how long you've spoken. When you say you are about to end, end.

Ways to End

There are almost as many ways to end a presentation as there are ways to begin one. Some methods can help you make that final connection between your purpose and your audience. Other methods can strengthen the audience's final impression of you and your message. Each method can be used separately or combined with others.

> **WAYS TO END**
> - Summarize
> - Quote someone
> - Tell a story
> - Share your personal feelings
> - Use poetic language
> - Call for action
> - Refer to the beginning

Summarize

Reinforcing your key points in a succinct summary is the most direct way to conclude a presentation. It's clear and brief. And if you pay enough attention to the words you select for your ending, it can be memorable. In the following example, the speaker has reviewed and repeated the main points of her presentation in the form of questions to emphasize her central idea that America needs more women in Congress.

> Now, if you ever hear someone question whether women are good enough, smart enough, and skilled enough to serve in the U.S. Congress, ask and then answer the three questions I posed today: Are women candidates caught in the "mommy trap"? Can women's issues attract big donors? And, are women too good to be "tough" in politics? Now that you know how to answer these questions, don't let doubters stand in the way of making a woman's place in the House.

Quote Someone

What is true about quoting someone in the beginning of your presentation is just as true about an ending quotation. Because quotations can be memorable, clear, and brief, people often use them as a finale to their presentations. Careful research can provide a quotation that will give your presentation a dramatic and effective ending.

Consider this example from the end of Barbara Jordan's keynote speech to the Democratic National Convention on July 12, 1976. Ms. Jordan, a congressional representative from Texas, was the first African American to deliver a keynote address at a major party's national political convention.

> I am going to close my speech by quoting a Republican President and I ask you that as you listen to these words of Abraham Lincoln, relate them to the concept of national community in which every last one of us participates: "As I would not be a slave, so I would not be a master." This expresses my idea of Democracy. "Whatever differs from this, to the extent of difference, is no Democracy."[8]

Tell a Story

Ending with a good story can be as effective as beginning with one. It can help an audience to visualize the outcome of your purpose. A well-told story can also

Texas congresswoman
Barbara Jordan, the keynote
speaker at the Democratic
National Convention in
1976, invoked the words of
Abraham Lincoln to con-
clude her speech.

help an audience to remember the main idea of your presentation. Dr. D. Stanley Eitzen, professor of sociology, delivered a speech at Bethell College in North Newton, Kansas, on September 25, 1989, about the dark side of competition. He left the audience with a story that summed up his central idea and message.

> Let me conclude with a special example from the Special Olympics. A friend of mine observed a 200-meter race among three evenly matched 12-year-olds at a Special Olympics event in Colorado Springs. About 25 yards from the finish line, one of the contestants fell. The other two runners stopped and helped their competitor to his feet, brushed him off, and jogged together, hand in hand to the finish line, ending the race in a three-way tie. The actions of these three, especially the two who did not fall, are un-American. Perhaps . . . they did not understand the importance of winning in our society. To them, the welfare of their opponent was primary. . . . My message is that the successful life involves the pursuit of excellence, a fundamental respect for others—even one's competitors, and enjoyment in the process. Competition as structured in our society with its emphasis on outcome undermines these goals. I enjoin you to be thoughtful about the role of competition in your life and how it might be restructured to maximize humane goals.[9]

Share Your Personal Feelings

One way of putting yourself into the ending of a presentation is to conclude by disclosing how you feel. Such an ending can touch the emotions of your audience and leave them with a strong memory of you, the speaker. People still remember how Martin Luther King Jr. closed the speech that he delivered on April 3, 1968. The next day King was assassinated.

I just want to do God's will, and He's allowed me to go up to the mountain, and I've looked over and I've seen the Promised Land. I may not get there with you, but I want you to know tonight that we as a people will get to the Promised Land. So I'm happy tonight, I'm not worried about anything, I'm not fearing any man. Mine eyes have seen the glory of the coming of the Lord.[10]

Use Poetic Language

Being poetic is one of the best ways to ensure that your conclusion is memorable. Being poetic doesn't mean ending with a poem. Rather, it means using language in a way that inspires and creates memorable images. Use of language strategies such as repetition and metaphor can affect an audience as much as a singer can delight one with a song. If Martin Luther King Jr. had said, "Things will improve," his speech would not have had the impact that his use of the lyrics of the "Battle Hymn of the Republic" does: "Mine eyes have seen the glory." Making your words "sing" can make your presentation more memorable and effective.

Before people used the written word, everything was communicated orally. Long epic poems and stories were passed down from generation to generation by the revered members of the community—the storytellers. How did these people remember thousands of lines of poetry? One way was by using rhyme and rhythm. It is much easier to remember lines that rhyme. Interestingly, as the written word has become the dominant form of transferring knowledge, rhyme has faded. Look at the poetry of a few hundred years ago—it is much more rhythmic than its modern counterparts. Rhyme and rhythm can make people remember what you said. Even during the O. J. Simpson trial, we heard, "If the glove don't fit, you must acquit."

One of the most dynamic American speakers is Jesse Jackson. On July 17, 1984, he concluded his speech at the Democratic National Convention poetically. Notice how he repeated the phrase "Our time has come" and the word *ground*. Reverend Jackson even adapted the beginning of the famous poem by Emma Lazarus carved into the base of the Statue of Liberty: "Give me your tired, your poor, Your huddled masses yearning to breathe free."

Our time has come. Our faith, hope and dreams will prevail. Our time has come. Weeping has endured for the night. And now joy cometh in the morning.

Our time has come. No graves can hold our body down. Our time has come. No lie can live forever.

Our time has come. We must leave racial battleground and come to economic common ground and moral higher ground. America, our time has come.

We've come from disgrace to Amazing Grace, our time has come.

Give me your tired, give me your poor, your huddled masses who yearn to breathe free, and come November, there will be a change because our time has come.

Thank you and God bless you.[11]

You don't have to be the leader of the Rainbow Coalition to be poetic at the end of your presentation. A young student ended a speech about respecting older people with the following short but poetic phrases:

For old wood best to burn, old wine to drink, old authors to read, old friends to trust, and old people to love.

Call for Action

One of the more challenging but effective ways to end a presentation is to call for action. Malcolm Kushner, a communication instructor and author, goes so far as to recommend that "every speech should end with a call to action. It doesn't have to be a call to action in the traditional sense (buy, give, vote), but it should ask every member of the audience to take some type of action. Because that's what really involves them."[12]

In a conclusion that calls for action, you are telling your audience to do more than merely listen to your presentation; you are asking them to *do* something. Even if you're just telling an audience to remember something, to think about a story you've told, or to ask themselves a question, you've asked them to become involved.

In the following example, Helen Keller ends a speech by calling for action. Born in 1880, Keller was left deaf, blind, and mute by disease at the age of nineteen months. With the help of Anne Sullivan, her dedicated teacher, she learned to read, write, and speak. In 1916, Helen Keller delivered an antiwar speech at Carnegie Hall in New York City. She ended her speech with this call for action:

> Strike against all ordinances and laws and institutions that continue the slaughter of peace and the butcheries of war. Strike against war, for without you no battles can be fought. Strike against manufacturing shrapnel and gas bombs and all other tools of murder. Strike against preparedness that means death and misery to millions of human beings. Be not dumb, obedient slaves in an army of destruction. Be heroes in an army of construction.[13]

WRITE OUT YOUR INTRODUCTION AND CONCLUSION

Unless you are very familiar with your audience or your topic, we recommend that you write out your introduction and conclusion word for word. In Chapter 13, "Performance and Practice," we recommend speaking from a brief outline or a list of key phrases for the entire presentation. However, the introduction and conclusion can be exceptions. Because the beginning and ending of a presentation matter so much, every word counts. But instead of reading from your manuscript, practice your introduction and conclusion so often that you won't need any notes (unless you're including a long quotation or complicated set of statistics). Because you will probably be most nervous at the beginning of your presentation, knowing your introduction by heart will also help you mask and minimize any nervous symptoms you may be feeling. Because you're not looking at notes, you can concentrate your full attention on your listeners rather than on your nervousness. As you close, you can again put aside your notes and deliver a well-crafted conclusion that allows you to focus on your audience and "clinch" your message.

Refer to the Beginning

If you can't decide which of the previously mentioned methods to use, consider ending your presentation with the same technique you used to begin it. We call this the *bookends method*. If you began your presentation with a quotation, end with the same or a similar quotation. If you began with a story, refer back to that story. If you began by referring to an event or incident, ask your audience to recall it.

When Rosharna Hazel prepared her persuasive presentation for an intercollegiate speaking contest (see Appendix A), she compared the human body to a machine in the introduction and conclusion of her speech.

> Our bodies are miraculous machines. We fuel them, tune them up, and "exercise" them so they don't rust. If we notice a problem, we put them in the shop for repair, just like our cars. There, you may think, the similarity ends here because most of us trust our medical system more than our mechanics. After all, mechanics make mistakes. "The clamp came off," your mechanic tells you. "Our mistake—we'll fix it for you free of charge."

After talking about the adverse effects of medical treatments in hospitals, she concluded her presentation this way:

Take care of your machine by demanding the same from your health care professionals as you would from your mechanic. When it comes to your body and your health, not everything can be fixed free of charge.

Mix Your Methods

As was the case with beginnings, many speakers rely on more than one way to conclude a presentation. Think about your audience's learning styles. Restate your main points or tell a story they can visualize depending on whether they are auditory, visual, or physical learners. For instance, note how this student speaker used statistics and a personal story to end a presentation on alcoholism.

> According to figures quoted in *Time* magazine, 18 million Americans are alcoholics, and that translates into better than one adult out of every ten. Very few, if any, of these people planned on becoming alcoholics. And many, like me, were well informed about the disease before falling victim. I've told you my story and alerted you to the role of denial in the hope that someday, if that doubt ever creeps into your mind and you find yourself asking whether you might have an alcohol problem, you'll remember my speech and take a harder, more objective look at that question. It could just save your life. It has saved mine.

The conclusion of your presentation puts the final touch on all that has come before. Regardless of which way you conclude, you should always ask yourself whether the method you have decided to use will be memorable, clear, and brief. No matter how poetic you try to be or how many statistics you can read in two minutes, you won't accomplish much unless you link your method to the goals of ending.

Ending Effectively

Many beginning speakers—and even some veterans—don't pay much attention to carefully crafting their conclusions. Why? What's left of a person's speaking anxiety at the end of a presentation offers a partial explanation. Once you've presented your message, you may want to flee the podium and escape. Taking time to present a well-planned, well-performed ending may be the last thing you want to worry about. But because last impressions linger, the last thing you say can be just as important as the first.

Knowing that you have a well-prepared and strong ending for your presentation can help calm your nerves. The most effective endings match the rest of a presentation and make realistic assumptions about the audience.

Make Sure It Matches

Sometimes we tell students, "Don't go for fireworks without a reason to celebrate." In other words, don't tack on an irrelevant or inappropriate ending. If you have given a serious presentation about the need for better childcare, don't end with a tasteless joke about naughty children. If you have explained how to operate a new and complicated machine, you probably shouldn't conclude your presentation with flowery poetry. Match the mood and method of your ending to the mood and style of your presentation.

Have Realistic Expectations

What if you issue a call for action, and no one in your audience acts? What if you end with your favorite joke, and no one laughs? Certainly, you don't want to embarrass yourself or your audience at the end of a presentation. Don't expect miracles. Only an inexperienced speaker would expect everyone in an audience to sign an organ donation card following a presentation on eye banks. Most audiences will not act when called upon unless the request is carefully worded, reasonable, and possible. Don't end by demanding something from your audience unless you are reasonably sure that you can get it.

There is no best way to begin or end a presentation. Deciding which methods to use depends on your purpose, the audience, and the occasion. Regardless of your chosen method, a good introduction should link you, your topic, and your audience. By gaining audience attention and interest, putting *you* in your presentation, introducing your purpose or topic, and setting the appropriate emotional tone, your introduction can get you off to a strong start. A good ending also should link you, your topic, and your audience by being memorable, clear, and brief. Introductions and conclusions are not ornaments or frills; they are essential to making good first and last impressions.

Summary

◆✦ Why do introductions matter so much?

The introduction of a presentation matters because that's when your audience creates and remembers its first impressions of you and your message. An effective introduction should attempt to focus audience attention and interest, put *you* in your presentation, preview the topic, and establish an appropriate emotional tone.

◆✦ How do I link my introduction to my topic?

Topic-specific methods include the use of interesting examples or statistics, quotations, stories, questions, and presentation aids.

◆✦ How can I acknowledge the speaking situation in my introduction?

Situation-specific methods include making references to the place or occasion, to a recent or well-known event, and to audience interests and needs as well as establishing a link between you and your audience.

◆✦ What do good conclusions do?

A good conclusion should be memorable, clear, and brief.

◆✦ What's the best way to end my presentation?

Methods include the use of summaries, quotations, stories, personal feelings, poetic language, calls for action, and references to the introduction.

Key Terms

Notes

1. See Douglas A. Bernstein et al., *Psychology,* 5th ed. (Boston: Houghton Mifflin, 2000), p. 227; and Lester A. Lefton, *Psychology,* 5th ed. (Boston: Allyn & Bacon, 1994), p. 218.
2. Patrick J. Collins, *Say It with Power and Confidence* (Paramus, NJ: Prentice-Hall, 1998), pp. 60–61.
3. *Baltimore Sun,* 2 February 1992, p. D1.
4. For the complete text of MacArthur's farewell address plus commentary, see James R. Andrews and David Zarefsky, *Contemporary American Voices: Significant Speeches in American History, 1945–Present* (New York: Longman, 1992), pp. 27–33.
5. For the complete text of King's "I Have a Dream" speech plus commentary, see Andrews and Zarefsky, 1992, pp. 78–81.
6. For the complete text of Roosevelt's war message plus commentary, see James Andrews and David Zarefsky, *American Voices: Significant Speeches in American History, 1640–1945* (New York: Longman, 1989), pp. 474–476.
7. Bernstein, p. 227, and Lefton, p. 218.
8. For the complete text of Jordan's keynote address plus commentary, see Andrews and Zarefsky, 1992, pp. 279–282.
9. For the complete text of Eitzen's speech plus commentary, see Owen Peterson, *Representative American Speeches, 1989–1990* (New York: H. W. Wilson, 1991), pp. 119–128.
10. For the complete text of King's "I've Been to the Mountaintop" speech plus commentary, see Andrews and Zarefsky, 1992, pp. 114–120.
11. For the complete text of Jackson's rainbow coalition address plus commentary, see Andrews and Zarefsky, 1992, pp. 355–362.
12. Malcolm Kushner, *Successful Presentations for Dummies* (Foster City, CA: IDG Books, 1997), p. 137.
13. For the complete text of Helen Keller's, *Strike Against War* speech, visit the Web site www.afb.org/afb/archives/papers/speeches/11speeches/11speech3.html.

PART IV

SPEAKER CREDIBILITY AND INTEREST

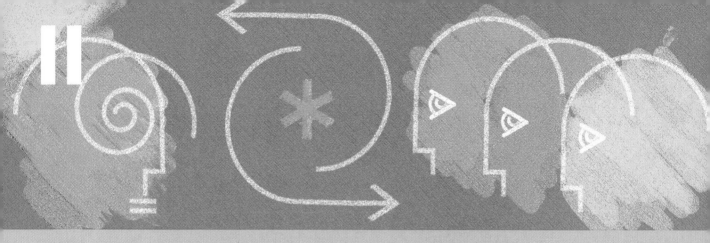

Speaker Credibility and Ethics

- ◆◆ What factors determine whether the audience will perceive me as a good speaker?
- ◆◆ How can I enhance my credibility as a speaker?
- ◆◆ How does my character influence the success of a presentation?
- ◆◆ How can I ensure that I am treating my audience fairly and ethically?
- ◆◆ What can audience members do to ensure that they are treating a speaker fairly and ethically?

Being well prepared and well rehearsed may not be enough to enable a speaker to achieve the purpose of a presentation. A well-prepared presentation and an effective speaker are not the same thing. If they were, you could hire a speechwriter and work with a speech coach to be guaranteed success. As we've indicated before, presentations differ from other forms of communication simply because *you are there.* Being willing to "put yourself on the line" can make your message more personal, more vital, and more effective. In this chapter, we emphasize how important you and your credibility are in determining whether an audience listens to, learns from, and responds to your presentation.

The concept of *speaker credibility* is over two thousand years old. Even in ancient times, speech coaches (yes, there were speech coaches way back then) recognized that the characteristics and qualities of a speaker were just as important as the speech. In his *Rhetoric,* Aristotle wrote about *ethos,* a Greek word meaning "character": "The character [ethos] of the speaker is a cause of persuasion when the speech is so uttered as to make him worthy of belief. . . . His character [ethos] is the most potent of all the means to persuasion."[1] Aristotle's concept of *ethos* has evolved into what we now call speaker credibility. In Chapter 18, "Understanding Persuasion," ethos will appear again as one of the most powerful ways to persuade an audience.

Studies of speaker credibility have demonstrated its significance. For example, in one study two different audiences listened to an audiotape of the same presentation. One audience was told that the speaker was a national expert on the topic. The other audience was told that the speaker was a college student. After listening to the presentation, each audience was asked for their reactions. Can you guess the results? The "national expert's" speech persuaded more audience members to change their minds than the speech by the "student" did.[2] Aristotle's contention about ethos is as true today as it was in ancient Greece. Audience perceptions about the speaker influence a presentation's success. Learning how to enhance your credibility is well worth the effort and is the topic of this chapter.

Components of Speaker Credibility

Speaker credibility represents the extent to which an audience believes you and the things you say. *The American Heritage Dictionary* defines *credibility* as the "quality, capability, or power to elicit belief."[3] In other words, the more credible you are in the eyes of your audience, the more likely you are to achieve the purpose of your presentation. If your audience rates you as highly credible, they may excuse poor delivery. They are so ready to believe you that the presentation doesn't have to be perfect.[4]

In order to become a more credible speaker, it's important to understand which qualities contribute to your credibility. Of the many factors researchers have identified as major components of speaker credibility, three have an especially strong impact on the believability of a speaker: character, competence, and charisma.[5]

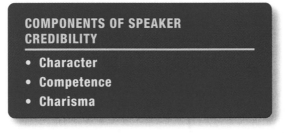

COMPONENTS OF SPEAKER
CREDIBILITY

- Character
- Competence
- Charisma

Character

Character relates to a speaker's honesty and goodwill. Are you a person of good character—trustworthy, sincere, and fair? Do you put the good of the audience above your own? When you speak, do you come across as friendly, sincere, and honest? When you're presenting an argument, is your evidence fair, are any reservations acknowledged, and is the conclusion warranted? Figure 11.1 on page 184

Figure 11.1   Character

Adjectives listed on the left side of the following word pairs describe a speaker of good character.

Honest	Dishonest
Kind	Cruel
Friendly	Unfriendly
Open	Closed
Fair	Biased
Respectful	Rude
Dedicated	Disloyal
Caring	Unconcerned

shows these and other aspects of character. Of the three components of speaker credibility, character may be the most important. If your listeners don't trust you, it won't matter if you are an international expert or the most exciting speaker that ever electrified an audience.

As shown later in this chapter, a speaker of good character is a good person. In this case, "good" means being ethical—doing what is right and moral when you speak in front of an audience. Unfortunately, a presentation can be used for unethical as well as ethical purposes. A speaker can help an audience or can take advantage of it, can present accurate information or can mislead an audience with false information, and can support a worthy cause or support a selfish one. In other words, the audience's opinion of your character determines whether they will believe you. If an audience *thinks* you are dishonest, you will have little chance of achieving your purpose. If you *are* dishonest, you don't deserve to achieve your purpose. But if you are honest, and the audience sees you as honest, their perception of you will help you to achieve your purpose.

Competence

Competence relates to a speaker's expertise and abilities, as the qualities in Figure 11.2 illustrate. In the best of all speaking situations, an audience will believe you are competent if you are a recognized expert. Proving that you are competent can be as simple as listing your credentials and experience. An audience is unlikely to question a recognized brain surgeon, a professional baseball player, or an international dress designer, as long as each sticks to discussing brain surgery, baseball, or dress design. Sometimes experts can use the prestige they have in one field and transfer it to another. A brain surgeon may speak about the need for national health care, a baseball player may warn youngsters about the dangers of drug abuse, and a dress designer may suggest inexpensive ways of looking stylish.

Figure 11.2   Competence

Adjectives listed on the left side of the following word pairs describe a competent speaker.

Experienced	Inexperienced
Well prepared	Unprepared
Qualified	Unqualified
Up-to-date	Out-of-date
Trained	Untrained
Informed	Uninformed
Intelligent	Unintelligent

If you were the captain of an eighty-foot sailboat that set a speed record sailing from Portugal to Boston, an audience will believe and probably will enjoy your tales of high-sea adventure. If a professor of oceanography describes Atlantic Ocean currents, an audience is likely to accept the information without question. Fortunately, you don't have to be a celebrated sea captain or have a Ph.D. to be an expert. A student, an auto mechanic, a waiter or waitress, a mother or father of six children, a minister, a chef, a nurse, and a government employee can all be experts. Such speakers can rely on their own life experiences and opinions to demonstrate competence.

But what happens when you aren't an expert? How can you demonstrate that you know what you're talking about? The answer lies in one word: research. As Chapter 7, "Supporting Material," discusses, you must thoroughly research the ideas and information you will need for your presentation. While skimming *The Joy of Cooking* will not make you an expert chef, thorough research can give you enough up-to-date content to become a well-informed speaker. Although you may only use a small percentage of the supporting materials you collect, you can rely on your hours of research to give you confidence. Letting an audience know how much time and effort you have put into researching your topic, or sharing your surprise at discovering new ideas and

In 1992, Rigoberta Menchú, a leader of the Committee of the Peasant Union in Guatemala, won the Nobel Peace Prize for her work as a leading advocate of Indian rights and ethnocultural reconciliation throughout the Western Hemisphere. Here, she brings enormous credibility and public visibility to a human rights symposium in Texas.

information, demonstrates that you have worked hard to become a qualified and competent speaker. If you don't have firsthand experience or cannot claim to be an expert, let your audience know what efforts you have made to be well prepared. The following are some examples: "We conducted a study of over 2,000 individuals and found. . . ." "After reviewing every textbook on this subject written after 1995, I was surprised that the authors didn't address. . . ." "I have spoken, in person, to all five of our county commissioners. They all agree that. . . ."

Charisma

Charisma is a quality reflected in your level of energy, enthusiasm, vigor, and commitment. A speaker with charisma is seen as dynamic, forceful, powerful, assertive, and intense. President John F. Kennedy and Martin Luther King Jr. were charismatic speakers who could motivate and energize audiences. So was Adolf Hitler. People can disagree about a speaker's message yet still find that speaker charismatic. Figure 11.3 on the right illustrates the elements of charisma.

Are you a dynamic speaker? Can you inspire and arouse the emotions of an audience with your words? Are you eager to share your opinions with other people? Is your delivery animated, energetic, and enthusiastic? If your answer is "yes" to any of these questions, *charisma* may be a component of your speaking style. If your answers to the previous questions are "no," do not despair. Charisma is a valuable characteristic for a speaker, but it is not essential for success. A gentle speaker who is competent and trusted can be more successful than a charismatic speaker of questionable motives. In fact, some speakers have too much energy and

Figure 11.3   Charisma

Adjectives listed on the left side of the following word pairs describe a charismatic speaker.

Active	Passive
Enthusiastic	Dull
Bold	Timid
Energetic	Tired
Confident	Hesitant
Stimulating	Boring
Dynamic	Lethargic

REAL WORLD, REAL SPEAKERS

Charisma does not have to rely on fireworks. Soft-spoken speakers can be very charismatic. Mother Teresa, the Catholic nun whose tireless work with the sick and poor in India earned her the Nobel Peace Prize, was one of these. Mother Teresa's words reached around the world. Her credibility was unimpeachable, her confidence unshakable. Yet she was "soft-spoken as a breeze. Her incredible intensity, her commitment, made her dynamic. She had that magical quality called charisma—drawing others to her and making them want to follow her lead." [1]

Peggy Noonan, one of Ronald Reagan's speechwriters, describes a National Prayer Breakfast in 1994 where Mother Teresa spoke:

> She was small and moved slowly, hunched forward slightly. . . . [She] looked weathered, frail, and tough as wire. . . . No thank you, no smile. She just stood there holding the speech and looking down at it. . . . For twenty-five minutes she just read . . . her text. . . . She finished her speech to a standing ovation and left as she had entered, silently, through a parted curtain, in a flash of blue and white. Her speech was a great success in that it was clear and strong, seriously meant, seriously stated, seriously argued and seriously received. . . . She softened nothing, did not deflect division but defined it. She came with a sword. She could do this, of course, because she had and has a natural and known authority. She had the standing of a saint." [2]

1. Gay Lumsden and Donald Lumsden, *Communicating with Credibility and Confidence* (Belmont, CA: Wadsworth, 1996), p. 37.
2. Peggy Noonan, *Simply Speaking: How to Communicate Your Ideas with Style, Substance, and Clarity* (New York: HarperCollins, 1998), pp. 197–204. Copyright © by Peggy Noonan. Reprinted by permission of HarperCollins Publishers, Inc.

intensity; they can frighten and exhaust an audience. Nevertheless, there is no question that an emotionally charged sermon or convention address can motivate thousands of people.

Despite Mother Teresa's soft-spoken intensity (see Real World, Real Speakers above), a key factor in determining whether a speaker has charisma is his or her delivery. Charisma often has more to do with how a speaker delivers a presentation than with what the person is saying. Speakers who have strong and expressive voices will be seen as having more charisma than speakers with hesitant or unexpressive voices. Speakers who gesture naturally and move gracefully will be perceived as having more charisma than those who look uncomfortable and awkward in front of an audience. Speakers who can look their audiences in the eye will be regarded as having more charisma than those who avoid any sort of contact with members of the audience. Practicing and developing your performance skills can enhance your charisma in the same way that preparation can help you become a more competent speaker.

Another way to enhance your charisma is to show an audience how committed you are to your purpose. Demonstrate that your actions speak louder than your words. Are you merely concerned about the homeless, or do you volunteer your time and energy at a local homeless shelter? Do you oppose nuclear energy, or do you demonstrate in front of nuclear power plants and donate one paycheck a year to antinuclear organizations? Do you complain about higher tuition and cutbacks in student services, or do you write to your college's board of trustees expressing your concerns? By showing that you are active and committed to your purpose, you can better stimulate an audience to join you.

Developing Credibility

You can develop or heighten your credibility, but please understand one very important fact: *Speaker credibility comes from your audience.* Only the audience decides whether or not you are believable. Several of our colleagues contend that credibility does not exist in any absolute or real sense; it is based solely on audience perceptions.[6] Thus, even if you are the world's greatest expert on your topic and deliver your carefully written and well-prepared presentation with skill, the ultimate decision about your credibility lies with your audience. Think of it this way: Credibility is "like the process of getting a grade in school. Only the teacher (or audience) can assign the grade to the student (or speaker), but the student can do all sorts of things—turn in homework, prepare for class, follow the rules—to influence what grade is assigned."[7] Teachers give grades, judges award prizes, reviewers critique books, and audiences determine your level of credibility. At the same time, there are things you *can* do—find out what you have to offer your audience, prepare an interesting presentation, and show your audience why you're uniquely qualified to deliver it—to influence your audience's opinion of you and your presentation.

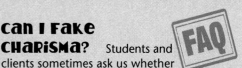

can I Fake CHaRiSMa? Students and clients sometimes ask us whether they should try to fake charisma. We answer this question with an absolute *no*. You either have charisma, or you don't. If being highly energetic and enthusiastic while you speak does not come naturally, don't fake it. You won't fool your audience and may even alienate it. "Faking" charisma is unethical. Pretending to be energetic and enthusiastic about a message you don't believe in deceives and misleads your audience.

However, any speaker can have charismatic moments. Think about your life experiences. Think of something you've done that will inspire people. Have you ever helped or saved someone in trouble? Have you ever faced down a threat? Have you ever succeeded when you thought you would fail? Have you heard an inspiring story about someone else? Use these examples and stories in your presentation. Tell them simply and sincerely, speaking from the heart. Let your enthusiasm for the story translate into energy. When you're telling a good story that's meaningful to you, a charismatic moment can materialize.

So should you fake charisma? No. You can, however, become charismatic when you carefully select and care about what you say.

DEVELOPING SPEAKER CREDIBILITY

Take a personal inventory

Be well prepared

Toot your own horn

Take a Personal Inventory

In order to enhance your credibility, you have to believe that you have something to offer an audience. We have worked with speakers who believed that they didn't have special skills or unique experiences, but such beliefs are usually unfounded. Every person can do or has done something that sets her or him apart from everyone else. It's just a matter of discovering what that something is. Chapter 4, "Purpose and Topic," explored aspects of the personal inventory for use in determining those two aspects of your speech. Here we use it to help you identify the unique gifts and talents that contribute to your credibility.

NAACP President Kweisi Mfume walks toward the podium at Baltimore City Community College. His competence, character, and charisma led Baltimore citizens and leaders to appeal to him to run for mayor. With regrets, he declined the honor.

Be Well Prepared

An effective presentation has a clear purpose, is adapted to the audience and occasion, is well prepared and organized, and is skillfully delivered. Your success as a speaker also depends on the relationship between you and your audience, and a well-prepared presentation gets that relationship off on the right foot. Likewise, lack of preparation communicates many negative messages to an audience. It says that you don't care enough about the audience to be well prepared. You didn't do enough research or didn't take enough time to organize your content. You didn't rehearse what you had prepared. If you don't have time to prepare for your audience, why should they have time for you? Conversely, a thoroughly researched, well-organized, and confidently delivered presentation conveys your respect for your audience. A respected audience will respond in kind.

Toot Your Own Horn

A presentation lets you show an audience that your ideas and opinions are based on more than good preparation. They are based on your experience, your accomplishments, and your special skills and traits. There's nothing wrong with using words such as *I, my,* and *me* if they are appropriate. But remember this: You can use too many *I, my,* and *me* words. You could step over the line and be accused of boasting. For example, one of us once sat through an honors student awards ceremony in which faculty members presented a variety of awards to outstanding students. Two of the almost three dozen presentations annoyed the audience. They were delivered by faculty members who used the word *I* instead of focusing on the student who was being honored: "As chairman of the department and an expert in this field of study, *I* decided. . . ." "As outgoing president of the association, *I* was the first person to. . . . " By using the awards presentation to spotlight themselves, the speakers undermined their own credibility.

FiNDiNG OUt ABOUt YOURSELF

If you doubt that you have the right stuff to become a highly credible speaker, we urge you to take a personal inventory. Find the answers to these three questions: (1) What are my experiences? (2) What are my achievements? (3) What are my skills and traits?

What are my experiences? An experience that seems routine to you may be a new experience for your listeners. Answer the following questions to help yourself identify those special experiences that make you unique.

▶ Where have I lived or worked (in another town, city, state, country)?

▶ What kinds of jobs or duties have I had (unusual, technical, dangerous, satisfying, interesting, unique)?

▶ What special events have I attended (legendary concerts, historic sporting events, special holiday celebrations, famous political marches, renowned speeches)?

▶ What experiences have had a great impact on my life (meeting a famous person, childbirth, the illness or death of a friend or family member, involvement in a dangerous situation, physical disability, drug or alcohol abuse, a religious conversion, a visit to a foreign country, combat experience, learning from a great teacher)?

Something as simple as living or working in a different state can add a dimension to your personality. Many audiences enjoy hearing stories about places they've never been and the kinds of people they rarely meet. You can use personal experiences in examples, stories, definitions, and analogies. Personal information can add character and interest to you and to your presentation.

What are my achievements? You don't have to land on the moon to achieve something important. What seems like an everyday accomplishment to you may be an impressive achievement to your listeners. The following questions may help you to identify those achievements that make you unique.

▶ What can I do that most people cannot (play the cello, manage a swimming pool, reconstruct a computer, write a song or a short story, raise money for charities, decorate cakes, train a horse, design clothing, speak Turkish)?

▶ What awards or contests have I won (a scholarship, a prize in an art show, an award for public service, a sporting championship, a cooking contest, a TV or radio quiz, the lottery)?

▶ What are my special hobbies or interests (mountain climbing, collecting autographs, playing the stock market, doing crossword puzzles, studying Buddhism, following a musical group or singer)?

What are my skills and traits? Once you have answered questions about your experiences and achievements, you can begin to uncover dozens of your skills and traits. You may not recognize some of your special skills and personality traits because you have been using them for so long. Go back to the list of your experiences and achievements and think about the skills that you have used, as well as the personality traits that have surfaced. For example:

▶ If you have won a sporting event, what qualities helped you to succeed (hard work, discipline, leadership, good sportsmanship, ability to learn the rules, accepting a coach's harsh criticism, analyzing the opponent, working well with team members, being competitive)?

▶ If you have organized a trip to a concert with a group of friends, what did you have to do to make it happen (coordinate schedules; research concert dates, times, and ticket prices; order or wait in line to buy tickets; collect money for tickets while remaining cheerful, helpful, enthusiastic, polite, and patient)?

You have unique qualities that can help enhance your credibility as a speaker. Take the opportunity of giving a presentation to use and display your experiences, accomplishments, skills, and traits.

As the Tip on page 190 notes, having someone else introduce you is one way to bolster your credibility. However, you can use your own introduction—and your entire presentation—to enhance your credibility by presenting your credentials during the presentation and by demonstrating a thorough understanding of your topic.[8] If you're an expert, find a way to tell the audience: "In my thirty years of college teaching. . . ." "When I was honored by the Chamber of Commerce. . . ." In none of these cases would you be exaggerating or boasting. Rather, you would be explaining how and why you know what you're talking about.

Every person has unique skills, experiences, outlooks, and drives. A presentation that emerges from those unique qualities reflects well on the person who gives it and enhances that speaker's credibility.

Ethos and Ethics

A discussion about speaker credibility would not be complete without giving attention to the relationship between ethos and ethics. The words *ethos* and *ethics* are very similar. Both come from the Greek word meaning "character." And as we indicated in our discussion of character as a component of credibility, the apparent "goodness" of a speaker is very important in determining whether that speaker will be believed by an audience. **Ethos,** Aristotle's term for speaker credibility, and *ethics*, however, are not the same thing. What makes them different is their sources.

Remember that the audience determines a speaker's credibility (*ethos*). A speaker's *ethics*, on the other hand, are personal. They are the speaker's beliefs about what is right or wrong, moral or immoral, good or bad. **Ethics** are a set of personal principles of right conduct, a personal system of moral values.[9] Only you can determine how ethical you are.

In Appendix B, the National Communication Association's *Credo for Ethical Communication*, we provide a summary of personal belief statements about what it means to be an ethical communicator. Each of the principles in this credo should be applied to how you communicate—whether you're talking to one person or to an audience of one thousand listeners. For example, the ethics credo states, "We believe that truthfulness, accuracy, honesty, and reason are essential to the integrity of communication." If you want to be a credible speaker, it is your responsibility to be truthful, accurate, honest, and reasonable when you prepare and deliver a presentation.

A very ethical speaker, however, may have low ethos because the audience perceives the speaker as uninformed, aloof, or boring or because the audience has no advance knowledge of the speaker's good reputation. Likewise, a speaker may be highly credible with one audience and yet be judged unethical by other observers on other occasions. Richard Johannesen, who studies communication ethics, uses Adolf Hitler to illustrate this point. Today, we assess Hitler as an unethical person and an unethical communicator, yet many of his contemporary Germans seemed to grant him a very high ethos level.[10] Because audiences will hold you accountable for what you say, ethical communication is *your* obligation.

Roger Ailes, a television producer and political media adviser, wrote a book titled *You Are the Message: Secrets of the Master Communicators*. His title sums up a lot of the research on speaker credibility. As Ailes says:

> When you communicate . . . , it's not just the words you choose to send the other person that make up the message. You're also sending signals of what kind of person *you* are—by your eyes, your facial expression, your body move-

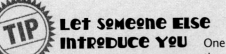

TIP **Let Someone Else Introduce You** One of the best ways to strengthen your credibility is to have someone introduce you to the audience. The introducer usually tells the audience something about the speaker's background, experiences, achievements, and skills—qualities and factors that demonstrate character, competence, and charisma. A good, well-delivered introduction can motivate an audience to listen to you. Like the first few moments of your own presentation, such an introduction can focus audience attention and interest, preview your topic area, establish an appropriate mood, and put *you* squarely into the presentation. In short, it can help you to achieve your purpose.

If the person who will be introducing you asks for information, don't be shy. Provide a list of your accomplishments. You can even write out what you would like the person to say, selecting those items most relevant to your purpose and audience. If you have the opportunity to craft one, a custom-made introduction can be an invaluable tool in creating an atmosphere that lets your character, competence, and charisma shine.

REAL WORLD, REAL SPEAKERS

Gary Reynolds, a manager for Amoco, told us about a successful presentation he made at a retirement dinner. Note how he enhanced his own credibility in front of an audience that knew him and his level of expertise very well. As he tells it, "I memorized a substantial [number] of facts and figures in an area that was widely known by the attendees and honoree but about which I had no knowledge. The area was of great interest to the honoree, and everyone else in the audience knew how ignorant I was about it. But because I spouted a myriad of facts and delivered my presentation without notes the honoree hugely appreciated the presentation, and my peers were humorously amazed."

Mr. Reynolds understood that his audience would be judging him and his message. He went to great lengths to ensure that he was respected for the effort that he had made (character), that he knew what he was talking about (competence), and that his delivery would help him to appear energetic and confident (charisma). Mr. Reynolds spent a great deal of time and effort creating an impressive and believable presentation.

ment, your vocal pitch, tone, volume, and intensity, your commitment to your message, your sense of humor, and many other factors. The [audience] is bombarded with symbols and signals from you. Everything you do in relation to other people causes them to make judgments about what you stand for and what your message is. . . . Unless you identify yourself as a walking, talking message, you miss that critical point.[11]

In other words, the total *you* affects every aspect of your presentation and how your audience feels about you and your message. Your success as a speaker is directly affected by your ethos and ethics. Your presence *does* make a difference.

Good Speeches by Good Speakers

We like to think of an ethical speaker as a good person who speaks well. Becoming a good speaker involves more than making decisions about your purpose, the audience, or your organizational pattern. A good speaker is also someone who is committed to being an ethical speaker and makes presentations that are true, fair, and beneficial to all.

A presentation can have significant and long-lasting effects on an audience. Like any tool, it can be applied with skill to achieve a useful purpose or it can be used to damage and destroy. Although a hammer can be used to build a home, it also can be used to punch holes in a wall. One unethical presentation can affect the way an audience sees you in all future encounters. Thus, we believe that a good speaker must ask and answer important ethical questions at every point in the speechmaking process. Ethical decision-making is more than a means of improving speaker credibility; it is a moral obligation of every good speaker.

ETHICAL DECISION-MAKING FOCUSES ON

Purpose

Audience

Logistics

Content

Organization

Performance

Ethical Decisions About Purpose

Who will benefit if you achieve your purpose—you, your audience, or you *and* your audience? If your public and private purposes conflict or undermine each other, you may be headed for an unethical decision. Unfortunately, audiences can be and are deceived by speakers who appear to be honest but whose private purposes are selfish and even harmful to their audiences. When Reverend Jim Bakker asked millions of TV viewers for contributions to support his religious work, he used their good-faith money to build a large personal financial empire. There was a conflict between his public and private purposes.

If your stated public purpose is to tell people to "join the Handy-Dandy Health Spa because it has the best equipment and trainers," but your private purpose is to get a fifty-dollar bonus for every member you recruit, you are standing on shaky ethical ground. If the spa does not have the best equipment and trainers, your need for fifty dollars should be weighed against your audience's right to know the truth. If you would be ashamed or embarrassed to reveal your private purpose to an audience, you should question the honesty and fairness of your public purpose. There's nothing wrong with having a private purpose such as wanting to get an A on your presentation or impressing the boss with your speechmaking success. On the other hand, there *is* something wrong when achieving your private purpose means deceiving your audience.

At a White House press conference on January 26, 1998, President Clinton said, "I did not have a sexual relationship with that woman, Ms. Lewinski. . . ." This famous statement contributed to the erosion of his credibility and ethical standing.

Ethical Decisions About the Audience

Are you being fair to your audience? Are you using the information that you have gathered about audience members to help or to harm them? The more you know about your listeners, the easier it is to tell them what they want to hear. However, telling an audience what they want to hear may not be the same as telling them what they *need* to hear. It may be difficult to convince audience members who want "no new taxes" that more money is needed for education and job training. Simultaneously promising "no new taxes" and a reduction of government waste to pay for education and public services can earn a politician votes but may not serve the public good.

Market researchers and political pollsters can tell their clients what an audience wants. A good speaker has the ethical responsibility to weigh what an audience wants to hear against what is truthful, fair, and beneficial. A good speaker also has the responsibility not to pander to audience wishes. You would rightly question the character of a politician who tells an audience of teachers and parents that education is her first priority and then tells a group of builders and bankers that tax breaks for developers come first. Changing your message as you move from group to group may demonstrate good audience analysis and adaptation, but it is unethical if the messages conflict with one another.

Ethical Decisions About Logistics

At first, where and when you speak may seem to have nothing to do with ethical decision-making. But just as decisions about your purpose and your audience can be used to manipulate or even to trick listeners, decisions about logistics can also be used unethically.

Time limits can be used as an excuse to withhold important information: "If time allowed, I could explain this in more detail, but trust me. . . ." An ethical speaker might say, "Because I have limited time, I've prepared a handout of well-respected sources that support my position. . . ." Uncomfortable physical conditions can also be used as an excuse for quick and uncritical decisions: "We've tried to get the air conditioner working, but since we can't, let's cut off debate and vote so we can get out of here." An ethical speaker might say, "I know it's hot, but considering how important this issue is, let's keep talking to ensure that we make a responsible decision." Good speakers should consider how their decisions about logistics and occasion may affect their messages and the audience's beliefs about their credibility.

Ethical Decisions About Content

You face many ethical choices as you research, select, and use supporting material in your presentation. As described in Chapter 7, the ethical speaker is responsible for ensuring the validity of all ideas and information used in a presentation. You must identify and qualify your sources. You should know whether the information is recent, complete, consistent, and relevant. You should be sure that statistics are valid. And you must not plagiarize. Ethical speakers never, ever represent someone else's words or ideas as their own.

SHOULD I IMITATE A SPEAKER WHOM I ADMIRE? There's nothing wrong with using a good speaker as a model. But don't get carried away. Don't try to mimic your idol. Only James Earl Jones can or should sound like James Earl Jones. Don't be too attached to beliefs you may have about what a "good" speaker looks and sounds like. It's much easier and more comfortable to let the real *you* come through. Say what you have to say, and trust your instincts.

Peggy Noonan, who was President Reagan's speechwriter, goes even further when she offers this advice: "Don't imitate the high oratory of past presidents and generals. Say it the way you'd say it if you were speaking, with concentration and respect, to a friend. Your own style will emerge with time as you write and speak. . . . And while it is good to be inspired by these speeches [by famous leaders], . . . it is not good to be daunted by them, to think, 'This isn't as good as Kennedy's inaugural [so] I might as well throw in the towel.'"[1]

What matters is that you sound like yourself, not like some famous actor, past president, or orator. Being an ethical speaker means being true to who you are and how you normally communicate.

1. Peggy Noonan, *Simply Speaking: How to Communicate Your Ideas with Style, Substance, and Clarity* (New York: HarperCollins, 1998), pp. 205 and 47. Copyright © 1998 by Peggy Noonan. Reprinted by permission of HarperCollins Publishers, Inc.

REAL WORLD, REAL SPEAKERS

By delivering his "I Have a Dream" speech in front of the Lincoln Memorial, Martin Luther King, Jr. linked himself and his message to the president who signed the Emancipation Proclamation. By campaigning at a company that manufactures American flags in 1988, presidential candidate George Bush, Sr. linked himself and his candidacy to the symbols connected with the flag—patriotism and American values. When President Clinton criticized powerful drug companies for pursuing "profits at the expense of our children," he did so during a visit to a local health clinic where children got free immunization shots. How did these speakers use the place and the occasion at which they were speaking to help them achieve their purposes? To what extent did these speakers succeed in enhancing their credibility and effectiveness by choosing where they were speaking? What did their decisions reveal about their character?

Ethical speakers learn as much as they can about their topics. They recognize that most controversial issues have good people and good arguments on both sides. Ethical speakers also demonstrate respect for those who disagree with them. By making ethical decisions about content, you ensure that your presentation will be forthright and fair.

Ethical Decisions About Organization

As Chapter 8, "Organization," and Chapter 9, "Organizational Tools," explain, good organization requires answering two basic questions: What should I include? and How should I organize my content? These may not seem like ethical issues, but deciding to leave out information can be as unethical and unfair as including false information. Should you add valid information that does not support your purpose? Should you include opponents' arguments that could damage your case? Should you present only one side of an argument when the other side is reasonable and well supported? Should you use emotional examples to cover up your lack of valid statistics? Unfortunately, there are no simple answers to these questions. As you will see in Chaper 18, "Understanding Persuasion," and in Chapter 19, "Developing Persuasive Presentations," acknowledging the other side of an argument can enhance your credibility by demonstrating your awareness of other points of view. Emotional examples can be powerful forms of supporting material as long as they complement other types of valid supporting material.

Deciding what to include and what to leave out of your presentation directly affects your credibility. While determining how to organize a presentation, an ethical speaker tries to be truthful and fair when deciding what to include and how to organize that material.

Ethical Decisions About Performance

Although the chapters on performance and delivery are yet to come, it's not too early to say a few words about ethical performance. The good speaker uses his or her performance to communicate, not to distract the audience from the truth. A highly emotional performance can be more convincing than sharing the most up-to-date and valid statistical information. If the emotions are real, they are appropriate. However, when an emotional response is inappropriate, it's unethical to fake emotions or to incite them in your audience.

Even a speaker's appearance can deceive an audience. A speaker could dress in poor-quality, threadbare clothing as part of a plea for money. A speaker can fake weakness or illness to gain sympathy. A phony accent can make a speaker appear to be a very different person. A good speaker uses an honest communication style and avoids acting out a false role.

The Good Audience

Throughout this chapter, we have emphasized the importance of being an ethical speaker. We've also seen how your success as an ethical speaker depends on the relationship between you and your audience. After all, it's the audience that either does or does not regard you as competent, charismatic, and of good character.

The ethical speaker has the responsibility of being honest, fair, and concerned about the audience, but audiences have important ethical responsibilities, too. Good audiences are good listeners. They listen for ideas and information with open minds. They withhold evaluation until they are sure that they understand what a speaker is saying. Good audiences are active listeners—they listen to understand, to empathize, to analyze, and to appreciate. They think critically about a speaker's message. However, not all audience members are "good" at these skills. Many don't or won't listen because they have decided, even before the presentation begins, that they don't like the message or the speaker. In Chapter 18, a major section is devoted to adapting to an audience that is unwilling to listen or hostile to your ideas.

Your audience is more likely to appreciate and listen to you if they think you have character, competence, and charisma. Although competence and charisma are important characteristics of a good (effective) speaker, character determines whether you are seen as a good (ethical) speaker. The audience has the final say, though, and also has an ethical responsibility to do unto the speaker as they would have the speaker do unto them. An open-minded, unprejudiced audience is essential in order for a genuine transaction to occur between speakers and listeners.

Summary

What factors determine whether the audience will perceive me as a good speaker?

The most important factors affecting the believability of a speaker are character, competence, and charisma.

How can I enhance my credibility as a speaker?

Three ways in which you can enhance your credibility are to take a personal inventory of your experiences, achievements, skills, and traits; to be well prepared; and to "toot your own horn."

How does my character influence the success of a presentation?

Speaker credibility (ethos) can be the most important factor in determining whether you achieve the purpose of your presentation.

(continued)

Summary (continued)

◆✦ **How can I ensure that I am treating my audience fairly and ethically?**

Good speakers make ethical decisions about all aspects of a presentation, including its purpose, audience, logistics, content, organization, and performance.

◆✦ **What can audience members do to ensure that they are treating a speaker fairly and ethically?**

Audience members should use effective listening and critical thinking skills when evaluating a speaker and his or her message.

Key Terms

character 183	competence 184	ethos 190
charisma 185	ethics 190	speaker credibility 183

Notes

1. Lane Cooper, *The Rhetoric of Aristotle* (New York: Appleton-Century-Crofts, 1932), pp. 8–9.
2. Dan O'Hair, Gustav W. Friedrich, and Linda Dixon Shaver, *Strategic Communication in Business and the Professions,* 3rd ed. (Boston: Houghton Mifflin, 1998), p. 498.
3. *The American Heritage Dictionary of the English Language,* 3rd ed. (Boston: Houghton Mifflin, 1992), p. 438. Copyright © 1996 by Houghton Mifflin Company. Reproduced by permission from *The American Heritage Dictionary of the English Language, Third Edition.*
4. Malcolm Kushner, *Successful Presentations for Dummies* (Foster City, CA: IDG Books Worldwide, 1997), p. 21.
5. The earliest and most respected source describing the components of a speaker's credibility is Aristotle's *Rhetoric.* As translated by Lane Cooper (New York: Appleton-Century-Crofts, 1932, p. 92), Aristotle identified "intelligence, character, and good will" as "three things that gain our belief." Aristotle's observations have been verified and expanded. In addition to those qualities identified by Aristotle, researchers have added variables such as objectivity, trustworthiness, coorientation, dynamism, composure, likability, and extroversion. Research has consolidated these qualities into three well-accepted attributes: competence, character, and dynamism. We have used the term *charisma* in place of *dynamism.*
6. O'Hair et al., p. 498.
7. Kushner, p. 21.
8. Jo Sprague and Douglas Stuart, *The Speaker's Handbook,* 4th ed. (Fort Worth; Harcourt Brace, 1996), p. 259.
9. *The American Heritage Dictionary,* p. 630. Copyright © 1996 by Houghton Mifflin Company. Reproduced by permission from *The American Heritage Dictionary of the English Language, Third Edition.*
10. Richard L. Johannesen, *Ethics in Human Communication,* 2nd ed. (Prospect Heights, IL: Waveland, 1983), p. 109. Also see Richard L. Johannesen, *Ethics in Human Communication,* 4th ed. (Prospect Heights, IL: Waveland, 1996), pp. 10–11.
11. Roger Ailes with Jon Kraushnar, *You Are the Message: Secrets of the Master Communicators* (Homewood, IL: Dow Jones-Irwin, 1988), p. 20.

Generating Interest

- Why do audiences lose interest?
- What language tools can help me engage my listeners?
- Why are stories so interesting?
- How do I integrate humor into my presentation?
- How can I directly involve my audience?

"How can I be more interesting when I speak?" It's understandable that many speakers ask this question. For one thing, novice speakers often *assume* they're not interesting; they can't imagine why an audience would want to listen to them talk about their topic. For another, they may have heard lots of boring presentations and may fear that theirs are doomed to the same fate. Rarely is either assumption true. There is no reason why a well-prepared, audience-focused speaker should be dull or boring.

Although everything in this textbook is designed to help you make your presentations interesting and memorable, we also know that giving special attention to this issue can improve your chances of preparing and delivering a more successful presentation. In this chapter, we revisit some of the key principles and techniques with one thing in mind: using them to gain audience attention and interest. This chapter also provides a bridge between the basic principles and the application of those principles to specific types of presentations. Whether you are presenting an informative briefing, advocating a persuasive position, or toasting a newlywed couple, there are many ways to make your presentation more interesting, more impressive, and more memorable.

A well-planned and well-rehearsed presentation that adapts to audience interests and needs is your best guarantee of success. If you have determined an appropriate purpose, collected relevant supporting material, carefully organized your content, crafted a compelling introduction and conclusion, and practiced your delivery, you should have nothing to worry about. There is, however, no harm in taking extra steps to enhance audience interest. Spending time thinking about additional ways to interest and motivate your audience can transform an interesting presentation into a captivating one, changing a presentation that enhances your credibility into one that also puts you in a superstar category.

Overcoming Boredom Factors

Effective speakers understand that audience analysis and adaptation are the keys to generating attention and interest in a presentation. While speaking, they can sense the audience's interest level and realize that any lack of interest means the audience won't remember or care about them or their messages. Some speakers get discouraged or flustered by negative feedback. However, immediate feedback is a unique opportunity that only speakers get. A writer cannot tell if a reader is bored, and what's more, a speaker can immediately adapt to feedback, while an author cannot.

Sometimes an audience's "I'm bored" feedback has little to do with you and your message. At other times, it's justified. To deliver an engaging presentation or to know when to modify a less-than-engaging one requires that you understand why audiences lose interest.

At the risk of simplifying a complex phenomenon, let's begin by acknowledging that bored audiences are often victims of two bad habits: short attention spans and poor listening skills. Two other bad habits can be attributed to the presenters: speaking too long and delivering poorly. Learning to compensate for these habits is the first step in ensuring an interesting presentation.

> **BOREDOM FACTORS**
> - Limited attention span
> - Poor listening habits
> - Length of presentation
> - Poor delivery

Limited Attention Span

Even the most interesting speaker and topic cannot command 100 percent of an audience's attention 100 percent of the time. Life isn't like that. Audience members drift in and out of presentations, paying more attention to some sections than to others. They may be diverted for as little as half a second to as long as several minutes while thinking about personal problems, their upcoming day, lunch, or something else. **Attention span,** the amount of time an audience member can be attentive to sensory stimulation, differs for each of us according to age, intelligence, health, past experience, and motivation.[1] How long do you think the average adult can sustain undivided attention? Fifteen minutes? No. Try fifteen seconds![2]

Effective speakers understand and adjust to an audience's attention span. You can do this as soon as you start to determine your purpose by linking it to attention-getting devices. This lets you shape your audience's attention.[3] For example, when giving factual or instructional material, plan to ease into your topic and to capture your audience's attention in the middle of your presentation with strong content. Then ease out with a review or summary. The best motivational speakers start out slowly but keep building and building to give an audience the most electrifying and memorable material at the end, thus leaving their listeners energized. If you're invited to make the opening address at a conference, plan to gain audience attention and interest right from the beginning. Your job is to set the mood and pace. Then, once you have their attention, you can gradually relax toward the end of your presentation. Your purpose can help you to determine the best way to generate and hold audience interest.

Poor Listening Habits

As noted in Chapter 2, "Critical Thinking and Listening," most audience members (and speakers) are not very good listeners. Therefore, it should not surprise you that an audience's listening ability is linked to its interest level. If an audience does not comprehend what you are saying, they may lose interest. If an audience does not appreciate what you are saying, they may tune out. If an audience is not analytical or empathic when they listen, your best arguments and stories will have little or no impact.

However, you can counteract the effects of poor listening. One way is to give your audience more than one opportunity to listen to your ideas. That doesn't mean simply repeating them. Rather, look for more than one way to make and support your key points. For example, in addition to citing a statistic, give an example or tell a relevant story. Try engaging more of the audience's senses. Use a presentation aid or provide a handout to visually reinforce your spoken message.

You can also use organizational strategies to drive your ideas home. A good introduction can provide both a statement of your central idea and a preview of the key points in your presentation. As you move from key point to key point, use connectives to reinforce your message. Another technique is to use internal previews and summaries to give the audience an additional opportunity to listen to each key point.

You can also help listeners by using a repetitive phrase to emphasize a point. For example, you may have heard politicians, members of the clergy, and motivational speakers repeat a word or phrase for this purpose. One of us heard a county executive do this to dispel an audience's negative perception of the police:

> Our crime rate? It's down. Car thefts? Down. Break-ins? Down. Assaults? Down. Rape and homicide? Down. And the number of complaints about police brutality? Down!

Most speakers can learn to adjust to an audience's attention span and listening habits. Some also need to break their own speaker-based habits that can cause boredom: making overly long presentations and using lackluster delivery.

IS IT TELEVISION'S FAULT? Some writers and researchers blame television for our short attention spans. Fifteen- and thirty-second commercials tell entire stories. Rarely does a television show go for more than fifteen minutes without a break. TV has taught our brains to disengage and think about something else. Consider the nightly TV news. How much time do most network news shows devote to a major story—a natural disaster, an economic crisis, a presidential scandal? Ten minutes? Five minutes? Guess again. News stories seldom get more than three minutes of air time. The entire day, around the world, is covered in about twenty minutes.[1]

Not only does television accommodate our short attention spans; programming is also designed to capture our attention with exciting videos and sound tracks. No speaker can compete with the technical whiz-bang of television. After all, what's the most boring thing on television? Talking heads. But no TV can do what live speakers do: engage and respond *personally* to their audiences.

1. Ron Hoff, *I Can See You Naked* (Kansas City, MO: Andrews and McMeel, 1992), pp. 75–76.

NOTE YOUR TIME AND VICE VERSA

Recently one of us helped a colleague adjust some testimony he was preparing for a legislative hearing. He was told he had five to seven minutes to testify. What he wrote filled four single-spaced pages. Using an unrelenting red pen, we cut more than half of the copy. But he still ran overtime.

How do you calculate, during the preparation process, how long a presentation will be? Depending on the complexity of the material, the mood of the message, and your natural speaking rate, five double-spaced pages of manuscript can equal anywhere from seven to ten minutes of speaking time. Keep in mind that it's more difficult to gauge speaking time when using notes. The key is to repeatedly practice out loud what you want to say, while your presentation is still in the early stages of development. Time yourself and indicate the results right on your notes. Use a stopwatch to gauge the length of each section; you may discover that some sections go on for too long while others are brief and clear. Soon you'll be quite comfortable estimating how long it will take to deliver a presentation using notes.

Length of Presentation

One reason why audience members dread presentations is that many of them just go on for too long. Peggy Noonan tackled the time issue as a presidential speechwriter. In the very beginning of her book, *Simply Speaking,* she puts this statement *first* on her list of preliminaries: "No speech should last more than twenty minutes."[4] She tells of learning that from President Ronald Reagan:

> [Reagan] knew that twenty minutes is more than enough time to say the biggest, most important thing in the world. The Gettysburg Address went three minutes or so, the Sermon on the Mount hardly more. . . . So keep in mind what [Senator] Hubert Humphrey's wife is said to have advised him: "Darling, for a speech to be immortal it need not be interminable."[5]

If you realize that your presentation will run long, how do you shorten it? Alan M. Perlman,[6] a professional speechwriter at Kraft Foods, recommends answering three questions:

▶ Will the audience be able to reach this conclusion without my help? If the answer is *yes,* don't overburden an audience with unnecessary explanations, stories, or visuals.

▶ Is the audience already inclined to believe this? Don't spend a lot of time on a point if the audience already shares your opinion or belief.

▶ Does the audience really need to know this? If the answer is *no,* delete or shorten any statement, idea, or piece of supporting material that isn't directly relevant to your purpose.

Although it can be hard to distance yourself from your material, you should realize that it's not all equally important. Learning to assess your material honestly in light of the three previous questions makes controlling your presentation's length relatively easy.[7]

Poor Delivery

As emphasized in Part V, "Performance," poor delivery can undermine even the best-prepared presentation. One performance component has a particularly strong impact on audience interest levels: expressiveness. We define **expressiveness** as the vitality, variety, and sincerity that a speaker puts into his or her delivery. It is more than enthusiasm or energy. It is an extension of the speaker's personality and attitude.[8] If you feel good about yourself, are excited about your message, and are truly interested in sharing your ideas with an audience, you are well on your way to being expressive. Speakers who care about their topics and their audiences are usually much more expressive than presenters who are struggling through presentations they don't want to give. Also, the more expressive you are, the more likely you will be seen as a highly credible, charismatic speaker.

You *can* become more expressive, although you may find it difficult to do so if you are very self-conscious about showing your emotions. If, on the other hand, you are comfortable injecting yourself and your feelings into your presentations, you will be rewarded with a more attentive and interested audience. Like so many other aspects of the presentation speaking process, becoming expressive requires you to know your material and to know yourself. And, of course, it requires practice.

Language

Well-chosen words lie at the heart of electrifying, memorable presentations. The right words teach, persuade, inspire, and delight audiences. How you use words can determine your ultimate success as a speaker. As Mark Twain, the great American humorist, observed, "The difference between the almost right word and the right word is really a large matter—'tis the difference between the lightning bug and the lightning."[9] Language can make the difference between a presentation that gets polite applause and one that gets people standing up and cheering. The best words can give a presentation a unique flavor, emotional excitement, and brilliant clarity.

> **BUILD YOUR LANGUAGE POWER**
>
> **Use an oral style**
> **Use active language**
> **Match your words to your listeners**
> **Use personal pronouns**
> **Spice up your speech**

Use an Oral Style

You must be comfortable saying the words and sentences you select for your presentation. There is a big difference in how we choose words for written documents and how we choose words for spoken presentations. Our advice: Say what you mean by speaking the way that you talk, not the way that you write.

Oral and written styles differ tremendously. Oral style uses shorter sentences, shorter words, more personal pronouns (such as *I, we, you, me,* and *they*), and more contractions (such as *don't, I'll,* and *she's*). Oral style is also less formal than written style and can even include incomplete sentences and colloquial expressions. For example, business letters sometimes begin with "Enclosed please find the document you requested" or end with "Thank you in advance for your assistance in this matter." Does anyone talk that way? Of course not. In person, you would say, "Here's the report you wanted" or "Thanks for helping me."

Say what you mean by forgetting about what you *think* is expected—formal language—and remembering what you *want* to achieve—memorability. Instead of looking for a big word, find one that says what you mean. Peggy Noonan reminds us why simple language works best: "Remember that speeches are words in the air. Your audience doesn't have a printed copy to which to refer to clear up any questions. All they have is you, speaking, up there, into a mike."[10] Two basic techniques will help you to say what you mean: using simple words and using short sentences.

Use Simple Words. Use the kinds of words that you would use in everyday talk. When practicing your presentation, question any complex words or phrases. Ask yourself, "Is this really what I want to say? Is this really what I mean?" Choosing short and simple words keeps your style plain and direct. "I didn't like it" may be better than "I was displeased." Clarity always beats formality, as the phrases in Figure 12.1 on page 202 show.

Use Short Sentences. Short sentences have more impact than long ones. Appendix A includes an informative presentation on using CliffsNotes by a former

Yes	No
I need help.	I require assistance.
I tried to find her.	I attempted to locate her.
This is a bad idea.	This idea represents an infeasible course of action.
He came back.	He returned to his point of departure.

student, John Sullivan. Note how John begins his presentation with a series of short sentences:

> Eight o'clock Wednesday night. I have an English exam bright and early tomorrow morning. It's on Homer's *Iliad*. And I haven't read page one. I forego tonight's beer drinking and try to read. Eight forty-five. I'm only on page 12. Only 482 more to go. Nine thirty, it hits me. Like a rock. I'm not going to make it.

Although short and grammatically incomplete, this series of sentences gives a vivid picture of an unprepared and somewhat desperate student who is facing a major exam.

Use Active Language

Strong, active verbs keep your presentation moving. Avoid passive verbs that take the focus away from the subject of your sentence. "The *Iliad* was read by the student" is passive. "The student read the *Iliad*" is active. Because active verbs require fewer words, they help to keep your sentences short. Tell us who did what, not what was done by whom.

Active verbs are vigorous verbs. They are much stronger expressions of meaning than their weaker counterparts—forms of the verb *to be* or verbs in the passive voice.[11] Let verbs do the work for you. Less confident speakers often have trouble using active phrasing because they worry about sounding too direct. Look at the differences in these sentences:

Active Verb: Sign my petition.

Passive Verb: The petition should be signed by you.

The more passive the sentence, the less powerful the message. Forms of the verb *to be* (*is, am, are, was, were, been, being*) lack action. With passive verbs, the subject is the recipient of the action. With active verbs, the subject *performs* the action.

Match Your Words to Your Listeners

If your audience can't understand your words, you won't achieve your purpose. The more you know about your audience

 How can I Plan Words Without a Manuscript? When we emphasize the importance of using an oral language style, we often are greeted with this challenge: "Unless I write out my presentation and read it, I can't choose my words in advance." We agree. You can, however, make sure that you phrase your key points carefully and that you choose supporting materials, such as testimony and examples, that both inform and inspire. You can also write out and even memorize your introduction and conclusion to make sure that you get the most out of every word. You can practice stories that you intend to tell, until the words become second nature to you. You can even identify and practice the key phrases that you will repeat throughout your presentation.

members' characteristics and learning styles (see Chapter 5, "Audience Analysis and Adaptation"), the better you can choose the most appropriate language for their needs. If you start praising the virtues of "boarding" to an audience of senior citizens, they may think you're talking about living arrangements, not a snow sport. Take your audience into account as you select key words for your presentation.

In 1989, Dr. Henry Louis Gates Jr., an African American scholar, delivered a speech at *The New York Times* President's Forum on Literacy.[12] What assumptions did Dr. Gates make about his audience by including the following quotation?

> In the resonant words of W. E. B. DuBois: "I sit with Shakespeare, and he winces not. Across the color line, I move arm in arm with Balzac and Dumas, where smiling men and welcoming women glide in gilded halls. . . . I summon Aristotle and Aurelius and what soul I will, and they come all graciously with no scorn or condescension."

Dr. Gates assumed that his audience was college educated and had read or would recognize the quotation from W. E. B. DuBois's 1903 book, *The Souls of Black Folk*. He also assumed that they understood DuBois's references to Shakespeare, Balzac, Dumas, Aristotle, and Aurelius. These assumptions were fine for his audience, but had he later been addressing a group of sixth-graders or recent Asian immigrants, many audience members would not have understood him:

At the beginning of the same presentation, Dr. Gates used a simpler style that made other assumptions about his audience:

> I grew up in a little town on the eastern panhandle of West Virginia, called Piedmont, population two thousand, supposedly (we could never find the other one thousand people). I started school in 1957, two years after the *Brown v. Board* decision, and in that year, 1957, my father bought a full set of the *World Book* encyclopedia.

Even though his words are less complex and the story more folksy, Dr. Gates assumed his audience knew the importance of the Supreme Court's *Brown v. Board of Education* decision. Dr. Gates's mixing of styles—simpler at the start of his speech, more elaborate in the middle—demonstrates another fact about audiences: Variety keeps them interested.

Use Personal Pronouns

Personal pronouns put *you* in your presentation and help you establish a connection with your audience. Using the pronouns *you* and *your* frequently—and focusing your attention on people in different parts of the room as you do so—make each audience member feel singled out. A personal message is always more interesting than one for the masses.

"Ask not what your country can do for you. Ask what you can do for your country." If John F. Kennedy had instead said, "People should not ask what their country can do for them. People should ask what they can do for their country," do you think people would still remember his words? The second version does not have the impact of the first. *You* and *your* speak directly to an audience. Because the word *you* can be singular or plural, it allows you to speak to an entire audience as well as to each individual. It's personal. It asks you for your attention.

Make sure to put *you* in your presentation by using self-referential pronouns such as *I, me,* and *my.* By taking responsibility for your message, you establish

TIP

REDUCE REDUN-DANT REPETITIONS

Be cautious with repetition and alliteration. These techniques lose their power if they're used excessively or haphazardly. Dr. Ronald Carpenter, a professor of English and communication studies, has cautioned: "Do not squander repetition on unworthy words!"[1] Here's an example of such overindulgence in these two sentences from President George Bush's acceptance speech at the Republican National Convention in 1992: "[Congress] is a body caught in a hopelessly tangled web of PACs, perks, privileges, partisanship, and paralysis. Every day, Congress puts politics ahead of principles and above programs." Rather than adding impact and motivation, the sentences sound a bit silly and are difficult to pronounce with dignity and style.

1. Ronald H. Carpenter, *Choosing Powerful Words* (Boston: Allyn & Bacon, 1999), p. 117

your credibility (see Chapter 11, "Speaker Credibility and Ethics"). Telling a story about the time you saved a choking victim's life will interest audiences more than describing how other people have used the Heimlich maneuver to dislodge objects from choking people's windpipes. First-person accounts engage audiences. Using pronouns such as *we, us,* and *ours* intensifies the connection by highlighting the links between you and your audience. "We shall overcome" has significantly more power than "You shall overcome" or "I shall overcome." Personal pronouns bring your topic closer to you and to your audience.

Spice Up Your Speech

Poets, playwrights, and politicians have long understood the power of repetition (words and sounds) and resemblances (similes, metaphors, and analogies) to make their words memorable. You can use these tools, too.

Repetition of Words. As we saw earlier in this chapter, repetition helps listeners stay attentive. It's also a great way to spice up a presentation. You can repeat a word, a phrase, a clause, or an entire sentence. Dr. Martin Luther King Jr. used the clause "I have a dream" nine times in his famous 1963 speech in Washington, D.C. He used "let freedom ring" ten times.

In 1996, Vice President Al Gore addressed the Democratic National Convention on the eve of Bill Clinton's renomination. Gore ended seven paragraphs with the clause "But we won't let them." For example, he said that the Republicans "want someone in that Oval Office who will rubber-stamp their plan. That's why they want to replace Bill Clinton. But we won't let them."[13] By the time Gore reached his third example, the audience was energized and eager to roar back, "But we won't let them!"

Dr. Martin Luther King, Jr. repeated the phrases "I have a dream" and "Let freedom ring" multiple times during his eloquent, powerful March on Washington speech, August 28, 1963.

You can also repeat words or short phrases within a single sentence. In President Abraham Lincoln's Gettysburg Address, the words *the people* are used three times in the famous concluding line: "and that government of the people, by the people, for the people, shall not perish from the earth."[14]

Repetition can drive home important ideas to the audience. Psychologists contend that repetition can help to evoke action.[15] Audience members will anticipate repeated phrases during a presentation and will remember them long afterwards. Also note that repetition within a single sentence often sounds better when used in groupings of three, as in Lincoln's conclusion about "the people."

Repetition of Sounds. Another type of repetition is of sounds rather than of words. **Alliteration** refers to beginning successive words (or words placed closely together) with the same sound. At the opening of Julie Borchard's presentation on Muzak (see Appendix A), she refers to Muzak as the sound of "*v*acant *v*olumes of *v*apid *v*iolins." The first part of Lincoln's Gettysburg Address—"*F*our score and seven years ago our *fa*thers brought *f*orth"[16]—includes three words beginning with the letter *f*. President Clinton used the same repetitive sound in his 1992 acceptance speech at the Democratic National Convention, in which he celebrated "*f*amily and *f*riends and a *f*aith that in America no one is left out."[17]

Resemblances. Similes, metaphors, and analogies are figures of speech that highlight resemblances. They compare two things that are usually quite different in most ways but have at least one quality in common. A **simile** makes a direct comparison between two things or ideas, usually by using the words *like* or *as*. **Metaphors** make comparisons between two things or ideas without directly connecting the resemblances with words such as *like* or *as*. When used creatively, both figures of speech can spice up a presentation by highlighting interesting and even eloquent resemblances.

Analogies (discussed in Chapter 7, "Supporting Material") can compare similar things or contrast dissimilar things. Analogies are, basically, extended metaphors or similes. For example, the analogy "If a copilot must be qualified to pilot the plane, a U.S. vice president should be qualified to govern the country" can be expressed as a simile: "The U.S. vice president is like a copilot." It could also work as a metaphor: "The U.S. vice president is our country's copilot." At the 1989 Congress of the Arts in California, Chilean novelist Isabel Allende used metaphors and similes to describe the arts: "Art is a rebellious child, a wild animal that will not be tamed. Like dreams, it obeys only its own rules."[18]

Metaphors and similes help to make an idea clear and dramatic. Many have become well-known phrases in our language. Muhammad Ali talked about his ability to "Float like a butterfly, sting like a bee." Poet Langston Hughes wrote: "What happens to a dream deferred? Does it dry up like a raisin in the sun? . . . Or does it explode?" Winston Churchill, Great Britain's wartime prime minister, coined a now common phrase when he said, "An iron curtain has descended across the continent of Europe."

USE LANGUAGE ETHICALLY Although words have the power to make a presentation more memorable, they also have the power to hurt, deceive, and belittle. The National Communication Association's Credo for Ethical Communication addresses the destructive power of communication (see Appendix B). It states, "We condemn communication that degrades individuals and humanity through distortion, intolerance, intimidation, coercion, hatred, and violence." These are strong words about the words that we use to communicate.

Inappropriate word choices can stereotype people on the basis of race, ethnicity, gender, age, religion, and background. For example, one of us attended a scholarship awards ceremony at which the president of a business organization's education foundation referred to the scholarship recipients as "underprivileged children." One look at his audience would have told him that the average scholarship recipient was a thirty-something adult who had his or her own children to support. The word *children* sent a chill through the audience that cooled their previously appreciative response to the speaker.

Language can be sexist and racist. Language can insult and offend audience members. In Chapter 5, "Audience Analysis and Adaptation," we described the dangers of stereotyping audience members. We also cautioned speakers to avoid all racial slang terms as well as gender, racial, and ethnic jokes. We have witnessed well-meaning speakers losing credibility and respect by using a word or phrase that insulted audience members' backgrounds and beliefs.

Telling Stories

Most of us are good storytellers in conversations. We can easily recount something that has happened to us or something that we have witnessed. Crafting and telling a story for a presentation, however, is not the same as describing the day's events. It requires giving attention to several features of a good story. Unlike the everyday stories we tell and hear, a story for a presentation must be carefully selected and well told. It should conform to the following storytelling guidelines.[1]

▶ *Simple Story Line.* First and foremost, use a simple story line. Long stories with complex themes and multiple events are difficult to follow and just as difficult to tell. Can you summarize your story in fewer than twenty-five words? If not, don't use it—it's too complex.[2] All good stories—no matter how short or how simple—share the same key elements: (1) an initial buildup that includes background information and character development; (2) action or conflict; (3) a high point of the story during which a discovery, decision, or outcome occurs; (4) a punch line in which a sentence or phrase communicates the climax of the story; (5) an ending or resolution of the story.[3] The punch line is perhaps the most

critical aspect since it pulls the other four elements together. You can determine which sentence or phrase is a punch line by leaving it out and seeing what the omission does to your story. Without the punch line, the story won't make any sense.[4]

▶ *Limited Characters.* Unless you are an accomplished actor or storyteller, limit the number of characters in your story. Good storytellers distinguish their characters by giving them unique voices—varying volume, rate, pitch, and tone. Doing this can be tough for the novice speaker. If your story has more than three or four characters, look for another story or drop the extra people. It can be difficult for both you and your audience to keep track of a lot of characters. As noted earlier, your story's characters must be consistent in the ways in which they behave and speak.[5] If they aren't, your listeners will lose trust in them and also lose trust in the story.

▶ *Exaggeration.* Exaggerate both content and delivery. Whether you are describing the whale of a fish that got away or the disaster that befell you on a vacation, the story will be more effective if you stretch reality. Exaggeration both makes a story vivid and helps you to highlight its message. The

The Power of Stories

All humans have responded to stories, whether depicted in prehistoric cave paintings, written in novels, or told to children.[19] Stories have the power to captivate and educate. Audiences remember stories because they create lasting images. Joanna Slan, author of *Using Stories and Humor,*[20] claims that the ability to tell stories separates great presenters from mediocre ones. Time after time, she contends, speakers who are invited to reappear before the same audience will be asked, "Are you going to tell us the story about . . . ?" In some cases, presenters are hired because a client wants the audience to hear a certain story that the speaker loves to tell.

Even corporations are learning the value of storytelling. *The New York Times* reported a rise in "executive storytelling" seminars, some of which can cost $3,000 to $4,000 for a personal two-and-a-half-hour session with a business executive. CEOs and corporate officers are mastering personal storytelling "as a way of enlivening speeches, sales pitches, training sessions, and other presentations on otherwise dry or technical topics."[21]

Stories also benefit speakers. If you're anxious, they can help to reduce your nervousness. Most of us find it relatively easy to tell stories, a situation which makes them less challenging to deliver. Most of us also find stories easy to remember, particularly when they relate events that we have experienced personally.

tone of your voice, the sweep of your gestures, and your facial expression add another layer of meaning and emphasis to your story. Think about the way in which you exaggerate your delivery when reading a story to a child. Use a similar kind of bigger-than-life performance for most stories. However, stay away from exaggeration when the story is very simple or very sad. Such stories should be told with simple dignity.

▶ *Audience Links.* Good stories provide a link to the audience. Stories don't work if the audience can't connect with the setting, characters, or topic. Even the most basic children's story about a barnyard full of animals can give us characters who share human feelings and experiences. If the audience can imagine themselves in a situation similar to that of a character in a story, they are much more likely to listen. Also, make sure that your story is appropriate for your audience. Be sensitive to what you have learned from your audience analysis. Don't tell stories that show insensitivity to audience members' ages, gender, race, religion, ethnic background, or income level. An insensitive, inappropriate story will sever your connection to the audience in an instant and will undermine your credibility.

▶ *Practice.* Don't wait until you are standing at a lectern to see if your story works. Most stories get better after you've told them a few times. Practice telling your story to someone else—a friend, neighbor, colleague, or family member. Practice until you can tell the story without notes. Both of us have a repertoire of stories that we tell in our classes year after year. We know how to time each part of the story and how to exaggerate a point or a character's voice. We even know exactly how long to pause before or after the punch line of a story. Our storytelling skills come from lots of practice.

Finally, know when not to tell a story. If the story won't help you achieve the purpose of a presentation, leave it out.

1. William Hendricks et al., *Secrets of Power Presentations* (Franklin Lakes, NJ: Career Press, 1996).
2. Hendricks et al., p. 80.
3. Joanna Slan, *Using Stories and Humor: Grab Your Audience* (Boston: Allyn & Bacon, 1998), pp. 88–95.
4. Slan, p. 94.
5. Hendricks et al., p. 81.

What Stories Are

Stories are accounts of real or imagined events. They can be success stories, personal stories, stories about famous people, humorous stories, or even startling stories. The clergy use parables, stories with a lesson or moral, to apply religious beliefs to everyday life. We read fables, fairy tales, and folktales to children to demonstrate that "slow and steady win the race" or that "there's no place like home." Ancient peoples have passed down stories—which we call *myths*—that commemorate famous events and people, explain natural and supernatural phenomena, and chronicle great adventures. Regardless of the type, however, stories must have a point that relates to your purpose, a reason for being told. Otherwise, you'll run the risk of annoying your audience with a pointless story.[22]

There are many sources for stories. You can find stories in children's books and in holy books. You can highlight the exploits of heroes from mythology or movies to make a point. Sports celebrities and historical figures often have life stories that you can use to inspire and teach. You can also relate personal incidents from your childhood or recount events that changed your life. We are surrounded by stories. Good speakers keep their eyes and ears open for the ones that can be used in presentations. When they read a story in a newspaper, magazine, or book that can help them make a point, they clip it. When they hear someone tell a story that illustrates or dramatizes a concept they will be discussing, they write it down.

Why Stories Work

Storytelling is the oldest art form in the world.[23] Dr. Walter R. Fisher, a well-respected communication scholar, has devoted significant energy and intellect to studying the nature and purpose of **narratives,** a term that encompasses the process, art, and techniques of storytelling. Fisher sees storytelling as an essential aspect of being human. Good stories possess two essential qualities: probability and fidelity.[24] Understanding these two qualities can help all storytellers improve their ability to select or write effective stories for a presentation.

Story probability refers to whether a story "hangs together" and makes sense. Stories that make sense have structural coherence (internal consistency—that is, one event leads to another) and character coherence (characters behave consistently). If you can't follow the events in a story, it probably lacks structural coherence. Likewise, if you can't tell why the characters do the things that they do, chances are the story doesn't have character coherence. Improbable stories are hard to follow and even harder to enjoy.

Story fidelity refers to the apparent truthfulness of a story. Speakers who fill their presentations with unbelievable stories will not earn their audience's respect. To test the fidelity of a story, ask the following questions:

▶ Do the facts and incidents in the story ring true and seem believable?

▶ Does the story address or support the speaker's point?

▶ Does the story omit, distort, or take out of context key facts and events?

▶ Does the story use logical arguments and patterns of reasoning?

▶ Does the story create the impact that the speaker intended?

Speakers whose stories pass this test are master storytellers. Former President Ronald Reagan was one such storyteller. Why is it, asks Walter Fisher, that President Reagan enjoyed a nearly unanimous evaluation as a "Great Communicator" despite the fact that he was also known for making factual errors, uttering inconsistent statements, reasoning in only a limited fashion, and frequently diverting attention from relevant issues?[25] One answer to this question is that Reagan's speaking talent was a triumph of acting, storytelling, presence, and performance.

A traditional Aleut storyteller and environmental activist uses drumming to enliven the tales he tells young people on the Bering Sea coast in Alaska.

The LibrarySpot Web site, www. libraryspot.com, is an excellent way to search a multitude of libraries for fascinating information on a variety of topics. Their online reference desk provides well-researched feature articles on many subjects, such as this one on the art of storytelling.

The Value of Humor

Injecting humor into a presentation can capture and hold an audience's attention and help listeners remember you and your presentation. Humor can defuse anger, ease tension, and stimulate action. Audience members tend to remember humorous speakers positively, even when they are not enthusiastic about the speaker's message or topic. Humor also encourages listeners to have a good time while learning (and thus enhances learning). Since it has so many advantages, why not sprinkle some humor into your presentation?

Gene Perret, author of *Using Humor for Effective Business Speaking,* claims that humor can generate audience respect for the speaker, attract and hold listeners' attention, clarify obscure or complicated issues, and help an audience remember your main points.[26] Most of Perret's claims are easy to accept—with one exception. How, you may be wondering, can humor clarify obscure or complicated issues? Good humor is clear and understandable (or it won't get a laugh). Thus, understanding the principles behind the joke can help a listener understand your point of view. For instance, Perret once listened to a manager give a pep talk to a production group that feared their entire line would be dropped and layoffs would begin. At the end of his talk, the manager "made his bottom line point empathetically. He said, 'I'm not saying all these things because your jobs are on the line. I'm saying them because mine is.'"[27]

Types of Humor

There are as many types of humor as there are funny speakers. The best humorous speakers know which type of humor to use in a particular situation in front of a particular audience. Some audiences respond well to one-liners, puns, funny stories, and goofy props. Others love funny quotations, cartoons, wacky definitions, lists, humorous letters, silly headlines, misspelled signs, absurd laws, funny song lyrics, and even light-bulb jokes. As is so often the case, the more you know about your audience, the better you can use humor to establish a connection with its members.

Using humor in a presentation does not necessarily mean telling jokes. It means poking fun and having fun. For example, in preparing the presentation about CliffsNotes that appears in Appendix A, John Sullivan worried because there was so little written about the topic. He had searched many sources and had even tried to interview Cliff Hillegass, the founder of CliffsNotes. In the following excerpt from his presentation, he poked fun at himself, at his sources of information, and at his discovery about the founder.

> Yet for all the trust I put into CliffsNotes, I couldn't have told you one thing about them. Even though, according to no less a prestigious source than *People* magazine, over 50 million of these yellow and black pamphlets have been sold, you probably don't know too much about them, either. After exhausting *People* magazine and the *Nebraska Sunday World Herald Magazine*, I had to turn to Cliff himself. Yes, there is a Cliff behind CliffsNotes, and no, his last name is not Notes.

Sometimes a humorous quotation or story can lighten up a presentation. In announcing the possibility of salary and budget freezes to a group of faculty members, an academic dean said, "In the immortal words of 'Peanuts,' There's no problem too big we can't run away from." She then reworded a Woody Allen line—"If my films make one more person feel miserable, I'll feel I've done my job"—by saying, "To paraphrase Woody Allen, if my announcement makes all of you as miserable as I am, I'll feel I've done my job." Although both quotations emphasized the seriousness of a problem, both were greeted with laughter.

Notice how the previous examples related directly to the speaker and topic. Humor is not dumping a bunch of jokes into a presentation; it *is* finding a way to have fun while you are informing or persuading an audience. Appropriate humor makes your presentation more enjoyable both to give and to receive.

Presenting humor is difficult. Most listeners will give you the benefit of the doubt if you don't hit their funny bone. And most audiences will forgive you if a joke or a humorous story doesn't come out as funny as was intended. There are, however, some approaches to humor that an audience will not and should not forgive. Offensive humor tops the list because it insults your audience and seriously damages your credibility. Irrelevant humor is a close second because it wastes the audience's time and makes you appear poorly organized. Stale, prepackaged humor comes in third. It's often irrelevant *and* offensive—a deadly combination. Chapter 20, "Special Presentations," explores these pitfalls in more detail. Here we offer some strategies for finding and inserting humor into a presentation.

Humor for Beginners

Explaining how to be humorous is something like explaining how to ice skate. You can read about ice skating, and you can watch videotapes of Olympic skaters, but nothing will replace putting on a pair of skates and getting on the ice. Of course, your first few steps may leave you flat on your face or rear end. But with practice and some coaching, you can become quite comfortable and even graceful on ice. You may not become a gold medal winner, but you can learn to enjoy yourself. The same is true about using humor in a presentation. You can read about it and borrow funny lines from books and comedians. However, nothing replaces trying it in front of a real audience.

You don't have to begin with an entire humorous presentation to be funny. A few humorous lines in almost any kind of presentation can get you started. One of the easiest ways to become a humorous speaker is to begin with humor that pokes fun at yourself. You don't have to worry about offending anyone if you are the butt or target of your joke. You don't have to worry as much about forgetting details of a humorous story if it is based on something that happened to you.

Real-life humorous stories are much easier to tell than stories you've made up or borrowed from a book.

Both of us take great delight in telling our students about presentation aids that didn't work, about audiences that didn't behave the way we expected them to, and about embarrassing goofs we've made while speaking. We don't embarrass anyone but ourselves, and our students love it. Vice President Al Gore, a man regarded as straight-laced and formal, started telling jokes about himself as a way to humanize his image. How, he would ask, can you pick Al Gore out from the Secret Service agents around him? The answer: Al Gore is the stiff one.

With just a little exaggeration about the dog that wouldn't perform, the power saw that didn't work, the fish tank that broke, the exercise outfit that split, and the handmade poster that spelled an innocent word in a way that cannot be printed in a textbook, you too can turn an amusing story into a very funny one.

In most cases, you are your own best source of humor. Although you can buy books of jokes and handbooks on humor, their contents will rarely match the effectiveness of **self-effacing humor**—your ability to direct humor at yourself. Poking fun at yourself can lower the barrier between speaker and audience by showing the audience that you are an ordinary, fallible human being—just like them. At first, you may be at a loss. What can you poke fun at that's personal? Your job, your family, your experiences, and even your near-misses or failures can be a source of humor. But be careful that you don't poke too much fun at yourself. If you begin to look foolish or less than competent, you will damage your credibility, reduce your level of confidence, and weaken the power of your message.

One of the guidelines we use when looking for the "lighter side" of life is remembering situations where we've said, "I can't believe this is happening to me" or "Someday we'll laugh about this." Such situations can later be retold as humor. U.S. presidents are often remembered for their self-effacing humor. Ronald Reagan was well known for making fun of his age, an approach that also defused controversy about his being the oldest president in U.S. history. Here are two examples:[28]

> I want to begin by saying how grateful I am that you've asked me here to participate in the celebration of the hundredth anniversary of the Knights of Columbus. Now, it isn't true that I was present at the first anniversary.

> There was a very prominent Democrat who reportedly told a large group, "Don't worry. I've seen Ronald Reagan, and he looks like a million." He was talking about my age.

The Benefits of Audience Participation

One of the most powerful ways to keep an audience alert and interested is to ask audience members to participate actively in a presentation. Most audiences remember speakers who include them in the action. When audiences members participate, they use more than their eyes and ears. They may speak, raise their hands, write, or reach out and touch someone or something. When a speaker interacts with audience members, they become more alert because they have to be prepared to participate.[29]

REAL WORLD, REAL SPEAKERS

Many respondents to our survey were eager to share their interest-generating techniques. Carol Herzog, an elementary school teacher in Warren, Indiana, often speaks to groups of educators and community members. She wrote, "I like to keep the audience actively involved during the presentation. My handouts are often an outline that needs filling in during the presentation. I have also done a personal growth speech where the audience writes themselves a postcard about a change they would like to make in their lives as a result of my talk. I mail the postcard six months later as a reminder of that change."

Dr. Rob Simpson, who works for the Salvation Army in Grand Rapids, Michigan, believes that he keeps audience attention by "beginning with humor, using professional visuals, including topics that require audience participation, linking theory to practical applications, using plain and simple language for all levels of audiences, and being thoroughly prepared." Note how these experienced speakers rely on varied techniques to keep their audiences interested and involved.

Audience participation is a common practice in religious services. Worshipers may engage in responsive reading, singing, kneeling, tithing, clapping, saying "amen," and going to the altar for special blessings or ceremonies. Great preachers know that audience involvement creates a sense of community and inspires loyalty to a congregation. The same kinds of involvement can be enlisted to serve a presenter. Audience participation involves audiences physically, verbally, and psychologically with your presentation. There are many ways to actively engage your audience.

> ### FORMS OF AUDIENCE PARTICIPATION
>
> **Ask questions**
> **Encourage interaction**
> **Do an exercise**
> **Ask for volunteers**
> **Invite feedback**

Ask Questions

One of the easiest ways to involve audience members is to ask questions, pose riddles, or ask for reactions. Even if audience members do little more than nod their heads in response, they will have become part of a transaction with the speaker. Also, when audiences know that they will be quizzed or questioned during or after a presentation, they will be more alert and interested in what is said.

One special type of audience question, the poll, combines involving listeners and doing a quick form of audience analysis. Ask for a show of hands in response to simple questions such as "How many of you know someone who . . . ?" "How many of you have visited . . . ?" "Have any of you heard of . . . ?" "Do we have anyone here who was born or raised in . . . ?" The responses will tell you something about your audience and will also let the audience members know whether they share common experiences, opinions, and beliefs.

REAL WORLD, REAL SPEAKERS

At a Virginia Press Association's Minority Job Fair in Richmond, Virginia, a speaker combined storytelling and audience participation into a highly effective presentation. Mr. Marvin Leon Lake, public editor of a Norfolk-based newspaper, the *Virginian-Pilot*, began his job fair presentation by announcing that he was going to tell a true story. And like all good stories, this one had a moral. But, he said, he wasn't going to tell his audience the moral. It was up to them to tell him what they thought the story meant.

He then told about a young journalism student who, at a previous job fair, had volunteered to be interviewed by a panel of strangers in front of an audience. The student went on to become a successful journalist. When he finished, Lake asked the audience: "What is the moral of this story?" One student raised her hand and said, "When given an opportunity—even in the face of public scrutiny—do it!" Another audience member said, "If you stand out in a crowd, you will be noticed." A third listener suggested that you should always be prepared, both physically and mentally, to accept a challenge. Lake said all of the answers were correct.

Lake engaged his audience by telling a relevant story and then involving them in a discussion about the story. The students attending the job fair had a lot to remember, but at the top of their list was Lake, his story, and its important lesson.

Encourage Interaction

As corny as it may seem, you can ask a general audience to shake hands or to introduce themselves to the people sitting on either side of them. Depending on the purpose of your presentation, you could add something beyond a handshake. For example, in a talk about childcare, you could request that audience members share the number, ages, and genders of their children with each other. If it's a business audience, ask members to exchange business cards. If you're addressing young college students, ask them to identify the high schools they attended or their career aspirations.

Do an Exercise

Both simple games and complex training exercises can involve audience members with your presentation and with each other. Most large bookstores have shelves filled with training manuals describing ways of involving audience members in games and exercises. They range from coming up with a name for a new product to suggesting solutions to hypothetical or real problems. Interrupting a presentation for a group exercise gives both the audience and the speaker a break during which they can interact in a different but effective way.

Ask for Volunteers

If you ask for volunteers from the audience, someone will usually offer to participate. Volunteers can help you demonstrate how to perform a skill or how to use a piece of equipment. They can engage in role-playing exercises. Some can even be persuaded to wear funny hats, sing songs, or leave the room. Most audiences love

REAL WORLD, REAL SPEAKERS

One of my most successful speaking experiences occurred when I gave a presentation to a group of public relations professionals. This was a group accustomed to PowerPoint presentations and slick delivery. I decided to break the rules as a way of gaining attention and interest. After I was introduced, I stood up and welcomed them to my "powerpoint" presentation. There was no projector, no screen, no computer. I looked pretty dumb, but I had their attention. Then I said, "I have three points I want to make today, and all of them are powerful." No fancy introduction, just a slight play on words. They smiled; a few applauded. Why? Because my beginning was unexpected, because it broke a mold, and because it put aside the fancy stuff and got right to the point.

Then I told them that each of my three points began with the letter M. Why? So that I wouldn't forget them and so that they could remember them. I wrote a key word that began with the letter M with a red marker on three 4 x 6-inch cards. My visuals were small and scrawled in a difficult-to-read color. Because I wanted them to see my "visual aids," I left the safety of the lectern and its microphone and walked into the audience holding up my little visual aid cards. I even left a card with an audience member who seemed unusually attentive.

When the presentation was over, I was applauded and spent several minutes answering questions and listening to comments from an enthusiastic audience. Several weeks later, I attended another meeting at which several of the same audience members made a point of telling me that my little 4 x 6 cards were impossible to forget and that they still remembered my three important and powerful points. The presentation could have been a disaster if I had not planned, very carefully, to break several well-known "rules" of presentation speaking. Instead, they remembered my presentation *because* I had broken several of the sacred rules that they knew so well.

Isa Engleberg

to watch a volunteer in action. If possible, find a way to reward volunteers—with a small prize or special thanks. Once audience members see that volunteering is a risk-free opportunity, they will be more willing to participate.

As long as everyone is involved, most audiences will go along with what they're asked to do. If you invite audience members to stand up and stretch, most of them will. If you ask them to write something down, most of them will pick up their pens. Both of us have learned that audiences will volunteer to do something as long as everyone is in it together. At the same time, don't force a volunteer or audience member to participate if you sense reluctance or apprehension. "Volunteers" who don't want to volunteer can become a hostile audience.

Invite Feedback

During or at the end of your presentation, you can invite questions and comments from the audience. Once interested audience members know that they can interrupt you with a question or comment, some will do just that. Of course, it takes a skillful presenter to allow this kind of interaction without losing track of a prepared presentation. Waiting until the end of a presentation for questions and comments is safer but doesn't involve the audience as much.

Encouraging audience participation requires skill and sensitivity. Respect any feedback from your audience. If audience members seem reluctant to participate, don't badger or embarrass them. If no one responds, go on and give your presentation without such involvement. In all likelihood, however, you will find most audiences ready, willing, and able to participate. The vast majority of audience members remember presentations in which they participated.

Break the Rules

Many successful speakers break lots of the "rules" and "guidelines" in this textbook. Mainly, they're highly experienced speakers who know how far to push the limits. In some rare cases, they are inexperienced but inspired speakers who, despite lack of organization or a weak speaking voice, rise to an occasion and move an audience to tears or action.

Rules are *not* made to be broken. This book includes rules that represent our best advice as well as scholarly research about preparing and delivering effective presentations. We encourage following the rules until you gain enough experience to tailor them to your own needs and abilities. Keep the length of your presentations under twenty minutes until you know for certain that you can keep an audience interested for twice that long. Tell brief, one-character stories until you know that you can skillfully juggle multiple characters and plots. Break the rules when you know yourself and your audience well enough to also know when some rules don't apply.

Summary

●▸ **Why do audiences lose interest?**

Audiences lose interest because they have short attention spans and poor listening skills. Speakers contribute to the problem of lost interest when they speak too long or deliver a presentation poorly.

●▸ **What language tools can help me engage my listeners?**

Use an oral style and active verbs, match your words to your listeners, use personal pronouns, and spice up your speech with repetitive words and phrases as well as with figures of speech.

●▸ **Why are stories so interesting?**

Well-delivered stories with simple story lines, limited characters, exaggeration, and audience links have the ability to captivate and educate because they create lasting images.

●▸ **How do I integrate humor into my presentation?**

Humor should be used to make a point, not for its own sake. Effective humor is usually well prepared and well rehearsed. The best humor often pokes fun at the speaker.

(continued)

◆◆ **How can I directly involve my audience?**

In addition to adapting to the results of audience analysis, ask questions, encourage interaction, do an exercise, ask for volunteers, and invite feedback.

Key Terms

alliteration 205	metaphor 205	self-effacing humor 211
attention span 198	narrative 208	story fidelity 208
expressiveness 200	simile 205	story probability 208

Notes

1. Florence I. Wolff and Nadine C. Marsnik, *Perceptive Listening,* 2nd ed. (Fort Worth, TX: Harcourt Brace Jovanovich, 1992), p. 176.
2. Wolff and Marsnik, p. 176.
3. William Hendricks et al., *Secrets of Power Presentations* (Franklin Lakes, NJ: Career Press, 1996), pp. 144–145.
4. Peggy Noonan, *Simply Speaking: How to Communicate Your Ideas with Style, Substance, and Clarity* (New York: HarperCollins, 1998), p. 9. Copyright © 1998 by Peggy Noonan. Reprinted by permission of HarperCollins Publishers, Inc.
5. Noonan, pp. 9–10. Copyright © 1998 by Peggy Noonan. Reprinted by permission of HarperCollins Publishers, Inc.
6. Alan M. Perlman, *Writing Great Speeches: Professional Techniques You Can Use* (Boston: Allyn & Bacon, 1998), p. 52.
7. Perlman, p. 53.
8. Thomas Leech, *How to Prepare, Stage, & Deliver Winning Presentations* (New York: AMACOM, 1993), p. 242.
9. Perlman, p. 129.
10. Noonan, p. 36. Copyright © 1998 by Peggy Noonan. Reprinted by permission of HarperCollins Publishers, Inc.
11. Diana Hacker, *The Bedford Handbook,* 5th ed. (Boston: Bedford Books, 1998), p. 231.
12. For the complete text of Gates' speech plus commentary, see Owen Peterson, *Representative American Speeches, 1989–1990* (New York: H. W. Wilson, 1991), pp. 163–168.
13. The complete text of Gore's address was obtained from The White House in 1999.
14. Garry Wills, *Lincoln at Gettysburg* (New York: Simon and Schuster, 1992), p. 263.
15. Ronald H. Carpenter, *Choosing Powerful Words* (Boston: Allyn & Bacon, 1999), p. 117.
16. Wills, p. 263.
17. Carpenter, p. 127.
18. For the complete text of Allende's address plus commentary, see Owen Peterson, *Representative American Speeches, 1989–1990* (New York: H. W. Wilson, 1991), pp. 71–82.
19. Walter R. Fisher, *Human Communication as Narration: Toward a Philosophy of Reason, Value, and Action* (Columbia: University of South Carolina Press, 1987), pp. 64–65.
20. Joanna Slan, *Using Stories and Humor: Grab Your Audience* (Boston: Allyn & Bacon, 1998), pp. 5–6.
21. Eric Quinones, "Companies Learn the Value of Storytelling," *New York Times,* 1 August 1999, p. 4.
22. Malcolm Kushner, *Successful Presentations for Dummies* (Foster City, CA: IDG Books, 1997), p. 79
23. Slan, p. 42.
24. Fisher, p. 68.
25. Fisher, pp. 145–157.
26. Gene Perret, *Using Humor for Effective Business Speaking* (New York: Sterling, 1989), pp. 19–26.
27. Perret, p. 25.
28. Malcolm Kushner, *Successful Presentations for Dummies* (Foster City, CA: IDG Books, 1997), p. 350.
29. Ron Hoff, *I Can See You Naked* (Kansas City, MO: Andrews and McMeel, 1992), p. 106.

PERFORMANCE

Performance and Practice

- ➤➤ **What is a good performance?**
- ➤➤ **Should I use an outline or read my presentation word for word?**
- ➤➤ **How should I use notes when I speak?**
- ➤➤ **What's the best way to practice?**

erform is a verb that has several meanings, two of which apply especially well to presentations. *Perform* can mean to accomplish, carry out, or do something, as in "She performed her job efficiently and effectively." In this sense, performing a presentation carries out your purpose. Your performance is the final product. *Perform* also can mean to demonstrate an art in front of an audience. Actors, singers, and dancers perform. In this sense, performance is the way in which you use your voice and body to deliver your presentation. Just as you made decisions about the purpose and content of your presentation, you will have to make performance decisions that will affect how well you deliver your presentation and how well you achieve or carry out your purpose.

We use the term **performance** to refer to the effective vocal and physical delivery of your presentation. You've probably been impressed by speakers whose performances seemed natural, confident, and clear. And you've probably been distracted or annoyed by speakers whose performances were stilted, rushed, or filled with inappropriate gestures. It's all too easy to be a distracting presenter. Being a poised and powerful performer, though, takes effort and practice. You need to decide how you can best apply the performance techniques we discuss in this chapter and in the next three to your presentation purpose, your audience, the logistics, and yourself. We discuss specific techniques in Chapter 14, "Vocal Delivery," Chapter 15, "Physical Delivery," and Chapter 16, "Presentation Aids." In this chapter, we focus on the preparation and practice needed to deliver a strong presentation.

Choosing How to Deliver Your Presentation

You know what you want to say; now it's time to decide how to deliver your message. Whether you choose to rely on a few note cards or to read from a manuscript, your decisions about delivery will affect how you perform your presentation. You will need to decide which form of delivery to use: impromptu, extemporaneous, manuscript, or memorized.

> **FORMS OF DELIVERY**
>
> **Impromptu**
> **Extemporaneous**
> **Manuscript**
> **Memorized**

Impromptu Speaking

Impromptu speaking, also known as "off-the-cuff" speaking, is when you give a presentation without advance preparation or practice. You're called upon in class to answer a question or to share your opinion. Your boss asks you to summarize a report without giving you advance warning. You're at a public meeting and decide to stand up and be heard on an important community issue. In impromptu situations like these, do you abandon all you've learned about preparing an interesting, well-organized presentation and blurt out whatever comes into your head? The answer is *no.* Even though you don't have enough time to stop and give a lot of thought to every detail of your presentation, you can very quickly think of a purpose and the ways in which you intend to organize and adapt your message to your audience. The more experience you have as a speaker, the more instinctive the "basics" become, even in impromptu speaking.

Although you can't prepare an impromptu presentation, you can *be prepared* by anticipating when you might have to give one. Most people do this kind of preparation when they are getting ready for an important job interview. Even if they don't know the

Cristina Saralegui (with microphone), a popular talk-show host on Univision, asks an audience member to speak impromptu.

Figure 13.1   Impromptu Delivery

Advantages	Disadvantages
1. Natural and conversational speaking style.	1. Speaker may have nothing to say on such short notice.
2. Maximum eye contact.	2. Presentation anxiety may be very high.
3. Freedom of movement.	3. Limited or no time to prepare.
4. Easier to respond and adjust to audience feedback.	4. Limited or no time for audience analysis.
5. Demonstrates speaker's knowledge and skill.	5. Limited or no supporting material.
6. Performance can exceed audience expectations.	6. Only rudimentary organizational format.
	7. Delivery may be awkward and ineffectual.
	8. Difficult to gauge time.

interview questions, they prepare responses for the ones that might be asked. When an interviewer says, "Tell me about yourself," or "What would you do if you were confronted with . . . ?" you are being asked to speak impromptu. Your impromptu speaking ability may be just as important for landing a good job as your credentials and references. Whether it's during an interview, an English class, or a staff meeting when you might have to speak, take a few minutes to consider what you may be asked to say or contribute. If you are going to a public meeting, give some thought to how you may want to respond if someone asks for questions or comments. As we explain in Chapter 20 "Developing Special Presentations," special techniques and standard organizational patterns can make an impromptu presentation a talk to be proud of.

Figure 13.1 lists the advantages and disadvantages of impromptu speaking as a form of delivery.

Extemporaneous Speaking

Extemporaneous speaking is the most common form of delivery. In **extemporaneous speaking,** you use an outline or a set of notes to guide yourself through your performance instead of reading aloud a written presentation word for word. Your notes can be a few key words on a single small card or a detailed outline on one or two sheets of paper. These notes will reflect the decisions you have made in the preparation process, but they will also give you the flexibility to quickly adapt your presentation to the audience and occasion.

In extemporaneous speaking you can combine the advantages of impromptu speaking (maximum eye contact, moving away from your notes, making mid-speech adjustments to the audience, setting, and occasion) with the advantages of a manuscript presentation (carefully planned organization, the opportunity to practice everything in advance, reduced nervousness). Classroom lectures, business briefings, and courtroom arguments are usually delivered extemporaneously. No other form of delivery gives you as much freedom and flexibility with pre-planned material. An extemporaneous speaker can make last-minute adjustments much more easily than a speaker saddled with an inflexible manuscript can. Later in this chapter, we describe techniques for using notes effectively during an extemporaneous presentation.

Advantages	Disadvantages
1. It allows more preparation time.	1. Presentation anxiety may increase for sections not covered by notes.
2. Speaker can pay attention to purpose, audience, logistics, content, organization, credibility, and delivery.	2. Too many or too few notes can hamper fluency and physical delivery.
3. It seems spontaneous but is actually well prepared.	3. Language may not be well chosen or vivid throughout the presentation.
4. Speaker can monitor and respond to audience feedback.	4. It can be difficult to make extensive last-minute changes.
5. Speaker can respond to unforeseen events or logistical problems.	5. It can be difficult to estimate speaking time.
6. It allows more audience interaction and eye contact than manuscript delivery does.	
7. Practice can build confidence.	
8. Audiences respond positively to this delivery style.	
9. Speaker can choose concise language for key points and important ideas.	
10. With practice, it becomes the most powerful form of delivery.	

Figure 13.2 lists the advantages and disadvantages of speaking extemporaneously, and as you can see, the advantages of extemporaneous speaking far outweigh the disadvantages. Extemporaneous speaking can give the audience the impression that you are speaking spontaneously. Because what you are saying is well planned and well rehearsed, you can change things around to adapt to the audience, the logistics, and the occasion. Because it's not restricted by a manuscript, a well-practiced extemporaneous presentation has an ease to it that makes both audience and speaker feel more comfortable.

Manuscript Speaking

Manuscript speaking involves writing your presentation in advance and reading it word for word. Using a manuscript allows you to choose each word carefully. You can plan every detail. Manuscript use also gives you time to practice the same presentation over and over. It ensures that your presentation will fit within your allotted speaking time. For very nervous speakers, a manuscript can be a lifesaving document that keeps them afloat throughout an entire presentation, even when they feel as though they're drowning. With all of these advantages, why do we discourage speakers from using manuscript delivery?

Manuscript presentations are hard for all but the most skilled and practiced speakers to deliver effectively. The most significant disadvantages of using a manuscript are inappropriate word choice, poor reading, and inflexibility. In manuscript delivery speakers often use the complex words, long sentences, formal style, and perfect grammar required for written reports and papers rather than the oral style that Chapter 12, "Generating Interest," recommends. *If you must use a*

At a rally supporting the Upward Bound program in Austin, Texas, a teenager clutches her handwritten manuscript. In such public settings, a set of notes on note cards would be easier to use and better suited to the setting and occasion.

manuscript, write it as though you are speaking. You may even want to try speaking into a tape recorder and then transcribing what you have said, in order to make appropriate decisions about the words you select. Although most speech instructors and coaches don't encourage their students or clients to use manuscript delivery, many speakers continue to rely on it for important presentations.

There are, however, occasions for which a word-for-word manuscript may be needed.[1] If the occasion is an important public event at which every word counts and time is strictly limited, you may have no choice but to use a manuscript. If your presentation might be quoted by reporters, you may want to make sure that they quote exactly what you say.

Figure 13.3 lists the advantages and disadvantages of using a manuscript to deliver a presentation. Learning how to read well from a manuscript lets you tap into the advantages and minimize the disadvantages of this form of delivery.

Even if you write your manuscript in an accessible oral style, it still may not sound that way when you read it. Lack of vocal expression and lack of eye contact with the audience can turn the reading of a manuscript into a dull and boring performance. Effective manuscript delivery requires a lot of practice. The better you know the words that you've written and the more comfortable you feel with them, the easier it will be to concentrate on how you deliver them.

Despite its disadvantages, manuscript delivery is a fact of life. For a variety of reasons, speakers continue to rely on manuscripts for important presentations. Learning how to read from a manuscript is as important as learning how to speak impromptu or extemporaneously.

Memorized Speaking

A **memorized presentation** offers a speaker one major advantage over manuscript delivery and a major disadvantage when compared with the other three

Figure 13.3   Manuscript Delivery

Advantages	Disadvantages
1. Speaker can pay attention to purpose, audience, logistics, content, organization, credibility, and delivery.	1. Delivery can be stilted and dull.
2. Speaker can choose concise and eloquent language.	2. Difficult to maintain sufficient eye contact.
3. Presentation anxiety may be eased by having a "script."	3. Limited gestures and movement.
4. Speaker can stay within the time limit.	4. Language can be too formal, lacking oral style.
5. Speaker can rehearse the same "script" every time.	5. Audience may conclude that the speaker has not adapted to them.
6. Speaker can ensure accurate reporting of speech content.	6. Difficult to modify or adapt to the audience or situation.

A few years ago a well-known Shakespearean scholar was invited to speak at a local college. His hosts' mistake was failing to find out ahead of time whether he was a good speaker. The man had been scheduled to talk for thirty minutes; instead, he talked for an hour . . . in a monotone. Although he had been asked to speak to a general audience, he behaved as though he were addressing an audience of university professors. He had been asked to keep his talk informal; instead, he read a lecture, and read it badly. He had said he would not need a microphone, but he could barely be heard. His voice had no expression, and he never varied his delivery speed. Furthermore, he never looked at his audience, and the only movement he made was to sway back and forth as he read. The lecture was a total and terrible disaster.

forms. The major advantage is physical freedom. You can look at your audience 100 percent of the time; you can gesture freely and even move around. There is no manuscript to keep you chained to a lectern or desk. The disadvantage, however, outweighs any and all advantages. What if you forget something? What if you go blank? If you can't remember your presentation and begin to rely on an impromptu style of delivery, the audience will know something is wrong. A bad situation will only feel worse. Unless you are a professional actor who can memorize a script and make it sound as if you just came up with the wording, forget about using the memorized style of delivering a presentation.[2]

Figure 13.4 lists the advantages and disadvantages of memorizing a presentation for delivery.

We strongly discourage memorizing *entire* presentations. However, there's nothing wrong with trying to memorize your introduction or a few key sections, as long as you still have your notes to fall back on. An audience may be impressed by your skill at reciting a few lines of poetry or by your ability to put aside your notes, look them in the eye, and deliver a powerful ending. But don't count on remembering everything; the likelihood is that you will fumble or forget something important.

Figure 13.4   Memorized Delivery

Advantages	Disadvantages
1. Incorporates the preparation advantages of manuscript speaking and the delivery advantages of impromptu speaking.	1. Extensive time required to memorize the presentation.
2. Allows maximum eye contact.	2. Disaster awaits if memory fails.
3. Allows freedom of movement.	3. Can sound "canned," stilted, and insincere.
	4. Very difficult to modify or adapt to the audience or situation.
	5. Lacks sense of spontaneity unless expertly delivered.

Mix and Match

Learning how to deliver a presentation in extemporaneous, impromptu, manuscript, and memorized forms lets you select the method that works best for you and for your purpose and lets you vary your delivery within a presentation. You don't have to stay within the bounds of one form. An impromptu speaker can recite a memorized statistic or a rehearsed argument in much the same way that a politician responds to press questions. An extemporaneous speaker may read a lengthy quotation or a series of statistics and then deliver a memorized ending. A manuscript reader may stop and tell an impromptu story or may deliver memorized sections that would benefit from direct eye contact with the audience. A speaker can pause in a memorized presentation to repeat a key phrase or to re-explain an idea. Your decision about which delivery form or forms to use is important, and under most circumstances, it will be yours to make.

Using Notes Effectively

Regardless of what form of delivery you select, you should be ready to use notes and to use them effectively. Even when you are speaking impromptu, you may find yourself using notes. A few quick words jotted down just before you stand to speak can help you through an unplanned talk. And if you are brave enough to try a memorized presentation, you should keep your manuscript nearby in case your memory or nerve fails you.

Not everyone can handle notes well. You've probably seen speakers lose the connection with their audience by awkwardly shuffling their pages or searching for a missing index card in the middle of a huge stack. You may have wished you could see a speaker whose face was buried in his notes! Fortunately, you can easily learn to use notes effortlessly and unobtrusively.

Some speakers prefer to put their manuscript or speaking notes on 8½ x 11-inch paper. If you do this, we recommend using large type fronts (14 or 16 point), double- or triple-spacing, and carefully numbering your pages. Type on only the top two-thirds of the page so that you don't have to bend your head to see the bottom of the page, a movement that will cause you to lose eye contact with your audience and will constrict your windpipe in such a way that your voice can sound muffled.[3] Use wide margins and make sure that none of your sentences run over to a new page. Some speakers like to incorporate special visual cues right on the manuscript—such as underlining important words, indicating with slash marks places where they want to pause or move to another position, or putting a star at a place where they intend to refer to a presentation aid. When we speak from a manuscript, our pages are filled with little marks as well as last-minute additions and cross-outs.

Other speakers prefer to put their notes on index cards, which work especially well for extemporaneous speaking. As you would for notes written on larger pa-

Karl Sprague of Corporate Finance Associates speaks about opportunities at his company to hundreds of business people at a seminar. Because his notes are placed on the lectern for easy reference, he can gesture naturally and establish direct eye contact with his audience.

per, number each note card and use large print so that you can read your words at a glance. It might help to think of each note card as a visual aid. Provide yourself with just enough information to trigger an idea or to supply a vital piece of supporting material. Figure 13.5 offers some tips for using note cards when making a presentation.

Regardless of what form your notes take, put them on the lectern if you are provided with one. And don't let your notes hang over the front of a lectern. If you don't have a lectern, put the notes on a table or hold them in one hand. Also, hand-held note cards work much better than hand-held floppy paper. Regardless of whether you use full-size paper or index cards, slip each page or card behind the others when you're finished with it so that you don't end up revisiting the same information by mistake.

Practice

Athletes and musicians practice, and so do the best and most experienced speakers. Practice involves translating the decisions you make about performance into action. Practice is your best guarantee that you will perform well—in every sense of the word. Practice requires more than repeating your presentation over and over again. You must also pay attention to the fine points of your performance. Practice can tell you whether there are words that you have trouble pronouncing or sentences that are too long to say in one breath. In addition, it may help you discover that what you thought was a ten-minute talk takes thirty minutes to deliver. Practicing with presentation aids is critical, particularly if you've seen the embarrassing results that befall speakers who don't have their visuals in order. It's not a question of whether you should practice; rather, it's deciding what aspects of your performance need the most practice. Practicing is the only way to make sure that you sound and look good in a presentation. To put it another way, "give your speech *before* you give it."[4]

NOTES ARE A SAFETY NET, NOT A CRUTCH
Some of the best speakers we know feel "naked" without their notes. Even though they are familiar with their material and have delivered the same message over and over, they still feel incomplete without a set of notes in hand. Great Britain's eloquent prime minister Winston Churchill was asked why he always had notes for his speeches, even though he rarely used them. He replied, "I carry fire insurance, but I don't expect my house to burn down."[1] Bringing notes with you is fine, particularly if you don't use them or only refer to them briefly. The problem occurs when well-prepared but insecure speakers bury their heads in their notes, even though the information is second nature to them.

1. Malcolm Kushner, *Successful Presentations for Dummies* (Foster City, CA: IDG Books, 1997), p. 204.

Figure 13.5   Using Note Cards

1. **Use key words.** Use only key words rather than complete sentences on each note card. Manuscripts do not fit or belong on note cards.

2. **Using fewer cards is better.** It's best when you can use one card for your introduction, one card for each key point, and one card for your conclusion.

3. **Using fewer words is better.** Don't overload the card with information or use small print.

4. **Use card stock.** Use sturdy card stock, not slips of paper.

5. **Use only one side of a note card.**

6. **Number the cards.** Doing this will keep the parts of your presentation in order or will allow you to rearrange key points at the last minute.

7. **Practice using your notes.** You may discover that you have too many cards or too much information on each card.

Rehearsing a presentation at home may feel awkward at first, but family and friends can offer useful suggestions and help you feel more confident about your upcoming talk.

Practice can take many forms. It can be as simple as closing your door and rehearsing your presentation in private or as complex as a full, on-stage, videotaped rehearsal. The ways in which you can practice range from a quick look at your notes to a major dress rehearsal.

Depending on how much time you have, the length and importance of your presentation, and your familiarity with your material, there are several different ways to practice.

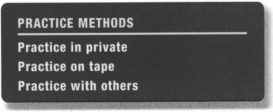

PRACTICE METHODS

Practice in private
Practice on tape
Practice with others

TIP **PRACTICE IN BITE-SIZE CHUNKS** Although it is important to do several complete run-throughs of your presentation, there is a lot to be said for breaking some of your practice sessions into smaller segments. Thomas Mira, author of *Speak Smart*, suggests using brief practice sessions during which you practice for only five or ten minutes at a time. He advises, "You can do anything for five or ten minutes. If you make practice a lengthy drudgery, you just won't do it. If you divide your practice time into manageable, bite-size chunks, you'll find yourself practicing more often and building confidence for each segment."[1]

1. Thomas K. Mira, *Speak Smart: The Art of Public Speaking* (New York: Random House, 1997), p. 91.

Practice in Private

Practice is usually a solo activity. You may go over your presentation as you drive your car, while you shower, behind a closed door in your home or office, or all by yourself in the room where you will be speaking. Regardless of where you practice, you should try to practice the way you want to sound and look in front of your audience. Speak at the volume and rate you intend to use, glance at your notes only occasionally, and use body movement that's appropriate for you and for your presentation. At first, you may feel a bit strange while talking to yourself. It may help to remember that musicians rehearse alone, athletes exercise alone, and actors recite their lines alone. Speakers must also learn to practice alone.

Practice on Tape

If you practice in private, it's difficult to concentrate on delivering your presentation and to evaluate it at the same time. How do you know whether you are speaking clearly, maintaining enough eye contact, or fidgeting? An audiotape recording of your practice session can tell you a lot about what you are saying and how you sound. A video recording can tell you even more. Not everyone has access to a video camera, but most speakers can record themselves on audiocassette.

One of the first things you will notice in an audio recording is that your voice doesn't sound the way you thought it would. But remember, you hear your voice from the inside; your audience hears it projected across a room. The outside sound will be different. So instead of focusing on yourself, try to listen as an audience member would. Do you understand what is being said—the ideas and information as well as the individual words and phrases? You can time your presentation, check your pronunciation, and monitor your fluency.

If you can record yourself on videotape, you will also be able to assess how you look. Again, be aware that in all probability, you won't like what you see. At first, you may be distracted by the way your hair looks, the way you gesture, or the extra ten pounds you'd like to lose. If you're going to use a videotape, try watching it alone at first and then with a friend. A videotape can help you practice if you are able to look at it objectively.

Videotaping your practice session can tell you how to polish and improve your presentation before you speak. Videotaping your actual performance can tell you a lot about why you did or didn't achieve your purpose.

Practice with Others

With or without audiotaping or videotaping, you can practice your presentation in front of someone else. Your listener doesn't have to be a public speaking instructor to say, "I couldn't hear you," "You didn't look at me during the last section," or "I'm not sure what you were trying to prove with those statistics." Equally important, a friendly listener can reassure you and give you an extra dose of confidence. We often are our own harshest critics. Someone else's reaction can help you put the finishing touches on a well-prepared and well-practiced presentation.

Mid-Performance Decisions

You've reached that crucial moment that you've been preparing and planning for. After hours, days, even weeks of work, you're about to make your presentation. Even the most experienced speakers and speechwriters have described how it often takes one hour of work to prepare for each minute of performance time. Is it worth it? You bet it is! You'll be so well-prepared that you will concentrate on communicating what you want to say, not on how you sound or look. You can concentrate your energy and will on achieving your purpose. You can put aside concerns about yourself and become an audience-focused speaker.

One of the most significant differences between good and great speakers is their ability to use audience feedback to make mid-performance adaptations. You don't have to wait until your presentation ends to get the audience's reactions. As

SHOULD I PRACTICE IN FRONT OF A MIRROR?

Some speakers report that they like to practice in front of a full-length mirror, and many popular public speaking books recommend this practice technique. We do not share the general enthusiasm for this method. In fact, we discourage it. Try it, and you will see why. When you start talking to a mirror, you'll notice your face, your hair, your clothes, and your eyes. You will notice your mouth moving, your hands gesturing, and your posture. As a result, you'll think very little about your presentation.

In Chapter 3, "Building Presentation Confidence," we discussed how being too self-focused can heighten presentation anxiety. Mirrors are the ultimate in self-focus. Staring at your performance in a mirror takes you away from your purpose, your audience, and your setting. All it does is reflect how you look to yourself in the confines of a bathroom or bedroom.

Malcolm Kushner, who once taught speech communication classes at the University of Southern California, is the author of an amusing but substantive book, *Successful Presentations for Dummies*. He's also "anti-mirror." Kushner argues that practicing in front of a mirror is distracting and very unnatural. How many people, he asks, look at themselves while they're talking (other than the evil queen from *Snow White*)?[1]

At the same time, we recognize that there are pro-mirror people. So if you have rehearsed in front of a mirror and believe that doing so improves your performance, don't abandon this technique. Just make sure that it doesn't divert your focus from your purpose, your audience, and your message.

1. Malcolm Kushner, *Successful Presentations for Dummies* (Foster City, CA: IDG Books, 1997), p. 212.

REAL WORLD, REAL SPEAKERS

A few years ago, I taught a graduate course to a group of experienced and would-be college teachers who wanted to improve their classroom communication skills. The participants let me videotape them giving a fifteen-minute lecture. No one else in the class viewed the tape. It was strictly for the private use of the speaker. In their final reports, even the most experienced professors made interesting and positive comments about the use of video as a practice tool.

Here's what one instructor wrote after viewing herself on video:

It took me three days to get up enough courage to watch my videotape. Then it took me three more days before I'd let my husband watch it. I guess I'll never be a TV personality. However, I really did learn a lot from the experience and from watching the tape. I never realized before how active my hands are while I'm lecturing. The gestures were appropriate, though, and I thought they helped me look at ease as I lectured. One problem I noticed after watching the video was that I focused more on the center of the room rather than on the sides. I will need to make a conscious effort to look around the entire classroom as I speak.

You, too, can learn more about yourself as a presenter by viewing yourself on tape.

Isa Engleberg

HOW MUCH SHOULD I PRACTICE?

Generally, it's a good idea to practice your entire presentation several different times rather than to devote one long session to the process. Plus, brief five- to ten-minute sessions in which you practice smaller segments should ensure a good performance. Schedule and use at least three, but no more than five, complete run-through sessions. The reason for the upper limit is that too much practice can make you sound *canned*, a term used to describe speakers who have practiced their presentation so often or who have given the same presentation so many times that they no longer sound spontaneous and natural. Both of us have had to tell students and corporate speakers to stop practicing because they looked and sounded like robots.

Rather than prescribe the number of practice sessions, we offer this advice: Keep practicing until you feel satisfied. Then, practice with the goal of improving the fine points of your presentation. Then, stop!

you speak, you can see and hear how audience members react to your presentation and performance. Their facial expressions, their levels of concentration, and their responses to suggestions and humor are forms of feedback. What you decide to do with this information is critical. You can ignore the feedback and continue giving your performance exactly the way you did when you practiced it. Or you can modify your presentation.

These adaptations can be minor. You might slow down, increase your volume, or leave out a controversial story, a long quotation, or a complicated statistic. Sometimes, though, feedback can lead to major changes. You might modify or leave out a major argument, ask for or suggest a course of action that you hadn't intended to mention, make your general presentation style more or less formal, or spend more time demonstrating your competence.

Don't be afraid to make mid-course adjustments and corrections. Watch and listen to your audience as they watch, listen, and respond to you. If there's a noisy disruption in the room or nearby, increase your volume or stop and wait for the noise to end. If your audience laughs at a comment or applauds, stop and accept their response. If your talk runs longer than you've planned, and the audience is getting restless, do some quick thinking and shorten your presentation. Mid-course corrections in sailing are an accepted safety precaution. Mid-performance adjustments are just as important in order to deal with unexpected audience responses.

As the creator of your presentation, you have the right and power to change it at every decision-making point in the process. And if audience feedback tells you that an adaptation is needed, decide how to change, and do it.

Summary

❖❖ What is a good performance?

A good performance helps you accomplish your purpose through the use of effective vocal and physical delivery and feedback-based adaptation.

❖❖ Should I use an outline or read my presentation word for word?

Decide which form of delivery best suits your purpose, the audience, the logistics, the nature of the occasion, and your speaking style. Then choose from among impromptu, extemporaneous, manuscript, memorized, or a combination of these delivery forms.

❖❖ How should I use notes when I speak?

If you are using notes or a manuscript, use them during every practice session. Make sure that your notes are easy to read, are in proper order, and suit the delivery form that you have chosen and the logistics of the setting.

❖❖ What's the best way to practice?

Try practicing in three ways: in private, on tape, and in front of others. Each form can help you improve your performance.

Key Terms

extemporaneous speaking 220
impromptu speaking 219
manuscript speaking 221

memorized presentation 222
performance 218

Notes

1. Laurie E. Rozakis, *The Complete Idiot's Guide to Speaking in Public with Confidence* (New York: Alpha Books, 1995), p. 221.
2. Marjorie Brody, *Speaking Your Way to the Top* (Boston: Allyn & Bacon, 1998), p. 113.
3. Rozakis, p. 222.
4. Peggy Noonan, *Simply Speaking: How to Communicate Your Ideas with Style, Substance, and Clarity* (New York: HarperCollins, 1998), p. 9. Copyright © 1998 by Peggy Noonan. Reprinted by permission of HarperCollins Publishers, Inc.

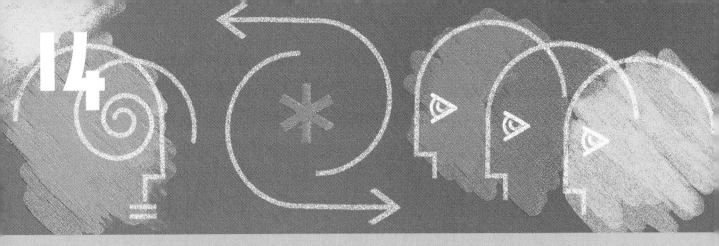

Vocal Delivery

▶▶ Can I improve my speaking voice?

▶▶ Can I speak loudly enough without feeling as though I'm shouting?

▶▶ Can I speak slowly enough to be understood without putting everyone to sleep?

▶▶ What's the best pitch for my voice?

▶▶ How can I avoid stumbling over words?

▶▶ How can I speak more clearly and accurately?

▶▶ How can I get rid of my accent?

Whether you like your speaking voice or not, it's *yours.* And like you, your voice is unique. Most of you can recognize your favorite singers or announcers on the radio because you know what their voices sound like. It's not unusual to telephone a friend and say, "Hi, it's me," and have that person recognize your voice.

Like fingerprints, each of our voices is one of a kind. As a result, there is little you can or should do to change it for a presentation. At the same time, you can *improve* your voice in order to make sure that your message is loud and clear. Although you must practice and want to improve, developing an effective speaking voice takes more than motivation and practice. You first must understand what it takes to make your voice an effective instrument for communication. In this chapter we start with the basics—the unique sound of your voice—and then move on to ways of improving its quality and effectiveness.

Developing an Effective Speaking Voice

Only a few lucky speakers are born with beautiful voices. Radio and television announcers often have natural voices that stand out in a crowd. Other speakers have learned Standard American English, the dialect used by the majority of outstanding educators, social and civic leaders, and prominent newscasters,[1] or grew up in an area of the country where it is spoken. Some people who do a lot of public speaking hire voice coaches for up to two hundred dollars an hour to help them improve the sound of their voices. In the musical *My Fair Lady,* professor Henry Higgins bets that he can change Eliza Doolittle's speech from that of a "gutter snipe" to that of a "lady" and thereby fool aristocratic society into thinking that she *is* a lady. Even with coaching, however, it can take years for a person to change the sound or quality of his or her voice.

Most of us don't have the money or time to hire a vocal coach, which is just as well. You probably don't need one anyway. What you *do* need is to know how to produce an effective voice and how you can monitor specific vocal qualities as you practice.

Think of your voice as the instrument that you use to produce sounds. Much like a musical instrument, the structure or anatomy of your vocal mechanism dictates the kind of sound you'll produce (see Figure 14.1). Men, for example, whose vocal cords are usually longer and thicker than women's, speak in a lower pitch. When your throat is swollen with a cold, your voice may be weaker or huskier. So before you try to sound like someone else, make sure that you comprehend the potential power and limits of your vocal instrument. Once you understand these factors, you can harness your vocal instrument for the task of producing clear and expressive speech.

Figure 14.1   Voice Mechanism

The intermittent force of exhaled air from the lungs through the larynx produces vocal fold vibration. Much like the lips of a trumpet player forcing air against a mouthpiece, a controlled breath stream sets the vocal folds in motion to produce a vocal sound. The interaction of your lips, teeth, tongue, and oral cavity modifies that vocal sound to create the unique sounds of speech.

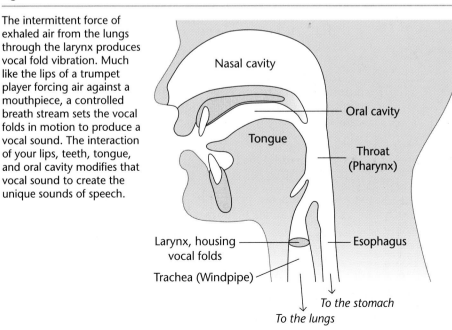

Components of an Effective Voice

Being able to make a sound on a musical instrument (striking the keys on a piano, banging on a drum, or plucking a violin string) is not the same as making music. Knowing the notes on a keyboard is not the same as playing a tune and making that tune loud or soft, fast or slow, crisp or *legato* (smooth and connected). The same is true of the instrument called your *voice*. There are ways of "playing" your voice that improve its quality and vocal characteristics that you can control and practice.

VOCAL CHARACTERISTICS

Breath
Volume
Rate
Pitch
Fluency

Developing a more effective speaking voice requires the same kind of time and effort that you would devote to improving any skill. You don't learn to be an accomplished carpenter, pianist, swimmer, writer, or speaker overnight. You need to learn the basics first.

Breath

Lyle Mayer, the well-respected author of a voice and articulation textbook, notes that "breathing to sustain life is primary and automatic—we're not always conscious of breathing."[2] Breathing for life, however, is not the same as breathing for speech. When we breathe to speak, we exercise conscious control of the processes of inhalation and exhalation. When we speak, we take in more air and control the release of air through exhalation. In fact, we control and expend air in much the same way that a trumpet player applies breath to the mouthpiece of a trumpet. Thus, the first step in producing an effective vocal sound is inhaling enough air and then exhaling it in a controlled manner to produce speech.

All of the sounds in spoken language are made during exhalation. The key to effective breathing for speech is controlling your outgoing breath, not just inhaling and holding more air in your lungs. Effective breath control improves the sound of your voice in several ways:[3]

▶ **Volume:** Effective breath control amplifies the loudness of your voice.

▶ **Duration:** Effective breath control lets you say more with a single breath.

▶ **Quality:** Effective breath control reduces the likelihood of vocal problems such as harshness or breathiness.

Voice coaches—whether they're teaching speakers or singers—always begin with breathing. Whether they call it "deep breathing," "abdominal breathing," or "diaphragmatic breathing," they insist that their students learn how to breathe more

USE YOUR OWN VOICE, NOT SOMEONE ELSE'S

In the hope of impressing an audience, inexperienced speakers sometimes try to imitate another speaker's voice. Trying to sound like a speaker you admire or a famous person can have disastrous results. If nothing else, you will spend too much energy and concentration trying to mimic the other person instead of working to improve your natural voice. Rather than impressing your audience, you are likely to sound phony and insincere. Be true to your own voice; train it properly, and it will serve you well.

efficiently and effectively. Your breathing may be shallow and inefficient now, but you can learn how to change it.

The first step in learning to breathe for speech is to note the difference between the shallow, unconscious breathing you do all the time and the deeper breathing that produces a strong, sustained sound quality. Many speech coaches recommend the following exercise to learn abdominal breathing.

1. Lie flat on your back on a comfortable surface. Support the back of your knees with a pillow.

2. Place a moderately heavy hardbound book on your stomach. The book should sit right over your navel.

3. Begin breathing through your mouth. The book should move up when you breathe in and sink down when you breathe out.

4. Place one of your hands on the upper part of your chest in a "Pledge of Allegiance" position. As you inhale and exhale, this area should not move in and out.

5. Now, take the book away and replace it with your other hand. Is your abdomen moving up when you breathe in and sinking down when you breathe out?

6. Once you're comfortable with step 5, try doing the same kind of breathing while sitting up or standing.

Once you've learned how abdominal breathing feels, you can begin to add sound.[4] For example, try sighing the vowel *ahh* with each exhalation. Sustain the vowel for five seconds. Once you have mastered *ahh,* try counting from one to five, holding each number for a full second. Your progress may be slow, but your efforts will reward you with a stronger and more controllable voice.

Volume

If your audience can't hear you, you won't achieve your purpose. One of the best ways to make sure that everyone in your audience can hear you is to practice your presentation *out loud,* using the voice and volume you intend to use when making your presentation. **Volume** measures your voice's degree of loudness. The key to producing adequate volume is knowing the size of the audience that you will be addressing and the dimensions of the room in which you will be speaking. Experienced speakers know how to use these factors to adjust their volume automatically. You can do the same. If there are only five people in an audience, and they are sitting close to you, you can speak at a normal, everyday volume. If there are fifty people in your audience, you will need more energy and force behind your voice. Once your audience exceeds one hundred people, you may be more comfortable using a microphone. However, a strong speaking voice can project to an audience of a thousand people without any electronic amplification. Professional speakers, actors, and classical singers do it all the time, but they also have spent years developing the power of their voices.

If you are not a trained speaker, actor, or singer, how can you make sure that your voice is loud enough? One thing you should *not* do is practice in your head or in a whisper, nor should you do all of your practicing in a small room. You can practice most vocal characteristics in a quiet voice, but not volume.

Try to practice in a room that is about the same size as the one in which you will be speaking. Ask a friend to sit in a far corner and report back on your volume level. If you are not loud enough, keep increasing your volume until your friend is satisfied. Also note that a room full of people absorbs sound; you will

James Carville, President Clinton's chief strategist in his 1992 campaign, speaks to students and professors at Jefferson Community College in Louisville, KY. Despite the large gathering, Carville's voice is strong enough that he can leave the lectern and microphone during his presentation.

have to turn up your volume another notch. Speakers who cannot be heard are a common problem. It's very rare, though, for a speaker to be too loud. Can we teach you to speak louder? The answer is, we don't have to; instead, let us convince you that it's okay to use your full voice. Have you ever yelled to someone in another room, called out to someone across campus, sung along full blast with a recording, or joined in a cheer at a game? Of course you have. Understand, however, that we are not suggesting that you yell at your audience. We're only pointing out that you already know how to speak loudly. The trick is finding and using the right volume level for your audience.

To reach all audience members, you need to learn to project. **Projection** is controlled vocal energy "that gives impact and intelligibility to sound. It involves a deliberate concentration and a strong desire to communicate with your listeners."[5] When you project, your voice will reach the audience members sitting furthest away. Like many other speakers, you may tend to speak to the people sitting right in front of you. You don't need a loud voice to be heard by someone five feet away. It's the person in the back row who will be straining to hear you. Simply looking at people in the back row and deliberately thinking about making them hear you can automatically increase your volume.

Here's an exercise that can help you learn to project. Ask someone to sit at the back of the room or auditorium in which you will be speaking. Then read a nonsense sentence in a voice that is loud and clear. The point, according to Lyle Mayer, is that by "practicing nonsense material, you'll quickly discover that loudness alone won't put it over."[6] You will need to tackle the consonants and vowels in the words with force and energy. Try to project your reading of the following sentences to someone sitting far away.

Samuel Hornsbee threw a turkey at the dragon's striped Chevrolet.

Karla Pavemore's heavy pen fell through the Earth's crust and reached New Zealand coated with magma.

Twenty-seven squirrels sang chants for the Christmas in April ball.

You may be thinking, "Well, if people can't hear me, why can't I just use a microphone to amplify my voice?" You can, but don't jump at every chance to use an amplification system. Most microphones don't reproduce a natural-sounding voice. Therefore, you may have to speak more slowly, articulate more clearly, and make sure that the system can accommodate changes in your volume. Microphones tend to be preset for one volume. If you speak too loudly, it may sound as though you are shouting at your audience. If you speak too softly, the "mike" may not pick up everything you say. An audience might forgive a few lost words under non-miked circumstances, but they will be less forgiving when you use a microphone, since they will expect to hear you very well.

Sometimes, though, a microphone is essential. An audience or a room may be so large that you won't be heard without one. Or you may find yourself in a situation where microphones have already been set up for each speaker. Regardless of how you end up in front of a microphone, make the most of the technology.

The trick is to go against your instincts. If you want to project a soft tone, speak closer to the microphone and lower your volume. Your voice will sound more intimate and will be able to convey subtle emotions. If you want to be more forceful, speak further away from the microphone and project your voice. This technique minimizes distortions and will make your presentation sound more powerful.

Familiarize yourself with the specific microphone you'll be using.

▶ If you can, test the mike ahead of time. Ask someone to sit at the back of the room and monitor your amplified voice. Can you speak at a normal volume, or do you need to be louder?

▶ Determine whether the microphone is sophisticated enough to capture your voice from various angles and distances or whether you'll need to keep your mouth close to it.

▶ Microphones work best when placed about five to ten inches from the speaker's mouth. If you are using a hand-held microphone, hold it below your mouth at chin level.

▶ If you are using a clip-on lavaliere microphone (wired or wireless), test it carefully. Once it's clipped on, it can be difficult to readjust.

▶ Focus on your audience, not on the microphone. Stay near the mike, but don't tap it, lean over it, keep readjusting it, or make the *p-p-p-p-p* "motorboat sound" as a test. Experienced speakers make all the adjustments they need during the first few seconds that they hear their own voices projected through an amplification system.

▶ When your microphone is well adjusted, and you're feeling comfortable, speak in a natural, conversational tone.

Sometimes the *p* sound comes popping through a microphone, particularly if you speak straight into it instead of at an angle. Adjusting the position of the microphone usually eliminates the popping sound. If you hear the painful squeal of sound system feedback, try moving away from the speakers; you may be too close to them. Last, keep in mind that a microphone will not only amplify your voice; it will also amplify other sounds—coughing, throat-clearing, the shuffling of papers, or the tapping of a pen.

Learn to avoid these common microphone problems, and you'll sound like a pro! Microphones can be a valuable tool once you learn how to use them effectively.

Using these nonsense sentences will ensure that your listener cannot anticipate the correct words. When asked to write down or repeat what you have said, your listener won't be able to guess a logical ending to your sentence. Thus, if you don't project with force and clarity, you won't be understood.

If your voice is too soft, you may need some direct coaching and confidence building before you speak. Don't wait until your presentation is over to find out that you couldn't be heard. Sometimes after a soft-spoken student has finished a presentation, we ask him or her to repeat the first ten seconds of the speech in a louder voice. After the student responds with some hesitancy and a slightly louder beginning, we ask for a louder one. And after that, we ask for an even louder one. In bewilderment, the student often says, "But I'm shouting." We then ask the class for a verdict and the answer is always the same: "You're not

FAST TALK IS BETTER THAN SLOW TALK In most cases, it's better to speak a little too fast than too slowly. Listeners perceive presenters who speak quickly *and* clearly as energized, competent, and interested.[1] Given the choice, we'd rather be accused of speaking too fast than run the risk of boring an audience. Too slow a rate can suggest that you are unsure of yourself or, even worse, that you are not very bright. Since audiences can listen faster than you can talk, it's better to keep the pace up than to speak at a "crawl." Familiarize yourself with how it feels to speak at 145 to 180 words a minute so that you can monitor your rate during your presentation.

1. Michael Argyle, "Nonverbal Vocalizations." In Laura K. Guerrero, Joseph A. DeVito, and Michael L. Hecht (Eds.), *The Nonverbal Communication Reader: Classic and Contemporary Readings*, 2nd ed. (Prospect Heights, IL: Waveland, 1999), p. 141.

shouting; your volume is just right. That's how you should always speak." A quiet person is comfortable using a soft voice. What seems like a shout may be the perfect volume level for a presentation.

Practice your presentation at full volume. Give your speech at the same volume, observe your audience's reactions, and ask a friend to signal you if you need to increase your volume.

Rate

We've all heard speakers who talked too fast or too slow. Your **rate** of speech equals the number of words you say per minute added to the number and length of pauses you use. There is no single "speed limit" for a presentation. But as in driving, for which there are different speed limits for different road and traffic conditions, there are various speech rates for various situations. Your natural speaking style, your presentation's mood, your vocabulary's complexity, and your audience's listening ability should affect your rate. Some general guidelines can help you determine whether you are speaking too slowly, too fast, or at just the right rate. First, you have to time yourself. This paragraph contains about 125 words. Read it out loud in the kind of voice you would use before an audience. How long did it take you to read it?

If it took you sixty seconds to read the previous paragraph, you're a slow speaker. If it took you thirty seconds, you are speaking at a rate of 250 words per minute (wpm), which is too fast for most audiences to follow easily.

Now read and time the previous two paragraphs. They contain about 170 words. Given that the material is fairly easy to read and unemotional, a total of sixty seconds (give or take a few) would be about right. Generally, anything below 125 wpm is too slow; 125 to 145 wpm is acceptable; 145 to 180 is better; 180 or higher exceeds the speed limit.[7] But don't carve these guidelines in stone. Your wpm depends on you, your message, and your audience.

Generally, presenters tend to speak too fast—they exceed the 180 wpm speed limit. Often speakers are so familiar with what they want to say that they forget that their audience is hearing it for the first time. Both of us have been accused of racing through presentations when we have had a lot to say. Even after years of making presentations, we still have to remind ourselves to slow down, slow down, slow down. Don't race; pace yourself.

Pitch

Just like the notes on a musical scale, **pitch** refers to how high or low your voice sounds. Most men speak at a lower pitch than women do. Most adults speak at a lower pitch than children do. Anatomy determines pitch. Men have longer and thicker vocal cords (also known as vocal folds) than women do. Just as the longer, thicker strings on a piano produce lower notes, longer, thicker vocal cords produce a lower vocal pitch.

Americans seem to prefer low-pitched voices. They think that men and women with deeper voices sound more authoritative and effective. Men with a naturally high pitch may be labeled effeminate or weak, and women with very high speaking voices may be labeled childish or silly. To compensate for a high natural voice, some speakers push their voices down into a lower range of notes. However, this practice limits the voice's expressiveness, can make it sound harsh, and damages the voice by putting a strain on the vocal cords.

Like everyone else, you have a natural or **optimum pitch** at which you speak most easily and expressively. The hard part is finding it. Like many other speakers, you may have the habit of speaking at a too-low or too-high pitch. You need to rediscover your optimum pitch so that you can produce the strongest and clearest sound with the least amount of effort and strain.

Finding Your Optimum Pitch. Although there are several ways to find your optimum pitch, a method called "Sing *Sol-La*" works for many speakers. This exercise requires the ability to sing a musical scale or access to a musical instrument (and someone who can play a scale). Sing the lowest note you can sing. Then, sing up the scale—*Do-Re-Mi-Fa-Sol-La-Ti-Do*. Next, go back to your lowest note and sing up to *Sol*. Can you easily sing an octave above *Sol*? Try *La*. If you have to strain a little to reach the octave above *La,* go back to *Sol*. Your best pitch is probably the fifth (*Sol*) or sixth (*La*) note above your lowest note. Test your *Sol* or *La* note to see if you can increase its volume with minimal effort and strain. Then, sing an octave higher than that note. The sound should be clear and unstrained.[8]

Now, try to say a nursery rhyme or the Pledge of Allegiance very quickly at your optimum pitch. Can you produce the sound easily? Do you feel any strain? Is the sound higher or lower than the pitch at which you usually speak? If it is higher than your normal pitch, try raising your overall pitch when you speak. Finding this pitch doesn't mean that you should speak at only that one note. Instead, think of this pitch as "neutral," and use it as your base line for increasing the expressiveness of your voice. Then, establish your optimum pitch in your auditory memory and use it to project a clear and powerful speaking voice.

HOW DO I PREVENT MY VOICE FROM SHAKING?

One of our survey respondents, an assistant superintendent of schools in New York, wrote: "My problem—my voice quivers!" Many speakers believe that their voices quiver, but in fact, the audience hears nothing like a shake, rattle, or roll. When you speak loudly and forcefully, you perceive the sound of any vocal variation more intensely because your speaking voice is amplified in your head. Most of the time, the audience does not hear anything distracting in your voice. If that's the case, then don't worry about it. If, however, the shaking in your voice is obvious, you can take a few steps to reduce this phenomenon.

- Make sure that your volume is adequate, a situation which, in turn, ensures a strong and steady stream of air.

- Make sure that you are speaking at your optimum pitch.

- Review ways of reducing presentation anxiety, which may cause a trembling voice (see Chapter 3, "Building Presentation Confidence").

THE BENEFITS OF USING OPTIMUM PITCH

- **Your voice will be stronger and less likely to fade at the ends of sentences.**

- **Your voice will not tire easily.**

- **You will be less likely to sound harsh, hoarse, breathy, or squeaky.**

- **You will have "room to move" above and below that pitch, an absolute must for an expressive and energetic voice.**

Varying Pitch for Emphasis. **Inflection** is the changing pitch within a syllable, word, or group of words. Inflection makes speech expressive; lack of it is the culprit for what most people call a "monotone voice." A **monotone** voice occurs not because you use the wrong pitch or speak slowly but rather because you don't change the pitch of sounds within words or the pitch of words within phrases and sentences. Speaking in a monotone limits your expressiveness. In English, we tend to use a rising inflection when we ask questions, express uncertainty, or stress a word or syllable.[9] We tend to use downward inflections at the ends of phrases and sentences or when we're depressed or under stress. "I can't cope anymore" would not end with a rising inflection unless you were doing a "Valley Girl" imitation, in which almost every statement would end on the upswing.[10]

Inflection both helps you to avoid having a monotone voice and allows you to emphasize an important or meaningful word or phrase. When you're speaking from a manuscript, we recommend that you underline words that should receive extra stress or emphasis. More often than not, varying pitch sets a word apart from the rest of a sentence. A single change in inflection can change the entire meaning of a sentence, as is illustrated in the following examples.

I was born in New Jersey.   (You, on the other hand, were born in Maryland.)

I **was** born in New Jersey.   (No doubt about it!)

I was **born** in New Jersey.   (So I know my way around.)

I was born in **New Jersey**.   (Not in New York.)

Inflection may not seem very important, since the resulting change in pitch can be a fraction of a note. Yet, like the effects of any strong spice in a recipe, a small rise or drop in inflection can change the entire meaning of a sentence or the quality of your voice. Inflection is a key ingredient in making your voice more interesting, exciting, emotional, and emphatic.

Fluency

Fluency is the ability to speak smoothly without tripping over words or pausing at awkward moments. Although an audience might not notice how fluent you are, they *will* notice when something interrupts the flow of your speech.

The more you practice your presentation, the more fluent you will become. Practice will alert you to words, phrases, and sentences that look good in your notes but sound awkward or choppy when spoken. You'll find out if you have included any words that you have trouble pronouncing. Practice lets you work on volume, rate, pitch, and articulation. With adequate practice, your voice will sound fluent.

Filler Phrases. Many people have the habit of using filler phrases, a very common fluency problem. Annoying filler phrases, you know, like a, okay, break up, um, your fluency and, uh, drive your audience, right, like crazy. Everyone knows how annoying and distracting it can be to listen to a presentation loaded with filler phrases. Who hasn't sat in the back of a classroom or auditorium and counted the number of times a speaker said, "You know" or "okay"? Unfortunately, most speakers don't even know they're doing it.

In addition to filler words and phrases such as "you know," "okay," "like," and "right," some speakers have their own personal phrases—"Got it?" "There!" "Yup," and the unwarranted giggle that appears when it absolutely shouldn't. It doesn't matter what the phrase is. It only matters that you become aware of how often you use it and then try to stop.

 HOW DO I AVOID SAYING *UM* AND *UH* SO OFTEN? First, let's get one misconception out of the way about *um*s and *uh*s. Not all filler phrases are equally bad. There is nothing wrong with an occasional *uh* or *um*, particularly when you're speaking informally or impromptu. Even the most eloquent and experienced speakers may insert an occasional *uh* or *um* into their presentations to make themselves sound more natural and spontaneous. In fact, *um* seems to become part of our vocabulary before the age of three.

An *um* can mean that you're thinking about the way to phrase the next sentence or that you're searching for a word. In a presentation, it is perfectly okay to have a few of these short filler phrases—not three or four per sentence, but an occasional interruption that makes your speech sound natural and conversational. With worries about using an occasional *uh* and *um* put aside, you can start eliminating some of your more annoying filler phrases as well as excessive use of *uh* and *um*.

The History Channel Web site,
www.historychannel.com/
speeches/index.html, invites you
to "hear the words that changed
the world." As you listen to some
of these famous broadcasts and
recordings, pay attention to the
speakers' volume, rate, pitch,
fluency, articulation, and
pronunciation.

Reprinted by permission of A & E Television Networks. www.historychannel.
com. Copyright © 200 A&E TELEVISION
NETWORKS. All Rights Reserved.

Tape-record one of your practice sessions or an actual presentation and listen for filler phrases. Sometimes they appear only during your actual presentation, when you are most nervous and least aware of the extra phrases that can sneak into your speech. Then comes the hard part. In order to break the filler phrase habit, you must slow down and listen to yourself as you practice. At first, you will be less fluent, stopping at almost every phrase, correcting yourself. Monitor your performance and practice as well as your everyday speech. Filler phrases cannot be turned off at the beginning of a presentation and allowed to reappear after- wards. As in breaking any habit, going "cold turkey" requires saying *no* to filler phrases in *all* speaking situations.

Run-on Sentences.   The second cousins of filler phrases are run-on sentences. Sometimes, because a speaker is nervous and is trying hard to maintain fluency, she or he may have a tendency to connect all sentences with *and* or *uh* and keep going, even though there may have been several natural places to stop and begin another sentence during the speech. Notice how the last sentence could have ended after *uh* but instead used the word *and* to keep going. In a few cases, stu- dent speakers have managed to utter a seven-minute sentence rather than give a seven-minute presentation.

As with breaking the filler phrase habit, you need to slow down and listen to yourself. Even better, tape-record your practice sessions and listen for run-on sen- tences. For practice purposes, write out a few sections of your presentation in manuscript form to make sure that your sentences are short. Practice those sec- tions in order to get a feel for speaking in smaller units. Then apply that feeling to your entire presentation.

Clarity and Correctness

A strong, well-paced, optimally pitched voice that is also fluent and expressive may not be enough to ensure the successful delivery of a presentation. Clarity and correctness also matter. A million-dollar vocal instrument will have little value if you mumble and mispronounce words. Proper articulation and pronun- ciation are just as important as volume, rate, pitch, fluency, and inflection.

**FACTORS AFFECTING CLARITY
AND CORRECTNESS**

Articulation
Pronunciation
Accents and dialects

Articulation

Articulation is a term that describes your diction or how clearly you make the sounds in the words of a language. Poor articulation is often described as "sloppy speech," "lazy tongue," or just plain mumbling. If friends ask, "What?" after you've said something, they are rarely asking you to speak louder; they are asking you to articulate.

You can improve and practice your articulation. Generally, it helps to speak a little more slowly and a bit more loudly and to open your mouth a little wider than you usually do. Speakers whose lips barely move and whose teeth barely part let their words get trapped and jumbled in their mouths. The result is mumbling.

Certain sounds account for most articulation problems. The culprits are combined words, "ing" endings, and final consonants. If someone said, "Firs, I'm gonna telya watsumata with sayin and readin thisenens," you might be able to translate it as "First, I am going to tell you what's the matter with saying and reading this sentence." Many of us combine words—"what's the matter" becomes "watsumata"; "going to" becomes "gonna." Some of us shorten the "ing" sound to an "in" sound: "sayin" instead of "saying." And others leave off final consonants such as the *t* in "first."

The final consonants that get left off most often are the ones that pop out of your mouth in a mini-explosion. Because these consonants—*p, b, t, d, k, g*—cannot be hummed like an "m" or hissed like an "s," it's easy to lose them at the end of a word. While you can hear the difference between "Rome" and "rose," poor articulation can make it difficult to hear the difference between "rack" and "rag," "hit" and "hid," or "tap" and "tab," to give a few examples. Make a note of words that end with these consonants and practice articulating the final sounds.

Pronunciation

Pronunciation refers to whether you say a word correctly—whether you put all the correct sounds in the correct order with the correct stress. It can be embarrassing to mispronounce a common word. Once one of us heard a speaker give a presentation on the importance of pronunciation, but she undermined her effectiveness by referring to "pro*nounc*iation" throughout her speech! Finding a word's correct pronunciation is not difficult; look it up in a dictionary or listen to someone who knows how to pronounce the word. Speakers who don't take the time to check their pronunciation may find themselves embarrassed in front of an audience.

Pronunciation errors fall into five general categories. Speakers add sounds, subtract sounds, substitute sounds, reverse sounds, and misplace stress. Figure 14.2 shows examples of each kind of error.

CREATE YOUR OWN PRONUNCIATION DRILLS One way to correct commonly mispronounced words is to create and practice saying a sentence that includes words that you have trouble pronouncing correctly. For example, read the following sentences out loud and ask a good listener to use the list of mispronounced words on page 241 to check your pronunciation.

Both Detroit police officers asked the deaf witness to gesture at the relevant suspect.

It's not surprising that the picture of a larynx was used to help the eager students pronounce words such as *nuclear, chasm,* and *theater.*

Create your own sentence and use it to practice the words you have difficulty pronouncing.

REAL WORLD, REAL SPEAKERS

A professional colleague of ours told us this story about the importance of correct pronunciation:

I once attended a critical meeting with officers from a large corporate foundation and staff members from my college. We were seeking a substantial grant for our institution. Admittedly, the name of the corporation was long and difficult to pronounce. However, when introductions were being made around the conference table, a college official mispronounced the name of the foundation. It got worse and worse as each of the corporate officers was introduced with his or her corporate title. Within seconds, the rest of us at the table knew that we had jeopardized our chance for a donation. One mispronounced word cost us thousands of dollars.

Pronunciations can and do change. According to most pronunciation dictionaries, the word *often* should be pronounced "ofen," but many people now accept "often" as an acceptable pronunciation. The word *a* should be pronounced "uh," not rhyme with "hay," but many people now use both versions. When the word *the* appears before the sound of a consonant as in "the table" or "the dog," it should be pronounced "thuh." When *the* comes before the sound of a vowel, as in "the apple" or "the ambulance," it should be pronounced "thee." However, many people no longer make these distinctions. One way to look at pronunciation is to

Figure 14.2   Common Mispronunciations

Correct Spelling	Correct Pronunciation	Incorrect Pronunciation	Type of Error
across	uh-kraws	uhkrawst	Added sound
nuclear	nooklear	nookyoolear	Added sound
pronounce	pronauns	pronaunseate	Added sound
surprise	serprize	suprize	Subtracted sound
shouldn't	shoud'nt	shount	Subtracted sound
picture	pikcher	picher	Subtracted sound
deaf	def	deef	Substituted sound
chasm	kazm	chazm	Substituted sound
both	both	bof	Substituted sound
Detroit	de*troit*	*de*troit	Misplaced stress
theater	theater	the*a*ter	Misplaced stress
police	po*lees*	*po*less	Misplaced stress
larynx	larinks	larniks	Reversed sound
ask	ask	aks	Reversed sound
relevant	relevant	revelant	Reversed sound

ask whether the way you pronounce a word will call attention to it. In front of a group of voice and diction teachers, "thuh apple" would be distracting and annoying. In front of a general audience, "thuh apple" might go unnoticed.

Accents and Dialects

When teaching or coaching speakers from other countries, we are often asked, "How can I get rid of my accent?" The honest answer to this question is that in most cases, you can't. The better answer is this: Why do you want to? An accent generally won't hinder your ability to communicate. Sometimes, in fact, an accent can add charm and interest to your presentation. In other cases, however, a heavy accent can distract an audience and can subsequently reduce your effectiveness. Before you try to change your accent, there a few things you should learn about accents and dialects.

An **accent** is the sound of one language imposed on another.[11] Some Asian speakers have difficult producing the "r" and "v" sounds in English. Spanish speakers often make the "i" sound in a word like *sister* sound like a long "e" sound, as in *see*. Eastern Europeans may substitute a "v" for the "w" sound. Many non-English speakers have difficulty making the "th" sound. While listening to two colleagues—one from Thailand, the other from the former Yugoslavia—we heard the Thai speaker say that he was "wehwee worried" about a student and the Yugoslavian saying that she was also "very vorried." It's important to note that both of these speakers were rated as excellent teachers and communicators. Their accents did not inhibit the speakers from expressing themselves; nor did they prevent us from understanding what the speakers said.

Dialects differ from accents because they represent regional and cultural differences within the same language. What people call a southern accent is really a southern dialect. The phrase "pahking the cah in the Hahvahd yahd" demonstrates a Boston dialect, not an accent. Is it acceptable to say, "Y'all" and "Sho 'nuf" if you are a southerner? Is it acceptable for some African Americans and speakers of street lingo to say, "My brother, he sick"? If you answer these questions according to the rules of Standard American English,[12] the answer is *no*. Does that mean a speaker should never use "Y'all" and "He sick"? Again, the answer is *no*.

Although we can't answer all the arguments or resolve the debate about accents and dialects, we will take a position regarding presentation speaking. Whether standard or nonstandard, the language you use is a means to an end, a way of achieving the purpose of your presentation. Because words are the basic building blocks of a presentation, it is your choice which building blocks to use. If "y'all" or "he sick" is difficult for you to change or is the way you *want* to be heard, you run a risk. An audience that doesn't like or has trouble listening to that particular dialect may be distracted or even turned off by your presentation. In fact, a consistent finding across many research studies is that Standard American English speakers are judged as more intelligent, ambitious, and successful, even when the judges themselves speak in a nonstandard American dialect.[13] On the other hand, an audience that expects to hear your natural dialect may think that you are talking down to

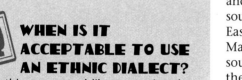

WHEN IS IT ACCEPTABLE TO USE AN ETHNIC DIALECT?

At first this may sound like a question that treads the dangerous territory of political correctness. After all, many southerners don't say, "Sho 'nuf," and most African Americans don't say, "My brother, he sick." Does that make southerners and African Americans who don't use these phrases better speakers than those who do?

For years a fierce debate has raged over whether there should be a standardized and official English language in the United States. It's not likely to be settled anytime soon. Those who want everyone to speak Standard American English argue that a common language will keep the country strong, literate, and unified. Those who argue against a common standard language recognize that such rules put immigrants and minority Americans at a significant disadvantage and take some of the richness out of our language. Didn't Lyndon Johnson, Martin Luther King Jr., and Jimmy Carter speak in southern dialects? Didn't John F. Kennedy speak with a Boston dialect?

In fact, it seems that some dialects are more acceptable than others. Is it okay to say, "Y'all come down now" but not acceptable to say, "He sick"? In the end, the answers depend on several factors. Ask yourself whether your decision to use an ethnic dialect in your presentation is suitable for the purpose, occasion, and audience. If you're not sure, monitor your presentation for "down-home" or "old-country" lingo that could offend or confuse your audience.

REAL WORLD, REAL SPEAKERS

I was born in Jersey City, New Jersey, and spoke in a very strong Jersey/New York dialect. When my family moved to a town where Standard American English was spoken, my speech was greeted with laughter. I decided that it was time for me to learn a second language—Standard American English. With the help of a tireless speech teacher, I learned the "proper" way to speak. But at the same time, I could speak pure Jersey whenever I was with my family and friends from New Jersey and New York.

I learned the same lesson when I spent a year teaching in Australia. I learned that a "subject" in Australian colleges is the same as a U.S. college course and a "course" is the same as a major or program. I learned to follow "timetables" instead of "schedules" and permitted my students to bring "rubbers" (erasers) to final exams. In order to be understood, I tried to speak Australian. Over time, even the sound of my American dialect changed. Although I will never sound like an Australian, at least I made the effort to sound less harsh to the Australian listener. So now I speak three "languages"—Standard American English, New Jersey, and a bit of Australian. Of course, all of these "languages" are different dialects of English. All of them are useful tools or building blocks that I can use in a presentation.

Isa Engleberg

them if you use Standard American English. As is so often the case, knowing your audience is the key to achieving your purpose.

If words are building blocks, the more blocks you have to choose from, the better. Just as you would dress differently for different speaking situations, you may sometimes want to change the way you use words. This can be a difficult but not impossible task, as both of us have learned during the course of living and working in many different places.

Having a strong accent or dialect does not stop anyone from being a strong speaker. Many years ago, one of us heard Dr. Elisabeth Kubler-Ross, who had a soft voice and a strong German accent, speak at a medical school graduation. Dr. Kubler-Ross's book *On Death and Dying* had brought her international attention and fame on the topic of caring for dying patients. During the first few minutes of her address, the audience strained to understand what she was saying. Yet her stories were so touching and her personality so compelling that the audience was soon captivated by her. Her accent made no difference at all.

At the same time, we don't want to minimize the importance of having an effective speaking voice. Esther-Ann Asch, a vice president with Federal Employment and Guidance Services in Manhattan, told us that she gives her voice credit for her success as a speaker: "My voice has always been the key to presenting. Because it is loud, forceful, and compelling, it gets and keeps the audience's attention."

You don't need a perfect voice to be a great speaker. You need a purposeful, well-organized message and a clear voice that helps you achieve the goal of your presentation. As long as your voice is loud enough and clear enough, you can concentrate your attention and energy on what you have to say.

Summary

Can I improve my speaking voice?

By further developing vocal characteristics that you already have—such as breath control, volume, rate, pitch, fluency, articulation, and pronunciation—you can improve the effectiveness of your speaking voice.

Can I speak loudly enough without feeling as though I'm shouting?

Yes, if you are willing to use your naturally loud voice and to project to the back of the room. Ask a friend or sympathetic listener to monitor your volume and to alert you to any problems.

Can I speak slowly enough to be understood without putting everyone to sleep?

Yes, if you time yourself and then try to adjust your speed to the message, room, and audience. Remember that most presenters speak too fast, not too slowly.

What's the best pitch for my voice?

Don't assume that a lower pitch is a better pitch. Instead, find your optimum pitch and try using it in all of your daily speaking situations. Make sure that syllables, words, and phrases receive the appropriate inflection and stress.

How can I avoid stumbling over words?

In addition to practicing your presentation, avoid using an excessive number of filler phrases and run-on sentences.

How can I speak more clearly and accurately?

Generally, you can improve your articulation by speaking a little more slowly and a bit more loudly and by opening your mouth a little wider than you usually do, while watching out for combined words, "ing" endings, and final consonants. Also, avoid mispronunciations by looking up questionable words in a dictionary before your presentation and by practicing words that are difficult to pronounce.

How can I get rid of my accent?

There is nothing wrong with having an accent or speaking in a dialect. If you speak clearly and accurately, your audience should understand you and your message.

Key Terms

accent 242	inflection 237	projection 234
articulation 240	monotone 237	pronunciation 240
dialect 242	optimum pitch 237	rate 236
fluency 238	pitch 236	volume 233

Notes

1. Lyle V. Mayer, *Fundamentals of Voice and Articulation*, 11th ed. (Madison, WI: Brown & Benchmark, 1996), p. 8.
2. Mayer, p. 18.
3. Ethel C. Glenn, Phillip J. Glenn, and Sandra Forman, *Your Voice and Articulation*, 4th ed. (Boston: Allyn & Bacon, 1998), pp. 30–31.
4. Jeffrey C. Hahner, Martin A. Sokoloff, and Sandra L. Salisch, *Speaking Clearly: Improving Voice and Diction*, 4th ed. (New York: McGraw-Hill, 1993), pp. 289–290.
5. Mayer, p. 61.
6. Mayer, p. 62.
7. Authors of voice and articulation textbooks generally agree that a useful, all-purpose speaking rate is around 145 to 180 words per minute. See Lyle V. Mayer, *Fundamentals of Voice and Articulation*, 11th ed. (Madison, WI: Brown & Benchmark, 1996); Jeffrey C. Hahner, Martin A. Sokoloff, and Sandra L. Salisch, *Speaking Clearly: Improving Voice and Diction*, 5th ed. (New York: McGraw-Hill, 1997); Ethel C. Glenn, Phillip J. Glenn, and Sandra Forman, *Your Voice and Articulation*, 4th ed. (Boston: Allyn & Bacon, 1998).
8. Comprehensive descriptions of and guidelines for achieving optimum pitch can be found in a classic voice and diction textbook: Hilda B. Fisher, *Improving Voice and Articulation* (Boston: Houghton Mifflin, 1966), pp. 162–174.
9. Hahner, Sokoloff, and Salisch, 4th ed. (1993), p. 339.
10. A glossary of "Valley Girl Speak" can be found in Jim Crotty, *How to Talk American: A Guide to Our Native Tongues* (Boston: Houghton Mifflin, 1997), pp. 166–167.
11. Glenn, Glenn, and Forman (p. 8) define a dialect as a "variation pattern of speech features within a given language that is characteristic of certain native speakers. By contrast, an accent usually refers to patterns from a speaker's native language spilling over into the production of a second language; thus, a person from Paris might speak English with a French accent. Dialects can vary on a number of features including vocabulary, rhythm, and pronunciation. These variations may mark certain geographic areas (New Orleans, Boston, Brooklyn), ethnic and national groups (Black, Hispanic, Eastern European), and socioeconomic distinctions (upper class, working class)."
12. Glenn, Glenn, and Forman (pp. 8–9) point out that "in the United States, one particular dialect—Standard American English—has gained widespread acceptance. . . . Standard American English is a dialect, and in this country it is the dialect most commonly accepted and employed in the entertainment, education, business, and political worlds."
13. Glenn, Glenn, and Forman, p. 10.

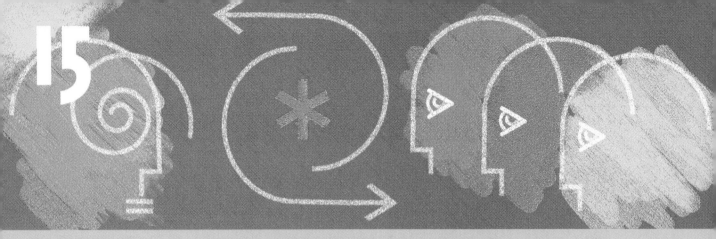

15

Physical Delivery

- ▸▸ Why is eye contact so important?
- ▸▸ Can I control my facial expressions?
- ▸▸ Which gestures work best during a presentation?
- ▸▸ How should I stand and move during a presentation?
- ▸▸ How do I deliver a presentation on radio, on camera, or online?

A natural delivery style tells your audience a great deal about who you are and how much you care about reaching them. An audience-centered speaker is a natural speaker, and naturalness makes your personality an integral part of your performance. Audiences feel comfortable when you seem comfortable. When you appear competent and confident, they can relax and listen. Naturalness lets the real you come through. However, being natural doesn't mean "letting it all hang out." Rather, it means being so well prepared and well practiced that your presentation is an authentic reflection of you. During such a presentation, your eye contact, facial expressions, gestures, posture, and movement will not draw attention to themselves. Your movement will support and highlight your presentation's important words and ideas. In this chapter, we explain how to achieve this natural physical delivery style.

Making a Good Physical Impression

Audience members jump to conclusions about speakers on the basis of first impressions of their appearance. Even though such snap judgments may seem unfair, you've probably made them yourself. The ways in which you stand, move, gesture, and make eye contact will have a significant impact on your presentation.

Although you can change these aspects of your physical delivery, there's one thing you cannot change: your body. However, you *can* compensate for or adapt to the place where you will be speaking. If you are short, a small platform behind the lectern can make the difference between being hidden and being seen and will also let you see your audience. If you need glasses, wear them. Accommodate to the things you can't change, but control those you can. As in the case of your voice, special skills and strategies can help you practice and improve the way that you physically deliver a presentation.

COMPONENTS OF PHYSICAL DELIVERY

Eye contact
Facial expression
Gestures
Posture and movement

Eye Contact

Eye contact may be the single most important component of effective physical delivery. Quite simply, **eye contact** is establishing and maintaining visual links with individual members of your audience. Communication scholars, speech teachers, authors of popular public speaking books, and experienced presenters overwhelmingly agree that eye contact is critical because it initiates and controls communication, affects speaker credibility, and provides the speaker with a means of assessing listener feedback.

Control. When you want to speak with someone, you "catch her eye" to initiate communication. The same is true in a presentation. When you establish initial eye contact with your audience, you indicate that you are ready to begin speaking and that they should get ready to listen. Lack of eye contact communicates a message, too: It says that you don't care to connect with your audience. After all, if you don't look at your audience, why should they look at you?

Not only does eye contact initiate communication; it also has the power to make people listen. Every good teacher, preacher, police officer, and political candidate knows that "giving the eye" to inattentive listeners is one of the best ways to get and keep their attention. Direct eye contact says, "I'm talking to *you*; I want *you* to hear this." Direct eye contact transforms the speaker from an impersonal messenger into someone worth listening to.

Credibility. Eye contact can also have a direct and positive effect on your credibility.[1] It says:

▶ *I'm of good character.* I care enough to share this important message with you.

▶ *I'm competent.* I know this subject so well that I can leave my notes and look at you.

▶ *I'm charismatic.* I want to energize and connect with everyone in this room.

SHOULD I IMAGINE MY AUDIENCE NAKED?

Despite and perhaps because of its importance, eye contact has inspired numerous myths. We've had clients say that they've been told to look over and between the heads of the people in their audiences. Others have been told to find a spot on the back wall or one friendly face to look at throughout a presentation. Some have even been given the absurd suggestion that they should imagine their audience members without their clothes on—the best argument we've ever heard for *not* looking at your audience. Coming closer to receiving good advice—but not yet there—are the speakers who have been trained to move their gaze by looking at groups of people in every section of the room (a tactic which works well with audiences of one thousand but not with twenty listeners). Then there are those who have been told to move their gaze up and down or across every row. In all of these situations, the speakers were told not to look directly at individual listeners or to look at them as inanimate objects.

These myths and misconceptions about eye contact border on the ridiculous. They just don't work. Staring at a clock at the back of a room can make you look like a zombie or a sleepwalker. Imagining an audience naked not only insults the people you want to influence but also can be terribly distracting. Looking up and down every aisle is more suitable for mowing the lawn than for making a presentation. There's no "trick" to eye contact. Just look at individual people in your audience—eye to eye.

In everyday conversation, avoiding eye contact can indicate disinterest, insincerity, or deception. By looking directly at your audience, you demonstrate your dedication to open and honest communication. People who seek and maintain eye contact while speaking, whether face to face or before an audience of thousands, tend to be more believable.

Feedback. Making eye contact is the best way to gauge audience feedback during your presentation. At first, looking at your audience members eye to eye may distract you. Some people may smile, others may look bored or confused, and some may be looking around the room or passing notes to friends. With all of this going on in the audience, it's easy for you to become sidetracked wondering why you're getting so many different reactions.

Receiving all of those different responses can be unsettling until you realize that being aware of those responses is the very reason why you must establish and maintain eye contact. By looking at the individual members of your audience, you can tell whether they are interested, bored, delighted, or displeased. Speakers who don't look at their audiences rarely have a clue about why their presentations succeed or fail. Yes, audience reactions can be distracting, but they also give back more than they take. Eye contact gives you a wealth of information about the audience's reactions to you and your presentation. Moreover, when you see that your audience is attentive and interested, you may gain more confidence and enthusiasm.

> **BENEFITS OF EYE CONTACT**
>
> Initiates and controls communication
> Enhances speaker credibility
> Provides feedback

Eye Contact Techniques. Talk to audience members in the same way that you would talk to a friend, coworker, client, or customer. This doesn't mean staring at them until they squirm in their seats; rather, it means catching their eye for a few seconds, saying something, and then moving on to someone else. Don't establish eye contact row by row as though you're taking roll. Move your gaze around the room, settle on someone, and establish direct eye contact. Then switch to someone else—someone sitting near the person whom you just looked at or someone all the way across the room.

Don't move your eyes in a rigid pattern but do try to establish eye contact with as many individual people as you can. It's very tempting to direct your eye contact at people sitting directly in front of you or at those who seem friendliest or most interested. Instead, try to look at the person seated farthest away from you just as often as you look at the person directly in front of you. Look at the people seated off to one side as often as you look at those in the center.

Amount of Eye Contact. Generally, the more eye contact you have with your audience, the more personal and responsive your presentation will be. So how much is enough? Ideally, you should maintain eye contact with your audience during most of your entire presentation. This is easiest to do in impromptu and extemporaneous presentations or in memorized speeches. Note that we said *most;* it would be unnatural to keep your eyes glued to your audience 100 percent of the time. An occasional look around the room, a glance at your hands, a peek at the clock, or a reference to a presentation aid adds naturalness and gives your eyes a brief rest.

Even when using a set of notes, you should maintain as much eye contact as you can—at least 75 percent of your speaking time. If you are using a manuscript, you should know your script so well that you can glance at the page, see a whole line of words, look up, and say them without having to read from the script word for word.

One useful method for maximizing eye contact when using detailed notes or a manuscript is called **eye scan.** Eye scan involves training your eyes to glance at a specific section of your notes or manuscript, to focus on a phrase or sentence, to glance back up at your audience, and to speak. Begin by placing your thumb and index finger on one side of the page to frame the section of your notes or the manuscript that you are using, to make sure that you don't lose your place on the page.[2] Then, as you approach the end of a phrase or sentence within that section, glance down again and visually grasp the next phrase to be spoken. Keep moving your thumb and index finger down the page as you move through each section. Eye scanning helps you maintain maximum eye contact without losing your place. Even when discussing a highly technical or complex topic, you should practice enough beforehand in order to be able to look at your audience most of the time.

With an audience of thirty or fewer people, it's usually possible to make eye contact with each person. In most cases, limit your eye contact to three to five seconds with any one person. Otherwise, the listener may become uncomfortable and feel singled out. If your audience is much larger than thirty or forty people, you may find it necessary to look instead at different sections of the audience. Focus on one or two individuals in the group of people closest to you; then look at a few people in the far corners of the room—to the right, center, and left. Even if the glare of stage lights prevents you from seeing anyone's face clearly, do your best to direct your eyes to different parts of the audience as if you could zero in on a single person. Many successful performers and public officials have mastered this technique. They appear to establish eye contact even when the spotlights are virtually blinding them. Making eye contact reassures listeners that you are trying to reach them with your message.

Various Cultures View Eye Contact Differently While many cultures place a high value on establishing and maintaining eye contact, not all do. For example, intercultural communication experts Guo-Ming Chen and William Starosta note that "direct eye contact is a taboo or an insult in many Asian cultures. Cambodians consider direct eye contact as an invasion of one's privacy. In ancient China, only a 'bad' girl or a prostitute would look straight into the eyes of males, whereas the English consider such gazing attentive listening." Likewise, they discuss how one source of racial tension in the United States may be differences in eye contact. They contend, "White Americans tend to look at their communication partner more when they are listening than talking, but African Americans use more eye contact when they are talking, than when they are listening."[1]

1. Guo-Ming Chen and William J. Starosta, *Foundations of Intercultural Communication* (Boston: Allyn & Bacon, 1998), p. 91.

Facial Expression

Whether you are speaking to one person or to one hundred people, your audience will be watching your face, trying to read your facial expression. According to Mark Knapp and Judith Hall, experts in nonverbal communication, your face reflects your attitudes and emotional states, provides nonverbal feedback, and next to the words that you speak, is the primary source of information about you.[3]

Despite the enormous consequences of facial expression, it is difficult to control. Generally, we tend to display a particular style of facial expression. Some people show little expression—they have a serious, "poker" face most of the time. Others are "like an open book"—you have little doubt about how they feel. It's very difficult, therefore, to make a poker face into an open book—or vice versa.

Adding to the difficulty are the effects of nervousness. A nervous speaker may be too distracted to smile, too frightened to stop smiling, or too giddy to register displeasure or anger when it's appropriate.

Unless your topic is very solemn or serious, we recommend that you try to smile. A smile shows your listeners that you are comfortable and eager to share your ideas and information. Smiles can even change behavior.[4] Audience members are more likely to smile if *you* smile. By smiling back, they reciprocate the positive bond that you, the speaker, have established.

Try this exercise. Read this short paragraph aloud while frowning. Then read it over again with a small smile on your face. Which version sounded better? In most cases, it's much easier to speak while smiling. So smile!

While we sincerely recommend smiling, a smile can be inappropriate if it does not reflect what you feel or if it contradicts your message. A big goofy smile would clash with a presentation on the crisis of AIDS in prisons. At the same time, a small smile might relieve tension if you're talking about the discipline it takes to study for exams, lose weight, or stop smoking. But if you can't seem to smile naturally, don't. An artificial smile is worse than no smile at all. In *Speak Smart*, Thomas Mira puts it simply and well when he writes: "If you're happy, it's important to smile. If you're sad, it's OK to look sad. If you're angry, it's fine to look angry. If you're frustrated, you should look frustrated. If you allow your face to communicate your feelings, . . . your audience will appreciate that you are being honest with them, even if they disagree with you."[5] In the end, the best advice we can offer is this: Let your face do what comes naturally. If you communicate your message honestly and sincerely, your facial expression will be appropriate and effective.

Gestures

A **gesture** is a body movement that conveys or reinforces a thought, an intention, or an emotion. Most gestures are made with the hands and arms, but the shrug of a shoulder, bending of a knee, and tapping of a foot are gestures, too.

Gestures can clarify and support your words, help you relieve nervous tension, arouse audience attention, and function as a visual aid. Gestures make you more interesting to watch and therefore more interesting to listen to.

We can't really tell you how to gesture, in part because you already know how to do it. You gesture every day—when you speak to friends, family members, coworkers, and even perfect strangers. Sure, you may say, but that's not the same kind of gesture you need for a presentation. Remember, though, that a presentation is, first and last, speaking. Nevertheless, we've often seen naturally graceful and energetic people become stiff and straight as a stick when they speak in front of a group. Why? They become so worried about how they look and how to gesture that they stop doing what comes naturally. Sometimes we'll ask a stiff speaker a few easy questions at the end of a presentation, such as "Could you tell me more about this?" or "How did you first become interested in that?" In the blink of an eye, the speaker will start gesturing, moving naturally, and showing a lot of expression. This person will have stopped thinking about how he or she looks in order to answer our question.

WHAT SHOULD I DO WITH MY HANDS?

We hear this question all the time, and our answer is deceptively simple: Do what you normally do with your hands. If you gesture a lot, keep doing what comes naturally. If you rarely gesture, don't try to invent new and unnatural hand movements. Steve Allen, the comedian, songwriter, and author, put it this way:

Simply do with your hands what you would if you were talking to members of your family. Put one hand in your jacket pocket and gesture with the other. . . . Scratch your nose if it itches, make a gesture if it illustrates a story or point, or clasp both hands behind your back. It's not a big deal unless you make it one.[1]

1. Steve Allen, *How to Make a Speech* (New York: McGraw-Hill, 1986), p. 67.

Effective Gestures. Despite our advice about "doing what comes naturally," there are some techniques that can liberate

Energy Secretary Bill Richardson gestures and smiles while discussing his priorities and goals during an address to Energy Department employees on August 24, 1998, his first official day on the job.

and animate your hands during a presentation. Begin by linking your gestures to a specific word, concept, or object. For example, introduce the number of main points in your presentation by holding up the correct number of fingers. Then, lift one finger for the first point, two fingers for the second, and so on. If you are describing an object, you can use your hands to trace its shape or size in the air. If you are telling a story in which someone scratches his head, points in a direction, or reaches into his pocket, you can do the same. If you're talking about alternatives, illustrate them on one hand and then on the other hand. But remember, if none of these gestures come naturally or improve with practice, avoid them.

Finally, try to adjust your gestures to the space in which you are speaking. If you are being videotaped close up or are talking to a small group, your gestures should be smaller and closer to your face. If you are speaking to a large audience in a large space, make your gestures bigger, broader, and more vigorous. An audience member a hundred feet away will have trouble seeing a small gesture. Conversely, an audience member sitting three feet away from you may have to duck if your gesture is too sweeping.

Peggy Noonan, former speechwriter for Ronald Reagan, describes a whole industry that exists to tell people how to move their hands while giving a presentation. It's one of the reasons, she maintains, why so many politicians and TV journalists look and gesture alike. "You don't have to be smooth; your audience is composed of Americans, and they've seen smooth. Instead, be you. They haven't seen that yet."[6]

Effective gestures are a natural outgrowth of what you feel and what you have to say. If you start thinking about your gestures, you are likely to appear awkward, unnatural, and forced. Rather than thinking about your hands, think about your message. In all likelihood, your gestures will join forces with your emotions in a natural and spontaneous mixture of verbal and nonverbal communication.

Ineffective Gestures.   Unless you have a lot of speaking or acting experience, it's very difficult to plan your gestures. In fact, it's downright dangerous because most preplanned gestures look artificial and awkward. When speakers try to preplan their gestures in the same way that they would plan a dance step, the

Figure 15.1   Problem Gestures

The fig leaf	Hands gripped together in front of the groin
The handcuffs	Hands gripped together behind the back
The banker	Rattling coins or keys in your pocket
The beautician	Twirling a lock of hair or continuously pushing hair away from your face
The gunfighter	Both arms hanging stiffly away from both sides
The death grip	White-knuckled grip on the lectern, pointer, or notes
The optician	Constantly adjusting eyeglasses
The toy maker	Playing with pointers, pens, markers
The church builder	Keeping hands in a steeple position in front of your face

results can be ineffective and even comical. Figure 15.1 lists some common problem gestures.

Almost any gesture is acceptable if it occurs occasionally and appropriately. Clasping your hands in front of your body is okay if it isn't the only way you position your hands. Adjusting your glasses is fine if they need adjusting. The problem arises when you don't vary your gestures. If you use the same gestures over and over, your audience may begin counting them. As soon as your gestures fall into a pattern, your physical delivery becomes distracting.

As difficult as planned gestures are to execute well, becoming aware of unplanned, distracting ones can be even harder. A **fidget** is a small, repetitive movement, a physical filler phrase. Constantly pushing up on your eyeglasses, tapping a lectern with a pencil, jingling change or keys in your pocket, playing with a necklace or tie, swaying back and forth, repeatedly hiking up your pants and tucking in your shirt, and pulling on a favorite ear lobe or hair curl are all fidgets. One of the easiest ways to stop fidgeting is to videotape and then watch your practice session. Once you see how often you jingle change or sway back and forth, you'll never want to inflict your fidgets on an audience again.

Posture and Movement

Posture and movement involve how you stand and move and whether your movements add to or detract from your presentation. Inexperienced speakers rarely worry about posture and movement because they believe that once they get behind a lectern, they are there to stay. They give little thought to whether they should move from behind the lectern. However, the authors of public speaking books written for the general public urge speakers to move away from the lectern. Author Ron Hoff says, "Podiums are poison. Lecterns are lethal."[7] We don't agree. Podiums and lecterns serve important functions but must be used appropriately and with skill.

Posture.   Your posture communicates. If you stand comfortably and confidently, you will radiate alertness and control. If you are stooped and unsure on your feet, you will communicate apprehension or disinterest. Not only does good posture add to your credibility, it also aids proper breathing and gives you a strong stance from which to gesture. We recommend that you stand straight but

John Ghidiu, a skating instructor and rep for Rollerblade, uses "body language" in his lesson to would-be rollerbladers in the parking lot at the State University of New York, Oswego.

not rigidly. If you lock your knees, you may become lightheaded. Your feet should be about one foot apart. Lean forward just a little instead of rocking back on your heels. And then, like a good soldier—chest out, stomach in—you'll be ready to begin. And as long as we're using clichés, don't forget to keep your chin up. Doing so will open your airways and help make your voice both clear and loud.

Movement. Generally, a certain amount of movement is a good thing during a presentation. Although it's been said that "there's nothing more boring than something that never moves,"[8] we have listened to great speakers who plant their feet on the floor, practically glue their notes or manuscript to the lectern, and proceed to captivate and delight their listeners.

At the same time, you can move around the podium or occasionally around the room to attract attention, support and emphasize a point you are making, or channel nervous energy. Movement even gives you short pauses during which you can collect your thoughts or give the audience a moment to ponder what you have said. Both of us have used movement to direct attention to an important idea or piece of information.

Delivering Mediated Presentations

Not that long ago, the average speaker would probably not have had to consider giving **mediated presentations** on the radio or on camera. Times have changed. Although it's still unlikely that the average speaker will "go prime time," the rise of local radio stations, public access cable, video presentations, teleconferencing, and distance learning means that you should know what to do if you end up in the studio or in front of the camera.

SHOULD I SIT OR STAND? When it's your turn to speak, you may or may not be able to choose whether you sit or stand. For panel discussions, participants often sit behind a table at the front of a room. Nervous students often ask whether they can sit during their presentations. There are good reasons why we say *no*. First and foremost is this: You are your own best visual aid. Why hide that advantage under a table? Standing up is a way of taking charge. It's also easier to breathe for speaking if you stand. It's easier to see your audience and maintain eye contact if you stand. And it's easier to gesture if you have your full body's length to use. In addition, it's easier to move from a standing position than to get up from a chair.

We even recommend that you find a way to stand when other speakers are sitting. Get up and use a flip chart or move to the head of a conference table. By standing when everyone else is sitting, you become the focus of attention. And that's exactly what you want to be during a presentation.

Making Lecterns Work For You

If your presentation is formal or your audience large, you will probably have a lectern. For more informal talks and presentations to small groups, you may have nothing more than a place to stand. Given the choice, however, most presenters prefer and ask for a lectern. The key, of course, is learning how to take advantage of a lectern without falling prey to its perils. President Clinton has two distracting lectern habits. In his desire to connect with an audience, he often leans far forward over his lectern. Unfortunately, it looks as though he and the lectern are about to come crashing down into the audience. Even more distracting is his habit of pounding the lectern while he speaks. Since his microphone is often attached to the lectern, the pounding becomes a deafening and distracting noise.

Although a lectern can become a crutch or a protective barrier between the speaker and the audience, it offers many advantages if it's used well. We like lecterns because they give us a place to put our notes, a spot to focus audience attention, and even an electrical outlet for a light and microphone.

Coaches and consultants often advise their clients to speak without a lectern or to come out from behind the lectern and speak at its side. In this way, speakers remain close to their notes but also get closer to their audience.[1] We agree. Although you may begin your talk behind a lectern, there is nothing wrong with moving to one side of the lectern as you speak. At the same time, we recognize that audiences rarely remember whether a speaker stood behind, to the side, or in front of a lectern.

If you're going to move from behind a lectern, do it for a reason. After speaking from behind a lectern, we often move to its side or move out in front of it and toward the audience. Then we deliver an important part of our message: "And remember this . . ." or "Think about the impact of . . ." or "Let me say this again. . . ." If you do this, your movement will put a huge exclamation point on your message.

Twenty years ago, a speaker could make camp and be quite comfortable behind a lectern. Today it is more difficult, given the extensive use of presentation aids and presentation software. Nowadays you may need to walk over and point to something on a screen or to get out of the way of a slide. Presentation aids in all of their forms have liberated speakers who at other times would have stayed behind a lectern. But as Chapter 16, "Presentation Aids," discusses, these tools must be used effectively so that they don't steal the show from the presenter.

If you're very nervous or feel more comfortable behind a lectern, then use one. The key is using it well. Don't be afraid to gesture when you're behind a lectern. Don't stay glued to your notes; make sure that you look up and establish eye contact. Don't grip the lectern as if it were the top railing of the sinking *Titanic.* Use it as it was intended to be used: as a center of focus where you and your notes can be stationed.

1. Thomas Leech, *How to Prepare, Stage, & Deliver Winning Presentations* (New York: AMACOM, 1993), p. 174.

Before suggesting delivery techniques for each of these media, we do want to note their one common characteristic: Despite the fact that radio and television can reach huge audiences, they are still very personal and even intimate forms of communication. Most people listen to the radio or watch TV on their own turf—in their cars, living rooms, or bedrooms—so the voice from the speaker or the face on the screen seems to talk directly to them. In addition, the audience at the other end of the radio or television set is as close as a good friend or colleague. Consequently, mediated presentations can be more relaxed and conversational.

Radio

Speaking on the radio is, in a sense, easier than speaking in front of a television camera. Obviously, you don't have to worry about your appearance. You don't have to worry about the amount of eye contact you maintain with audience members. And you don't have to worry about having adequate volume—that's adjusted for you electronically.

Christina Stuart, a speech consultant and author, rightfully notes that the most important factor on radio is your voice and its ability to communicate enthusiasm, sincerity, and vitality.[9] Just because an audience can't see you doesn't mean that your attitude or level of commitment changes. If you are being interviewed or are on a panel, speak to the interviewer or panelists in a conversational tone, the way you would if there weren't a microphone in front of each speaker. If you apply the Chapter 14, "Vocal Delivery," techniques for developing an effective speaking voice (well, most of them—you won't need to project your voice), your radio delivery will sound clear and natural.

Rely on the radio staff to show you how to use the microphone (the mini-module in Chapter 14 gives some tips, too). Some staffers will tell you to keep your elbows and forearms on the table as a way of keeping yourself from leaning into the mike. Other production engineers will tell you to ignore the microphone. Follow their advice. Radio technicians are there to make you and the radio show sound good.

Television

Being on TV adds the elements of physical delivery to those of vocal delivery. Because TV is primarily a visual medium, how you look matters a lot. Don't be surprised if a studio's makeup artist pays you a backstage visit. Both men and women on television wear makeup. It helps reduce shine and can highlight facial features. As odd as you may think you look after a makeup session, you will be surprised by the positive results you will see on screen.

As we've indicated, radio and television are personal media. Of the two, television is the most intimate. Why? Because the camera can zoom in for a close-up. A full close-up of someone's face on television reveals every flicker of a smile, flinch, raised eyebrow, frown, or wince. Trying to hide those minute details will only result in an uninterested, deadpan look.

When you're on camera, your face is the main focus of attention—not your gestures, not your hands, not even your voice. If you gesture a great deal while you speak, remember that the television camera may be too close to pick up your hand movements. Consider gesturing closer to your face, being careful not to hide your face behind your hands. You may want to have a friend videotape you in close-up so that you can get a sense of how—or if—your gestures appear on-screen.

Whether you're part of a panel or appearing alone, make sure that you're dressed appropriately for television. Generally, this means wearing rather formal business attire, but if you're not sure, ask your contact at the station for advice. Because of the way that cameras work, some colors and patterns should be avoided.

- Black, dark gray, or midnight blue come out very dark on camera and can look too somber, even for a business program. Instead, choose a paler gray, gray-blue, or mid-blue.

- Bright white can be blinding. Choose cream, beige, or pale blue instead.

- Material with narrow stripes, small checks, or large patterns tends to vibrate or look jumpy. Plain colors look best on camera.

- Dangling earrings and fussy necklines tend to be distracting. Remember that most of the camera shots will be of your head and shoulders, so aim for a simple, plain, uncluttered look.[10]

SHOULD I LOOK AT THE CAMERA? If you have never been on TV, it can be confusing when the cameras start rolling. The key thing to remember is TV's intimate nature. If you are being interviewed, act as though you are having a conversation with that person and no one else. If you are on a panel, talk to the panel members, not to the camera. When other panelists are speaking, look at them. The camera may be shooting the entire panel at any time, so don't decide to adjust your clothes or look around the studio while you're not speaking.

The only time when you should look at the camera is when you are the only person on the set or when you are addressing the viewing audience directly, as candidates do in a political forum or debate. In these cases, talk directly to the camera as though it is a person rather than a machine connected to thousands of viewers. If you will be reading from a TelePrompTer, make sure that you have practiced reading your manuscript thoroughly and know which key words and phrases to emphasize. To keep your delivery natural and sincere, treat the TelePrompTer screen as you would your notes rather than following every word with your eyes.

If you know that you are going to be on television, you already have easy access to the best resource available on how to behave, how to move, where to look, and what to wear. Watch television. Watch news anchors. Watch Sunday morning news shows. Watch the weather channel. Watch shows in which real persons (talk-show guests and game-show contestants), not your favorite actors or sit-com characters, are talking.

Videotape and Videoconferences

The use of videotape is no longer confined to broadcast and cable television. Many businesses—both large and small—now commonly videotape presentations for in-house use and videoconferences with colleagues at different locations. Regardless of whether you are being taped for an in-house video newsletter or are participating in an international videoconference, the "rules" are the same as those for appearing on television. One difference is that the equipment, the studio, and the technical support may not be broadcast quality. There is not a great deal you can do about technical quality. So if your presentation comes out looking a little grainy, and the camera never moves from a straight-on, medium shot, don't worry. As video presentations and videoconferencing become more common, knowing how to be comfortable while using and appearing on video will serve you well.

Online Presentations

The world of cyberspace has given us a new arena for speaking in front of audiences—online presentations. Many universities and corporations have turned to online training as an efficient way to reach students and employees all over the

Tennessee Senator Bill Frist and NASA Administrator Daniel Goldin take part in a teleconference call with shuttle astronauts Michael Gernhart, Roger Crouch (upside down!) and Janice Voss, demonstrating that today's mediated presentations know no bounds.

REAL WORLD, REAL SPEAKERS

A colleague of ours provided us with her recollection of an online presentation, on behalf of a major computer company, that she had to prepare and deliver:

> Once I had to deliver the keynote address to a conference of five hundred senior military and government officials attending a conference on learning, in Singapore. To make matters more interesting, I was in New York at the time delivering the address online. I had to select the mix of learning activities and supporting technologies to make this a high energy distance-learning experience. I wanted to have a different visual every three minutes and to vary the format of my presentation several times. I combined slides, live camera shots of myself, audience pools (we had a camera in the conference room in Singapore that fed to a monitor in New York), and still pictures. I also reserved about fifteen minutes after the speech for audience questions, which really made it feel as if we were in the same room. I built a Web site for the presentation with hundreds of links and resources so audience members could also follow up at their leisure.
>
> I was struck by how much energy it took to do the presentation online. I had to produce my own presentation as I was giving it by pointing and clicking the mouse on my laptop. Yet it paid off. I saved twenty-eight hours of travel for a forty-minute presentation. I saved our hosts a lot of money. Most important, though, the online format drove home the message about the power of technology-assisted learning.

world. What makes online presentations different from other types of mediated presentations is the level of preparation needed for coordinating and operating complex equipment while delivering a media-adapted presentation. Giving a successful online presentation takes more than just computer skill. The basic requirements of any good presentation still apply—you need a clear purpose, audience analysis, logistical planning, thorough preparation, good organization, and well-rehearsed delivery.

Putting It All Together

In order to understand how all of the elements of your physical delivery (eye contact, facial expression, gestures, posture, and movement) work together, let's follow you from the beginning to the end of a presentation.

First, you have to get to the place where you will speak or make your mediated presentation. You may be called on, introduced, take your turn, or just walk up and begin talking. When you stand up and walk to the lectern, desk, table, microphone, or open space, walk with confidence. Don't wince or make a face that says, "I'd rather not be doing this." Remember that your audience will "read" your posture and expression before they hear a word of your presentation. Let that first impression be positive!

In Chapter 3, "Building Presentation Confidence," we saw how visualization can help reduce presentation anxiety. Visualization also can help improve your performance. Take a few minutes during the course of every practice session to imagine yourself giving your presentation from start to finish. If visualization works for Olympic and other topnotch athletes, it can work for speakers.

The key, writes Jean Williams, a sports psychologist at the University of Arizona, "is to engage all the senses in the imaging process."[1] As you visualize your presentation, imagine how you look, the way you gesture and move, the sound of your voice, the feel of your notes, even the smell of the room and the taste of the cold water you will sip between major sections of your presentation. Then go one step beyond your five senses and focus on positive emotions: how wonderful and exhilarating it feels to be a successful speaker. The more vivid you make your visualization, the more focused you can be on improving and controlling every detail of your performance.

1. Wendy DuBow, "Do Try This at Home," *Women's Sports and Fitness* 19 (May 1997):78.

Don't start speaking right away. Take a few seconds to get ready by rechecking your notes and scanning the room for potential problems such as a group of late arrivals. This pause also will give your audience a few seconds to settle down and prepare to listen to you. When you're ready, establish eye contact with several audience members. And then, start speaking without looking at your notes. The first few words of your presentation should be delivered to your audience, not to your note cards. To maintain maximum contact with your audience, refer to your notes as little as possible throughout the presentation. Let yourself become totally involved in your message.

As you deliver your presentation, visualize yourself reaching out to the audience with your message. Hear yourself emphasizing important words and ideas. Feel yourself gesturing and moving with confidence and ease. Notice how the audience looks at you when you look at them. See them nod in agreement, smile, and sit forward to concentrate. Feel the growing excitement that comes with knowing that you are making the most of your presentation.

Once you have finished your presentation, make a graceful and confident exit. Too often, nervous speakers are halfway to their seats before the last word has had time to reach the audience's ears. Just as you got ready before you began speaking, pause after you have finished, look at your audience, and then turn your gaze away from them and walk off with confidence.

After reading the previous few paragraphs, you may be thinking that we have described the perfect performance. In truth, we have also described a good practice session. You should practice every step of your presentation. A play director blocks a scene by telling the actors where, when, and even how to move. You can do the same thing. Practice walking to the podium. Practice the way in which you will handle your notes. Practice your presentation as though an audience were present. Only this kind of practice can give you the added confidence you can rely on when it's time for the real thing.

Summary

Why is eye contact so important?

Eye contact may be the single most important element of physical delivery. Effective eye contact helps to initiate and control communication, enhances speaker credibility, and provides useful feedback.

Can I control my facial expressions?

Controlling your facial expressions is difficult because, in most cases, they naturally reflect what you are thinking and feeling. At the same time, something as simple as a smile can relax both you and your audience while also conveying your sincere interest in communicating your message.

◆◆ Which gestures work best during a presentation?

Gestures that reinforce a thought, an intention, or an emotion add to the effectiveness of a presentation. Usually, if you stop thinking about how to gesture and instead concentrate on your message, your gestures will be natural and communicative.

◆◆ How should I stand and move during a presentation?

An erect and confident posture and purposeful movements can enhance your credibility; give you a strong stance from which to gesture, support, and emphasize important ideas and information; and channel nervous energy.

◆◆ How do I deliver a presentation on radio, on camera, or online?

Remember that radio and television are very personal forms of communication. Speak as though you're talking to one other person rather than orating to thousands of listeners. Mediated presentations require practice and technical know-how as well as a thorough understanding of the basic principles of presentation speaking.

Key Terms

eye contact 247
eye scan 249
fidget 252

gesture 250
mediated presentation 253

Notes

1. Steven A. Beebe, "Eye Contact: A Nonverbal Determinant of Speaker Credibility," *The Speech Teacher* 23 (1974): 21–25.
2. Marjorie Brody, *Speaking Your Way to the Top* (Boston: Allyn & Bacon, 1998), p. 113.
3. Mark L. Knapp and Judith A. Hall, *Nonverbal Communication in Human Interaction,* 4th ed. (Fort Worth, TX: Harcourt Brace, 1997), p. 332.
4. Knapp and Hall, p. 360.
5. Thomas K. Mira, *Speak Smart* (New York: Random House, 1997), pp. 25–26.
6. Peggy Noonan, *Simply Speaking: How to Communicate Your Ideas with Style, Substance, and Clarity* (New York: HarperCollins, 1998), p. 206. Copyright © 1998 by Peggy Noonan. Reprinted by permission of HarperCollins Publishers, Inc.
7. Ron Hoff, *I Can See You Naked* (Kansas City, MO: Andres & McMeel, 1992), p. 80.
8. Hoff, p. 83.
9. Christina Stuart, *How to Be an Effective Speaker* (Lincolnwood, IL: NTC, 1996), p. 213.
10. Stuart, p. 216.

Presentation Aids

- ◆◆ How can presentation aids help me as a speaker?
- ◆◆ What kinds of presentation aids should I use?
- ◆◆ What medium should I use?
- ◆◆ How do I design effective presentation aids?
- ◆◆ Are there tips for using my presentation aids?

Not that long ago, a speaker needed two things for a successful presentation: a good speech and a strong voice. Today you can use dozens of tools to enhance your presentation—ranging from scale models, flip charts, slide projectors, and overheads to multimedia presentations. In fact, in many business settings you are expected to use visual images throughout a briefing. From chalked notes on a blackboard to computer animation, a speaker's options seem endless. Deciding how to take advantage of such technologies, however, must be considered as part of your overall strategy for achieving the purpose of your presentation.

How Presentation Aids Can Help You

Like a picture, a chart, a map, a computer-generated slide, or a videotape may also be "worth a thousand words." The reason why this old saying carries so much weight is that the brain processes most of the information that it receives visually. From early childhood on, humans rely on visual stimulation. Think of the books you "read" as a child. They were filled with pictures. Adult minds still prefer visual images. Most of us spend more time watching television than reading books. Waiting rooms are cluttered with photo-filled magazines, not journals.

Benefits of Presentation Aids

Although you can describe the car of your dreams in great detail, the color photos in a car dealer's brochure probably can do it better. Although you may be able to describe a good tennis serve, a live demonstration or a training videotape will be more useful to a player. You can try to persuade an audience that your chocolate chip cookie recipe is the greatest, but a sample taste can convince them in seconds.

Presentation aids are the many supplementary resources available to a speaker for presenting key ideas and supporting material. They give your audience an additional sensory contact with your presentation. Whether you intend to engage their sense of sight, hearing, touch, taste, or smell, presentation aids encompass a wide range of items and media—from homemade cookies to PowerPoint presentations.

Research studies conducted for the 3M Corporation found that when presenters used overhead transparencies, the audience remembered up to 10 percent more of the information presented. Subsequent research at the University of Minnesota showed that presenters who used computer-generated visual aids were 43 percent more persuasive.[1] In both of these studies, presenters who used some form of visual aid were perceived as better prepared, more professional, more credible, and more interesting than speakers who used no aids. Only a dozen or so years ago, a hand-drawn poster would have been an acceptable presentation aid in most situations. This is no longer the case. Learning to create and use sophisticated presentation aids is the responsibility of every effective speaker.

Functions of Presentation Aids

Presentation aids are more than a pretty picture or a "gee-whiz" graphic. They serve several functions, all of which support you and your message. Presentation aids can attract attention and can clarify, reinforce, supplement, compare, and illustrate information. They can help an audience understand, learn, and remember what you say. Thus, it's no surprise that some speakers claim as much as a 40 to 50 percent increase in communication effectiveness when they're using presentation aids. At the same time, the 40 to 50 percent gain can be reversed if those aids are poorly prepared or used.[2]

FUNCTIONS OF PRESENTATION AIDS

Gain attention

Clarify and reinforce ideas

Improve efficiency

Senator Dianne Feinstein of California grabs attention by holding a modified AK-47 to emphasize her call for a ban on high-capacity ammunition clips.

Gain Attention. Presentation aids attract attention. A clever cartoon, a bold headline, a soundtrack, an attractive or shocking picture, or any other compelling visual can gain and hold an audience's attention. Attention can wane, however, if the visuals are poorly prepared or irrelevant to the presentation. Margaret Rabb, an expert in designing presentation aids, writes that presentation aids "clarify the spoken word, help the audience identify the most important points, and rivet attention on the topic at hand. Subject matter is often more interesting and easier to understand when illustrated. . . . Colors, motion, and visual organization bring facts and figures to life."[3]

TIP **Appeal to Varied Learning Styles** As the discussion of learning styles in Chapter 5, "Audience Analysis and Adaptation," pointed out, some audience members learn better by seeing and reading, some by listening, and some by doing. Using presentation aids adds a second channel of communication to your message and helps you adapt to your audience's different learning styles by engaging more of their senses. For audience members who learn better by seeing, you have many choices—ranging from charts to demonstrations. For physical learners, you may want to allow time for some hands-on experience. Let them sort through samples, help you demonstrate a product, or try out a technique or an exercise. Use a variety of presentation aids to ensure that you reach all kinds of learners.

Clarify and Reinforce Ideas. Depending on the subject, presentation aids can be more effective than words in conveying meaning. Complicated directions to a destination are often easier to give if you can point to a map. The intricacies of a business plan can be more simply explained if the plan can be charted. One of us once observed a benefits consultant helping a large group fill out a complicated preretirement form. His first presentation aid was a slide of the entire form. His second presentation aid zeroed in on the first two lines with an example of how to complete them. The third slide showed the next group of lines filled in—and so on through the last lines. Using a series of slides to move through the form in stages clarified and reinforced his verbal instructions.

In addition to clarifying and reinforcing a message for the audience, presentation aids can serve the same purpose for a speaker. If your visual aids follow an outline or the order of key points in your presentation, they can also function as speaking notes. Instead of using paper notes, you can speak from the visuals. You won't forget what you want to say, and your audience can follow along as you talk.[4]

Improve Efficiency. Presentation aids can save time, particularly when you use a graph, drawing, or chart to summarize a complex process or a set of statistics. As instructors and consultants, we often use overhead transparencies or computer-generated visuals to highlight important ideas. This way, we don't need to spend time writing on a board or flip chart, and we also save time by being able to point to the critical section of a pie chart or the key variable on a graph. If we give our listeners copies of our visuals, we will also save them the time it would have taken to write down what we said. By giving everyone the same material in written form, we have more confidence that the audience will "get" the message as we intend it.

The Basic Principle

As you consider the benefits and functions of presentation aids, keep in mind the most basic principle of all: *Presentation aids are aids.* They are not your presentation. Unfortunately, when some inexperienced speakers find out that they have to make a presentation, they immediately turn on their computers and start churning out PowerPoint slides. They have not yet determined their purpose, analyzed their audience, nor looked for or selected relevant supporting material. Just because they're using their favorite graphics template doesn't mean they're creating a cohesive, understandable presentation.

A presentation aid is something that "aids" the speaker. You and your presentation come first; the aid helps you to achieve your purpose by supporting and supplementing your message. Don't let your aids and their technical razzle-dazzle steal the show. Today many business and professional presentations have become nothing more than narrated slide shows. The presenter simply reads what appears on a slide or transparency. By not taking the opportunity to connect with their audiences, such presenters have missed the point of making a live presentation in the first place.

Try this exercise the next time you have prepared a set of visuals for a presentation. Imagine that just as you are about to give your presentation, you misplace your visual aids, or the equipment breaks down. What would you do? Could you still communicate your message without the presentation aids? If the answer is *no,* or even "I'm not sure," then you're relying too much on your visuals.

Presentation aids should not be the centerpiece of or reason for your presentation. Don't become one of those speakers who prepare their presentations by preparing their images. Because of time pressure, workload, or simply bad habits, these speakers make their visuals first. They begin at the computer, creating slides as they come up with ideas for their presentations. After a few hours of work, they save or print out their slides and feel fully prepared to speak. The process we've just described is totally and absolutely backwards.

Outstanding speakers thoroughly prepare their presentations *before* creating their presentation aids. Only after carefully considering what they want to say and what they want their audience members to understand and remember do they prepare visuals. Your visuals are there to support you, not to take your place.

Messages and Media

Given the many different types of presentation aids and the enormous benefits of using them, it's important to understand how to select, shape, and use them effectively. When asked, "What kind of presentation aid should I use? Should I use slides? overhead transparencies? flip charts? scale models?" we answer, "Use whatever works best to communicate your message." As obvious as this response may be, it masks a complex decision-making process.

Not only do you need to decide what type of aid will work best, but you also need to decide which medium you want to create it in. For example, you could draw a graph on a blackboard or flip chart, display it on a transparency or computer screen, or distribute it as a handout. You could describe an accident with words or show a photograph or videotape of it. First, then, select the most appropriate and effective form to display your ideas and supporting material as presentation aids. Second, select the most appropriate media for sharing those presentation aids with your audience.

Types of Presentation Aids

Presentation aids are a means of displaying supporting materials—facts, examples, statistics, and testimony—that clarify or reinforce your message. Presentation aids can take many forms: photographs, maps, diagrams, drawings, graphs, charts, tables, lists, models, and objects. Before deciding whether to power up your computer or buy a set of new markers, make sure that you have selected the most appropriate type of presentation aid.

Choosing the right form for a presentation aid is not as simple as choosing an item from a menu: "Should I use a single chart, a couple of graphs, or three drawings?" Your decision should be strategic. Which type of presentation aid will best achieve your purpose? Which type will be best for gaining and keeping audience attention, clarifying and reinforcing your message, and saving time? The first step in selecting an appropriate graphic is understanding that certain types of graphics work best for specific purposes. The following descriptions and guidelines can help you choose the most appropriate form for your presentation aid.[5]

HEADLINE YOUR VISUALS Although a picture may be worth a thousand words, a picture can lose its impact if it doesn't have a title or headline. Gene Zelazny, a visual designer, writes, "Don't keep it a secret; let your message head the chart. In so doing, you reduce the risk that the reader will misunderstand, and you make sure he or she focuses on the aspect of the data you want to employ."[1] Zelazny uses the following pie chart to make his point.

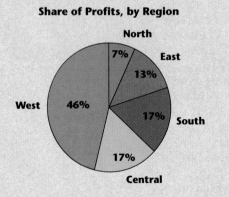

Share of Profits, by Region

What is the significance of this pie chart? Most viewers would probably focus on the West, believing the message to be "West Accounts for Half of Profits." However, that may not be the point. Perhaps the reason the chart was developed was to show that the "North Generates Smallest Profits." Putting a more specific title on your visuals reinforces your message and ensures that your audience focuses on the aspect of the data you want to emphasize.[2]

1. Gene Zelazny, *Say It with Charts: The Executive's Guide to Successful Presentations* (Homewood, IL: Dow Jones--Irwin, 1985), p. 18.
2. Zelazny, pp. 18–19.

TYPES OF PRESENTATION AIDS

Pie charts
Graphs
Text charts
Tables
Drawings
Maps
Photographs

Pie Charts.   Pie charts show *how much*. They show proportions in relation to a whole, or they depict relationships among related items. Each wedge of the pie usually represents a percentage, as in Figure 16.1. Most audiences comprehend pie charts quickly and easily.

When using a pie chart, try not to use more than six components. Why? Gene Zelazny, who advises executive-level presenters about the best ways to use presentation aids, notes that the pieces of the pie will be difficult to distinguish if you go beyond six. If you must have more than six pieces, select the most important components and group the remainders into an "oth-

Figure 16.1   Pie Chart

The pie chart shows that 5,311 students attending a local community college who also intend to transfer to a four-year college or university are enrolled in one of six program areas.

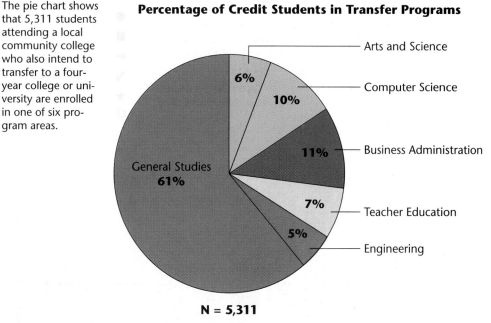

Percentage of Credit Students in Transfer Programs

Arts and Science — 6%

Computer Science — 10%

Business Administration — 11%

Teacher Education — 7%

Engineering — 5%

General Studies 61%

N = 5,311

ers" category. Also, because the eye is accustomed to measuring in a clockwise motion, begin the most important segment of your pie chart against the 12 o'clock line. To add emphasis, use the most contrasting colors or the most intense shading pattern for consecutive slices of the pie chart to make sure that they are clearly separated.[6]

Graphs.   Graphs also show *how much,* but they are primarily used to demonstrate comparisons. In addition, they can illustrate trends and can clearly show increases or decreases. Graphs, which can be displayed using bars or lines (see Figures 16.2a and 16.2b on p. 266), usually represent countable things such as the number of different responses to a survey question or the number of products manufactured over a period of time. Stock market summaries on the nightly news are often presented in the form of graphs that extend over a week, a year, or even a decade.

Dennis McBride, author of *How to Make Visual Presentations,* notes that although "charts and graphs are the most widely used form of graphic visual display, . . . anyone who wishes to make the most of these forms must first find the one that precisely fits the information to be presented. Otherwise, they can hurt a presentation more than help it."[7]

When using a bar graph, make the space separating the bars smaller than the width of the bars. Also, use the most contrasting color or shading to emphasize the most important item on the graph.[8]

Text Charts.   Text charts list ideas or key phrases, often under a title or headline. Most of the "slides" in this book are text charts. They depict goals, functions, types of formats, recommendations, and guidelines. Items listed on a text chart may be numbered, "bulleted," or simply set apart on separate lines.

"BULLETS" TAKE MANY FORMS

- • Circle
- ■ Box
- → Arrow
- ✔ Check mark
- ★ Star
- ☺ Happy face

Both bar graphs (a) and line graphs (b) chart trends over time. The bar graph tracks the number of high school graduates enrolled at a local community college. The line graph shows that the number of students enrolled in occupational programs exceeds the number of students intending to transfer to a four-year college or university.

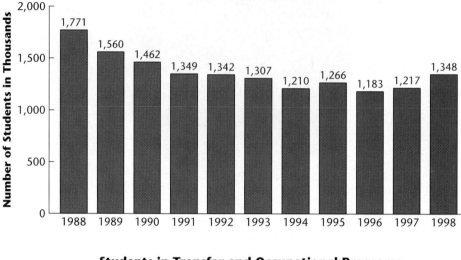

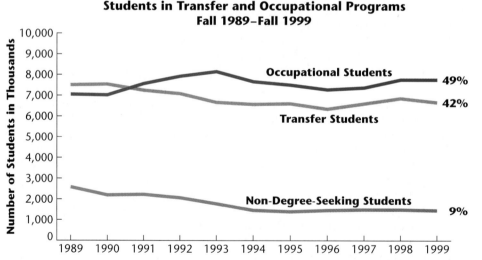

Tables.   Tables summarize and compare data. In *The Presentation Design Book*, Margaret Rabb offers the cautionary note, "When graphs aren't specific enough and verbal descriptions are too cumbersome, tables offer elegant solutions for showing exact numeric values."[9] Tables also can summarize and compare key features, as in the table on p. 268 that summarizes the types of media most appropriate for small, medium, and large audiences.

Drawings.   Drawings show *how things work*. They can also be used to explain relationships or processes. They can be highly abstract, in the form of flow charts or organizational diagrams. In addition, they can chart a process—the steps in-

Figure 16.3   Enrollment Map

By using census-tract areas as a basis for tabulating student enrollment, a local college demonstrates that students in the northern and southern parts of the county are less likely to attend the college, which is located in the center of the county. The concentration of students in the southwest portion of the county reflects the location of the college's large extension center on an Air Force base.

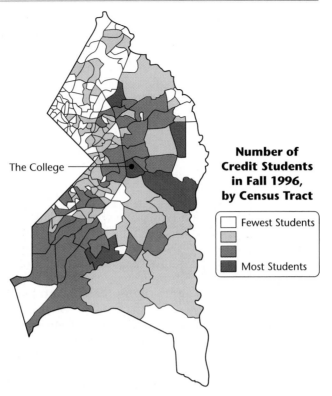

The College

Number of Credit Students in Fall 1996, by Census Tract

☐ Fewest Students
▨
▨
■ Most Students

volved in making a product, a cake, or even a presentation. Drawings also can chart timelines, and can even "explode" a physical object so that you can see the inside of an engine, a heart, or a flower. The drawing in Chapter 1, "Presentation Speaking," of the Dynamic Model of Presentation Speaking (see Figure 1.1 on page 13) shows how the presentation speaking process works, for example.

Drawings can also depict physical objects and areas in the form of simple line drawings and scale drawings or as detailed schematics and blueprints. In Chapter 6, "Logistics and Occasion," we included a simple floor plan of a room to illustrate the proper placement of a screen for presentation aids (see Figure 6.2 on page 97). Even cartoons are a type of drawing that can be used to poke fun at or ridicule a real-life situation or issue highlighted in a presentation.

Maps.   Maps show *where;* they "translate data into spatial patterns."[10] They also can be used to give directions or compare locations. Maps have more uses than those of your glove-compartment highway map or a geography textbook map. In presentations, maps can be used to locate and direct an audience's attention to a troubled traffic intersection, a complex battle scene, a proposed office complex, or a vacation destination. Maps can be divided into sections that link statistical data to population characteristics. For example, in making the case for building two satellite campuses of a community college, a college president used a map of the county to show the number of students attending the college from each electoral district. In a presentation to county council members, the map in Figure 16.3 demonstrated that the further a council member's district was from the college's main campus, the fewer students it served. All the talk in the world could not equal the impact of showing a single map to the county council.

Photographs. Photographs portray reality. A real face or place is easily recognized through a photograph. Photographs also have the advantage of capturing emotions. Words such as *beautiful, dramatic, funny, heartbreaking,* and *awesome* can register in audience members' minds when a photograph is displayed.

Beyond Visual Aids. There are other forms of presentation aids—audio recordings, objects, handouts, and physical demonstrations. Regardless of the form or type, the key to selecting effective presentation aids is to make sure that they are relevant to your topic and purpose and that they have the potential to save time, gain attention, and clarify or reinforce your presentation's content.

Selecting the Media

Once you decide which type of presentation aid would best support your message, you can begin to consider which medium to use. Visual media fall into two basic types, projected and nonprojected. Projected, electronic media include overhead transparencies, 35mm slides, videotapes, presentation software, and multimedia presentations. Nonprojected, hard-copy media include more traditional types of displays such as flip charts, poster board, handouts, and chalk or marker boards.

The first and most important decision to make when preparing presentation aids is selecting the right media for the message you are supporting. Consider your purpose, the audience, the setting, and the logistics of the situation. As much as you may want to make a multimedia presentation, you may find that the room in which you're scheduled to speak cannot be darkened or that the facility cannot provide the hardware you need for the presentation. Writing detailed notes on a board or flip chart for an audience of hundreds will not make you any friends in the back row.

Figure 16.4 does not include all possible media, but it can help you understand how to select appropriate media for your audience.

Like all other recommendations, these have exceptions. A corporation's team presentation to a small group of prospective clients may require a multimedia presentation to compete with other team presentations. A predesigned flip chart with huge one- or two-word messages on each page can work in front of an audience of three hundred people. (An overhead transparency with too much data or

Figure 16.4   Selecting the Appropriate Medium

Media	Small Audience (50 or fewer)	Medium Audience (50–150)	Large Audience (150 or more)
Chalk/white board	✓		
Flip chart	✓		
Hand-held object	✓	✓	
Overhead transparencies	✓	✓	✓
35mm slides	✓	✓	✓
Presentation software slides	✓	✓	✓
Videotapes	✓	✓	✓
Multimedia	✓	✓	✓

Holding a remote control device, Steve Jobs enlists presentation software to display Apple Computer's year-end results.

tiny type would not.) But in general, certain media are better suited for certain types and sizes of audiences.

Criteria for Media Selection

Although there are many tips to offer about choosing the best medium for your presentation aids, we consolidate this advice into four key criteria: ease of use, audience expectations, availability, and adaptability.

Ease of Use. How familiar are you with the medium? If you love computers and understand software, then a computer-assisted medium such as PowerPoint or Astound may be a good choice. If, on the other hand, you are not comfortable or experienced with computer hardware, try overheads or flip charts. The day before a presentation is not the time to learn how to use new software or hardware.

Audience Expectations. Does your audience expect to see a computer-assisted multimedia presentation, or are they accustomed to flip charts? What have other speakers used when presenting to this audience? If your audience is expecting a presentation software slide show, make sure you can justify using something else.

Availability. Can you get the equipment you will need to the place where you will be speaking? Is the equipment available at the site? How much will it cost? Is the cost worth it? Recently one of our colleagues called to request a video playback unit from the hotel at which he was scheduled to make a professional presentation. He was told that it would cost one hundred dollars an hour to rent and set up the equipment.

Adaptability. If things go wrong, how quickly can you adapt? For example, if your computer shuts down, will you have time to get it going again? If the bulb on the projector blows, will there be a replacement handy? If your marker runs out of ink, will you have spare markers with you?

OVERHEADS CAN CAUSE HEADACHES

Slide and overhead projectors can be quite noisy. Often when we turn off an overhead projector in class, there's a brief and wonderful silent moment in which everyone enjoys the disappearance of the background hum. Try to approximate how loudly you'll need to speak over the noise of the projector. And if you're using a microphone, remember that the noise of the projector fan may be amplified just as much as your voice is. Also, make sure that you know where the vent on your overhead projector is located. Then be careful what you lay in front of it. Too often, speakers who are unaware of the powerful breeze caused by this fan can be unhappily surprised when their notes or transparencies sail off the table on which the projector rests.

Figure 16.5   Matching the Presentation Aid to Your Purpose

Purpose	Presentation Aids
Purpose: To explain the parts of an internal combustion engine	Drawing of an engine Pieces of an engine Animated cartoon of engine operation
Purpose: To compare rap music and talking blues	Audio excerpts of each musical form Live performances Chart listing music's characteristics
Purpose: To demonstrate how to separate egg whites from egg yolks	Live demonstration Still photos or slides Audience participation
Purpose: To learn the causes and symptoms of sickle cell anemia	Chart listing symptoms Drawing of blood-cell action Family tree tracing inheritance of the disease

Match the Medium to the Message

Some presentations are almost impossible to give without presentation aids. Try giving an informative talk on the sign language of the deaf without demonstrating a few signs. Try explaining the difference between major and minor musical keys without at least humming a tune. Figure 16.5 matches topics with some of the presentation aids that a speaker could use to achieve his or her purpose.

Almost any kind of presentation can be supplemented by the use of a presentation aid. Deciding which kind of aid to use requires both creative and strategic thinking.

Visual Design Principles

Regardless of the type of supporting material or the medium you choose to display, you can apply certain design principles to creating your presentation aids. In the following section, we use the general term *visual* to apply to any words or image that you put on a flip chart, slide, or computer-software template. In this way, we can generalize about design without referring to a specific medium.

> **VISUAL DESIGN PRINCIPLES**
>
> **Preview and highlight**
>
> **Exercise restraint**
>
> **Choose readable typefaces and suitable colors**
>
> **Use appropriate graphics**
>
> **Build sequentially**
>
> **Create an overall look**

Preview and Highlight

Use your visuals to preview and highlight the most important and most memorable components of your message. The slides that accompany your presentation should not include every fact, statistic, and quotation that you include in your talk. What slides should do is preview what you want to say and highlight the most important facts and features of your presentation.

The RAND Corporation's guidelines for preparing briefings recommend using an outline slide near the beginning of a presentation and repeating it at transition points during the presentation. An outline slide gives a visual preview of your presentation. It is your presentation's table of contents. "When the slide first appears, it telegraphs the structure of the presentation, thereby increasing the audience's ability to understand and remember. When the outline slide reappears in the briefing, it reminds the audience of where they are in the structure. It can also underscore a substantive point by repetition."[11] Depending on how sophisticated your equipment is, you can incorporate a marker or change in color that moves down the outline as the presentation progresses.

Exercise Restraint

Presentation software has made it possible for speakers to use a dazzling array of graphics, fonts, colors, and other visual elements. At first, it's tempting to use them all. Resist that temptation. More often than not, a simple slide will be much more effective than a complex one.

We offer two general recommendations that apply to almost all types of presentation aids:

1. Make only one point on each chart or slide, and make sure the title of the slide states that point. Everything else on the visual should support the main point. It takes more time to explain one slide with a muddled message than to present two well-structured slides.[12]

2. Follow the six-by-six rule. Aim for no more than six lines of text with no more than six words per line. This rule of thumb allows your slide to contain the main heading and several bulleted lines below it without your having to fear information overload.[13]

These recommendations apply equally to the most sophisticated, computer-generated multimedia presentations and to hand-drawn posters and flip charts.

Please remember that an aid is only an aid; slides are not a presentation. They are not meant to be a script read word for word. In his book *TechEdge: Using Computers to Present and Persuade,* William Ringle recommends balancing "tersity" and diversity. By *tersity,* he means making visuals compact and concise while using them to add variety and interest. Finding this balance depends on understanding both the value of presentation aids and the pitfalls to avoid when adding technical "sizzle" to your presentation.[14]

Not only should you exercise restraint when creating each visual; you should also limit the number of presentation aids you use. Even the most alert and

TiPS FOR FLiPS Amidst all the high-tech options for presentation aids, flip charts—a large pad of paper on an easel—remain one of the most common media for displaying ideas and information. Not only do they work without electricity or software, but they also provide enormous flexibility. You can prepare your flip chart in advance or write on it as you speak. This flexibility allows you to involve the audience in generating ideas or filling in blanks. Flip charts also allow you to tear off pages and post them on walls as reminders or as templates for recording additional ideas. Both of us have participated in strategic planning sessions in which we were encouraged to add items to flip chart pages posted on the walls of a room. Marjorie Brody, a presentation speaking consultant and author, offers the following additional tips for using flip charts:[1]

- Flip charts work best during small-group presentations.

- Leave your flip chart covered until you are ready to use it.

- Black or dark blue markers are best—use a color like red only for emphasis.

- Write large enough so that those in the back of the room can read your words. Although your print size should vary with the room size, we recommend at least three-inch letters.

- Prewrite your flip chart pages lightly with pencil before you fill in with markers.

You can even use flip charts as a form of speaker notes. Not only does the material on a flip chart serve as a master outline, but you can also write additional notes on a flip chart in light pencil in order to remind yourself to tell a story, share some statistics, or ask a particular question.

1. Marjorie Brody, *Speaking Your Way to the Top: Making Powerful Business Presentations* (Boston: Allyn & Bacon, 1998), p. 92.

IF It's Not Relevant, Don't Use It Don't use presentation aids unless they are relevant to your topic. Presentation aids are a means of sharing supporting material; they are not the reason why you are speaking. For example, one of our students once asked to rehearse a presentation that she was scheduled to give at work to an important group of clients. She had an absolutely stunning multimedia presentation filled with animation, bright colors, extraordinary sound effects, and delightful, even funny, pictures. When it was over, the class had only one criticism. Most of her visuals had little to do with what she was talking about. She had fallen in love with her visuals and was committed to using them— even when they weren't relevant.

interested audience has its limits. Fifty slides do not necessarily hold more information than ten carefully selected and explained ones. Six pamphlets on energy conservation are not necessarily more persuasive than one. A musical excerpt may be enough; the entire song may be too much. Most audiences cannot absorb and retain a great deal of complex information, no matter how important it may be. In the end, do you want your audience to remember you and your message? Or do you want them to remember a blur of charts and outlines? The choice is yours.

Choose Readable Typefaces and Suitable Colors

After deciding what you want to put on a visual, you will need to select a typeface or font. Again, exercise restraint. Using too many typefaces on a single slide will make your visual look amateurish. As a general rule, never use more than two different fonts on a single slide. As much as you may be tempted, avoid fancy but difficult-to-read fonts. You will be better off choosing common typefaces such as Helvetica, Arial, or Times Roman.

Type size is as important as font selection. Set up your visuals in the room where you will be speaking and walk to the back and sides of the room to determine whether your type is large enough and clear enough. When using computer-generated slides, try to avoid selecting type that is smaller than 24 points. If you find that you have more text than will fit on a slide, don't reduce the size of the type. Instead, reduce the amount of text on a slide. Remember the six by six rule. Reducing the size of the type to include more text not only results in a poor visual but also makes it less legible.

Choose colors with an eye to legibility, too. Contrast heightens legibility. If you use a light background, use dark text and vice versa. If your visuals are going to be projected on overhead transparencies or slides, it is often better to use a dark background with light text. Otherwise, the text tends to visually melt together, creating eyestrain for your audience.[15] No matter how sublime light blue letters on a lavender background may appear at your desktop, they will become nearly invisible when projected onto a screen.[16]

Also consider whether the color scheme will be appropriate for the situation and your purpose. If you are making a presentation on behalf of your college, using your school colors may be appropriate if they provide sufficient contrast. If you are making a presentation to a conservative business group, a very bright color scheme may not be appropriate unless you are trying to emphasize that your ideas are "not the same old thing." If you're in doubt about color, stick to proven color schemes. Most graphic software packages recommend colors that will sharply contrast with a background.

Use Appropriate Graphics

When choosing graphics, first ask yourself whether your audience really needs to see the picture you want to use. If you are making a presentation about a new medical device, showing the actual device or a drawing of the device would help your audience understand it. On the other hand, including a picture of a hospital would add little to your presentation.

In fact, artwork that doesn't have a specific purpose can get in the way of your presentation. Resist the temptation to use graphic elements just because you

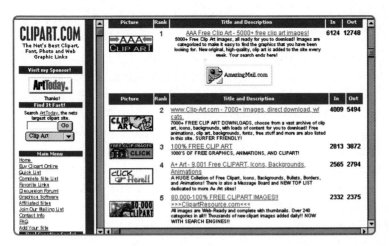

The ClipArt homepage, www. clipart.com, has links to more than 5000 free clip art images, which you can download and use in your presentations.

can. Not only does presentation software come with numerous clip-art images, but you also can buy clip-art books and software that specialize in certain types of images—such as job-related, sports, holidays, or around-the-world famous sites. However, more often than not, a clip-art graphic can get in the way of your message if the clip-art image doesn't reinforce the slide's meaning.

Build Sequentially

William Ringle, a presentation speaking consultant, refers to building sequentially as "progressive disclosure" and advises speakers to show relevant portions of material on a slide as seems appropriate.[17] For example, if you have a list of bulleted or numbered items and want to control how much the audience sees at one time, use progressive disclosure. If you want to build a chart or table by adding sections to it in a sequence, use progressive disclosure. By building your visual sequentially, you can build audience anticipation, focus on the point you are talking about, and save a "punch line" or conclusion until it is appropriate.

Create an Overall Look

Using presentation software to generate slides has become so common that many audience members can recognize many common templates (backgrounds) by name. Your presentation software will let you select any of several dozen backgrounds or templates, too. Restraint is the key. A fireworks background can overpower your message. An under-the-sea template can drown your words. In most cases, it's better to choose a modest background that will spruce up your slides but not compete with your words, charts, or graphics. Use a consistent style and background from slide to slide.

Handling Your Presentation Aids

Using presentation aids well can make a dull topic interesting, a complex idea understandable, or a long presentation endurable. On the other hand, using presentation aids poorly can bore, confuse, and annoy your audience. Having spent the time and effort to plan and prepare presentation aids to enhance your message,

REAL WORLD, REAL SPEAKERS

A friend of ours told a story about a young attorney who made a presentation to a group of prospective clients. He gave all his slides different backgrounds. He reasoned that since he wasn't that interesting a speaker, his slides would have to be really dazzling. Unfortunately, his listeners thought that the slides had been pulled from a number of prior presentations. Consequently, they were annoyed because they thought he hadn't taken the time or effort to prepare a presentation specifically for them.

When your slides have a consistent style, they convey a professional image and add credibility to your presentation. There's a saying in advertising: "It's a look." What this means is that it's better to have a consistent and identifiable "look" than to have an undistinguishable mishmash of images. The same is true of presentations. Keep the look of your visuals consistent.

you should make sure you handle your aids smoothly and professionally. Certain delivery issues arise when speakers use presentation aids.

HANDLING YOUR PRESENTATION AIDS

Focus on your audience, not on your aids

Timing is everything

Begin with *you*, not your visual

Be prepared to do without

Focus on Your Audience, Not on Your Aids

Always focus on your audience, not on your presentation aids. Some speakers get so involved with their presentation aids that they forget they have an audience. Don't, for example, turn your back to the audience. Not only does this movement put you in a potentially unattractive pose and eliminate eye contact, but listeners also may not be able to hear you very well.

Remember that you control the presentation aid; it shouldn't control you. If you're explaining a chart or reviewing something on a screen (appropriately placed to the right of the audience), stand to its side, face your audience, and point with your left hand. Although this movement may feel awkward, it ensures that your audience can see both you and your aid. Also, don't stand in front of your screen or flip chart. Inexperienced presenters often forget that their audience cannot see through them.

If you're displaying an object or demonstrating a procedure, hold your head up as much as possible. Watch how the people who appear in commercials do it.

*O*ne of us once worked with an administrator who loved putting everything on transparencies. But as soon as she'd project something onto the screen, she'd turn around and point out the numbers she thought were important. She'd stand right between the screen and the overhead projector. As a result, most of the information was projected on her back. It was all we could do to keep from laughing at the way the numbers would move all over her back. It's an unflattering image that is difficult to forget.

They hold their products up near their faces. They wash floors, mow lawns, and eat candy with their eyes on the camera and its audience. They talk to you, not to their product. Please note, however, that we are not suggesting that you rigidly plant your feet and never move. In fact, turning toward your visuals can add emphasis. Generally, people will instinctively look wherever you are looking. Selecting one or two moments to "talk to your visual" can add emphasis, but it should not become the focus of your presentation.[18]

Timing Is Everything

There is a right time and place for each type of presentation aid. Appropriate background music before a presentation can set the right mood. Turning the music off right before you speak can signal to the audience that it's time for their attention. Setting up a photo display can provide an interesting introduction to your presentation, but you also should move the audience and their attention away from the display when your presentation begins.

It's equally important to know when to introduce your presentation aids, how long to leave them up, and when to remove them. Unfortunately, presenters often rush though their materials, forgetting that audience members would like to see them, study them, and understand them. Here's a rule of thumb: Any chart or slide needs to be displayed for at least the length of time it would take an average reader to read it twice. In other words, give your audience time to digest the message on your aid before you take it away. You should usually let the audience read the visual themselves—don't read your presentation from the screen or flip chart. The one exception to this rule is that when you want to underscore a specific aspect of your visual, it's appropriate to read those words out loud.

Try to avoid long pauses between slides. If you speak while showing a chart or graph and stop while changing the visual, you will send a signal that your presentation aids are driving the presentation, not you. Keep talking as you move from one visual to another—it's a great time to make transitions or to give mini-summaries or previews.

Finally, when you've finished talking about a visual, get rid of it. Don't leave it on the screen or displayed on a flip chart as you move on to a new point. Likewise, don't reveal a new visual until you are ready to talk about it. When using electronic projection equipment, you may even want to insert or program a blank slide during the sections of your presentation that don't need visuals. And when

REAL WORLD, REAL SPEAKERS

A few years ago, I went to a very creepy presentation at a conference. The meeting room was nearly dark. At the front of the room was a large screen with the word *Welcome* in huge letters. After sitting for a few minutes, I spied a shadow in the front corner of the room. Through the sound system an amplified voice boomed, "I'm glad all of you could be here today. My name is Sandra James [the name has been changed], and what we will discuss today is. . . ." At that point, a bright slide appeared with the words *Sandra James* on the first line and the title of the presentation on the second line. The presentation continued like this until the end, when the final side popped up and said—you guessed it—"The End"! The room lights never came on, and the speaker never stepped forward to be seen, so the audience slowly left. To this day, some of us wonder who the speaker *really* was.

Isa Engleberg

you're nearly finished with your presentation, don't start to pack up your overheads, shut off your equipment, or take down your flip chart. Finish with a strong conclusion. You can clean up later.

Begin with *You*, Not Your Visual

Always establish rapport with your audience before your start using presentation aids. The audience should know whom they are going to be listening to during the presentation. Your introduction should be you talking. After the audience has settled in and is comfortable with you, you can use your presentation aids.

Unfortunately, the increased use of computer-controlled presentations has made the "voice-from-the-darkness" delivery technique more common in professional settings. We worry that too many presentations by disembodied speakers hiding in the dark corners of rooms will make presentations dull and tiresome rather than interesting and energizing experiences. Unless your only purpose is to narrate, don't leave your audience in the dark. That doesn't mean turning the lights on and off for a few seconds between each visual—that would be worse. It means dividing your presentation into sections so that you can speak in the light and, when appropriate, narrate in a dimmed room.

The disembodied speaking voice can result in several problems:

▶ The presenter loses the principle advantage of a live presentation—the presence of a real speaker connecting with an audience.

▶ Speaker credibility can be eroded.

▶ Audience members may have more trouble comprehending the presentation because most of the speaker's nonverbal communication channels (eye contact, appearance, physical delivery) have been removed.

▶ A presenter can alienate an audience by seeming to be disconnected from his or her message.

Our advice: Always start and end your presentation by making direct and personal contact with your audience.

USING a Pointer

Pointers have become nifty high-tech toys. You can choose from among old-fashioned rubber-tipped wooden pointers; compact, retractable pointers; and illuminated laser-light pointers. Pointers can be very useful if you want to highlight or focus audience attention on a particular portion of your presentation aid. There are, however, some words of caution to consider when wielding a pointer.

▶ As a general rule, the "laser" pointers that flash a very small beam of light on a screen are not very effective. One of the respondents to our survey told us that he couldn't hold the pointer steady and ended up trying to circle the items with the light. The audience ended up feeling dizzy rather than enlightened.

▶ If you're using a rigid pointer, rest the pointer gently on the screen or flip chart at the place you want the audience to note. That way it won't move as you are talking. When using an overhead, use a sharpened pencil as your pointer. Point to the item right on the overhead, not on the screen. Lay the pencil down on the overhead, with the point aimed directly at the material you want your audience to note.

▶ When you have finished pointing, put the pointer down. Don't hold it in your hand as you continue to talk. Don't use it to point at the audience. Don't wave it about. Use it to point; then put it away. Almost nothing is more distracting than a speaker's gesturing into the air with a pointer or slapping it against his or her hand. Even worse, one of our classes was reduced to tears from laughing at a student who closed his retractable pointer against himself and got it caught in his belt buckle.

Marjorie Brody suggests a simple way to remember how to use a pointer. "Touch, turn, talk," she advises.[1] Use the pointer to touch the material on which you want your audience to focus its attention. Next, turn toward your audience. Then talk to your audience.

1. Marjorie Brody, *Speaking Your Way to the Top: Making Powerful Business Presentations* (Boston: Allyn & Bacon, 1998), p. 96.

Be Prepared to Do Without

The reason why we can tell sad tales about speakers using presentation aids is that no matter how well you plan and practice, something can always go wrong. Televisions can break, slide projectors can burn out, computers can lock up, and transparencies can be left at home. You can run out of pamphlets, samples, or chalk. Your faithful dog can refuse to perform its tricks. Your scale model can fall apart. Your assistant may forget to show up. Many speakers learn this lesson the hard way.

Consider the new architect who was giving her first presentation to her firm's partners. Her talk began confidently until she got to the first slide. It was upside down. She passed it off with a funny remark and went on to the next slide. Upside down again. This time she stopped and, with some embarrassment, took three minutes to turn all fifty slides right-side up. The third slide displayed a company's name. It came up backwards—totally unreadable, and unforgivable.

One way to avoid presentation aid disasters is to do a dry run, a special practice just to check your aids. A dry run would have averted the architect's problems with her upside-down and backwards slides. But practice cannot guarantee that a piece of equipment will work properly, nor will it create new transparencies. It will not change small visuals into large ones for a bigger-than-expected audience. So what should you do? You should have a "Plan B." Think about whether you could deliver your presentation without your presentation aids. In many cases you can. After all, if used properly, presentation aids are not the presentation. They are only there to help and assist you. You and your message should always come first.

Putting the message first was beautifully illustrated in a multimedia presentation one of us saw at an international convention of university planners. The team presentation wowed an audience of educators and architects who had become accustomed to slick computer-generated presentations. A university dean, an internationally respected campus designer, and two architects had choreographed a brilliant presentation on how they had planned and were building a new private university in California.

The architectural firm had assigned the development of the multimedia presentation to one of its architectural associates who was highly skilled in the technical aspects of computer-generated presentations. As each member of the four-person presentation team spoke, the architectural associate advanced the slides. There was music in the background when the speakers were silent. During presentations, each slide appeared and disappeared at the perfect moment. There were preview slides as well as slides that built sequentially and highlighted important statements and data. Integrated into the presentation were photographs of happy multicultural students (all were models, since the campus was still under construction) studying, talking, and having fun.

After the speakers had completed their individual presentations, a brilliantly choreographed computer-generated animation sequence gave the audience a bird's-eye tour through the new campus-to-be. The final sequence ended with swelling music and the university's logo emblazoned on the screen. The audience gave the presentation a standing ovation—a first for such a program.

Do you think you could pull off a similar victory with your presentation aids? Probably not. Unless, that is, you have a full-time assistant who can devote a month's time to developing the slides and thousands of dollars to invest in a computer-generated animation sequence. And you must make sure that all members of the presentation team are willing to spend days developing, coordinating, and practicing their parts. However, you don't need the resources of Bill Gates or the Disney Corporation to develop effective presentation aids. Decide what will make *your* presentation more effective rather than worrying whether you can compete with high-tech experts. The presentation comes first. Presentation aids merely *aid*. When well planned and well presented, the simplest of presentation aids can make your presentation more interesting, dynamic, and successful.

Summary

How can presentation aids help me as a speaker?

Research has found that speakers who use appropriate presentation aids are perceived as more persuasive, better prepared, more professional, more credible, and more interesting. In addition, presentation aids can gain audience attention, clarify and reinforce ideas, and improve a speaker's efficiency.

What kinds of presentation aids should I use?

Use the presentation aids that are most appropriate for you, your audience, your setting, and your message. Presentation aids include pie charts, graphs, text charts, tables, drawings, maps, and photographs as well as audiotape recordings, objects, handouts, and physical demonstrations.

◆✦ What medium should I use?

You may choose from a variety of media such as flip charts, slides, video-tapes, or multimedia. Make sure that your choice matches the type of presentation aid that you are using and that it is appropriate for the setting and size of the audience.

◆✦ How do I design effective presentation aids?

When preparing presentation aids, you should keep several principles in mind: preview and highlight, exercise restraint, choose readable typefaces and suitable colors, use appropriate graphics, build sequentially, and create an overall look.

◆✦ Are there tips for using my presentation aids?

When delivering a presentation, remember to focus on the audience, not on your aids; to time your presentation aids for the appropriate moments; to begin with *you,* not with your visual; and to be prepared to do without the aids.

Key Terms

drawings 266	**pie charts** 264	**text charts** 265
graphs 265	**presentation aids** 261	
maps 267	**tables** 266	

Notes

1. The 3M Meeting Management Team with Jeannine Drew, *Mastering Meetings: Discovering the Hidden Potential of Effective Business Meetings* (New York: McGraw-Hill, 1994), p. 140.
2. Thomas Leech, *How to Prepare, Stage, & Deliver a Winning Presentation* (New York: AMACOM, 1993), p. 128.
3. Margaret Y. Rabb, *The Presentation Design Book,* 2nd ed. (Chapel Hill, NC: Ventana, 1993), pp. 2–3.
4. Malcolm Kushner, *Successful Presentations for Dummies* (Foster City, CA: IDG Books, 1997), p. 159.
5. There are several useful guides for selecting effective types of visual aids. The following references were used to support this section of the chapter: Dennis McBride, *How to Make Visual Presentations* (New York: Art Direction Book Co., 1983); Margaret Y. Rabb, *The Presentation Design Book,* 2nd ed. (Chapel Hill, NC: Ventana, 1993); 3M Meeting Management Team with Jeannine Drew, *Mastering Meetings: Discovering the Hidden Potential of Effective Business Meetings* (New York: McGraw-Hill, 1994).
6. Gene Zelazny, *Say It with Charts: The Executive's Guide to Successful Presentations* (Homewood, IL: Dow Jones-Irwin, 1985), p. 28.
7. Dennis McBride, *How to Make Visual Presentations* (New York: Art Direction Book Co., 1985), p. 39.
8. Zelazny, p. 33.
9. Rabb, p. 154.
10. Rabb, p. 210.
11. RAND, *Guidelines for Preparing Briefings* (Santa Monica, CA: Rand, 1996), pp. 5 and 9. Also see *www.rand.org/publications/electronic/.*
12. RAND, p. 10.

13. William J. Ringle, *TechEdge: Using Computers to Present and Persuade* (Boston: Allyn & Bacon, 1998), p. 125.
14. Ringle, pp. 125–126.
15. Hinkin, p. 35.
16. Ringle, pp. 127–128.
17. Ringle, pp. 130–131.
18. Kushner, p. 173.

APPLICATIONS

Chapter 17
Developing Informative Presentations

Chapter 18
Understanding Persuasion

Chapter 19
Developing Persuasive Presentations

Chapter 20
Developing Special Presentations

Chapter 21
Speaking in Groups

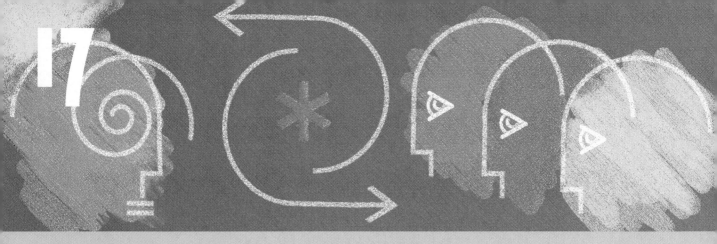

17

Developing Informative Presentations

▶▶ How do informative and persuasive presentations differ?

▶▶ How can I respond to the unique challenges of informative speaking?

▶▶ What strategies can make my informative presentation more effective?

▶▶ How can I make my informative presentation stand out?

O f all the different types of presentations, informative speaking is the most common. Businesses use informative presentations to orient new employees, to present company reports, and to explain new policies. Colleges use informative presentations to advise new students, to teach classes, and to report to boards of trustees and funding agencies. Television presents news, documentaries, and "how-to" shows. Whether it's called an informative presentation, a corporate briefing, or an oral report, people speak to inform others in just about every context.

What Is an Informative Presentation?

The primary purpose of an **informative presentation** is to instruct, explain, describe, enlighten, demonstrate, clarify, correct, or remind. An informative presentation can provide new information, explain complex concepts and processes, or clarify and correct misunderstood information. You will be asked to prepare and deliver informative presentations throughout your life and career, so learning how to do them well can give you a competitive edge.

Many of the speaking situations that our survey respondents described were informative. For example:

▶ Katie Smith Poole, a funeral director in Sandersville, Georgia, was invited by a church group to present a workshop on planning funerals.

▶ John Paguaga, a vice president and account executive at Fleet Bank in New York City, gave a presentation in England in which he explained the U.S. banking system to a large audience of executives from over one hundred British-owned banks.

▶ Captain Dr. Rob Simpson, a divisional finance secretary for the Salvation Army in Grand Rapids, Michigan, presented a paper titled "Enhancing Program Design Through Research" at a national social service conference.

▶ Ray Johnston, president of Top Hat Chimney Sweeps, Inc., in Altoona, Pennsylvania, talked about his background and professional experience in the chimney-sweep business to a group of insurance adjusters.

▶ Deanna Wolf, an assistant vice president of Platte Valley Bank in North Bend, Nebraska, gave a bank tour to a group of elementary school children.

▶ Joseph T. Mares, the director of Specialty Insecticide Development for Griffin L.L.C. in Valdosta, Georgia, gave a talk on fire ants at the local Rotary Club.

▶ Wendy Friedland, director of general accounting for Marriott International in Washington, D.C., made a presentation on new aspects of the accounting system to her colleagues.

As you can see, informative presentations can address a wide range of purposes and topics. Whether you're speaking to an audience of third-graders or an audience of CEOs, you can develop an informative presentation that helps them learn and understand.

Informative Versus Persuasive Speaking

The primary purpose of an informative presentation is to inform. As obvious as this may seem, it can be difficult to determine where an informative presentation ends and a persuasive presentation begins. Most informative presentations contain an element of persuasion. An informative presentation explaining the causes of acid rain may convince an audience that the problem is serious and should be addressed with stricter air pollution laws. Even an informative presentation demonstrating the proper way to change a tire can persuade an audience member not to call the local garage because changing a tire isn't as difficult as it looks. There is, however, a clear dividing line between informative and persuasive presentations: your purpose. As soon as you ask listeners to change their opinions or behavior, your presentation becomes persuasive.

The issue becomes even more complicated when your *private* purpose is considered. For example, if your presentation compares different brands of tires, it may slip over the boundary between informative and persuasive presentations if you manage a tire store that sells what you identify as the best brand. Advertisers often straddle this border. Statements such as "Laboratory tests show . . . ," "Three out of four doctors recommend . . . ," or "America's number one–selling brand . . ." may be true, but their primary purpose is persuasive, not informative. Information can be persuasive. A persuasive presentation can and usually does inform. The factor that separates the two types of presentations is the speaker's purpose.

The Special Challenge of Informative Speaking

In many cases, persuasive presentations more easily capture and maintain interest than do informative ones. Controversy can arouse an audience. Listeners may be more alert when a speaker is trying to change their opinions or behavior. Informative speaking often requires a concerted effort to gain and then keep the audience's attention. In a speech class, students can choose exciting and interesting topics to involve their audiences. Most real-world informative speakers don't have this advantage. Imagine the awesome task confronting presenters with the following assignments:

▶ Explain a new piece of federal legislation to a group of city government workers.

▶ Instruct senior executives on the techniques for using a new phone system.

▶ Describe the procedures for preparing an audit report.

▶ Teach the names and functions of the cranial nerves.

▶ Compare the features of the health insurance policies offered by a company to new employees.

There's little that's inspiring here! In fact, it's probably easier to present such information in written form. Audience disinterest can make an informative presentation particularly difficult to prepare and give. The informative speaker must consider every way of gaining and keeping the audience's attention and interest.

KNOW IF YOU'RE ASKING OR TELLING

Your presentation's purpose directly relates to what you expect of your audience. If you're *telling* them something, it's informative. If you're *asking* them to change their opinions or behavior, it's persuasive. Michael Hattersley, a contributor to Harvard University's *Management Update,* suggests that the answer to "Are you telling them or asking them?" usually falls somewhere in between. His guideline for choosing the correct approach is to *tell*—in a polite way, of course—when you are in complete control of the necessary information and authority and to *ask* when you're in command of the information, but your audience retains the ultimate decision-making power.[1]

1. Michael Hattersley, "The Key to Making Better Presentations: Audience Analysis," *Management Update: A Newsletter from Harvard Business School Publishing,* Vol.1, no. 5 (Oct. 1999): 5.

Pick a Purpose That Addresses Audience Needs. Selecting an appropriate purpose for your informative presentation can help you meet the challenge of overcoming audience disinterest. Begin by asking yourself what your audience may already know about your topic; then tailor your purpose accordingly. Suppose you were going to give a presentation on how to write a résumé but then determined that your audience of college seniors had already written theirs. You might change your presentation to one that focuses on making sure that a résumé uses words that will stand out in an electronic résumé keyword search. Once you know what you want to accomplish by making your presentation, make sure that your goal is achievable given your time limit, the audience whom you will be addressing, and their prior knowledge level.

Also, be sure to link your purpose and central idea. In a presentation on creating a searchable résumé, a central idea that addresses the strategies to use in a job interview would not match. The information you want to share should be directly related to your purpose, and your purpose should likewise be developed with your audience's needs in mind. Otherwise, you may make a well-organized and perfectly delivered presentation that doesn't engage the audience.

Include Content That Motivates the Audience. You can also overcome the challenge of audience disinterest by including specific motivational elements in your presentation. Explaining to audience members why your topic should matter to them and how it can affect their success may be just as important as making sure that your presentation is well organized and well delivered.

James A. McComb, a senior consultant for the Centre for Strategic Management in Colorado, makes presentations for a living. Here's his advice about audience motivation: "I judge success the same way every time—did the majority of the audience leave having received value (as they perceive it) for the time and money they invested in me." Your audience will be ready, willing, and able to listen to information that's needed and highly relevant.

A **value step,** which uses the presentation's introduction to tell an audience why the information is valuable or important to them, is a powerful motivational tool. The value step gives your audience a reason to listen to the entire presentation. As described in Chapter 10, "Introductions and Conclusions," you can use your introduction to refer to the place or occasion—the reason why they are assembled. You can show them how a recent event has affected or will affect them directly. You can involve the audience by asking questions about their needs or telling a story about people just like them. If you decide to begin by describing a problem, make sure that your audience understands how that problem directly and significantly affects their lives.

Note how this presenter uses a value step to motivate her audience to listen to a presentation about new evaluation plan forms, a topic that on first mention seems pretty dull:

> Last year one of your colleagues was denied promotion. She was well qualified—better than most applicants. She received the highest recommendations. But she wasn't promoted. She didn't get her well-deserved raise. Why? Because she didn't use the new evaluation plan forms and missed the new deadlines. When it was time to give out promotions, her application wasn't in the pool of candidates. Don't let this happen to you.

If there's a good reason for you to make a presentation, there should be a good reason for your audience to listen to it. Don't rely on the audience to figure it out, though. Tell them. Make it clear that the information has value. A value step may not be necessary in all informative presentations, but it can motivate a disinterested audience to listen to you.

Enhance Your Credibility. Sometimes audience disinterest is really audience distrust in disguise. As Chapter 11, "Speaker Credibility and Ethics," notes, several factors determine whether the audience sees you as competent, charismatic, and of good character. Listeners are more likely to appreciate and listen to you if they trust you and believe that you know what you're talking about. As you prepare an informative presentation, think about ways to enhance your own credibility. How can you let the audience know that you're an expert or that you've done considerable research on your topic? How can you show them that your primary purpose is to help them understand the material? How can you assure them that your purpose is exactly what it seems

Home Depot employees receive training in roof coating and driveway sealers in order to become more credible salespeople who can provide well-informed customer service.

to be—that you don't have any ulterior motives? Audiences are much more likely to listen and learn from a speaker they respect, trust, and like.

Informative Strategies

While each informative presentation you prepare may have a unique purpose, all will share the same goal: to help your audience better understand and become better informed about your topic. Informative goals are best achieved through a strategy that matches specific types of supporting material and organizational tools to audience characteristics.[1] That's why audience analysis is so critical to the success of an informative presentation. Katherine Rowan, a professor of communication at Purdue University, suggests that there are two types of informative communication—informatory and explanatory. **Informatory communication** is similar to news reporting—it creates awareness by presenting the latest information about some topic. **Explanatory communication** goes beyond reporting "the facts" and helps audiences understand, interpret, and evaluate them. Good explanatory presentations answer questions such as "Why?" or "What does that mean?"[2] Effective informative speakers understand when they need to report information and when they need to explain a more complicated concept or process. Not surprisingly, different types of informative messages require different communication strategies.

> **INFORMATIVE PRESENTATION STRATEGIES TO**
>
> Report new information
> Explain difficult concepts
> Explain complex processes
> Overcome confusion and
>   misunderstanding

Reporting New Information

Reporting new information can be the easiest informative presentation to prepare and present, particularly when an audience is eager to learn. As a type of informatory communication, sharing new information is much easier than struggling to explain a difficult, complex, or misunderstood concept. In informatory communication, listeners need only the facts. How you present those facts, however, will make a difference in how much the audience learns and remembers.

As Rowan notes in her explanation of informatory communication, reporting new information is what most news reporters do.[3] They report the *who, what, where, when, how,* and *why* of an event. They write about *who* is doing *what* to *whom*. They describe *how* or *why* something happened. You can find new information in daily newspapers and popular magazines, in textbooks and classroom lectures, and in encyclopedias and on specialized Web pages.

When college students are asked to prepare and deliver an informative presentation in a speech class, they often choose topics that report new information. They try to find a topic that they, rather than the audience, know a lot about: the life of a great-grandmother, fly-fishing lures, shoeing a horse, fixing warped table tops.

You face two major challenges when reporting new information in a presentation. First, if your information is very new or unexpected, an audience may have trouble grasping your central idea. Second, you need to give the audience a reason to listen, learn, and remember such information. Why and what do they really need to know about your great-grandmother or about unwarping a table?

Four strategies can help you overcome the challenges of sharing new information with an audience. First, include a value step in your introduction. Second, use a clear and, if possible, creative organizational pattern to help your audience learn and remember what you say. Third, use a variety of types of supporting material to present the information in different forms. Use facts, statistics, testimony, definitions, analogies, descriptions, examples, and stories as described in Chapter 7, "Supporting Material." Fourth, relate the new information to audience interests and needs *throughout* the presentation. If they see no reason to learn or use the information, they are likely to stop listening.

STRATEGIES FOR REPORTING NEW INFORMATION

1. **Include a value step in the introduction**
2. **Use a clear organizational pattern**
3. **Use various types of supporting material**
4. **Relate information to audience interests and needs**

Informative presentations that report new information fall into several subtypes. Choosing one can help you clarify your purpose, select appropriate supporting material, and decide how to go about organizing your presentation. Informative presentations can report new information about objects, people, procedures, and events.

Informing Audiences About Objects.   Students in public speaking classes often choose objects as the topic of their informative presentations. It's easy to see why: A tangible object can be described, touched, and even brought to the presentation, either in visual aid form or in the "flesh." Objects are often items very familiar to the speaker—a computer keyboard, a set of tools, or a favorite fishing pole. We've heard students report on their stamp collections, full-dress military uniforms, fishing lures, and exotic pets.

However, a topic alone is not a purpose statement or a central idea. Moreover, you won't have time to tell your audience everything there is to know about stamp collecting or fishing lures. So, as is the case in every presentation, you will need to focus your message on the characteristics that match your purpose, central idea, and organizational format. For example, this student used a spatial arrangement to develop an informatory presentation about fire-ant anatomy:

Topic Area: Fire ants

Purpose: To familiarize audience members with the external anatomy of a fire ant

Central Idea: A tour of the fire ant's external anatomy will help you understand why these ants are so hard to get rid of.

Linda Watson, a science resource materials specialist, explains her method of replenishing science kits to educators from the New England area.

Value Step: Besides inflicting painful, sometimes deadly, stings, fire ants can eat up your garden, damage your home, and harm your pets and local wildlife.

Organization: Spatial—a visual tour of the fire ant's external anatomy

Key Points: A. Integument (exoskeleton)

B. Head and its components

C. Thorax

D. Abdomen

Informing Audiences About People. Informatory presentations about people share common characteristics with presentations about objects. Like an object, people are tangible—in this case, flesh-and-blood personalities. A presentation about a person can focus on a historical or literary figure, a famous living individual, or someone whom you know. Regardless of whether you're developing an informatory presentation about a historical figure or about the person standing next to you, describe that person's life and accomplishments or select special stories about the person to tap audience interests and emotions. However, you need to be selective and focus your presentation on the personal characteristics or achievements that match your purpose and support your central idea. The following example presents a focused plan.

Topic Area: Early female blues singers

Purpose: To demonstrate the influence of four female blues singers of the 1920s on musicians in later eras

Central Idea: In the 1920s, Sippie Wallace, Edith Wilson, Victoria Spivey, and Alberta Hunter paved the way for other female blues singers.[4]

Value Step:	If you call yourself an honest-to-goodness blues fan, you should know more about the major contributions made by the early *female* blues singers.
Organization:	Stories and examples—brief biographies of four blues singers
Key Points:	A. Sippie Wallace
	B. Edith Wilson
	C. Victoria Spivey
	D. Alberta Hunter

Explaining Procedures to an Audience.   Presentations about procedures can be among the easiest to plan and present—or they can be the hardest. It depends on the topic and whether your communication purpose is informatory or explanatory. If you are describing a fairly simple procedure, an informatory demonstration may be all that's necessary to achieve your purpose. If the procedure is complex and requires considerable expertise, you may have trouble deciding on the best way to approach and organize your explanation. Here are some sample topics that are well suited for an informatory presentation based on procedures:

How to complete an evaluation form

How to draw blood

How to prepare a meeting agenda

How to prune a tree

How to boil an egg

Note the use of the word *how*. Procedures focus on *how* to do something rather than on *what* to do or *why* to do it. Changing a tire, filling out a form, and sewing on a button are not necessarily easy procedures, but at least there are accepted and proper sets of steps for each of them. On the other hand, transplanting a heart and docking a space shuttle are highly complex procedures. There are no do-it-yourself manuals or "simple tips" to follow. These challenging topics require explanatory communication as well as information.

Make sure you know enough about your topic, particularly if it's a complex procedure, to properly explain it to your audience. If it's a simple procedure, make sure that you provide enough information to cover each step adequately. For example, anyone who has ever tried to cook a perfect hard-boiled egg knows that following the right procedure can make the difference between getting a hard egg and creating a mess of white albumen floating around in a pot of boiling water.

Topic:	Cooking hard-boiled eggs
Purpose:	To teach listeners how to make foolproof hard-boiled eggs
Central Idea:	There are four steps to cooking perfect hard-boiled eggs.
Value Step:	Rather than wasting or throwing away cracked eggs, you can use the proper procedure to make sure your hard-boiled egg is perfect.
Organization:	Time Arrangement—step-by-step instructions
Key Points:	A. Cold-water start
	B. Stopping the boil
	C. The fifteen-minute stand
	D. The cold-water rinse

REAL WORLD, REAL SPEAKERS

One of us once heard Dr. Christiaan Barnard, the first surgeon to perform a heart transplant, speak to a group of university physicians and medical students. During his introduction he took a long time telling a joke about how his secretary could give his presentation better than he could. This was a way of assuring his audience that he would not be giving a highly technical presentation. Then, slowly and carefully, he led his audience through a series of detailed photographic slides showing the procedures that he had followed during a series of early heart transplants. "Don't try this at home," he joked in a lighter moment as a way of breaking up the explanation of a complex technical procedure.

Informing Audiences About Events. You can base an informatory presentation on historical or recent events. History professors often center their lectures on an important event. Business executives may discuss a critical event to demonstrate how to handle a crisis. Politicians are often invited to commemorate an event. An event can be a single incident—such as the anniversary of the Columbine High School shootings, the winning of an Olympic gold medal by a particular athlete, or the dedication and opening of a new building. An event can also be a series of incidents or milestones that have become a historical phenomenon or institution—such as the Civil War, the race to the moon, or the founding of a company. Regardless of the date, size, or significance of the event you select, the purpose of your informatory presentation will determine how you talk about that event.

The following example presents an approach to informatory speaking about an event.

Topic: Our company's fiftieth anniversary

Purpose: To preview the events scheduled for the company's upcoming fiftieth anniversary

Central Idea: The premiere events for our fiftieth anniversary will have something for everyone.

Value Step: Making our fiftieth anniversary celebration a success can bring more attention and—as a result—more business and profits to the company.

Organization: Topical—four major events

Key Points:
  A. Dedication of the new office annex
  B. Employee picnic and baseball game
  C. Presentation by a nationally recognized speaker
  D. Fiftieth anniversary gala

Explaining Difficult Concepts

Explaining a difficult concept presents special challenges for informative speakers. Unlike an object, person, procedure, or event, a concept is abstract—rarely can you touch it, demonstrate it, or easily define it in simple terms. You may be perplexed and bewildered for days trying to discover the essence of a concept and the most effective ways to explain it to an audience. Trying to explain quantum mechanics, the basic tenets of Islam, the relationship between nutrition and chronic disease, or the distinguishing characteristics of Karl Marx's theory of dialectical materialism would be a difficult task for any speaker.

Explaining a difficult concept requires more than reporting. It requires explanatory communication in which a speaker helps audience members understand and separate essential characteristics from nonessential features. What, for example, is the difference between concepts such as *validity* and *reliability, blues* and *jazz, ethos* and *ethics*? Why are corals classified as animals and not as plants?[5]

Shepherds looking at a flock of sheep will see things that we cannot see. They will be able to separate the old and young sheep, the males and the females, the healthy and the sick, the strong and the weak. With inexperienced eyes, we see only sheep. Your job as an informative presenter is to guide your audience to the distinctions that will help them better understand your topic.

If you are trying to explain a difficult concept to an audience, we recommend four strategies. First, define or list the concept's essential features. Whether you are using a presentation aid or are carefully defining the essence of a concept, make sure that you explain how it differs from other related concepts. Second, give typical examples of the concept. Third, use a variety of examples and counterexamples. Can you show the audience that chaos theory is not the same as complete disorder or randomness? Can you explain that the opposite of communism is capitalism, not democracy? Finally, consider quizzing your audience's understanding. We aren't talking about a paper-and-pencil test (although you could, at the end of your presentation, give an anonymous quiz to see if you've made your point). Rather, pose questions about the concept and, after giving the audience time to think about answers, provide the answers yourself. You also may want to include a question-and-answer session at the end of your informative presentation to give the audience a chance to ask you questions.

Learning a difficult concept is just that—difficult. It's a challenge for both speaker and audience. By employing some of the strategies we've recommended, you are more likely to leave your audience with an accurate understanding of a concept that's difficult to grasp.

WHAT'S A BRIEFING?

The word *briefing* should be familiar to those of you working in or seeking a career in business or government. A **briefing** is a type of informative presentation in which a speaker *briefly* reports about the status of an upcoming or past event or project in a business or organizational setting. In a business setting, you might be asked to present a short report to your colleagues or managers on what you learned at a recent conference or meeting. In a government setting, you might be asked to provide a brief update to staff members on the public response to an elected official's tax initiative or speech. The White House press secretary can often be seen on television providing a briefing to the press about the activities and reactions of the president.

Although briefings are—by their very definition—short, they may be the only way to inform an audience about a very important issue. Both of us have participated in briefings that were scheduled right before important events to make sure that all people involved were clear about their responsibilities and that any previously unforeseen problems were resolved before the event began.

STRATEGIES FOR EXPLAINING DIFFICULT CONCEPTS

1. **Define essential features**
2. **Use typical examples**
3. **Contrast examples and counter-examples**
4. **Quiz the audience**

In the following example, a biology student tried to explain the meanings of the terms *diversity* and *disparity* as they are used in studying animal species.

Topic Area: Biological diversity and disparity

Purpose: To explain how the differences between diversity and disparity of species account for a central fact of life's evolutionary history[6]

291

Central Idea: A realistic picture of evolution requires an understanding of the distinction between biological diversity and disparity.

Value Step: What you learned in high school biology may have distorted the true nature of life's history.

Organization: Topical plus questions to audience

Key Points: A. Diversity

       (High diversity: 1,500 species of rats versus low diversity: 10 species of horses)

       B. Disparity

       (Minor differences in body plans of "three blind mice" versus major differences in body plans of insect species)

       C. Quiz about diversity and disparity

The previous example may not have clarified or explained the concepts of diversity and disparity sufficiently for you as a reader, but it is a good basis for developing an explanatory, informative presentation. When he gave his talk, the speaker used typical examples throughout his presentation (rats, horses, mice, insects), contrasted examples and nonexamples ("three blind mice" may be diverse but do not have disparate body plans as insects do), and quizzed audience members (Are elephant and ant species highly diverse or highly disparate? Which disparate body plans have survived millions of years of evolution?).

Explaining Complex Processes

Explaining a complex process is not the same as explaining a difficult concept. In the case of difficult concepts, you are asking an audience to master the meaning and use of a certain term or principle. Processes tend to be multidimensional and have multiple steps. With complex processes, you are asking audience members to unravel something that is complicated.

The first challenge when making an explanatory presentation is identifying the key components of the process. What's the "big picture"? We offer four recommendations that can help you find and describe the big picture to your audience. First, make sure that you are very well organized. Provide clear and well-supported key points. Second, use analogies to compare the unfamiliar concept you're presenting to something the audience already understands. Third, use presentation aids such as models and drawings to help your audience visualize or experience the process. Finally, use connectives frequently within your presentation. Transitions, internal previews, internal summaries, and signposts can reinforce and help your audience understand the interrelationship among key components (see Chapter 9, "Organizational Tools").

**STRATEGIES FOR EXPLAINING
COMPLEX PROCESSES**

1. Provide clear key points
2. Use analogies
3. Use presentation aids
4. Use connectives—transitions, previews, summaries, signposts

Mitchell Waldrop, author of *Complexity: The Emerging Science at the Edge of Order and Chaos*,[1] gave a guest lecture on complexity theory at my college. The lecture hall was packed with faculty and students eager to understand this much-talked-about but complex scientific process. Waldrop's talk was a great success. Why? Because he used several strategies to ensure that his explanation of "self-organizing systems" was clear and comprehensible.

He began by describing the essence of complexity theory by linking several well-known and intriguing events (the collapse of the Soviet Union, hurricanes, air traffic controller decision-making) to three key points about complexity theory. Then he used an analogy to compare and contrast his key points about order, complexity, and chaos to different states of water: ice, liquid, and steam. By displaying simple drawings of an ice cube, a country lake, and a steam bath, he reinforced the essential features of his key points. Finally, he used the example of national economies to illustrate order (economic stagnation), chaos (economic collapse), and a complex economy (strong and flexible).

Throughout his presentation, he linked his three key points to one another by using a variety of previews, transitions, and summaries and consequently led his audience to an understanding of a fascinating process.

Isa Engleberg

1. M. Mitchell Waldrop, *Complexity: The Emerging Science at the Edge of Order and Chaos* (New York: W. W. Norton, 1989).

In the following example, the process of breathing for speech is outlined for a presentation designed to teach audience members how to improve the quality and strength of their voices.

Topic Area: Breathing for speech

Purpose: To explain how to breathe for speech in order to be a more effective and audible speaker

Central Idea: The ability to produce a strong and expressive voice requires an understanding and control of the inhalation/exhalation process.

Value Step: Learning to breathe for speech will make you a more effective and confident speaker.

Organization: Compare/Contrast—three components of the breathing process

Key Points: A. Active vs. passive exhalation

       B. Deep diaphragmatic vs. shallow clavicular breathing

       C. Quick vs. equal time for inhalation

By comparing something well known (breathing for life) to something less well known (breathing for speech), the speaker can help an audience understand this process. Throughout the presentation, the importance of breathing for speech can be explained by comparing it to playing a wind or brass instrument, by using presentation aids and demonstrations, and by making sure that transitions, previews, summaries, and signposts are used to connect the three key points.

HANDLING HANDOUTS

Handouts can be a huge help when you're trying to explain difficult concepts and complex processes. Handouts have the potential to enhance listener attention and understanding, keep the audience focused on the subject, present more information than can be covered in the presentation, and strengthen the speaker's credibility.[1] Generally, it's a good idea to use handouts if your presentation contains a lot of technical information or if you want your audience to take notes.[2] The problem with handouts is that many speakers don't know what to put in them or when to hand them out.

You can use handouts for many things: biographical information about yourself, copies of your presentation aids, checklists, drawings, references, article reprints, workshop exercises, an outline of your presentation, an evaluation form, and more. The nature and content of your handout should determine at what point you share it with audience members. Usually, distributing a handout during a presentation distracts the audience and takes their attention away from you.

In general, we recommend giving your audience handouts before you begin speaking or very near the beginning of your presentation—but not if your handout is a word-for-word copy of your presentation or if it outlines your ideas in minute detail. Both of us have left conference programs seconds before they began because presenters distributed and intended to read their papers to the audience. What keeps us in a room are handouts that help us follow the presentation and/or provide additional information about the topic. Handouts that contain a skeleton outline of the presentation on which listeners can take notes can also be helpful. If you want audience members to have copies of your handout before you begin speaking, place them on each seat in the room, distribute them at the door as audience members enter, or place a stack on a table at the entrance to the room and tell them to pick one up before your presentation begins.

Distributing handouts at the end of a presentation can be awkward. Robert Pike, a nationally known communication consultant, describes a common and unfortunate scenario: "I've heard presenters say, 'Don't worry about taking notes. It's all in the handout you'll get at the end.' As the presentation continues and I see various visuals, I find myself wondering (meanwhile, not listening to the presentation), 'Will this be in the handout?' Not wanting to take a chance, I become more preoccupied with trying to copy all the visuals than I am in relating the visuals to the content being presented."[3]

There are only a few circumstances in which we'd recommend distributing a handout at the end of a presentation. As noted earlier, if your handout repeats your presentation, save it for the end. When the information or the handout is not an integral part of the presentation—such as publications or names and addresses to file for future reference—it can be passed out once you've finished speaking. Another appropriate circumstance is when the directions for an exercise, recipe, or procedure are written out in detail for future use. Notice that these are examples of information that will be useful in the future, not information that was needed to understand and appreciate a presentation. Handouts can make a difference if they are used wisely and well.

1. Robert W. Pike, *High-Impact Presentations* (Des Moines, IA: American Media, 1995), pp. 74–77.
2. Marjorie Brody, *Speaking Your Way to the Top: Making Powerful Business Presentations* (Boston: Allyn & Bacon, 1998), p. 104.
3. Pike, p. 78.

Overcoming Confusion and Misunderstanding

In addition to instructing, explaining, and demonstrating, informative presentations can also help overcome confusion or misunderstanding. Why do people believe that going out into the cold without a hat will make them sick or that all dietary fat is harmful? People often cling to strong beliefs, even ones that are wrong. Informative speakers face the challenge of replacing old, erroneous beliefs with new, more accurate ones. The strategy is to first state the misconception; then acknowledge why it is believed; next, reject the misconception supported by evidence; and last, describe and explain the more acceptable belief. Let's keep it simple with an example about the fat content of our diets.

Topic:	Fat in foods
Purpose:	To explain that fat is an important element of everyone's diet
Central Idea:	Our health-conscious society has all but declared an unwinnable and unwise war on food with high fat content.
Value Step:	Eliminating fat from your diet can hurt you rather than help you lose weight.
Organization:	Problem (misinformation)/Solution (accurate information)
Key Points:	A. Many people believe that eliminating all fat from their diets will make then thinner and healthier.
	B. This belief is understandable, since fat is the very thing we're trying to reduce on our bodies.
	C. Fat is an essential nutrient.
	D. Fats are naturally occurring components in all foods that, in appropriate quantities, make food tastier and bodies stronger.

If you're thinking that an explanatory presentation designed to overcome confusion and misunderstanding is more persuasive than informative, you may be right. At the same time, it clearly fits within our definition of an informative presentation: one that seeks to instruct, explain, enlighten, demonstrate, clarify, correct, remind, or describe. If it's successful, a presentation about fat in the diet will encourage an audience to rethink what they believe. The presentation does not advocate a change in diet, nor does it provide a chart spelling out recommended fat intake. Its primary purpose is to provide accurate information in the hope that an erroneous belief will be corrected. However, the borderline between informative and persuasive speaking can be elusive. As noted on page 283 what matters is your purpose. In this case, you're *telling* audience members about the beneficial role of dietary fat, not *asking* them to change their diets.

STRATEGIES FOR OVERCOMING CONFUSION AND MISINFORMATION

1. State the misconception
2. Acknowledge its believability
3. Reject the misconception by providing evidence
4. State and explain the more acceptable belief

Informative Strategies, Organization, and Supporting Material

Effective informative speakers do not assume that their favorite organizational pattern will work with all presentations or that telling good stories and sharing dramatic statistics will make an audience understand new information, difficult concepts, or complex processes. Instead, an effective speaker considers the nature of the information, audience values, organizational options, and the different kinds of supporting material that can be used to achieve his or her purpose. Figure 17.1 on page 296 links each type of informative presentation to some of the organizational formats and types of supporting material that best suit the presentation's general purpose.

Figure 17.1   Organizing and Supporting Informative Presentations

Type of Information	Organizational Formats	Supporting Materials
Report new information (primarily informatory)	topical, time, space, cause/effect, comparison/contrast, stories and examples, memory aids	facts, statistics, testimony, definitions, analogies, descriptions, examples, stories
Explain difficult concepts (explanatory)	topical, space, comparison/contrast, stories and examples, memory aids	facts, definitions, analogies, descriptions, examples, counterexamples
Explain complex processes (explanatory)	topical, time, space, comparison/contrast	facts, analogies, descriptions, examples, presentation aids
Overcome confusion and misunderstanding (explanatory)	topical, causes/effects, comparison/contrast, problem/solution, stories and examples, memory aids	facts, statistics, testimony, definitions, analogies, descriptions, examples, stories

Insider Secrets of Informative Presentations

By following the principles explained in this chapter, you can develop a successful informative presentation. However, you can apply some special techniques to take it to the next level. As teachers and presenters, we have listened to and evaluated thousands of informative presentations by students, colleagues, and corporate clients. We have vivid and long-lasting memories of some of them and absolutely no recollection of others. What made the memorable presentations exceptional? We're going to share some insider secrets of exceptional informative speaking.

> **INSIDER SECRETS OF INFORMATIVE SPEAKING**
>
> - "KISS"
> - One sensory image
> - Avoiding information overload

"KISS"

Keep it simple, speaker! Most audiences cannot absorb and retain complex information, no matter how important it may be. Can you identify the problem in the following exchange between a speaker and a listener?

Listener: I heard your presentation on the new employee evaluation plan.

Speaker: What do you remember about what I said?

Listener: Well, you went through the plan page by page, explaining how the new provisions would apply.

Speaker: What was one of the new provisions?

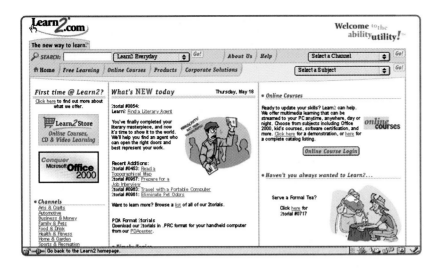

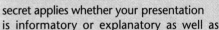

If you want to find examples of clear explanations, try www.learn2.com. Whether you are trying to understand a complex scientific principle or learn how to hold a tennis racket, this Web site prides itself on its accuracy and clarity.

Listener: Ah . . . well, . . . there was something about new forms, I think. I don't know—I'll look it up when I have to use it.

Exactly. The listener will look it up. The speaker's purpose—explaining the whole plan—was much too ambitious for a single, short presentation. Keep it simple, speaker! Audiences are intelligent, but they won't remember everything you say. In addition, most audience members are not highly skilled listeners. They can absorb only a few key ideas and facts during one sitting. Psychologists who study the capacity of short-term memory have concluded that most people can hold between five and nine chunks of information in their short-term memory.[7] Thus, an audience is unlikely to remember twelve recommendations or even ten good stories. Keep it simple if you want the audience to remember you and your message.

How could this speaker have presented the new evaluation plan more simply? First, she should have made sure that all employees already had a copy of the plan in their offices. Since many people don't read what they're given, the speaker would then have had to choose the essential elements to focus on during the presentation. She might have opted to explain the differences between the new and old plans or displayed the new forms that must be submitted at every deadline. Either option would have focused on one part of the plan only, but that would have been enough for a presentation. Keep it simple. Let the audience read the details.

One Sensory Image

What do you think of when you read the words *Ice Hockey* in the FAQ to the right? Fights, penalty boxes, screaming fans, chaos on ice, and body checks? Could one presentation incorporate all of these images? What do you start to imagine when you read *The Goalkeeper's Protective Equipment*? Perhaps you see a person bundled to near immobility or a

HoW Do I SiMPLiFy a COMPLEX ToPiC?   The "KISS"

secret applies whether your presentation is informatory or explanatory as well as whether you're in a corporate setting or a speech class because most audience members don't have the listening skills or patience to accommodate every detail. Keep your topic tightly focused. Concentrate on one or two important details, not ten. The following examples illustrate how students narrowed their informative speech topics into simpler messages by concentrating on just one aspect of a broader topic.

Broad Topic Area	*Narrow Topic Area*
Herbal Medicines	Camomile
Mediation	Prehearing Preparation
The Vatican	The Vatican's Swiss Guard
Ice Hockey	The Goalkeeper's Protective Equipment
Islam	Sunnites and Shiites
Auto Maintenance	Changing the Oil
Insects	Fire Ants

Present More Message and Less Information Thomas Leech, a communication consultant and author, offers this tip for creating presentation aids: Present more message and less information. It applies equally well to developing informative presentations. Leech writes that "information overload is universally hated and, unfortunately, extremely common. The value of a presentation is to help listeners understand the essence of the subject."[1] Keeping your informative presentation simple and focused on the essentials helps you and your audience communicate successfully. You have a clear message you want to convey, and your audience receives that message.

1. Thomas Leech, *How to Prepare, Stage, & Deliver Winning Presentations* (New York: AMACOM, 1993), p. 139.

menacing-looking face mask. A topic like "Herbal Medicines" can conjure up a witch's brew of images. "Chamomile" is easier to imagine—a strongly scented herb with tiny yellow blossoms.

You can make your informative presentation more interesting and memorable by focusing on one sensory image. Choose a topic that taps one of five senses. When one of our students chose garlic as the subject of her informative presentation, she worried that there wouldn't be enough to say about her topic. After completing some initial research, she was overwhelmed with information, so she narrowed her topic to garlic's powerful odor. Although this topic can stimulate a visual image, the characteristic we all know and remember is garlic's strong and easily recognized odor. Her presentation focused on garlic's powerful smell and ways to get rid of that smell after eating a large dose. Even a talk on something as uninspiring as a new evaluation plan can benefit from the one-sensory-image tip. Visualizing a sample evaluation form with a deadline stamped across it is enough to provide the speaker with a clear central idea—and a memorable presentation aid. Choose one sensory impression—sight, sound, taste, smell, or touch—as the focus of your informative presentation.

Looking for one sensory image takes some creative thinking. If you wanted to give a presentation on baking chocolate chip cookies, you could begin by thinking of one sensory image for each of the five senses, then develop a central idea based on each.

Sight: A thick brown cookie with visible chips

Sound: A cookie that doesn't snap when it's broken

Taste: A sweet cookie dough mixed with strong chocolate

Smell: A cookie that smells good while and even after baking

Touch: A soft and chewy cookie

An informative presentation could focus on how to make sure cookies are moist and chewy. Or you could emphasize the different tastes of different chocolates. Or you could identify the ingredients that make a cookie smell so good. How many of the five senses can you apply to the following topics: buying a new car, fire ants, explaining a company's mission statement, a school's discipline policy, the battle of Gettysburg, fighting oil well fires?

Avoiding Information Overload

We're all surrounded by too much information. We can subscribe to dozens of magazines, watch hundreds of shows on television, read thousands of books, spend hours surfing the Net, and retrieve millions of pieces of information from a single compact disc. Every job and profession is becoming more specialized. Instead of general practitioners, we have doctors who specialize in everything from hair implants to ingrown toenails. Lawyers, scientific researchers, builders, professors, and engineers must specialize. With so much information and specialization around us, it's easy to get overloaded. However, effective informative presentations ease this problem rather than add to it.

Whether you're explaining a new office procedure or a new dance step, your audience is unlikely to remember all the details of a complex set of instructions the first time that they hear them. Does this mean you should never try to explain anything complicated? No, but it does mean that you have to be especially careful as you prepare and plan your presentation. Have you adapted your message to your audience? Have you chosen clear and interesting examples to support your ideas? Have you selected language that will reinforce your message and make it more memorable? Have you practiced your delivery in front of others and asked for feedback? The best chef on earth can ruin a magnificent meal by serving too much food. Music fans can damage their hearing by listening to hours of very loud music. And speakers can overload their audience with too much information.

The final insider secret is that there isn't just one secret, any more than there's only one secret to the art of good painting, effective management, or skilled dancing. Insider secrets are nothing more than a series of good decisions that you make at key points in any process. First, you start with the basics. In dance, the basics involve a well-coordinated body, a sense of rhythm, and mastery of basic steps. In informative presentations, the basics involve all that we have discussed in the preceding chapters—clear purpose, audience analysis and adaptation, good research, effective organization, and skilled delivery. With these fundamentals well in hand, and with an understanding of informative speaking strategies and insider secrets, you can master the art of making interesting and effective informative presentations.

Summary

❖❖ How do informative and persuasive presentations differ?

Although there can be a thin dividing line between informing and persuading, the speaker's purpose determines the difference. The primary purpose of an informative presentation is to instruct, explain, describe, enlighten, demonstrate, clarify, correct, or remind by sharing information with an audience. As soon as you ask listeners to change their opinions or behavior, your purpose becomes persuasive.

❖❖ How can I respond to the unique challenges of informative speaking?

You should think critically about your purpose, your audience, and your credibility before making decisions about how to organize or strategically give an informative presentation.

❖❖ What strategies can make my informative presentation more effective?

Decide whether the information you want to share requires informatory or explanatory communication. Then use appropriate supporting material and organizational tools, depending on whether you want to share new information, explain a difficult concept or complex process, or correct misinformation.

❖❖ How can I make my informative presentation stand out?

After incorporating as many interest factors as you can, fine-tune your informative presentation by incorporating several insider secrets: (1) "KISS" ("Keep it simple, speaker!"), (2) highlight one sensory image, and (3) avoid information overload.

Key Terms

Notes

1. We are indebted to Katherine E. Rowan, who has proposed a new pedagogy for informative speaking, one which focuses on understanding reasons for misunderstandings or confusion on the part of audience members. With such an understanding, a speaker can develop a more responsive and successful informative speaking strategy. See Katherine E. Rowan, "A New Pedagogy for Explanatory Public Speaking: Why Arrangement Should Not Substitute for Invention," *Communication Education* 44 (1995): 236–250.
2. Rowan, pp. 241–247.
3. Rowan, p. 242.
4. See Daphne Duval Harrison, *Black Pearls: Blues Queens of the 1920s* (New Brunswick, NJ: Rutgers University Press, 1993).
5. Rowan, p. 241.
6. Based on the work of Stephen Jay Gould, *Wonderful Life: The Burgess Shale and the Nature of History* (New York: W. W. Norton, 1989), p. 49.
7. Douglas A. Bernstein et al., *Psychology,* 5th ed. (Boston: Houghton Mifflin, 2000), p. 223.

18

Understanding Persuasion

- ➡➡ What is persuasion?
- ➡➡ Will all audiences react to persuasive presentations in the same way?
- ➡➡ What's the best route to persuasion?
- ➡➡ How much persuasion can I achieve in a single presentation?
- ➡➡ How can marketing strategies be used to enhance persuasion?

Persuasive messages bombard us all from the time we wake up until the moment we end each day. Sometimes the persuasion is obvious—a commercial, a sales call, a political campaign speech. At other times it's less obvious—an inspirational sermon, an investment newsletter, a product sample in the mail. Businesses use persuasion to sell products. The armed forces use persuasion to justify their military budgets. Colleges use persuasion to recruit students and faculty. Even children use persuasive speaking to convince their parents to let them stay up late or to buy them the newest toy or breakfast cereal. In this chapter we explore how and why persuasion works. In the next chapter, "Developing Persuasive Presentations," we help you use this information to develop your own persuasive presentations.

What Is Persuasion?

Persuasion encourages audience members to change their opinions (what they think) or behavior (what they do). Figure 18.1 shows some opinions people may hold and the behaviors related to them. In informative presentations, a speaker tries to *tell* something to an audience by giving directions, advice, explanations, or insights. In persuasive presentations, a speaker tries to *ask* for something from the audience—their agreement or a change in their opinions or behavior. Just as information can be persuasive, a persuasive presentation can also inform. As we noted in Chapter 17, "Developing Informative Presentations," the speaker's purpose will determine which type of presentation he or she makes.

Figure 18.1   Opinions and Behavior

Opinion	Behavior
Nike makes the best athletic shoes.	Buy Nike shoes.
Vegetarian diets are good for your body—and good for the planet.	Cut red meat from your diet.
Your family is more important than your job.	Eat dinner with your family at least five times a week.
Stricter drunk driving laws and punishments are needed.	Write a letter to your state legislator supporting stricter drunk driving laws.

The Dynamics of Persuasion

Figuring out how to persuade audience members to change their opinions or behavior requires understanding why they may resist your efforts. Why don't you vote for the first candidate who asks for your support? Why don't you buy the cereal that a sports hero recommends? Why don't you change your job to one that offers more money? There are good answers to all of these questions, and that's the problem. All of the members of your audience can give you reasons why they *won't* vote, buy, quit, or do any of the things you ask them to do. It's up to you to address these reasons.

Classify Audience Attitudes

Audience members vary greatly in their characteristics, learning styles, opinions, and behavior, as Chapter 5, "Audience Analysis and Adaptation," discusses. Therefore, no matter what your persuasive purpose is, you must understand and adapt to the people in your audience. For persuasive presentations, your audience analysis should pay special attention to people's attitudes. Whether their attitudes are positive, negative, or mixed, audience members will hold opinions about current issues such as abortion rights, affirmative action, and gun control as well as opinions about personal issues such as child rearing, religion, and patriotism. One way to clarify audience attitudes is to place the members of your audience along a spectrum of attitudes such as this one:

Strongly agree with me	Agree	Neutral	Disagree	Strongly disagree with me

Once you understand where audience members stand, you can develop persuasive strategies adapted to the people you're trying to persuade.

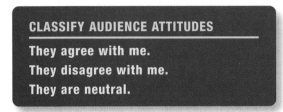

CLASSIFY AUDIENCE ATTITUDES

They agree with me.

They disagree with me.

They are neutral.

When Audience Members Agree with You

You may wonder if you even need to persuade an audience that already agrees with you. Although you don't have to sway them to your way of thinking, you can strengthen their existing agreement or use it to encourage behavioral change. Many audience members will agree that pollution is a problem, but most of them probably don't spend an hour a week cleaning up their neighborhoods or volunteering at a local recycling center. Persuasion can transform opinions into behavior. Several strategies can help you achieve your purpose with an audience that already agrees with you.

**WHEN AUDIENCE AND SPEAKER
AGREE, PERSUASION**

- Presents new information
- Strengthens audience resistance to counterpersuasion
- Excites the audience's emotions
- Provides a personal model
- Advocates a course of action

At the Barton W. Stone Christian Home in Jacksonville, Florida, Representative Ray LaHood addresses senior citizen concerns. In order to achieve his persuasive purpose, Representative LaHood must adapt his message and delivery style to the attitudes, needs, and listening ability of his audience.

PREACH TO THE CHOIR

People often use the expression "preach to the choir" to imply that speakers should avoid talking to friendly, supportive audiences. If they already agree, why preach to the choir? Yet members of the clergy preach to the choir all the time. In fact, choir members are often a congregation's truest believers. Every time a minister, priest, or rabbi delivers a sermon, he or she speaks to an audience that shares many of the same beliefs and agrees with most of what the sermon says. So why preach? It's because the strength and survival of a religious institution and its values lie with the faithful members—those who already believe. A preacher strengthens that bond by reassuring loyal members that their faith is well founded, encouraging them to stand by their religious beliefs and/or advocating good works. In much the same way, a persuasive presentation to an audience of "true believers" can build even stronger agreement with the speaker.

An audience that already agrees with you will welcome new information that reminds them why they do and thus reinforces their agreement. In essence, the information persuades these audience members that they're "right" to feel the way they—and you—do.

Give them answers to the questions asked by those who disagree or those who can't decide. Show them the strengths of their position and the weaknesses of the positions of those who disagree. If, for example, your audience agrees that more regulations are needed to control air pollution, you can show them how to answer and even how to criticize industry denials.

Excite audience members by being a cheerleader, a preacher, or a coach. Use examples and stories that demonstrate why they should feel pride, anger, happiness, or excitement about their shared opinions or behavior.

Also, be a model of the behavior you're advocating. Tell your audience what you've seen or done. Explain why and how they should pursue a similar course of action. Your example can persuade them to act—to sign a petition, write to a government official, report an incident to authorities, change their buying habits, or vote for a specific candidate.

When Audience Members Disagree with You

Audiences who completely agree with you are at one end of the spectrum; at the other end are audiences that don't agree with you at all. However, this disagreement doesn't mean that they will be hostile or rude. It *does* mean, though, that effecting a change in opinions or behavior becomes more challenging. In the face of disagreement, attempt to change only what *can* be changed.

WHEN AUDIENCE AND SPEAKER DISAGREE, PERSUASION

- **Sets reasonable goals**
- **Finds common ground**
- **Accepts differences of opinion**
- **Uses fair and respected evidence**
- **Builds personal credibility**

As much as you may want an audience that doesn't agree with you to come over to your way of thinking, a modest goal is more reasonable and realistic. You are unlikely to convince an audience full of avid meat-eaters to give up their steaks and become strict vegetarians. At best, you may be able to convince them that eating smaller meat portions is healthier. That alone would be a great accomplishment. Every small step taken in your direction can, in the long run, add up to a big change.

You also need to work on getting an audience that disagrees with you to listen. After all, you can't persuade an audience to change if they won't hear your recommendations. A good strategy here is to seek common ground with your audience. **Common ground** is a place where you and your audience can stand without disagreeing—it's a belief, value, attitude, or behavior that you and your audience share. Even pro-life and pro-choice opponents often agree that abortions should be considered if they're necessary to save the life of the mother. Smokers and nonsmokers may agree that smoking should be prohibited in and around schools. Literary and rhetorical scholar Kenneth Burke describes successful persuasion as the process of **identification,** in which the speaker and audience come to see that they share attitudes, ideas, feelings, values, and experiences.[1] Try to determine what you and your audience have in common. Identify with your audience by beginning on common ground before moving into potentially unfriendly territory.

You may not always find common ground. When you can't, persuasion may rest on accepting and adapting to differences of opinion. If your audience opposes censorship of any kind (and you're advocating curbs on hate speech), give them credit for defending the principle of freedom of speech. If your audience opposes a tax increase (and you're advocating one to build more elementary schools), acknowledge how difficult it can be to give up hard-earned money to the government.

An audience that disagrees with you will be highly critical, so it's vital that your supporting material be flawless. Choose your evidence from the most respected sources available and let your audience know where you found your information (see Chapter 7, "Supporting Material"). Also, make sure your sources aren't biased.

If you seek a reasonable goal, establish common ground, give the audience credit for their beliefs, and use fair and respected sources of information, your audience may come to like and respect you. Positive feelings about you may rub off on your arguments and help you to achieve your persuasive purpose. Your credibility can be a powerful tool to persuade an audience that disagrees with you.

When Audience Members Are Neutral

Some people may not have an opinion about a topic, or they may not be able to decide whether they agree or disagree. Audiences may be neutral or uncommitted for many reasons. Sometimes they're uninformed; at other times, they're unconcerned. Sometimes they're even adamantly undecided. Persuasion takes different courses, depending on the source of the neutrality.

Uninformed Audiences. An audience that doesn't know anything about a topic and hasn't formed an opinion about it is one of the easiest to persuade. All they need is information presented clearly and convincingly. Letting an uninformed audience know that Lyme disease and Rocky Mountain spotted fever are carried by ticks can persuade them to be more careful while walking in woods and fields. Telling uninformed employees that their credit union offers lower interest rates on loans than banks do can increase credit union membership. Sometimes information alone can persuade an uninformed audience.

HOW DO I FIND COMMON GROUND?

Brainstorming can help you identify a belief or behavior that you share with your audience—a place where you both can stand without disagreement. Listed next are several controversial topics. Complete each sentence by stating an issue on which a speaker and audience would find common ground. For example, "Free speech advocates and antipornography groups would probably agree that . . . pornography should not be available to children."

1. Pro-capital-punishment and anti-capital-punishment groups would probably agree that _____ _____.

2. Opera lovers and rap music fans would probably agree that _____ _____.

3. Antitaxation groups and pro-education groups would probably agree that _____ _____.

4. National health insurance supporters and the American Medical Association would probably agree that _____ _____.

5. The National Rifle Association and gun control groups would probably agree that _____ _____.

The next time that you anticipate audience disagreement, write a similar fill-in-the-blank statement representing your position and your audience's viewpoint. Then generate as many endings for the sentence as you can. Did you find common ground?

WHEN AUDIENCE MEMBERS ARE NEUTRAL:

Persuade the uninformed by	• providing information.
Persuade the unconcerned by	• gaining their attention and interest.
	• giving them a reason to care.
	• presenting relevant information.
Persuade the undecided by	• acknowledging both sides of the argument.
	• providing new information.
	• reinforcing old arguments.

Unconcerned Audiences.   When audience members see no reason to care or to have an opinion, the first step is getting their attention. Why should they listen to you if your topic doesn't affect them? If you can show them how the topic affects them personally, you are more likely to persuade them. Observe how this student speaker prepared her audience for a speech on the importance of voting and taking political action:

> How many of you applied for some form of financial aid for college? (More than half of the class raised their hands.) How many of you got the full amount you applied for or needed? (Fewer than one-fourth of the class members raised their hands.) I have some bad news for you. Financial aid may be even more difficult to get in the future. But the good news is that there's something you can do about it.

This opening captured the audience's attention by asking them two questions about a situation that had affected many of them. Next, the speaker presented her arguments urging students to be more active in the political system. Once you have their attention and can arouse their motivation, you can use information to persuade an unconcerned audience.

Undecided Audiences.   Neutral but undecided audiences can be difficult to persuade. Why? Because they've given the topic lots of thought. They understand both sides of the issue and either can't make up their minds or want to stay right where they are—in the middle. Some people can't or won't take a position for or against affirmative action, nuclear energy, capital punishment, or abortion. Because these are "hot" topics, this kind of audience knows the arguments on both sides. For example, audience members may be worried about the negative effects of television violence on children. At the same time, they oppose the censorship of program content by government agencies. They are caught between the pros and cons and, as a result, they cannot decide what should be done.

The first step with such an audience is to acknowledge how difficult it is to make a decision. Because this audience is already familiar with the issue, you should find *new* information that supports your position. Your task is to tip the balance. Maybe they don't know that the fears induced by scary television shows can spill over into a child's everyday life and interfere with otherwise normal activities.[2] No matter what side you're on, the key to persuading an undecided audience is to find something new. Then you can give new strength and force to your position by reminding them of all the other supporting arguments. Giving an undecided audience new information and then reinforcing old arguments leads to persuasion.

Why Does Persuasion Work?

More than in any other area of presentation speaking, researchers have devoted significant attention to developing theories that explain why persuasion works. One of the motives for this focus is using the information in the world of marketing and advertising. Theories of persuasion help advertisers develop effective marketing and sales campaigns. They also help speakers understand why enhancing their credibility can persuade some audiences while reinforcing logical arguments can persuade others. We know a lot about what does and doesn't work when messages are designed to persuade.

Next, we offer three schools of thought about the nature of persuasion. Each one tries to explain why and how a particular persuasive strategy affects an audience.

Persuasive Proof

Skilled workers master the tools of their trades. A carpenter knows that nails and screws serve different functions. A good cook knows when to boil a sauce and when to turn off the heat. Just as there are tools of the trade for most tasks, the persuasive speaker has several basic tools that can be used to persuade an audience. Among the most critical is knowing why, when, and how to use persuasive proof to make an argument.

Like a lawyer arguing before a jury, the persuasive speaker must prove his or her case. The lawyer decides how to argue a case, but it's up to the jury to determine the argument's success. In the same way, when you try to persuade an audience, your success depends on whether or not the audience believes what you say. **Proof,** then, consists of the arguments you select and use to persuade an audience. Since audiences and persuasive situations differ, so should your proof.[3] Thus, selecting the most appropriate forms of proof is just as important as developing valid arguments.

In the early fourth century B.C., Aristotle's *Rhetoric* proposed a theory that is still used as the basis for persuasion. By observing many persuaders at work in ancient Athens—in the law courts, the government, and the marketplace—Aristotle focused on what he called *artistic proofs* that a speaker could use to persuade.[4] Aristotle identified three major types of proof, which he labeled *ethos*, *pathos*, and *logos*. To that list we have added a fourth type of proof—*mythos*.

WHAT IF THERE'S A WIDE RANGE OF OPINIONS IN MY AUDIENCE? In the real world of presentation speaking, audience opinion will not be perfectly homogeneous. Rather, you're far more likely to face audiences consisting of some members who agree with you, others who don't, and still others who just aren't sure. Now what? You might want to focus your persuasive efforts on just one group—the largest, the most influential, or perhaps the easiest to persuade. Advertisers call this *targeting*. Or you might want to seek common ground among all three types of audience members. You could also try the persuasive strategy of providing *new* information from highly respected sources. Although especially suited to neutral, undecided audience members, this strategy can also encourage those who agree or disagree with you to change their opinions or behavior. But perhaps the best strategy of all is to acknowledge that you can't please everyone all of the time and to keep your persuasive message clear and consistent. Some members from each group will find your honesty, integrity, and resolve persuasive.

FOUR FORMS OF PROOF

Logos: Logical Proof
Pathos: Emotional Proof
Ethos: Personal Proof
Mythos: Narrative Proof

Logos: Logical Proof. **Logos** or **logical proof** asks if your arguments are reasonable and if your presentation makes sense. Logical arguments appeal to listeners' intellect, that is, their ability to think rationally and critically in order to arrive at a justified conclusion or decision. Note how the following speaker uses facts and statistics to prove logically that health care is too expensive for many Americans.

> Many hard-working Americans cannot afford the most basic forms of health care and health insurance. Some 41 million Americans, 15.5 percent of the population, most of them lower-income workers or their families, live without health insurance—a necessity of modern American life. In New Mexico and Texas, 25 percent of the population is not covered by any form of health insurance. And contrary to popular belief, most of the uninsured are jobholders or their family members—the working poor.[5]

The facts and statistics drive home the speaker's conclusion that the high cost of health insurance is seriously affecting the health and prosperity of many working Americans.

Logical proof, however, does not have to depend on supporting material. Often, appealing to your audience's common sense may be the best way to prove your point. Most audiences would accept the argument that everyone, whether rich or poor, needs good health care. As we noted in our discussion of Stephen Toulmin's model of an argument in Chapter 2, "Critical Thinking and Listening," using audience beliefs as evidence can help you support a claim. Reasonable people will agree with reasonable arguments.

Logical proof can be divided into two major categories—deductive logic and inductive logic. Understanding each form can help you develop stronger arguments for your persuasive presentations.

▶ **Deductive logic.** When using deductive logic, you make your case by moving from accepted general premises to a specific conclusion. Consider this deductive argument for improving a company's customer service program:

Premise: Successful companies emphasize customer service.

Premise: We want to be a successful company.

Conclusion: We should improve our customer service program.

You can find well-argued position papers on a variety of issues at the www.intellectualcapital.com Web site. On this page, the pros and cons of open adoption records are debated by experts. Not only can you find useful position papers on this site, but you can also use what you've learned about persuasion to assess the validity of their arguments.

If the audience agrees with the general premise, it is likely they will also agree with the conclusion. Many smart persuaders use deductive logic by convincing an audience that there are certain criteria that ought to be applied to any proposed solution. For example, they may say, "Don't we all agree that any proposal ought to be cost-effective? Don't we also all agree that any proposal should build from our current strengths? And don't we all agree that any proposal should be easily implemented?" Because our savvy presenter just happens to have a proposal that meets all of these criteria, the audience is likely to be persuaded.

▶ **Inductive logic.** Whereas deductive proof moves from the general to the specific, inductive logic does just the opposite, moving from specific instances to a general conclusion.

Instance: Our error rate is increasing monthly.

Instance: Our competitors have new quality-control programs.

Instance: Our customers are complaining that some of our products are shoddy.

Conclusion: We need to develop a quality-control program.

Here you are building your argument piece by piece. If your audience agrees with each of your instances, they are likely to agree with your final conclusion.

Pathos: Emotional Proof.   **Pathos** or **emotional proof** asks audience members to get in touch with their feelings. Audiences can experience various emotions—desire, anger, fear, pride, envy, joy, love, hate, regret, jealousy, or pity. Persuasion can be aimed at deep-seated feelings about qualities such as justice, generosity, courage, forgiveness, and wisdom.[6]

The following speaker uses a true story to touch the audience's emotions:

Kevin was twenty-seven years old and only two months into a new sales job when he began to lose weight and feel ill. After five weeks of testing and finally surgery, he was diagnosed with colon cancer. The bills were more than $100,000. But after his release from the hospital, he found out that his insurance benefits had run out.

As Kevin recalls, "Five weeks into the chemotherapy, I walked into my doctor's office, and he sat me down, put his hand on my knee, and told me there had been no payment. . . . Then he said that he could no longer bankroll my treatment. At one point in the middle of the whole thing, I hit bottom; between having cancer and being told that I had no insurance, I tried to commit suicide."

Instead of using logos to prove that many Americans suffer because they don't have dependable health insurance, the speaker tells a story of one person's suffering. Stories like this can persuade an audience that lack of health insurance can seriously affect the health and prosperity of many Americans in situations like Kevin's. Because audience members also know that the same thing *could* happen to them or someone they love, they are more likely to agree with the argument. Vice President Gore used pathos to great effect when, at the 1996 Democratic Convention, he described his sister's final moments of life before dying of lung cancer (see Appendix A). Also in Appendix A is Rosharna Hazel's presentation, "Victims of the Cure," in which she tells a series of tragic stories about medical errors.

Many television commercials appeal to audience emotions. Telephone companies and fast-food restaurants use human interest stories and gentle humor.

DOES PATHOS ALWAYS TAP INTO "NOBLE" EMOTIONS? Many advertisements, public service announcements, political ads, and magazine articles "go negative" as a persuasive technique. They try to persuade us by suggesting how bad things might be if we fail to take their advice. Do these fear appeals work? Yes. But they should be used both correctly and ethically. When a fear appeal is well justified, we are more open to being persuaded by it.

Fear appeals directed toward people we care about can also work well. Think of how many advertisements use this type of appeal. Life insurance ads suggest that you invest not for yourself but for those you love. Political ads tell you to vote for particular candidates because they will make the world better for your kids.

Fear appeals work best when they offer a way of avoiding the harms that are the centerpiece of the appeal. Consider public service announcements about AIDS. They don't say: "You will die of AIDS!" Instead, they say, "If you don't practice safe sex, you *may* die." An effective fear appeal tells listeners that they can do something to avoid what they fear.

Insurance companies may dramatize human tragedies to persuade you to buy more insurance protection. Perfect-looking people in beautifully filmed commercials may convince you to try a beauty product or a prepackaged diet. Whether we like it or not, commercials work because their creators understand the power of emotional proof.

Don't avoid emotional appeals because they seem to be illogical or irrational. Most of us have emotional responses to events and people, even though we cannot always provide a rational explanation for our reactions. The reasons why we are angry or sad or sympathetic or delighted can be quite understandable and justified.

Ethos: Personal Proof. As Chapter 11, "Speaker Credibility and Ethics," has noted, audiences form an impression of each speaker they see and hear. This impression is based on many factors—the content of the speaker's message, the speaker's ability to effectively deliver that message, and the speaker's reputation and expertise on the topic. Remember, **ethos** has three major dimensions: competence, character, and charisma. Each of these dimensions can be enhanced as a form of **personal proof** in a persuasive presentation.

Audiences tend to be more easily persuaded by speakers with whom they can identify—people who are *similar* to them in attitude or background. You can build this perceived similarity in a number of ways. Try to dress in a way similar to your audience's style. If you are addressing a group of bankers, don't show up in jeans. Use examples and stories to demonstrate the similarity between your values and background and those of your audience. Highlight similarities, not differences.

In order to use personal proof, you can't just *tell* an audience to trust or to like you. Remember our pronouncement in Chapter 11: *Speaker credibility comes from your audience.* Only the audience can decide whether you are believable. Thus, you need to demonstrate that you are competent and of good character. Deliver your presentation with conviction. Audiences are more likely to be persuaded when the speaker seems committed to the cause.

Mythos: Narrative Proof. During the second half of the twentieth century, **mythos** or **narrative proof** has emerged as a fourth and significant form of persuasive proof. According to the communication scholars Michael and Suzanne Osborn, mythos addresses the values, faith, and feelings that make up our social character and is most often expressed through traditional stories, sayings, and symbols.[7] The Osborns maintain that the "unique function of mythos is to help listeners understand how the speaker's recommendations fit into the total belief and value patterns of their group."[8] In other words, narrative proof appeals to the ingrained beliefs and myths that audience members hold about themselves.

In America we are raised on mythic stories that teach us about patriotism, freedom, honesty, and national pride. President George Washington's admission—"I cannot tell a lie"—after cutting down the family's cherry tree may be a myth, but it has helped teach millions of young Americans about the value of honesty. The request "Give me your tired, your poor" from the Emma Lazarus poem inscribed on the base of the Statue of Liberty, the "Women and children first" directive for passengers on sinking ships, and the civil rights speech and song refrain "We shall overcome" are phrases that have become part of American beliefs and values. Speakers who tap into the mythos of an audience form a powerful identification with their listeners.

REAL WORLD, REAL SPEAKERS

I once heard an executive at a large manufacturing firm use a story to create a new company value. He told how he had recently been to Greece, where he visited an old monastery that stood at the top of a mountain. The mountain had sheer cliffs on every side. The monastery had been built there many centuries ago because it offered perfect protection for the monks. The executive discovered, however, that the only way to visit the monastery was to get into a large basket and have a monk slowly use pulleys to draw up the basket. He got in, he said, and as the monk pulled him up, he noticed that the rope was quite frayed. A little worried, he turned to the monk and asked, "When do you decide to change the rope?" The monk responded, "Whenever it breaks."

After the laughter died down, the executive became more serious and said, "In this company, we don't wait until the rope breaks. We don't even let it fray. We fix things before they become hazards." The story was used to create a new belief and value: Fix it before it frays. The hope was that every time an employee came across a potential hazard, she or he would recall the story of the monk and report or fix the problem. The story and the statement "Fix it before it frays" became a form of mythos at the company. And it made the executive's presentation more persuasive and memorable than any simple declarative sentence about safety could ever do.

John Daly

One of the best ways to enlist mythos when trying to persuade is to tell stories. Religions teach many values through parables. Families bond through stories shared across generations. Effective leaders who inspire others are almost always excellent storytellers. Remember the two characteristics of a successful story that we described in Chapter 12, "Generating Interest"? A story that has both coherence (the story hangs together and has meaning) and fidelity (it's truthful or believable) can be applied to logical and emotional causes and will appeal to our imagination and feelings. And when told well, a story can be one of the most powerful persuasive tools we have.

The Elaboration Likelihood Model of Persuasion

Which forms of proof are the most effective—those based on emotion, those based on substantive evidence and logic, those centered on speaker credibility, or those built on stories? The answer is . . . it depends. Two other factors, listeners' thinking abilities and motivations, became the focus of research by two social psychologists, Richard Petty and John Cacioppo. They developed the **Elaboration Likelihood Model of Persuasion,** which says that there are two "routes" to persuasion, depending on how able and willing an audience is to process a message.[9]

The term *elaboration* refers to whether an audience can engage in "elaborative" or critical thinking (see Chapter 2). Will they listen comprehensively and analytically to a message? Are they capable of analyzing the arguments in a message? Are they motivated to listen to a presentation about the issue? Do they see the issue as relevant to their lives? A presenter's answers to these questions can help him or her determine which route or persuasive strategy to follow.

Routes to Persuasion. Persuasion can take a central route or a peripheral route. When people are highly involved in an issue and when they are capable of thinking critically, the central route to persuasion is best. Highly involved critical thinkers do a lot of counterarguing when listening to a persuader. They may think, "I just read an article that proves the opposite" or "That may be fine in Arkansas, but it won't work in South Dakota." Thus, the best form of proof with these involved listeners is a logical one in which a speaker's claims are backed by strong and believable **evidence.** When audiences are highly involved, persuasion using the central route tends to be enduring, resistant to counterpersuasion, and predictive of future behavior.

When audiences are less involved or aren't interested in an issue, you're better off taking the peripheral route. Interestingly, these types of listeners are highly influenced by whether they like the speaker and whether they think the speaker is credible.[10] The peripheral route involves focusing on cues that aren't directly related to the substance of a message—catchy phrases, dramatic stories or statistics, the quantity (rather than quality) of arguments and evidence, and the credibility and attractiveness of the speaker. Figure 18.2 shows key aspects of both routes.

To better understand the two routes to persuasion, consider the Elaboration Likelihood Model from the listener's perspective. Let's suppose that you're very

Figure 18.2   The Elaboration Likelihood Model of Persuasion

When your audience is motivated and able to think critically, the central route to persuasion works well. The peripheral route is better suited to less motivated, less critical audiences.

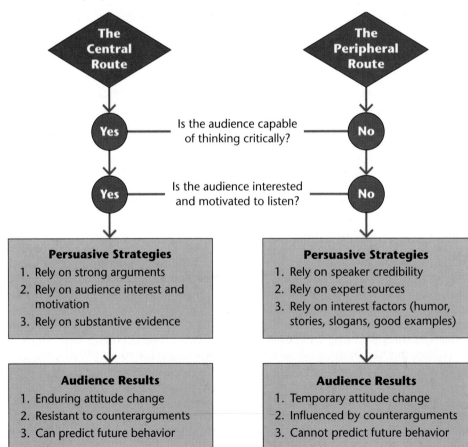

concerned about the traffic patterns in your neighborhood. You're tired of long waits at lights and slow-moving traffic. You attend a meeting where a county official is trying to convince the audience that traffic will not get worse in the future and that available funds would be better spent on parks and recreation. Since you're a good critical thinker and care about this issue, you're listening carefully and are probably generating a lot of counterarguments—traffic is awful, it's going to get worse, we need to spend money to alleviate traffic problems right now.

If the presenter wants to persuade you to adopt her point of view, she is going to have to come up with some good, logical arguments that take the central route to persuasion. Why? Because you're questioning almost everything she says. The only way that she can create a lasting change in your opinion is to present logically persuasive arguments that address your internal counterarguments directly.

Now, let's suppose that the person who's sitting next to you doesn't care that much about the traffic. He works at home and rarely drives during the busiest commuting hours. He's not very involved and is unlikely to do much critical thinking about this issue. How would the county official persuade him? The Elaboration Likelihood Model suggests that a peripheral route would be more effective. While logic and good evidence may be useful, the uninvolved listener might be more attuned to the speaker's emotional appeals as well as to her credibility and attractiveness ("she seems like a nice person," "she sounds as if she knows what she's talking about"). Interestingly, you often get only short-term attitude changes when using the peripheral route.

Inoculate Your Audience When you get a flu shot or smallpox vaccination, you are being inoculated against a harmful illness. According to social psychologist William McGuire, protecting audience attitudes from counterpersuasion by the "other side" is like inoculating the body against disease.[1] By exposing the flaws in the arguments opposing your persuasive message, you can increase audience resistance to those arguments. By presenting the arguments of the opposition *and* then showing your audience how to refute them, you build up their resistance to counterpersuasion and create a more enduring change of attitude or behavior. **Inoculation** is most effective when audience members are highly involved critical thinkers because it first makes them aware that their attitudes are vulnerable to attack, then provides ammunition against or resistance to the attack.[2]

1. William J. McGuire, "Inducing Resistance to Persuasion: Some Contemporary Approaches," in *Advances in Experimental Psychology*, ed. L. Berkowitz (New York: Academic Press, 1964), pp. 192–229.
2. Robert H. Gass and John S. Seiter, *Persuasion, Social Influence, and Compliance Gaining* (Boston: Allyn & Bacon, 1999), pp. 195–196.

Applying the Elaboration Likelihood Model of Persuasion. Using the Elaboration Likelihood Model of Persuasion requires a deep understanding of your audience. As we've indicated, you begin by assessing their levels of personal involvement and their ability to think critically. If you think the majority of people in your audience are highly involved and will respond to the central route, develop a well-organized presentation with strong arguments buttressed by good evidence and sound reasoning. Imagine all the different objections and reservations that audience members may raise as they think critically about your message. Consequently, when you do address these reservations in your presentation, you are more likely to be persuasive than if you ignore them.

Alternatively, if you think your audience members are far less involved and thus more responsive to the peripheral route to persuasion, concentrate your attention on your own credibility and attractiveness, emotional appeals, and the power of stories and traditions. Try to demonstrate how and why the issue affects each and every audience member. Something as simple as asking a rhetorical question—a technique that roughly one-third of all radio commercials use[11]—can motivate people to give more attention and thought to a message.

Many audiences, however, are composed of different people with different levels of interest in a topic or issue—and with different critical thinking and listening abilities. It may be necessary to use both routes to persuasion in a single presentation, even though the highly involved critical thinkers may become impatient with your peripheral strategies, while less involved audience members may become lost or bored when you present detailed argumentation. If you must take both routes, be sure to balance the strategies.

Social Judgment Theory

Choosing the best proof or route to persuasion rests on understanding your audience, as we've seen. Yet a team of psychologists claims that you cannot really understand how people feel about an issue just by asking them about their attitudes. Even if two people say that they agree, you still can't conclude that they share identical attitudes. Why not? Because one person may hold that position more intensely than the other person. The first person strongly agrees and doesn't accept any alternative. The second person agrees but is not highly committed to the position. Although both hold the same position, one holds it more intensely.

According to the **Social Judgment Theory** proposed by psychologists Muzafer Sherif, Carolyn Sherif, and Robert Nebergall, people's reactions to persuasive statements are best reflected by ranges—what they call *latitudes of acceptance* (statements they agree with), *rejection* (statements they can't agree with), and *noncommitment* (statements that are neither acceptable nor nonacceptable).[12] Earlier in this chapter, we recommended ways to persuade audience members who agree, disagree, or are neutral. Social Judgment Theory highlights one very important and additional aspect of the persuasive process: the possibility that audience members who hold the *same* position on an issue might have very different views and tendencies for changing their opinions.

Consider two audience members, Charlene and Alonia. A local pollster asks their opinion about county funding and support for the public library system. Their response choices range from 1 (cut funding by 5 percent and close two library branches) to 7 (increase funding by 10 percent and build a new branch library). Both choose 4 (increase funding by 2 percent). They agree, right? Not necessarily. Figure 18.3 looks at their latitudes of acceptance, noncommitment, and rejection.[13]

Figure 18.3   Social Judgment Theory

Since listeners are easier to persuade within their latitudes of acceptance, almost impossible to persuade in their latitudes of rejection, and open to persuasion in their latitudes of noncommitment, what should a speaker do when trying to gain more support for the public library system?

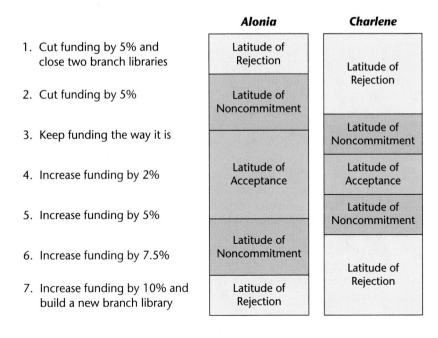

Members of a citizens group
take turns speaking against
radar microwaves at Camp Ed-
wards on Cape Cod, Massachu-
setts. Given that the military's
latitude of acceptance is small
on this issue, the citizens group
needs to mount a continuous
persuasive campaign that focuses on a series of small gains
in acceptance.

Latitude of Acceptance.   Charlene has a very narrow latitude of acceptance—
she cannot agree with any response other than 4. Why? Although she frequently
uses the library to borrow books and attend meet-the-author programs, she also
feels overburdened by the county's property tax rate and doesn't want to see her
taxes go up. Thus, even though she wants to support the library system, she cannot endorse anything more than a 2 percent increase in funding.

Alonia, on the other hand, has a large latitude of acceptance. If given good reasons, she could change her response to a 2 or 3—or even to a 5 or 6. She doesn't use
the library very much, and because she rents her apartment, she doesn't feel the direct sting of property taxes. Because she wants to support what seems like a good
cause, she joins Charlene at the 2 percent funding level.

Latitude of Noncommitment.   Charlene, the tax-weary library patron, has a
narrow latitude of noncommitment. A highly skilled persuader might get her to
accept a 3 or 5, but doing so would be hard work. Alonia is different. Her latitude
of noncommitment is larger. She's okay with a 2 or even a 6. Give her a good reason to change her mind, and she will.

Latitude of Rejection.   Their latitudes of rejection include all statements Charlene and Alonia cannot agree with. Charlene has a large one. She rejects almost
everything but the choice she has made. She doesn't want to support a significant
increase in funding but also doesn't want the library system to suffer or to cut
services. On the other hand, Alonia's latitude of rejection is comparatively small.
The only positions she can't imagine supporting would be 1 and 7. Charlene is
far more emphatic about her position than Alonia.

Applying Social Judgment Theory.   What does all this mean for you, the persuader? It means that in addition to having to address a range of opinions, you
also may need to make sure that you don't give listeners grounds for rejecting
your message. If you find yourself advocating a position that's in your listeners'
latitude of rejection, try to establish some common ground, respect differences of

opinion, and build your credibility by using fair and respected evidence. Both Charlene and Alonia would probably reject attending a public rally supporting the construction of a new library building, but they might be willing to join you in signing a petition urging elected officials to study the feasibility of expanding the library system. In general, try to advocate a position closer to your listeners' latitude of acceptance. Don't push too hard for a position that's too far from your listeners' current attitudes and feelings.

Social Judgment Theory also tells us that effective persuaders try to gradually broaden their listeners' latitudes of acceptance. Although this takes time and effort, it is a very realistic approach. Think about how your attitudes have changed over time. You probably find some things far more acceptable today than you did ten years ago. Did your attitudes change overnight? No. Rather, you were probably exposed to a variety of persuasive messages over the years. Your latitude of acceptance slowly widened, and the range of what you found objectionable narrowed. Social Judgment Theory thus gives one reason why persuasive campaigns—series of persuasive presentations—tend to be more effective than one-time messages.[14]

Applying Marketing Concepts to Persuasion

The idea of a persuasive campaign comes to us from the world of marketing. In fact, a great deal of our practical knowledge about persuasion comes from market researchers who study how to influence buyers in the marketplace. It's amazing how successful some marketing campaigns are in today's competitive business world. They succeed because their creators understand how persuasion works. Of the many strategies used by advertisers, five apply especially well to persuasive speaking.

> **MARKETING PRINCIPLES FOR PERSUASION**
>
> Create memorable slogans
> Generate strong images
> Focus on benefits
> Address audience needs
> Enlist celebrities

Create Memorable Slogans

We associate many products with their slogans: "Quality is job 1" (Ford), "A mind is a terrible thing to waste" (the United Negro College Fund), "breakfast of champions" (Wheaties), and "Be all you can be" (U.S. Army). The word *slogan* comes from the Gaelic phrase *slugh gairm*, which means "battle cry." The best slogans are a product's battle cry in the marketplace. They are strong, are easily remembered, and conquer the competition. Slogans briefly summarize the message about a product's benefits in a short, easy-to-remember phrase.[15]

There is almost a magical quality to some advertising slogans. When we think of a product name or a slogan, all sorts of images and feelings come to mind. Marketers spend millions of dollars trying to create and get consumers to identify with the labels and slogans for their products. Good slogans "imbue the products with the positive qualities which, over time, become embedded in receivers'

REAL WORLD, REAL SPEAKERS

A friend of mine was quite successful using images in a speech he gave to endorse a political candidate. He started by creating an image of an idyllic place for families to live. "Imagine," he said, "a county where children play freely and safely in every neighborhood. Imagine towns with clean streets, modern schools, and communities where you feel at home. Imagine a place where people are real neighbors—borrowing cups of sugar, celebrating the holidays together, and helping each other in tough times. Nice dreams, right? Well these dreams can come true if we all get out and support. . . ."

John Daly

minds."[16] A slogan can even affect people's perceptions of a concept. For example, groups on both sides of the abortion debate call themselves "Pro-." After all, few people would want to be identified with an anti-choice or anti-life group.

Great persuaders understand the potential and power of words. They create and use memorable slogans with the hope that listeners will be persuaded when they are moved or inspired by a turn of phrase. When Dr. Martin Luther King Jr. proclaimed, "I have a dream," and when his supporters sang, "We shall overcome," both statements became battle cries for the civil rights movement.

A memorable phrase or statement can become a form of mythos—a way of proving an argument. Whether it's President Abraham Lincoln's "government of the people, by the people, for the people" or President John F. Kennedy's statement "Ask not what your country can do for you—ask what you can do for your country," the effect of the words can be powerful and persuasive.

Generate Strong Images

Ever notice how sleek the cars look in television ads? A car ad may show a new vehicle driving over dusty hills, through blizzards, and across streams. But at the end of the ad, the car is always perfectly clean. Does this look like your car? Probably not. Ads are designed to create an image. People buy images. So do audiences.

According to Karen Lawson, a communication consultant and instructor, "imagery is the use of words to create pictures in the minds of the audience. Good speakers draw the picture very carefully so that audience members can share the speaker's experience and remember the speaker's message."[17] Images do not have to be beautiful to be memorable and effective. When organizations are raising funds or recruiting volunteers for charitable causes, we often see or hear detailed descriptions of needy families, ill children, diseased or starving animals, drought-stricken states, hurricane-damaged communities, and war-torn countries. The more vivid the images you create—whether positive or negative—the more persuasive you can be.

Focus on Benefits

Think about the image of a car you'd like to own. Like any other car, it has four wheels, doors, a hood, and bumpers, among other parts. But is that why you want to buy this car? Few people buy a car because of its basic features. What, then, prompts them to want one car more than another? For one buyer, safety, affordability, and a minimal need for repairs might matter most. For another, gaining

317

status among colleagues and friends could be more important than anything else. Having "made it" both socially and professionally, both buyers are now focusing on the benefits they associate with purchasing a particular car.

In marketing there are distinctions drawn between features, functions, and benefits. *Features* allow you to perform a *function* that generates certain *benefits*. When you are marketing an item, "you're not selling the product; you're selling the benefits of the product."[18] Effective persuasive speakers do the same. Audiences respond positively to presentations when they want the benefits you are describing. Skilled persuaders answer their listeners' most basic question: "What's in it for me?"

Address Audience Needs

Most of the purchases we make satisfy some need. We buy food for sustenance, homes for shelter, jewelry to give pleasure to ourselves or to the one we love, a car for transportation (and perhaps also for status), and designer clothing to make an impression. Effective persuaders understand that if their proposals satisfy audience needs, they are more likely to succeed. Although there may be an infinite number of individual needs, we can classify most people's needs in terms of a few major types.

Psychologist Abraham Maslow has suggested one way of thinking about these needs: as a hierarchy (see Figure 18.4).[19]

At the lowest, most basic level of **Maslow's Hierarchy of Needs,** people have physiological needs. They need food and shelter. Beyond physiological needs are safety needs—a desire for protection and security. At the next level, there are social needs—a desire for affection and acceptance. These three levels are often called *deficiency needs* because if they are not met, we have difficulty surviving.

Beyond the three deficiency needs are two *fulfillment needs*—esteem needs (self-worth, prestige, status) and a need for self-actualization (for becoming self-fulfilled). When trying to persuade, you may think about these needs and use them as justification for the case you are making. For instance, a speaker making a presentation about exercise might note the value of exercise for health (physiological need), for the pleasant company of others (social needs), and for building confidence (esteem needs).

Another psychologist, William Schutz, has offered a second theory that focuses on psychological needs.[20] He proposes three basic needs in his **Fundamental Interpersonal Relationship Orientation (FIRO) Theory.**

Figure 18.4   Maslow's Hierarchy of Needs

Persuasive speakers should appeal to deficiency needs when listeners are faced with threats to their physical survival, personal safety, and social development. When these needs have been met in an audience, speakers can then appeal to their listeners' fulfillment needs—their desires for esteem and self-actualization.

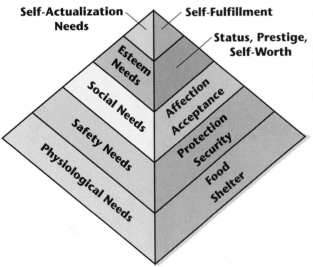

▶ *Need for Inclusion:* To some extent, all of us have a need to be included. For instance, if we feel we've been excluded from a meeting, we may interpret any statement about the results of that meeting negatively. Effective persuaders make audience members feel included. They use plural pronouns such as *we, our,* and *us* rather than *I* and *my.* They ask audience members to *share, join,* and *participate.*

▶ *Need for Control:* Most of us think of ourselves as independent people. No one controls us; if anyone tries, we may rebel. The expression "I've gotta be me" is really everyone's theme song. Persuaders know this. If they push too hard, they will create resistance in their audiences. In fact, telling an audience that you're going to change their minds about something can make them more resistant to persuasion. You are threatening their sense of control. Using statements such as "It's your decision," "You can make a difference," and "It's up to you" can speak to listeners' control needs.

▶ *Need for Openness:*[21] Most of us want to be liked and appreciated. Usually, when someone doesn't like you, it bothers you. And you're not likely to listen or be persuaded by this person. Effective persuaders try to make sure that audience members feel well liked and respected. Speakers who communicate openly with genuine affection for their audiences are more likely to be successful persuaders.

Enlist Celebrities

Celebrity endorsements work in advertising. In one study, ads with testimonials from celebrities scored 11 percent higher than the average in terms of whether potential buyers noticed the ad and its product.[22] On the other hand, testimonials from noncelebrities actually earned below-average scores in terms of whether they were noticed. Thus, Jane and John Doe's endorsement of milk will not have the same impact as the entire cast of "Frasier" posing with milk "mustaches" on their upper lips.

What do such research findings mean for you as a speaker? First, they should encourage you to use testimony from famous people who, at the very least, can attract listener attention. As we noted when explaining the Elaboration Likelihood Model of Persuasion, endorsements by celebrities work best when you're using the peripheral route to persuasion, but the results may not be long-lasting. Finding a respected celebrity who agrees with your position will enhance your persuasiveness. Thus, when President Clinton was trying to move the proposal to join NAFTA (the North Atlantic Free Trade Alliance) through Congress, he called on every living president—both Republicans and Democrats—to publicly support the proposed trade agreement. Bipartisan "endorsements" from such esteemed figures left Congress little choice but to give in and join the alliance.

Aristotle's forms of proof, the Elaboration Likelihood Model of Persuasion, Social Judgment Theory, hierarchical and psychological needs theories, and marketing research all try to explain why and how persuasion works. Although such theories and research do not tell you *what* to say in a specific persuasive presentation, they can help you identify the most effective persuasive strategies. In Chapter 19, "Developing Persuasive Presentations," these models and theories will serve as the foundation for choosing specific strategies and speaking techniques that will help you become a more effective persuasive speaker.

Muhammad Ali with a display of the special edition Muhammad Ali Wheaties box that marks the cereal's 75th anniversary. The slogan "The Breakfast of Champions" and celebrity endorsements have sold millions of boxes of cereal for General Mills.

Summary

◆✦ What is persuasion?

Persuasion attempts to change opinions (what people think) and/or behavior (what people do) by using effective logical, emotional, personal, and/or narrative appeals.

◆✦ Will all audiences react to persuasive presentations in the same way?

Audience reactions to persuasive presentations can vary significantly, depending on the differences and strengths of their attitudes, their abilities and willingness to listen critically, their basic and psychological needs, and whether their opinions are narrowly focused or open to change. Effective persuaders use their understanding of audience attitudes to select the most appropriate persuasive strategies.

◆✦ What's the best route to persuasion?

According to the Elaboration Likelihood Model of Persuasion, there are two routes to persuasion. For audience members who are able and motivated to listen critically, a carefully constructed, logical presentation will produce long-lasting results. For audiences unable or unmotivated to listen critically, a presentation that relies on speaker credibility and attractiveness, celebrity endorsements, and numerous arguments will persuade an audience in the short run but may not sustain long-lasting results.

◆✦ How much persuasion can I achieve in a single presentation?

According to Social Judgment Theory, listeners' reactions to persuasive messages are reflected in varying degrees of acceptance, rejection, and noncommitment. A series of persuasive presentations designed to broaden listeners' latitudes of acceptance may be more effective than a single presentation.

◆✦ How can marketing strategies be used to enhance persuasion?

Marketing strategies such as creating slogans, presenting vivid images, focusing on benefits rather than on features, addressing audience needs, and enlisting celebrity testimony can enhance persuasion.

Key Terms

common ground 305
deductive logic 308
Elaboration Likelihood Model of Persuasion 311
emotional proof 309
ethos 310
evidence 312
Fundamental Interpersonal Relationship Orientation (FIRO) Theory 318
identification 305
inductive logic 309
inoculation 313

logical proof 308
logos 308
Maslow's Hierarchy of Needs 318
mythos 310
narrative proof 310
pathos 309
personal proof 310
persuasion 302
proof 307
Social Judgment Theory 314

Notes

1. Kenneth Burke, *A Rhetoric of Motives* (New York: Prentice-Hall, 1950).
2. Joanne Cantor, *Mommy, I'm Scared: How TV and Movies Frighten Children and What We Can Do to Protect Them* (San Diego: Harcourt Brace, 1998), p. 20.
3. Charles U. Larson, *Persuasion: Reception and Responsibility,* 8th ed. (Belmont, CA: Wadsworth, 1998), p. 180.
4. Larson, p. 58.
5. U.S. Bureau of the Census, *Statistical Abstract of the United States: 1997*, 117th ed. (Washington, D.C.: U.S. Bureau of the Census, 1997).
6. Larson, p. 60.
7. Michael Osborn and Suzanne Osborn, *Public Speaking,* 4th ed. (Boston: Houghton Mifflin, 1997), pp. 458–460.
8. Osborn and Osborn, p. 460.
9. Richard Petty and John Cacioppo, *Communication and Persuasion: Central and Peripheral Routes to Attitude Change* (New York: Springer-Verlag, 1986). For a detailed explanation of the Elaboration Likelihood Model of Persuasion, see Daniel J. O'Keefe, *Persuasion: Theory and Research* (Newbury Park, CA: Sage, 1990), Chapter 6.
10. Daniel J. O'Keefe, *Persuasion: Theory and Research* (Newbury Park, CA: Sage, 1990), p. 97.
11. Sharon S. Brehm, Saul M. Kassin, and Steven Fein, *Social Psychology,* 4th ed. (Boston: Houghton Mifflin, 1999), p. 183.
12. See Muzafer Sherif and Carolyn Sherif, *Attitude, Ego Involvement and Change* (New York: Wiley, 1967); Muzafer Sherif, Carolyn Sherif, and Roger Nebergall, *Attitude and Attitude Change: The Social Judgment–Involvement Approach* (Philadelphia: W. B. Saunders, 1965). A detailed explanation of Social Judgment Theory can be found in Daniel J. O'Keefe, *Persuasion: Theory and Research* (Newbury Park, CA: Sage, 1990), Chapter 2.
13. Robert H. Gass and John S. Seiter, *Persuasion, Social Influence, and Compliance Gaining* (Boston: Allyn & Bacon, 1999), p. 106.
14. Gass and Seiter, p. 107.
15. J. Thomas Russell and W. Ronald Lane, *Kleppner's Advertising Procedure*, 14th ed. (Upper Saddle River, NJ: Prentice-Hall, 1999), p. 462.
16. Gass and Seiter, p. 59.
17. Karen Lawson, *Involving Your Audience: Making It Active* (Boston: Allyn & Bacon, 1999), p. 95.
18. Russell and Lane, p. 465.
19. Abraham H. Maslow, *Motivation and Personality* (New York: Harper & Row, 1954).
20. William C. Schutz, *FIRO: A Three-Dimensional Theory of Interpersonal Behavior* (New York: Holt, Rinehart, & Winston, 1958).
21. Since publishing his three-dimensional theory of interpersonal behavior (FIRO-B) in 1958, Schutz has renamed the third dimension. Instead of *affection,* he uses the term *openness.* Thus, like inclusion and control, openness is a behavior (rather than an emotion) which, when enacted, can convey feelings of likability and affection. See Will Schutz, *The Human Element* (San Francisco, CA: Jossey-Bass, 1994), pp. 49–70.
22. Russell and Lane, p. 466.

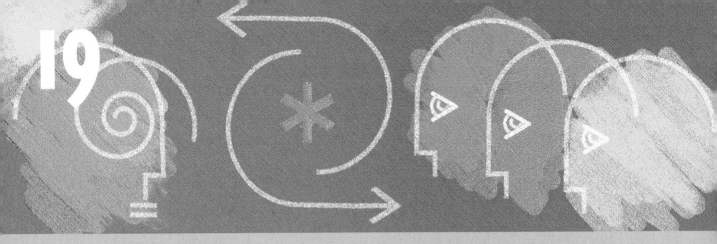

19

Developing Persuasive Presentations

- ◆▶ What constitutes a good persuasive presentation?
- ◆▶ What's the best type of evidence to use in a persuasive presentation?
- ◆▶ What's the best way to organize a persuasive presentation?
- ◆▶ What are the common fallacies of argument?

As we saw in Chapter 18, "Understanding Persuasion," persuading people to change their attitudes or behavior is among the more complex challenges of presentation speaking—and is certainly among the most widely studied. Communication scholars, psychologists, and master marketers all offer theories and research to explain why people react to persuasive messages in so many ways. In this chapter, we help you put these theories into practice in your own persuasive presentations.

Purposeful Persuasion

In order to prepare and deliver an effective persuasive presentation, you must know *why* you are speaking. Taking three initial steps can help ensure that your persuasive presentation achieves a specific purpose. You need to determine *what* you want your audience to believe after hearing your presentation, *why* your audience should believe it, and *what evidence* supports the belief you're advocating.

PURPOSEFUL PERSUASION

- **Matches your purpose to your passion**
- **Clarifies your arguments**
- **Bolsters your arguments with persuasive evidence**

Match Your Purpose to Your Passion

What are you trying to achieve when you make a persuasive presentation? This question involves more than asking which attitudes or behaviors you are trying to change. It asks *why* you are trying to change them.

Are you making a persuasive presentation because you believe the audience needs changing or because you have been asked to give a persuasive speech? If you believe that people who take a CPR course will be able to save more lives, you can justify the time needed to prepare a talk on this topic. If you decide to make a presentation on the need for CPR training because you think it will be an easy topic to research, your presentation may not be very convincing to your audience. A health insurance manager told us she speaks two or three times a month to a variety of audiences. Here's how she describes the link between purpose and passion: "I believe the success of any speaking engagement is to *love* and *believe* what you are talking about. In my case, it's my company's Healthy Lifestyles Program."

Choose a topic you care about. It will be hard to convince your audience that they should change their opinions or behavior if you don't believe in the change yourself. Even though there may be plenty of information available on topics such as capital punishment, abortion, gun control, cigarette smoking, and the need for regular exercise, don't select one of them unless you have strong feelings about it and are willing to do a lot of thorough research. The most effective presentations are often the most personal: "Contribute to the local charity that helped my family after Hurricane Floyd." "Stay out of the harmful sun so you don't get melanoma like I did." "Help clean up the neighborhood we all call home." A passion for your topic will give you a real-world reason for addressing an audience. Most audiences can tell if you honestly care about your topic; your passion can help convince them. At the same time, Social Judgment Theory cautions that no matter how passionately *you* feel about a topic, you may not be able to persuade your audience if your purpose lies deep in their latitudes of rejection.

A student with a megaphone voices her objections to the 1997 visit of China's President Jiang Zemin to Harvard University. Public rallies give protesters a way to make their feelings known, though they aren't the best forums for presenting detailed arguments. Given that such protests take a peripheral rather than a central route to persuasion, with whom are they more likely to be effective?

Note how the following student speaker directly addresses the question about the purpose of his presentation.

> I am tired of being called a monster and murderer because I'm a deer hunter. Most people think I'm out there killing cute little Bambi when, in fact, I'm helping to protect the deer herds from disease and starvation. Sure, I enjoy hunting, but I do it safely and legally. If people knew more about deer hunting, they might not be so critical of it.

A speaker who cares about a topic will work harder to prepare an effective presentation. A speaker with strong feelings about a topic will spend hours practicing because the outcome matters to her or him.

Clarify Your Arguments

Having decided how to approach the purpose and topic of your persuasive presentation, you can now develop and clarify your arguments in light of their persuasive potential. Remember that an **argument** consists of a claim supported by evidence and reasons for accepting it (see Chapter 2, "Critical Thinking and Listening"). Good arguments explain and justify why audience members should change their attitudes or behavior. Good speakers develop and select the arguments most likely to achieve their purposes.

As you begin planning a persuasive presentation, list all the possible arguments you could use—all the reasons why the audience should agree with you. The speaker who was planning a presentation on hunting as a means of controlling the growing deer population listed several reasons:

The enormous deer population
> is starving and dying of disease.
> is eating up crops, gardens, and forest seedlings.
> is carrying deer ticks that cause Lyme disease in people.
> is causing an increase in the number of highway accidents.

Although there may be several arguments for advocating hunting to reduce the deer population, the speaker should use only the arguments that, based on an analysis of his audience, would most likely persuade that audience. Whatever arguments you choose, ask yourself whether they answer questions of fact, value, conjecture, or policy. The answers will help you determine how best to make your case.

> **CLARIFY YOUR ARGUMENTS**
>
> Do they address questions of fact?
> Do they address questions of value?
> Do they address questions of conjecture?
> Do they address questions of policy?

Questions of Fact. An argument based on a **question of fact** addresses beliefs about whether something is true or false, whether an event did or didn't happen, or whether a circumstance was caused by one thing or another. Even though questions of fact are not concerned with whether something is good or bad, or likely or unlikely, they are not easy to answer, particularly when audience members are neutral or disagree with your position. Most friendly audiences will accept what you say as fact. On the other hand, skeptical audience members will want you to demonstrate that your facts are accurate and true.

The factual question "How has enrollment changed at your college during the past ten years?" can require answers to a series of subquestions about the enrollment of women and ethnic groups or the status of part-time and full-time students. When you are trying to develop an argument that answers questions of fact, you must look for the best evidence you can find and then closely scrutinize that information. If you are trying to persuade an audience that something is true or that evidence points to a particular conclusion, be sure that your facts are accurate, credible, and relevant. Use the tests of evidence that we offered in Chapter 7, "Supporting Material."

Questions of Value.   An argument based on a **question of value** makes judgments about whether something is worthwhile—is it good or bad; right or wrong; moral or immoral; best, average, or worst? It's hard to address questions of value because your success hinges on your ability to modify well-established attitudes and beliefs of audience members. In many cases, the answer to a question of value may be "It depends." Is a public college a better place to begin higher education than a prestigious private university? It depends on a student's financial situation, professional goals, academic achievement record, work and family situation, and beliefs about the quality of education offered at each type of institution. Convincing an audience of parents who hold advanced degrees from Ivy League schools that their children would be better off beginning their higher education at the local community college requires more than presenting facts about the quality of schooling available at a particular two-year college. It requires changing their attitudes about the value and benefits of attending a less prestigious school. Changing listeners' perceptions about strongly held values requires an understanding of and respect for your audience and—depending on the critical thinking ability and motivation of your audience—requires either a central or a peripheral route to persuasion.

Questions of Conjecture.   An argument based on a **question of conjecture** asks whether something will or will not happen. Unlike a question of fact or value, only the future holds the answer to this type of question. Instead of focusing on *what is,* you are asking the audience to consider possibilities: *what could be* or *what will be.* Will John Doe be the next president? Will the stock market go up? Will our hometown get an expansion football team? Even though it's impossible to know what the future will bring, you can address questions of conjecture by basing your predictions as much as possible on statistical trends, past history, and expert opinion.[1] Answers to questions of conjecture should also consider the values held by audience members. A stockbroker trying to convince an audience to invest in mutual funds or in a particular company is dealing with facts about the past and present as well as audience hopes and fears about the future. The key to convincing an audience about arguments based on questions of conjecture is to discover how to use facts and scenarios that touch their interests, needs, and values.

USE ALL FOUR TYPES OF QUESTIONS   Basing arguments on all four types of questions within a single presentation can be especially effective! For example, whether you are supporting or condemning capital punishment, you might start with questions of fact: How many people are executed in the United States each year? What crimes are punishable by death? Which state leads the nation in executions? Then you could move to questions of value: Is it right for a state to take the life of a prisoner regardless of how serious the crime? Is capital punishment cruel? Is "a life for a life" a moral position? Questions of conjecture, the third type, require predictions about the future: Will the number of executions increase in the future? Will criminals be deterred from committing crimes if all states have mandatory capital punishment laws for similar crimes? Finally, you could ask a question of policy: Should capital punishment be expanded (or curtailed or abolished)?

Most persuasive presentations deal with more than one type of question. If you don't adequately address the questions about the facts of a situation, the values held by your audience, future implications, and possible audience reactions to a proposed course of action, you may get a disappointing reaction to your persuasive presentation.

Questions of Policy.   An argument based on a **question of policy** asks whether or not to take a particular course of action. A persuasive presentation that looks at a policy question focuses on the issues that arise when people are asked to change how things are or should be done. We often ask ourselves questions of policy when trying to make difficult decisions. We weigh the pros and cons of choosing a particular college, accepting a new job, or making a major purchase.[2] When used for a persuasive presentation, arguments based on policy questions ask an audience to do something or to support a course of action. Should you vote for Jane Doe? Should you speak out against the college's proposed tuition increase? Should you spend more time with your family and less overtime on the job? Should you support more funding for the public library system?

When asking an audience to take action, try to determine whether your listeners are able and willing to think critically about your arguments. If they are, using a central route to persuasion is more likely to produce long-lasting behavioral change. For less critical and less motivated audience members, taking a peripheral route to persuasion may be the only way to induce even a temporary change in their behavior.

Find Persuasive Evidence

In Chapter 2 we defined *evidence* as the information, data, or audience beliefs used to support and prove the claim of an argument. In Chapter 7 we illustrated how to use valid supporting material to help explain and/or advance a central idea and main points. When supporting material is used to strengthen the persuasive claim of an argument, it becomes evidence.

In persuasive speaking, evidence verifies and strengthens the proof you use to secure belief in an argument. It is the backup material that justifies why an audience should accept or reject an idea. If you claim that millions of Americans cannot afford health insurance, a statistic from a reputable source can help to justify your claim. If you argue that responsible environmentalists support deer hunting, you'd better have a reputable quotation or survey to prove your point. If you are trying to demonstrate the benefits of early diagnosis of diabetes, you may want to tell two contrasting stories—one about a person who was diagnosed early and one who wasn't diagnosed until the disease had ravaged her body. Be strategic. Select your evidence according to the type of argument you are trying to prove, the attitudes and needs of your audience, and whether you're seeking a central or a peripheral route to persuasion.

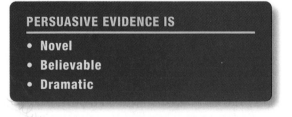

PERSUASIVE EVIDENCE IS
- Novel
- Believable
- Dramatic

Novel Evidence.   Very often the best persuasive evidence is information that is new to your audience. If they have heard a piece of evidence before, they've already considered its implications when forming an attitude. The best persuaders constantly look for new evidence to support their arguments. How many times have you seen someone at a swimming pool stand next to a sign that reads, "No diving" and then dive right into the pool? Overly familiar evidence just doesn't work that well. By the way, this is one of the reasons why advertisements on television keep changing: Once an ad is familiar, viewers don't pay as much attention to it.

The theories of persuasion that we discussed in Chapter 18 reinforce the value of novel evidence. When you're speaking to a primarily friendly audience, new evidence can strengthen their resolve and provide answers to any questions asked by audience members who disagree. When audience members are uninformed or undecided, new evidence can tip the balance in favor of your position. And if you are seeking a central route to persuasion, audiences will expect to hear new, well-researched evidence to support your arguments.

Believable Evidence.   Even if the evidence is completely accurate, well understood, and novel, it still will not be persuasive if people don't believe it. If your audience doubts the believability of your evidence, take the time to explain why it's true or provide other sources of evidence that support the same conclusion. If you think the source of your evidence has high credibility, you should mention that source *before* presenting your evidence. On the other hand, if you think that naming the source will not add to the evidence's believability, mention it *after* you've presented the evidence.

As we noted in Chapter 18, if an audience disagrees with your position, it is vital that your evidence be fair and respected. Establish the credibility of your evidence in order to strengthen your own credibility. If you demonstrate that the sources of your evidence are highly respected, you will have found a way to take both the central and the peripheral routes to persuasion.

Dramatic Evidence.   When using evidence, especially statistics, for a persuasive presentation, find ways to make it memorable. Instead of saying that your proposal will save the organization $250,000 dollars during the next year, you could say that it will save a quarter of a million dollars next year, the equivalent of the entire travel budgets of the three largest divisions of the company.

EVIDENCE CAN CHANGE ATTITUDES

TIP

According to Martin Fishbein, an expert in how people form attitudes, evidence can affect attitude change in three ways.[1] First, information can alter the believability, or weight, of a particular belief: "Given this evidence, I will now believe it or reject it more strongly than ever." Second, information can change the direction of a belief: "The evidence supports just the opposite belief. I've been wrong about this." Third, information can add new beliefs: "I had no idea that was the case! But I believe it now."[2]

1. Martin Fishbein, *Readings in Attitude Theory and Measurement* (New York: Wiley, 1967). Also see Martin Fishbein and Icek Ajzen, *Belief, Attitude, Intention, and Behavior* (Reading, MA: Addison-Wesley, 1975).
2. Steven W. Littlejohn, *Theories of Human Communication*, 5th ed. (Belmont, CA: Wadsworth, 1996), p. 140.

Senator Tom Harkin of Iowa (on the left) went ballistic in 1995 when he learned from the Government Accounting Office that Medicare paid $2.32 for surgical gauze that could be bought wholesale for 19 cents. To dramatize his criticism of Medicare payment practices, the senator had an aide dress himself in surgical gauze.

Statistics are often more dramatic when they are used in attention-getting comparisons. For instance, a study by an advocacy group for better road maintenance reported that motorists spend twice as much to repair cars damaged by potholes and pavement cracks as governments spend to fix the same holes and cracks. Why not save motorists a lot of money, they proposed, by investing in better road repair?[3] Or consider this comparison made by Robert Reich, former secretary of labor in the Clinton administration. Writing about the increasing income disparity between the rich and the poor in the United States, Reich noted that Bill Gates's net worth roughly equaled the combined net worth of the least wealthy 40 percent of American households.[4] That comparison brings home the point far better than relying solely on statistical evidence would. Presenting such statistical comparisons visually can heighten their impact. Imagine the chart or graph Reich could have used to dramatize his evidence!

Organizing Your Persuasive Presentation

You have a topic you care about; a list of potential arguments; an understanding of how your arguments answer questions of fact, value, conjecture, and policy; and evidence to support your arguments. You've reached a key decision-making point. It's time to put these elements together to form an effective persuasive message.

In addition to the organizational patterns discussed in Chapter 8, "Organization," there are some additional formats particularly suited to persuasive presentations.

> **PERSUASIVE ORGANIZATIONAL PATTERNS**
>
> Problem/Cause/Solution
> Better Plan
> Overcoming Objections
> Monroe's Motivated Sequence
> Persuasive Stories

Problem/Cause/Solution

A **Problem/Cause/Solution organizational pattern** is exactly what its name implies. First, you describe a serious problem, explain why the problem continues (the cause), and offer a solution. The basic outline for a Problem/Cause/Solution presentation looks like this:

I. There is a problem.
   A. The problem is serious and/or
   B. The problem is widespread.

II. The problem is caused by . . .

III. There is a solution to the problem.
   A. This solution can and will work.
   B. This solution will not create new problems.

In the following outline, the speaker uses a Problem/Cause/Solution organizational pattern to propose a national health care system for all U.S. citizens.

I. Americans are not getting needed medical care.

   A. Serious diseases (cancer, heart disease, diabetes, sexually transmitted diseases) are going undetected and untreated.

   B. Millions of Americans do not see a doctor for regular checkups.

II. The high costs of health care and health insurance prevent a solution.

III. A national health care system can guarantee medical care for all citizens by providing free health care for those in need without eliminating private care for those who can and want to pay extra.

   A. This plan works well in other modern countries.

   B. This plan will not cause problems such as low-quality care or long waiting lines.

The Problem/Cause/Solution pattern of organization works best when you are proposing a specific course of action to solve a serious problem. The previous outline's primary arguments addressed a question of policy: What should be done to guarantee medical care for all citizens? Depending on the results of audience analysis, the speaker would use logical arguments and substantive evidence if the audience was able and motivated to think and to listen critically. However, with an unmotivated audience that would be unwilling to listen, personal stories and the opinions of well-known, respected experts would be more likely to persuade. Regardless of the type of evidence, however, the basic outline for the Problem/Cause/Solution pattern works well for many kinds of audiences.

Better Plan

If a problem is complex and difficult to solve, a **Better Plan organizational pattern** may be a better way to structure your persuasive presentation. In this pattern, you present a plan that will improve a situation or help to solve a problem while acknowledging that a total solution may not be possible. The basic outline for a Better Plan follows.

I. There is a plan.
   A. What is it?
   B. How will it work?

II. This plan will be better than current plans.
   A. It will be better because . . .
   B. It will be better because . . .
   C. It will be better because . . .

In the following outline, the speaker contends that more hunting is a Better Plan for alleviating the serious problems caused by the growing deer population. The speaker is arguing that hunting is a better way to control deer populations than letting them die of starvation and disease. Although animal rights and anti-hunting advocates may disagree, the speaker is trying to show that increasing deer hunting is a better plan than doing nothing.

I. There is a plan that will help to reduce the deer population.

    A. The deer hunting season should be extended.

    B. States should allow hunters to kill more female than male deer.

II. This plan will reduce the problems associated with a large deer population.

    A. It will reduce the number of deer deaths from starvation and disease.

    B. It will save millions of dollars now being spent to repair crop, garden, and forest seedling damage.

    C. It will reduce the number of deer ticks carrying Lyme disease, which endangers humans.

The strategic advantage of using a Better Plan organizational pattern is that it can anticipate audience resistance and inoculate them against counterarguments. Unlike the Problem/Cause/Solution pattern—which says, "Here's the solution to the problem"—the Better Plan pattern offers a course of action acknowledging that it may be difficult, if not impossible, to "solve" the problem. Audience members who engage in critical thinking may respond positively to a speaker who admits that he or she doesn't have all of the answers. Audience members who are neutral or who disagree may find the Better Plan easier to accept as an option and easier to adopt as a reasonable solution.

Overcoming Objections

Sometimes an audience agrees that there is a problem and even knows what should be done to solve it. Yet they do not act because the solution is frightening, expensive, or difficult to implement. At other times, an audience disagrees with a speaker and comes prepared to reject the message before hearing it. With both types of audiences, you must deal with and try to overcome their objections. The basic outline for an **Overcoming Objections organizational pattern** has three sections.

I. People should do X.
    A. Most people know that doing X is a good idea.
    B. Many people don't do X.

II. There are several reasons why people don't do X.
    A. Reason #1
    B. Reason #2
    C. Reason #3

III. These reasons can and should be overcome.
    A. Overcoming Reason #1
    B. Overcoming Reason #2
    C. Overcoming Reason #3

In the following example, the speaker uses the Overcoming Objections organizational pattern to encourage listeners to donate blood. The audience already knows about the need for well-stocked blood supplies. They also know that people's donating more blood is the best way to solve the blood shortage problem. However, the speaker needs to overcome the audience's barriers to giving blood, deal with their counterarguments, and persuade them to act.

I. People should give blood but often don't.
   A. Most people think that giving blood is a good idea, but . . .
   B. Most people don't give blood.

II. There are several reasons why people don't give blood.
   A. They're afraid of pain and needles.
   B. They're afraid that they could get a disease from giving blood.
   C. They claim that they don't have time or know where to go to give blood.

III. These reasons can and should be overcome.
   A. There is little or no pain involved in giving blood.
   B. You can't *get* a blood disease by *giving* blood. You can get one only by *receiving* blood carrying a disease.
   C. The Red Cross makes it easy and convenient to give the gift of life.

Remember the Elaboration Likelihood Model of Persuasion from Chapter 18? Logical proof backed by strong evidence is effective when well-informed audience members are likely to do a lot of counterarguing. If you ignore their objections and concerns, you are not likely to persuade them. Take the central route to persuasion by addressing their reservations head-on and inoculating them against counterpersuasion. Overcoming Objections is also a useful pattern for strengthening the resolve of audience members who agree but still need motivation before they will take action.

Monroe's Motivated Sequence

In 1935, a communication scholar and teacher named Alan Monroe took the basic functions of a sales presentation (attention, interest, desire, and action) and transformed them into a step-by-step method of organization that could be used for all kinds of speeches.[5] The five basic steps in **Monroe's Motivated Sequence** have been used quite successfully by many persuasive speakers.

I. *The Attention Step:* Get the audience's attention.

II. *The Need Step:* Show the audience that there is a problem related to their individual interests and needs that should be solved.

III. *The Satisfaction Step:* Propose a plan of action that will solve the problem and satisfy audience needs.

IV. *The Visualization Step:* Describe what the audience's life and/or the lives of others will be like once the plan of action is implemented.

V. *The Action Step:* Ask the audience to act in a way that demonstrates their personal commitment to the solution.

In the following example, a student used Monroe's Motivated Sequence to focus on the problem of geographic illiteracy and to urge listeners to support the teaching of geography in public schools.

I. The Attention Step: Half of all Americans don't know where Columbus landed.

II. The Need Step
   A. Americans need to know more about geography for environmental, economic, and political reasons.

Using Language Persuasively

Effective persuaders select their words very carefully because they understand the impact language can have on an audience. A poorly chosen word or an inaccurate description can have dire results. In Chapter 12, we discussed the ways in which carefully selected words can make your presentation more interesting. Here we focus on other ways in which words can make your presentation more persuasive.

▶ *Use simple and direct words.* Don't let long, fancy words get in the way of your persuasive message. Be straight with your audience. Marketing expert Jerry Della Femina, chairman of the board of Della Femina, Travisano & Partners, wrote: "Nobody has the time to try and figure out what you're trying to say, so you need to be direct. Most great advertising is direct. That's how people talk. That's the style they read. That's what sells products or services or ideas."[1] Direct language persuades audiences.

▶ *Include descriptive details.* Don't load your presentation with adjectives and adverbs just to provide more detail. Instead, be specific and use language to create accurate and interesting images. Unless you use a presentation aid, language is the only means you have for providing details. Choose your words carefully and try to make them work for you to create images and emotional reactions. Several years ago, one of our students began an award-winning persuasive speech with a story. Her clear and specific language created a powerful and unforgettable image. Try reading the following introduction out loud. You don't have to be dramatic—just let the words do it for you.

> Picture two-year-old Joey. A hole in his throat so he can breathe. A tube jutting out of his stomach so he can be fed. Angry red scar marks where a surgeon implanted a new esophagus. It all began when Joey found an open can of drain cleaner and swallowed some of its contents. However, this is not going to be a speech about poisoning and how to prevent it, because Joey's tragedy was not caused by the drain cleaner. It occurred because Joey's mother followed an old set of first aid instructions. She gave him vinegar. But instead of neutralizing the poison, the vinegar set off a chemical reaction that generated heat and turned Joey's tiny digestive tract into an inferno of excruciating pain.

The student graduated many years ago, yet faculty members still refer to the "poor Joey" introduction as a model of effective language use.

▶ *Vary language intensity.* **Language intensity** refers to the degree to which your language deviates from bland, neutral terms.[2] You might say that your vacation was "okay," or that it was "good," or

---

    B. Citizens of other countries are much more literate about geography than Americans are.

III. The Satisfaction Step

    A. Integrate geography into the curriculum.

    B. Offer geography workshops for teachers.

    C. Reinstate geography as a separate subject.

IV. The Visualization Step

    A. Heather Hill Elementary School's successful geography classes.

    B. U.S. students would know as much about geography as foreign students now do.

V. The Action Step

    A. Increase parent-student involvement.

    B. Put pressure on local and national education agencies.

The unique visualization step in Monroe's Motivated Sequence makes this organizational pattern particularly suitable for neutral audience members who are uninformed, unconcerned, and unmotivated to listen or for listeners who are skeptical of or opposed to the proposed course of action. By encouraging listeners

that it was "great!" Good persuaders use intense language to get attention and signal their commitment. Instead of using a word like *nice*, try *captivating*. *Disaster* is a much more powerful word than *mistake*. A *vile* meal sounds much worse than a *bad* one. But don't go overboard—being too intense can boomerang. Listeners may feel that you've lost control. Effective persuaders vary language intensity to get attention. On an important issue, they're more intense. Then they take a breather by using more neutral language so that the audience will be ready for the next important idea.

▶ *Mean it!* Have you ever heard a person say something like "I guess we should probably adopt the proposal" or "It's a good idea, I think. Don't you agree?" or "Um . . . I don't mean to be negative, but I wonder if, possibly, we might be making the wrong move here"? What's your reaction to these kinds of statements? Are they persuasive? Why not? Because making such cautious, qualified statements undercuts their meaning. Consider these alternative statements: "We should adopt the proposal." "It's a good idea!" "We're making the wrong move." These statements sound confident. You'll be a better persuader if you put aside qualifying words and phrases (*maybe, sort of, possible*) and say what you mean.

▶ *Avoid filler phrases.* Try to avoid using using filler words or sounds such as *um, uh,* and *you know*. Although they're short, they are not persuasive because they create the perception of powerlessness. How? Sounds such as *um* and *uh* are hesitations and can signal uncertainty or anxiety. As we noted in Chapter 14, "Vocal Delivery," even though it can be very hard to break an *um* or *you know* habit, there is a major benefit to doing so: Audience members will see you and your message as more powerful and credible.

▶ *"Punch" important words.* Your words can sound as if you really mean them if you vocally emphasize or "punch" the important words and phrases. Professional speechwriters often underline in speech manuscripts the words and phrases that the speaker should punch. You can do the same. In fact, one of the reasons why we recommend practicing your presentation out loud (see Chapter 13, "Performance and Practice") is that it gives you a chance to identify which words to emphasize.

1. A. Jerome Jewler, *Creative Strategy in Advertising*, 2nd ed. (Belmont, CA: Wadsworth, 1985), p. 41.
2. John W. Bowers, "Some Correlates of Language Intensity," *Quarterly Journal of Speech* 50 (1964): 415–420.

to project themselves into the future to "see" the results of taking or failing to take a particular course of action, you can strengthen the impact of your message. The more you involve your listeners' senses in the visualization and the more realistic you make that future scenario, the more likely you will be able to persuade them.[6] The visualization step intensifies the audience's willingness and motivation to believe, feel, or act in a certain way.

An added advantage of Monroe's Motivated Sequence is its focus on audience needs. We noted in Chapter 18's discussion of Maslow's Hierarchy of Needs and Schutz's FIRO Theory that appealing to the deficiency, fulfillment, or psychological needs of audience members can enhance the persuasiveness of a message. Monroe's organizational pattern is perfectly suited to that purpose.

Persuasive Stories

Stories are a powerful type of supporting material (see Chapter 7) that can capture and hold audience interest (see Chapter 12, "Generating Interest") and serve as a persuasive form of proof (see Chapter 18). So why not use stories that represent the central idea of your persuasive presentation as an organizational format? When using a **Persuasive Stories organizational pattern,** you rely on narrative proof (mythos) to organize your presentation along with emotional proof (pathos) to show how people, events, and objects are or can be affected by the change you are seeking. The Persuasive Stories outline is fairly simple:

I. The following stories show why people should change their opinions and/or behavior about X.
   A. Story A
   B. Story B
   C. Story C

II. Unless people change their opinions and/or behavior about X, there will be more (or fewer) stories like A, B, and C.

Note how the following speaker uses a series of persuasive stories to convince an audience to support programs designed to help political refugees. By telling real stories about refugee families, the speaker relies on emotional proof, going beyond logical appeals based on newspaper summaries and government statistics about the refugee problem.

I. The stories of three refugee families demonstrate the need for and the value of migration ministries.
   A. Story of Letai Teku and her family (Cambodia)
   B. Story of Peter Musooli and his family (Ethiopia)
   C. Story of Nasir Rugova and his family (Kosovo)

II. More support for migration ministries can save even more families who are fleeing foreign tyranny and persecution.

The Persuasive Stories organizational pattern may not be very effective for convincing those audience members who are well informed about this topic, opposed to extending more aid to refugees, or critical thinkers. Their counterarguments may range from "The speaker has used only three examples—maybe it's not such a big problem" to "The speaker is trying to manipulate me by using emotional appeals."

The Persuasive Stories organizational pattern, however, can be a very effective way of delivering a persuasive message to neutral audience members who are uninformed or are unable or unwilling to listen critically. By adding your personal reactions to and involvement in these stories, you can use the Persuasive Stories organizational pattern as an effective peripheral route to persuasion.

Fallacies of Argument

Critical thinking is essential for both persuasive speakers and effective listeners. If you are preparing a presentation, you must understand and be on guard against obstacles to clear thinking and purposeful persuasion. If you are listening to a presentation, you must be alert for unsound or unfair arguments. Although poor organization, uninspired language, and weak delivery can reduce the power of a persuasive presentation, the fallacies of argument can totally derail a speaker from achieving his or her purpose.

According to the *American Heritage Dictionary of the English Language,* a fallacy is "a statement or an argument based on a false or an invalid inference." It also is "incorrectness of reasoning or belief" and "the quality of being deceptive."[7] The word *fallacy* comes from the Latin verb *fallere,* which means "to deceive." **Fallacies,** then, are invalid arguments or misleading statements that can deceive an audience. Fallacies can be intentional or unintentional. However, whether an unethical speaker misuses evidence or reasoning for the purpose of deceiving an audience or whether a well-meaning speaker misinterprets evidence or draws erroneous conclusions, the result is still the same: A deceived audience is led to believe something that is not true or justified.

One way to keep fallacies from creeping into your presentations (with or without your knowledge) is to become familiar with them. Once you are, you'll start noticing fallacies everywhere—in product advertisements, in political campaign commercials, and in everyday conversations!

COMMON FALLACIES

Faulty cause
Attacking the person
Hasty generalization
Selected instances
Bandwagon
Begging the question
Victory by definition

Faulty Cause

The **faulty cause** fallacy has a Latin name: *Post hoc, ergo propter hoc* or, in shortened form, the *post hoc* fallacy. It means "After this; therefore, because of this." Think of it as the superstition fallacy. If you walk under a ladder, you will have bad luck. In politics, the *post hoc* fallacy is often used to blame elected officials for problems that they didn't cause: When Juan Diaz became our mayor (after this), juvenile delinquency increased (because of this). College students are not immune to this fallacy: Just because you spent four hours in the library (after this) does not mean that you are ready for the test (because of this).

Unfortunately, the *post hoc* fallacy is often difficult to detect, in part because it is so common. When you are constructing an argument for your presentation or listening to a speaker making claims about causality, make sure that the *post hoc* fallacy isn't clouding the issue. Here are some questions to ask about faulty causality:

▶ Have you or the speaker identified the real cause?

▶ What else could explain why this has happened?

▶ Are there multiple causes instead of just one?

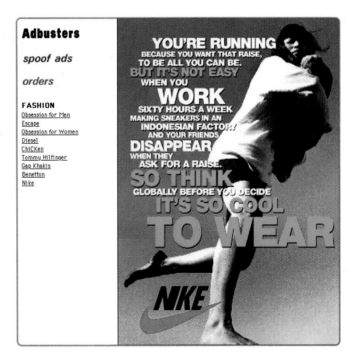

By spoofing well-known advertisements, Adbusters, www.adbusters.org/spoofads, tries to highlight the persuasive techniques used by marketers as well as the controversies surrounding certain corporate practices. What first appears to be a regular Nike ad is an Adbuster spoof focused on Nike's use of low-paid workers in Indonesia. What fallacies of argument can you find in this Adbuster spoof or in the real Nike ad it attempts to make fun of?

Attacking the Person

The fallacy of **attacking the person** also has a Latin name: *ad hominem,* which means "against the man." Thus, the *ad hominem* fallacy involves attacking a person rather than the substance of that person's argument. Attacking a person diverts audience attention from the person's argument and damages the person's credibility. Calling someone a cheat or a racist doesn't make the charge true, but it does plant seeds of doubt. Negative campaign ads take advantage of this phenomenon. Making *ad hominem* attacks on a rival candidate rather than addressing the issues has helped many politicians get elected. Name calling, labeling, and attacking a person rather than the substance of his or her argument are unethical practices as well as fallacies of argument. Here are some questions to ask about the *ad hominem* fallacy:

▶ Does the person deserve this negative criticism?

▶ Is the person's character linked in any way to the substance of the issue?

▶ Is the argument valid and justified regardless of who supports it?

Hasty Generalization

All of us occasionally make hasty generalizations. We go to a restaurant with a friend and have a good meal, so we recommend the restaurant to a colleague. A few days later she comes to work with a tale of terrible service and tasteless food. It's possible we might have made a hasty generalization. Because we had liked the dishes we ate at our first and only meal at the restaurant, we assumed that all of the dishes were excellent. All it takes to commit a **hasty generalization** fallacy is to jump to a conclusion based on too little evidence. For example, you could be making a mistake if you avoid taking a class from a certain professor just because you've heard a disgruntled student complain about that professor. When developing a persuasive presentation, make sure that you have surveyed the research and opinions on your topic. If the first study or opinion you find supports your position, do more research to make sure that other studies and experts also agree. Here are some questions to ask, to ensure against making hasty generalizations:

▶ Is the conclusion based on enough or typical examples?

▶ Are there more comprehensive studies or surveys that arrive at the same conclusion?

▶ Are there a significant number of exceptions to this conclusion?

Selected Instances

The fallacy of **selected instances** is the opposite of a hasty generalization and more sinister because the speaker usually knows exactly what she or he is doing. This fallacy occurs when a speaker purposely picks atypical examples to prove an argument. Let's say that you are trying to convince a pro-environmental group that they should help elect a candidate to Congress. You know that the candidate whom you support has had an anti-environmental voting record in the state legislature, yet you choose to tell the audience only about the one time he voted *yes* on a pro-environmental bill. You are using the fallacy of selected instances.

When issues are highly controversial, some speakers will go out of their way to prove a point by using only selected instances. A speaker who's against gun control may tell carefully selected stories about gun owners who thwarted robbers rather than sharing the many more documented stories about accidental shootings and crimes of passion committed with guns in the home. Here are some questions to ask about the use of selected instances:

▶ Are these rare or infrequent examples?

▶ How many times has the opposite occurred?

▶ Why did the speaker choose these particular stories or examples?

Bandwagon

The **bandwagon** fallacy is an appeal to popularity. Its Latin term is the *ad populum* fallacy, which claims that something is good, right, or desirable because it is popular. "Join the smart crowd" and "Everyone's doing it" are typical bandwagon appeals. Whether you were buying the latest fashion or wishing for the newest hot car, at some point you probably have succumbed to the bandwagon fallacy. In a persuasive presentation, a speaker may state or imply that audience members are "out of it," "behind the times," or "not in step" if they fail to join the majority and support a particular issue. Sadly, the bandwagon appeal has been used to justify and recruit people for hate groups, unscrupulous financial schemes, and illegal "thrills." Here are some questions to ask about a bandwagon appeal:

▶ Is this proposal right or best just because it's popular?

▶ Is popularity a relevant criterion for making a decision?

▶ What are the disadvantages of following the crowd in this case?

Begging the Question

The **begging the question** fallacy assumes that an unproven fact in an argument is true. Here are some examples: Have you stopped cheating on your spouse? When did you first smoke marijuana? How did you manage to deceive the IRS? These questions assume you did cheat on your spouse, smoke marijuana, and deceive the IRS. In *Begging the Question*, Douglas Walton writes that this fallacy uses "deceptive tactics to try to get a respondent to accept something as a legitimate premise that is really not, and to slur over the omission, to disguise the failure of any genuine proof."[8] Here are some questions to ask about begging the question:

▶ Does the question assume that something unproven is true?

▶ Does any direct answer to the question get the subject into trouble?

▶ Does the speaker presume to know what you think or what you have done?

AM I COMMITTING A FALLACY IF I PRESENT ONLY ONE SIDE OF AN ARGUMENT? This question often comes up when speakers realize that presenting only one side of an argument may appear manipulative. It may seem as though the speaker isn't telling the audience good reasons why there is disagreement on an issue. For example, advertisers rarely present both sides of an argument—TV ads won't tell you that the active ingredient in Bayer aspirin is exactly the same as the one in less expensive generic aspirin.

At first glance, you may be tempted to tell an audience only your side of the story. Don't give in, though. Deceiving an audience by presenting only one side of an argument is unethical. There may be good reasons why several members of your audience cannot or should not change their opinions or behavior. The wisest move is to acknowledge both sides of an issue.[1] Both the Better Plan and the Overcoming Objections organizational patterns acknowledge that there are other viewpoints and other approaches to an issue.

When you present the other side, though, also refute it. Inoculate your listeners with a refutational message: "Here is my position. My opponent will tell you this, but let me tell you why I think my opponent's position is incorrect or misleading." (Of course, your "opponent" would likewise explain why your position is just as incorrect or misleading.) Because you have acknowledged that legitimate differences of opinion exist, your audience will see you as more credible for mentioning other points of view. Also, remember that when audience members are well informed but undecided about an issue or are likely to engage in counterarguing, it's a good idea to acknowledge both sides of the issue. When your arguments are strong, a two-sided approach will enhance your persuasiveness.

1. Robert H. Gass and John S. Seiter, *Persuasion, Social Influence, and Compliance Gaining* (Boston: Allyn & Bacon, 1999), pp. 191–193.

Victory by Definition

Victory by definition is a fallacy that makes the definition of a word self-serving. For instance, during the 1998 impeachment proceedings against him, President Clinton's definition of the term *sexual relations* provided him with a way of "telling the truth" about his inappropriate encounters with Monica Lewinsky. The more abstract or emotional a term, the easier it is to make its definition suit a persuasive purpose. For example, when asked whether a marketing campaign had been successful, a manager reported that the competition had seen only a 2 percent rise in sales compared with his company's 4 percent. Therefore, the campaign worked. Unfortunately, though, the marketing department had predicted an 8 percent increase! By defining *success* as an increase "twice as high as that of any competitor," the manager was able to avoid mentioning that the marketing department had missed its projected mark by half. Here are some questions about victory by definition:

▶ Is this the accepted definition of the word?

▶ Is this the definition that the speaker used at other points in this argument?

▶ Would using other definitions change the speaker's conclusion?

Knowing that so many fallacies exist should forewarn you that speakers with the best of intentions can still fall prey to a lurking fallacy. Whether you're a speaker or an audience member, do your best to test what you say or hear before delivering or believing a message. The tests of evidence that we discussed in Chapter 7, "Supporting Material," can be applied to arguments, too. Use the checklist in Figure 19.1 to test an argument's overall validity.

When a fallacy unintentionally enters a persuasive presentation, we can usually forgive the speaker and hope that she or he will recognize the error and avoid making it in the future. What we should not forgive is the intentional use of fallacies. Being able to identify the fallacies of arguments is the first step in making sure that we avoid using them and condemn them when we hear them being used.

Figure 19.1   Testing Arguments

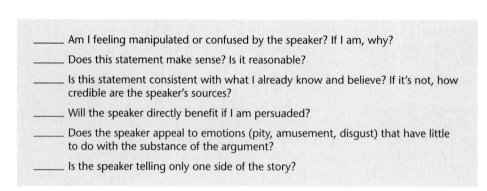

_____ Am I feeling manipulated or confused by the speaker? If I am, why?

_____ Does this statement make sense? Is it reasonable?

_____ Is this statement consistent with what I already know and believe? If it's not, how credible are the speaker's sources?

_____ Will the speaker directly benefit if I am persuaded?

_____ Does the speaker appeal to emotions (pity, amusement, disgust) that have little to do with the substance of the argument?

_____ Is the speaker telling only one side of the story?

Summary

◆◆ What constitutes a good persuasive presentation?

Begin with a topic and purpose that are important to both you and your audience. Then develop your arguments while considering whether they are asking the audience to believe questions of fact, value, conjecture, and/or policy.

◆◆ What's the best type of evidence to use in a persuasive presentation?

Assuming that you have already collected valid supporting material for your presentation, select evidence that is novel, believable, and dramatic.

◆◆ What's the best way to organize a persuasive presentation?

Adapt your persuasive organizational pattern to the beliefs and needs of your audience. In addition to standard formats, consider the following organizational patterns: Problem/Cause/Solution, Better Plan, Overcoming Objections, Monroe's Motivated Sequence, and Persuasive Stories.

◆◆ What are the common fallacies of argument?

Some of the most common fallacies of argumens include faulty cause, attacking the person, hasty generalization, selected instances, bandwagon, begging the question, and victory by definition. Regardless of their names, fallacies are invalid arguments or misleading statements, made during a persuasive presentation, that intentionally or unintentionally deceive an audience.

Key Terms

Notes

1. Dennis S. Gouran, "Effective Versus Ineffective Group Decision Making," in *Managing Group Life: Communicating in Decision-Making Groups,* ed. Lawrence R. Frey and J. Kevin Barge (Boston: Houghton Mifflin, 1997), p. 139.
2. David L. Vancil, *Rhetoric and Argumentation* (Boston: Allyn & Bacon, 1993), p. 26.
3. *Washington Post,* 6 November 1998, p. F3.
4. *New Yorker,* 30 November 1998, p. 32.
5. Alan H. Monroe, *Principles and Types of Speech* (Chicago: Scott, Foresman, 1935), pp. vii–viii, x. Various applications of Monroe's Motivated Sequence can be found in Bruce E. Gronbeck et al., *Principles and Types of Speech Communication,* 13th ed. (New York: Longman, 1997).
6. Gronbeck et al, pp. 186–187.
7. *The American Heritage Dictionary of the English Language,* 3rd ed. (Boston: Houghton Mifflin, 1992), p. 658. Copyright © 1996 by Houghton Mifflin Company. Reproduced by permission from *The American Heritage Dictionary of the English Language, Third Edition.*
8. Douglas N. Walton, *Begging the Question: Circular Reasoning as a Tactic of Argumentation* (New York: Greenwood, 1991), p. 285.

20

Developing Special Presentations

- ●▸ What kinds of special presentations should I know how to make?
- ●▸ How do I introduce a presenter?
- ●▸ How should I welcome an audience or a group of guests?
- ●▸ What's the best way to make a toast?
- ●▸ What should I do if I'm asked to make a humorous presentation?
- ●▸ How do I handle question-and-answer sessions?
- ●▸ Can I *prepare* for impromptu presentations?

Although most presentations inform, persuade, and/or entertain, a special group of presentations resists such strict classification. Sometimes called special occasion speeches or ceremonial speaking because of the unique occasions that prompt their use, special presentations have specific names that tell you a great deal about their unique purpose, audience, setting, and preparation requirements. For example, a toast celebrates someone at a special event, humorous comments can lighten the atmosphere at a retirement dinner, and welcoming remarks at a ribbon cutting ceremony can kick off the dedication of a building or monument. This chapter focuses on how to prepare and deliver several kinds of special presentations that you are likely to encounter as a speaker and listener.

Special Presentations

The purpose of most **special presentations** is to bring people together, to create social unity, to build goodwill, to answer questions, or to celebrate.[1] There are many types of special presentations.

> **SPECIAL PRESENTATIONS COME IN MANY FORMS**
>
> Welcomes   Nominations
> Acceptance speeches   Toasts
> Award presentations   Dedications
> Eulogies   Commencement addresses
> After-dinner speeches   Question-and-answer sessions
> Impromptu remarks   Retirement roasts

At this point you may be wondering why the chapters on informative and persuasive speaking won't provide you with enough strategies to master these forms of presentation speaking. Actually, they will—if you are a quick-thinking, highly adaptable speaker who has tremendous confidence. If you're at a wedding or a retirement dinner, and someone asks you to offer a toast, you will have to think quickly and adapt your toast to what you know about the bride and groom or about the retiree. It also helps to have a great deal of confidence if you're confronted with such a speaking opportunity. Most guests can't pull a toast out of their hats with ease.

Special presentations often come with their own sets of rules—rules that a speaker is expected to follow. If you're asked to make a toast, nominate a candidate, or present an award, many of your decisions will have already been made for you. If you're presenting an award, for example, you can't choose the person or organization that will receive the award—that will already have been done. The audience and the place where you will be speaking will also have been predetermined. And you will have a very specific purpose that will require specific types of preparation and planning. Generally, you will be expected to praise the award recipient, cite reasons why the recipient deserves the award, and deliver your presentation in a positive, uplifting style.

Most of you will never nominate a presidential candidate at a national convention (see Al Gore's nomination speech in Appendix A), but you might nominate a classmate or coworker for an office in your student government or a professional association. Most of you will never have to dedicate a public memorial or building, but you may be asked to say a few words at the opening of a new branch office. We don't have enough space in this text to give you specific advice for every type of special presentation. However, if you apply the basic principles of presentation speaking, you can adapt to any type of situation, no matter how monumental or modest the occasion may be.

Introducing a Presenter

When you're invited to **introduce a presenter,** you are being asked to make brief remarks about the speaker and the presentation in order to motivate the audience to listen. You are the warm-up act for the speaker who follows you. Introducing a speaker, a very common type of special presentation, is, unfortunately,

*O*nce, before a large audience of students, I introduced the president of a college at which I was working on a one-year faculty contract. I used words such as *extraordinary, the best, beyond compare,* and *brilliant* to describe my new boss. When he stood up to speak, he threw me a friendly glance and then told the audience that he would have to check the personnel records to see if I had applied for a promotion. The audience burst out laughing. I had clearly gone overboard with the praise. Fortunately, the president used my comments to begin with a friendly joke in order to come across as a real person rather than as the superman I had described.

Isa Engleberg

often dismissed as an easy chore by those who do it. After all, it's the presentation that's given *after* the introduction that everyone has come to hear. Instead of thinking about introducing a speaker as a necessary but unimportant trifle, you should look upon your comments as a golden opportunity to prepare an audience for the main event and as a way of enhancing your own credibility.

When you introduce a presenter, your purpose is to make listeners *want* to hear the person being introduced. You can share information that makes listeners interested in and curious about the person or give details that can create admiration and respect for him or her. Your introductory comments will also set the stage for the upcoming presentation. Remember the goals of a presentation's introduction from Chapter 10, "Introductions and Conclusions"? They can be exactly the same for introducing a presenter except that you are achieving these goals for someone else rather than for yourself. Introducing a presenter can (1) gain audience attention and interest, (2) enhance the presenter's credibility, (3) introduce the presenter's purpose or topic area, and (4) set the appropriate mood for the upcoming presentation.

The introduction of a presenter should "warm up" an audience and make the speaker seem interesting and human. Sometimes, however, an introducer can go overboard and heap so much praise on a speaker that he or she would have a lot of trouble living up to the introduction. (See Real World, Real Speakers above.)

Creating effective remarks to introduce a presenter takes preparation. Let's consider some of the basic decisions you'll need to make and a few guidelines specific to this type of special presentation.

Basic Decisions About Introducing a Presenter

Although on the one hand, you can view an introduction of a presenter as a presentation's introduction, on the other hand, it helps to consider it as a complete mini-presentation. You can apply the seven basic principles of presentation speaking to your introductory comments, making a few adjustments for this type of special presentation.

Purpose: Your purpose is quite clear-cut: to introduce a particular presenter to a specific audience. In addition, ask yourself, "How can I make the listeners respect and want to hear the person being introduced?"

Audience: As with any other presentation, you'll need to research the characteristics and needs of your audience. In particular, ask yourself, "What do the listeners already know or need to know about the presenter?"

Logistics: A presentation that calls for a formal introduction by someone else—you!—will already have had many of its logistic decisions made. It's up to you to find out what they are. Ask yourself, "How formal is the occasion, and how formal should the introduction be?"

Content: The content of your introduction needs to include details about the person you're introducing. Ask yourself, "What background information do I need to have about the presenter (accomplishments, experiences, education, titles, personal information, and so on)?"

Organization: Even though the introduction of a presenter should be brief, it needs to be well organized instead of being a random collection of unrelated comments. Ask yourself, "How can I review, regroup, reduce, and refine the key points I want to make in a well-organized introduction?"

Credibility: Because your introduction should focus the audience's attention on the presenter, not on you, your comments should likewise bolster the presenter's credibility—although one of the best ways to do this is to transfer some of your own credibility to the speaker. Ask yourself, "What can I say that will impress the audience about the presenter's competence and character?"

Performance: Once you have prepared your introduction, you'll need to decide what's the best way to deliver it. Ask yourself, "What form of delivery—other than impromptu—is best for this occasion and presenter?" Then, practice! At this point, one of your most critical questions will be "Can I pronounce the presenter's name correctly and easily?"

Guidelines for Introducing a Presenter

Your answers to the previous questions will help you introduce a presenter. We also offer the following guidelines, developed over years of hearing wonderful and not-so-wonderful introductions.

1. An introduction should be carefully prepared; don't try to make one impromptu.

2. An introduction should *appear* to be spontaneous and natural. If you're using a manuscript, practice your delivery in order to maximize eye contact instead of reading it word for word.

3. When making an introduction, look at the audience. Don't talk to the person being introduced.

4. The introduction should be short. You aren't the main attraction; the speaker is. In most cases a one- or two-minute introduction will be enough. If the audience knows the presenter very well, it can be even shorter.

5. Don't speak at length on the presenter's subject; that's the speaker's job.

6. Play a supportive role. Don't steal the show or embarrass the presenter with extravagant compliments.

7. Avoid using clichés such as "Tonight's speaker needs no introduction" or "So without further ado. . . . "

8. Make sure that your introduction is appropriate for the presenter. If the speaker is not your close friend, don't describe him or her as one.

9. At the end of your introduction, begin applauding until the presenter reaches the lectern or podium. Then, when the speaker begins the presentation, listen closely. You might have to respond to a thank-you for a great introduction!

10. Ask the presenter what she or he wants you to say. Doing this can save you a lot of preparation time and can answer most of your questions.

Interview the Presenter

Because including good information is the key to making a good introduction, it's better to collect too much information about the person whom you will be introducing rather than not enough. Often the best source of this information will be the speaker, and the best way to get that information is to conduct an interview (see the mini-module in Chapter 7, "Supporting Material"). You can ask the presenter one or more of the following questions:[1]

- What do you hope to accomplish with your presentation?

- How did you become interested in your topic?

- What are the two or three most important things that the audience should know about you or your topic?

- Whom should I contact to hear some good stories about you?

- Is there anything that you specifically want me to mention or not to mention?

- Is there anything else that you thought I was going to ask?

1. Malcolm Kushner, *Successful Presentations for Dummies* (Foster City, CA: IDG, 1997), p. 310.

Welcoming an Audience

Welcoming remarks are one of the most common and most underappreciated forms of special presentations. Although making them may look easy, they require significant preparation and thought. You may be asked to welcome a speaker or a special guest, which is not the same as introducing a presenter. Rather, you will be welcoming that person on behalf of the audience. Welcoming remarks also kick off special events. For instance, when a group visits a college, company, or organization, someone usually has been asked to welcome the audience.

What makes giving this type of special presentation difficult is that there isn't much to say if you haven't done your homework. You stand up, look at the audience, and say, "We are delighted to welcome you to (insert the name of the event)." Now what? "On behalf of the entire organization, we are pleased you chose (insert the name of your organization) to host your meeting." Now what? "Thank you, and have a great day." Those three sentences may constitute a welcome, but they won't do much for you or your organization—or for your credibility as a speaker.

When you welcome an audience, you create a critical first impression of yourself and your organization. If your welcome is dull, the audience may regard *you* as dull. If your welcome says nothing about the audience or their organization, your listeners may decide that you are a poor speaker who has no interest in whether or not they are there. Although welcoming remarks can be brief, they can provide a lot of benefits for speakers and their organizations.

Basic Decisions About Welcoming Remarks

Effective decisions about welcoming an audience are based on the material you know or have collected about a group or the reason why audience members have been assembled. Paying attention to a series of basic questions can help you make your remarks memorable.

Purpose: How can I link my welcoming remarks to the goals of the organization that *I* represent?

Audience:	What are the audience's expectations and interests? What is the organization's goal or history? What kind and size of audience will attend?
Logistics:	How formal is the occasion, and how formal and long should my welcome be?
Content:	What specific content should I include that relates to the assembled group, its purpose, and the occasion?
Organization:	How can I use a simple organizational pattern to accomplish my purpose?
Credibility:	What can I say to demonstrate that I share the audience's interests, beliefs, or values?
Performance:	What form of delivery is best for this occasion? Regardless of what form I choose, can I deliver my remarks naturally, with maximum eye contact?

Guidelines for Effective Welcoming Remarks

Your answers to the previous basic questions will help you prepare and present successful welcoming remarks. The following guidelines can help you make them even better.

1. Don't throw your welcoming remarks together at the last minute. If you do, you run the risk of making a "one-size-fits-all-groups" welcome that basically says, "I don't know anything and didn't have time to learn anything about you, but in any event, I'm glad you're here."

2. Link your own or your organization's goals to those of the group. If you can, show that you share their interests and values. Also, use the opportunity to share information about your own organization.

3. Acknowledge the group's leader or leaders by name somewhere in your welcoming remarks.

4. Make sure that you correctly pronounce the name of the group that you are welcoming.

5. Stick around after you finish your welcoming remarks. Don't rush out the door. Someone may have a question or need your help. Even if you do nothing more than stand at the back of the room for a few minutes, you will be further extending the goodwill created by your welcome.

Making a Toast

If you've ever been at a wedding, retirement party, or special banquet, you've probably been asked to lift your glass and toast the newlyweds, guest of honor, retiree, employee, or family member. A **toast** consists of remarks that accompany an act of drinking to honor a person, a couple, or a group. Most of you, at some point, will be asked or inspired to make a toast. Whether you're drinking champagne or orange juice, a toast is a way to publicly honor, recognize, or thank someone or something. Yes, you can make a toast to a thing: Here's a toast to our tenth anniversary in business!

Basic Decisions About Toasts

Even though many toasts are impromptu in form, you can still prepare and practice them. Here, too, there are basic decisions to make. Some of them involve the basic principles of presentation speaking. However, the answers to some additional questions can help you to prepare and present a successful toast.

Purpose: How can I help the audience join in and celebrate the reason why we are here?

Audience: What do the listeners already know and feel about the person or object being honored?

Logistics: How formal is the occasion, and how formal should my toast be?

Content: What can I discover or share in my toast that will celebrate the person, group, or occasion (special stories, accomplishments, personal experiences)?

Organization: How can I use a series of stories or experiences to support the key points in my toast?

Credibility: What can I say that will show the audience how wonderful this person or cause is?

Performance: What style of delivery would best suit this occasion?

WHY IS IT CALLED A TOAST? Apparently the term *toast* comes from an old English tradition of putting a spiced piece of toast in an alcoholic drink to add more flavor. In speaking situations, the toast brings attention to something special at an event—it "spices up" and adds a joyous flavor to a celebration. Thus, a toast is a way of focusing on a special guest or event. From the word *toast,* we have *toastmaster,* a term that has come to mean the person who introduces a speaker or who serves as a master or mistress of ceremonies at a special event.

Guidelines for Great Toasts

A toast can be as solemn as a prayer or as risqué as a wedding-night joke. A toast can remind an audience why they are celebrating or remind a person why he or she is being honored. Because toasts are supposed to make everyone feel good, they can be more emotional, inspiring, and joyful than other types of presentations. Toasts can be memorable and great fun if you take the time to make appropriate decisions and follow a few simple guidelines.

1. Carefully prepare your toast. Don't try to make it impromptu if you know in advance that you will be expected to make a toast.

2. A toast should sound and look spontaneous and natural; never *read* a toast unless you are reading a special poem or quotation.

3. When making a toast, look at the audience *and* at the person or group whom you are toasting. This isn't an introduction—it's a celebration.

4. Keep it short and simple; your audience will get tired of holding their glasses up.

5. Be direct and sincere; your job is to say what everyone else is feeling.

6. Make sure your comments are appropriate for the person, group, or occasion you are honoring.

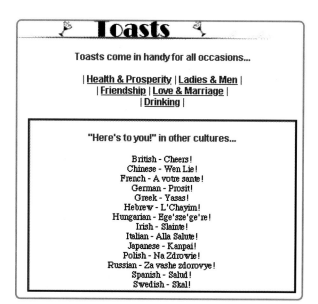

Toasts

Toasts come in handy for all occasions...

| Health & Prosperity | Ladies & Men |
| Friendship | Love & Marriage |
| Drinking |

"Here's to you!" in other cultures...

British - Cheers!
Chinese - Wen Lie!
French - A votre sante!
German - Prosit!
Greek - Yasas!
Hebrew - L'Chayim!
Hungarian - Ege'sze'ge're!
Irish - Slainte!
Italian - Alla Salute!
Japanese - Kanpai!
Polish - Na Zdrowie!
Russian - Za vashe zdorovye!
Spanish - Salud!
Swedish - Skal!

If you want to read a host of toasts as model presentations, try the Web site www.cocktails.about.com/home/cocktails/library/bltoasts.htm. But be careful—a toast is a very personal message. The best toasts come from real stories about people you respect or love.

Humorous Presentations

What's the most difficult kind of presentation to prepare and present? As you might guess from the location of this question, our vote goes to the **humorous presentation,** sometimes called an after-dinner speech, a "roast" of a friend, or a speech to entertain. Following the basic principles of presentation speaking requires a lot of work; trying to be funny at the same time requires even more work—with a dash of talent added to the mix.

Life without humor would be pretty dull. Some researchers even claim that humor can prevent or cure illness. The saying "laughter is the best medicine" may have some basis in fact. We do know that humor can reduce stress. In fact, it's so effective at relieving muscle tension that people often fall down laughing.

As we noted in Chapter 12, "Generating Interest," a little humor in an otherwise "straight" presentation can relax the speaker as well as ease audience tensions. It can also capture and hold an audience's attention. It can even defuse anger and stimulate action. Audience members tend to remember humorous speakers positively, even when they aren't enthusiastic about the speaker's message. In this chapter, we look at making humor the centerpiece of a presentation.

With so much to be said about the advantages of using humor as a component of a presentation or as the centerpiece of a talk, why don't more speakers give humorous presentations? For one thing, many presenters don't think they can deliver a humorous presentation well. For another, many people have no idea how to go about being funny. However, it's easy to learn what pitfalls to avoid and what guidelines to follow for using humor well.

The Pitfalls of Humorous Speaking

What are some of the mistakes that speakers make when they're trying to be funny? A few common pitfalls stand out.

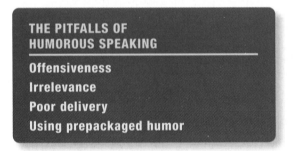

THE PITFALLS OF
HUMOROUS SPEAKING

Offensiveness

Irrelevance

Poor delivery

Using prepackaged humor

Offensive Humor.   We shouldn't have to say this, but we will: Don't use humor that has the potential to offend your audience. Avoid telling stories or jokes that could be interpreted as racist or sexist. We are astounded at how many speakers think it's okay to tell stories or jokes about a "priest, minister, and rabbi," "a ditzy blond," or a trio of "deaf, blind, and crippled" people. This point is not about political correctness. It's about common courtesy and audience sensibilities. There are plenty of ways to be funny without being insulting or offensive. Don't even think about using humor if there's any chance that it would offend your audience.

Deciding whether a one-liner, story, or joke is offensive or inappropriate isn't always easy. Most of us can recognize a joke that is blatantly racist or in poor taste. But it's harder to make a call on the borderline ones. If you have any doubts, heed them! Malcolm Kushner, a speaker, author, and former communication instructor, provides this simple test for making sure that your humor is ap-

When Roberto Benigni's "Life Is Beautiful" won him Oscars for Best Foreign Language Film and Best Actor, he climbed over the seats in joy and delivered one of the funniest acceptance speeches on record. Who but Benigni could have said, "I would like to be Jupiter! And kidnap everybody and lie down in the firmament making love to everybody, because I don't know how to express."

propriate for an audience: "Picture a front-page headline in your hometown newspaper describing your use of the joke in a presentation. Would you be embarrassed? If the answer is 'yes,' then don't use the joke."[2]

One of the reasons why ethnic and sexist jokes are popular is that they're based on very funny ideas. One way to take advantage of such humor—and to make it less offensive—is to tailor the object of the joke to the audience or occasion. For example, try filling in the blanks for jokes such as "How many _____s does it take to _____?" or "What do you call a _____?" With apologies to our academic colleagues, we offer a couple of examples: "How many professors does it take to change a curriculum?" (We don't know. They're still in committee.) "What do you call a professor who yells at the dean?" (Tenured.) If you don't get these feeble jokes, don't worry. They're aimed at an academic audience. They're also a good example of the self-effacing humor we discuss in Chapter 12. By making fun of yourself, you can use humor to make a serious point. Depending on where you work or live, you can substitute any group you work with or belong to. At the same time, make sure you don't make *too* much fun of the group and its members. They may not be amused.

Irrelevant Humor. Why do speakers often begin or end a presentation with a joke? We guess that there are two major reasons. One is that they don't know how to create an effective introduction or conclusion. The other is that they think they're expected to begin and end with a joke—even if it has nothing to do with the presentation. We dislike pointless humor. When a humorous story or joke is irrelevant to your message, it can distract an audience and waste their time. And what happens if the audience doesn't find your opening or closing statement funny? Just when you should be making a good first and last impression, you've bombed! Humor—regardless of its form—should support your presentation by tying in to a specific point. Just because you've heard a good joke, don't assume that's any reason to share it with the world—particularly in a presentation that has nothing to do with the characters or topic of the joke.

Poorly Delivered Humor. Don't use humor unless you feel comfortable telling jokes and humorous stories. Do you have trouble remembering a joke or the punch line of a funny story? Are you confident enough to tell a long joke without jumping over some parts of the story ("So, anyway, this happens four or five more times and then . . . ")? Do you ramble through a joke ("And then this guy says, . . . and then she says, . . . and then the guy says, . . . and then . . . ")? Do you laugh at your own humor before you get to the funny part? Do you apologize for lacking the skill to tell a good joke? Do you spoil the joke by telling everyone when the funny parts are coming up? If you aren't skilled at delivering humorous material, think twice before taking on the challenge of creating and delivering a humorous presentation.

Prepackaged Humor. Some speakers use other people's humor. You can buy books on humor and look up jokes in alphabetized categories such as *Advertising, Age, Television, Unions,* or *Women.* Many of the jokes, stories, and one-liners in these books are funny, but they may not be appropriate for your audience. They can't possibly reflect the specifics of the audience you're addressing. Or you may not feel comfortable telling them. Many of these jokes are dated and stale. Despite these cautions, speakers persist in using prepackaged jokes without realizing how obvious it is that they're telling jokes that they found in a book.

Guidelines for Humorous Presentations

Before you turn in your jokes at the door and avoid using humor at all, be reassured that humor can be delivered easily if you use it in a way that's appropriate for you and for your presentation. Very few people can tell a lengthy joke well, but most people can deliver meaningful one-liners, tell humorous stories, or make fun of themselves. For those of you who want to use humor but are nervous about giving it a try, we offer some guidelines to help you decide when and how to prepare and deliver a humorous presentation.

> **GUIDELINES FOR HUMOROUS PRESENTATIONS**
>
> Focus on one humorous idea
> Let the humor suit you
> Practice until you drop

Focus on One Humorous Idea. Whether you are inserting humor into a presentation or preparing an entire speech to entertain, you can develop quite a few funny lines by focusing on and researching one humorous idea. One student decided to meet the challenge of creating an entire presentation about what would happen if doctors decided to advertise. The following excerpt was part of it:

> Since no healthy, red-blooded American can resist a bargain—a rash of sales will develop. Surgeons could have grand opening sales. Of course, the same is true of obstetricians and Labor Day sales—20 percent off on all deliveries. And, of course, if you're going to run sales, that means advertising in the print media. Organ donor banks might have their own section in the classified ads, right behind "Used Parts—Auto."

The previous examples illustrate an idea allowed to run wild. The result, by the way, was a presentation that won first place at a national speech tournament.

Let the Humor Suit You.   Some speakers are good storytellers; others are known for their ability to tell jokes. Some presenters are masters at making puns; others do great imitations of friends and famous people. When you use humor, make sure it suits you and your speaking style. If you're not good at delivering one-liners, don't use them. If you can take a common situation and exaggerate it into a hilarious episode, you have found your niche.

Gene Perret, author of *Using Humor for Effective Business Speaking,* strongly believes that humor should begin with the speaker, not the joke. "Rarely will you find a chunk of comedy that you can retell as is. A joke or a story is a naked thing. It has no relation to you, to your audience, or to your message. You have to work to make it personal."[3] In other words, don't contort yourself to fit your material; adapt the material to fit your personality and your style.

Practice Until You Drop.   Of all the forms, types, kinds, and styles of presentation speaking, humorous speaking needs to be practiced the most in order to ensure a good performance. It involves more than just knowing the content of your presentation. It requires comic timing—knowing when and how forcefully to say a line, when to pause, and when to look at the audience for their reactions. To pull off a humorous presentation, you have to practice, practice, and then practice some more. The result will be a very funny speech that looks as if it's easy and enjoyable to perform.

Answering Audience Questions

At first, answering audience questions may not seem like a type of special presentation, but it qualifies in every way. The **question-and-answer session** (often called "Q-and-A") is a special type of impromptu talk that is limited and directed by questions. Other types of presentations may have planned or spur-of-the-moment Q-and-A sessions that follow them. Very often, audiences report that they liked the Q-and-A sessions better than the presentations. Why? As Chapter 13, "Performance and Practice," notes, speakers often talk and move more naturally while answering audience questions because they have stopped thinking about how they sound and look. Instead, they are thinking about how to answer the questions. Some speakers report that they don't think of a question-and-answer session as a presentation or speech, so they have less to be nervous about.

Audiences often like these sessions because they can get their specific questions answered and can interact directly with the speaker instead of remaining quiet and passive. If some speakers like this form of speaking, why don't other speakers? The reason is that some speakers are afraid of answering or don't know how to answer questions. The key to making a question-and-answer session a positive experience is to be prepared.

Be Prepared

Did you know that U.S. presidents take days to prepare for press conferences? Certainly, they have other important things to do, yet no one argues about the need to prepare and practice for a press conference. All speakers should heed the advice of press conference veterans. Advance preparation is the best way to ensure that you can and will answer questions effectively. Here's how you do it:

PREPARING FOR A QUESTION-AND-ANSWER SESSION

Predict and practice
Have ready-made remarks
Have a ready-made closing

Job interviews are question-and-answer sessions that require impromptu speaking. In this photograph, members of a program that helps people on welfare to get jobs are practicing their job interview skills.

Predict and Practice.   Predict which issues you think will be most important to your audience. Ask your friends or coworkers what questions they would ask or what kinds of questions have been asked in similar situations. Ask the chairperson of the meeting or the person who invited you to speak what questions the audience might have. Once you have identified these questions, practice answering them.

Also, you may want to announce the fact that there will be a question-and-answer session at the end of your presentation (and how long it will be). This announcement can affect the way in which an audience listens to you. If audience members don't understand something you say or feel you've left out something that concerns them, they know they can ask you questions about it later.

Have Ready-Made Remarks.   Be prepared with a few interesting statistics, stories, examples, and quotations that you can use in an answer. You may not use any of them, but at least you will know that you'll have something in reserve to support the ideas you express.

Have a Ready-Made Closing.   When audience questions begin winding down or when it's time to stop the Q-and-A session, make a concluding remark that you've prepared in advance. Saying "thank you" is polite, but it doesn't take advantage of the opportunity to end with a memorable statement. Marjorie Brody, author of *Speaking Your Way to the Top,* suggests that you return to the central idea, make references to the conclusion of your presentation, or talk about next steps.[4] Even if your concluding statement is short, it can neatly and professionally wrap things up.

Answer the Question

Once you feel well prepared for a question-and-answer session, the most important piece of advice we can offer is this: Answer the questions. Unless a question is technical and demands a lengthy response, each answer should be no longer than three sentences, and we don't mean run-on sentences. Be direct. Don't ramble or change the subject. Be honest. Audiences can tell if you're dodging an issue

Handling Hostile Questions

Depending on your topic and the people in your audience, you may be faced with one or more hostile questions. Although this is a rare occurrence, it does happen. Before you panic, think about this: Even when an audience doesn't agree with you, they will usually be sympathetic and supportive if one of their members badgers you or asks hostile questions. They wouldn't want to be in your shoes and therefore may become your best allies if someone goes after you. Fortunately, there are strategies to help you deal with a hostile question from an antagonistic audience member.

▶ Take your time before answering. Listen carefully. And don't strike back. Don't get drawn into a raging argument with one person. Taking a few seconds to think first can help you stay under control and avoid an embarrassing response. Hostile questioners are trying to provoke you. Don't let them. Be diplomatic and keep your cool.

▶ Paraphrase the question. Rephrasing the question, even when it's a friendly one, is not a bad idea. Making sure you understand the question also gives you time to think of an appropriate answer. When rephrasing a hostile question, don't repeat it word for word. Instead, try to put the question in more neutral or even positive terms.

▶ If you don't know the answer, or you aren't sure how to answer, admit it. Audience members are more likely to respect speakers who admit that they can't answer a question, rather than those who try to derail a hostile question by faking their way through an answer.

▶ If possible, try to empathize with a hostile questioner. Very often hostile questions come from frustrated audience members. If a questioner has been treated poorly, has a personal stake in the outcome of your presentation, or is offended by something you have said, you shouldn't dismiss that person's feelings.

▶ Perhaps the best suggestion for dealing with a hostile questioner is to seek common ground with the questioner (see "When Audiences Disagree" in Chapter 18, "Understanding Persuasion"). Find an area in which you and the questioner agree and build your answer from there: "Then we both agree that customers are waiting much too long in line with their purchases. We just differ on how to speed up the checkout process." In addition, use fair and respected evidence when you support the answer to a question. Accept differences of opinion. Work to build personal credibility by treating your audience with respect and by answering their questions as specifically as you can.

▶ Finally, there may come a point at which you have to be more assertive with a hostile questioner. As we indicated, an audience will become just as tired of listening to a harangue as you will. When a questioner is being abusive, offensive, or threatening, it's often effective to suggest that the person talk to you after the presentation and then to quickly move on to the next person who has a question. And don't let a hostile questioner ask a follow-up question. Again, move on to other audience members who have questions.

---

or fudging an answer; they won't like you any better if you evade their questions. Be specific but be brief. That doesn't mean giving superficial answers. It means answering a question directly without using up so much time that no other listener has a chance to ask you anything else.

Respect Your Questioners

Most questioners are good people seeking answers to their questions. Even if they don't word their questions well, you will sense what they want or need to know. A few questioners, however, fall into a different category. They can be highly opinionated or incomprehensible. Nevertheless, you should treat all of your questioners with respect. The following suggestions can help you give questioners the respect they deserve.

1. Don't make the questioner feel embarrassed or stupid. Even if you think the question is absurd, foolish, or just plain dumb, treat the questioner with respect.

2. Assist a nervous questioner. Like speakers, audience members may experience speech anxiety when they get up to ask a question. Help them through their nerve-wracking moment in the spotlight. Encourage, praise, and thank them.

3. One very common problem is the overexcited questioner who tries to give a speech rather than ask a question. After a minute or two of the questioner's speech, interrupt (if you can) and politely ask what the question is. If the speaker keeps going, you may find audience members joining you and asking the questioner: "What's your question?"

4. Recognize questioners by name. If you know a questioner's name or can see it on a name tag, use it. Saying their names when you answer their questions personalizes the exchanges.

5. Control your body language. Looking bored, annoyed, impatient, or condescending while a questioner is speaking sends a negative nonverbal message. If the questioner or audience senses your negative response, your credibility will be damaged. To avoid this, make full eye contact, smile, and lean toward the questioner.

Because Q-and-A sessions are so common, being well prepared for them is just as important as being well prepared to make a full-scale presentation.

Impromptu Speaking

In much the same way that you can prepare for a Q-and-A session without knowing precisely what questions you may have to answer, you can prepare to speak impromptu whenever the opportunity arises. As we noted in Chapter 13, "Performance and Practice," **impromptu speaking** calls on you to present without advance practice and with little or no preparation time.

Of all the forms of speaking, impromptu speaking has the potential to be the most nerve-wracking. Also known as "off-the-cuff" speaking, this type of special presentation shouldn't be feared. In fact, Laurie Rozakis, a professor and communication consultant, contends that "being a good impromptu speaker is very beneficial because of its everyday usefulness. Mastering this skill will help you feel more comfortable thinking—and speaking—on your feet."[5]

In many ways, preparing to speak impromptu is similar to preparing for a question-and-answer session. You may be called on to share your opinion in class, be asked by your boss to summarize a report with no advance warning, be moved to speak at a public forum, or be asked during a job interview to describe your accomplishments to a panel of interviewers. In each case, the response you make will be a mini-impromptu speech. You can apply many of the same techniques to a variety of off-the-cuff speaking situations. Try to predict the topic you may be called upon to discuss. Then practice speaking on that topic. Know as much as you can about the topic and have a few ready-made remarks handy.

In addition to taking these preparation steps, you will have to make some important decisions right before or during an impromptu presentation. Speakers who sound as fluent during an impromptu presentation as they do during a memorized presentation have mastered two techniques. They have come equipped with ready-to-use organizational patterns, and they know how to make the best use of their time.

Ready-to-Use Organizational Patterns

Successful impromptu speakers always have a handful of standard organizational patterns to fall back on. In an impromptu situation, you won't have a lot of time to think about which pattern is best suited to your topic. So try fitting your response into a simpler pattern, one that clearly separates the key points. Suppose someone asked you to talk about the value of a college education. How would you structure your ideas and opinions with one of these ready-to-use organizational patterns?

> **ORGANIZATIONAL PATTERNS FOR IMPROMPTU SPEAKING**
>
> Past, Present, Future
> Me, My Friend, and You
> Yes/No: Here's Why

Past, Present, Future. This pattern is a variation of the time arrangement discussed in Chapter 8, "Organization." In such a pattern, you could begin by explaining that at the turn of the twentieth century, a college education was not necessary for most jobs and was something that only the rich and gifted could afford to pursue. By the end of the last millennium, jobs that once required only a high school diploma required at least an A.A. or a B.A. degree. In this century, our best hope for prosperity in a more competitive world will be a better educated work force. As you can see, time arrangement can be as focused as yesterday, today, and tomorrow or as long-reaching as from the Stone Age to the "dot com" era.

Me, My Friend, and You. In this pattern, you begin by explaining how the topic affects or has affected you, tell how it affects or has affected another person, and conclude with how it can affect everyone in your audience. When advocating a college education, you can start with your own story—why you went to college, what you have gained from your experience, and why you like or liked it. Then you can tell a story about someone else who did or didn't go to college. Finally, you can draw general conclusions about the importance of a college education for everyone in your audience. The key in this pattern is moving from your personal experiences to establishing common ground with your audience.

Yes/No: Here's Why. In this pattern, you state your position and then preview the reasons why you have taken that position. A college education can prepare you for a career, can inspire you to become a lifelong learner, and can help you meet interesting people who will be your good friends for the rest of your life. You can give numerous reasons without many details, or you can focus on one or two reasons and emphasize their importance.

Time Management

Time is precious to the impromptu speaker. If you're lucky, you may have a minute to collect your thoughts and jot down a few ideas before speaking. In most cases, though, you will only have a few seconds to prepare. Manage the brief amount of time you have to your advantage.

Use Your Thought Speed. This technique is borrowed from the listening research we discussed in Chapter 2, "Critical Thinking and Listening." Remember that most people can think much faster than they can speak. If you speak at 150 words per minute, your brain can race ahead of what you are saying because you can think as fast as 500 or 600 words per minute. The very fact that you can listen to a speaker while writing a note or thinking about something else demonstrates your ability to think faster than a person can speak.

The best impromptu speakers think ahead. As they get up to speak, they're deciding on their two or three key points and which organizational pattern they will use. When they reach the podium or lectern, they're formulating an attention-getting beginning. As they start talking, they're thinking ahead to their first key point. They trust that the words will come out right, even though their thinking is divided between what they are saying now and what they want to say in the next few seconds. No wonder impromptu speakers feel exhausted after a successful presentation!

The best way to master using your thought speed to full advantage is to get plenty of impromptu speaking practice. While you are alone, with no pressures from an audience, practice your impromptu speaking with one part of your thinking focused on what you are saying and another part focused on what you will say next. Make sure to practice out loud—you won't become comfortable using this technique any other way.

Buy Time. In the few seconds between the time you're asked to make impromptu remarks and the moment when you start speaking, you have to plan and organize your entire presentation. You can stretch those seconds by following a few suggestions.[6]

1. *Pause thoughtfully.* Give yourself a few seconds to think before you speak. This technique can enhance your credibility. As Malcolm Kushner, a communication consultant and author, notes, "The audience assumes that your words will now be carefully considered rather than the first thoughts that flew into your head."[7] Of course, your audience may now expect something better than random thoughts.

2. *Rephrase the question.* As we suggested in our discussion of Q-and-A sessions, paraphrasing serves many functions. In addition to ensuring that you heard and understood the question or topic for comment, it also gives you more time. As the questioner answers you, you can be thinking ahead to your next response.

3. *Use all-purpose quotations.* Most of us know a few quotations by heart—from the Bible, from Shakespeare or a favorite poet, from song lyrics, or the tag lines from famous commercials. Try memorizing a few all-purpose quotations that can apply to almost any speaking situation. Not only does quoting someone make you sound intelligent; it also gives you a little extra time to think about what you want to say. Both of us have our own stockpile of quotations to call up when we have to speak off-the-cuff.

Throughout your life you will make many different kinds of presentations. You will give informative and persuasive presentations, and you will be asked to introduce speakers, welcome guests, offer toasts, answer questions, and speak impromptu. The strategies and skills that you use for such presentations can also be applied to other situations in which you are asked to give and accept awards, speak at special events, deliver eulogies and tributes, or nominate a colleague for a professional office. The key to success in any speaking situation is understanding how to apply the basic strategies and skills you have learned from this textbook to the unique characteristics of each presentation you will make. As these strategies and skills become second nature, you will improve your speaking ability and will become a more polished and successful presenter.

Summary

◆✦ What kinds of special presentations should I know how to make?

Some of the most common special presentations include introducing a presenter, welcoming an audience, making a toast, entertaining an audience, answering audience questions, and speaking impromptu.

◆✦ How do I introduce a presenter?

Think of the introduction of a presenter as being similar to the introduction to a presentation. Try to gain audience attention and interest, indicate the topic of the presentation, enhance the presenter's credibility, and set the appropriate tone for the presentation. Remember that your purpose is to motivate the audience to respect and listen to the person whom you are introducing.

◆✦ How should I welcome an audience or a group of guests?

Apply the basic principles of presentation speaking in such a way that you link yourself and your organization's goals to the characteristics, interests, needs, and expectations of the group that you are welcoming.

◆✦ What's the best way to make a toast?

Because toasts are more emotional, inspiring, and joyous than other types of presentations, you should be more personal in both the content and the delivery style used for this special presentation.

◆✦ What should I do if I'm asked to make a humorous presentation?

Unless you're comfortable making this type of presentation, avoid them. If you want to ensure your success, use humor that is relevant, appropriate, and well delivered.

◆✦ How do I handle question-and-answer sessions?

Preparation is the key. Predict and practice answering possible questions. Plan ready-made responses and have a ready-made closing. Make sure that you answer the questions and show respect for your questioners.

◆✦ Can I *prepare* for impromptu presentations?

Effective impromptu speakers employ ready-to-use organizational patterns and use what little time they have to plan and organize their remarks.

Key Terms

humorous presentation 348

impromptu speaking 354

introducing a presenter 342

question-and-answer session 351

special presentations 342

toast 346

welcoming remarks 345

Notes

1. Laurie E. Rozakis, *The Complete Idiot's Guide to Speaking in Public with Confidence* (New York: Alpha, 1995), p. 181.
2. Malcolm Kushner, *Successful Presentations for Dummies* (Foster City, CA: IDG, 1997), p. 327.
3. Gene Perret, *Using Humor for Effective Business Speaking* (New York: Sterling, 1989), p. 88.
4. Marjorie Brody, *Speaking Your Way to the Top: Making Powerful Business Presentations* (Boston: Allyn & Bacon, 1998), p. 158.
5. Rozakis, p. 193.
6. Kushner, pp. 315–316.
7. Kushner, p. 315.

Speaking in Groups

- ◆◆ What kind of speaking will I have to do in groups?
- ◆◆ How do I prepare for a group presentation?
- ◆◆ What's the best way to organize group decision making?
- ◆◆ How can I become a more effective group member?
- ◆◆ How can I become an effective group leader?

U p to now, we've been exploring the strategies and skills you need for preparing and making *presentations,* which we defined in Chapter 1 as any time speakers use verbal and nonverbal messages to generate meanings and establish relationships with audience members. We have focused on your role as a single speaker trying to achieve a specific purpose in front of a particular audience. We now turn our attention to the speaking skills needed to be successful in small group settings. Understanding how the basic principles of presentation speaking apply to this setting is critical in the world of work as well as to social and civil harmony.[1]

What Are Groups?

No matter what you do or where you go, you feel the influence of people who join groups to make decisions, solve problems, share information, and build friendships. Think of how many groups you belong to. Depending on your current situation in your college or professional career, you may list family, friends, study groups, car pools, roommates, class project groups, sports teams, coworkers, campus clubs, religious groups, neighborhood groups, service clubs, management teams, governing boards, political committees, or professional association memberships.

We use the term **small group communication** in this chapter to refer to the interaction of three or more interdependent people working toward a common goal.[2] The expression "Two's company; three's a crowd" recognizes that a conversation between two people is quite different from a three-person discussion. In fact, each person who is added to a group significantly affects the interaction. We believe that the ideal size for a group is five to seven members.

Group members come together for a reason. It is this collective reason or goal that defines and unifies a group. The label doesn't matter—*goal, objective, purpose, mission,* or *assignment.* Without a common goal, groups wonder: Why are we meeting? Why should we care or work hard? The importance of a group's goal can't be underestimated. If there is one single factor that separates successful from unsuccessful groups, it's having a clear goal.[3] Small groups achieve their goals by talking and working together.

Types of Groups

The interpersonal interactions that occur among group members are vital to achieving a group's goals, and so too are presentation skills. We use these speaking skills to give reports at staff meetings, present recommendations to organizational groups, and offer remarks at family gatherings. We inform, persuade, and entertain our supervisors, colleagues, associates, friends, and families in settings in which the "audience" can be as small as two or three people.

In order to understand how the purpose and setting of small groups can affect your communication, consider three types: public groups, teams, and working groups. As you will see, each type of group has a particular mission that requires particular communication strategies and skills.

Public Groups

Most groups function in private. Although a group and its product may be visible to the public, members usually meet, discuss, and make decisions in private. There is, however, one type of group that is seen and heard by public audiences. **Public groups** engage in discussion in front of and for the benefit of the public. Their meetings usually occur in open settings in which group participants can be judged by an audience of listeners.

> **TYPES OF PUBLIC GROUPS**
>
> Panel discussions
> Symposiums
> Forums

A group of teachers discusses ways to improve student proficiency in writing.

Panel Discussions.   A **panel discussion** involves several people who interact with one another about a common topic for the benefit of an audience. Panel discussions are very common on television and range from tabloid-style talk shows to heated discussions of current events. The participants in such discussions talk with one another in the hope that they will educate, influence, or entertain an audience. A moderator usually tries to control the flow of communication.

Symposiums.   In a **symposium,** group members present short, uninterrupted presentations on different aspects of a topic for the benefit of an audience. For example, a college may sponsor an AIDS symposium in which a doctor, medical researcher, AIDS activist, and health department official each give uninterrupted talks about the status of AIDS research and treatment. Symposium members apply the strategies and skills of presentation speaking to prepare their contributions.

Forums.   A **forum,** which provides an opportunity for audience members to comment or ask questions, frequently follows a panel or symposium. Some forums invite open discussions, letting audience members share their concerns about a specific issue. Other forums give the public an opportunity to ask questions of and express concerns to elected officials and experts. A strong moderator may be needed to ensure that all audience members have an equal opportunity to speak. In Chapter 20, "Developing Special Presentations," we discuss a variety of techniques for responding to audience questions. You can apply these strategies and skills to participating in forums, too.

When participating in any public group—whether it's a panel discussion, symposium, or forum—remember that you are "on stage" all the time, even when you aren't speaking. If you look bored while another member is presenting, the audience may question your commitment to the group's goals. If one member of a panel or symposium rolls his eyes every time another group member speaks, it sends the audience a mixed message about the credibility and civility of the speakers. Try to look at and support the other members of your group when they speak—and hope that they will do the same for you.

Participating in panel discussions, symposiums, or forums gives you an opportunity to advance yourself and your group. Making an effective presentation as a member of a public group is something you can learn to do with skill and confidence by employing the presentation speaking strategies and skills described in this textbook.

Team Presentations

When a person prepares a presentation, he or she must make dozens of decisions. When an entire group has to prepare a presentation together, the task becomes much more complex. Unlike panel discussions, symposiums, or forums—which are designed to inform general audiences—team presentations tend to have different goals. A **team presentation** is a well-coordinated, persuasive presentation made by a cohesive group of speakers who aim to influence an audience of key decision makers. Organizations as diverse as nonprofit agencies and international corporations rely on team presentations to offer marketing proposals, to compete for major contracts, and to request funding. In many ways, the team presentation is the ultimate group challenge because it requires efficient and effective decision-making as well as coordinated performances.

Team presentations can demonstrate whether a group or company is competent enough to perform a task or take on a major responsibility. When organizations seek support and endorsements, they must present a united front. Team presentations often have high stakes.[4]

Fortunately, the presentation speaking strategies and skills in this textbook can direct a group through the critical decision-making steps needed to develop an effective team presentation. Much as a single speaker does, a team should apply the basic principles of presentation speaking:

▶ *Purpose:* Determine the team presentation's overall purpose or theme.

▶ *Audience:* Adapt the presentation to a specific group of decision makers.

▶ *Logistics:* Adjust to the time limits and the place where the team presentation will be delivered.

▶ *Content:* Prepare and share appropriate supporting materials.

▶ *Organization:* Plan the introduction, body, and conclusion for each team member's presentation as well as those for the entire team's presentation.

▶ *Credibility:* Enhance the team's credibility by demonstrating the team's expertise and trustworthiness.

▶ *Performance:* Practice until the team's performance approaches perfection.

Team presentations require a great deal of time, effort, and money to prepare and make. Marjorie Brody, author of *Speaking Your Way to the Top*, writes:

> To be effective, team presentations must be meticulously planned and executed. They must be like a ballet, in which each dancer knows exactly where to stand, when to move, and when to exit from the stage. . . . If a team works like a smooth, well-oiled machine, if one member's presentation flows into the next presentation, and if all members present themselves professionally and intelligently, the impression left is one of confidence and competence.[5]

High-stakes team presentations can have equally high payoffs. For instance, Thomas Leech, a management communication consultant, reports that in 1992, following team presentations by several companies, the Department of Energy awarded a $2.2 billion contract for environmental cleanup to a team headed by Fluor Corporation. Assistant Energy Secretary Leo P. Duff said Fluor made the best impression. "All the firms had capabilities, but how the team works as a team in the oral presentations is a key determining factor."[6] The awarding of a $2.2 billion contract should convince anyone who doubts the value of effective team presentations.

Working Groups

Despite the importance of presentation speaking in, to, and on behalf of groups, most communication within small groups is more interactive. Although you *may* be asked to be part of a public group or a team presentation, you *will* be a member of many working groups. **Working groups** exert collective effort to achieve a shared goal. They work in private settings and in order to benefit the group rather than to benefit a public audience or external decision makers. Working groups can range from the most personal and informal types of groups to more formal types. And like their individual members, each type of group has different characteristics and concerns. As Figure 21.1 shows, each type of group can be recognized by its membership (who is in the group) and by its function.

The communication strategies, skills, and styles of working groups can differ, depending on the group's membership and its function. At the same time, all of these groups require dedicated and cooperative members who can communicate effectively as they work together toward a common goal.

Figure 21.1   Types of Working Groups

The common goal of each type of working group determines its membership and function.

Type of Working Group	Membership	Function
Primary Group (family, friends)	People who are close, intimate friends or relatives	Provides members with affection, support, and a sense of belonging
Social Group (athletic teams, hobby groups, sororities, fraternities)	People who enjoy interacting with others while pursuing social or recreational goals	Allows members to share common interests in a friendly setting or participate in social activities
Self-Help Group (therapy groups, Weight Watchers, Alcoholics Anonymous)	People who hope to overcome problems by sharing their personal concerns with people who have similar concerns	Offers advice and encouragement to members who want or need support with personal problems
Learning Group (study groups, book groups, fitness classes)	People who share an interest in understanding concepts or mastering particular skills	Helps members acquire information and develop skills
Service Group (labor unions, Kiwanis, civic associations)	People who see value in using a group to help themselves or others	Dedicated to worthy causes that help people both within and outside the group
Work Group (committees, work teams, task forces)	People who work in groups in order to make decisions, solve problems, and carry out assigned tasks	Responsible for performing specific tasks and routine duties on behalf of a business or organization

REAL WORLD, REAL SPEAKERS

Rosa Vargas, Human Resources Manager for The Topps Company in New York City, was introduced to team presentations in graduate school. She wrote:

> During my MBA studies, I was part of a team, and our purpose was to launch a new product to market. I feel that preparation and rehearsal are key to a successful team presentation. I was nervous in the beginning of our presentation (we presented to a panel of professors and students), but as the presentation progressed, I relaxed a bit. Our group had practiced, and I know this helped us give a more focused presentation.

Another respondent was less fortunate. She wrote that her work-based team presentation was unsuccessful because "people hadn't gotten together beforehand, and hence there was unnecessary repetition in the group presentation." Successful team presentations must be meticulously planned and practiced.

Communicating in Small Groups

Most of the time you spend in groups will be taken up in discussion focused on achieving a common goal. Regardless of whether you are in a task force, a learning group, or a staff meeting, asking group-focused questions about the basic principles of presentation speaking can help ensure that your group both is productive and provides a positive experience for all members.

> ### GROUP COMMUNICATION PRINCIPLES
>
> - *Purpose:* What is the group's goal?
> - *Audience:* Who will benefit from the discussion?
> - *Logistics:* Where and when does the group do its work?
> - *Content:* What does the group need to know?
> - *Organization:* How should the group organize its task and its meetings?
> - *Credibility:* How can members enhance their believability?
> - *Performance:* What delivery skills will enhance the group's performance?

Purpose

As we indicated earlier in this chapter, successful groups clearly understand their goals. A group's goal is similar to a speaker's purpose and asks this question: What does the group want to achieve?

The 3M Meeting Network, www.3m.com/meetingnetwork, provides a
wealth of material on small group communication. The subjects range
from improving basic communication skills, to interviews with small group
communication experts, to advice about overcoming common obstacles
to meetings' efficiency and effectiveness.

The first and most important task all groups face is to make sure that everyone agrees with and understands the group's purpose. One way to develop a
group's purpose is to word it as a question. In Chapter 19, "Developing Persuasive
Presentations," we suggested framing your arguments as questions of fact, value,
conjecture, or policy. The same advice holds true in groups. Not only do such
questions identify the discussion topic, but the answers to the questions also become clear statements of the group's goal.

Note how the following questions give you a clear idea of the topic that the
group will be discussing, as well as an understanding of the group's ultimate goal.

Questions of Fact:	What foods have the highest fat content?
Questions of Value:	Is a community college a better place to begin higher education than a prestigious university?
Questions of Conjecture:	Will inflation increase by 5 percent next year?
Questions of Policy:	How should we improve our customer service?

Whether you're leading a strategic planning team for a major corporation or
trying to choose a topic for your classroom discussion, make sure that everyone
in your group understands the group's goal.

Audience

Like all audiences, group members have demographic characteristics, motives, interests, knowledge, attitudes, and learning styles. You are part of that "audience"
when the other group members speak. They become the "audience" when you
speak. However, your relationship with listeners in a working group differs from
that of a speaker addressing a one-time audience. In most working groups, you
can count on the same people attending every meeting. Your ability to get along
with these members matters as much as your ability to adapt to them as listeners.

BRAINSTORMING IN GROUPS

When students have trouble coming up with a topic for an in-class group discussion, we suggest that they brainstorm for ideas. When working groups need to generate ideas for a project—determining the goal of a fundraising campaign, choosing possible themes for an advertising campaign, nominating members for a special committee assignment, selecting reasonably priced holiday gifts for support staff—they often begin by brainstorming for ideas. **Brainstorming** is a tool for generating as many ideas as possible in a short period of time.[1] When a group is asked to generate a list of suggestions, explanations, or solutions, brainstorming can be used to increase the number and creativity of suggestions. The following guidelines can help.

▶ *The more, the better:* Suggest as many ideas as you can. Quantity is more important than quality.

▶ *Be creative:* Free your imagination. Wild and crazy ideas are welcome and often generate breakthroughs.

▶ *Never criticize:* During the brainstorming session, don't analyze, oppose, praise, or laugh at another member's ideas. Also, don't discuss, defend, clarify, or comment upon your own suggestions. Evaluation occurs only *after* the brainstorming session is over.

▶ *Hitchhike:* Build on or modify ideas presented by others. Someone else's wild ideas can trigger a creative suggestion.

▶ *Combine and extend:* Combine two or more ideas into a new idea.

Although groups often use brainstorming, its success depends on the nature of the group and the characteristics of its members. If a group is self-conscious and sensitive to implied criticism, brainstorming can flop. If a group is comfortable with such a freewheeling process, brainstorming can enhance creativity and produce valuable ideas and suggestions.

1. Alex F. Osborn, *Applied Imagination,* rev. ed. (New York: Scribner's, 1957).

In addition to having all the characteristics of any group of listeners, group members assume group roles. Very often, by understanding the roles they play within your group, you can predict how members will react to what you say. Figure 21.2 shows two categories of roles found in most groups.[7] Group **task roles** affect a group's ability to achieve its goals by focusing on behaviors that help get the job done. Group **maintenance roles** affect how group members get along with one another while pursing a shared goal.

Depending on your group's goal, the nature of its task, and the characteristics of its members, you could function in several different roles. When each of the roles is assumed by at least one group member, the group is more likely to achieve its goal.

Logistics

Although the logistics of working groups differ from those individual speakers face, they require just as much attention if a group expects to achieve its purpose. Answering two basic questions can help a group begin the process of planning an effective meeting: When should we meet? Where should we meet? In many cases, a group will meet at the same time in the same room, one that already contains the furniture and equipment the group needs. In other cases, a group will first have to find out when members are available, then reserve a room that matches the purpose and size of the meeting. The room should be large enough, clean, comfortable, and far from distractions such as ringing phones or noisy conversations.

Once the group has secured a comfortable and quiet place to work, someone should be responsible for distributing necessary reading material and an agenda far enough in advance so that everyone has time to prepare. Also plan on having

Figure 21.2   Group Task Roles and Group Maintenance Roles

Group Task Roles

Initiator: Proposes ideas and suggestions, provides direction

Information Seeker: Asks for needed facts, requests explanations

Information Giver: Researches, provides, and presents needed information

Opinion Seeker: Asks for others' opinions, tests validity of group opinions

Opinion Giver: States personal beliefs, shares feelings, offers analysis

Clarifier: Explains ideas to others, reduces confusion, summarizes

Evaluator: Assesses ideas, arguments, and suggestions; diagnoses problems

Energizer: Motivates group members, helps create enthusiasm

Group Maintenance Roles

Encourager: Praises and supports group members, listens empathically

Harmonizer: Helps resolve conflicts, emphasizes teamwork

Compromiser: Offers suggestions that minimize differences, helps the group reach decisions

Tension Releaser: Alleviates tension with friendly humor, relaxes the group

Gatekeeper: Monitors participation, encourages equal participation

Observer: Explains and interprets what others are trying to say, paraphrases

Follower: Supports the group and its members, accepts assignments

extra copies available at the meeting. In addition, make sure that supplies and equipment such as flip charts or projectors are available and in working order.

Content

Researchers investigating the reasons why some groups achieve their goals while others fail emphasize that the quantity and quality of information available to a group is a critical factor in predicting its success. Randy Hirokawa, a group communication researcher, concludes that "the ability of a group to gather and retain a wide range of information is the single most important determinant of high-quality decision making."[8] Sometimes, when group members have preconceived notions about which decision is best, they may reject information that does not support their conclusions. As a result, the group will fail to fully understand an issue or to consider other options. Overlooking useful information or accepting inaccurate information will produce poor decisions and frustrated group members.[9]

If you want your group to succeed—regardless of its purpose, audience, or setting—make sure that you have collected appropriate ideas and information from credible sources. Chapter 7, "Supporting Material," covers how to research and use supporting material. All of these strategies and skills apply equally to small group communication as well as to individual presentations.

Organization

Some groups have tasks that are fairly easy to accomplish—deciding when to meet again, what to include in a monthly report, or to whom to assign a routine job. Other group tasks are much more complex and difficult—determining the group's common goal, whom to hire or fire, where to hold a major convention, or how to solve a serious problem. As difficult as it can be to make a personal decision or solve a personal problem, these challenges are much more complex for groups. On the other hand, achieving a group's goal through a well-organized decision-making process can be highly satisfying and worthwhile. Although there are many different ways to organize a group discussion, we have narrowed our focus to two: the standard problem-solving agenda and the working agenda.

The Standard Problem-Solving Agenda. The founding father of problem-solving procedures was a U.S. philosopher and educator named John Dewey. In 1910, Dewey wrote a book titled *How We Think,* in which he described a set of practical steps that a rational person should follow when trying to solve a problem. These guidelines have come to be known as *Dewey's reflective thinking process.*[10]

Dewey's ideas have been adapted to the process of solving problems in groups. The reflective thinking process begins with a focus on the problem itself and then moves on to a systematic consideration of possible solutions. Figure 21.3 shows an expanded, modified approach to this process—the **Standard Problem-Solving Agenda**—developed by three communication scholars, Julia Wood, Gerald Phillips, and Douglas Pedersen.[11]

Before a group can solve a problem, members must understand the group's assignment. The task clarification step answers questions such as these: What are we being asked to do? Why is it important to do this? What are we trying to achieve? During the second step—problem identification—the group should make sure that everyone understands the nature of the problem, possibly by wording the issue as a question of fact, value, conjecture, or policy. During the fact-finding and problem-analysis step, group members should investigate facts,

Figure 21.3   The Standard Problem-Solving Agenda

Problem-Solving Steps	Goals
1. Task Clarification	*Goal:* To make sure that everyone understands the group's task or assignment
2. Problem Identification	*Goal:* To make sure that everyone understands the nature of the problem and why it must be solved
3. Fact Finding and Problem Analysis	*Goal:* To collect and analyze facts, claims about causes and effects, and value judgments about the seriousness of the problem
4. Solution Criteria and Limitations	*Goal:* To develop realistic criteria for a solution, including an understanding of solution limitations, be they financial, institutional, practical, political, and/or legal in scope
5. Solution Suggestions	*Goal:* To generate a list of possible solutions
6. Solution Evaluation and Selection	*Goal:* To discuss the pros and cons of each suggestion in light of the agreed-upon criteria for a solution and to select the solution that rises to the top of the list
7. Solution Implementation	*Goal:* To plan the implementation of the decision, including an assignment of responsibilities

opinions, and value judgments about the seriousness and causes of the problem. At this point, group members may be tempted to skip the fourth step—solution criteria and limitations. But if the group has a limited budget or short time period for implementation, some proposed solutions may not be reasonable or even possible.

Once a group has analyzed a problem in light of realistic criteria, members can become fully involved in step five—suggesting as many solutions as possible. Then comes the hard part. The sixth step of the standard problem-solving agenda requires group members to discuss the pros and cons of each suggestion in light of their agreed-upon criteria for a solution. Some solutions will be rejected quickly, but others may be argued until one or more rise to the top of the list. Agreeing on a solution, however, is not the end of the process. At this point, the group has one more challenge: How should they implement the solution? Despite all the time a group spends trying to solve a problem, it may take even more time to organize the task of implementing the solution. Fortunately, groups that follow the seven steps in the standard problem-solving agenda will have a much better solution to implement.[12]

Working Agendas. In *Effective Meetings: The Complete Guide*, Clyde Burleson maintains that two of the most powerful tools in meeting management are agendas and minutes.[13] A **working agenda** is the outline of items to be discussed and the tasks to be accomplished during a discussion or meeting. A well-prepared working agenda can serve many purposes. First and foremost, it's a road map for the discussion and helps group members focus on their task. When used properly, a working agenda helps participants get ready for a meeting by telling them what to expect and even how to prepare. Most important of all, an agenda provides a detailed outline for a discussion, indicating what issues will be discussed and in what order. By following a well-constructed agenda, a group is much more likely to reach its goal. In fact, the 3M Management Team states that a "written agenda, distributed in advance, is the single best predictor of a successful meeting."[14] There are two basic types of working agendas, a business meeting agenda and a task-specific agenda. Each type has a specific purpose and a specific format.

Business meeting agendas follow a standardized format that lists, in a specified order, several items for discussion and/or decision. The meeting's chairperson or convener usually prepares and distributes the agenda to all members in advance. The following example shows a formal business meeting agenda. The notes in parentheses explain the functions of particular agenda items.

Business Meeting Agenda

    I. Call to order (The chairperson officially opens the meeting.)

    II. Approval of meeting agenda (Members may vote to add, subtract, or modify agenda items.)

    III. Approval of previous meeting's minutes

    IV. Officers' reports

    V. Committee reports

    VI. Unfinished business (issues and business from previous meetings)

    VII. New business (new issues and business to consider)

    VIII. Announcements

    IX. Adjournment

While business meeting agendas offer a general framework on which to build any formal meeting, a task-specific agenda helps a working group share complex information, discuss a problem, or make a decision about one particular issue.

Working groups use such agendas for project planning, decision making, and team meetings. Students in communication classes use this type of agenda to organize their in-class discussions. The following agenda could be used by a management team to discuss a company's Web site problem.

Task-Specific Agenda

    I. The current situation
       A. Current responsibility for Web site
       B. Existing Web policy and procedures
    II. The problem
       A. Poor quality of the Web site
       B. Out-of-date and erroneous information
    III. The possible causes
       A. Lack of authority and assigned responsibility
       B. Inadequate maintenance staff
       C. Poor design
    IV. Solution criteria
       A. Cost
       B. Speed of response
       C. Quality control of content
    V. Solutions
       A. Option A: Hire full-time Web master and assign support staff
       B. Option B: Contract Web design and maintenance to outside sources
       C. Other options
    VI. Decision
    VII. Implementation

Notice how this agenda includes every component of the standard problem-solving agenda. Ensuring that a group understands the nature of a problem as well as the criteria or limitations affecting its solution makes the successful implementation of an agreed-upon solution much more likely.

Taking Minutes.   The **minutes** of a meeting are the written record of a group's discussion and decisions. Instead of describing a group's discussion in detail, minutes include brief, clear statements that summarize the main ideas and actions. In many cases, an hour's worth of discussion may be recorded as only a few statements in the minutes. Despite their brevity, minutes must record decisions and task deadlines in the exact wording that the group uses, in order to avoid future disagreements and misunderstandings. In formal meetings, minutes are legal documents as well as part of the historical record of an organization.[15] If there is any question about what to include in the minutes or how to word an item, the person taking the minutes should ask the group for clarification.

Most important of all, the minutes of a meeting must be objective. They should neutrally report the facts and accurately represent all sides of a discussion. They should never include the minutes-taker's personal opinions.[16] Minutes should reflect the experience of the entire group, not just that of the person chosen to document it.

Credibility

When group members communicate with one another, their comments and behavior determine how credible they are in the eyes of other members. Chapter 11,

"Speaker Credibility and Ethics," notes that audiences believe and trust credible speakers more often. The same holds true for groups. Highly credible groups exhibit the three components of ethos we described in Chapter 11: competence, character, and charisma.

Competence.   *Competence* means being prepared, in advance, for a discussion or group assignment. You wouldn't make a presentation without preparing for it. Why, then, do some group members show up for meetings with little or no preparation? Participants in group discussions must be well prepared to deal with a host of predictable as well as unpredictable issues and people. Depending on the topic of a group discussion or meeting, preparation may involve reviewing documents, drafting a proposal, or doing library or online research. All of the research strategies and skills described in Chapter 7, "Supporting Material," can help you prepare for a group discussion or meeting.

Character.   Having *character* means making a commitment to act and accept responsibility before, during, and after a group discussion or meeting. Whereas competence requires planning, critical thinking, and time, character depends on your attitude toward and commitment to the group's goal and its members. Assuming appropriate task and maintenance roles is one way to demonstrate your support for and dedication to your group and its goal.

Charisma.   *Charisma* refers to your ability to communicate both your message (a product of your competence) and your commitment to the group (a product of your character). Being prepared and committed to your group may have little effect if you do not communicate effectively. Group members must be able to speak and listen during a discussion. At a more personal level, they need to be able to relate to the feelings and needs of others. And, of course, group members must be able to make effective presentations in, for, and with their group.

Performance

When we talked about performance in Chapter 13, "Performance and Practice," we noted that *perform* is a verb that has several meanings. Although it can refer to the way in which a speaker delivers a presentation, it also can mean to accomplish, carry out, or do something. The same applies to the way in which you perform during a group discussion. Certainly the vocal and physical delivery skills you would use in a presentation also have value in groups. Although you may not speak with as much volume, you still should speak clearly and with appropriate vocal emphasis. Although you may not gesture broadly and walk around a stage, your eye contact and gestures will still communicate a significant portion of your meaning.

Performing well in a group also means knowing how to deal with the inevitable obstacles that prevent a group from achieving its goal. Rarely do the biggest obstacles arise from technical problems—short deadlines, technical errors, or limited resources. Rather, the biggest problems in groups relate to their members' behavior. Next, we offer some suggestions for overcoming two common obstacles: difficult members and hidden agendas.

Difficult Members.   Although most groups can handle an occasional encounter with a difficult member, constant problems caused by such people can be disruptive. The negative group roles listed in Figure 21.4 on page 372 depict a few of the most common "people" problems encountered in groups.[17]

Several strategies can help a group deal with difficult people. A group can accept, confront, or even exclude a troublesome member. If the behavior won't

Figure 21.4   Negative Group Roles

> ▶ *The Aggressor* puts down other members, is sarcastic and critical, and takes credit for other people's work or ideas.
>
> ▶ *The Blocker* stands in the way of progress, presents uncompromising positions, and uses delay tactics to derail ideas or proposals.
>
> ▶ *The Dominator* prevents others from participating, interrupts others, and tries to manipulate others.
>
> ▶ *The Recognition Seeker* boasts about personal accomplishments, tries to be the center of attention, and pouts if he or she doesn't get enough attention.
>
> ▶ *The Clown* interjects inappropriate humor, seems more interested in goofing off than in working, and distracts the group from its task.
>
> ▶ *The Deserter* withdraws from the group, appears to be "above it all" by acting annoyed or bored with the discussion, and stops contributing.

detract from the group's ultimate success or if the member's positive contributions far outweigh the inconvenience or annoyance of putting up with the negative behavior, a group may tolerate the behavior and allow it to continue. For example, a "clown" may be disruptive on occasion but may also be the group's best report writer. A person who is often late for meetings may put in far more than her fair share of work during or after the meeting.

When it becomes impossible to accept or ignore behavior that threatens the effectiveness of the group and its members, the group must take action. At first, it may try to reason with the wayward member. Group members may even talk about him or her during the discussion: "If we disregard Barry's objections, I think the rest of us are ready to decide." In a moment of extreme frustration, one member may say what everyone else is thinking: "Darn it, Lisa. Why can't you let me finish a sentence?" Although such a confrontation may make everyone uncomfortable, it can put a stop to disruptive behavior.

Finally, when all else fails, a group may exclude a difficult member. A group can ignore what a disruptive member says or does. The member may be assigned a solo task to keep her or him away from everyone else. Finally, a group may expel a member to be rid of the troublemaker. Being asked to leave a group or being barred from participating is a humiliating experience that all but the most stubborn members would prefer to avoid.

Hidden Agendas.   Most groups have a shared goal or clear agenda. They know what they want and how they intend to go about achieving their goal. When, however, a member's private goals conflict with the group's goals, that member has a **hidden agenda.** Hidden agendas represent what people *really* want instead of what they *say* they want. When people's hidden agendas become more important than a group's agenda or goal, the situation can lead to frustration and failure.

For example, someone serving on a selection committee may dislike a job applicant for very personal reasons that he may not want to share with the group. Instead, he will look for ways to criticize the candidate for things that have nothing to do with his reason for disliking the person. Another member of the selection committee may be a good friend of the candidate but may not want anyone to know it. Instead, she will look for ways to heap praise on the candidate and will refute any suggested weaknesses. Both of these committee members' agendas bury the real issues and concerns and let pseudo-issues dominate the discussion.

Recognizing the existence of hidden agendas can make groups more effective. When group members refuse to compromise, or if group progress is unusually slow, look for hidden agendas. Groups can resolve some of the problems caused by hidden agendas through early agreement on the group's goal and careful planning of the discussion process. Rodney Napier and Matti Gershenfeld, experts in group behavior, suggest that up-front answers to three questions can help counteract the blocking power of hidden agendas:

1. What are the open and shared goals of the discussion?

2. Do any members have any up-front personal concerns or possible hidden goals?

3. What does each participant want from the discussion?[18]

Discussing these questions openly can be productive if a group recognizes the inevitability and purpose of hidden agendas. Hidden agendas don't always cause problems or prevent a group from achieving its goal. However, recognizing and understanding them can help explain why some members are not ready, willing, or able to participate in a group discussion.

Group Leadership

All groups need leadership. Without it, a group may be nothing more than a collection of people lacking the coordination to achieve a common goal. **Leadership,** the ability to make strategic decisions and use communication to mobilize group members toward achieving a shared goal,[19] is a talent and a skill. However, a leader and leadership are not the same thing. *Leader* may be the title given to a person with the most status in the group or to someone appointed or elected to a leadership position; *leadership* refers to the action that a leader takes to help group members achieve a goal.

Becoming a Leader

In some situations you may be hired for a job that gives you authority over others, or you may be promoted or elected to a leadership position. However, that doesn't make you a leader. Very often, the most effective leadership occurs when a leader emerges naturally from a group rather than being promoted, elected, or appointed. Although there is no foolproof method for becoming a leader, small group communication research suggests several strategies to follow that may improve your chances.[20] These include:

▶ *Talking early and often—and listening.* Generally, the person who speaks first and most often in a group is more likely to emerge as the group's leader. The quality of your contributions will become more significant after you become a leader.

▶ *Learning more—and sharing what you learn.* Leaders often emerge because they are experts. Groups want well-informed leaders; they don't need know-it-alls.

▶ *Offering your opinion—and welcoming constructive disagreement.* When groups are having trouble making decisions or solving problems, they appreciate someone who can offer good ideas and informed opinions. Aspiring leaders should also welcome constructive disagreement and discourage hostile confrontations.

373
Group Leadership

▶ *Volunteering for meaningful roles—and following through.* The person who is willing to take on and complete the tough tasks is more likely to become a leader. If, however, you volunteer for a task but then fail to follow through, you will only succeed in demonstrating why you shouldn't be the group's leader.

Once you become a leader, your ultimate success in the leadership position will depend on matching your leadership style to group needs while earning the members' confidence and trust.

Know Your Leadership Style

What kind of leader are you? Understanding the style you prefer to use as a leader has implications for the kinds of group situations in which you will be most successful.

Autocratic Leader.   An autocrat is a person who has a great deal of power and authority. **Autocratic leaders** maintain strict control over a group and its discussions. They know exactly what they want and demand compliance from group members. An autocratic leader tries to control the direction and outcome of a discussion, makes many of the group's decisions, gives orders, expects to be obeyed, and focuses on achieving results. Although this description may sound harsh, circumstances often call for such a leader. During a serious crisis there may not be enough time to do anything other than follow a leader's orders.

Democratic Leader.   Other leaders are more democratic in style. **Democratic leaders** share decision-making with the group, help members chart a plan of action, focus on group morale as well as on tasks, and give the entire group credit for its success. As much as you may want to be a democratic leader, the role may not suit your style. Democratic leaders spend a lot of time meeting with group members. In deferring to a group, democratic leaders don't always get what they want. In the long run, however, members of groups with democratic leaders are often more satisfied with their group experience, more loyal to their leader, and more productive in the long run.

Laissez-faire Leader.   The French phrase *laissez faire* means "to let people do as they choose." Thus, a **laissez-faire leader** lets the group take charge. In highly productive groups, a laissez-faire style may be a perfect match. The leader just gets out of the way of the group and lets it succeed. Unfortunately, laissez-faire leaders do little to help a group when it needs decisive leadership.

Assess your own leadership style. If you understand the ways in which your style affects the members of a group, you can better gauge whether you are a good match to lead a particular group and to direct its task.

Leadership and Trust

In their book *Learning to Lead*, Warren Bennis and Joan Goldsmith claim that highly effective leaders inspire trust by demonstrating vision, empathy, consistency, and integrity.[21]

▶ *Vision:* We trust leaders who involve group members in the creation of shared visions instill trust. Leaders who impose a vision may not be trusted to pursue the group's shared goal.

▶ *Empathy:* We trust leaders who have empathy for group members. Even when trusted leaders have points of view or backgrounds that differ from those of other group members, they try to understand how the group members see situations and how individual members feel about matters.

▶ *Consistency:* We trust consistent leaders who know where they stand. There is almost nothing as unsettling as a leader who has one position this week and another position next week, especially when each position requires group members to expend both time and energy in meeting the leader's expectations.

▶ *Integrity:* We trust moral and ethical leaders. Applying high moral and ethical standards to their own behavior empowers leaders to apply the same standards to everyone in a group.

Effective leaders must balance the requirements of the task with the social and emotional needs of group members. Achieving balanced leadership does not depend on developing a particular style. Rather, it depends on a leader's ability to analyze a situation and select appropriate leadership strategies to help mobilize a group to achieve its goal.

Summary

◆◆ What kind of speaking will I have to do in groups?

In addition to interacting as a member of small working groups, you may have to make presentations to group members during meetings, make presentations on behalf of a group to public audiences, or be part of a team presentation directed to a group of important decision makers.

◆◆ How do I prepare for a group presentation?

You use the presentation speaking principles described in this textbook while also making sure that you help your group achieve its shared goal. In the case of a team presentation, you should pay meticulous attention to individual presenters and to the team's presentation as a whole.

◆◆ What's the best way to organize group decision making?

Using the standard problem-solving agenda and using a working agenda are two ways to ensure that your group will make a better-informed and better-reasoned decision. Group members must understand the nature of an issue or problem that they are discussing before they make a decision or select a solution to a problem.

◆◆ How can I become a more effective group member?

Develop your credibility by being well prepared (competence), willing to make a commitment to the group and its task (character), and skilled at communicating your message and commitment (charisma).

◆◆ How can I become an effective group leader?

Adapt your leadership style to the situation and group. Effective leaders also demonstrate vision, empathy, consistency, and integrity as they help group members achieve their shared goals.

Key Terms

autocratic leader 374
brainstorming 366
democratic leader 374
forum 361
hidden agenda 372
laissez-faire leader 374
leadership 373

maintenance roles 366
minutes 370
panel discussion 361
public group 360
small group
    communication 360
standard problem-
    solving agenda 368

symposium 361
task roles 366
team presentation 362
working agenda 369
working groups 363

Notes

1. A significant portion of the material in this chapter is based on or selected from Isa N. Engleberg and Dianna R. Wynn, *Working in Groups: Communication Principles and Strategies,* 2nd ed. (Boston: Houghton Mifflin, 2000), by permission of the authors and publisher.
2. Engleberg and Wynn, pp. 4–6.
3. Carl E. Larson and Frank M. J. LaFasto, *TeamWork: What Must Go Right/What Can Go Wrong* (Newbury, CA: Sage, 1989), p. 27.
4. Thomas Leech, *How to Prepare, Stage, & Deliver Winning Presentations* (New York: AMACOM, 1993), p. 278.
5. Marjorie Brody, *Speaking Your Way to the Top: Making Powerful Business Presentations* (Boston: Allyn & Bacon, 1998), p. 81.
6. Leech, p. 288.
7. In 1948, K.D. Benne and P. Sheats published in the *Journal of Social Issues* an essay, "Functional Roles of Group Members," which labeled and described the functional roles they had observed in groups. The list in this textbook is based on a modification of the Benne and Sheats list. See Isa N. Engleberg and Dianna R. Wynn, *Working in Groups: Communication Principles and Strategies,* 2nd ed. (Boston: Houghton Mifflin, 2000), pp. 72–74.
8. Randy Y. Hirokawa, "Communication and Group Decision-Making Efficacy," in *Small Group Communication: Theory and Practice,* 7th ed., ed. R. S. Cathcart, L. A. Samovar, and L. D. Henman (Madison, WI: Brown & Benchmark, 1996), p. 108.
9. Randy Y. Hirokawa and Dirk R. Scheerhorn, "Communication in Faulty Group Decision-Making," in *Communication and Group Decision Making,* ed. R. Y. Hirokawa and M. S. Poole (Beverly Hills, CA: Sage, 1986), pp. 73–74.
10. John Dewey, *How We Think,* Revised and Expanded Edition (Boston: Houghton Mifflin, 1998).
11. Julia Wood, Gerald Phillips, and Douglas Pedersen, *Group Discussion: A Practical Guide to Participation and Leadership,* 2nd ed. (New York: Harper & Row, 1986).
12. Engleberg and Wynn, pp. 191–195.
13. Clyde W. Burleson, *Effective Meetings: The Complete Guide* (New York: Wiley, 1990), p. 25.
14. 3M Management Team with Jeannine Drew, *Mastering Meetings: Discovering the Hidden Potential of Effective Business Meetings* (New York: McGraw-Hill, 1994), p. 26.
15. Engleberg and Wynn, p. 306.
16. Burleson, p. 88.
17. Engleberg and Wynn, pp. 74–75. Engleberg and Wynn have modified a list of negative, self-centered roles that first appeared in K. D. Benne and P. Sheats, "Functional Roles of Group Members," *Journal of Social Issues* 4 (1948): 41–49.
18. Rodney W. Napier and Matti K. Gershenfeld, *Groups: Theory and Experience,* 6th ed. (Boston: Houghton Mifflin, 1999), p. 182. Napier and Gershenfeld's questions have been modified to suit the specific nature of a group discussion.
19. Engleberg and Wynn, p. 47.
20. Engleberg and Wynn, pp. 50–55.
21. Warren Bennis and Joan Goldsmith, *Learning to Lead: A Workbook on Becoming a Leader* (Reading, MA: Addison-Wesley, 1997), pp. 87–88.

Appendix A: Sample Presentations

Student Presentations

Real World, Real Speakers

Informative Presentation

The Sound of Muzak

JULIE BORCHARD, STUDENT

Julie Borchard, who now works as a public education specialist for the U.S. Treasury Department, developed the following informative presentation when she was still in college. She was looking for a topic that would provide new and interesting information about a subject familiar to everyone. She found such a topic in Muzak. In addition to conducting library research, Julie visited a large Muzak franchise, where she interviewed the company's president and collected a wide variety of supporting materials from its library and marketing department. Her use of language is powerful because it is clear and simple, as well as direct and vivid, through her use of personal pronouns and alliteration. In Chapter 9, we present the mind map Julie used to organize her presentation, as well as her complete outline.

Julie Borchard is a graduate of Prince George's Community College and the University of Iowa. (Editorial Note: Some of the information in The Sound of Muzak *has been updated to reflect the company's current status.)*

It's been referred to by its creators as "sonorous design" and "sound energy, attractively arranged." On the other hand, to much of the American public, this product conjures up images of "spineless melodies" with "vacant volumes of vapid violins." In short, it's Muzak. And what you're now hearing is an actual demonstration tape of Muzak. But Muzak isn't just any old song. According to its creators, it can reduce your stress, boredom, fatigue, and increase your productivity.

Julie began her presentation by turning on a demonstration tape that played excerpts of music from Muzak. After a few opening bars, she began speaking carefully chosen words that described people's positive and negative reactions to Muzak. This paragraph also introduced her first use of alliteration ("vacant volumes of vapid violins"), many more of which would follow.

---

*Ms. Anderson talks about "what it means to be Indian," as well as "why you should care about all this." By providing information about the differences between Indians and non-Indians, she fulfills both an informative and a persuasive purpose.

Muzak is actually a trademarked brand name for background music, much like Kleenex is for facial tissue. Although the background music industry is composed of several independent companies, according to Allen Smith, president of Muzak's Washington, D.C., franchise, "Muzak dominates the field by over 70 percent."

By understanding how pervasive Muzak is, how it originated, and how it supposedly lifts your spirits and productivity, you can become a little more enlightened next time it's playing your song.

Now, even if you don't care to lend Muzak a thoughtful ear, it may interest you to note that this $200 million a year business can be heard in over 250,000 locations in the United States and in 15 foreign countries. Each day, more than 80 million people listen to Muzak in one form or another. And amazingly, according to independent surveys reported in *USA Today,* at least 90 percent of these people actively like what they hear. A recent list of the 150 largest industrial corporations, retail companies, and commercial banks in this country showed that only seven were not plugged into Muzak somewhere within their organization. In short, you may be able to avoid the IRS, outwit the FBI, and even fool Mother Nature, but you can't escape the sweet strains of Muzak.

Before explaining how Muzak claims to put a smile on your face, energy in your work effort, and a song in your heart, let's step back in time to 1922 to see how this dynasty developed. Muzak was the creation of Major George O. Squier, Chief Signal Office of the U.S. army during World War I. Before the success of commercial radio, he patented a plan to use electric power lines for transmitting news, music, and advertising directly into homes—the same idea being used today for cable television. In the 1930s Muzak began piping in music—via telephone lines—to hotels and restaurants. But the big break came in 1937 when two British industrial psychologists, S. Wyatt and J. Langdon, released a study called "Fatigue and Boredom in Repetitive Work." Their studies contained evidence that music cheers up workers sapped by the monotony of the assembly line. Muzak had found its niche. According to Professor Russell Nye of the University of Southern Florida, by 1945, 75 percent of the war industry had Muzak in its plants. The U.S. Army claimed Muzak helped spur defense workers onto new heights of wartime productivity. And as postwar industry boomed, so did Muzak.

In slightly more recent history, a 1972 controlled experiment was conducted at a Manhattan Blue Cross and Blue Shield Company, where workers were processing an average of 90,000 Medicare claims by computer each week. A little mind-boggling, wouldn't you say? But nothing that Muzak couldn't handle. After Muzak was installed, Blue Cross reported a 100 percent jump in worker productivity. In a major cosmetics firm, Muzak is credited with decreasing errors by 16.4 percent and lowering absenteeism by 29.9 percent.

Thus, to many office and factory subscribers, Muzak is as beneficial to their work environment as good lighting and air conditioning. Now, if all this is true—and dozens of studies have verified these results—why don't companies just install their own stereo systems and play a local radio station or an old Lawrence Welk album? The reason they don't is that Muzak does something unique to its music, and thus does something unique to you. In order to appreciate how Muzak works, it's necessary to understand what happens to a worker on the job.

This paragraph represents a transition from one section to another. It was used to introduce the characteristics that explain Muzak's unique form and function.

Researchers have concluded that most of us arrive at work in the morning at a certain energy level, which drops in mid-morning and picks up with thoughts of lunch. This pattern is repeated in the afternoon. To counteract these sluggish periods, Muzak designed what they call "stimulus progression." Stimulus progression involves alternating 15 minutes of music with 15 minutes of silence to offset periods of fatigue in listeners. According to *USA Today*, Muzak's stimulus progression nudges workers during the 11 A.M. droop and perks them up in the later afternoon. These 15-minute segments are selected from a computerized music library housing more than 200,000 recorded melodies, each with an assigned "stimulus quotient" of between 0 and 7. These values are determined by such factors as the music's tempo and intensity. A typical music segment might start with a soothing song that would rate a 1 or 2, and end with a toe-tapping rendition of a popular tune rating of 6 or 7. Thus we can see how Muzak carries and maintains a worker's energy level throughout the course of the day.

The next two paragraphs covered the more technical sections of the presentation in which Julie explained the "stimulus progression" and "dulled" features of Muzak. By now, she had warmed up her audience, involved them, and could let her performance style and personal credibility (character, competence, and charisma) serve her and her purpose.

In addition to subjecting you to these mood-enhancing progressions, Muzak's music takes a distinct musical form. It is more than just adding violins. The arrangements are "dulled" by electronically chopping off the high and low tones in a recording. The sharp contrasts and other techniques used by composers and musicians to catch your attention are smoothed over so the music slips by with little notice. Janis Jarvis, a Muzak executive, explains: "If listeners say they like a song it means the presentation has been too distracting and it is taken out of circulation right away." All that matters to Muzak is that you experience increased energy, higher productivity, and improved morale. No wonder Muzak has so many fans—fans like AT&T, IBM, and Xerox, who use it in their paper processing divisions. It's also big in the federal bureaucracy where it not only soothes stressed file clerks but aids in drowning out CIA spy talk.

Beginning with the phrase "In addition to . . .," Julie made a smooth transition to her next key point. By using a quotation and brief examples, she explained how and why Muzak "dulls" its sound.

Muzak isn't restricted to the office, however. Restaurants employ it to drown out the buzzing of competing dinner table conversations, and supermarkets use Muzak to encourage shoppers to linger and buy on impulse. Even hospitals have introduced Muzak to their sterile corridors. Dr. Frank B. Flood, Chief of Cardiology at St. Joseph's Hospital in Yonkers, New York, reported that "recovery rates among coronary patients improved when the intensive-care unit was bathed in homogenized Beatles and Bacharach."

Julie provided additional examples in this section to extend the range and influence of Muzak.

However, not only clients are soothed by Muzak. John Mose, Professor of Industrial and Organizational Psychology at George Washington University, separates people into two categories—those who crave external stimulation, "like the people you see jogging around the streets with headphones," and those capable of entertaining themselves with private reverie. For the second group, Muzak can be an annoyance. And although *The New York Times* subscribes to Muzak, many of the editors turned it off in their area. One savings and loan officer told me, "Most managers don't like Muzak." Nor, studies conclude, do most people with relatively interesting jobs.

But the president of Muzak, "Bing" Muscio, has little difficulty defending the sound of his music. Muzak is used by more than 100,000 organizations. There are some 250 franchises around the world and a Muzak franchise can sell for as much as $2 million. But Mr. Muscio's plans extend even further.

> We know it can affect the heartbeat and the pulse rate. We know it can be effective in dealing with people under stress. Just think what it might mean if we could begin to substitute music for the incredible number of invasive drugs we put into our systems.

Imagine Vic Damone instead of Valium. Paul Simon instead of penicillin. Impossible? Well, given what you've just heard about Muzak's pervasiveness, development, and techniques, nothing should surprise you. Yes, the sound of Muzak is here to stay.

Informative Presentation

CliffsNotes

JOHN SULLIVAN, STUDENT

"For all the trust I put in CliffsNotes, I don't know one thing about them" was the sentence that inspired this informative presentation on CliffsNotes. John Sullivan, who now works for the American Association of Retired Persons as director of Information Technology, External Partner Solutions, translated his very personable speaking style into a delightful and interesting presentation. When he discovered that very little had been written about CliffsNotes, he phoned the company's headquarters in Lincoln, Nebraska, and interviewed the managing editor, Gary Carey. John Sullivan graduated from Prince George's Community College and the University of Maryland. (Editorial Note: Some of the information in CliffsNotes has been updated to reflect the company's current status.)

Eight o'clock Wednesday night. I have an English exam bright and early tomorrow morning. It's on Homer's *Iliad*. And I haven't read page one. I forego tonight's beer drinking and try to read. Eight forty-five. I'm only on page 12. Only 482 more to go. Nine thirty, it hits me. Like a rock. I'm not going to make it.

The way I see it I have three options. I can drop the class, cheat, or go ask Cliff. Because I'm not a quitter, and because I don't think cheating is the right thing to do, I borrow a copy of the CliffsNotes from a friend.

Yet for all the trust I put in CliffsNotes, I couldn't have told you one thing about them. Even though, according to no less a prestigious source as *People Mag-*

azine, over fifty million of these yellow and black pamphlets have been sold, you probably don't know too much about them either. After exhausting *People Magazine,* the *Nebraska Sunday World Herald Magazine,* and *Forbes Magazine,* I had to turn to Cliff himself. Yes, there is a Cliff behind CliffsNotes and no, his last name is not Notes. After two interviews with Gary Carey, the managing editor of CliffsNotes, it became clear to me that CliffsNotes was truly an American success story.

At one time, the notes were nothing more than simple plot summaries. But today, they offer the reader much more in terms of character analysis and literary criticism. To better appreciate this unique publishing phenomenon, it is necessary to trace the history of CliffsNotes, note some of the changes they have undergone, and finally, understand why Cliff and his notes get put down by teachers and praised by students.

Mr. Cliff Hillegass, owner and founder of CliffsNotes, literally started the business in the basement of his home as a mail-order company. As an employee of the Nebraska Book Company, he happened upon a Canadian publisher who had a full line of study guides. Upon returning home from a trip to Canada, he brought with him the notes to sixteen Shakespearian plays. He immediately made three thousand copies of each and sent them throughout the U.S. Book store managers were very receptive to the idea and put the Notes on sale.

When CliffsNotes first splashed onto the scene in 1958, 18,000 copies were sold. By 1960 sales had increased to 54,000. By the mid-60s, the magic number was two million and soon everyone wanted a piece of the action. By 1968, no less than thirteen other companies were in the market. Mr. Hillegass was confident through it all that none could overtake him. He told his sales staff not to worry. He said, "I believe most of our competition are large publishers for whom the study guides would never be more than one item in their line."

He couldn't have been more correct. By 1968, just two years later, only three competitors were left. And as competition went down, sales went up. By the mid-1980s, CliffsNotes was grossing over $4 million a year with over 200 titles in print. In 1988, CliffsNotes sold 5 million copies and brought in revenues of $11 million. By 1992, sales exceeded $13 million.

Even with 200-plus titles, it is the original 50 titles that constitute 70 percent of sales. Obviously certain titles have remained relatively constant through the years. In fact, Cliff keeps a top ten for every year. The following list represents the Top Ten in 1992. As I list them in descending order, try and think what might be number one. And, as a hint, keep in mind that most CliffsNotes are sold to high school juniors and seniors.

10. *To Kill a Mockingbird*
 9. *The Scarlet Letter*
 8. *Great Expectations*
 7. *A Tale of Two Cities*
 6. *Romeo and Juliet*
 5. *The Great Gatsby*
 4. *Julius Caesar*
 3. *Macbeth*
 2. *Huckleberry Finn*
 1. *Hamlet*

According to Mr. Carey, CliffsNotes first went intercontinental in 1983. In Europe they were first sold in France and Italy—in the land down under, in Australia and New Zealand. They entered the Chinese market in Beijing and Hangzhou. CliffsNotes are now sold in thirty-eight foreign countries.

What next, you may wonder. Well, in another interview with Mr. Carey, he told me that the next development will be the expansion of CliffsNotes into several new languages. In addition to Spanish, Portuguese, and Greek, CliffsNotes will soon be read right to left, in Hebrew. In 1998, IDG Books Worldwide, Inc., the people who publish the . . . *for Dummies* books, acquired the little company that Cliff built. CliffsNotes now takes on other challenges, such as how to prepare for the GMAT test, how to master computer technology, and how to manage your finances.

Yet despite international inroads and domestic success, CliffsNotes has its critics. Questions have been raised concerning the quality of the literary criticism within CliffsNotes, the claims of copyright infringements, and the academic ethics of using CliffsNotes in place of the real thing.

Mr. Hillegass, no writer himself, commissions the writing of the notes to scholars and teachers. At the college level, he uses Ph.D.'s or grad students who have experience with the work. For example, the notes on *The Iliad* were penned in 1986 by Dr. Elaine Strong Skill of the University of Oregon. The consulting editor was Dr. James L. Roberts from the University of Nebraska.

Cliff did find, however, that Ph.D.'s and grad students sometimes write above the level of high school students. As a result, many of the high school notes are written by secondary school teachers who use the work in question, year in and year out.

Cliff also has had his share of problems with publishers. In 1966 Random House filed suit against CliffsNotes for quoting too extensively from some of its copyrighted Faulkner titles. Both sides had lawyers poised and ready to do combat. It could have become a landmark case. Instead Cliff and some of the people from Random House solved their problems out of court.

Cliff believes that this was a turning point for both himself and his company. It forced them to take a fresh look at the notes. As a result, the classics were revamped to the point that they are now approximately 50 percent text summary and 50 percent critical analysis.

For example, the notes on *Macbeth,* Act I, scene 1, discuss the witches' famous lines "When shall we three meet again" and "In thunder, lightening, or in rain?" These lines take up only two lines in the play. The CliffsNotes analysis is many times that length, with commentary on such things as the dramatic creation of mood, the use of time as a key theme, and the language of paradox and prophecy.

Cliff no longer has problems with publishers, but his academic critics are still there. Certainly you have heard (or can easily imagine) teacher complaints that CliffsNotes allows students to avoid reading the original text.

In an article about CliffsNotes published in the *Nebraska Sunday World Herald Magazine,* one educator said, "Reading CliffsNotes is like letting someone else eat your dinner. They deprive students of the pleasure of discovering literature for themselves."

Mr. Carey countered such criticism in the same article by stating: "Teachers' apprehensions concerning CliffsNotes may have been well founded twenty years ago when they were simple plot summaries. But, today, they are mainly composites of mainstream literary criticism that are of little value to students who have not read the book."

An informal survey at Creighton University and the University of Nebraska has indicated that Mr. Carey may be correct. Where students' older brothers and sisters may have used CliffsNotes in place of the real thing, more than 80 percent of those students interviewed said they never used CliffsNotes by themselves. They only used them to accompany the reading of the required text. If anything, the CliffsNotes helped them discover the pleasure of reading the literature.

But then again . . . I did pass my exam, and I have yet to read *The Iliad*. And I'm sure there are plenty of students out there who have missed the delights of *Huckleberry Finn* or the pathos of *The Grapes of Wrath*. "To be or not to be," "Friends, Romans, Countrymen," and "Out out damn spot" very well could be the only lines of Shakespeare that some students know.

So the controversy continues. But at least you know that, unlike Ronald Mc-Donald, Cliff is a real person and he has not dodged the issues. He will go on explaining the finer points of his 200-plus titles. Because as long as teachers assign the classics of literature, the racks of yellow and black will continue to grow and prosper.

Persuasive Presentation

Victims of the Cure

ROSHARNA HAZEL, STUDENT

Victims of the Cure *is based on a persuasive presentation written by Rosharna Hazel, a student who was on the forensics team at Morgan State University in Baltimore, Maryland. The speech was coached by Dr. J. B. Bury and appeared in Winning Orations.[1] (Editorial Note: Victims of the Cure has been updated and edited for this textbook with permission from the Interstate Oratorical Association.)*

Rosharna's introduction opens with a metaphor ("Our bodies are miraculous machines"). She compares our bodies to cars in order to set up her Central Idea that going to the hospital for a "repair" may result in illness, injury, or even death. The organizational pattern is problem-cause-solution. After documenting the problem of iatrogenic injuries with a definition, descriptions, examples, quotations, tragic stories, and plenty of statistics, she discusses the causes and recommends several actions that can protect patients before, during, and after a hospital stay. Her conclusion returns to the body/machine metaphor she used in her introduction.

O ur bodies are miraculous machines. We fuel them, tune them up, and "exercise" them so they don't rust. If we notice a problem, we put them in the shop for repair, just like our cars. There, you may think, the similarity ends because most of us trust our medical system more than our mechanics. After all, mechanics make mistakes. "The clamp came off," your mechanic tells you. "Our mistake; we'll fix it for you free of charge."

But some things can't be fixed free of charge, and tragically, some things can't be fixed at all. According to a 1992 study from Harvard University's School of Public Health, "1.3 million Americans may suffer unexpected, disabling injuries in hospitals each year, and 198,000 may die as a result." A second Harvard study, reported in a 1999 *USA Today* article, notes that researchers estimate more than 120,000 preventable deaths and one million injuries that occur during the course of medical treatment each year. These statistics tell a sad tale: Going to the hospital for a cure may result in illness, injury, or even death.

In all likelihood, you or someone you love will need medical attention in a hospital. Before crossing that threshold, be prepared to combat the serious

---

[1] *Winning Orations* (Northfield, MN: The Interstate Oratorical Association, 1995).

problem known as iatrogenic injuries or adverse effect. To help you prepare for such combat, I want to take a few minutes to explain the scope and types of iatrogenic injuries and help you arm yourself with ways to protect yourself and others who may become victims of the cure.

Let's begin by looking at the scope and types of iatrogenic injuries. According to Dr. Lucien Leape, director of Harvard University's School of Public Health study, "medical injury is indeed a hidden epidemic." So hidden that all of you are probably unfamiliar with the term. The term iatrogenic means caused by medical treatment and is used especially for unintended infections or complications. So, the victim of an iatrogenic injury may have had successful surgery to correct a birth defect but later had to be treated for an iatrogenic infection caused by an improperly sterilized scalpel or a sponge left in the body.

Iatrogenic injuries are frequent and sometimes deadly. The Harvard study conducted in 1992 showed that nearly 155,000 Americans die in hospitals each year as the result of medical accidents such as drug overdoses and infected wounds. This is three times higher than the number of people killed each year in traffic accidents. Sadly, iatrogenic injuries are not a new problem. It is just well-hidden. Dr. Lucien Leape of Harvard University maintains that "hundreds of mistakes occur every day in a major hospital," and many of them go unreported, unrecognized, and uninvestigated.

How bad is this problem? According to a 1997 study, observers who spent nine months at a large urban hospital found errors occurred in the care of nearly half the patients. More than one out of six patients experienced a serious medical error that caused harm ranging from temporary disability to death. In 1997, Doug Cook, Florida's top healthcare regulator, called iatrogenic injuries a "ticking time bomb." "Patients are being harmed needlessly," he said "and no one is being held responsible."

The human cost of iatrogenic injuries is evident throughout the medical system. Let's look at some of the most frequent types. According to a report by the Center for Disease Control, there is a "strong rise in the incidence of hospital-induced infections in the last two decades. . . . The most common injury is wound infection, nearly 90 percent of which is preventable." The 1992 Harvard study reports that infections due to surgery account for 48 percent of iatrogenic injuries. Invasive technologies, such as urinary catheters, are another cause of hospital-induced infections. These technologies "are overused and often used only for the convenience of hospital staff," says Dr. Robert Haley at the University of Texas Southwestern Medical Center.

Next and perhaps more deadly is the incorrect dispensing of medication. *The American Association of Retired Persons Bulletin* tells the story of Martha, a woman who entered a New York hospital to receive one of her last chemotherapy treatments. She was beating cancer and looking forward to the end of her long struggle. Unfortunately, it was over much sooner than she thought. She received the wrong drug, which was far more powerful than what was prescribed. A few days later, she died.

In February of 1995, my hometown *Baltimore Sun* reported a serious case at an Annapolis hospital. Morphine was given to four newborns instead of the prescribed hepron solution. None of the babies died but medical experts fear that consequences may result later.

A third type of hospital-induced injury, but certainly not the last or least, is the performance of incompetent or incorrect surgery. *The Providence Sunday Journal* ran a three-part series in 1999 cataloguing numerous cases of iatrogenic injuries running the gamut from benign to fatal. Among the listed injuries were eight surgical patients requiring second operations to retrieve sponges, cotton, or metal instruments left inside their bodies. In one case, a fifty-six-year-old woman was admitted to a suburban hospital for a routine D&C. A hospital clerk incorrectly scheduled her for a full hysterectomy. "Everyone makes mistakes?" "We'll fix it free of charge?" Luckily, the error was recognized and the surgeon performed the correct operation. But others are not as fortunate. Willie King was scheduled to have his right leg amputated below the knee. But, according to *The Baltimore Sun,* February 20, 1995, . . . you guessed it. The surgeon incorrectly amputated his left leg instead. The irony of the situation could be humorous if it were not for the tragic, irreparable results. Dr. Robert Brook, a professor of Medicine at the University of California at Los Angeles, agrees. "It's really a joke to worry about the occasional plane that goes down when we have thousands of people who are killed in hospitals every year."

Despite these tragic stories and words of warning, there are several things you can do to make sure that you leave a hospital infection-free, that you are given and take the correct medication, that your surgeon and physicians are treating you correctly. Be alert and prepared to protect yourself before, during, and after a hospital stay.

First, do the obvious. Try to stay out of the hospital. Begin by getting a second opinion when a doctor recommends hospitalization or surgery. On two occasions, my own doctor, a man with a sense of humor, has recommended office treatments and procedures rather than a hospital stay. Hospitals, he says, are a dangerous place; you can get sick there.

Second, if you must be admitted to the hospital, be assertive. Ask questions and don't be afraid of hurting a nurse or doctor's feelings. When medication is prescribed, ask your doctor to spell the name, write it down, and write down the dosage you should be taking. When a nurse brings you the medication, make sure you're getting the right product and dose before you take it. And don't sign away your rights by allowing the hospital to use substitute surgeons or physicians without your knowledge. Let the medical students and first-time surgeons practice on someone else.

Third, if you don't think you are well enough to stand up for your own rights, ask a friend or family member to become a patient advocate. If you're not capable or confident enough to make demands or ask questions, they can do it for you. They can also monitor your treatment to make sure you're not fed something you're allergic to or forgotten in a hallway waiting for a test. Some enlightened hospitals are hiring and training their own patient advocates—employees who monitor your progress and speak for you when you can't.

Fourth, take the advice of the American Iatrogenic Association, an organization dedicated to promoting accountability for medical professionals and institutions. If you observe or experience bad practices at a hospital, file a complaint with the state's medical board. Although the American Iatrogenic Association's Web page acknowledges that the odds are small that your complaint will result in a physician being disciplined, it will alert future patients and the hospital of a doctor's bad practices. Documenting your experience might help prevent others from being injured or victimized. The best weapon against bad medicine is public disclosure and awareness.

Finally and most obviously, there is something you can't do but that others can do. It is the professional, ethical, and moral responsibility of the medical profession to expose and treat this "hidden epidemic." With one in twenty-five hospital patients suffering from iatrogenic injuries and with more than two-thirds of those injuries preventable, the authors of the Harvard study suggest that "it is time for the medical professional to become as concerned about safety as about a cure." Fortunately, a recent and well-publicized report on iatrogenic injuries by the Institute of Medicine has stepped up pressure to revamp a health care system that hides and ignores mistakes that kill tens of thousands of patients a year. The medical community knows about the problem and now, so do you. You can share this message and its advice with others. You also know that every one of us must become more vigilant and aggressive when it comes to our health care.

Several years ago there was a Ford commercial that asked, "Would you like your car fixed by someone named Earl or Bud?" I'd like to ask you a similar question. Do they become any more conscientious and risk-free because they are Drs. Earl and Bud? Take care of the most precious machine you own by demanding the same from your health care professionals as you would from your trusted mechanic. When it comes to your body and your health, not everything can be fixed free of charge.

Source: Rosharna Hazel, "Victims of the Cure." Reprinted by permission of the Interstate Oratorical Association.

Looking Through Our Window: The Value of Indian Culture

MARGE ANDERSON, CHIEF EXECUTIVE, MILLE LACS BAND OF OJIBWE

Ms. Anderson's March 5, 1999, presentation on the value of Indian culture reflects many of the strategies for generating interest discussed in Chapter 12. It was delivered to the First Friday Club of the Twin Cities and sponsored by the St. Thomas Alumni Association, St. Paul, Minnesota. As you read Ms. Anderson's words, analyze how she:

- *Accommodates the audience's attention span by limiting the length of her presentation.*
- *Adapts to the audience's level of motivation and listening habits.*
- *Enlists the power of language. Look, for example, at her second paragraph and note the simple words, short sentences, active voice, numerous personal pronouns, and repetition of the word* about.
- *Tells two stories — one real, one mythic.*

Ms. Anderson delivers a highly informative presentation that also persuades. By explaining "what it means to be Indian," "how my People experience the world," and "the ways in which our culture differs from yours," she uses interesting information to take a peripheral route to persuasion (see the Elaboration Likelihood Model of Persuasion in Chapter 18). Thus, she informs her audience about her culture and helps them understand why they "should care about all this." For example, note how she:

- *Relies on her competence, character, and charisma to enhance her credibility.*
- *Uses St. Thomas Aquinas and the story of Jacob wrestling with the angel as a theme and a form of mythos.*
- *Avoids statistics and a "laundry list" of Indian problems and complaints.*
- *Lists ways the Indians have "given back."*
- *Uses mythos as persuasive proof.*
- *Acknowledges and respects differences between Indians and non-Indians.*

Aniin. Thank you for inviting me here today. When I was asked to speak to you, I was told you are interested in hearing about the improvements we are making on the Mille Lacs Reservation, and about our investment of casino dollars back into our community through schools, health care facilities, and other services. And I do want to talk to you about these things, because they are tremendously important, and I am very proud of them.

But before I do, I want to take a few minutes to talk to you about something else, something I'm not asked about very often. I want to talk to you about what it means to be Indian. About how my People experience the world. About the fundamental way in which our culture differs from yours. And about why you should care about all this.

The differences between Indians and non-Indians have created a lot of controversy lately. Casinos, treaty rights, tribal sovereignty — these issues have stirred such anger and bitterness.

I believe the accusations against us are made out of ignorance. The vast majority of non-Indians do not understand how my People view the world, what we value, what motivates us.

They do not know these things for one simple reason: they've never heard us talk about them. For many years, the only stories that non-Indians heard about my People came from other non-Indians. As a result, the picture you got of us was fanciful, or distorted, or so shadowy, it hardly existed at all.

It's time for *Indian* voices to tell *Indian* stories.

Now, I'm sure at least a few of you are wondering, "Why do I need to hear these stories? Why should I care about what Indian People think, and feel, and believe?"

I think the most eloquent answer I can give you comes from the namesake of this university, St. Thomas Aquinas. St. Thomas wrote that dialogue is the struggle to learn from each other. This struggle, he said, is like Jacob wrestling the angel — it leaves one wounded and blessed at the same time.

Indian People know this struggle very well. The wounds we've suffered in our dialogue with non-Indians are well-documented; I don't need to give you a laundry list of complaints.

We also know some of the blessings of this struggle. As *American* Indians, we live in two worlds — ours, and yours. In the 500 years since you first came to our lands, we have struggled to learn how to take the best of what your culture has to offer in arts, science, technology and more, and then weave them into the fabric of our traditional ways.

But for non-Indians, the struggle is new. Now that our People have begun to achieve success, now that we are in business and in the headlines, you are starting to wrestle with understanding us.

Your wounds from this struggle are fresh, and the pain might make it hard for you to see beyond them. But if you try, you'll begin to see the blessings as well — the blessings of what a deepened knowledge of Indian culture can bring to you. I'd like to share a few of those blessings with you today.

Earlier I mentioned that there is a fundamental difference between the way Indians and non-Indians experience the world. This difference goes all the way back to the bible, and Genesis.

In Genesis, the first book of the Old Testament, God creates man in his own image. Then God says, "be fruitful, multiply, fill the earth and conquer it. Be masters of the fish and the sea, the birds of the heaven, and all living animals on the earth."

Masters. Conquer. Nothing, *nothing* could be further from the way Indian People view the world and our place in it. Here are the words of the great nineteenth century Chief Seattle:

"You are a part of the earth, and the earth is a part of you. You did not weave the web of life, you are merely a strand in it. *Whatever you do to the web, you do to yourself.*"

In our tradition, there is no mastery. There is no conquering. Instead, there is kinship among all creation — humans, animals, birds, plants, even rocks. We are all part of the sacred hoop of the world, and we must all live in harmony with each other if that hoop is to remain unbroken.

When you begin to see the world this way — through Indian eyes — you will begin to understand our view of land, and treaties, very differently. You will begin to understand that when we speak of Father Sun and Mother Earth, these are not new-age catchwords — they are very real terms of respect for very real beings.

And when you understand this, then you will understand that our fight for treaty rights is not just about hunting deer or catching fish. It is about teaching our children to honor Mother Earth and Father Sun. It is about teaching them to respectfully receive the gifts these loving parents offer us in return for the care we give them. And it is about teaching this generation and the generations yet to come about their place in the web of life. Our culture and the fish, our values and the deer, the lessons we learn and the rice we harvest — everything is tied together. You can no more separate one from the other than you can divide a person's spirit from his body.

When you understand how we view the world and our place in it, it's easy to appreciate why our casinos are so important to us. The reason we defend our businesses so fiercely isn't because we want to have something that others don't. The reason is because these businesses allow us to *give back* to others — to our People, our communities, and the Creator.

I'd like to take a minute and mention just a few of the ways we've already given back:

- We've opened new schools, new health care facilities, and new community centers where our children get a better education, where our Elders get better medical care, and where our families can gather to socialize and keep our traditions alive.
- We've built new ceremonial buildings, and new powwow and celebration grounds.
- We've renovated an elderly center, and plan to build three culturally sensitive assisted living facilities for our Elders.
- We've created programs to teach and preserve our language and cultural traditions.
- We've created a small Business Development Program to help Band members start their own businesses.
- We've created more than twenty-eight hundred jobs for Band members, people from other tribes, and non-Indians.
- We've spurred the development of more than one thousand jobs in other local businesses.
- We've generated more than fifty million dollars in federal taxes, and more than fifteen million dollars in state taxes through wages paid to employees.
- And we've given back more than two million dollars in charitable donations.

The list goes on and on. But rather than flood you with more numbers, I'll tell you a story that sums up how my People view business through the lens of our traditional values.

Last year, the Woodlands National Bank, which is owned and operated by the Mille Lacs Band, was approached by the city of Onamia and asked to forgive a mortgage on a building in the downtown area. The building had been abandoned and was an eyesore on Main Street. The city planned to renovate and sell the building, and return it to the tax rolls.

Although the Band would lose money by forgiving the mortgage, our business leaders could see the wisdom in improving the community. The opportunity to help our neighbors was an opportunity to strengthen the web of life. So we forgave the mortgage.

Now, I know this is not a decision everyone would agree with. Some people feel that in business, you have to look out for number one. But my People feel that in business — and in life — you have to look out for *every* one.

And this, I believe, is one of the blessings that Indian culture has to offer you and other non-Indians. We have a different perspective on so many things, from caring for the environment, to healing the body, mind and soul.

But if our culture disappears, if the Indian ways are swallowed up by the dominant American culture, no one will be able to learn from them. Not Indian children. Not your children. No one. All that knowledge, all that wisdom, will be lost forever.

The struggle of dialogue will be over. Yes, there will be no more wounds. But there will also be no more blessings.

There is still so much we have to learn from each other, and we have already wasted so much time. Our world grows smaller every day. And every day, more of our unsettling, surprising, wonderful differences vanish. And when that happens, part of each of us vanishes, too.

I'd like to end with one of my favorite stories. It's a funny little story about Indians and non-Indians, but its message is serious: you can see something differently if you are willing to learn from those around you.

This is the story: Years ago, white settlers came to this area and built the first European-style homes. When Indian People walked by these homes and saw see-through things in the walls, they looked through them to see what the strangers inside were doing. The settlers were shocked, but it makes sense when you think about it: windows are made to be looked through from both sides.

Since then, my People have spent many years looking at the world through your window. I hope today I've given you a reason to look at it through ours.

Mii gwetch.

Source: Reprinted with the permissions of Chief Executive Marge Anderson and the Mille Lacs Band of Ojibwe Indians.

Source: Reprinted with the permissions of Chief Executive Marge Anderson and the Mille Lacs Band of Ojibwe Indians.

Special Presentation

Commencement Address

VIVIAN HOBBS, ATTORNEY

Vivian Hobbs, an alumnus of Prince George's Community College, was invited to be the 1991 Commencement Speaker. In 1972, at the age of seventeen, Ms. Hobbs was involved in an automobile accident that left her paralyzed from the neck down. Her doctors told her that she would never be able to move, talk, or breathe without a respirator. Since this pronouncement, Vivian Hobbs became a prominent Washington attorney and partner in the law firm of Arnold and Porter and raised three children. She passed away in 1997 from complications related to her disability.

Ms. Hobbs's commencement address was a moving testament to her college. Not only was she a celebrated alumnus, her presentation earned her enormous credibility with the audience. Her competence was unquestioned, her character was unassailable, and her quiet, heartfelt delivery bestowed on her an inspiring form of charisma.

Good evening. My name is Vivian Hobbs. I can't begin to tell you how honored I am to have been asked to speak at this commencement ceremony.

Prince George's Community College has played a very special part in my life and holds a very special place in my heart.

I was in an automobile accident just after high school, which left me in a wheelchair. I was trying to deal with that, a new marriage, and other personal and financial problems, not the least of which was an uncertainly about what I could do, about the extent of my own potential.

Even then, in 1975, Prince George's Community College took a real leadership position in serving the community and meeting the special needs of each student. In my case, this did not stop with meeting the basic obligation of making the campus accessible to a wheelchair. Professors helped me study and gave me oral exams because I cannot use my hands to write. New rules and procedures were developed to help me get through lab courses. Many other adjustments were made to help me succeed.

But, most of all, I received support and encouragement from every staff member, every member of the administration, and every one of my professors. They made me feel that my problems were their problems—that their mission was to help me and all of this college's students to realize our full potential, whatever the obstacles.

For example, my biology professor spent a great deal of time and patience helping me to get slides just right under a microscope so that I could see various organisms and processes. My chemistry professor showed equal patience in helping me through chemistry lab experiments. My history professor allowed me to tape, rather than to write, my exams. This required him to spend much longer grading my examinations, because it takes longer to listen to a tape than to read a written exam. Other professors let me take exams orally, instead of having to write them. And some professors even allowed me to take my exams home on an honor system.

Ultimately, I left Prince George's Community College with a renewed confidence in myself, with a stronger sense of purpose, and with a greater awareness of my own potential. This has helped hold me together as I have gone on in life through less supportive institutions and tougher problems, both personal and in my career.

I finished my Bachelor of Science degree at the University of Maryland. I went to Georgetown Law Center, and I'm now a partner at the biggest and, I think, the best law firm in Washington, D.C.

Prince George's Community College was the first and most important step in my career and in my adult life. I succeeded largely because of the support and help I got here. This college provides all kinds of special help and support for all kinds of special problems. So much so, that it's not even special. Here it's just routine. Child care for students who are parents, financial aid to those who need it, evening and weekend classes for those who work, developmental classes for those who may not have been given the academic background they need, counseling and career planning as well as tutorial programs for those who need extra guidance and assistance.

I feel that I have a lot in common with many of you. Many of you have had to struggle with other problems and obligations while earning your degree. Many of you have families—spouses or children—who take up a lot of your time. You may have had to work while going to college to support yourself or your family. Many of you have had to go to school at night after working long, hard days, or have had to come on weekends or give up time with your family. You may have found it difficult to afford the time, money, and energy that has been required of you.

Some of you have started your college careers with doubts about the extent of your own potential. Like me, many of you have come from families where no one else has had a college degree.

But you hung in there. You kept working and learning and growing, because you knew you deserved the better life that this degree can give. Some of you will leave here for careers in nursing, computer technology, accounting, business, education, engineering, law enforcement or other professions or careers. Others will transfer to four-year colleges or universities. Still others will leave the job market to raise families. But, wherever you choose to go from here, you will take a new, stronger sense of your own value and potential.

Through your work and success at Prince George's Community College, you have set yourselves apart from the vast majority of people who just didn't have the right stuff to get this far. Many of you have done this despite tremendous obstacles and at great personal cost. You have proved that you do have the right stuff. From here, you can, and will go on to do anything, to make and live your lives according to your own dreams.

I hope that you will remember Prince George's Community College. You will go on to other endeavors and higher achievements. Many of you will go on to earn degrees at more prestigious colleges and universities. But Prince George's Community College is the place where we all got our start—the place where we changed our lives and goals forever.

I am very honored and humbled to have been asked to share this celebration with each of you, in this new beginning. And I do honor each and every one of you. Thank you.

Drunk, Dangerous, and Deadly

Herb Simpson, Ph.D., President and CEO, Traffic Injury Research Foundation

Dr. Simpson's persuasive presentation, delivered to the American Legislative Exchange Council's annual meeting on August 12, 1999, resembles some of the better student presentations we have heard about drunk driving. It is well organized in a problem-cause-solution organizational format. Part of what makes Dr. Simpson's talk different, however, is that he does not document every piece of supporting material he uses. As president and CEO of the Traffic Injury Research Foundation, he relies on his authority and expertise to make claims about the problem, its causes, and potential solutions. The presentation is heavy with statistics, but that is what a research foundation provides to the public and policy makers. Yet by including four brief stories, he puts a human face on the numbers. His language is direct and his presentation of statistics is clear. Dr. Simpson openly acknowledges that some of his foundation's research has been supported by grants from the Anheuser-Busch Corporation. His introduction begins with a blunt statement of the problem rather than leading up to his Central Idea with an attention-getting device. His conclusion is just as blunt.

Despite the impressive gains that have been made in the fight against drunk driving, a dangerous minority, called the Hard Core, keeps bucking the trend. This group repeatedly takes to the road after consuming large amounts of alcohol, placing themselves and others at very great risk. They often have blood alcohol concentrations (BACS) that are double or triple the legal limit, causing a majority of drinking and driving deaths.

As a result, they continue to make headlines in the most regrettable ways: A Florida man was convicted of driving under the influence (DUI) manslaughter in the deaths of five people. He had a BAC of .25—a level that is two and a half times the legal limit in most states. His license had been suspended and even revoked in three states for prior drinking and driving offenses.

Or consider the case of a North Carolina man who was recently convicted of second-degree murder in the death of a young woman who was a sophomore in college and also the mother of a two-year-old. He had a BAC of .26 and had two previous drunk driving convictions.

In another tragic case, a thirty-one-year old Tennessee woman and her unborn child were killed when a drunk driver ran his truck up on a curb, pinning the woman against a light pole. The man driving the car had a BAC of .28. His license had already been revoked because of two previous drunk driving convictions.

Unfortunately, these are not rare, isolated events but all too familiar. However, it is only in recent years that hard core drinking drivers have received serious attention by policy makers. Contemporary focus on the problem began in the U.S. at the beginning of this decade with the publication of what has become an internationally acclaimed study entitled *The Hard Core Drinking Driver.* Conducted by the Traffic Injury Research Foundation (TIRF), under a grant from Anheuser-Busch, this research documented the extent of the problems caused by this group and identified it as a target for special attention by policy leaders.

Several years later, TIRF, again with support from Anheuser-Busch, provided a comprehensive review of effective and promising programs and policies for dealing with hard core drinking drivers. This study urged lawmakers to better enforce laws already on the books and use proven methods to deal with these troublemakers.

Since then, many organizations, both public and private, have joined the fight in dealing with these extremely dangerous drivers. Recognition is growing, not only of the severe threat they pose to public safety but the challenge they present. This is underscored by the fact that they have numerous convictions. This is a double-edged sword from a public policy standpoint. The system is obviously having some success because hard core drinking drivers keep getting caught; at the same time, the system is failing because the same offenders are frequently caught again and again. Obviously, they are not receptive to traditional appeals and are even resistant to changing their behavior in the face of usual sanctions. New approaches are needed.

In part, the challenge presented by this group lies in identifying them. Studies have shown that the hard core represents less than one percent of all night-time drivers. Being such a small group, it can be very challenging to target them through traditional enforcement.

However, this small group is a significant threat, causing as many as 65 percent of the serious collisions. The major reason for this is that they drive with very high BACS, which has a profound effect on their risk of being in a serious traffic accident. A driver with a BAC of .20 or higher is 460 times more likely to be involved in a fatal crash than a driver with no alcohol, or very low amounts of alcohol, in their system.

But as indicated earlier, the hard core does fall into the arms of the criminal justice system with great regularity, so it is imperative that the most be made of these opportunities to address them with effective policies. And, research shows that that there are very real limits to the ability of stiffer monetary fines and longer jail sentences to induce changes in their drinking and driving behavior. Fortunately, there is an emerging consensus that the strategic application of a diversity of proven measures can have a significant positive impact. And, there are proven measures at our disposal. Let me briefly describe a few of them.

At the top of the list is rehabilitation. Because so many of the hard core are alcohol abusers or dependent—up to 75 percent of second time offenders—there is a need to get offenders into treatment. To ensure that officials prescribe the most appropriate treatment for offenders, a reliable screening and assessment technique should be used to identify the nature and severity of their problems.

And, treatment works. It has a significant impact on re-offense rates and alcohol-related crashes. But a note of caution is warranted. Because it is a long-term process and by no means perfectly effective, treatment should be provided in combination with other sanctions and not used as a substitute for, or a means to circumvent them.

One of those other sanctions is license suspension. It has been one of the most popular and effective sanctions for drunk driving. However, many offenders are not deterred by the loss of their license; up to 75 percent drive anyway. And, some continue to drive and drink. This behavior can be remarkably persistent. For example, a motorist in New York City was recently stopped making an illegal U-turn. During this, the police discovered the driver was the "phantom motorist" whose license had been suspended 633 times since 1990. This motorist had eluded capture for four years, and it took the computer nearly two hours to generate a written report of the motorist's driving record.

For such hard core offenders, the next logical step is to deny them access to their vehicle, or to ensure that if they do drive, they have not been drinking. Actions against the vehicle have been gaining popularity in the past few years.

In general, these vehicle-based measures are designed to limit the mobility of the offender. At one end of the spectrum is the alcohol-ignition interlock, a device that still allows offenders and their family to use the vehicle but only if they are sober. At the other end of the spectrum is vehicle immobilization, which denies the offender and family access to the vehicle.

The ignition interlock is a small breath test device installed in the vehicle to measure the driver's BAC. The driver is required to provide a zero or low-BAC breath sample to operate the vehicle. Technological improvements in these devices over the past several decades prevent virtually all of the known ways to "fool" the system.

Ignition interlocks work. Evaluation studies have consistently demonstrated that interlocks are effective—the re-arrest rate among offenders with an interlock device has been found to be as much as 75 percent lower than among those without the device.

Obviously, with an interlock on the vehicle, family members and the offender can drive. But some vehicle sanctions allow only the family to use it, not the offender. These typically involve special license plates, such as blaze-orange or zebra-striped, primarily to alert police to the fact that this is the vehicle of a convicted drunk driver. Ideally, the legislation that permits the use of these plates empowers the police to stop such a vehicle and verify that the drive is not the offender.

The most severe form of vehicle-based sanctions includes immobilization or impoundment, and forfeiture. Depending on the jurisdiction, the vehicle can be seized by the police if the driver is under suspension for any reason, or for an alcohol-related offense, or is driving under the influence of alcohol. The vehicle is then either placed in a secure compound for a period of usually one or two months or is immobilized with a device such as a "club" on the steering wheel, often in the offender's driveway.

There is solid evidence that these programs have a significant impact on the prevalence of driving while under suspension as well as on alcohol-related collisions. In Canada, a federally funded study by TIRF showed there was a 12 percent decrease in drunk driving fatalities when vehicles were impounded, along with a 50 percent decrease in DUI offenses. Most importantly, there was a 27 percent decrease in repeat driving while suspended offenses, a category that many hard core drinking drivers all fall into. Evaluations of programs in California, Ohio and Minnesota have also produced positive results.

The toughest vehicle sanction program was recently introduced in New York City. The ordinance began making headlines because the vehicle of anyone stopped for drunk driving, most of whom do not fit the hard core drunk driving descriptions, was seized and forfeited. This very aggressive approach has not yet been evaluated but the attention the law has gathered, from both fans and critics, underscores an important lesson we should not forget in dealing with this problem. Too frequently countermeasures are embraced as the silver bullet, magic elixir or panacea for the problem. If we have learned one lesson in the long struggle to deal with this problem, it is that there is no single solution. It requires a diversity of complementary measures. License suspension became for many "the solution" of the 80s; hopefully, vehicle forfeiture will not become "the solution" of the 90s. Both work but they are only part of the puzzle.

Drinking and driving declined dramatically during the 1980s and has continued to show some, albeit more modest, progress in the 90s. Many have argued that we've already achieved the easy gains because responsible, social drinkers have gotten the message. Hard core drinking drivers have not. Many do not care about the threat they pose to others, or even about being punished. They are the single largest challenge in the continuing battle against impaired driving and must be a priority if further meaningful progress is to be made. A key to that progress is the widespread use of effective measures for dealing with hard core drinking drivers.

Source: Reprinted by permission of Dr. Herb Simpson, President & Ceo, Traffic Injury Research Foundation

1996 Democratic National Convention

VICE PRESIDENT AL GORE

Albert Gore's address at the Democratic National Convention (August 28, 1996) was a make-or-break speech. Given his reputation as a dull speaker, he needed to demonstrate his ability to rouse the audience on behalf of President Clinton's candidacy for a second term. He also had to demonstrate that he had the "right stuff" to become Clinton's successor. Very few audience members expected the speech to be energizing or emotional. Gore showed them otherwise. By beginning with self-effacing humor, moving on to a call-and-response refrain ("But we won't let them") that involved audience members, and ending with the highly personal and poignant story about his sister's cancer death, Gore became a contender. Ironically, although this emotional account of his sister's death from lung cancer brought tears to the eyes of his audience, the Republicans and media were quick to point out that Gore continued to favor (and his family continued to profit from) tobacco farming price supports long after he claimed that the fight against tobacco companies was a moral crusade.

Thank you very much. Thank you. Thank you very much. Thank you very much, ladies and gentlemen. Thank you very much.

Four years ago, four years ago, you gave me your nomination to be vice president. And tonight I want to say, from the bottom of my heart: Thank you for the opportunity to serve our country, and for the privilege of working beside a president who has done so much to lift the lives of America's families.

Tradition holds that this speech be delivered tomorrow night. But President Clinton asked me to speak tonight. And you can probably guess the reason why.

My reputation for excitement.

I'd—this is some crowd. I've been watching you doing that macarena on television. And if I could have your silence, I would like to demonstrate for you the Al Gore version of the macarena.

Would you like to see it again?

Four years ago, America faced a set of problems our leaders had lost the courage to confront. Our nation was not creating jobs. Our jobs were not increasing pay. Our people were running in place. Our nation was falling behind.

Four years later, we meet in this great city of Chicago, the place Carl Sandburg called the "city of the big shoulders . . . with lifted head so proud to be alive . . . and strong." Four years later, Democrats are proud. Our hopes are alive. And America is strong.

Bill Clinton's leadership is paying off. How can you tell? By what the American people have achieved themselves. Just look at what all of us have created together these last four years:

Ten million new jobs; a deficit cut in half; a smaller, leaner re-invented government working better and costing less; unemployment and inflation both down; record exports; wages on the rise; an economy moving forward; empowerment zones bringing neighborhoods back to life; classrooms connected to the information superhighway; communities given the right to know about environmental dangers; toxic wastes being cleaned up; rivers and lakes reclaimed and thriving; an America not just better off, but better.

And our strength at home has led to renewed respect abroad, nuclear missiles no longer targeted at our cities, democracy replacing tyranny in Haiti, peace replacing war in Bosnia, leadership toward reconciliation in Northern Ireland and the Middle East. While our nation has made great progress, we have much more to do, and we are here to declare that the man who can help us fashion this better future is President Bill Clinton.

The president's opponent, Senator Bob Dole, is a good and decent man. We honor his service to America and his personal courage in fighting back from injuries sustained in battle. Though we disagree with his ideas, only the unknowing would deny him the respect he deserves.

But make no mistake: there is a profound difference in outlook between the president and the man who seeks his office. In his speech from San Diego, Senator Dole offered himself as a bridge to the past. Tonight, Bill Clinton and I offer ourselves as a bridge to the future.

Ralph Waldo Emerson once said, "Humanity is divided between the past and the future . . . between memory and hope." It is easy to understand the nostalgic appeal of the party of memory and the men who lead it. But let there be no doubt: the future lies with the party of hope and the man from Hope who leads it.

We Americans write our own history. And the chapters of which we're proudest are the ones where we had the courage to change. Time and again, Americans have seen the need for change, and have taken the initiative to bring that change to life. But always with a struggle. Always with opponents. Senator Dole was there. We remember. We remember that he voted against the creation of Medicare, against the creation of Medicaid, against the Clean Air Act, against Head Start, against the Peace Corps in the '60s and AmeriCorps in the '90s. He even voted against the funds to send a man to the moon.

If he's the most optimistic man in America, I'd hate to see the pessimists.

That pessimistic view of America is very different from ours. And we saw it in the budget that Senator Dole and Speaker Gingrich tried to slip past the American people last fall. Their budget doubled Medicare premiums while slashing benefits, wiped out nursing home care for seniors, ended the guarantee of decent medical care for disabled children, rolled back protections for our air and water, increased the cost of college while making student loans harder to get, terminated anti-drug programs for our schools, and raised taxes on the hardest-hit working families.

They passed their reckless plan, and then demanded that President Clinton sign it. They shut the government down. Twice. Because they thought Bill Clinton would buckle under the pressure, wither in the face of their attacks, cave in to their demands.

But they did not know the true measure of this man. He never flinched or wavered. He never stooped to their level. And, of course, he never attacked his opponent's wife.

Let me tell you what Bill Clinton did do. Bill Clinton took Speaker Newt Gingrich and Senator Bob Dole into the Oval Office. I was there. I remember. And he said, President Clinton said: "As long as I occupy this office, you will never enact this plan. Because as long as I am president, I won't let you."

That's why they want to replace Bill Clinton. But we won't let them.

They want someone in that Oval Office who will rubber-stamp their plan. That's why they want to replace Bill Clinton. But we won't let them.

They want a president who will appoint the next three justices of the Supreme Court so they can control all three branches of government and take away a woman's right to choose. That's why they want to replace Bill Clinton. But we won't let them.

They want to give health insurance ripoff artists a license to change Medicare, to let this program for our seniors wither on the vine. That's why they want to replace Bill Clinton. But we won't let them.

They want to outlaw all affirmative action and many other measures to reach out to those who want to reach up. That's why they want to replace Bill Clinton. But we won't let them.

They want to cut education and undermine our schools—put down teachers instead of lifting up students. That's why they want to replace Bill Clinton. But we won't let them.

They want to give free reign to lobbyists for the biggest polluters in America to rewrite our environmental laws, allowing more poison in our air and water, and then auction off our natural wonders piece by piece. That's why they want to replace Bill Clinton. But we won't let them.

We will not; we cannot; we must not let them.

And you know what? We can make Bill Clinton's job a lot easier by making Dick Gephardt speaker of the House and Tom Daschle Senate majority leader.

You can judge a president by the enemies he is willing to make. You know that someone who's been attacked as much as Bill Clinton is doing something right. America has never changed without a president willing to confront the status quo and take on the forces of greed and indifference. It has changed only when we have had a president with the vision to tackle the real problems that really matter to our families. That's what this president has done.

Because families don't eat or breathe political slogans. They thrive or fail according to how they handle each day's challenges.

When your alarm goes off in the morning, if your family is like mine, everybody starts rushing around, getting ready for school and work. When one of your children reaches for cereal and fruit, you shouldn't have to worry about whether the food is safe. That's why just this month, President Clinton brought farmers and environmentalists together and signed an historic law to keep dangerous pesticides off our fruits and vegetables.

When you pour a glass of water for each member of the family at the table, you shouldn't have to wonder: "Should I buy bottled water? We really can't afford it." That's why President Clinton signed the Safe Drinking Water Act, to give families more peace of mind that their water will be pure and safe.

When you notice your child staring at a television set and watching violent and explicit images he or she is not old enough to handle, you shouldn't be forced to choose between throwing the TV out of the house and monitoring every second that child watches.

That is why, last month, the president persuaded the broadcasters to agree to air three hours of quality children's educational programming each week. And that's why we're giving parents a new tool, the V-chip, to keep violent and explicit programming out of their homes and away from their children. When our children turn on the TV, let them learn how to read and add and spell and think, not how to kill.

If one of your children has an operation or some other serious health problem, you shouldn't have to choose between taking care of that child or keeping your job. That is why Bill Clinton fought to pass the Family and Medical Leave Act—so parents can get time off work to care for a sick child, bond with a newborn, or tend to an aging relative.

When your children do well in school and head toward graduation, they shouldn't have to wonder about whether their family can afford to send them to college. That's why President Clinton expanded scholarships, student loans, and Pell Grants. And that's why he wants to give a tax credit to pay $1,500 per year for tuition to make college more affordable for every single American family.

If the business where you work is changing in ways that cause you to think about getting a different kind of job, you ought to be able to get the training and education you need to learn new skills and plan for the future. That's why President Clinton is proposing a tax credit so if you go to a community college, you can take every single dollar you pay right off your taxes. If you take responsibility, President Clinton will give you the opportunity to learn.

And if you see an opportunity to move to a better job, you shouldn't feel forced to stay in your old job just because that's the only way you can keep your health insurance. Even if you have some pre-existing condition, you ought be able to change jobs and not loose your coverage. That is why President Clinton passed the Kennedy-Kassebaum law.

Americans shouldn't have to feel imprisoned in their homes because of crime. We have a right to streets and neighborhoods that are safe. That is why President Clinton fought for the Brady Bill and the assault weapons ban. And that is why President Clinton is putting 100,000 new community police officers on our streets and sidewalks.

These problems are real, and they must be addressed. It's been a long time since we've had a president so in tune with the issues that touch the real lives of America's families. It's been a long time since we've had a president willing to fight the powerful forces that often seem to stand in the way.

Some of the most powerful forces that do the most harm are often hard to see and even harder to understand. When I was a child, my family was attacked by an invisible force that was then considered harmless. My sister Nancy was older than me. There were only the two of us and I loved her more than life itself. She started smoking when she was thirteen years old. The connection between smoking and lung cancer had not yet been established but years later the cigarettes had taken their toll.

It hurt very badly to watch her savaged by that terrible disease. Her husband, Frank, and all of us who loved her so much, tried to get her to stop smoking. Of course she should have, but she couldn't.

When she was forty-five years old, she had a lung removed. A year later, the disease had come back and she returned to the hospital. We all took turns staying with her. One day I was called to come quickly because things had taken a turn for the worse.

By then, her pain was nearly unbearable, and as a result, they used very powerful painkillers. And eventually it got so bad they had to use such heavy doses that she could barely retain consciousness. We sometimes didn't know if she could hear what we were saying or recognize us.

But when I responded to that call and walked into the hospital room that day, as soon as I turned the corner—someone said, "Al's here"—she looked up, and from out of that haze her eyes focused intensely right at me. She couldn't speak, but I felt clearly I knew she was forming a question: "Do you bring me hope?"

All of us had tried to find whatever new treatment or new approach might help, but all I could do was to say back to her with all the gentleness in my heart, "I love you." And then I knelt by her bed and held her hand. And in a very short time her breathing became labored and then she breathed her last breath.

Tomorrow morning another thirteen-year-old girl will start smoking. I love her, too. Three thousand young people in America will start smoking tomorrow. One thousand of them will die a death not unlike my sister's, and that is why, until I draw my last breath, I will pour my heart and soul into the cause of protecting our children from the dangers of smoking.

And that is also why I was intensely proud last week when President Clinton stood up for American families by standing up to tobacco advertising aimed at getting our children addicted. He proposed the first-ever comprehensive plan to protect children from smoking; to ban tobacco advertising aimed at our children, and to ban it for good.

It took courage for Bill Clinton to take on the tobacco companies. I promise you it is no accident that no president has ever been willing to do it before.

But coming from him, that's no surprise. I've seen him get up day after day and make the toughest decisions, and always by asking, "What is right for the American people?"

As a result, with Bill Clinton's leadership, our nation is moving forward with confidence. Americans don't believe our best days are behind us. We see better days ahead because we have the courage to meet our challenges and protect our values. And now, once again, in pursuit of the American dream, we are crossing the bridge to the future.

By shepherding, guiding and protecting our children's souls, we build a better America. The American spirit lives within that child. The child will grow up to believe in it, to add new vision to it.

It's not a vision of a distant future, nor of a remote past, but a constant accumulation of our best instincts and our noblest aspirations. From the spirit of our Founding Fathers, to the courage of today's families, it is one vision. It is an American vision. It is the vision of President Bill Clinton.

Thank you, God bless you, and God bless America.

Appendix B: National Communication Association Credo for Ethical Communication

(approved by the NCA Legislative Council in 1999)

Questions of right and wrong arise whenever people communicate. Ethical communication is fundamental to responsible thinking, decision making, and the development of relationships and communities within and across contexts, cultures, channels, and media. Moreover, ethical communication enhances human worth and dignity by fostering truthfulness, fairness, responsibility, personal integrity, and respect for self and others. We believe that unethical communication threatens the quality of all communication and consequently the well-being of individuals and the society in which we live. Therefore we, the members of the National Communication Association, endorse and are committed to practicing the following principles of ethical communication:

- We advocate truthfulness, accuracy, honesty, and reason as essential to the integrity of communication.
- We endorse freedom of expression, diversity of perspective, and tolerance of dissent to achieve the informed and responsible decision making fundamental to a civil society.
- We strive to understand and respect other communicators before evaluating and responding to their messages.
- We promote access to communication resources and opportunities as necessary to fulfill human potential and contribute to the well-being of families, communities, and society.
- We promote communication climates of caring and mutual understanding that respect the unique needs and characteristics of individual communicators.
- We condemn communication that degrades individuals and humanity through distortion, intimidation, coercion, and violence, and through the expression of intolerance and hatred.
- We are committed to the courageous expression of personal convictions in pursuit of fairness and justice.
- We advocate sharing information, opinions, and feelings when facing significant choices while also respecting privacy and confidentiality.
- We accept responsibility for the short- and long-term consequences of our own communication and expect the same of others.

Source: Used by permission of the National Communication Association.

Glossary

Accent. The sound of one language imposed on another. (242)

Acoustics. The science of sound; the sound characteristics of the room in which you will be speaking. (96)

Alliteration. A figure of speech in which a series of words all begin with the same sound. (205)

Analogy. Identifies similarities in things that are alike or similar in function and highlights similarities in things that don't initially seem alike. (113)

Analytical listening. A type of listening that focuses on evaluating whether a message is reasonable and/or whether an argument is valid. (30)

Appreciative listening. A type of listening that focuses on how well a person expresses an idea or opinion. (31)

Argument. A claim supported by evidence and reasons for accepting it. (23, 324)

Articulation. How clearly you make the sounds in the words of a language; your diction. (240)

Attack the person fallacy. Criticizing or attacking a person instead of the substance of the argument. (336)

Attention span. The amount of time audience members can be attentive to sensory stimulation. (198)

Audience analysis. The ability to understand, respect, and adapt to audience members before and during a presentation. (76)

Audience attitudes. A measure of whether audience members agree or disagree with a speaker's purpose statement as well as how strongly they agree or disagree. (81)

Autocratic leader. A leader who relies on power and authority to control a group and its discussions. (374)

Backing. The component of the Toulmin model of an argument that provides support for an argument's warrant. (24)

Bandwagon fallacy. An appeal to popularity. (337)

Begging the question fallacy. An unproven assertion, in an argument, that is assumed to be true. (337)

Better Plan organizational pattern. Presenting a plan that will improve a situation or help to solve a problem while acknowledging that a total solution may not be possible. (329)

Biased. A source whose opinion is so slanted or self-serving that it may not be objective or fair. (115)

Boolean search. A research technique that helps you focus and narrow a computerized search by using terms such as *AND, OR,* and *NOT* as well as other term-limiting techniques. (122)

Brainstorming. A technique that encourages group members to generate as many ideas as possible in a nonevaluative atmosphere. (366)

Briefing. A type of informative presentation in which a speaker briefly reports about the status of an upcoming or past event or project in a business or organizational setting. (291)

Causes and effects arrangement. An organizational format that identifies a situation, object, or behavior and then describes the results of that situation, object, or behavior. (138)

Central idea. A sentence or thesis statement that summarizes the key points of a presentation. (134)

Channel. The medium in which a message exists; using the senses of sight, hearing, touch, taste, and/or smell as a medium for transferring messages. (12)

Character. A component of speaker credibility that relates to a speaker's honesty and goodwill. (183)

Charisma. A speaker's level of energy, enthusiasm, vigor, and/or commitment; a speaker's dynamic qualities. (185)

Claim. The conclusion or position a speaker is advocating. (23)

Cognitive restructuring. A presentation anxiety therapy that attempts to change the way a speaker thinks about speaking, so that positive thinking replaces worrisome, irrational, nonproductive thoughts. (51)

Common ground. A belief, attitude, or experience shared by the speaker and the audience; a "place" where both the speaker and the audience can stand without disagreeing. (171, 305)

Communication model. An illustration that shows the interactions of essential components of the communication process in order to clarify relevant relationships and to help predict outcomes. (12)

Communication transaction. Communication in which speakers and listeners exchange messages in order to share meaning. (12)

Comparison-contrast arrangement. An organizational format that uses similarities and differences between two things or concepts as a method of arranging ideas. (140)

Competence. A component of speaker credibility that relates the speaker's expertise and abilities. (184)

Comprehension questions. Questions asked of an audience by a speaker during a presentation as a way of involving the audience, assessing their understanding, and maintaining control of the situation. (90)

Comprehensive listening. A type of listening that focuses on accurately understanding spoken and nonverbal messages. (29)

Connectives. Devices that link key points, remind the audience of the speaker's direction, and preview or summarize major sections of a presentation. (155)

Context. The surrounding environment—both physical and psychological—that can affect every aspect of a presentation. (12)

Creativity. The process of searching for, separating, and connecting thoughts as a way of combining previously unrelated elements. (159)

Critical thinking. The particular kind of thinking we use to analyze what we read, see, or hear in order to arrive at a justified conclusion or decision. (22)

Decoding. The process of comprehending a message as influenced by audience characteristics, motives, interests, knowledge, attitudes, and learning styles. (12)

Deductive logic. Proving a persuasive argument by moving from accepted general premises to a specific conclusion. (308)

Definition. A statement that explains or clarifies the meaning of a word, phrase, or concept. (112)

Democratic leader. A leader who seeks input from followers and shares the decision-making process with group members. (374)

Demographic information. Information about audience characteristics such as age, gender, marital status, race, religion, place of residence, ethnicity, occupation, education, and income. (77)

Description. A statement that creates a mental image of a scene, concept, event, object, or person. (113)

Dialect. Regional and cultural differences within the same language. (242)

Documentation. The practice of citing the sources of supporting material used in a presentation. (124)

Drawings. Presentation aids that show *how things work;* can explain relationships or processes. (266)

Elaboration Likelihood Model of Persuasion. Persuasive proof should be selected based on considering "two routes to persuasion"—a central route and a peripheral route. The central route requires strong, logical arguments; the peripheral route depends on simpler cues based on emotional, personal, and narrative proofs. (311)

Emotional proof. Proof that appeals to the audience's emotions and feelings. (309)

Empathic listening. A type of listening that focuses on understanding and identifying with a person's situation, feelings, or motives. (29)

Encoding. The process of making decisions about how to create and send a message. (12)

Entertainment speaking. A presentation designed to amuse, interest, divert, or "warm up" an audience. (70)

Ethics. A speaker's moral values and personal principles of correct conduct. (190)

Ethos. Aristotle's term for personal proof. Proof that relies on the competence, character, and charisma of a speaker. See *personal proof.* (190, 310)

Evidence. The information, data, or audience beliefs used by a speaker to support or to prove the claim of an argument. (23, 312)

Example. A reference to a specific case or instance; examples are often items, facts, or instances that represent an entire group. (113)

Explanatory communication. Communication that enhances understanding of a topic the audience may be aware of but does not or cannot fully comprehend. (286)

Expressiveness. The vitality, variety, and sincerity that you put into the delivery of your presentation. (200)

Extemporaneous speaking. A well-prepared presentation delivered from an outline or set of notes. (220)

Eye contact. The establishment and maintenance of visual contact with individual members of your audience. (247)

Eye scan. A method for establishing maximum eye contact while using detailed notes or a manuscript form of delivery. (249)

Fact. A verifiable observation, experience, or event. (111)

Fallacy. An invalid argument or misleading statement that deceives an audience. (334)

Faulty cause fallacy. An erroneous claim that something was caused by an event or action that preceded it. (335)

Feedback. The verbal and nonverbal responses made by audience members as they listen to and interpret the meaning of a presentation. (14)

Fidget. Small, repetitive body movements that function as physical filler phrases. (252)

Figurative analogy. A way to compare two things that are not in the same class but that have basic attributes in common. (140)

Fluency. The ability to speak smoothly without tripping over words or pausing at awkward moments. (238)

Formal outline. A comprehensive written framework for a presentation that follows established conventions of content and style. (151)

Forum. A public meeting in which audience members express their concerns and address questions to public officials and/or experts. (361)

Fundamental Interpersonal Relationship Orientation (FIRO) Theory. Three interpersonal needs (inclusion, control, and openness) that can be addressed in a persuasive presentation. (318)

Gesture. A body movement, usually made by the hands and arms, that conveys or reinforces a thought, an intention, or an emotion. (250)

Golden listening rule. The principle that you should listen to others as you would have them listen to you. (33)

Graphs. Presentation aids that show comparisons and trends. (265)

Hasty generalization fallacy. Drawing a conclusion from relevant but insufficient evidence or examples. (336)

Hidden agenda. An individual group member's private motives and goals that may conflict with and affect the achievement of a group's common goal. (372)

Humorous presentation. A presentation in which the speaker's primary purpose is to entertain the audience or to use humor as a means of making a serious point. (348)

Identification. A persuasive strategy in which the speaker encourages the audience to see how he or she and they all share common attitudes, ideas, feelings, values, and experiences. (305)

Impromptu speaking. A presentation for which the speaker has little or no time to prepare or practice. (219, 354)

Inductive logic. Proving a persuasive argument by moving from specific instances to a general conclusion. (309)

Inflection. A change of pitch, within a word or group of words, that adds emphasis or meaning. (237)

Informative presentation. A presentation designed to instruct, enlighten, explain, share, demonstrate, clarify, remind, or interpret. (69, 283)

Informatory communication. Creates awareness of the latest information about a topic; news reports are informatory. (286)

Inoculation. A persuasive strategy in which a speaker presents the opposition's argument *and* then refutes them in order to build audience resistance to counterpersuasion. (313)

Internal preview. A connective phrase or sentence that introduces the key points of a presentation or tells an audience what will be covered in what order. (157)

Internal summary. A connective phrase or sentence that concludes a section of a presentation, summarizes major ideas, or reinforces important ideas and information. (157)

Introducing a presenter. A presentation in which a speaker provides information about a presenter who is about to speak, as a means of motivating the audience to listen. (342)

Key points. The most important issues or the main ideas that you want your audience to understand and remember during and after your presentation. (132)

Laissez-faire leader. A leader who lets the group take charge of all decisions and actions. (374)

Language intensity. The degree to which your language deviates from bland, neutral terms. (332)

Leadership. The ability to make strategic decisions and to use communication to mobilize a group toward achieving a shared goal. (373)

Lectern. A stand that serves as a support for the notes of a speaker. (254)

Listening. The ability to understand, analyze, respect, and respond to the meaning of another person's spoken and nonverbal messages. (28)

Logical proof. Proof that appeals to the intellect; proof appealing to the rational side of an audience. (308)

Logistics. The strategic planning, arranging, and use of people, facilities, time, and materials relevant to a presentation. (94)

Logos. Aristotle's term for logical proof. See *logical proof.* (308)

Maintenance roles. Group roles that affect how members get along with each other while pursuing a shared goal. (366)

Manuscript speaking. A presentation written out in advance and delivered word for word. (221)

Maps. Presentation aids that show *where;* translate data into spatial patterns. (267)

Maslow's Hierarchy of Needs. A specific sequence of needs (physiological, safety, social, esteem, and self-actualization) that can be addressed in a persuasive presentation. (318)

Mediated Presentation. A presentation that relies on electronic media to support or convey the speaker's message.

Memorized presentation. A presentation for which the speaker memorizes a manuscript and then delivers it without notes. (222)

Memory aids arrangement. An organizational format that uses easily remembered letters of the alphabet, words, or common phrases to arrange the key points of a presentation. (142)

Message. The content of a presentation; the way a speaker's purpose is transformed into words and action. (12)

Metaphor. A figure of speech that makes a comparison between two things or ideas without directly connecting the resemblances with words such as *like* or *as.* (205)

Mind map. An organizational technique for discovering the key points and connections among the ideas in a presentation without forcing a predetermined organizational scheme on them. (147)

Minutes. The written record of a group's discussions and decisions that occur during a meeting. (370)

Monotone. A voice with very little variety in pitch. (237)

Monroe's Motivated Sequence. Alan Monroe's five-step sequence for motivating an audience to change its opinions or behavior: attention, need, satisfaction, visualization, and action steps. (331)

Mythos. A term used to denote various forms of narrative proof. See *narrative proof.* (310)

Narrative. The process, art, and techniques of storytelling. (208)

Narrative proof. Proof that appeals to the values, faith, and feelings that make up our social character and is most often expressed through traditional stories, sayings, and symbols. (310)

Noise. In the communication process, anything that inhibits a message from reaching and being understood by its listeners as it was originally intended. (15)

Nonverbal communication. Messages we send using means other than words. (35)

Occasion. The reason why an audience assembles at a particular place and time. (100)

Optimum pitch. The natural pitch at which you speak most easily and expressively. (237)

Organization. A strategy or method that determines what to include in a presentation as well as how to arrange the ideas and information in an effective way. (131)

Organization tree. An organizational technique that puts ideas and information in a hierarchical order, shows whether there is adequate supporting material for each key point, and ensures that key points are directly related to the central idea. (149)

Overcoming Objections organizational pattern. Each key point attempts to overcome an objection or to refute an argument that prevents the audience from accepting the speaker's position. (330)

Panel discussion. A group discussion in which participants interact with one another on a common topic for the benefit of an audience. (361)

Paraphrasing. Rephrasing what a person has said as a way of indicating that the listener has understood what the speaker means and feels. (35)

Pathos. Aristotle's term for emotional proof. See *emotional proof.* (309)

Performance. The effective vocal and physical delivery of a presentation. (218)

Personal proof. Proof that relies on the credibility and attractiveness of the speaker. (310)

Persuasion. Communication that seeks to change audience attitudes or behavior by using logical, emotional, personal, and/or narrative appeals. (302)

Persuasive presentation. A presentation designed to change or to influence an audience's opinion and/or behavior. (69)

Persuasive Stories organizational pattern. Using stories to illustrate each key point of the central idea of a persuasive presentation. (333)

Pie charts. Presentation aids that show *how much;* show proportions in relation to a whole or to comparable items. (264)

Pitch. How high or low your voice sounds. (236)

Plagiarism. Using or passing off the ideas or writing of another person as your own. (125)

Podium. An elevated platform on which a speaker stands. (99)

Preliminary outline. An initial planning outline that puts the major pieces of a message in a clear and logical order. (146)

Presentation aids. Mediated ways of sharing key ideas and supporting material during a presentation. (261)

Presentation anxiety. A speaker's individual level of fear or anxiety that is associated with either real or anticipated communication to a group of people or an audience. (43)

Presentation software. Software designed to help presenters prepare visual aids for projection or distribution. (153)

Presentation speaking. Occurs when speakers use verbal and nonverbal messages to generate meanings and to establish relationships with audience members, who are usually present at the delivery of a presentation. (5)

Primacy effect. An audience is more likely to recall what speakers say in an introduction than what they say in the body of a presentation. (163)

Primary source. The document, testimony, or publication in which information first appeared. (121)

Private purpose. The personal goal of your presentation. (64)

Problem/Cause/Solution organizational pattern. Describing a problem and its possible causes and then offering a solution. (328)

Problem-solution arrangement. An organizational format that describes a situation that is harmful (the problem) and then offers a plan to solve the problem (the solution). (137)

Projection. Controlled vocal energy that gives impact and intelligibility to sound. (234)

Pronunciation. Putting all the correct sounds in the correct order with the correct stress in a word. (240)

Proof. The strategies, evidence, and/or arguments you select in order to persuade an audience. (307)

Protocol. The expected format of a ceremony or the etiquette observed at a particular type of ceremony or event. (103)

Public group. A group that engages in discussion in front of or for the benefit of the public. (360)

Public purpose. The publicly stated goal of your presentation. (64)

Public speaking. A type of presentation speaking that occurs when speakers address public audiences in community, government, and/or organizational settings. (5)

Purpose. The outcome that you are seeking as a result of making your presentation. Purpose answers the question "What do I want my audience to know, think, feel, or do as a result of my presentation?" (61)

Purpose statement. A sentence that clearly states the specific, achievable, and relevant goal of your presentation. (66)

Qualifier. The component of the Toulmin model of an argument that states the degree to which a claim appears to be true. (25)

Question of conjecture. Asks whether something will or will not happen. (325)

Question of fact. Asks whether something is true or false, whether an event did or did not happen, or whether a circumstance was caused by one thing or by another. (324)

Question of policy. Asks whether a particular course of action should be taken. (326)

Question of value. Asks whether something is worthwhile—is it good or bad; right or wrong; moral or immoral; best, average, or worst? (325)

Question-and-answer session. A situation in which a speaker responds to audience questions. (351)

Rate. Your speaking speed; the number of words you say per minute added to the number and length of pauses that you use. (236)

Receiver. The communicator who interprets a message and responds to its perceived meaning. (12)

Recency effect. An audience is more likely to recall what speakers say in a conclusion than what they say in the body of a presentation. (172)

Research. A search or investigation designed to find useful and appropriate ideas, opinions, and information. (116)

Reservation. The component of the Toulmin model of an argument that recognizes exceptions to an argument or indications that a claim may not be true under certain circumstances. (25)

Search engine. A Web service that matches key words to Web sites that include those terms. (122)

Secondary source. A source that reports, repeats, or summarizes information from one or more other sources. (121)

Selected instances fallacy. A speaker chooses atypical examples to prove an argument. (336)

Self-effacing humor. The ability to direct humor at yourself; to poke fun at yourself. (211)

Signposts. Short phrases that tell or remind an audience of the speaker's current place in the organizational scheme of a presentation. (158)

Simile.   A figure of speech that makes a direct comparison between two things or ideas, usually by using words such as *like* or *as*. (205)

Situation-specific introductory methods.   Ways of beginning a presentation that adapt to the interests and concerns of a specific audience in a particular setting or situation. (165)

Skills.   The most basic abilities needed to prepare and to perform a presentation. (17)

Small group communication.   The interaction of three or more interdependent people working toward a common goal. (360)

Social Judgment Theory.   Audience reactions to persuasive statements are best reflected by *latitudes of acceptance* (statements they agree with), *latitudes of rejection* (statements they cannot agree with), and *latitudes of noncommitment* (statements that are neither acceptable nor unacceptable). (314)

Source.   The communicator who creates a message and sends it to one or more receivers. (12)

Space arrangement.   An organizational format that arranges ideas, objects, events, people, and/or places in a physical pattern, location, or space. (137)

Speaker credibility.   Ethos; the characteristics of a speaker that determine whether the audience believes the speaker and the message. (183)

Special presentations.   Unique types of presentations that are used to bring people together, to create social unity, to build goodwill, to answer questions, or to celebrate. (342)

Standard problem-solving agenda.   A procedure that guides a group through problem solving by using the following steps: clarifying the task, understanding and analyzing the problem, assessing possible solutions, and implementing a decision or plan. (368)

Statistics.   A system of organizing, summarizing, and analyzing numerical data that has been collected and measured. (112)

Stereotypes.   Oversimplified conceptions, opinions, or images of a person or a group of people that are often based on demographic characteristics. (78)

Stories.   Accounts or reports about some things that have happened. (114)

Story fidelity.   Refers to whether a story seems truthful and believable. (208)

Story probability.   Refers to whether a story "hangs together"; whether it is coherent and makes sense. (208)

Strategy.   A plan of action selected to help achieve the purpose of a presentation. (17)

Supporting material.   Ideas, opinions, and information that help explain and/or advance a presentation's key points and purpose. (111)

Survey.   A series of written questions designed to gather information about audience characteristics and opinions. (86)

Symposium.   A group presentation in which participants give short, uninterrupted presentations on different aspects of a topic for the benefit of an audience. (361)

Systematic desensitization.   A presentation anxiety therapy that teaches speakers how to relax before and during a stressful speaking situation. (49)

Tables.   Presentation aids that summarize and compare data; can show exact numeric values. (266)

Task roles.   Group member roles that affect a group's ability to achieve its goals by focusing on behaviors that help get the job done. (366)

Team presentation.   A presentation by a cohesive group of speakers trying to influence an audience of decision makers. (362)

Testimony.   Statements or opinions that someone has said or written. (112)

Text charts.   Presentation aids that list ideas or key phrases, often under a title or headline. (265)

Theory.   A principle that tries to explain and to predict events and behavior. (16)

Thought speed.   The speed (words per minute) at which most people can think, as contrasted with the slower speed at which most people speak. (32)

Time arrangement.   An organizational format that orders ideas and information according to time or calendar dates. (136)

Toast.   Spoken remarks that accompany an act of drinking to honor a person, a couple, or a group. (346)

Topic.   The subject matter of a presentation. (67)

Topical arrangement.   An organizational format that divides a large topic into small subtopics. (135)

Topic-specific introductory methods.   Ways of beginning a presentation that rely on topic-related supporting material. (165)

Transitions.   A connective in the form of a word, phrase, number, or sentence that helps a speaker move from one key point or section to another. (157)

Tree outline.   An organizational technique that compares the central idea, key points, and supporting materials to the trunk, limbs, and branches of a tree. (148)

Valid. Ideas, information, or opinions that are well founded, justified, and true. (114)

Value step. A section in the introduction of a presentation that explains why the information is valuable or important to the audience. (285)

Victory by definition fallacy. A self-serving definition of a word is used to benefit the speaker and the speaker's argument. (338)

Visualization. A procedure that encourages people to think positively about presentation speaking by imagining what it would be like to go through an entire and successful speechmaking process. (52)

Volume. Your voice's degree of loudness. (233)

Warrant. The part of an argument that explains why the evidence supports a claim. (24)

Welcoming remarks. A presentation in which a speaker representing one organization welcomes the public or a group from another organization to an event or place. (345)

Working agenda. An outline of the items to be discussed and the tasks to be accomplished during a meeting or discussion. (369)

Working groups. Private groups in which members exert collective effort to achieve a shared goal. (363)

Index